WordPress®

ALL-IN-ONE

5th Edition

by Lisa Sabin-Wilson

for dummies®
A Wiley Brand

WordPress® All-in-One For Dummies®, 5th Edition

Published by: **John Wiley & Sons, Inc.,** 111 River Street, Hoboken, NJ 07030-5774, www.wiley.com

Published simultaneously in Canada

For general information on our other products and services, please contact our Customer Care Department within the U.S. at 877-762-2974, outside the U.S. at 317-572-3993, or fax 317-572-4002. For technical support, please visit https://hub.wiley.com/community/support/dummies.

Wiley publishes in a variety of print and electronic formats and by print-on-demand. Some material included with standard print versions of this book may not be included in e-books or in print-on-demand. If this book refers to media such as a CD or DVD that is not included in the version you purchased, you may download this material at http://booksupport.wiley.com. For more information about Wiley products, visit www.wiley.com.

Library of Congress Control Number: 2023951276

ISBN: 978-1-394-22538-5 (pbk); 978-1-394-22540-8 (ebk); 978-1-394-22539-2 (ebk)

SKY10063513_122823

Contents at a Glance

Table of Contents

Introduction

WordPress is the most popular online content management software on the planet. Between the hosted service at `WordPress.com` and the self-hosted software available at `WordPress.org`, millions of bloggers use WordPress, and to date, WordPress powers over 45 percent of the Internet. That's impressive! With WordPress, you can truly tailor a website to your own tastes and needs.

With no cost for using the benefits of the WordPress platform to publish content on the web, WordPress is as priceless as it is free. WordPress makes writing, editing, and publishing content on the Internet a delightful, fun, and relatively painless experience, whether you're a publisher, a business owner, a designer, a developer, or a hobbyist blogger.

About This Book

The fact that WordPress is free and accessible to all, however, doesn't make it inherently easy for everyone to use. For some people, the technologies, terminology, and coding practices are a little intimidating or downright daunting. That's where this book comes in. *WordPress All-in-One For Dummies*, 5th Edition, eases any trepidation about using WordPress. With a little research, knowledge, and time, you'll soon have a website that suits your needs and gives your readers an exciting experience that keeps them coming back for more.

WordPress All-in-One For Dummies is a complete guide to WordPress that covers the basics: installing and configuring the software, using the Dashboard, publishing content, utilizing the site and block editor, and using plugins. Additionally, this book provides advanced information about security, the WordPress tools, the Multisite features, and search engine optimization (SEO).

Foolish Assumptions

I make some inescapable assumptions about you and your knowledge, including the following:

- You're comfortable using a computer, mouse, and keyboard.
- You have a good understanding of how to access the Internet, use email, and use a web browser to access webpages.
- You have a basic understanding of what a website is; perhaps you already maintain your own.
- You want to use WordPress for your online publishing, or you want to use the various WordPress features to improve your online publishing.

If you consider yourself an advanced user of WordPress, or if your friends refer to you as an all-knowing WordPress guru, chances are good that you'll find some of the information in this book elementary. Although this book is aimed toward beginner users, intermediate and advanced users will also find useful information. There's something here for everyone.

Icons Used in This Book

The little pictures in the margins of the book emphasize a point to remember, a danger to be aware of, or information that you may find helpful. This book uses the following icons:

TIP

Tips are little bits of information that you may find useful — procedures that aren't necessarily obvious to a casual user or beginner.

WARNING

When your mother warned you, "Don't touch that pan; it's hot!" but you touched it anyway, you discovered the meaning of "Ouch!" I use this icon for situations like that one. You may very well touch the hot pan, but you can't say that I didn't warn you!

TECHNICAL STUFF

All geeky stuff goes here. I use this icon when talking about technical information. You can skip it, but I think that you'll find some great nuggets of information next to these icons. You may even surprise yourself by enjoying them. Be careful — you may turn into a geek overnight!

REMEMBER

When you see this icon, brand the text next to it into your brain so that you remember whatever it was that I thought you should remember.

Beyond the Book

On the web, you can find some extra content that's not in this book. Go online to find

- The Cheat Sheet for this book is at `www.dummies.com/cheatsheet`. In the Search field, type **WordPress All-in-One For Dummies Cheat Sheet** to find the Cheat Sheet for this book.
- Updates to this book, if any, are at `www.dummies.com`. Search for the book's title to find the associated updates.

Where to Go from Here

From here, you can go anywhere you please! *WordPress All-in-One For Dummies* is designed so that you can read any or all of the minibooks between the front and back covers, depending on what topics interest you.

- Book 1 is a great place to get a good introduction to the world of WordPress if you've never used it before and want to find out more.
- Book 2 gives you insight into the programming techniques and terminology involved in running a WordPress website — information that's extremely helpful when you move forward to the other minibooks.
- Book 3 is a good place to jump in and start exploring the WordPress Dashboard, with all of the different settings available for you to start making your website unique and tailored to your needs.
- Book 4 digs into using the block editor in order to create posts and pages, and gives you good information on working with media within your content (images, video, audio, and documents).
- Book 5 takes you through some great information about using tracking tools, such as Google Analytics, to understand how visitors are using your website, as well as some important SEO information and tools you can use to improve your search engine presence.

- Book 6 gives you an understanding of finding and installing WordPress themes, as well as information about block themes, the site editor, and block patterns, and how you can use those tools to customize the look of your site.
- Book 7 introduces you to WordPress plugins, and how to find and install them in order to extend and increase the features and functionality of WordPress.
- Book 8 introduces you to the Multisite feature in WordPress, and how you can set it up and use it to run multiple websites with just one installation of the WordPress software.

Above all else, have fun with the information contained within these pages! Read the minibooks on topics you think you already know; you might just come across something new. Then dig into the minibooks on topics that you want to know more about.

1

Understanding WordPress Basics

Contents at a Glance

IN THIS CHAPTER

» Discovering content publishing

» Publishing and archiving content

» Interacting through comments

» Using WordPress as a content management tool to create different types of sites

Chapter 1

Exploring Basic WordPress Concepts

Blogging gives regular, nontechnical Internet users the ability to publish content on the World Wide Web quickly and easily. Consequently, blogging became extremely popular very quickly, to the point that it's now considered to be mainstream. In some circles, blogging is even considered to be passé, as it has given way to publishing all types of content freely and easily with WordPress. Regular Internet users are blogging, and Fortune 500 businesses, news organizations, and educational institutions are using WordPress to publish content on the web. Today, more than 45 percent of all sites on the web have WordPress behind them.

Although you can choose among several software platforms for publishing web content, for many content publishers, WordPress has the best combination of options. WordPress is unique in that it offers a variety of ways to run your website. WordPress successfully emerged as a favored blogging platform and expanded to a full-featured content management system (CMS) that includes all the tools and features you need to publish an entire website on your own without a whole lot of technical expertise or understanding.

In this chapter, I introduce you to such content basics as publishing and archiving content, interacting with readers through comments, and providing ways for readers to access your content through social media sharing. This chapter also helps you sort out the differences between a blog and a website, and introduces how WordPress, as a CMS, can help you build an entire website. Finally, I show you some websites that you can build with the WordPress platform.

Discovering Blogging

A *blog* is a fabulous tool for publishing your diary of thoughts and ideas. A blog also serves as an excellent tool for business, editorial journalism, news, and entertainment. Here are some ways that people use blogs:

- **Personal:** You're considered to be a personal blogger if you use your blog mainly to discuss topics related to you or your life: your family, your cats, your children, or your interests (such as technology, books, music, politics, sports, art, or photography). I maintain my own personal blog at `https://lisasabin-wilson.com`.
- **Business:** Blogs are very effective tools for promotion and marketing, and business blogs usually offer helpful information to readers and consumers, such as sales events and product reviews. Business blogs also let readers provide feedback and ideas, which can help a company improve its services. I run a global WordPress design and development agency called WebDevStudios, and we maintain an active business blog at `https://webdevstudios.com/blog`.
- **Media/journalism:** Popular news outlets such as Fox News, MSNBC, and CNN are using blogs on their websites to provide information on current events, politics, and news on regional, national, and international levels. *Variety* magazine hosts its entire website on WordPress at `https://variety.com`.
- **Government:** Governments use blogs to post news and updates to the web quickly and to integrate social media tools as a means of interacting with their citizens and representatives. In the United States, the White House is using WordPress to power its official website at `https://whitehouse.gov`, where the executive branch of the government provides policy statements and updates on the economy, national security, the budget, immigration, and other topics. (See Figure 1-1.)

- **Citizen journalism:** Citizens are using blogs with the intention of keeping the media and politicians in check by fact-checking news stories and exposing inconsistencies. Major cable news programs interview many of these bloggers because the mainstream media recognize the importance of the citizen voice that has emerged via blogs. An example of citizen journalism is The Lincoln Project at `https://lincolnproject.us/latest-news/`.
- **Professional:** Professional blogs typically generate revenue and provide a source of monetary income for the owner through avenues such as advertising or paid membership subscriptions. Check out Darren Rowse's ProBlogger blog at `https://problogger.com/blog/`. Rowse is considered the grandfather of professional blogging.

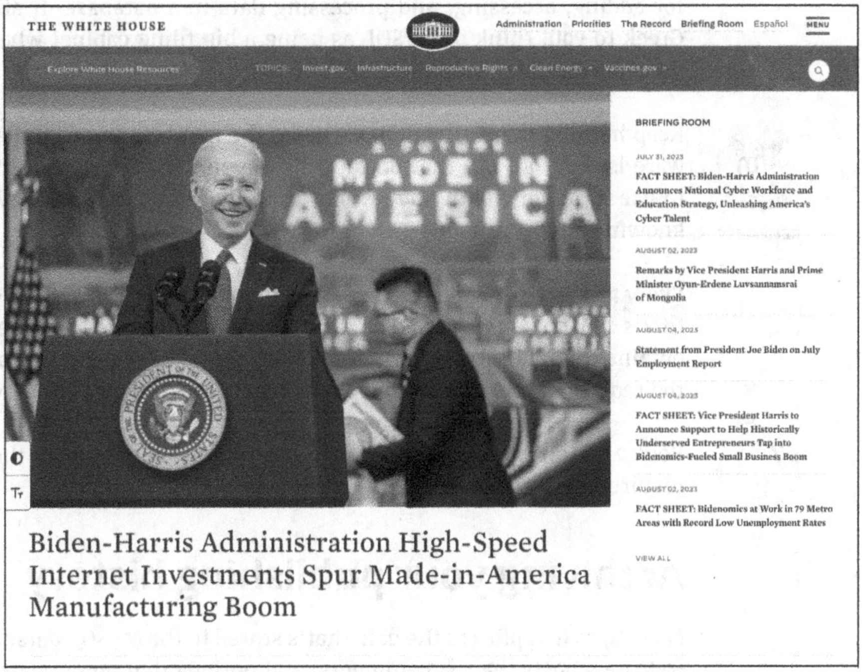

FIGURE 1-1: The official White House website is powered by WordPress.

The websites and blogs I provide in this list run on the WordPress platform. A wide variety of organizations and individuals choose WordPress to run their blogs and websites because of its popularity, ease of use, and large and active development community.

Understanding WordPress Technologies

The WordPress software is a personal publishing system that uses a PHP-and-MySQL platform, which provides everything you need to create your blog and publish your content dynamically without having to program the pages yourself. In short, with this platform, all your content is stored in a MySQL database in your hosting account.

TECHNICAL STUFF

PHP (which stands for *PHP Hypertext Preprocessor*) is a server-side scripting language for creating dynamic webpages. When a visitor opens a page built in PHP, the server processes the PHP commands and then sends the results to the visitor's browser. MySQL is an open-source relational database management system (RDBMS) that uses Structured Query Language (SQL), the most popular language for adding, accessing, and processing data in a database. If all that sounds like Greek to you, think of MySQL as being a big filing cabinet where all the content on your website is stored.

REMEMBER

Keep in mind that PHP and MySQL are the technologies that the WordPress software is built on, but that doesn't mean you need experience in these languages to use it. Anyone with any level of experience can easily use WordPress without knowing anything about PHP or MySQL.

Every time a visitor goes to your website to read your content, they make a request that's sent to your server. The PHP programming language receives that request, obtains the requested information from the MySQL database, and then presents the requested information to your visitor through their web browser.

TIP

Book 2, Chapter 1 gives you more in-depth information about the PHP and MySQL requirements you need to run WordPress.

Archiving your publishing history

Content, as it applies to the data that's stored in the MySQL database, refers to your website's posts, pages, comments, and options that you set up in the WordPress Dashboard or the control/administration panel of the WordPress software, where you manage your site settings and content. (See Book 3, Chapter 2.)

WordPress maintains chronological and categorized archives of your publishing history automatically. This archiving process happens with every post you publish to your blog. WordPress uses PHP and MySQL technology to organize what you publish so that you and your readers can access the information by date, category, author, tag, and so on. When you publish content on your WordPress site, you can file a post in any category you specify; a nifty archiving system allows you and your readers to find posts in specific categories. The archives page of my blog (`https://lisasabin-wilson.com/archives`), for example, contains a Category section, where you find a list of categories I created for my blog posts. Clicking the Music/Books link below the Categories heading takes you to a listing of posts on that topic. (See Figure 1-2.)

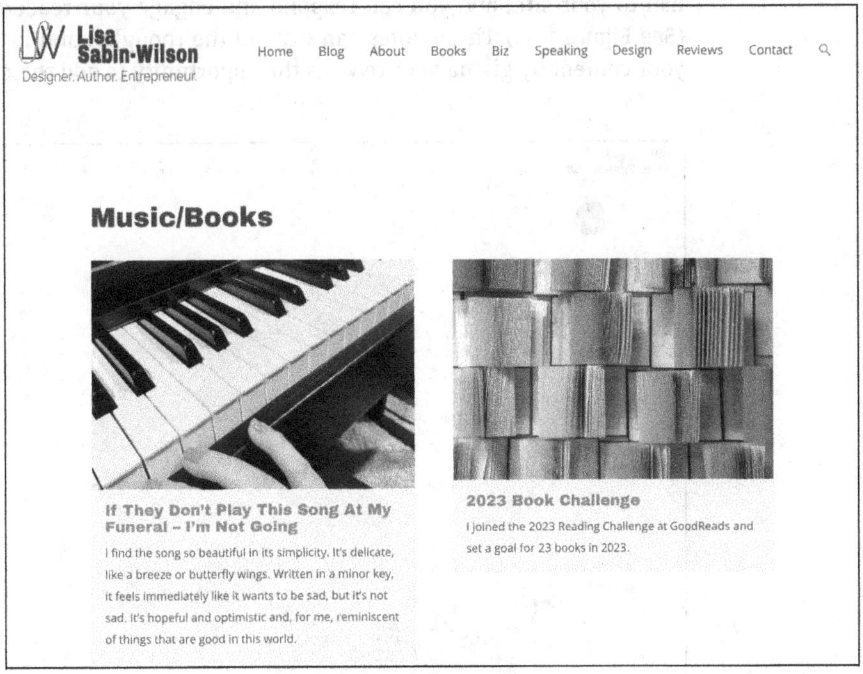

FIGURE 1-2: A page with posts in the Music/Books category.

WordPress lets you create as many categories as you want for filing your content. Some sites have just one category, and others have up to 1,800 categories. When it comes to organizing your content, WordPress is all about personal preference. On the other hand, using WordPress categories is your choice. You don't have to use the category feature if you'd rather not.

TIP

When you look for a hosting service, keep an eye out for hosts that provide daily backups of your site so that your content won't be lost if a hard drive fails or someone makes a foolish mistake. Web hosting providers that offer daily backups as part of their services can save the day by restoring your site to a previous form.

REMEMBER

The theme (design) you choose for your site — whether it's the default theme, one that you create, or one that you custom-design — isn't part of the content. Those files are part of the file system and aren't stored in the database. Therefore, it's a good idea to create a backup of any theme files you're using. See Book 6 for further information on WordPress theme management.

Interacting with your readers through comments

An exciting aspect of publishing content with WordPress is receiving feedback from your readers after you publish to your site. Receiving feedback, or *comments*, is akin to having a guestbook on your site. People can leave notes for you that publish to your site, and you can respond and engage your readers in conversation. (See Figure 1-3.) These notes can expand the thoughts and ideas you present in your content by giving your readers the opportunity to add their two cents' worth.

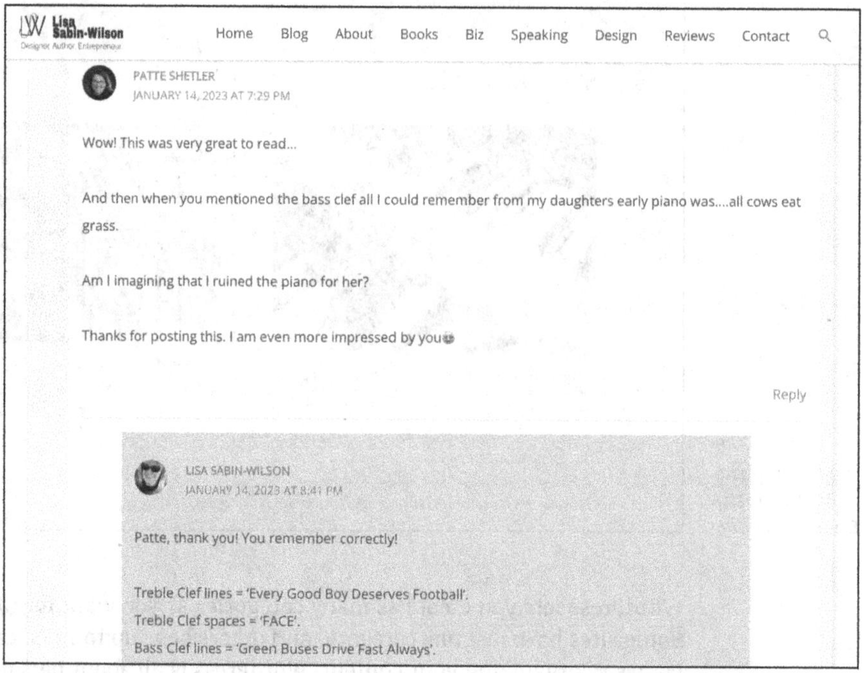

FIGURE 1-3: Blog comments and responses.

REMEMBER

The WordPress Dashboard gives you full administrative control over who can leave comments. Additionally, if someone leaves a comment with questionable content, you can edit the comment or delete it. You're also free to not allow comments on your site. (See Book 3, Chapter 4 for more information.)

Feeding your readers

RSS stands for *Really Simple Syndication*. An *RSS feed* is a standard feature that blog readers have come to expect. So what is RSS, really?

RSS is written to the web server in XML (Extensible Markup Language) as a small, compact file that can be read by RSS readers (as I outline in Table 1-1). Think of an RSS feed as a syndicated, or distributable, auto-updating "what's new" list for your website.

TABLE 1-1 Popular RSS Feed Readers

Reader	Source	Description
Feedly	`http://feedly.com`	RSS aggregator for websites that publish an RSS feed. It compiles published stories from various user-chosen sources and allows the Feedly user to organize the stories and share the content with others.
MailChimp	`https://mailchimp.com`	MailChimp is an email newsletter service. It has an RSS-to-email service that enables you to send your recently published content to your readers via an email subscription service.
dlvr.it	`https://dlvrit.com`	Use RSS to autopost to Facebook, Twitter, LinkedIn, Pinterest, and other social media sites.

TECHNICAL STUFF

Facebook is now called Meta, and as of this writing, Twitter is being rebranded as X. More name changes may be in the works. But because most readers will recognize Facebook and Twitter by those names, I've used them throughout this book.

Tools such as feed readers and email newsletter services can use the RSS feed from your website to consume the data and aggregate it into a syndicated list of content published on your website. Website owners allow RSS to be published to allow these tools to consume and then distribute the data in an effort to expand the reach of their publications.

Table 1-1 lists some popular tools that use RSS feeds to distribute content from websites.

For your readers to stay up to date with the latest and greatest content you post, they can subscribe to your RSS feed. WordPress RSS feeds are autodiscovered by the various feed readers. The reader need only enter your site's URL, and the program automatically finds your RSS feed.

WordPress has RSS feeds in several formats. Because the feeds are built into the software platform, you don't need to do anything to provide your readers an RSS feed of your content.

Tracking back

The best way to understand *trackbacks* is to think of them as comments, except for one thing: Trackbacks are comments left on your site by other sites, not by people. Sounds perfectly reasonable, doesn't it? After all, why wouldn't inanimate objects want to participate in your discussion?

Actually, maybe it's not so crazy after all. A trackback happens when you make a post on your site, and within the content of that post, you provide a link to a post made by another author on a different site. When you publish that post, your site sends a sort of electronic memo to the site you linked to. That site receives the memo and posts an acknowledgment of receipt in the form of a comment to the post that you linked to on the site. The information contained within the trackback includes a link back to the post on your site that contains the link to the other site — along with the date and time, as well as a short excerpt of your post. Trackbacks are displayed within the comments section of the individual posts.

The memo is sent via a *network ping* (a tool used to test, or verify, whether a link is reachable across the Internet) from your site to the site you link to. This process works as long as both sites support trackback protocol. Almost all major CMSes support the trackback protocol.

REMEMBER

Sending a trackback to a site is a nice way of telling the author that you like the information they presented in their post. Most authors appreciate trackbacks to their posts from other content publishers.

Dealing with comment and trackback spam

The absolute bane of publishing content on the Internet is comment and trackback spam. Ugh. When blogging became the "it" thing on the Internet, spammers saw an opportunity. If you've ever received spam in your email program, you know what I mean. For content publishers, the concept is similar and just as frustrating.

Spammers fill content with open comments with their links but not with any relevant conversation or interaction in the comments. The reason is simple: Websites receive higher rankings in the major search engines if they have multiple links coming in from other sites, like trackbacks. Enter software like WordPress, with comment and trackback technologies, and these sites become prime breeding grounds for millions of spammers.

Because comments and trackbacks are published to your site publicly — and usually with a link to the commenter's website — spammers get their site links posted on millions of sites. They do this by creating programs that automatically seek websites with open commenting systems and then hammering those systems with tons of comments that contain links back to their sites.

No one likes spam. Therefore, developers of CMSes such as WordPress spend untold hours trying to stop these spammers in their tracks, and for the most part, they've been successful. Occasionally, however, spammers sneak through. Many spammers are offensive, and all of them are frustrating because they don't contribute to the conversations that occur on the websites where they publish their spam comments.

TIP

All WordPress systems have one important thing in common: Akismet, which kills spam dead. Akismet is a WordPress plugin brought to you by Automattic, the creator of the `WordPress.com` service. I cover the Akismet plugin, and comment spam in general, in Book 3, Chapter 4.

Using WordPress as a Content Management System

A *content management system* (CMS) is a platform that lets you run a full website on your domain. This means that WordPress enables you to create and publish all kinds of content on your site, including pages, blog posts, e-commerce pages for selling products, videos, audio files, events, and more.

A *blog* is a chronological display of content — most often, written by the blog author. The posts are published and, usually, categorized into topics and archived by date. Blog posts can have comments activated so that readers can leave their feedback and the author can respond, creating a dialogue about the blog post.

A *website* is a collection of published pages with different sections that offer the visitor different experiences. A website can incorporate a blog but usually contains other sections and features. These other features include

- **Photo galleries:** Albums of photos uploaded and collected in a specific area so that visitors can browse through and comment on them
- **E-commerce stores:** Fully integrated shopping area into which you can upload products for sale and from which your visitors can purchase them

- **Discussion forums:** Where visitors can join, create discussion threads, and respond to one another in specific threads of conversation
- **Social communities:** Where visitors can become members, create profiles, become friends with other members, create groups, and aggregate community activity
- **Portfolios:** Sections where photographers, artists, or web designers display their work
- **Feedback forms:** Contact forms that your visitors fill out with information that then gets emailed to you directly
- **Static pages (such as Bio, FAQ, or Services):** Pages that don't change as often as blog pages, which change each time you publish a new post
- **Courses:** Where people can come to watch videos or read information to learn about a subject — sometimes this is behind a paywall to require someone to purchase access

This list isn't exhaustive; it's just a listing of some of the most common website sections.

Figure 1-4 shows what the front page of my business blog looked like at the time of this writing. Visit `https://webdevstudios.com/blog` to see how the site displays the most recent blog posts. Although my blog doesn't publish the dates of each blog post, I can personally attest that it is a chronological listing of our most recent posts.

My business website at `https://webdevstudios.com` also uses WordPress. This full site includes a static front page of information that acts as a portal to the rest of the site, on which you can find a blog; a portfolio of work; a contact form; and various landing pages, including service pages that outline information about the different services we offer (`https://webdevstudios.com/services`). Check out Figure 1-5 for a look at this website; it's quite different from the blog section of the site.

Using WordPress as a CMS means that you're creating more than just a blog; you're creating an entire website full of sections and features that offer different experiences for your visitors.

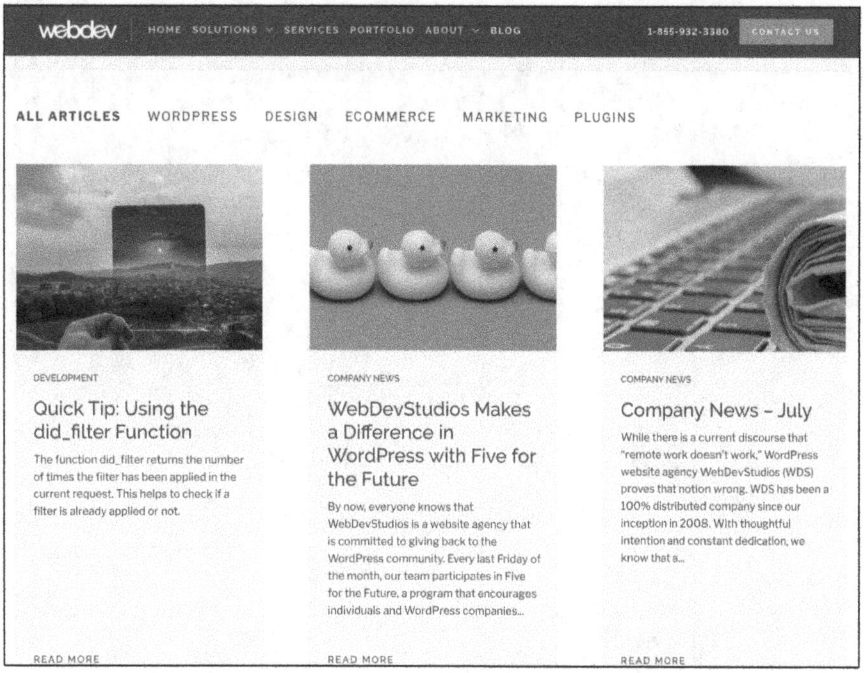

FIGURE 1-4: Visit my business blog at `https://webdevstudios.com/blog` to see an example of a chronological listing of blog posts.

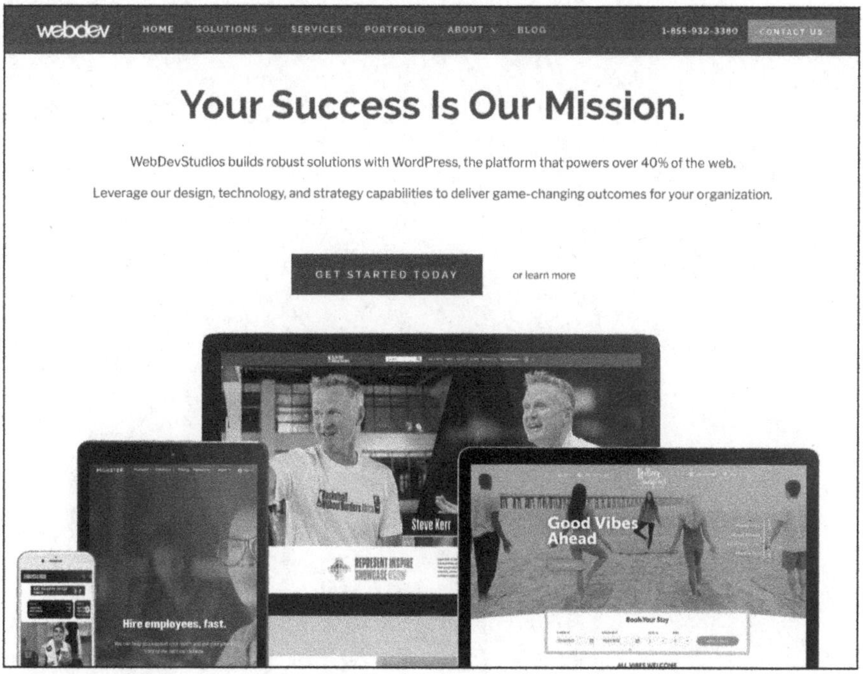

FIGURE 1-5: My business website uses WordPress as a CMS.

IN THIS CHAPTER

» Exploring open-source concepts

» Discovering examples of open-source projects

» Understanding WordPress licensing

» Applying WordPress licensing

Chapter 2

Exploring the World of Open-Source Software

Open-source software is a movement that started in the software industry in the 1980s. Its origins are up for debate, but most people believe that the concept came about in 1983, when a company called Netscape released its Navigator web browser source code to the public, making it freely available to anyone who wanted to dig through it, modify it, or redistribute it.

WordPress software users need a basic understanding of the open-source concept and the licensing upon which WordPress is built because WordPress's open-source policies affect you as a user — and greatly affect you if you plan to develop plugins or themes for the WordPress platforms. A basic understanding helps you conduct your practices in accordance with the license at the heart of the WordPress platform.

This chapter introduces you to open-source; the Open Source Initiative (OSI); and the GNU General Public License (GPL), which is the specific license that WordPress is built upon (GPLv2, to be exact). You also discover how the GPL license applies to any projects you may release (if you're a developer of plugins or themes) that depend on the WordPress software and how you can avoid potential problems by abiding by the GPL as it applies to WordPress.

REMEMBER

IANAL — *I Am Not a Lawyer* — is an acronym that you often find in articles about WordPress and the GPL. I use it here because I'm not a lawyer, and the information in this chapter shouldn't be construed as legal advice. Rather, you should consider the chapter to be an introduction to the concepts of open-source and the GPL. The information presented here is meant to inform you about and introduce you to the concepts as they relate to the WordPress platform.

Defining Open-Source

A simple, watered-down definition of open-source software is software whose source code is freely available to the public and that can be modified and redistributed by anyone without restraint or consequence. An official organization called the Open Source Initiative (OSI; `https://opensource.org`), founded in 1998 to organize the open-source software movement in an official capacity, has provided a very clear and easy-to-understand definition of open-source. During the course of writing this book, I obtained permission from the OSI board to include it here.

Open-source doesn't just mean access to the source code. The distribution terms of open-source software must comply with the following criteria:

1. **Free Redistribution**

   The license shall not restrict any party from selling or giving away the software as a component of an aggregate software distribution containing programs from several different sources. The license shall not require a royalty or other fee for such sale.

2. **Source Code**

   The program must include source code, and must allow distribution in source code as well as compiled form. Where some form of a product is not distributed with source code, there must be a well-publicized means of obtaining the source code for no more than a reasonable reproduction cost; preferably, downloading via the Internet without charge. The source code must be the preferred form in which a programmer would modify the program. Deliberately obfuscated source code is not allowed. Intermediate forms such as the output of a preprocessor or translator are not allowed.

3. **Derived Works**

   The license must allow modifications and derived works, and must allow them to be distributed under the same terms as the license of the original software.

4. **Integrity of the Author's Source Code**

   The license may restrict source code from being distributed in modified form only if the license allows the distribution of "patch files" with the source code for the purpose of modifying the program at build time. The license must explicitly permit distribution of software built from modified source code. The license may require derived works to carry a different name or version number from the original software.

5. **No Discrimination Against Persons or Groups**

   The license must not discriminate against any person or group of persons.

6. **No Discrimination Against Fields of Endeavor**

   The license must not restrict anyone from making use of the program in a specific field of endeavor. For example, it may not restrict the program from being used in a business, or from being used for genetic research.

7. **Distribution of License**

   The rights attached to the program must apply to all to whom the program is redistributed without the need for execution of an additional license by those parties.

8. **License Must Not Be Specific to a Product**

   The rights attached to the program must not depend on the program's being part of a particular software distribution. If the program is extracted from that distribution and used or distributed within the terms of the program's license, all parties to whom the program is redistributed should have the same rights as those that are granted in conjunction with the original software distribution.

9. **License Must Not Restrict Other Software**

   The license must not place restrictions on other software that is distributed along with the licensed software. For example, the license must not insist that all other programs distributed on the same medium must be open-source software.

10. **License Must Be Technology-Neutral**

    No provision of the license may be predicated on any individual technology or style of interface.

The preceding items comprise the definition of open-source as provided by the OSI. You can find this definition (see Figure 2-1) at `https://opensource.org/osd`.

Open-source software source code must be freely available, and any licensing of the open-source software must abide by this definition. Based on the OSI definition, WordPress is an open-source software project. Its source code is accessible and publicly available for anyone to view, build on, and distribute at no cost anywhere, at any time, or for any reason.

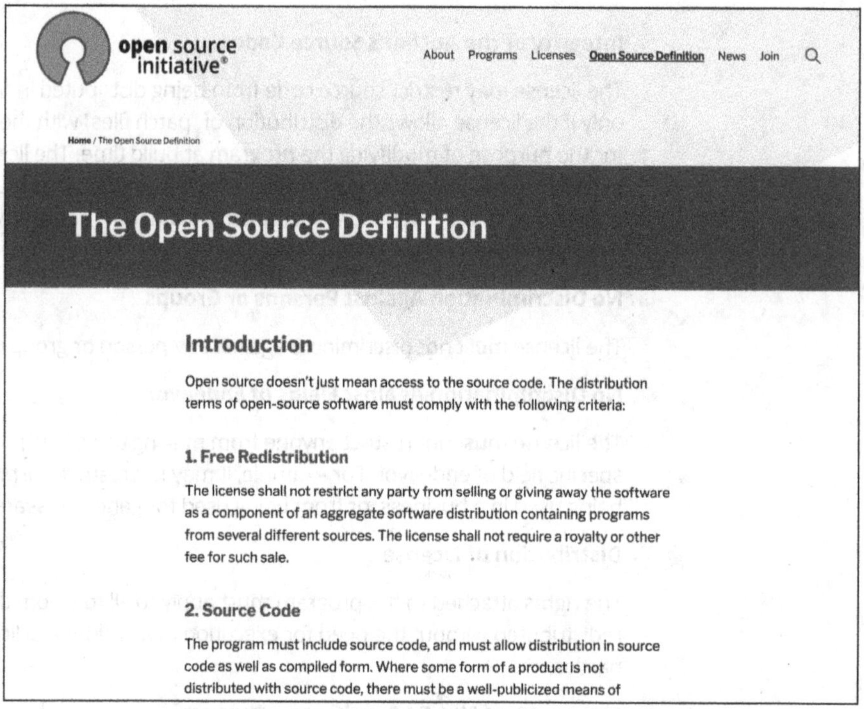
open source initiative®
About
Programs
Licenses
Open Source Definition
News
Join
Home / The Open Source Definition
The Open Source Definition
Introduction
Open source doesn't just mean access to the source code. The distribution terms of open-source software must comply with the following criteria:
1. Free Redistribution
The license shall not restrict any party from selling or giving away the software as a component of an aggregate software distribution containing programs from several different sources. The license shall not require a royalty or other fee for such sale.
2. Source Code
The program must include source code, and must allow distribution in source code as well as compiled form. Where some form of a product is not distributed with source code, there must be a well-publicized means of

FIGURE 2-1: Definition of open-source from the OSI.

Several examples of high-profile software enterprises, such as the ones in the following list, are also open-source. You'll recognize some of these names:

- **Mozilla (`https://www.mozilla.org`):** Community whose projects include the popular Firefox Internet browser and Thunderbird, a popular email client. All projects are open-source and considered to be public resources.
- **PHP (`http://php.net`):** An HTML-embedded scripting language that stands for PHP Hypertext Preprocessor. PHP is popular software that runs on most web servers today; its presence is required on your web server for you to run the WordPress platform successfully on your site.
- **MySQL (`https://www.mysql.com`):** The world's most popular open-source database. Your web server uses MySQL to store all the data from your WordPress installation, including your posts, pages, comments, links, plugin options, theme option, and widgets.
- **Linux (`https://www.linux.org`):** An open-source operating system used by web hosting providers, among other organizations.

As open-source software, WordPress is in some fine company. Open-source itself isn't a license; I cover licenses in the next section. Rather, open-source is a movement — some people consider it to be a philosophy — created and promoted to provide software as a public resource open to community collaboration and peer review. WordPress development is clearly community-driven and focused. You can read about the WordPress community in Book 1, Chapter 4.

Understanding WordPress Licensing

Most software projects are licensed, meaning that they have legal terms governing the use or distribution of the software. Different kinds of software licenses are in use, ranging from very restrictive to least restrictive. WordPress is licensed by the GNU General Public License version 2 (GPLv2), one of the least restrictive software licenses available.

If you're bored, read the GPL text at `www.gnu.org/licenses/gpl-2.0.html`. Licensing language on any topic can be a difficult thing to navigate and understand. It's sufficient to have a basic understanding of the concept of GPL and let the lawyers sort out the rest, if necessary.

TIP

A complete copy of the GPL is included in every copy of the WordPress download package, in the `license.txt` file. The directory listing of the WordPress software files shown in Figure 2-2 lists the `license.txt` file.

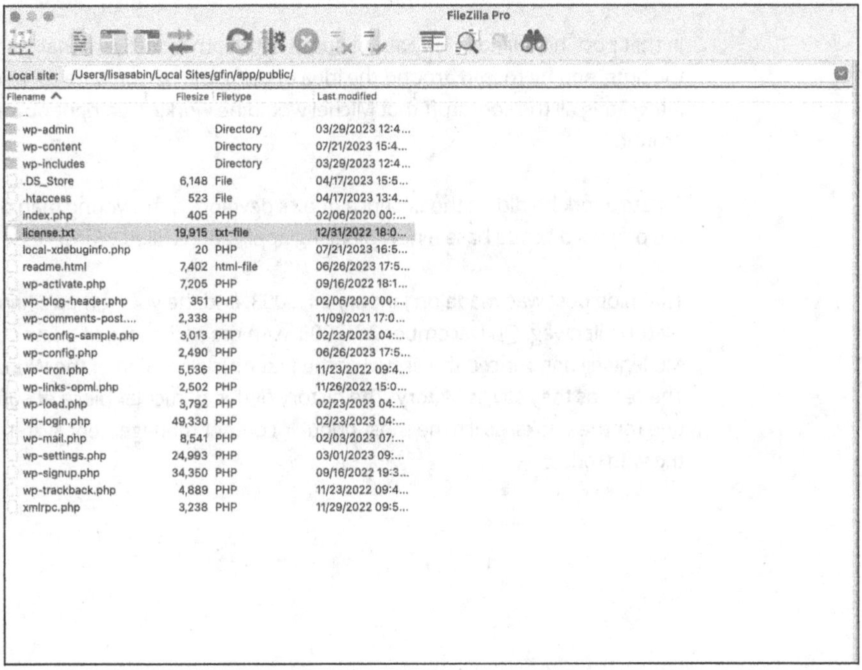

FIGURE 2-2: The GPL text is included in every copy of WordPress.

Simply put, any iteration of a piece of software developed and released under the GPL must be released under the very same license in the future. Check out the nearby sidebar "The origins of WordPress," which tells the story of how the WordPress platform came into existence. Essentially, the software was *forked* — meaning that the original software (in this case, a blogging platform called b2 — `https://cafelog.com`) was abandoned by its original developer and adopted by the founders of WordPress, who took the b2 platform, called it WordPress, and began a new project with a new plan, outlook, and group of developers.

THE ORIGINS OF WORDPRESS

Once upon a time, there was a simple PHP-based blogging platform called b2. This software, developed in 2001, slowly gained a bit of popularity among geek types as a way to publish content on the Internet. Its developer, Michel Valdrighi, kept development active until early 2003, when users of the software noticed that Valdrighi seemed to have disappeared. They became a little concerned about b2's future.

Somewhere deep in the heart of Texas, one young man in particular was very concerned, because b2 was his software of choice for publishing his own content on the World Wide Web. He didn't want to see his favorite publishing tool become obsolete. You can view the original post to his own blog in which he wondered what to do (`https://ma.tt/2003/01/the-blogging-software-dilemma`).

In that post, he talked briefly about some of the other software that was available at the time, and he tossed around the idea of using the b2 software to "to create a fork, integrating all the cool stuff that Michel would be working on right now if only he was around."

Create a fork he did. In the absence of b2's developer, this young man developed from the original b2 code base a new blogging application called WordPress.

That blog post was made on January 24, 2003, and the young man's name was (and is) Matt Mullenweg. On December 26, 2003, with the assistance of a few other developers, Mullenweg announced the arrival of the first official version of the WordPress software. The rest, as they say, is history. The history of this particular piece of software surely is one for the books, as it's the most popular content management system available on the web today.

Because the b2 platform was originally developed and released under the GPL, by law the WordPress software (all current and future iterations of the platform) must also abide by the GPL. Because of the nature of the GPL, you, your next-door neighbor, or I could do the very same thing with the WordPress platform. Nothing is stopping you, or anyone else, from taking WordPress, giving it a different name, and rereleasing it as a completely different project. Typically, open-source projects are forked when the original project development stalls or is abandoned (as was the case with b2), or (in rare cases) when the majority of the development community is at odds with the leadership of the open-source project. I'm not suggesting that you do that, though, because WordPress has one of the most active development communities of any open-source project I've come across.

Applying WordPress Licensing to Your Projects

Regular users of WordPress software need never concern themselves with the GPL of the WordPress project at all. You don't have to do anything special to abide by the GPL. You don't have to pay to use the WordPress software, and you aren't required to acknowledge that you're using the WordPress software on your site. (That said, providing on your site at least one link back to the WordPress website is common courtesy and a great way of saying thanks for the really great, and free, software!)

Most people aren't even aware of the software licensing because it doesn't affect the day-to-day business of publishing with the platform. It's not a bad idea to educate yourself on the basics of the GPL, however. When you try to be certain that any plugins and themes you use with your WordPress installation abide by the GPL, you have peace of mind that all applications and software you're using are in compliance.

Your knowledge of the GPL must increase dramatically, though, if you develop plugins or themes for the WordPress platform. (I cover WordPress themes in Book 6 and WordPress plugins in Book 7.)

The public licensing that pertains to WordPress plugins and themes wasn't decided in a court of law. The current opinion of the best (legal) practices is just that: opinion. The opinion of the WordPress core development team, as well as the opinion of the Software Freedom Law Center (`https://www.softwarefreedom.org/services`), is that WordPress plugins and themes are derivative works of WordPress and, therefore, must abide by the GPL by releasing the development works under the same license that WordPress has.

A *derivative work*, as it relates to WordPress, is a work that contains programming whose functionality depends on the core WordPress files. Because plugins and themes contain PHP programming that call WordPress core functions, they rely on the core WordPress framework to work properly and, therefore, are extensions of the software.

TECHNICAL STUFF

The text of the opinion by James Vasile from the Software Freedom Law Center is available at `https://wordpress.org/news/2009/07/themes-are-gpl-too`.

To maintain compliance with the GPL, plugin or theme developers can't release development work under any (restrictive) license other than the GPL. Nonetheless, many plugin and theme developers have tried to release material under other licenses, and some have been successful (from a moneymaking standpoint). The WordPress community, however, generally doesn't support these developers or their plugins and themes. Additionally, the core WordPress development team considers such works to be noncompliant with the license and, therefore, with the law.

WordPress has made it publicly clear that it won't support or promote any theme or plugin that isn't in 100 percent compliance with the GPL. If you're not 100 percent compliant with the GPL, you can't include your plugin or theme in the WordPress Plugin Directory hosted at `https://wordpress.org/plugins`. If you develop plugins and themes for WordPress, or if you're considering dipping your toe into that pool, do it in accordance with the GPL so that your works are in compliance and your good standing in the WordPress community is protected.

Table 2-1 provides a brief review of what you can (and can't) do as a WordPress plugin and theme developer.

TABLE 2-1 **Development Practices Compliant with GPL License**

Development/Release Practice	GPL-Compliant?
Distribute to the public for free with GPL.	Yes
Distribute to the public for a cost with GPL.	Yes
Restrict the number of users of one download with GPL.	No
Split portions of your work among different licenses. (PHP files are GPL; JavaScript or CSS files are licensed with the Creative Commons license.)	Yes (but `WordPress.org` won't promote works that aren't 100 percent GPL across all files)
Release under a different license, such as the PHP license.	No

The one and only way to make sure that your plugin or theme is 100 percent compliant with the GPL is to do the following before you release your development work to the world:

- Include a statement in your work indicating that the work is released under the GPLv2 license in the `license.txt` file, which WordPress does. (Refer to Figure 2-2.) Alternatively, you can include this statement in the header of your plugin file:

```
<?php
This program is free software; you can redistribute it and/or modify it
   under the terms of the GNU General Public License, version 2, as
   published by the Free Software Foundation.
This program is distributed in the hope that it will be useful,
but WITHOUT ANY WARRANTY; without even the implied warranty of
MERCHANTABILITY or FITNESS FOR A PARTICULAR PURPOSE. See the
GNU General Public License for more details.
You should have received a copy of the GNU General Public License
along with this program; if not, write to the Free Software
Foundation, Inc., 51 Franklin St., Fifth Floor, Boston, MA 02110-1301 USA
*/
?>
```

- Don't restrict the use of your works by the number of users per download.
- If you charge for your work, which is compliant with the GPL, the licensing doesn't change, and users still have the freedom to modify your work and rerelease it under a different name.
- Don't split the license of other files included in your work, such as CSS or graphics. Although this practice complies with the GPL, it won't be approved for inclusion in the WordPress Plugin Directory.

IN THIS CHAPTER

» Delving into WordPress release cycles

» Exploring betas, release candidates, and final release versions

» Navigating WordPress release archives

» Tracking WordPress development

» Using bleeding-edge builds

Chapter 3

Understanding Development and Release Cycles

If you're planning to dip your toe into the WordPress waters (or you've already dived in and gotten completely wet), the WordPress platform's development cycle is really good to know about and understand, because it affects every WordPress user on a regular basis.

WordPress and its features form the foundation of your website. WordPress is a low-maintenance way to publish content on the web, and the software is free in terms of monetary cost. WordPress isn't 100 percent maintenance-free, however, and part of maintenance is ensuring that your WordPress software is up to date to keep your website secure and safe.

This chapter explains the development cycle for the WordPress platform and shows you how you can stay up to date and informed about what's going on. This chapter also gives you information on WordPress release cycles and shows you how you can track ongoing WordPress development on your own.

Discovering WordPress Release Cycles

Book 1, Chapter 2 introduces you to the concept of open-source software and discusses how the WordPress development community is primarily volunteer developers who donate their time and talents to the WordPress platform. The development of new WordPress releases is a collaborative effort, sometimes requiring contributions from more than 300 developers.

The public schedule for WordPress updates is a goal of roughly one new release every 4 months. This doesn't include *patches* — smaller fixes for security or similar reasons. As a user, you can expect a new release of the WordPress software about three times per year. The WordPress development team sticks to that schedule closely, with exceptions only here and there. When the team makes exceptions to the 4-month rule, it usually makes a public announcement so that you know what to expect and when to expect it.

Mostly, interruptions in the 4-month schedule occur because the development of WordPress occurs primarily on a volunteer basis. A few developers — employees of Automattic, the company behind `WordPress.com` — are paid to develop for WordPress, but most developers are volunteers. Therefore, the progress of WordPress development depends on the developers' schedules.

REMEMBER

I'm confident in telling you that you can expect to update your WordPress installation at least three, if not four, times per year.

Upgrading your WordPress experience

Don't be discouraged or frustrated by the number of times you'll upgrade your WordPress installation. The WordPress development team is constantly striving to improve the user experience and to bring exciting, fun new features to the WordPress platform. Each upgrade improves security and adds new features to enhance your (and your visitors') experience on your website. WordPress also makes the upgrades easy to perform, as I discuss in Book 2, Chapter 5.

The following list gives you some good reasons why you should upgrade your WordPress software each time a new version becomes available:

- **Security:** When WordPress versions come and go, outdated versions are no longer supported and are vulnerable to malicious attacks and hacker attempts. Most WordPress security failures occur when you're running an outdated version of WordPress on your website. To make sure that you're running the most up-to-date and secure version, upgrade to the latest release as soon as you can.

- **New features:** Major WordPress releases offer great new features that are fun to use, improve your experience, and boost your efficiency and productivity. Upgrading your WordPress installation ensures that you always have access to the latest, greatest tools and features that WordPress has to offer. (I discuss the difference between major and minor, or point, releases later in this chapter, in the sidebar titled "Major versus point releases.")
- **Plugins and themes:** Most plugin and theme developers work hard to make sure that their products are up to date with the latest version of WordPress. Generally, plugin and theme developers don't worry about backward compatibility, and they tend to ignore out-of-date versions of WordPress. To be sure that the plugins and themes you've chosen are current and not breaking your site, make sure that you're using the latest version of WordPress and the latest versions of your plugins and themes. (See Book 6 for information about themes and Book 7 for details about plugins.)

Understanding the cycles of a release

By the time the latest WordPress installation becomes available, that version has gone through several iterations, or *versions*. This section helps you understand what it takes to get the latest version on your website and explains some of the WordPress development terminology.

The steps and terminology involved in the release of a new version of WordPress include

- **Alpha:** This phase is the first developmental phase of a new version. Alpha typically is the "idea" phase in which developers gather ideas, including those from users and community members. During the alpha phase, developers determine which features to include in the new release and then develop an outline and a project plan. After features are decided, developers start developing and testers start testing until they reach a "feature freeze" point in the development cycle, at which all new features are considered to be complete. Then development moves on to perfecting new features through user testing and bug fixes.
- **Beta:** This phase is for fixing bugs and clearing any problems that testers report. Beta cycles can last four to six weeks, if not longer. WordPress often releases several beta versions with such names as WordPress version 5.0 Beta, WordPress version 5.0 Beta 1, and so on. The beta process continues until the development team decides that the software is ready to move into the next phase in the development cycle.
- **Release candidate:** A version becomes a release candidate (RC) when the bugs from the beta versions are fixed and the version is nearly ready for final

release. You sometimes see several RC iterations, referred to as RC-1, RC-2, and so on.

» **Final release:** After a version has gone through full testing in several (ideally, all) types of environments, use cases, and user experiences; any bugs from the alpha, beta, and RC phases have been squashed; and no major bugs are being reported, the development team releases the final version of the WordPress software.

After the WordPress development team issues a final release version, it starts again in the alpha phase, gearing up and preparing to go through the development cycle for the next major version.

REMEMBER

Typically, a development cycle lasts 4 months, but this figure is an approximation, because any number of things can happen (from developmental problems to difficult bugs) to delay the process.

Finding WordPress release archives

WordPress keeps a historical archive of all versions it has ever released at `https://wordpress.org/download/releases`, as shown in Figure 3-1. On that page, you find every release of the WordPress software for which a record exists.

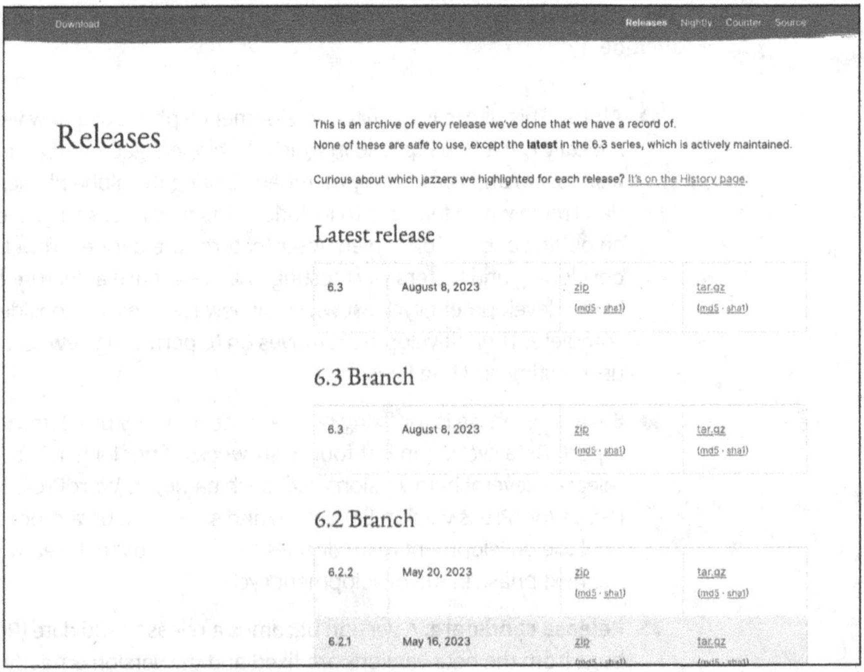

FIGURE 3-1: The archive of every WordPress release on record.

MAJOR VERSUS POINT RELEASES

You may have noticed that WordPress versions are numbered. These numbers show the progress of the development of the software, and they also tell you something else about the version you're using. *Software versioning* is a method of assigning unique numbers to each version release. Generally, the two types of versioning are

- **Point release:** Point releases usually increase the numbered version only by a decimal point or two, indicating a relatively minor release. Such releases include insignificant updates or minor bug fixes. When the version number jumps from 6.2 to 6.2.2, for example, you can be certain that the new version was released to fix minor bugs or to clean up the source code rather than to add new features.
- **Major release:** A major release most often contains new features and jumps by a more seriously incremented version number. In 2023, when WordPress went from 6.2 to 6.3 (release 6.2 versioned into 6.2.2 before jumping to 6.3), that release was considered to be a major release because it jumped a whole number rather than a decimal point. A large jump is a sign to users that new features are included in this version, rather than just bug fixes or cleanup of code. The bigger the jump in the version number, the more major the release is. A release jumping from 6.3 to 7.0, for example, would be an indication of major new features.

WARNING

None of the releases on the WordPress website is safe for you to use except the latest release in the 6.0.x series. Using an older version leaves your website open to hackers. WordPress just likes to have a recorded history of every release for posterity's sake.

Keeping Track of WordPress Development

If you know where to look, keeping track of the WordPress development cycle is easy, especially because the WordPress development team tries to make the development process as transparent as possible. You can track updates by reading about them at various spots on the Internet and by listening to conversations between developers. If you're so inclined, you can jump in and lend the developers a hand, too.

You have several ways to stay up to date on what's going on in the world of WordPress development, including blog posts, live chats, development meetings, tracking tickets, and bug reports, just to name a few. The following list gives you a solid start on where you can go to stay informed:

- **WordPress development updates (`https://make.wordpress.org/core`):** The WordPress development team's blog, Make WordPress Core, is where you can follow and keep track of the progress of the WordPress software project while it happens. (See Figure 3-2.) You find agendas, schedules, meeting minutes, and discussions surrounding the development cycles.

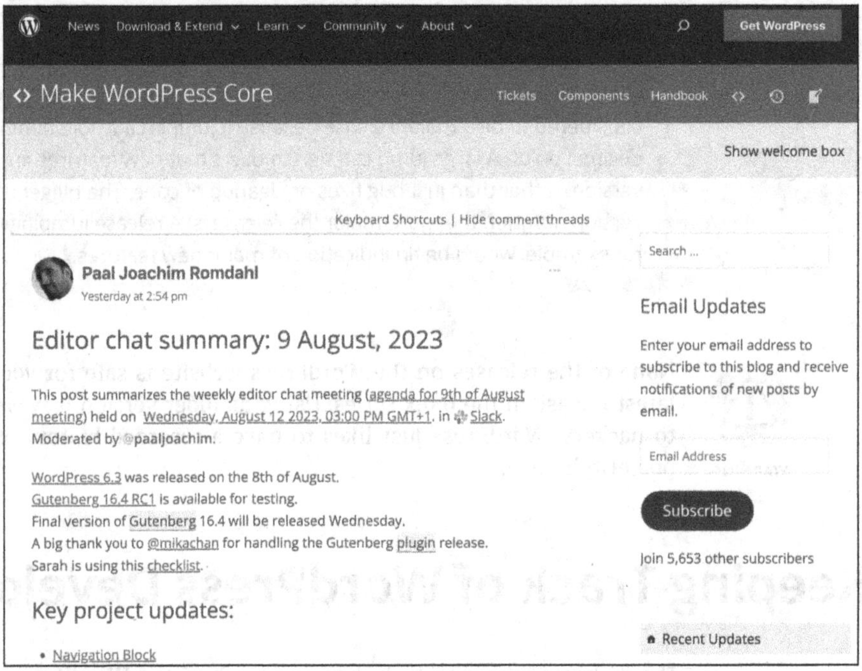

FIGURE 3-2: The WordPress development blog.

- **WordPress developers' chats (`https://make.wordpress.org/chat`):** Developers who are involved in development of WordPress core use a real-time communication platform called Slack (`https://slack.com`). You can easily participate in any of the scheduled meetings listed on `https://make.wordpress.org/core`. Regular scheduled chats are listed on the right sidebar of the site.

- **WordPress Trac (`https://core.trac.wordpress.org`):** Here are ways to stay informed about the changes in WordPress development:
  - Follow the timeline: `https://core.trac.wordpress.org/timeline`
  - View the road map: `https://core.trac.wordpress.org/roadmap`
  - Read reports: `https://core.trac.wordpress.org/report`
  - Perform a search: `https://core.trac.wordpress.org/search`
- **WordPress mailing lists (`https://codex.wordpress.org/Mailing_Lists`):** Join mailing lists focused on different aspects of WordPress development, such as bug testing, documentation, and hacking WordPress. (For specific details about mailing lists, see Book 1, Chapter 4.)

Downloading Nightly Builds

WordPress development moves pretty fast. Often, changes in the software's development cycle occur daily. While the developers are working on alpha and beta versions and release candidates, they commit the latest core changes to the repository and make those changes available to the public to download, install, and test on individual sites. The changes are released in a full WordPress software package called a *nightly build*. This nightly build contains the latest core changes submitted to the project — changes that haven't yet been released as full and final versions.

WARNING

Using nightly builds isn't a safe practice for a live site. I strongly recommend creating a test environment to test nightly builds. Many times, especially during alpha and beta phases, the core code breaks and causes problems with your existing installation. Use nightly builds in a test environment only, and leave your live site intact until the final release is available.

Hundreds of members of the WordPress community help in the development phases, even though they aren't developers or programmers. They help by downloading the nightly builds, testing them in various server environments, and reporting to the WordPress development team by way of Trac tickets (shown in Figure 3-3; check out `https://core.trac.wordpress.org/report`) any bugs and problems they find in that version of the software.

You can download the latest nightly build from the WordPress repository at `https://wordpress.org/download/beta-nightly`. For information about installing WordPress, see Book 2, Chapter 3.

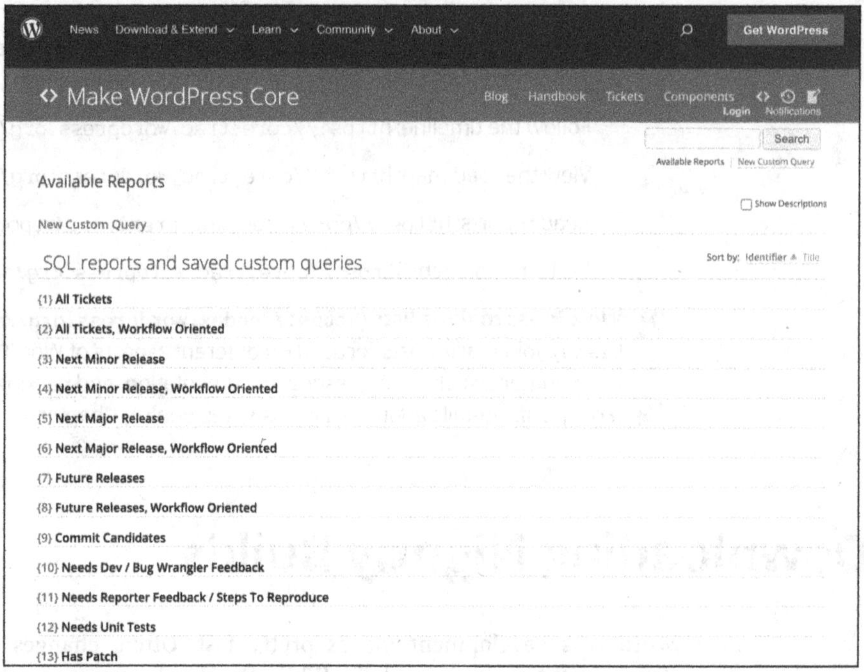

FIGURE 3-3: WordPress Trac tickets.

REMEMBER

Running the latest nightly build on your website is referred to as using *bleeding-edge* software because the software is an untested version, requiring you to take risks just to run it on your website.

TIP

WordPress Beta Tester (`https://wordpress.org/plugins/wordpress-beta-tester`), by the WordPress Upgrade/Install Team, is a super plugin that enables you to use the automatic upgrade tool in your WordPress Dashboard to download the latest nightly build. For information about installing and using WordPress plugins, check out Book 7, Chapter 2.

IN THIS CHAPTER

- Finding WordPress users
- Locating users on social networks
- Getting help in the support forums
- Participating in testing and bug squashing
- Discovering professional consultants and services
- Attending and organizing local WordCamps and other events

Chapter 4
Meeting the WordPress Community

Allow me to introduce you to the fiercely loyal folks who make up the WordPress user base, better known as the WordPress community. These merry ladies and gentlemen come from all around the globe, from California to Cairo, Florida to Florence, and all points in between.

Early on, in March 2005, Matt Mullenweg of WordPress proudly proclaimed that the number of WordPress downloads had reached 900,000 — an amazing landmark in the history of the software. By contrast, in 2023, the download counter for WordPress version 6.3 had exceeded 18 million times in the first week after its release in August 2023. The World Wide Technology Surveys (`https://w3techs.com`) published results showing WordPress to be the most popular content management system (CMS) being used on the web today. An astounding 43.1 percent of all sites on the Internet that use a CMS use WordPress. This popularity makes for a large community of users, to say the least.

This chapter introduces you to the WordPress community and the benefits of membership within that community, such as finding support forums, locating other WordPress users on various social networks, getting assistance from other users, participating in WordPress development, and hooking up with WordPress users face to face or virtually at WordPress events such as WordCamp.

Finding Other WordPress Users

Don't let the sheer volume of users intimidate you: WordPress has bragging rights to the most helpful blogging community on the web today. Thousands of websites exist that spotlight everything, including WordPress news, resources, updates, tutorials, and training. The list is endless. Do a quick Google search for *WordPress*, and you'll get about 1.7 billion results.

My point is that WordPress users are all over the Internet, from websites to discussion forums and social networks to podcasts and more. For many people, the appeal of the WordPress platform lies not only in the platform itself, but also in its passionate community of users.

Finding WordPress news and tips on community websites

WordPress-related websites cover an array of topics related to the platform, including everything from tutorials to news and even a little gossip, if that's your flavor. The Internet has no shortage of websites related to the popular WordPress platform. Here are a few that stand out:

- **WP Tavern (`https://wptavern.com`):** A site that covers everything from soup to nuts: news, resources, tools, tutorials, and interviews with standout WordPress personalities. You can pretty much count on WP Tavern to be on top of what's new and going on in the WordPress community. WP Tavern is owned by Automattic, the parent company of `WordPress.com`.
- **Smashing Magazine (`https://www.smashingmagazine.com/category/wordpress/`):** A very popular and established online design magazine and resource that has dedicated a special section of its website to WordPress news, resources, tips, and tools written by various members of the WordPress community.
- **Make WordPress Core (`https://make.wordpress.org/core`):** A website that aggregates content from all the "Make WordPress" websites built and

maintained by the WordPress.org community. It includes resources for contributing to WordPress core, making plugins and themes, planning WordPress events, supporting WordPress, and more.

Locating users on social networks

In addition to WordPress, many website owners use microblogging tools and social media networks such as Facebook (https://www.facebook.com) to augment their online presence and market their blogs, services, and products. Within these networks, you can find WordPress users, resources, and links, including the following:

- **WordPress Twitter lists:** Twitter allows users to create lists of people who have the same interests, such as WordPress. When you are logged into your Twitter account, you can find a few of these lists here:
  - *Twitter Search:* https://twitter.com/search?q=WordPress
  - *Twitter Hashtag:* https://twitter.com/hashtag/WordPress
- **Facebook Pages on WordPress:** Facebook users create pages and groups around their favorite topics of interest, such as WordPress. Log in to your Facebook account, and you can find some interesting WordPress pages and groups here:
  - WordPress.org: https://www.facebook.com/WordPress
  - *Advanced WordPress:* https://www.facebook.com/groups/advancedwp
  - *Matt Mullenweg* (founder of WordPress): https://www.facebook.com/matt.mullenweg

TIP

You can embed a custom Facebook feed on your site by using the handy Smash Balloon Social Post Feed widget for WordPress at https://wordpress.org/plugins/custom-facebook-feed/.

Users Helping Users

Don't worry if you're not a member of the WordPress community. Joining is easy: Simply start your own website by using the WordPress platform. If you're already publishing on a different platform, such as Drupal or Tumblr, WordPress makes migrating your data from that platform to a new WordPress setup simple. (See Book 2, Chapter 6 for information on migrating to WordPress from a different platform.)

WordPress support forums

You can find the WordPress Support Forums page (shown in Figure 4-1) at `https://wordpress.org/support/forums/`. This page is where you find users helping other users in their quest to use and understand the platform.

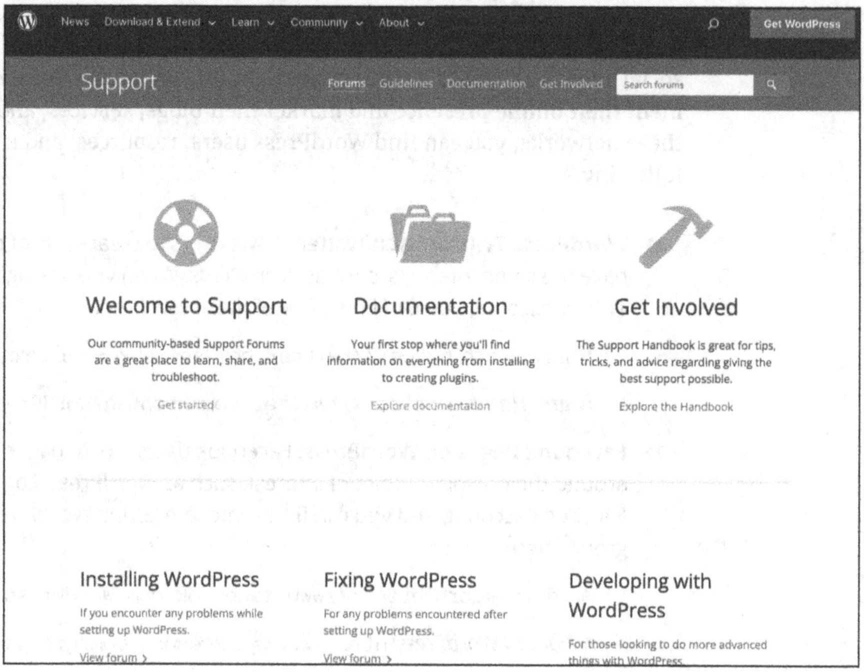

FIGURE 4-1: WordPress Support Forums page.

REMEMBER

The support forums are hosted on the `WordPress.org` website, but don't expect to find any official form of support from the WordPress developers. Instead, you find a large community of people from all walks of life seeking answers and providing solutions.

Users from beginner level to the most advanced level browse the forums, providing support for one another. Each user has their own experiences, troubles, and knowledge level with WordPress, and the support forums are where users share those experiences and seek out the experiences of other users.

REMEMBER

It's important to keep in mind that the people you find and interact with on these official forums are offering their knowledge on a volunteer basis only, so as always, common-courtesy rules apply. "Please" and "Thank you" go a long way in the forums.

TIP

If you find solutions and assistance in the WordPress support forums, consider browsing the forum entries to see whether you can help someone else by answering a question or two.

WordPress user manual

You can find users contributing to the very helpful WordPress Codex (a collection of how-to documents) at `https://codex.wordpress.org`. *Codex*, by the way, is Latin for *book*.

The WordPress Codex is a collaborative effort to document the use of the WordPress software. All contributors are WordPress users who donate their time as a way of giving back to the free, open-source project that has given them a dynamic piece of software for publishing freely on the web.

Make WordPress

If you'd like to get involved in the WordPress project, Make WordPress is the place to go. The Make blogs in this community offer you the opportunity to become involved in various aspects of the WordPress community as well as future development of the software. All the available WordPress Make blogs are on the WordPress website at `https://make.wordpress.org`. The most popular ones include the following:

- **Core (`https://make.wordpress.org/core`):** Subscribe and participate on the Make Core blog list to interact and talk to the WordPress core development team — keep up to date on the status of the project, and get involved in discussions about the overall direction of the project.
- **Accessibility (`https://make.wordpress.org/accessibility`):** The Make WordPress Accessible blog is an area to get involved in if you're interested in helping improve the accessibility of WordPress to (among others) people who can't see or use a mouse, people who can't hear and/or who use sign language as a primary means of communication, users and visitors whose primary language isn't your primary language, people who use special assistive devices to access the Web, and people who are color-blind.
- **Support (`https://make.wordpress.org/support`):** The Make WordPress Support blog is where you should go if you have an interest in helping other users. Answering questions in the support forums is one of the easiest ways to contribute to the WordPress project.
- **Community (`https://make.wordpress.org/community/`):** The Community team is a great place to go if you want to help organize a meetup or WordCamp

(which I discuss in the section "Participating in Live and Virtual WordPress Events," later in this chapter). They work to support events, outreach, and training programs for the WordPress community.

- **Training (`https://make.wordpress.org/training/`):** The Training team helps teach people how to use, contribute to, and extend WordPress through lessons and other learning opportunities. If you love teaching people, this is a great team to join!

Discovering Professional WordPress Consultants and Services

You have big plans for your website, and your time is valuable. Hiring a professional to handle the backend design and maintenance of your website enables you to spend your time creating the content and building your readership on the front end.

Many website owners who decide to go the custom route by hiring a design professional do so for another reason: They want the designs/themes of their website to be unique. Free themes are nice, but you run the risk that your website will look like hundreds of other websites.

A *brand* (a term often used in advertising and marketing) refers to the recognizable identity of a product — in this case, your website. Having a unique brand or design for your site sets yours apart from the rest. If your website has a custom look, people will associate that look with you or your company. You can accomplish branding with a single logo or an entire layout and color scheme of your choosing.

Many consultants and design professionals put themselves up for hire. Who are these people? I get to that topic in a second. First, you want to understand what services they offer, which can help you decide whether hiring a professional is the solution for you.

Here are some of the many services available:

- Custom graphic design and CSS styling for your website
- Custom templates
- WordPress plugin installation and integration

- Custom WordPress plugin development
- WordPress software installation on your web server
- Upgrades of the WordPress software
- Web hosting and domain registration services
- Search engine optimization and site marketing

REMEMBER

Some website owners take advantage of the full array of services provided, whereas others use only a handful. The important thing to remember is that you aren't alone. Help is available for you and your website.

Table 4-1 pairs the three types of website experts — designers, developers, and consultants — with the services they typically offer. Many of these folks are free-lancers with self-imposed titles, but I've matched titles with typical duties. Keep in mind that some of these professionals wear all these hats; others specialize in only one area.

TABLE 4-1 Types of WordPress Professionals

Title	Services
Graphic Designers	These folks excel in graphic and layout design using software like Adobe Photoshop for the purpose of creating a unique visual design for your website.
Developers	These guys and gals are code monkeys. Some of them don't know a stitch about graphic design, but they pair up with a graphic designer to provide custom code to make your website do things you never thought possible. Usually, you'll find these people releasing plugins in their spare time for the WordPress community to use for free.
Consultants	If you have a website for your business, these folks can provide you with a marketing plan for your site or a plan for using your site to reach clients and colleagues in your field. Many consultants also provide search engine optimization to help your domain reach high ranks in search engines.

I wish I could tell you what you could expect to pay for any of these services, but the truth is the levels of expertise — and expense — vary wildly. Services can range from $5 per hour to $300 or more per hour. As with any purchase, do your research and make an informed decision before you buy.

Listing all the professionals who provide WordPress services is impossible, but Tables 4-2 through 4-4 list some of the most popular ones. I've tried to cover a diverse level of services so that you have the knowledge to make an informed decision about which professional to choose.

TABLE 4-2 Established WordPress Designers

Who They Are	Where You Can Find Them
WebDevStudios	`https://webdevstudios.com`
Freshy Sites	`https://freshysites.com/`
GB Digital	`https://greenbay.digital`

TABLE 4-3 Established WordPress Developers

Who They Are	Where You Can Find Them
WebDevStudios	`https://webdevstudios.com`
Bill Erickson	`https://www.billerickson.net/`
WPRiders	`https://wpriders.com/`

TABLE 4-4 Established Blog Consultants

Who They Are	Where You Can Find Them	Type of Consulting
The Bryan Agency	`https://www.thebryanagency.net/`	Search engine optimization (SEO), digital marketing
Pam Ann Marketing	`https://pamannmarketing.com`	SEO
WordPress 101	`https://www.wp101.com`	WordPress training

WordPress designers

WordPress frontend designers can take a simple website and turn it into something dynamic, beautiful, and exciting. These people are experts in the graphic design, CSS styling, and template tagging needed to create a unique theme for your website. Often, WordPress designers are skilled in installing and upgrading WordPress software and plugins; sometimes, they're even skilled in creating custom PHP or plugins. These folks are the ones you want to contact when you're looking for someone to create a unique design for your website that's an individual, visual extension of you or your company.

Some website designers post their rates on their websites because they offer design *packages*, whereas other designers quote projects on a case-by-case basis because every project is unique. When you're searching for a designer, if the prices aren't displayed on the site, drop the designer an email and ask for an estimate.

Armed with this information, you can do a little comparison shopping while you search for just the right designer.

The designers and design studios listed in Table 4-2 represent a range of styles, pricing, services, and experience. All of them excel in creating custom WordPress websites. This list is by no means exhaustive, but it's a good starting point.

Developers

The WordPress motto sits at the bottom of the WordPress home page:

> Code is poetry.

No one knows this better than the extremely talented developers in the core WordPress development team. A developer can take some of the underlying code, make a little magic happen between PHP and the MySQL database that stores the content of your website, and create a dynamic display of that content for you. Most likely, you'll contact a developer when you want to do something with your site that's a little out of the ordinary, and you can't find a plugin that does the trick.

If you've gone through all the available WordPress plugins and still can't find the exact function that you want your WordPress blog to perform, contact one of these folks. Explain what you need. The developer can tell you whether it can be done, whether they are available to do it, and how much the job will cost. (Don't forget that last part!) You may recognize some of the names in Table 4-3 as developers/authors of some popular WordPress plugins.

Consultants

Website consultants may not be able to design or code for you, but they're probably connected to people who can. Consultants can help you achieve your goals for your website in terms of online visibility, marketing plans, and search engine optimization. Most of these folks can help you find out how to make money with your website and connect you with various advertising programs. Quite honestly, you can do what website consultants do by investing a little time and research in these areas. As with design and coding, however, figuring everything out and then implementing it takes time. Sometimes it's easier — and more cost-effective — to hire a professional than to do the work yourself.

Who hires website consultants? Typically, businesses that want to take their websites to the next level through expert consulting, and new businesses that want to launch new websites and need some help with marketing, branding, and search engine optimization (SEO). Table 4-4 lists some people and organizations that offer this kind of consulting.

Contributing to WordPress

Contributing code to the core WordPress software is only one way of participating in the WordPress project. You don't need to be a coder or developer to contribute to WordPress, and it's easier than you might think. Here are several ways you can contribute to the project, including (but not limited to) code:

- **Code:** One of the most obvious ways you can contribute to WordPress is providing code to be used in the core files. The WordPress project has several hundred developers who contribute code at one time or another. You submit code through the WordPress Trac at `https://core.trac.wordpress.org`. Within the Trac, you can follow current development and track changes. To contribute, you can use the Trac to download and test a code patch or look at reported bugs to see whether you can offer a fix or submit a patch. Required skills include, at the very least, PHP programming, WordPress experience, and MySQL database administration. (That list isn't exhaustive, mind you.)
- **Testing:** You can join the Make WordPress Test blog (`https://make.wordpress.org/test`) to test beta versions of WordPress and report your own user experience. WordPress developers monitor this Make Blog and try to fix any true bugs or problems.
- **Documentation:** Anyone can submit documentation to the WordPress Codex (the user documentation for WordPress). All you need to do is visit `https://codex.wordpress.org`, create an account, and dig in!

  TIP

  Be sure to check out the article titled "Get Involved" (`https://make.wordpress.org/docs/handbook/get-involved`), which provides good tips on how to get started, including guidelines for documentation contributions.
- **Tutorials:** Do you have a few tips and tricks you want to share with other WordPress users? Take them to your blog! What better way to contribute to WordPress than sharing your knowledge with the rest of the world? Write up your how-to tutorial, publish it on your website, and then promote your tutorial on Twitter and Facebook.
- **Support forums:** Volunteer your time and knowledge on the WordPress support forums at `https://wordpress.org/support/forums`. The involvement of the WordPress users who donate their time and talents in the support forums is an essential part of the WordPress experience.
- **Presentations:** In the next section, I discuss live WordPress events where users meet face to face and virtually. Consider offering to speak at one of those events to share your knowledge and experience with other users — or hosting one in your area.

- **Video/live-streaming:** If you're comfortable in front of a camera, consider creating video tutorials or live-streams on WordPress. A picture is worth a thousand words, and since most videos have several pictures per second . . . well, you do the math!

Participating in Live and Virtual WordPress Events

You can not only find out about WordPress and contribute to the project online via the Internet, but also get involved in WordPress offline. Live WordPress events, called WordPress Meetups and WordCamps, are where users and fans get together in personal or virtually to discuss, learn, and share information about their favorite platform. The two events are somewhat different:

- **WordPress Meetups:** Generally, these events involve small groups of people from the same geographical location. Recently, some meetups have transitioned to an online format, so anyone can join from anywhere in the world. Typically, these speakers, organizers, and attendees enjoy gathering on a monthly or bimonthly basis.

  You can find a WordPress Meetup near your community by visiting the Meetup website at `https://www.meetup.com/topics/wordpress/`, or by performing a search, using the keyword *WordPress* and your city or zip code.

- **WordCamps:** These annual events are usually much larger than Meetups and are attended by people from all over the country. WordCamps are hosted in almost every major city in the United States and abroad. Usually, WordCamps cost a small amount to attend, and speakers at WordCamps are well-known personalities from the WordPress community.

  Some WordCamps recently have gone to a "virtual format," allowing people to attend from the comfort of their own living rooms. The event details usually have information about a "virtual ticket" that can be purchased to access the content live and after the WordCamp.

  You can find a WordCamp event close to you by visiting the WordCamp Central website at `https://central.wordcamp.org` and browsing the upcoming WordCamps.

TIP

If there isn't a Meetup or WordCamp scheduled in your area, consider getting involved and organizing one! You can find some great tips and information about organizing WordCamps at `https://central.wordcamp.org`.

IN THIS CHAPTER

- **Getting hosted with `WordPress.com`**
- **Self-hosting with `WordPress.org`**
- **Running a network of blogs with the Multisite feature**
- **Exploring enterprise options and VIP services**

Chapter 5
Discovering Different Versions of WordPress

Website publishers have a wealth of software platforms to choose from. You want to be sure that the platform you choose has all the options you're looking for. WordPress is unique in that it offers two versions of its software. Each version is designed to meet the various needs of publishers.

One version is a hosted platform available at `WordPress.com` that meets your needs if you don't want to worry about installing or dealing with software; the other is the self-hosted version of the WordPress software available at `https://wordpress.org`, which offers you a bit more freedom and flexibility, as described throughout this chapter.

This chapter introduces you to both versions of the WordPress platform so you can choose which version suits your particular needs the best.

Comparing the Two Versions of WordPress

The two versions of WordPress are

- The hosted version at `WordPress.com`
- The self-installed and self-hosted version available at `WordPress.org`

Certain features are available to you in every WordPress site setup, whether you're using the self-hosted software from `WordPress.org` or the hosted version at `WordPress.com`. These features include (but aren't limited to):

- Quick, easy installation and setup
- Full-featured publishing capability, letting you publish content to the web through an easy-to-use web-based interface
- Topical archiving of your posts, using categories
- Monthly archiving of your posts, with the capability to provide a listing of those archives for easy navigation through your site
- Comment and trackback tools
- Automatic spam protection through Akismet
- Built-in gallery integration for photos and images
- Media Manager for managing video and audio files
- Great community support
- Unlimited number of static pages, letting you step out of the blog box and into the sphere of running a fully functional website
- RSS capability with RSS 2.0, RSS 1.0, and Atom support
- Tools for importing content from different content management systems (such as Blogger and Movable Type)

Table 5-1 compares the two WordPress versions.

Choosing the hosted version from `WordPress.com`

`WordPress.com` (see Figure 5-1) is a free service. If downloading, installing, and using software on a web server sound like Greek to you and are chores you'd rather avoid, the WordPress folks provide a solution for you at `WordPress.com`.

TABLE 5-1 **Exploring the Differences between the Two Versions of WordPress**

Feature	WordPress.org	WordPress.com
Cost	Free	Free
Software download required	Yes	No
Software installation required	Yes	No
Web hosting required	Yes	No
Custom CSS control	Yes	Available in the Premium or Business plan starting at $96/year
Template access	Yes	No
Block editor	Yes	Yes
RSS syndication	Yes	Yes
Access to core code	Yes	No
Ability to install plugins	Yes	Available in the Business plan starting at $300/year
WP themes installation	Yes	Available in the Business plan starting at $300/year
Multiauthor support	Yes	Yes
eCommerce Store	Yes	Available in the Commerce plan starting at $540/year
Unlimited number of site setups with one account (multisite)	Yes*	Yes
Community-based support forums	Yes	Yes

** Only with the Multisite feature enabled*

`WordPress.com` is a *hosted solution*, which means that it has no software requirement, no downloads, and no installation or server configurations. Everything's done for you on the back end, behind the scenes. You don't even have to worry about how the process happens; it happens quickly, and before you know it, you're making your first blog post.

`WordPress.com` offers several upgrades (see Figure 5-2) to help make your publishing life easier. Here's a list of package upgrades you can purchase to enhance your `WordPress.com` account, with prices reflecting the annual cost:

- **Personal:** This plan allows you to add your own domain name to your `WordPress.com` account; see Book 2, Chapter 1. This service also provides you email and live chat support, basic design, and 6GB of storage space. For the additional fee, your site also becomes ad-free. (With the free plan, `WordPress.com` advertisements are part of your experience.) This plan costs $4 per month, billed annually at $48 per year.

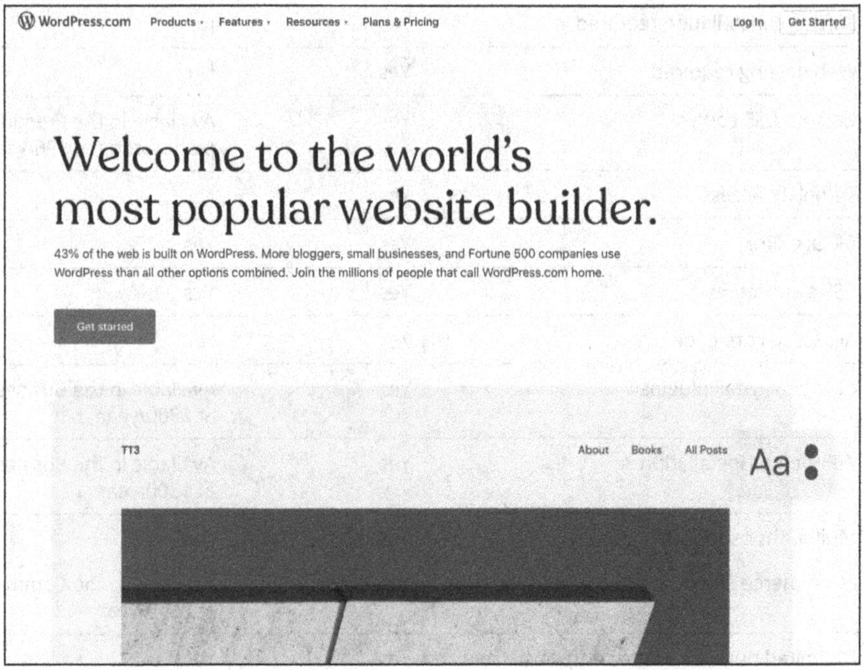

FIGURE 5-1: The `WordPress.com` website.

- **Premium:** This plan provides you everything included in the Personal plan and also includes access to premium themes, full control of the CSS for style customizations, increased storage space at 13GB, the ability to monetize your site, and VideoPress support. This plan costs $8 per month, billed annually at $96 per year.

TIP

The VideoPress service is described in the "Discovering WordPress VIP Services" section at the end of this chapter.

- **Business:** This plan provides you everything included in both the Personal and Premium plans. In addition, you have access to 50GB of storage, unrestricted bandwidth, plugin and theme installations, automated updates, Google Analytics integration, and the removal of all `WordPress.com` branding — all for the cost of $25 per month, billed annually at $300 per year.

- **Commerce:** This plan allows you to create a robust online storefront, and offers several features that enhance the e-commerce experience on WordPress. This includes several store themes, product and inventory management tools, payment options (fee-free), and a few marketing features to help you promote your store. This package costs $45 per month, billed annually at $540.

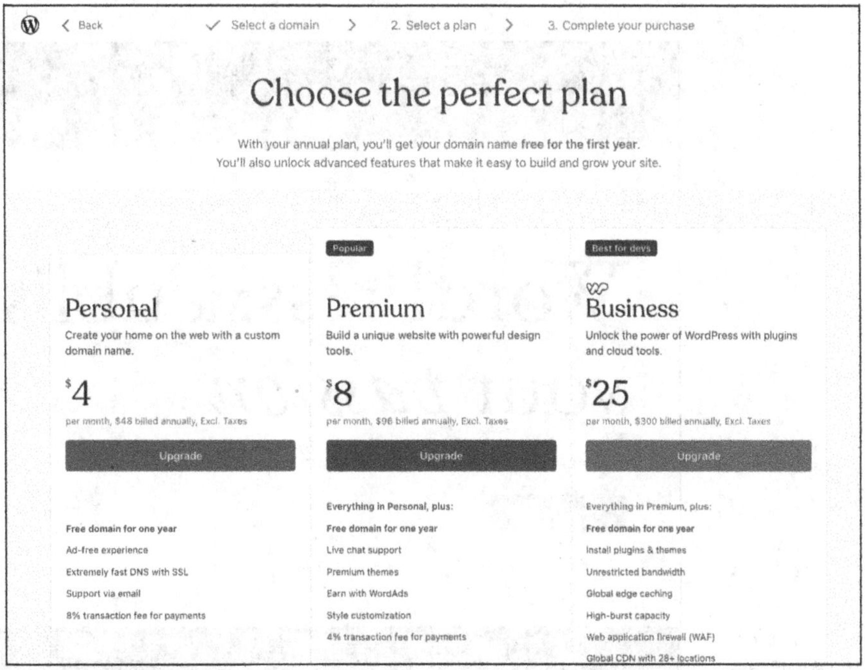

FIGURE 5-2: Several paid upgrades available on the `WordPress.com` free service.

TIP

`WordPress.com` has some limitations. You can't install plugins or custom themes, for example, unless you have the business plan. Neither can you can customize the base-code files, sell advertising, or monetize your site without upgrading to a paid plan. But even with its limitations, `WordPress.com` is an excellent starting point if you're brand-new to Internet publishing and a little intimidated by the configuration requirements of the self-installed `WordPress.org` software.

The good news is that if you outgrow your `WordPress.com`-hosted site and want to move to the self-hosted `WordPress.org` software, you can. You can even take all the content from your `WordPress.com`-hosted site with you and easily import it into your new setup with the `WordPress.org` software. (In Book 2, Chapter 6, I cover the steps you need to take to move a `WordPress.com` website to a self-hosted one using the `WordPress.org` software.)

In the grand scheme of things, your options aren't really that limited.

Self-hosting with WordPress.org

The self-installed version from WordPress.org is the primary focus of *WordPress All-in-One For Dummies.* Using WordPress.org requires you to download the software from the WordPress website at https://wordpress.org (shown in Figure 5-3); then you need to install it on a server from which your website operates.

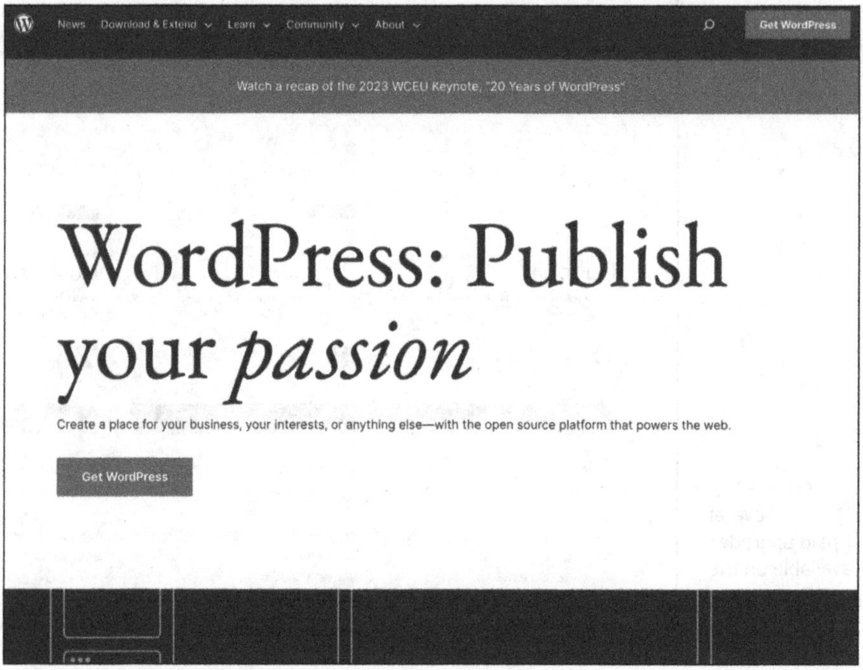

FIGURE 5-3: The WordPress.org website.

The WordPress.org website is an excellent repository of tools and resources for you throughout the lifespan of your WordPress-powered website, so be sure to bookmark it for future reference! Here's a list of helpful things that you can find on the website:

- **Plugins (https://wordpress.org/plugins):** The WordPress Plugins page houses a full directory of plugins available for WordPress. You can search for and find the plugins you need for search engine optimization (SEO) enhancement, comment management, and social media integration, among many others.
- **Themes (https://wordpress.org/themes):** The theme directory page, shown in Figure 5-4, is a repository of WordPress themes that are free for the taking. In this section of the WordPress.org website, you can browse more than 11,000 themes to use on your site to dress up your content.

- **Codex (`https://codex.wordpress.org`):** Almost every piece of software released comes with documentation and user manuals. The Support section of the `WordPress.org` website contains the WordPress Codex, which tries to help you answer questions about the use of WordPress and its various features and functions.
- **Forums (`https://wordpress.org/support/forums`):** The support forums at `WordPress.org` involve WordPress users from all over with one goal: finding out how to use WordPress to suit their particular needs. The support forums are very much a community of users (from beginners to experts) helping other users, and you can generally obtain a solution to your WordPress needs here from other users of the software.
- **Roadmap (`https://wordpress.org/about/roadmap`):** This section of the `WordPress.org` website doesn't contain support information or tools that you can download; it offers an at-a-glance peek at what's new and upcoming for WordPress. The Roadmap page gives you a pretty accurate idea of when WordPress will release the next version of its software; see Book 1, Chapter 3 for information about versions and release cycles.

TIP

Click the version number to visit the WordPress Trac and see what features developers are working on and adding.

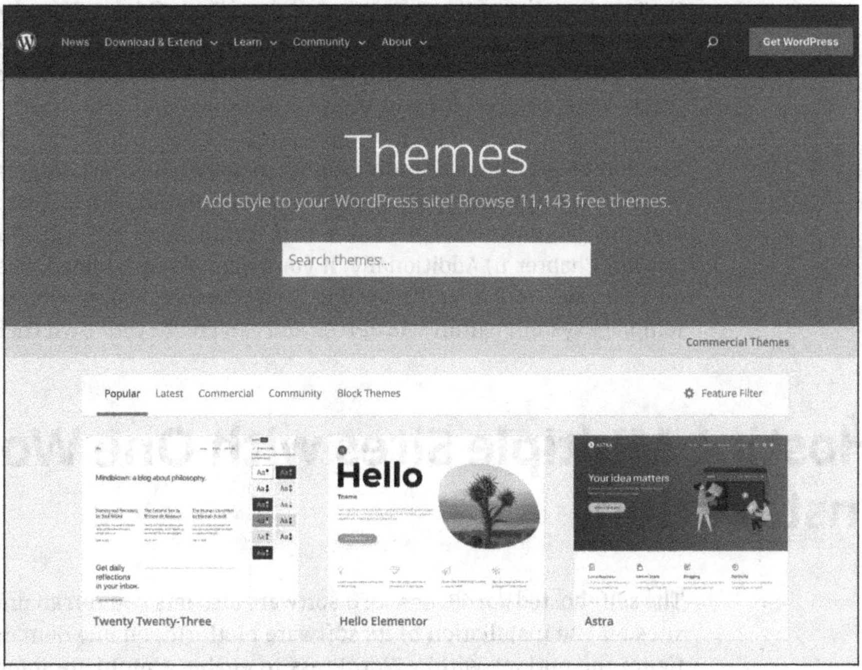

FIGURE 5-4: Theme directory page on `WordPress.org`.

WordPress.org is the self-installed, self-hosted software version of WordPress that you install on a web server you've set up on a domain that you've registered. Unless you own your own web server, you need to lease one. Leasing space on a web server is *web hosting,* and unless you know someone who knows someone, hosting generally isn't free.

That said, web hosting doesn't cost a whole lot, either. You can usually obtain a good, basic web hosting service for anywhere from $10 to $15 per month. (Book 2, chapters 1 and 2 give you some great information on web hosting accounts and tools.) You need to make sure, however, that any web host you choose to work with has the required software installed on the web server. The recommended minimum software requirements (which you can view at `https://wordpress.org/about/requirements`) for WordPress include

- PHP version 7.4 or later
- MySQL version 5.7 or later *or* MariaDB version 10.4 or later
- HTTPS support

After you have WordPress installed on your web server (see the installation instructions in Book 2, Chapter 3), you can start using it to publish to your heart's content. With the WordPress software, you can install several plugins that extend the functionality of the software, as I describe in Book 7. You also have full control of the core files and code that WordPress is built on. If you have a knack for PHP and knowledge of MySQL, you can work within the code to make changes that you think would be good for you and your website.

You don't need design or coding ability to make your site look great. Members of the WordPress community have created more than 1,600 WordPress themes (designs), and you can download them free and install them on your WordPress site. (See Book 6, Chapter 1.) Additionally, if you're creatively inclined, like to create designs on your own, and know Cascading Style Sheets (CSS), you have full access to the template system within WordPress and can create your own custom themes.

Hosting Multiple Sites with One WordPress Installation

The self-hosted WordPress.org software also lets you run an unlimited number of sites on one installation of its software platform, on one domain. When you configure the options within WordPress to enable a multisite interface, you become administrator of a network of sites. All the options remain the same, but with the multisite options configured, you can add more sites and domains, as well as allow registered users of your website to host their own sites within your network. For more information about the Multisite feature in WordPress, see Book 8.

The following types of sites use the Network options within WordPress:

- **Site networks,** which can have hundreds of sites. Boise State University uses WordPress to power hundreds of sites for their degrees and certifications at its website: `https://www.boisestate.edu/`.
- **Newspapers and magazines,** such as *The New York Times,* and universities, such as Harvard Law School, use WordPress to manage the blog sections of their websites.
- **Niche-specific blog networks,** such as `Edublogs.org`, use WordPress to manage their full networks of free sites for teachers, educators, lecturers, librarians, and other education professionals.

TIP

Extensive information on running a network of sites by using the Multisite feature in WordPress is available in Book 8. The chapters there take you through everything: setup, maintenance, and the process of running a network of sites with one WordPress installation.

With the Multisite features enabled, users of your network can run their own sites within your installation of WordPress. They also have access to their own Dashboards with the same options and features you read about in Book 3. Heck, it probably would be a great idea to buy a copy of this book for every member of your network so everyone can become familiar with the WordPress Dashboard and features, too. At least have a copy on hand so people can borrow yours!

If you plan to run a few of your own sites with the WordPress Multisite feature, your current hosting situation is probably well suited to this purpose. (See Book 2, Chapter 1 for information on web hosting services.) If you plan to host a large network with hundreds of sites and multiple users, however, you should consider contacting your host and increasing your bandwidth and the disk space limitations on your account.

The best example of a large site network with hundreds of blogs and users (actually, more like millions) is the hosted service at `WordPress.com`, which I discuss earlier in this chapter. At `WordPress.com`, people are invited to sign up for an account and start a site by using the Multisite feature within the WordPress platform on the WordPress server. When you enable this feature on your own domain and enable the user registration feature, you invite users to:

- » Create an account.
- » Create a site on your WordPress installation (on your domain).
- » Create content by publishing posts and pages.
- » Upload media files, such as photos, audio, and video.
- » Invite their friends to view their blogs or sign up for their own accounts.

WARNING

In addition to the necessary security measures, time, and administrative tasks that go into running a community of sites, you have a few things to worry about. Creating a community increases the resource use, bandwidth, and disk space on your web server. In many cases, if you go over the allotted limits given to you by your web host, you incur great cost. Make sure that you anticipate your bandwidth and disk-space needs before running a large network on your website! (Don't say you weren't warned.)

REMEMBER

Many WordPress network communities start with grand dreams of being large and active. Be realistic about how your community will operate to make the right hosting choice for yourself and your community.

Small Internet communities are handled easily with a shared-server solution; larger, more active communities should consider a dedicated-server solution for operation. The difference between the two lies in their names:

- » **Shared server:** You have one account on one server that has several other accounts on it. Think of this as apartment living. One building has several apartments under one roof.
- » **Dedicated server:** You have one account on one server. The server is dedicated to your account, and your account is dedicated to the server. Think of this as owning a home where you don't share your living space with anyone else.

A dedicated-server solution is a more expensive investment for your community; a shared-server solution is more economical. Base your decision on how big and how active you estimate that your community will be. You can move from a shared-server solution to a dedicated-server solution if your community becomes larger than you expect, but starting with the right solution for your community from day one is best. For more information on hosting WordPress, see Book 2, Chapter 1.

Discovering WordPress VIP Services

The company behind the Automattic `WordPress.com` service is owned and operated by the WordPress cofounder, Matt Mullenweg. Although Automattic doesn't own the `WordPress.org` software, Automattic is a driving force behind all things WordPress.

REMEMBER

As an open-source platform, `WordPress.org` is owned by the community and hundreds of developers that contribute to the core code.

Have a look at the Automattic website at `https://automattic.com` (shown in Figure 5-5). The folks behind WordPress own and operate several properties and services that can extend the features of your WordPress site, including:

- **`WordPress.com` (`https://wordpress.com`):** A hosted WordPress blogging service, discussed previously in this chapter.
- **Jetpack (`https://jetpack.com`):** A suite of plugins that can be installed on a `WordPress.org` self-hosted site.
- **JetPack VaultPress Backup (`https://vaultpress.com`):** Premium backup and restoration service for your blog.
- **Akismet (`https://akismet.com`):** Spam protection for your blog. This service comes with every `WordPress.org` installation, but there are different levels of service, as discussed in Book 3, Chapter 4.
- **Crowdsignal (`https://crowdsignal.com`):** A polling and survey software that easily plugs into the WordPress platform.
- **VideoPress (`https://videopress.com`):** Video hosting and sharing application for WordPress.
- **Gravatar (`https://gravatar.com`):** Photos or graphical icons for comment authors (discussed in Book 3, Chapter 2).
- **Longreads (`https://longreads.com`):** Great examples of storytelling on the Internet.
- **Simplenote (`https://simplenote.com`):** An easy way to keep notes across various iOS, Android, Mac, and Windows devices.
- **`WordPress.com` VIP (`https://wpvip.com`):** Enterprise-level web hosting and WordPress support starting at $15,000 per year (usually reserved for heavy-hitters such as CNN, BBC, and *Time* magazine, for example).
- **Cloudup (`https://cloudup.com`):** Easy sharing of media, including videos, music, photos, and documents.

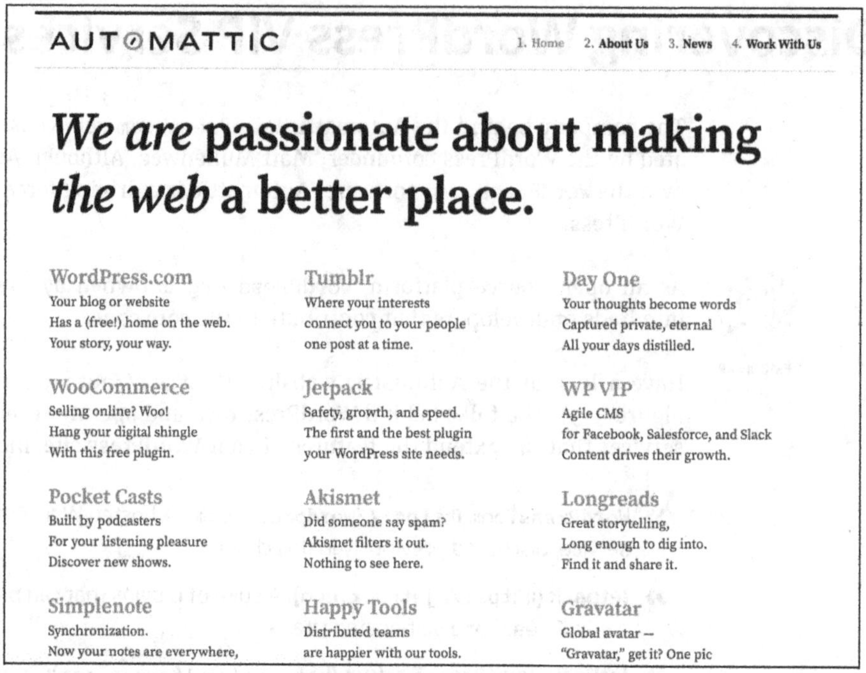
AUTOMATTIC
1. Home 2. About Us 3. News 4. Work With Us
We are passionate about making the web a better place.
WordPress.com
Your blog or website Has a (free!) home on the web. Your story, your way.
Tumblr
Where your interests connect you to your people one post at a time.
Day One
Your thoughts become words Captured private, eternal All your days distilled.
WooCommerce
Selling online? Woo! Hang your digital shingle With this free plugin.
Jetpack
Safety, growth, and speed. The first and the best plugin your WordPress site needs.
WP VIP
Agile CMS for Facebook, Salesforce, and Slack Content drives their growth.
Pocket Casts
Built by podcasters For your listening pleasure Discover new shows.
Akismet
Did someone say spam? Akismet filters it out. Nothing to see here.
Longreads
Great storytelling, Long enough to dig into. Find it and share it.
Simplenote
Synchronization. Now your notes are everywhere,
Happy Tools
Distributed teams are happier with our tools.
Gravatar
Global avatar — "Gravatar," get it? One pic

FIGURE 5-5: The Automattic website.

2 Setting Up the WordPress Software

Contents at a Glance

IN THIS CHAPTER

» Registering a domain name

» Exploring web hosting environments

» Knowing the basic requirements for PHP and MySQL

» Getting web hosting recommendations for WordPress

» Understanding bandwidth and disk space needs

Chapter 1
Understanding the System Requirements

Before you can start creating content with WordPress, you have to set up your foundation. Doing so involves more than simply downloading and installing the WordPress software. You also need to establish your *domain* (your website address) and your *web hosting service* (the place that houses your website). Although you initially download your WordPress software onto your hard drive, you install it on a web hosting server.

Obtaining a web server and installing software on it are things you may already have done on your site, in which case you can move on to the next chapter. If you haven't installed WordPress, you must first consider many factors, as well as cope with a learning curve, because setting up your website through a hosting service involves using some technologies that you may not feel comfortable with. This chapter takes you through the basics of those technologies, and by the last page of this chapter, you'll have WordPress successfully installed on a web server with your own domain name.

Establishing Your Domain

You've read all the hype. You've heard all the rumors. You've seen the flashy websites powered by WordPress. But where do you start?

The first steps in installing and setting up a WordPress site are deciding on a domain name and then purchasing the registration of that name through a domain registrar. A *domain name* is the *unique* web address that you type in a web browser's address bar to visit a website. Some examples of domain names are `WordPress.org` and `Google.com`.

REMEMBER

I emphasize *unique*, because no two domain names can be the same. If someone else has registered the domain name you want, you can't have it. With that in mind, it sometimes takes a bit of time to find a domain that isn't already in use.

Understanding domain name extensions

When registering a domain name, be aware of the *extension* that you want. The `.com`, `.net`, `.org`, `.info`, or `.biz` extension that you see tagged onto the end of any domain name is the *top-level domain extension*. When you register your domain name, you're asked to choose the extension you want for your domain (as long as it's available, that is).

A word to the wise here: Just because you registered your domain as a `.com` doesn't mean that someone else doesn't, or can't, own the very same domain name with a `.net`. Therefore, if you register `MyDogHasFleas.com`, and the site becomes hugely popular among readers with dogs that have fleas, someone else can come along, register `MyDogHasFleas.net`, and run a similar site to yours in the hope of riding the coattails of your website's popularity and readership.

DOMAIN NAMES: DO YOU OWN OR RENT?

When you "buy" a domain name, you don't really own it. Rather, you're purchasing the right to use that domain name for the time specified in your order. You can register a domain name for one year or up to ten years. Be aware, however, that if you don't renew the domain name when your registration period ends, you lose it — and most often, you lose it right away to someone who preys on abandoned or expired domain names. Some people keep a close watch on expiring domain names, and as soon as the buying window opens, they snap the names up and start using them for their own websites, in the hope of taking full advantage of the popularity that the previous owners worked so hard to attain for those domains.

If you want to avert this problem, you can register your domain name with all available extensions. My business website, for example, has the domain name `webdevstudios.com`, but we also own `webdvstudios.net` just in case someone else out there has the same combination of names.

Considering the cost of a domain name

Registering a domain costs you anywhere from $5 to $300 per year or more, depending on what service you use for a registrar and what options (such as storage space, bandwidth, privacy options, search engine submission services, and so on) you apply to your domain name during the registration process.

REMEMBER

When you pay the domain registration fee today, you need to pay another registration fee when the renewal date comes up again in a year, or two, or five — however many years you chose to register your domain name for. (See the nearby "Domain names: Do you own or rent?" sidebar.) Most registrars give you the option of signing up for a service called Auto Renew to automatically renew your domain name and bill the charges to the credit card you set up on that account. The registrar sends you a reminder a few months in advance, telling you that it's time to renew. If you don't have Auto Renew set up, you need to log in to your registrar account before it expires and manually renew your domain name.

TIP

When choosing a domain name for your website, you may find that the domain name you want isn't available. You know if it's available when you search for it at the domain registrar's website (listed in the next section). Have some backup domain names prepared just in case the one you want isn't available. For example, if your chosen domain name is `cutepuppies.com`, but it's not available, you could have some variations of the domain ready to use, such as `cute-puppies.com` (notice the dash), `mycutepuppies.com`, `reallycutepuppies.com`, or go with a `.net` domain like `cutepuppies.net`.

Registering your domain name

Domain registrars are certified and approved by the Internet Corporation for Assigned Names and Numbers (ICANN). Although hundreds of domain registrars exist, the ones in the following list are popular because of their longevity in the industry, competitive pricing, and variety of services they offer in addition to domain name registration (such as web hosting and website traffic builders):

- **GoDaddy:** `https://www.godaddy.com`
- **Register.com:** `https://www.register.com`

- **Network Solutions:** `https://www.networksolutions.com`
- **Namecheap:** `https://www.namecheap.com`

No matter where you choose to register your domain name, here are the steps you can take to accomplish this task:

1. **Decide on a domain name.**

   A little planning and forethought are necessary here. Many people think of a domain name as a *brand* — a way of identifying their websites or blogs. Think of potential names for your site and then proceed with your plan.

2. **Verify the domain name's availability.**

   In your web browser, enter the URL of the domain registrar of your choice. Look for the section on the registrar's website that lets you enter the domain name (typically, a short text field) to see whether it's available. If the domain name isn't available as a `.com`, try `.net` or `.info`.

3. **Purchase the domain name.**

   Follow the domain registrar's steps to purchase the name, using your credit card. After you complete the checkout process, you receive an email confirming your purchase, so be sure to use a valid email address during the registration process.

The next step is obtaining a hosting account, which the next section covers.

REMEMBER

Some of the domain registrars have hosting services that you can sign up for, but you don't have to use those services. Often, you can find hosting services for a lower cost than most domain registrars offer. It just takes a little research.

Finding a Home for Your Site

After you register your domain, you need to find a place for it to live: a web host. Web hosting is the second piece of the puzzle that you need to complete before you begin working with `WordPress.org`.

A *web host* is a business, group, or person that provides web server space and bandwidth for file transfer to website owners who don't have it. Usually, web hosting services charge a monthly or an annual fee — unless you're fortunate enough to know someone who's willing to give you server space and bandwidth free. The cost varies from host to host, but you can usually obtain quality web hosting services for $10 to $50 per month to start.

REMEMBER

When discussing web hosting considerations, it's important to understand where your hosting account ends and WordPress begins. Support for the WordPress software may or may not be included in your hosting package.

Some web hosts consider WordPress to be a *third-party application*. This means that the host typically won't provide technical support on the use of WordPress (or any other software application) because software support generally isn't included in your hosting package. The web host supports your hosting account but typically doesn't support the software you choose to install.

On the other hand, if your web host supports the software on your account, it comes at a cost: You have to pay for that extra support. To find whether your chosen host supports WordPress, ask first. If your host doesn't offer software support, you can still find WordPress support in the support forums at `https://wordpress.org/support/view/all-topics/`, as shown in Figure 1-1.

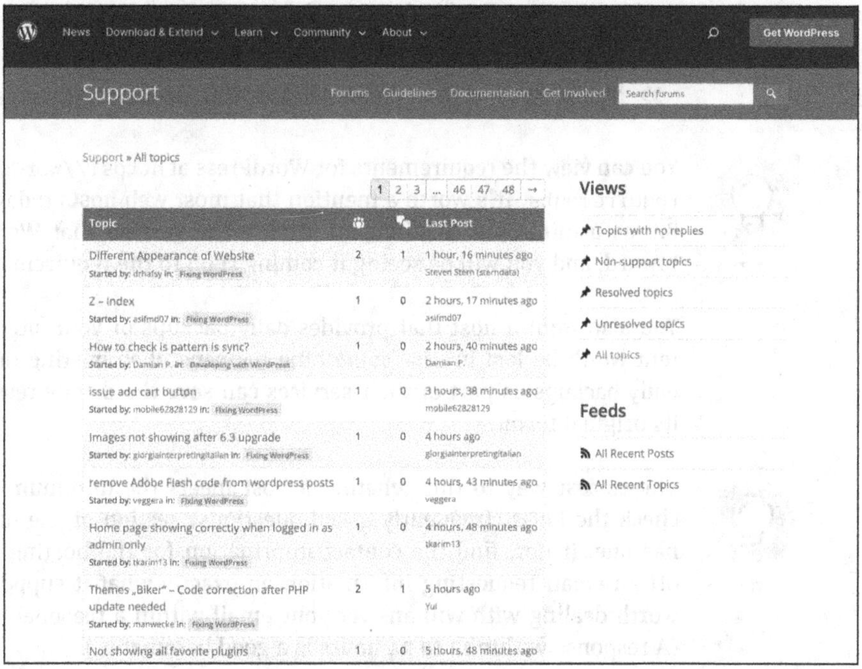

FIGURE 1-1: The WordPress support forums.

TIP

Several web hosting providers also have WordPress-related services available for additional fees. These services can include technical support, plugin installation and configuration, and theme design.

Generally, hosting services provide (at least) these services with your account:

- Hard drive space
- Bandwidth (transfer)
- Domain email with web mail access
- Secure File Transfer Protocol (SFTP) access
- Comprehensive website statistics
- MySQL database(s)
- PHP

Because you intend to run WordPress on your web server, you need to look for a host that provides the *minimum* requirements needed to run the software on your hosting account, which are

- PHP version 7.4 (or greater)
- MySQL version 5.7 (or greater) *or* MariaDB version 10.4 (or greater)

TIP

You can view the requirements for WordPress at `https://wordpress.org/about/requirements`. It's worth a mention that most web hosts today recommend PHP 8.0 as a minimum requirement. That's the version that WordPress is moving toward, and you will be seeing it coming soon to the requirements page.

You also want a host that provides daily backups of your site so that your content won't be lost in case something happens. Web hosting providers that offer daily backups as part of their services can save the day by restoring your site to its original form.

TIP

The easiest way to find whether a host meets the minimum requirement is to check the FAQs (frequently asked questions) section of the host's website, if it has one. If not, find the contact information for the hosting company and fire off an email requesting information on exactly what it supports. Any web host worth dealing with will answer your email within a reasonable amount of time. (A response within 12 to 24 hours is a good barometer.)

TIP

If the technojargon confuses you — specifically, all that talk about PHP, MySQL, and SFTP in this section — don't worry! Book 2, Chapter 2 gives you an in-depth look at what SFTP is and how you use it on your web server; Book 2, Chapter 3 introduces you to the basics of PHP and MySQL. Become comfortable with these topics, because they're important when using WordPress.

Getting help with hosting WordPress

The popularity of WordPress has given birth to web services — including designers, consultants, and (yes) web hosts — that specialize in using WordPress.

Many web hosts offer a full array of WordPress features, such as an automatic WordPress installation included with your account, a library of WordPress themes, and a staff of support technicians who are very experienced in using WordPress.

Here are a few of those providers:

- **Pagely:** `https://pagely.com`
- **WP Engine:** `https://wpengine.com` (shown in Figure 1-2)
- **Pantheon:** `https://pantheon.io`

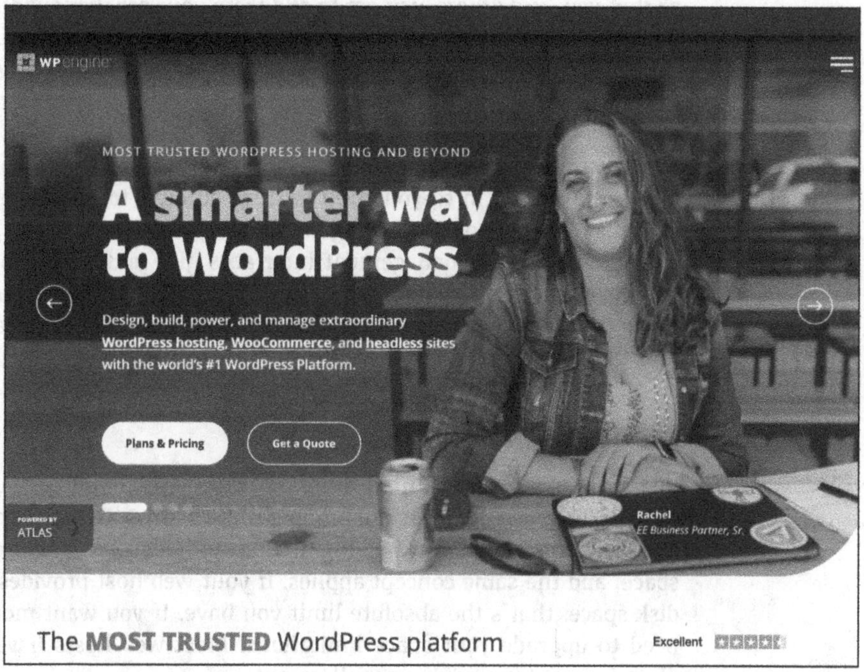

FIGURE 1-2: The WP Engine WordPress hosting provider.

WARNING

A few web hosting providers offer free domain name registration when you sign up for hosting services. Research this topic and read the terms of service, because that free domain name may come with conditions. Many clients have gone this route only to find out a few months later that the web hosting provider has full control of the domain name and the client can't move that domain off the host's servers, either for a set period (usually, a year or two) or for infinity. You need control in *your* hands, not someone else's, so stick with an independent domain registrar, such as Network Solutions.

Dealing with disk space and bandwidth

Web hosting services provide two very important things with your account:

- **Disk space:** The amount of space you can access on the web servers' hard drive, generally measured in megabytes (MB) or gigabytes (GB).
- **Bandwidth transfer:** The amount of transfer your site can do per month. Typically, traffic is measured in gigabytes.

Think of your web host as a garage that you rent to park your car in. The garage gives you the place to store your car (disk space). It even gives you the driveway so that you, and others, can get to and from your car (bandwidth). It won't, however, fix the rockin' stereo system (WordPress or any other third-party software application) that you've installed — unless you're willing to pay a few extra bucks for that service.

TIP

Most web hosting providers give you access to a hosting account manager that allows you to log in to your web hosting account to manage services. cPanel is perhaps the most popular management interface, but Plesk and NetAdmin are still widely used. These management interfaces give you access to your server logs, where you can view such things as bandwidth and hard disk use. Get into the habit of checking those things occasionally to make sure that you stay informed about how much storage and bandwidth your site is using. Typically, I check monthly.

Managing disk space

Disk space is simply the hard drive on your own computer. Each hard drive has *capacity*, or space, for a certain number of files. An 80GB hard drive can hold 80GB of data — no more. Your hosting account provides you a limited amount of disk space, and the same concept applies. If your web host provides you with 10GB of disk space, that's the absolute limit you have. If you want more disk space, you need to upgrade your space limitations. Most web hosts have a mechanism in place for you to upgrade your allotment.

Starting with a self-hosted WordPress website doesn't take much disk space at all. A good starting point for disk space is 20GB to 50GB. If you find that you need additional space, contact your hosting provider for an upgrade.

Choosing the size of your bandwidth pipe

Bandwidth refers to the amount of data that's carried from point A to point B within a specific period (usually, only a second or two). I live out in the country — pretty much in the middle of nowhere. The water that comes to my house is provided by a private well that lies buried in the backyard somewhere. Between my house and the well are pipes that bring the water to my house. The pipes provide a free flow of water to our home so that everyone else can enjoy long, hot showers while I labor over dishes and laundry, all at the same time. Lucky me!

The same concept applies to the bandwidth available with your hosting account. Every web hosting provider offers a variety of bandwidth limits on the accounts it offers. When I want to view your website in my browser window, the bandwidth is essentially the "pipe" that lets your data flow from your "well" to my computer. The bandwidth limit is similar to the pipe connected to my well: It can hold only a certain amount of water before it reaches maximum capacity and won't bring the water from the well any longer. Your bandwidth pipe size is determined by how much bandwidth your web host allows for your account. The larger the number, the bigger the pipe. A 50MB bandwidth limit makes for a smaller pipe than a 100MB limit, for example.

Web hosts are pretty generous with the amount of bandwidth they provide in their packages. Like disk space, bandwidth is measured in gigabytes. Bandwidth provision of 50GB to 100GB is generally a respectable amount to run a website and/or a blog.

WARNING

I've found that if your website exceeds its allowed bandwidth, the web host won't turn off your website or limit traffic. The host will continue to allow inbound web traffic to your site, but will bill you at the end of month for any bandwidth overages. Those charges can get pretty expensive, so if you find that your website is consistently exceeding the bandwidth amount every month, contact your web host to learn whether you can get an upgrade to allow for increased bandwidth.

REMEMBER

Websites that run large files — such as video, audio, or photo files — generally benefit from higher disk space compared with sites that don't involve large files. Keep this point in mind when you're signing up for your hosting account. Planning will save you a few headaches down the road.

Be wary of hosting providers that offer things like unlimited bandwidth, domains, and disk space. Those offers are great selling points, but what the providers don't tell you outright (you may have to look into the fine print of the agreement) is that although they may not put those kinds of limits on you, they will limit your site's CPU usage.

CPU (which stands for *central processing unit*) is the part of a computer (or web server, in this case) that handles all the data processing requests sent to your web servers whenever anyone visits your site. Although you may have unlimited bandwidth to handle a large amount of traffic, if a high spike in traffic increases your site's CPU use, your host will *throttle* — significantly slow down — your site because it limits the CPU use. The shutdown isn't permanent, though; it lasts maybe a few minutes to an hour. The host does this to kill any connections to your web server that are causing the spike in CPU use. Your host eventually turns your site back on — but the inconvenience happens regularly with many clients across various hosting environments.

TIP

When looking into different web hosting providers, ask about their policies on CPU use and what they do to manage a spike in processing. It's better to know about it up front than to find out about it after your site's been throttled.

IN THIS CHAPTER

» Discovering SFTP

» Understanding secure file transfer

» Exploring easy-to-use SFTP clients

» Making sense of SFTP terminology

» Editing files by using SFTP

» Changing file permissions

Chapter 2

Using Secure File Transfer Protocol

Throughout this book, you run into the term *SFTP*. SFTP (Secure File Transfer Protocol) is a network protocol used to copy files from one host to another over the Internet. With SFTP, you can perform various tasks, including uploading and downloading WordPress files, editing files, and changing permissions on files.

Read this chapter to familiarize yourself with SFTP; understand what it is and how to use it; and discover some free, easy-to-use SFTP clients and programs that make your life as a WordPress website owner much easier. If you run across sections in this book that ask you to perform certain tasks by using SFTP, you can refer to this chapter to refresh your memory on how to do it, if needed.

Understanding SFTP Concepts

This section introduces you to the basic elements of SFTP, which is a method of transferring files in a secure environment. SFTP provides an additional layer of security beyond what you get with regular FTP, as it uses SSH (Secure Shell) and encrypts sensitive information, data, and passwords. Encrypting the data ensures that anyone monitoring the network can't read the data freely — and, therefore, can't obtain information that should be secured, such as passwords and usernames.

TIP

I highly recommend using SFTP instead of FTP because SFTP provides a secure connection to your web host. If your web hosting provider doesn't provide SFTP connections for you, strongly consider switching to a hosting provider that does. Almost all hosting providers these days provide SFTP as the standard protocol for transferring files. In fact, if your hosting provider does not offer SFTP as an option, find a new host that does. Almost all web hosts offer SFTP; I would be surprised to find one that didn't.

The capability to use SFTP with your hosting account is a given for almost every web host on the market today. SFTP offers two ways of moving files from one place to another:

- **Uploading:** Transferring files from your local computer to your web server
- **Downloading:** Transferring files from your web server to your local computer

You can do several other things with SFTP, including the following, which I discuss later in this chapter:

- **View files.** After you log in via SFTP, you can see all the files that are located on your web server.
- **View date modified.** You can see the date when a file was last modified, which can be helpful when trying to troubleshoot problems.
- **View file size.** You can see the size of each file on your web server, which is helpful if you need to manage the disk space on your account.
- **Edit files.** Almost all SFTP clients allow you to open and edit files through the client interface, which is a convenient way to get the job done.
- **Change permissions.** You can control what type of read/write/execute permissions the files on your web server have. This feature is commonly referred to as *Chmod,* which is the command that you use to change the permissions. (You learn more about Chmod in the "Changing file permissions" section, later in this chapter.)

SFTP is a convenient utility that gives you access to the files located on your web server, which makes managing your WordPress website a bit easier.

Setting Up SFTP on Your Hosting Account

Many web hosts today offer SFTP as part of their hosting packages, so confirm that your hosting provider makes SFTP available to you for your account. In Book 2, Chapter 1, I mention the hosting account management interface called cPanel. It's cPanel, or your hosting account management interface, that allows you to set up an SFTP account for your website.

TIP

In this chapter, I use my account management interface at WP Engine (`https://wpengine.com`) as the example. If your hosting provider gives you a different interface to work with, the concepts are still the same, but you need to refer to your hosting provider for the specifics to adapt these directions to your specific environment.

In the WP Engine interface, the SFTP for your hosting account is set up automatically. Figure 2-1 shows the SFTP Users page, where you set up user accounts for SFTP access.

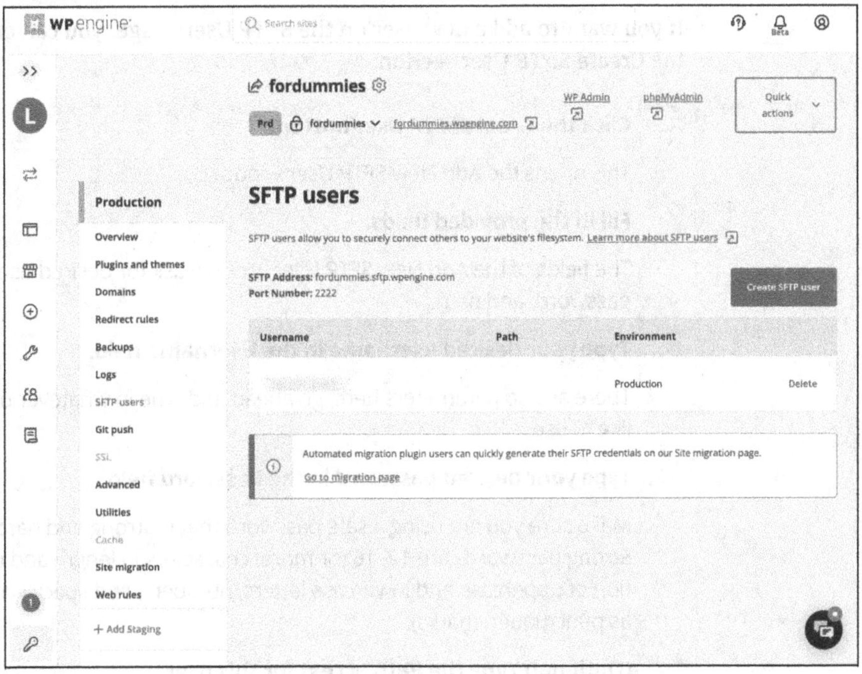

FIGURE 2-1: The SFTP Users page within the WP Engine account dashboard.

Follow these steps to get to this page and set up your SFTP account:

1. **Log in your account at WP Engine.**

   Typically, you browse to `http://my.wpengine.com` to bring up the login screen for your account. Enter your specific account username and password in the login fields, and click OK.

2. **Select the site on which you want to set up an SFTP account.**

   If you have multiple sites hosted on WP Engine, you need to select the site you want to work with by clicking it and accessing the settings for that site.

3. **Browse to the SFTP Users page.**

   Click the SFTP Users link in the left navigation menu to open the SFTP Users page (refer to Figure 2-1).

4. **View the existing SFTP account.**

   WP Engine automatically sets you up with an SFTP account, which you see listed on the SFTP Users page.

If you want to add a new user on the SFTP Users page, you can create one easily in the Create SFTP User section:

1. **Click the Create SFTP User button.**

   This opens the Add New SFTP User window.

2. **Fill in the provided fields.**

   The fields of the Add New SFTP User window ask for desired username, password, and path.

3. **Type your desired username in the Username field.**

   There are no parameters here, go ahead and type in whatever username you'd like to use.

4. **Type your desired password in the Password field.**

   Make sure you are using a safe password that is strong and hard to guess. Strong passwords are 12–16 (or more) characters in length and use a combination of uppercase and lowercase letters, numbers, and special characters (such as punctuation marks).

5. **(Optional) Type the Path access for this user.**

   Leaving this field blank gives this new user access to the root level of your hosting account — which, as the site owner, you want, so leave this field blank. In the future, if you set up accounts for other users, you can lock down their access to your hosting directory by indicating which directory the user has access to.

6. **Click the Add SFTP User button.**

   You see a new screen with a message that the SFTP User was added successfully. Additionally, you see the settings for this new user account; copy and paste them into a blank text editor window (such as Notepad for PC or TextEdit for Mac users). The settings for the user account are the details you need to connect to your web server via SFTP.

7. **Save the following settings.**

   Username, Password, and SFTP Server are specific to your domain and the information you entered in the preceding steps.

   - Username: *yourusername-sftpusername*
   - Password: *sftpuserpassword*
   - Host name: *yourdomain.com*
   - SFTP Server Port: 2222

TIP

Most of the time, the SFTP Server Port will be 22. But be sure to double-check your SFTP settings to make sure that this is the case, because some hosting providers have different port numbers for SFTP. WP Engine, used in this example, uses 2222 for the SFTP Server Port.

REMEMBER

At any time, you can revisit the User Accounts page to delete the user accounts you've created, change the quota, change the password, and find the connection details specific to that account.

Finding and Using Free and Easy SFTP Programs

SFTP programs are referred to as SFTP *clients* or SFTP *client software*. Whatever you call it, an SFTP client is software that you use to connect to your web server to view, open, edit, and transfer files to and from your web server.

Using SFTP to transfer files requires an SFTP client. Many SFTP clients are available for download. Here are some good (and free) ones:

- **SmartFTP (PC):** `https://www.smartftp.com/download`
- **FileZilla (PC or Mac):** `https://sourceforge.net/projects/filezilla`
- **Transmit (Mac):** `https://panic.com/transmit`
- **WinSCP (PC):** `https://winscp.net`

In Book 2, Chapter 1, you discover how to obtain a hosting account, and in the previous section of this chapter, you discover how to create an SFTP account on your web server. By following the steps in the previous section, you also have the SFTP username, password, server, and port information you need to connect your SFTP client to your web server so you can begin transferring files. In the next section, you discover how to connect to your web hosting account via SFTP.

Connecting to the web server via SFTP

For the purposes of this chapter, I use the FileZilla SFTP client (`https://sourceforge.net/projects/filezilla`) because it's easy to use and free.

Figure 2-2 shows a FileZilla client that's not connected to a server. By default, the left side of the window displays a directory of files and folders on the local computer.

The right side of the window displays content when the FileZilla client is connected to a web server; specifically, it shows directories of the web server's folders and files. (The right side is blank in Figure 2-2 because it is not yet connected to a web server.)

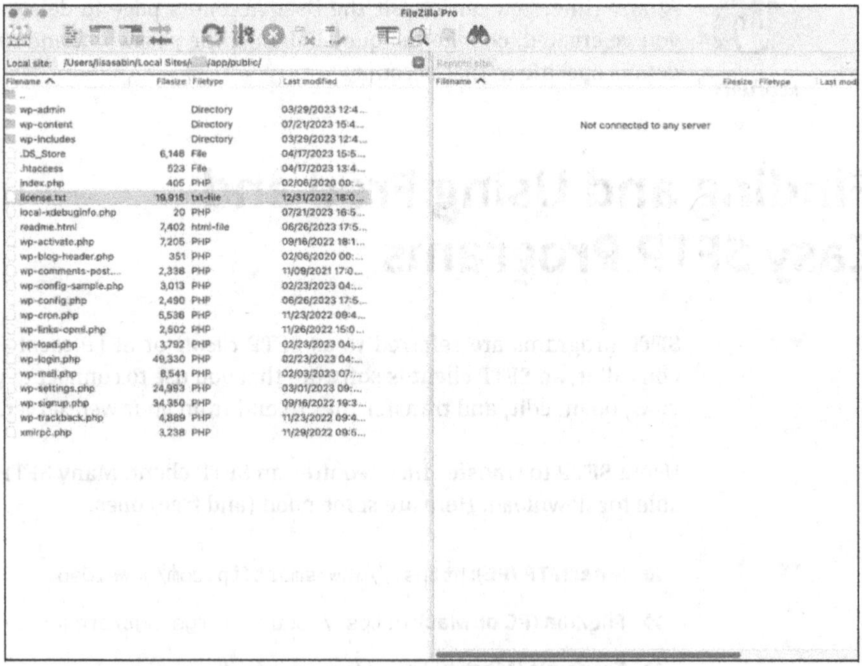

FIGURE 2-2: Mozilla FileZilla SFTP client software.

REMEMBER

If you use different SFTP client software from FileZilla, the steps and look of the software will differ. You need to adapt your steps and practice for the specific SFTP client software you're using.

Connecting to a web server is easy. The SFTP settings you saved from Step 7 in the "Setting Up SFTP on Your Hosting Account" section, earlier in this chapter, are also the same settings you see in the SFTP Users page if your SFTP was set up automatically for you:

- Username: *youraccount-sftpusername*
- Password: *sftpuser-password*
- Host name: *yourdomain.com*
- SFTP Server Port: 2222

This process is where you need that information. To connect to your web server via the FileZilla SFTP client, follow these few steps:

1. **Open the SFTP client software on your local computer.**

   Locate the program on your computer and click (or double-click) the program icon to launch the program.

2. **Choose File ⇨ Site Manager to open the Site Manager utility.**

   Site Manager appears, as shown in Figure 2-3.

3. **Click the New Site button.**

4. **Type a name for your site that helps you identify the site.**

   This site name can be anything you want it to be because it isn't part of the connection data you add in the next steps. (In Figure 2-4, you see ForDummies — which is the name I chose to name the site.)

5. **Select the Protocol.**

   FileZilla asks you to select a Protocol (as do most SFTP clients). Choose SFTP – SSH File Transfer Protocol from the Protocol drop-down menu, as shown in Figure 2-4.

6. **Enter the SFTP server in the Host field.**

   Host is the same as the SFTP server information provided to you when you set up the SFTP account on your web server. In the example, the SFTP server is `wordpress,sftp.wpengine.com`, so that's entered in the Host field, as shown in Figure 2-4.

7. **Enter the SFTP port in the Port field.**

   Typically, in most hosting environments, SFTP uses port 22, and this setting generally never changes. My host, on the other hand, uses port 2222 for SFTP. In case your host is like mine and uses a port other than 22, double-check your port number and enter it in the Port field, as shown in Figure 2-4.

8. **Select the logon type.**

   FileZilla gives you several logon types to choose from (as do most SFTP clients). Choose Normal from the Logon Type drop-down menu.

9. **Enter your username in the User field.**

   This username is given to you in the SFTP settings.

10. **Type your password in the Password field.**

    This password is given to you in the SFTP settings.

11. **Click the Connect button.**

    This step connects your computer to your web server. The directory of folders and files from your local computer displays on the left side of the FileZilla SFTP client window, and the directory of folders and files on your web server displays on the right side, as shown in Figure 2-5.

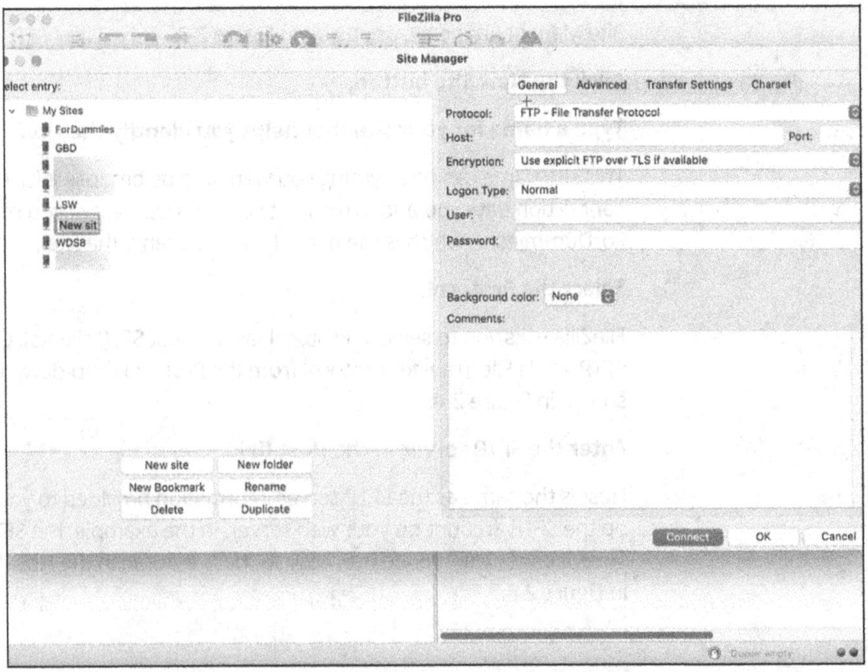

FIGURE 2-3: The Site Manager utility in the FileZilla SFTP client software.

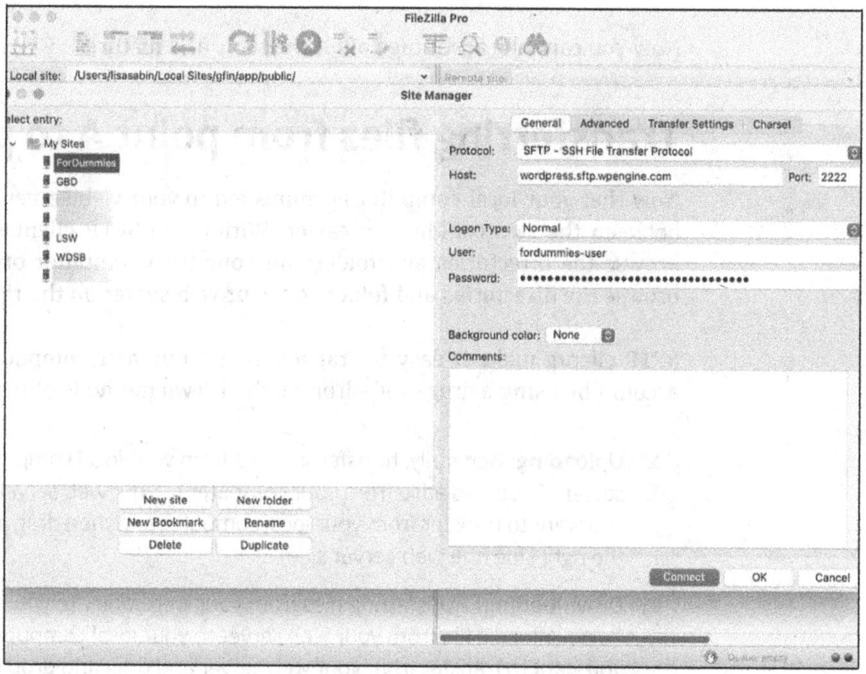

FIGURE 2-4: FileZilla Site Manager utility with SFTP account information filled in.

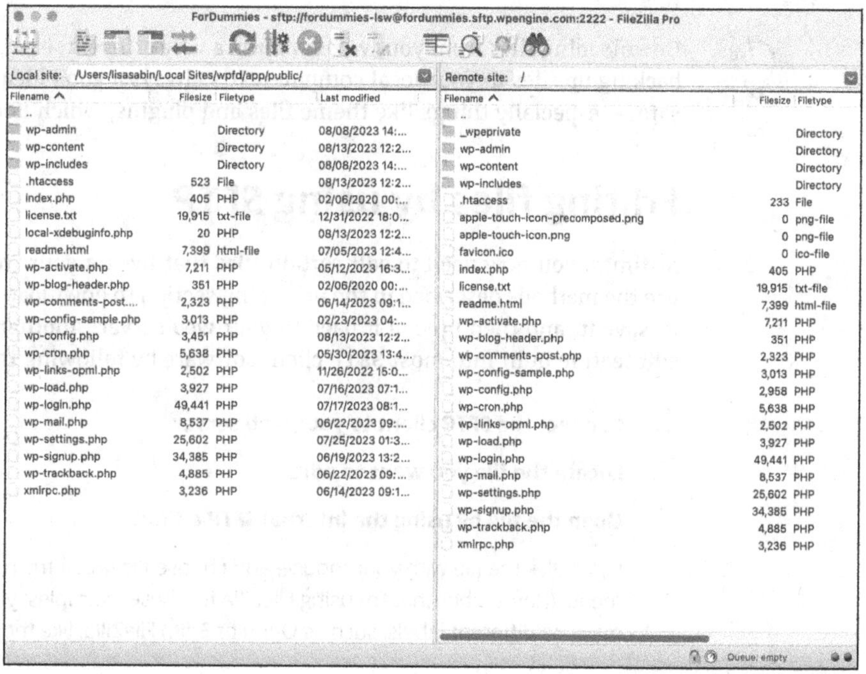

FIGURE 2-5: FileZilla displays local files on the left and server files on the right.

Now you can take advantage of all the tools and features SFTP has to offer you!

Transferring files from point A to point B

Now that your local computer is connected to your web server, transferring files between the two couldn't be easier. Within the SFTP client software, you can browse the directories and folders on your local computer on the left side and browse the directories and folders on your web server on the right side.

SFTP clients make it easy to transfer files from your computer to your hosting account by using a drag-and-drop method. Two methods of transferring files are

- **Uploading:** Generally, transferring files from your local computer to your web server. To upload a file from your computer to your web server, click the file you want to transfer from your local computer and then drag and drop it on the right side (the web-server side).
- **Downloading:** Transferring files from your web server to your local computer. To download a file from your web server to your local computer, click the file you want to transfer from your web server and drag and drop it on the left side (the local-computer side).

TIP

Downloading files from your web server is a very efficient, easy, and smart way of backing up files to your local computer. It's always a good idea to keep your files safe — especially things like theme files and plugins, which Books 6 and 7 cover.

Editing files by using SFTP

At times, you may need to edit certain files that live on your web server. You can use the methods described in the preceding section to download a file, open it, edit it, save it, and then upload it back to your web server. Another way is to use the edit feature built into most SFTP client software by following these steps:

1. **Connect the SFTP client to your web server.**
2. **Locate the file you want to edit.**
3. **Open the file by using the internal SFTP editor.**

   Right-click the file with your mouse, and choose View/Edit from the shortcut menu. (Remember that I'm using FileZilla for these examples; your SFTP client may use different labels, such as Open or Edit.) FileZilla, like most SFTP clients, uses a program (such as Notepad for a PC or TextEdit for Mac) designated for text editing that already exists on your computer. In some rare cases, your SFTP client software may have its own internal text editor.

4. **Edit the file to your liking.**
5. **Save the changes you made.**

   Click the Save icon or choose File ⇨ Save.
6. **Upload the file to your web server.**

   After you save the file, FileZilla alerts you that the file has changed and asks whether you want to upload the file to the server. Click the Yes button. The newly edited file replaces the old one.

That's all there is to it! Use the SFTP edit feature to edit, save, and upload files as you need to.

WARNING

When you edit files by using the SFTP edit feature, you're editing files in a "live" environment, meaning that when you save the changes and upload the file, the changes take effect immediately and affect your live website. For this reason, I strongly recommend downloading a copy of the original file to your local computer before making changes. That way, if you happen to make a typo in the saved file and your website goes haywire, you have a copy of the original to upload to restore the file to its original state.

TECHNICAL STUFF

Programmers and developers are people who generally are more technologically advanced than your average user. These folks typically don't use SFTP for editing or transferring files. Instead, they use a version-control system called Git. Git manages the files on your web server through a versioning system that has a complex set of deployment rules for transferring updated files to and from your server. Most beginners don't use such a system for this purpose, but Git *is* a system that beginners can use. If you're interested in using Git, you can find a good resource to start with at W3Schools (`https://www.w3schools.com/git/`).

Changing file permissions

Every file and folder on your web server has a set of assigned attributions, called *permissions*, that tells the web server three things about the folder or file. On a very simplistic level, these permissions include

- **Read:** This setting determines whether the file/folder is readable by the web server.

- **Write:** This setting determines whether the file/folder is writable by the web server.
- **Execute:** This setting determines whether the file/folder is executable by the web server.

Each set of permissions has a numeric code assigned to it, identifying what type of permissions are assigned to that file or folder. There are a lot of permissions available, so here are the most common ones that you run into when running a WordPress website:

- **644:** Files with permissions set to 644 are readable by everyone and writable only by the file/folder owner.
- **755:** Files with permissions set to 755 are readable and executable by everyone, but they're writable only by the file/folder owner.
- **777:** Files with permissions set to 777 are readable, writable, and executable by everyone. For security reasons, you shouldn't use this set of permissions on your web server unless absolutely necessary.

Typically, folders and files within your web server are assigned permissions of 644 or 755. Usually, you see PHP files — files that end with the `.php` extension — with permissions set to 644 if the web server is configured to use PHP Safe Mode.

TIP

This section gives you a very basic look at file permissions, because usually you won't need to mess with file permissions on your web server. In case you do need to dig further, you can find a great reference on file permissions from WPMU DEV at `https://wpmudev.com/blog/understanding-file-permissions/`.

You may find yourself in a situation in which you're asked to edit and change the permissions on a particular file on your web server. With WordPress sites, this situation usually happens when you're dealing with plugins or theme files that require files or folders to be writable by the web server. This practice is referred to as *Chmod* (an acronym for Change Mode, commonly pronounced "shmod"). So now, when someone says "You need to Chmod that file to 755," you'll know what that person is talking about.

Here are some easy steps for using your SFTP program to Chmod a file or edit its permissions on your web server:

1. **Connect the SFTP client to your web server.**
2. **Locate the file you want to Chmod.**

3. **Open the file attributes for the file.**

   Right-click the file on your web server, and choose File Permissions from the shortcut menu. (Your SFTP client, if not FileZilla, may use different terminology.)

   The Change File Attributes window appears, as shown in Figure 2-6.

4. **Type the correct file permissions number in the Numeric Value field.**

   This number is assigned to the permissions you want to give the file. Most often, the plugin or theme developer tells you which permissions number to assign to the file or folder — typically, 644 or 755. (The permissions in Figure 2-6 are assigned the value 644.)

5. **Click OK to save the file.**

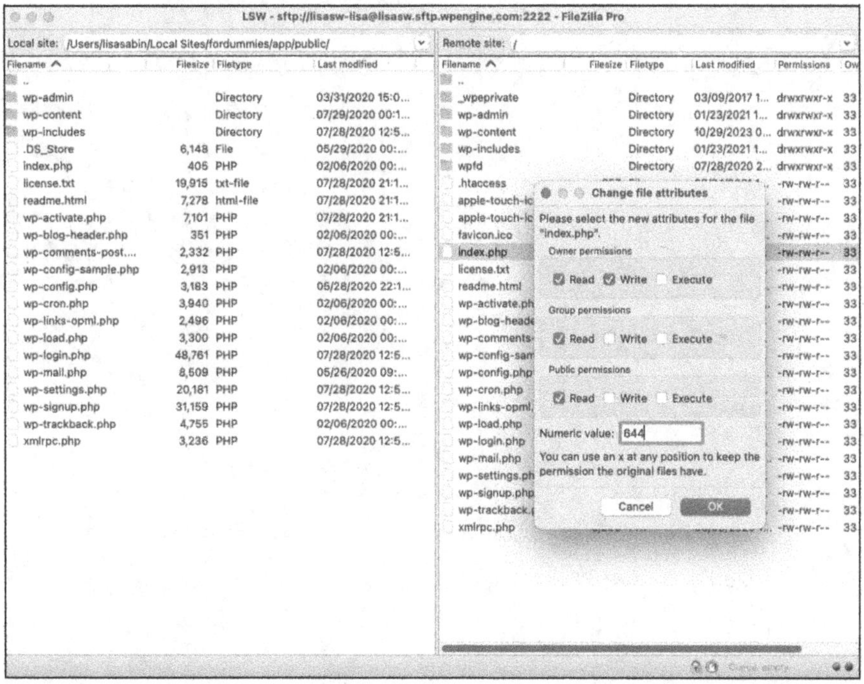

FIGURE 2-6: The Change File Attributes window in FileZilla.

IN THIS CHAPTER

» Discovering preinstallations by your host

» Manually installing WordPress

» Running installation scripts

Chapter 3

Installing WordPress on Your Web Server

This chapter takes you through two installation methods for WordPress: automatic installation with an installer provided by a managed web hosting service, which is available from your web hosting provider, and manual installation.

I also show you how to set up a MySQL database by using the cPanel web hosting management interface. By the time you're done reading this chapter, you'll be logged in to and looking at your brand-spanking-new WordPress Dashboard, ready to start publishing content right away. (If you already have WordPress installed, go ahead and skip to Book 2, Chapter 4, which contains great information about configuring WordPress for optimum performance and security.)

REMEMBER

Before you can install WordPress, you need to complete the following tasks:

- Purchase the domain-name registration for your account (Book 2, Chapter 1).
- Obtain a hosting service on a web server for your website (Book 2, Chapter 1).
- Establish your hosting account username, password, and Secure File Transfer Protocol (SFTP) address (Book 2, chapters 1 and 2).
- Acquire an SFTP client for transferring files to your hosting account (Book 2, Chapter 2).

If you omitted any of the preceding items, flip to the chapters listed to complete the step(s) you're missing.

Exploring Preinstalled WordPress

The WordPress software has become such a popular publishing tool that almost all hosting providers available today provide WordPress for you in a couple of ways:

- Already installed on your hosting account when you sign up
- A user dashboard with a utility for installing WordPress from within your account management

TIP

If your hosting provider doesn't give you access to an installation utility, skip to the next section, "Installing WordPress Manually," for the steps to install WordPress manually via SFTP.

One of the most popular web hosts for managed WordPress hosting is a service called WP Engine, which you can find at `https://wpengine.com`. The service provides a handy, easy-to-use installation utility that's built right into your account dashboard at WP Engine to allow you to get up and running with WordPress right away.

You may not be using WP Engine, so your host may have a slightly different utility, but the basic concept is the same. Be sure to apply the same concepts to whatever kind of utility your hosting provider gives you.

To install WordPress from within the account dashboard of WP Engine, follow these steps:

1. **Log in to the WP Engine user dashboard.**

   (a) *Browse to* `https://my.wpengine.com` *to bring up the login screen.*

   (b) *Enter the email address you used to sign up, enter your password, and then click Log In.*

   The page refreshes and displays the dashboard for your account.

2. **Click the Sites link on the left menu.**

   The My Sites page displays in your browser window, as shown in Figure 3-1.

3. **Click the Add Site button.**

   A small window labeled Add Site opens.

4. **Type the name of your new WordPress installation in the Site Name field.**

   This name is the temporary domain name of your new website. As shown in Figure 3-2, I'm using *wpfordummies,* which stand for WordPress For Dummies, which stands for *WordPress For Dummies*. This step creates the domain name `wpfordummies.wpenginepowered.com`.

5. **Choose Ungrouped from the Site Group drop-down menu.**

   This step ensures that your new WordPress installation isn't associated with any other sites that you may already have set up within your WP Engine account.

6. **Leave the Transferable check box unselected.**

   There may come a day where you want to create a WordPress installation that can be transferred between two WP Engine accounts, but today isn't that day. You can read about the process at `https://wpengine.com/support/transfer-wp-engine-environment/`.

7. **Click the Add Site button.**

   This step creates the WordPress installation in your account and takes you to the Overview page, where a message states that your WordPress installation is being created. When the installation is ready to use, you receive an email from WP Engine that contains the link to your new installation, along with login information.

   TIP

   In my experience, WP Engine always has the most up-to-date version of WordPress available for installation. Be sure to check that your hosting provider is supplying the latest version of WordPress with its installation utility.

Your WordPress installation via your provider's utility is complete, and you're ready to start using WordPress on your web server.

FIGURE 3-1: The My Sites page at WP Engine.

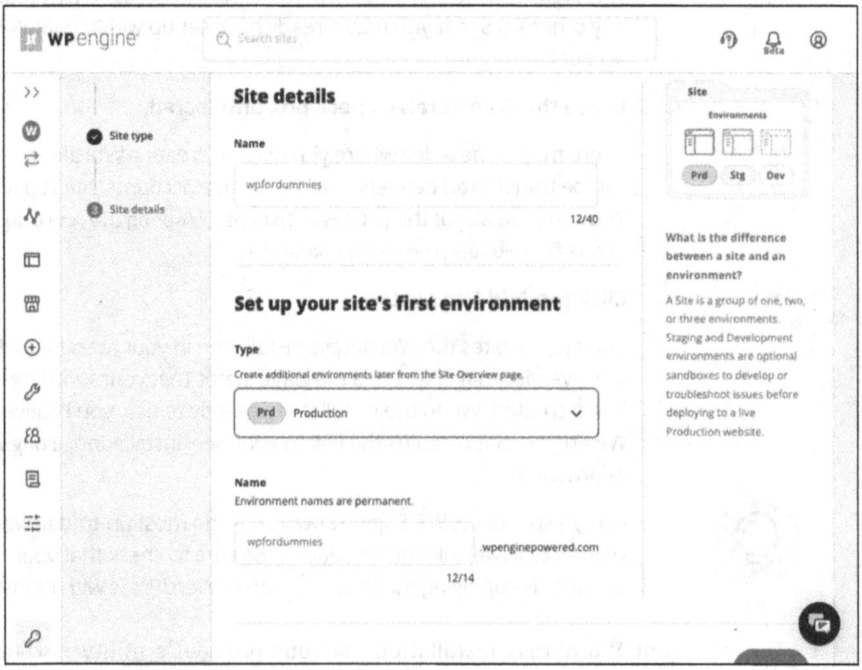

FIGURE 3-2: The Site Details window at WP Engine.

Installing WordPress Manually

Depending on where you host your WordPress website, you may never need to go through the steps of manually installing WordPress, as many web hosts have automated the process of installing WordPress on your server. If you installed WordPress by using your provider's utility method and don't want to review the steps to install WordPress manually, flip to Book 2, Chapter 4 for the steps to optimize your WordPress installation for performance and security.

If you do install WordPress manually, here's where the rubber meets the road — that is, where you're putting WordPress's famous 5-minute installation to the test. Set your watch, and see whether you can meet the 5-minute goal.

REMEMBER

The famous 5-minute installation includes only the time it takes to install the software — not the time it takes to register a domain name; obtain and set up your web hosting service; or download, install, configure, and figure out how to use the SFTP software.

Setting up the MySQL database

The WordPress software is a personal publishing system that uses a PHP/MySQL platform, which provides everything you need to create your own website and publish your own content dynamically without knowing how to program those pages. In short, all your content (options, posts, comments, and other pertinent data) is stored in a MySQL database in your hosting account.

Every time visitors go to your website to read your content, they make a request that's sent to your server. The PHP programming language receives that request, obtains the requested information from the MySQL database, and then presents the requested information to your visitors through their web browsers.

Every web host is different in how it gives you access to set up and manage your MySQL database(s) for your account. In this section, I use cPanel, a popular hosting interface. If your host provides a different interface, the same basic steps apply, but the setup in the interface that your web host provides may be different.

To set up the MySQL database for your WordPress site with cPanel, follow these steps:

1. **Log in to the cPanel for your hosting account:**

   (a) *Browse to* `http://yourdomain.com/cpanel` *(where* `yourdomain.com` *is your actual domain name) to bring up the login screen for your cPanel.*

(b) *Enter your specific hosting account username and password in the login fields, and then click OK.*

The page refreshes and displays the cPanel for your account.

2. **Locate the MySQL Databases icon.**

   Click the MySQL Databases icon to load the MySQL Databases page in your cPanel.

3. **Enter a name for your database in the Name text box.**

   Be sure to make note of the database name, because you need it to install WordPress.

4. **Click the Create Database button.**

   A message appears, confirming that the database was created.

5. **Click the Back button on your browser toolbar.**

   The MySQL Databases page displays in your browser window.

6. **Locate MySQL Users on the MySQL Databases page.**

   Scroll approximately to the middle of the page to locate this section.

7. **Choose a username and password for your database, enter them in the Username and Password text boxes, and then click the Create User button.**

   A confirmation message appears, stating that the username was created with the password you specified.

TIP

For security reasons, make sure that your password isn't something that sneaky hackers can easily guess. Give your database a name that you'll remember later. This practice is especially helpful if you run more than one MySQL database in your account. If you name a database *WordPress* or *wpsite*, for example, you can be reasonably certain that a year from now, when you want to access your database to make some configuration changes, that you know exactly which credentials to use.

WARNING

Make sure that you note the database name, username, and password that you set up during this process. You need them in the section "Running the installation script" later in this chapter before officially installing WordPress on your web server. Jot these details down on a piece of paper, or copy and paste them into a text editor window; either way, make sure that you have them handy.

8. **Click the Back button on your browser toolbar.**

   The MySQL Databases page displays in your browser window.

9. **In the Add User to Database section of the MySQL Databases page, choose the user you just set up from the User drop-down menu and then choose the new database from the Database drop-down menu.**

   If the user and/or database you created in the earlier steps don't display in these drop-down menus, you've done something wrong and should start over from Step 1.

10. **Click the Add button.**

    This step displays the Manage User Privileges page in your browser window.

11. **Assign user privileges by selecting the All Privileges check box.**

    Because you're the *administrator* (or owner) of this database, you need to make sure that you assign all privileges to the new user you just created.

12. **Click the Make Changes button.**

    The resulting page displays a message confirming that you've added your selected user to the selected database.

13. **Click the Back button on your browser toolbar.**

    You return to the MySQL Databases page.

The MySQL database for your WordPress website is complete, and you're ready to proceed to the final step of installing the software on your web server.

Downloading the WordPress software

Without further ado, get the latest version of the WordPress software at `https://wordpress.org/download`.

TIP

WordPress gives you two compression formats for the software: `.zip` and `.tar.gz`. Use the `.zip` file because it's the most common format for compressed files and because both Windows and Mac operating systems can use the format. Generally, the `.tar.gz` file format is used for Unix operating systems.

Download the WordPress software to your computer and then *decompress* (unpack or unzip) it to a folder on your computer's hard drive. These steps begin the installation process for WordPress. Having the program on your own computer isn't enough, however. You also need to *upload* (or transfer) it to your web server account (the one discussed in Book 2, Chapter 1).

Before you install WordPress on your web server, you need to make sure that you have the MySQL database set up and ready to accept the WordPress installation. Be sure that you've followed the steps to set up your MySQL database before you proceed.

Uploading the WordPress files via SFTP

To upload the WordPress files to your host, return to the `/wordpress` folder (shown in Figure 3-3) on your computer, where you unpacked the WordPress software that you downloaded earlier. If you need a review on using SFTP (Secure File Transfer Protocol) to transfer files from your computer to your web server, see Book 2, Chapter 2.

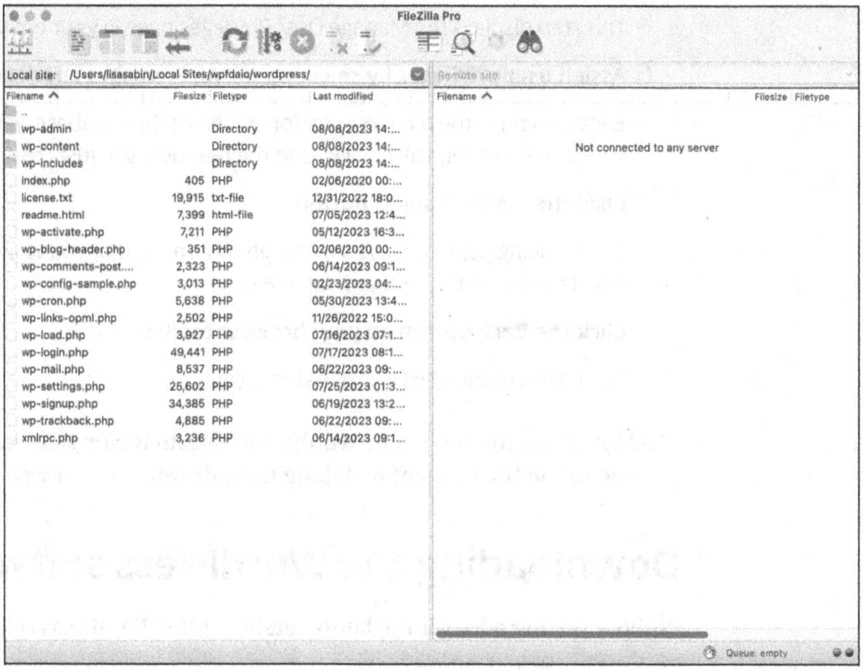

FIGURE 3-3: WordPress installation files to be uploaded to your web server.

Using your SFTP client, connect to your web server and upload all these files to the root directory of your hosting account.

TIP

If you don't know what your root directory is, contact your hosting provider and ask, "What is my root directory for my account?" Every hosting provider's setup is different. The root directory is most often the `public_html` folder, but you may find an `httpdocs` folder. The answer depends on what type of setup your hosting provider has. When in doubt, ask!

Here are some things to keep in mind when you upload your files:

- **Upload the *contents* of the /wordpress folder to your web server — not the folder itself.** Most SFTP client software lets you select all the files and drag and drop them to your web server. Other programs have you highlight the files and click a Transfer button.

- **Choose the correct transfer mode.** File transfers via SFTP have two forms: ASCII and binary. Most SFTP clients are configured to autodetect the transfer mode. Understanding the difference as it pertains to this WordPress installation is important so that you can troubleshoot any problems you have later:
  - *Binary transfer mode* is how images (such as JPG, GIF, BMP, and PNG files) are transferred via SFTP.
  - *ASCII transfer mode* is for everything else (text files, PHP files, JavaScript, and so on).

  For the most part, it's a safe bet to make sure that the transfer mode of your SFTP client is set to autodetect. But if you experience issues with how those files load on your site, retransfer the files by using the appropriate transfer mode.
- **You can choose a different folder from the root.** You aren't required to transfer the files to the root directory of your web server. You can choose to run WordPress on a subdomain or in a different folder on your account. If you're running just a blog (without a full accompanying website) and want your blog address to be `http://yourdomain.com/blog`, you transfer the WordPress files into a `/blog` folder (where *yourdomain* is your domain name).
- **Choose the right file permissions.** *File permissions* tell the web server how these files can be handled on your server — whether they're files that can be written to. Generally, PHP files need to have a permission (Chmod is explained in Book 2, Chapter 2) of 666, whereas file folders need a permission of 755. Almost all SFTP clients let you check and change the permissions on the files, if you need to. Typically, you can find the option to change file permissions within the menu options of your FTP client.

TECHNICAL STUFF

Some hosting providers run their PHP software in a more secure format: *Safe Mode.* If this is the case with your host, you need to *Chmod* the PHP files to 644. If you're unsure, ask your hosting provider what permissions you need to set for PHP files.

Running the installation script

The final step in the installation procedure for WordPress is connecting the WordPress software you uploaded to the MySQL database. Follow these steps:

1. **Type the URL of your website in the address bar of your web browser.**

   If you chose to install WordPress in a different folder from the root directory of your account, make sure you indicate that in the URL for the install script. If you transferred the WordPress software files to the `/blog` folder, for example, point your browser to the following URL to run the installation: `http://yourdomain.com/blog/wp-admin/install.php`. If WordPress is in the root directory, use the following URL to run the installation: `http://yourdomain.com/wp-admin/install.php` (where *yourdomain* is your domain name).

Assuming that you did everything correctly, you should see the first step in the installation process that you see in Figure 3-4. (See Table 3-1 for help with common installation problems.)

2. **Select your preferred language from the list provided on the setup page, shown in Figure 3-4.**

   At this writing, WordPress is available in 116 languages. For these steps, I'm using English (United States).

3. **Click the Continue button.**

   You see a new page with a welcome message from WordPress and instructions that you need to gather the MySQL information you saved earlier in this chapter.

4. **Click the Let's Go button.**

   A new page loads and displays the fields you need to fill out in the next step, shown in Figure 3-5.

5. **Dig out the database name, username, and password that you saved in the earlier section, "Setting up the MySQL database," and use that information to fill in the following fields, as shown in Figure 3-5:**

   - *Database Name:* Type the database name you used when you created the MySQL database before this installation. Because hosts differ in configurations, you need to enter the database name by itself or a combination of your username and the database name, separated by an underscore (_).

     If you named your database *wordpress,* for example, you enter that in this text box. If your host requires you to append the database name with your hosting account username, you enter ***username*_wordpress**, substituting your hosting username for *username.* My username is *lisasabin,* so I enter **lisasabin_wordpress**.

   - *Username:* Type the username you used when you created the MySQL database before this installation. Depending on what your host requires, you may need to enter a combination of your hosting account username and the database username separated by an underscore (_).
   - *Password:* Type the password you used when you set up the MySQL database. You don't need to append the password to your hosting account username here.
   - *Database Host:* Ninety-nine percent of the time, you leave this field set to `localhost`. Some hosts, depending on their configurations, have different

hosts set for the MySQL database server. If `localhost` doesn't work, you need to contact your hosting provider to find out the MySQL database host.

- *Table Prefix:* Leave this field set to wp_.

  You can change the table prefix to create an environment that's secure against outside access. See Book 2, Chapter 4 for more information.

6. After you fill in the MySQL database information, click the Submit button.

You see a message that says, `All right, sparky! You've made it through this part of the installation. WordPress can now communicate with your database. If you're ready, time to run the install!`

7. Click the Run the Install button.

Another page appears, welcoming you to the famous 5-minute WordPress installation process, as shown in Figure 3-6.

8. Enter the following information:

- *Site Title:* Enter the title you want to give your site. The title you enter isn't written in stone; you can change it later, if you like. The site title also appears on your site.
- *Username:* Enter the name you use to log in to WordPress. By default, the username is *admin,* and you can leave it that way. For security reasons, however, I recommend that you change your username to something unique. This username is different from the one you set for the MySQL database in previous steps. You use this username when you log in to WordPress to access the Dashboard (which is covered in Book 3), so be sure to make it something you'll remember.
- *Password:* Type your desired password in the text box. If you don't enter a password, one is generated automatically for you. For security reasons, it's a good thing to set a different password here from the one you set for your MySQL database in the previous steps; just don't get the passwords confused.

  TIP

  For security reasons (and so other people can't make a lucky guess), passwords should be at least seven characters long and use as many different characters in as many combinations as possible. Use a mixture of uppercase and lowercase letters, numbers, and symbols (such as ! " ? $ % ^ &).
- *Your Email:* Enter the email address you want to use to be notified of administrative information about your blog. You can change this address later, too.
- *Search Engine Visibility:* By default, this option isn't selected, which lets the search engines index the content of your website and includes your site in search results. To keep your site out of the search engines, select this check box. (See Book 5 for information on search engine optimization.)

9. **Click the Install WordPress button.**

   The WordPress installation machine works its magic and creates all the tables within the database that contain the default data for your blog. WordPress displays the login information you need to access the WordPress Dashboard. Make note of this username and password before you leave this page. Scribble them on a piece of paper or copy them into a text editor, such as Notepad.

   REMEMBER

   After you click the Install WordPress button, you're sent an email with the login information and login URL. This information is handy if you're called away during this part of the installation process. So go ahead and let the dog out, answer the phone, brew a cup of coffee, or take a 15-minute power nap. If you somehow get distracted away from this page, the email you receive contains the information you need to log in to your WordPress blog.

10. **Click the Log In button to log in to WordPress.**

   TIP

   If you happen to lose this page before clicking the Log In button, you can always find your way to the login page by entering your domain followed by the call to the login file (such as `http://`*`yourdomain.com`*`/wp-login.php`, where *yourdomain* is your domain name).

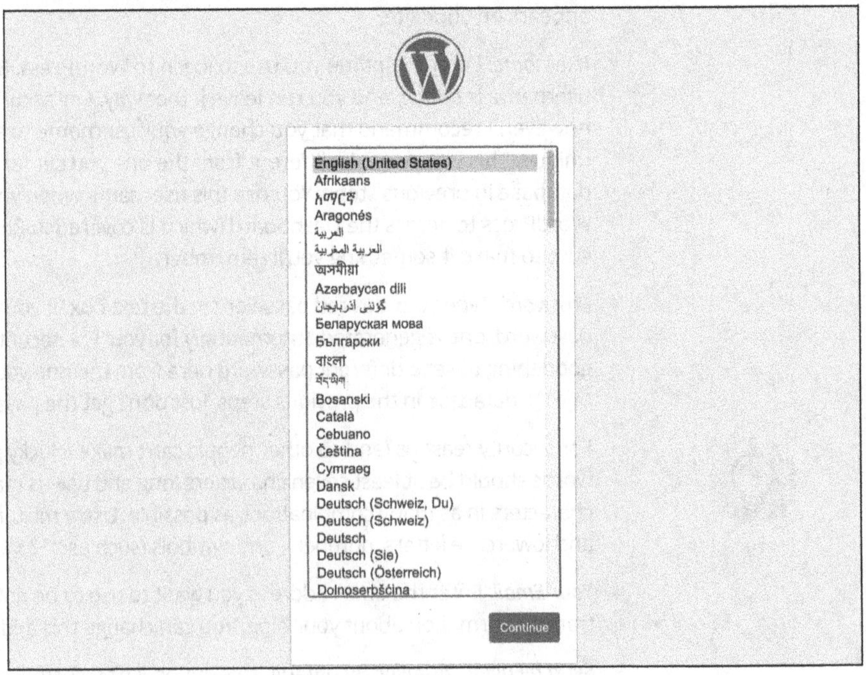

FIGURE 3-4: Choose the language for your installation.

TABLE 3-1 Common WordPress Installation Problems

Error Message	Common Cause	Solution
Error Connecting to the Database	The database name, username, password, or host was entered incorrectly.	Revisit your MySQL database to obtain the database name, username, and password and then reenter that information.
Headers Already Sent	A syntax error occurred in the wp-config.php file.	Open the wp-config.php file in a text editor. The first line needs to contain only this line: <?php. The last line needs to contain only this line: ?>. Make sure that those lines contain nothing else — not even white space. Save the file changes.
500: Internal Server Error	Permissions on PHP files are set incorrectly.	Try setting the permissions (Chmod) on the PHP files to 666. If that change doesn't work, set them to 644. Each web server has different settings for how it lets PHP execute on its servers.
404: Page Not Found	The URL for the login page is incorrect.	Double-check that the URL you're using to get to the login page is the same as the location of your WordPress installation (such as `http://`*`yourdomain.com`*`/wp-login.php`).
403: Forbidden Access	An index.html or index.htm file exists in the WordPress installation directory.	WordPress is a PHP application, so the default home page is index.php. Look in the WordPress installation folder on your web server. If an index.html or index.htm file is there, delete it.

Below you should enter your database connection details. If you are not sure about these, contact your host.
Database Name
lisasabin_wordpress
The name of the database you want to use with WordPress.
Username
lisasabin
Your database username.
Password
Show
Your database password.
Database Host
localhost
You should be able to get this info from your web host, if localhost does not work.
Table Prefix
wp_
If you want to run multiple WordPress installations in a single database, change this.
Submit

FIGURE 3-5: Entering the database name, username, and password.

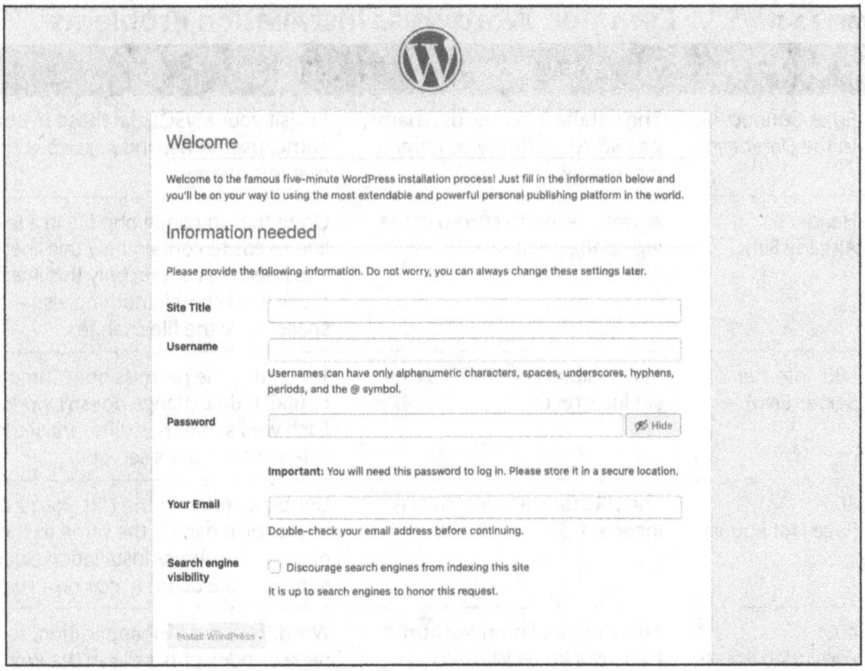

FIGURE 3-6: Finishing the WordPress installation.

You know that you're finished with the installation process when you see the login page, shown in Figure 3-7. Check out Table 3-1 if you experience any problems during this installation process; it covers some of the common problems users run into.

So do tell — how much time does your watch show for the installation? Was it 5 minutes? Stop by my website sometime at `https://lisasabin-wilson.com/#contact` and let me know whether WordPress stood up to its famous 5-minute installation reputation.

The good news is — you're done! Were you expecting a marching band? WordPress isn't that fancy . . . yet. Give it time, though. If anyone can produce it, the folks at WordPress can.

Let me be the first to congratulate you on your newly installed WordPress blog! When you're ready, log in and familiarize yourself with the Dashboard, which I describe in Book 3.

FIGURE 3-7: You know you've run a successful WordPress installation when you see the login page.

IN THIS CHAPTER

- **Understanding today's web threats and how you can protect yourself**
- **Using sources you can trust**
- **Managing users and passwords effectively**
- **Reducing the risk of attack**

Chapter 4

Configuring WordPress for Optimum Security

In this chapter, you deal with web security and how it pertains to WordPress. There are a lot of scary threats on the Internet, but with this chapter — and WordPress, of course — you'll have a much better chance at keeping your website safe and secure.

Part of being a website owner is keeping your website and subscribers safe from hackers. You can't ever be 100 percent secure. But with a WordPress website, you're in good hands. The WordPress developers understand the importance of security, and they built a highly effective system to address any vulnerabilities you'll run across.

TIP

Always have a reliable backup system in place so if something goes wrong with your website, you can reset it to the last version that you know worked. Book 2, Chapter 6 shows you how to back up your website.

Understanding the Basics of Web Security

Information security is the act of protecting information and information systems from unwanted or unauthorized use, access, modification, and disruption. Information security is built on principles of protecting confidentiality, integrity, and availability of information. The ultimate goal is managing your risk.

REMEMBER

No silver bullet can ensure that you're never compromised. Consider your desktop: The idea of running an operating system (whether it be Windows or MacOS) without antivirus software is highly impractical. The same principle applies to your website. You can never reduce the percentage of risk to zero, but you can implement controls to minimize impact and to take a proactive approach to threat preparedness.

You need to be familiar with six distinct types of risk (or threats):

- **Defacements:** The motivation behind most defacements is to change the appearance of a website. Defacements are often very basic and make some kind of social stance, such as supporting a cause or bringing attention to your poor security posture. If you visit your website, and it doesn't look anything like you expect it to, contact your host to find out whether it has been defaced, and if so, ask for assistance in restoring it.
- **Search engine optimization (SEO) spam:** This kind of attack sets out to ruin your search engine results; search engines can warn viewers away from your website. The most popular one is the Pharma hack, which injects code into your website and search engine links to redirect your traffic to pharmaceutical companies and their products. If you find that your website listing disappears from major search engines such as Google, you should be concerned that your website has been a victim of SEO spam and contact your hosting provider for assistance.
- **Malicious redirects:** Malicious-redirect attacks direct your traffic somewhere else, most likely to another website. If your domain is `domain.com`, for example, a malicious redirect might redirect it to: `adifferentdomain.com`. Malicious redirects are often integrated with other attacks (SEO spam being one). If you visit your website and discover that your domain redirects to a different domain that you don't recognize, your website has been a victim of a malicious-redirect attack, and you should contact your hosting provider for assistance.
- **iFrame injections:** This kind of attack embeds a hidden iFrame in your website that loads another website onto your visitor's browser (like a pop-up ad). These embedded websites or ads can lead to malicious websites that carry a multitude of infections.

- **Phishing scams:** Phishing scams used to belong only to the world of email: You get an email from your bank asking you to confirm your login information, but if you follow the instructions, your information actually goes to the attacker's servers rather than the legitimate site.

  WordPress websites are sometimes used for the distribution of these attacks. Attackers develop malicious files and code that look like plugins and themes and then exploit credentials on a server or WordPress site, or the attackers use a known vulnerability to infect the plugins and themes. Then they use the bait-and-hook approach through ads or emails to redirect traffic to these fake pages stored on legitimate websites. Keep an eye out for abnormal behavior on your website, such as the display of ads that you didn't insert yourself or the redirect to domains you're not familiar with. If at any time you suspect that your website and underlying files have been tampered with, contact your web hosting provider for assistance.
- **Backdoor shells:** With a backdoor shell, an attacker uploads a piece of PHP code to your website, which allows them to take control of it, download your files, and upload their own. This kind of attack is more difficult to discover because it doesn't always change the appearance of your site or your experience with it. You typically discover this kind of attack by noticing new files in your file system or a marked increase in your bandwidth use.

The rest of this chapter shows you how you can prevent any of these nasty attacks against your WordPress website so that you can keep yourself and your visitors safe.

Updating WordPress

The first way to prevent hackers is to keep your WordPress website up to date. The quick-and-easy way to do so is through the automatic update feature. Book 2, Chapter 5 takes you through the process of updating WordPress step by step.

REMEMBER

The beauty of applying updates is that they often introduce new streamlined features, improve overall usability, and work to patch and close identified or known vulnerabilities.

Unfortunately, as technology and concepts evolve, so do attackers and their methods for finding new vulnerabilities. The farther behind you get, the harder it is to update later and the more your risk increases, which in turn affects how vulnerable you are to attacks. So it's important to update WordPress as soon as an update becomes available.

Installing patches

All WordPress updates are not created equal, but you should pay special attention to a few updates of the WordPress core software.

Updates include *major releases,* which contain feature additions, user interface (UI) changes, bug fixes, and security updates. You can always tell what major release you're on by the first two numbers in the version number (as in 5.0). See Book 1, Chapter 3 for more information about the difference between major and minor releases.

Then you have *point releases,* which are minor releases that can be identified by the third number in the version number (as in 5.0.1). These releases contain bug fixes and security patches but don't introduce new features.

TIP

When you see a point release, apply it. Point releases rarely cause issues with your site, and in many cases they help close off vulnerabilities.

Using a firewall

A firewall builds a wall between your website and the much larger Internet; a good firewall thwarts a lot of attacks.

Your web server should also have a good firewall protecting it. Every day, countless visits, good and bad, are made to every website. Some visits are by real visitors, but many are by automated bots. A web application firewall (WAF) helps protect your WordPress installation from those bad visitors.

REMEMBER

WAFs don't offer 100 percent protection, but they're good deterrents for everyday attacks.

If you're using a managed hosting solution, you're probably in luck, because most of these solutions offer built-in WAF-like features.

TECHNICAL STUFF

If you plan to manage and administer your own server, install and configure a tool such as Cloudflare (`https://www.cloudflare.com`), an open-source, WAF-like solution that lives at the web server level as an Apache module. Cloudflare provides the best available WAF-like features for your WordPress website on a managed hosting solution. If you'd like to use the Cloudflare plugin on your WordPress website, you need to have a Cloudflare account at `https://www.cloudflare.com`. You can open a free account or upgrade to a paid account that includes more features. After you've installed the plugin on your website, follow the instructions on the Cloudflare configuration page to connect your WordPress blog to your Cloudflare account.

Using Trusted Sources

One of the simplest things you can do to keep your website secure is vet all the people who work on your website: website administrators, website designers, developers, and web hosts. If you're running a self-hosted WordPress website, this could be quite a few people.

Be sure to use trusted themes, plugins, and applications. If you're using themes or plugins, use the `WordPress.org` Theme and Plugin directories (`https://wordpress.org/themes` and `https://wordpress.org/plugins`, respectively). Each theme and plugin you find in those directories has gone through a documented review process, which reduces the risk of your downloading dangerous code.

Engage the WordPress user community. The WordPress forums (`https://wordpress.org/support/forums`) are great places to start. Ask for community references, and identify the support mechanisms in place to support the theme or plugin over the long term.

Managing Users and Passwords

The concept of *least privilege* has been in practice for ages: Give someone the required privileges for as long as they need it to perform their job or a task. When the task is complete, reduce the privileges.

REMEMBER

Apply this safeguard not just to your WordPress Dashboard, but also to your website host's control panels and server transfer protocols. (See Book 2, Chapter 2 for information on Secure File Transfer Protocol.)

Password management is perhaps the simplest of tasks, yet it's the Achilles' heel of all applications, including desktop and web-based apps. You can keep your files and data on your web server safe and secure through these simple password-management techniques:

- **Length:** Create passwords that are more than 16 characters long, including special characters, to make it more difficult for harmful users to guess your password.
- **Uniqueness:** Don't use the same password across all services. That way, if someone does discover the password for one of your applications or services, they won't be able to use it to log in to another service.

You can find detailed information on each of the roles in Book 3, Chapter 3. You can also discover more information on users and roles in the `WordPress.org`

Documentation at https://wordpress.org/documentation/article/roles-and-capabilities/.

TIP

Create a separate account with a lower role (such as Author) and use that account for everyday posting. Reserve the Administrator account purely for administration of your website.

Hardening WordPress

When you *harden* (or secure) your WordPress installation, you reduce your risk of being hacked by malicious attackers. Hardening your website involves following these five steps:

1. **Enable multifactor authentication using the Two Factor Authentication plugin.**
2. **Limit login attempts.**
3. **Disable theme and plugin editors.**
4. **Filter by IP (Internet Protocol) address.**
5. **Kill PHP execution.**

You'll learn more about each of these steps in the following sections. Also check out the nearby sidebar, "Website hardening resources," for more information.

WEBSITE HARDENING RESOURCES

I recommend the following website resources for your WordPress hardening and security needs:

- **Hardening WordPress:** https://wordpress.org/documentation/article/hardening-wordpress
- **The Definitive WordPress Security Guide:** https://sucuri.net/guides/wordpress-security
- **WordPress Hardening: 18 Ways to Harden Security of Your Website:** https://www.malcare.com/blog/wordpress-hardening
- **WordPress Security – 19+ Steps to Lock Down Your Site:** https://kinsta.com/blog/wordpress-security

Enabling multifactor authentication using the Two Factor Authentication plugin

Authentication, in this case, refers to confirming the identity of the person who is attempting to log in and obtain access to your WordPress installation — just like when you log in to your WordPress website by using a username and password. The idea of multifactor authentication stems from the idea that one password alone isn't enough to secure access to any environment. *Multifactor authentication* (also called *strong authentication*) requires more than one user-authentication method. By default, WordPress requires only one: a username with password. Multifactor authentication adds layers of authentication measures for extra security of user logins.

To enable multifactor authentication, you can use a free plugin called Two Factor Authentication, which provides two-factor user authentication through an application on your mobile or tablet device (iPhone, iPad, Android, and so on). For this plugin to work, you need the following:

- **Authentication app:** Use either Google Authenticator or Authy; you can find them both in the App Store for iOS devices or the Google Play Store for Android devices.
- **Multi-Factor Authentication plugin:** You can find this plugin in the Plugin list at `https://wordpress.org/plugins/miniorange-login-security/`. See Book 7, chapters 1 and 2 for details on finding, installing, and activating plugins.

When you have both of those tasks accomplished, you can configure the Two Factor Authentication plugin for use on your website. Follow these steps to configure the plugin for each user on your site:

1. **Click the Two Factor link on the Multi-Factor Authentication menu on your Dashboard.**

   The Setup Two Factor page opens.

2. **Download the authenticator app to your smartphone (Android or iPhone).**

   The authenticator app on your phone is required to complete the two-factor authentication. I've chosen the Authy app, downloaded to my iPhone.

3. **Scan the QR code in the Google Authenticator, or Authy, application on your phone.**

   Point your device camera at your computer screen, and line up the QR code within the camera brackets of your mobile device. The application automatically reads the QR code as soon as it's aligned correctly and displays a six-digit code identifying your blog. The six-digit code refreshes on a time-based interval. After you scan the QR code, you receive a message on your mobile device that contains a unique numeric code.

4. **Enter the six-digit code generated by the Google Authenticator, or Authy, app in the Code field.**
5. **Click the Verify and Save button.**

   A window pops up titled 2FA Setup Successful (see Figure 4-1).
6. **Click the Got It! button to close the setup window.**

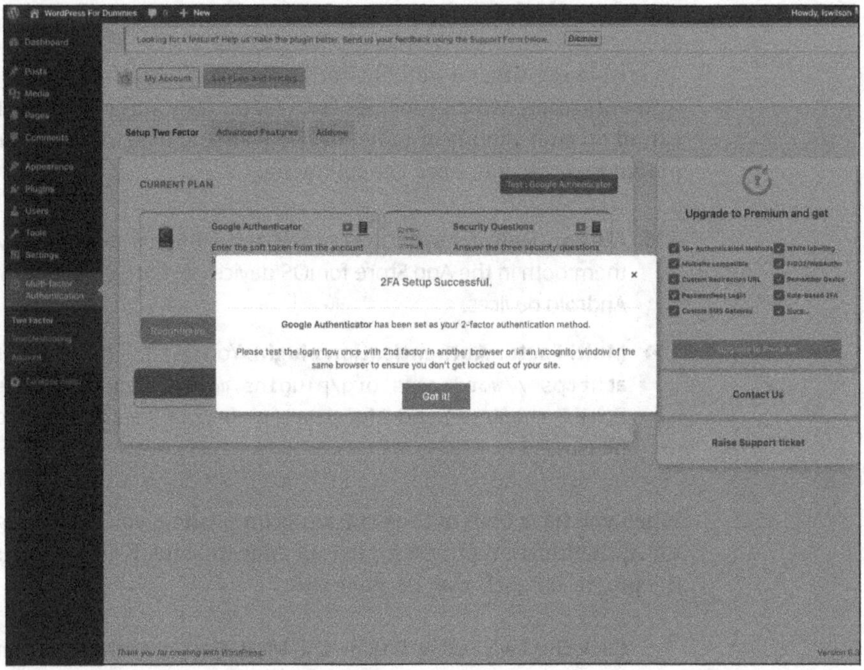

FIGURE 4-1: The 2FA Setup Successful setup window.

Now, with the Two Factor Authentication plugin in place, whenever anyone tries to log in to your WordPress Dashboard, they have to fill in their username and password, as usual, but with multifactor authentication in place, they also need to enter the authentication code that was sent to their mobile device. Without this unique code, the user can't log in to the WordPress Dashboard.

WARNING

The Google Authenticator application verification code is time-based, which is why it's very important that your mobile phone and your WordPress site are set to the same time zone. If you get the message that the Google Authentication verification code you're using is invalid or expired, you need to delete the plugin and then go to your WordPress Dashboard to make sure that the time zone is set to the same time zone that your mobile or tablet device uses. See Book 3, Chapter 2 for information on time settings for your WordPress site.

TIP

If you don't have access to a mobile device, there is a plugin you can use called Loginizer, which you can find here: `https://wordpress.org/plugins/loginizer`. The Loginizer plugin protects your site from brute-force attacks (see the next section).

Limiting login attempts

Limiting the number of times a user can attempt to log in to your WordPress site helps reduce the risk of a brute-force attack. A *brute-force attack* happens when an attacker tries to gain access by guessing your username and password through the process of cycling through combinations.

To help protect against brute-force attacks, you want to limit the number of times any user can try to log in to your website. You can accomplish this task in WordPress easily enough by using the Limit Login Attempts plugin. You can find this plugin in the WordPress Plugin list: `https://wordpress.org/plugins/limit-login-attempts-reloaded/`. See Book 7, chapters 1 and 2 for information on finding, installing, and activating it.

When you have the Limit Login Attempts plugin installed, follow these steps to configure the settings:

1. **Click the Limit Login link on the Settings menu of your Dashboard.**

   The Limit Login Attempts Reloaded page opens on your Dashboard (see Figure 4-2).

2. **Configure the settings.**

   With the free version of this plugin, you can configure the following settings by scrolling to the bottom of the page under App Settings:

   - *Allowed Retries:* This setting is the maximum number of times users are allowed to retry failed logins. The default is 4 retries.
   - *Minutes Lockout:* This setting is the length of time a user is prevented from retrying a login after they reach the maximum allowed number. The default is 20 minutes.
   - *Lockouts Increase Lockout Time To:* This option sets the number of times a user can be locked out before the default lockout time increases. The default number of times is 4 and the default length of time is 24 hours.
   - *Hours Until Retries Are Reset:* This is the length of time before login retries are reset. The default is 24 hours.

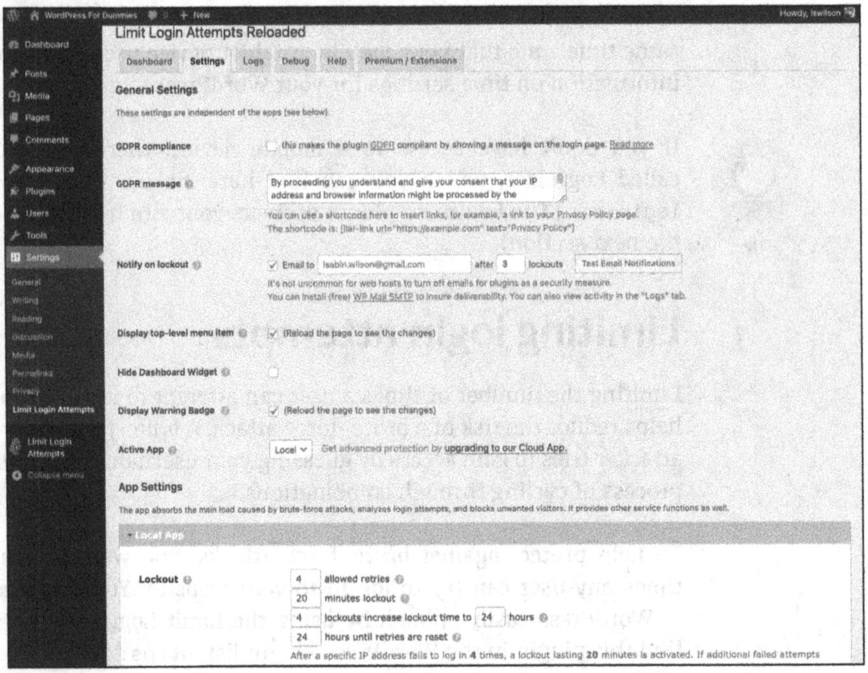

FIGURE 4-2: The Limit Login Attempts Reloaded page.

TIP

If you're managing your own server, monitor your login attempts to see whether a malicious attacker is making repeated attempts to obtain passwords and usernames. Keep track of those IP addresses from your logs, and if an address repeatedly attempts to log in, add it to your server firewall to prevent it from burdening your server access points.

Disabling theme and plugin editors

By default, when you log in to the WordPress Dashboard, you can edit any theme and plugin file by using the Theme Editor (click the Appearance link on the Editor menu) and the Plugin Editor (click the Plugins link on the Editor menu). The idea makes a lot of sense; it gives you the ability to do everything within your Admin panel without having to worry about logging in to your server via SFTP to edit files.

Unfortunately, having the theme and plugin editors available also gives any attacker who gains access to the Dashboard full rights to modify any theme or plugin file. This is very dangerous, because even one line of malware code embedded within any file can grant an attacker remote access to your environment without ever having to touch your Dashboard.

You can prevent this situation by disabling the Theme Editor and Plugin Editor. To do so, add a WordPress *constant* (or rule) to the WordPress configuration file (`wp-config.php`), which is in the installation folder on your web server. Download the `wp-config.php` via SFTP (see Book 2, Chapter 2), and open the file in a text editor, such as Notepad (PC) or TextEdit (Mac). Look for the following line of code:

```
define( 'DB_COLLAT', '' );
```

Add the following constant (rule) on the line directly below the preceding line:

```
define( 'DISALLOW_FILE_EDIT',true );
```

Although adding this constant won't prevent an attack, it helps reduce the impact of a compromise. You can find information about other constants you can add to the wp-config.php file at `https://wordpress.org/documentation/article/editing-wp-config-php/`.

TIP

You can also disable the automatic updates in WordPress (the feature in place that automatically updates WordPress core and WordPress plugins) to include the administrator. If you do, you'd have to do everything manually, via SFTP. To disable automatic updates, use the following constant in your `wp-config.php` file:

```
define( 'DISALLOW_FILE_MODS',true );
```

Filtering by IP address

Another option is to limit access to the Dashboard to specific IP addresses. This method is also referred to as *whitelisting* (allowing) access, which complements *blacklisting* (disallowing) solutions.

Everything that touches the Internet — such as your computer, a website, or a server network — has an IP address. An IP is like your home address; it uniquely identifies you so that the Internet knows where your computer is located. An example of an IP is 12.345.67.89 — a series of numbers that uniquely identifies the physical location of a computer or network.

You can edit the `.htaccess` file on your web server so that only IPs that you approve can access your Admin Dashboard, thereby blocking everyone else from having Dashboard access.

The lines of code that define the access rules get added to the `.htaccess` file located on your web server where WordPress is installed, in a folder called `/wp-admin`. Download that file to your computer via SFTP; open it with a text editor such as Notepad (PC) or TextEdit (Mac); and add the following lines to it:

```
order allow,deny
deny from all
allow from 12.345.67.89
```

In this example, the order defines what comes first. An IP that follows the `allow` rules is given access; any IP that doesn't follow the `allow` rules is denied access. In this example, only the IP 12.345.67.89 can access the Admin Dashboard; all other IPs are denied.

TIP

If the `/wp-admin` folder in your WordPress installation doesn't contain a file called `.htaccess`, you can easily create one using your SFTP program. Open the `/wp-admin` folder, right-click with your mouse in the SFTP program window to open a shortcut menu, and choose New File. Give that new file the name `.htaccess`, and make sure to add the new rules from the "Disabling theme and plugin editors" section, earlier in this chapter. This applies only if you are using a web server that is running Apache, not Nginx. If you are not sure which platform your web host is running, send them an email and ask.

Killing PHP execution

For most backdoor intrusion attempts to function, a PHP file has to be executed. The term *backdoor* describes ways of obtaining access to a web server through means that bypass regular authentication methods, such as file injections through programming languages such as PHP and JavaScript. Disabling PHP execution prevents an attack or compromise from taking place because PHP can't executed at all.

To disable PHP execution, add four lines of code to the `.htaccess` file on your web server:

```
<Files *.php>
Order allow,deny
Deny from all
</Files>
```

By default, you have an `.htaccess` file in the WordPress directory on your web server. You can also create an `.htaccess` file in other folders — particularly the folders in which you want to disable PHP execution.

To disable PHP execution for maximum security, create an `.htaccess` file with those four lines of code in the following folders in your WordPress installation:

- `/wp-includes`
- `/wp-content/uploads`
- `/wp-content`

This WordPress installation directory (the directory WordPress is installed in) is important because it's the only directory that has to be writeable for WordPress to work. If an image is uploaded with a modified header, or if a PHP file is uploaded and PHP execution is allowed, an attacker could exploit this weakness to create havoc in your environment. When PHP execution is disabled, however, an attacker is unable to create any havoc.

Disabling PHP execution only works if you are using a web server that is running Apache, not Nginx. Again, if you're not sure which platform your web host is running, send them an email and ask.

IN THIS CHAPTER

» Finding upgrade notifications

» Backing up your database before upgrading

» Upgrading from the Dashboard

» Upgrading manually

Chapter 5

Updating WordPress

As I discuss in Book 1, Chapter 3, the schedule of WordPress development and release cycles shows you that WordPress releases a new version (upgrade) of its platform roughly once every 120 days (or every 4 months). That chapter also explains why you need to keep your WordPress software up to date by using the most recent version — mostly for security purposes, but also to make sure you're taking advantage of all the latest features the WordPress developers pack within every major new release.

In this chapter, you discover the WordPress upgrade notification system and find out what to do when WordPress notifies you that a new version is available. This chapter also covers the best practices for upgrading the WordPress platform on your site to ensure the best possible outcome (that is, how not to break your website after a WordPress upgrade).

REMEMBER

The upgrade process occurs on a regular basis — at least three or four times per year. For some users, this process is a frustrating reality of using WordPress. This active development environment, however, is part of what makes WordPress the most popular platform available. Because WordPress is always adding great new features and functions to the platform, upgrading always ensures that you're on top of the game and using the latest tools and features.

Getting Notified of an Available Update

After you install WordPress and log in for the first time, you can see the version number on the WordPress Dashboard in the bottom-right corner, shown as "Version 6.3" in Figure 5-1. Therefore, if anyone asks what version you're using, you know exactly where to look to find out.

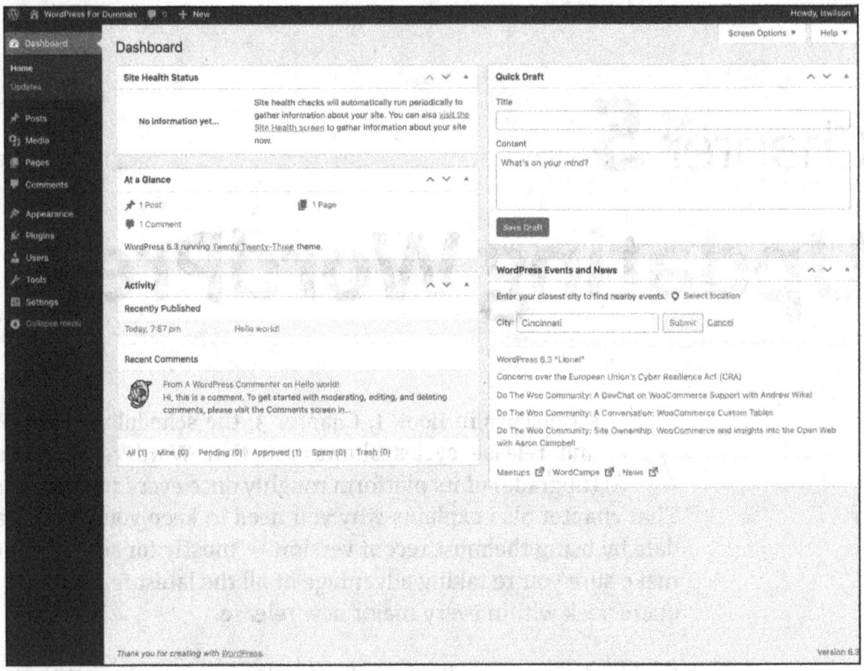

FIGURE 5-1: The WordPress version displayed on the Dashboard.

Suppose that you have WordPress installed, and you've been happily publishing content to your website with it for several weeks, maybe even months. Then one day, you log in to your Dashboard and see a message at the top of your screen you've never seen before: `WordPress X.X.X is available! Please update now.` Figure 5-2 displays the update alert message on the Dashboard, as well as a small bubble next to the Dashboard Updates links that indicates how many updates are available.

Both the message at the top of the page and the notification bubble on the Dashboard menu are visual indicators that you're using an outdated version of WordPress and that you can (and need to) upgrade the software.

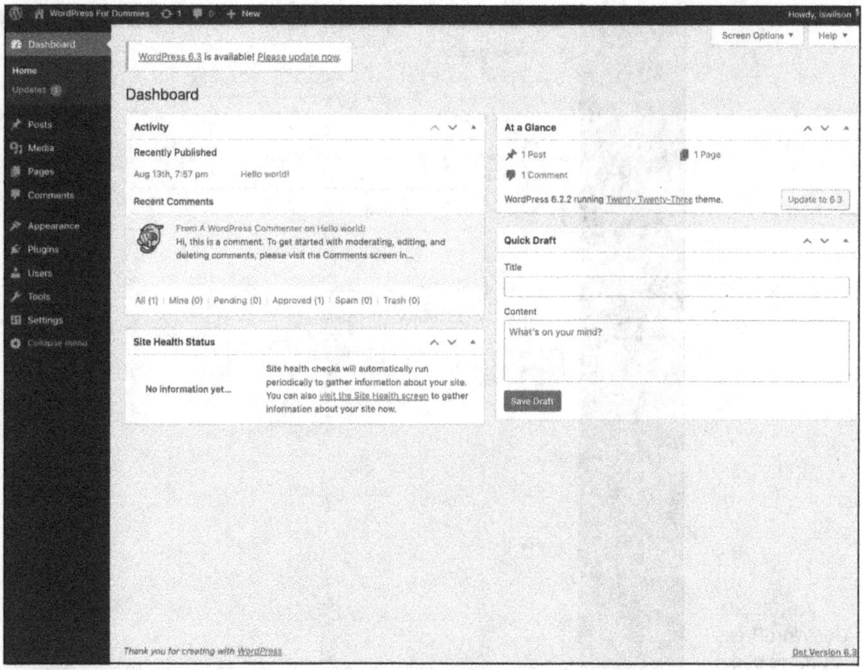

FIGURE 5-2: A Dashboard notification of an available WordPress upgrade.

The message at the top of your Dashboard includes two links that you can click for more information. (Refer to Figure 5-2.) The first is a link called `WordPress 6.3`. Clicking this link takes you to the WordPress documentation page titled Version 6.3 (`https://wordpress.org/documentation/wordpress-version/version-6-3/`), which is filled with information about the version upgrade, including

- Installation/upgrade information
- Highlights about the release
- Summary of the development cycle for this version
- List of files that have been revised

The second link, `Please update now`, takes you to another page of the WordPress Dashboard: the WordPress Updates page, shown in Figure 5-3.

In the middle of the WordPress Updates page is another important message for you:

```
Important: Before updating, please back up your database and
files. For help with updates, visit the Updating WordPress
documentation page.
```

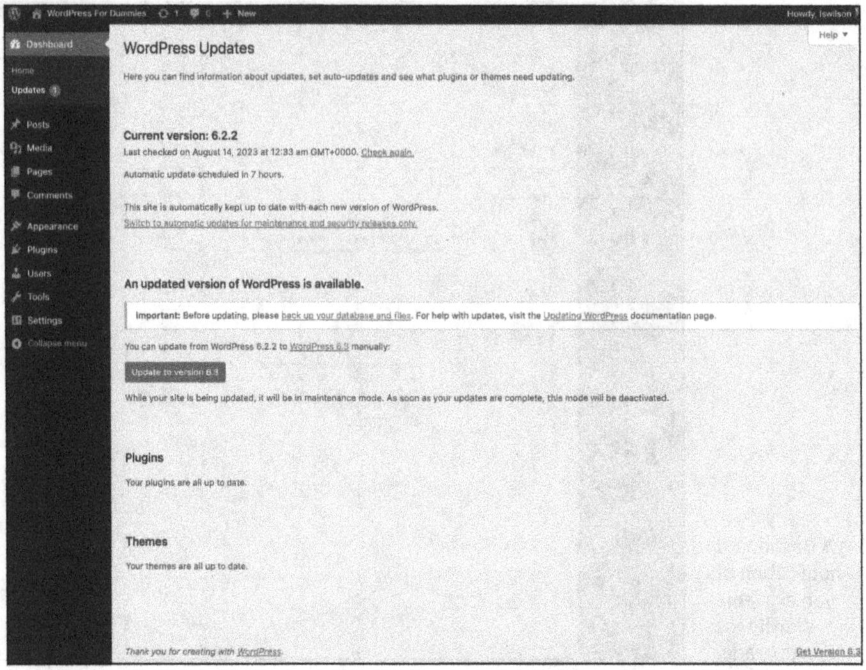

FIGURE 5-3: The WordPress Updates page.

Both links in the message take you to pages in the WordPress documentation that contain helpful information on creating backups and updating WordPress.

TIP

Book 2, Chapter 6 has extensive information on how to back up your WordPress website, content, and files.

The WordPress Updates page tells you that an updated version of WordPress is available. You can update in two ways:

- Automatically, by using the built-in WordPress updater
- Manually, by downloading the files and installing them on your server

These two ways to update are discussed later in the chapter.

Backing Up Your Database

Before upgrading your WordPress software installation, make sure that you back up your database. This step isn't required, of course, but it's a smart step to take to safeguard your website and ensure that you have a complete copy of your website data in the event that your upgrade goes wrong.

The best way to back up your database is to use the MySQL administration interface provided to you by your web hosting provider. Book 2, Chapter 3 takes you through the steps of creating a new database by using cPanel.

TIP

cPanel is a web hosting interface, provided by many web hosts as a web hosting account management tool, that contains phpMyAdmin as the preferred tool for managing and administering databases. Not all web hosts use cPanel or phpMyAdmin, however, so if yours doesn't, you need to consult the user documentation for the tools that your web host provides. The instructions in this chapter use cPanel and phpMyAdmin.

Follow these steps to create a database backup by using the phpMyAdmin interface:

1. **Log in to the cPanel for your hosting account.**

   Typically, you browse to http://*yourdomain.com*/cpanel to bring up the login screen for your cPanel. Enter your specific hosting account username and password in the login fields, and click OK to log in.

2. **Click the phpMyAdmin icon.**

   The phpMyAdmin interface opens and displays your database.

3. **Click the name of the database that you want to back up.**

   If you have more than one database in your account, the left-side menu in phpMyAdmin displays the names of all of them. Click the one you want to back up; the database loads in the main interface window.

4. **Click the Export tab at the top of the screen.**

   The page refreshes and displays the backup utility page.

5. **Choose the SQL option from the Format drop-down menu.**

6. **Click the Go button.**

   A pop-up window appears, allowing you to select a location on your computer to store the database backup file.

7. **Click the Save button to download the backup file and save it to your computer.**

TIP

Book 2, Chapter 6 contains in-depth information on making a complete backup of your website, including all your files, plugins, themes, and images. For the purposes of upgrading, a database backup is sufficient, but be sure to check out that chapter for valuable information on extensive backups, including how to restore a database backup in case you ever need to go through that process.

TIP

Almost all web hosting companies have a built-in backup feature and back up your website on a daily basis, as well as on demand. You don't always have to go into your database to back up your data if your hosting provider has a reliable backup tool that's ready for you to use. Also, there are a few WordPress plugins that help you get the backup job done, including the All-in-One WP Migration plugin (`https://wordpress.org/plugins/all-in-one-wp-migration`).

Updating WordPress Automatically

WordPress provides an easy, quick, and reliable method to update the core software from within your Dashboard. I recommend using this option whenever possible to make sure that you're accurately updating the WordPress software.

To update WordPress automatically, follow these steps:

1. **Back up your WordPress website.**

   REMEMBER

   Backing up your website before updating is an important step in case something goes wrong with the upgrade. Give yourself some peace of mind by knowing that you have a full copy of your website that can be restored, if needed. My advice is not to skip this step under any circumstances. If you're not sure how to back up, back up (pun intended!) to the preceding section.

2. **Deactivate all plugins.**

   This step prevents any plugin conflicts caused by the upgraded version of WordPress from affecting the upgrade process, and it ensures that your website won't break after the upgrade is completed. Find more information on working with and managing plugins in Book 7. For the purposes of this step, you can deactivate plugins by following these steps:

   (a) *On the Dashboard, hover your mouse pointer over Plugins on the navigation menu and then click the Installed Plugins link.*

   The Plugins page appears.

   (b) *Select all plugins by selecting the check box to the left of the plugin names listed on that page. (See Figure 5-4.)*

   (c) *From the drop-down menu at the top, choose Deactivate.*

   (d) *Click the Apply button.*

3. **Choose Dashboard ⇨ Updates.**

   The WordPress Updates page appears. (Refer to Figure 5-3.)

4. **Click the Update Automatically button.**

   The Update WordPress page appears with a series of messages, as shown in Figure 5-5.

5. **Wait for the Dashboard to refresh, or click the link in the last update message to visit the main Dashboard screen.**

   The Dashboard page appears in your web browser. Notice that both the update alert message at the top of the site and the notification bubble on the Dashboard menu are no longer visible. Your WordPress installation is now using the latest version of WordPress.

After you complete the WordPress software upgrade, you can revisit the Plugins page and reactivate the plugins you deactivated in Step 2 of the preceding list. (Refer to Figure 5-4.)

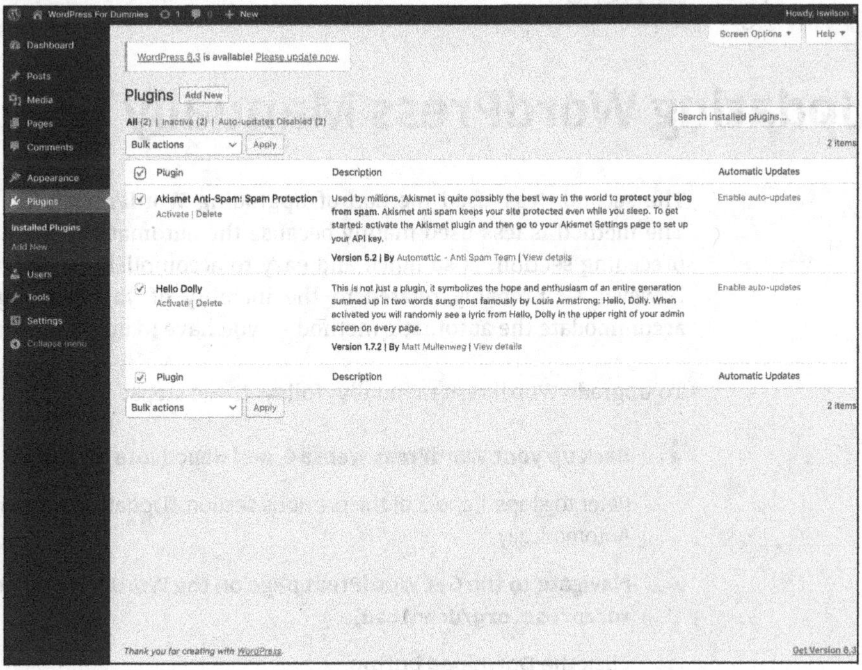

FIGURE 5-4: The Plugins page with all plugins selected, ready to deactivate.

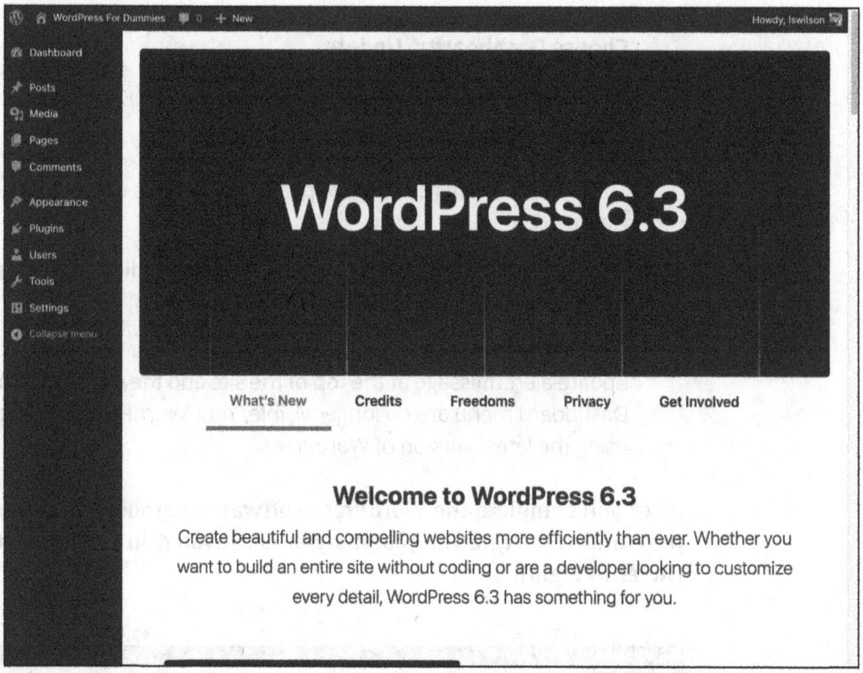

FIGURE 5-5: WordPress update messages.

Updating WordPress Manually

The second, less-used method of upgrading WordPress is the manual method. The method is less used mainly because the automatic method, discussed in the preceding section, is so quick and easy to accomplish. In certain circumstances, however — probably related to the inability of your hosting environment to accommodate the automatic method — you have to upgrade WordPress manually.

To upgrade WordPress manually, follow these steps:

1. **Back up your WordPress website, and deactivate all plugins.**

   Refer to steps 1 and 2 of the previous section, "Updating WordPress Automatically."

2. **Navigate to the Get WordPress page on the WordPress website (`https://wordpress.org/download`).**

3. **Click the Download button.**

   A dialog box opens that allows you to save the `.zip` file of the latest WordPress download package to your computer, as shown in Figure 5-6.

4. **Select a location to store the download package and click Save.**

   The `.zip` file downloads to the selected location on your computer.

5. **Browse to the `.zip` file on your computer.**
6. **Unzip the file.**

   Use a program like FileZilla (`https://filezilla-project.org`).

7. **Connect to your web server via SFTP.**

   See Book 2, Chapter 2 for details on using SFTP.

8. **Delete all the files and folders in your existing WordPress installation directory *except* the following:**
   - `/wp-content` folder (contains all your themes, plugins, and media uploads)
   - `.htaccess`
   - `wp-config.php`
9. **Upload the contents of the `/wordpress` folder to your web server — not the folder itself.**

   Most SFTP client software lets you select all the files to drag and drop them to your web server. Other programs have you highlight the files and click a Transfer button.

10. **Navigate to the following URL on your website: http://*yourdomain.com*/wp-admin.**

    Don't panic — your database still needs to be upgraded to the latest version, so instead of seeing your website on your domain, you see a message telling you that a database update is required, as shown in Figure 5-7.

11. **Click the Update WordPress Database button.**

    WordPress initiates the upgrade of the MySQL database associated with your website. When the database upgrade is complete, the page refreshes and displays a message that the process has finished.

12. **Click the Continue button.**

    Your browser loads the WordPress login page. The upgrade is complete, and you can continue using WordPress with the upgraded features.

TIP

If you're uncomfortable with performing administrative tasks, such as upgrading and creating database backups, you can hire someone to perform these tasks for you — either an employee of your company (if you run a business) or a WordPress consultant who's skilled in the practice of performing these tasks. Book 1, Chapter 4 includes a list of experienced consultants who can lend a hand.

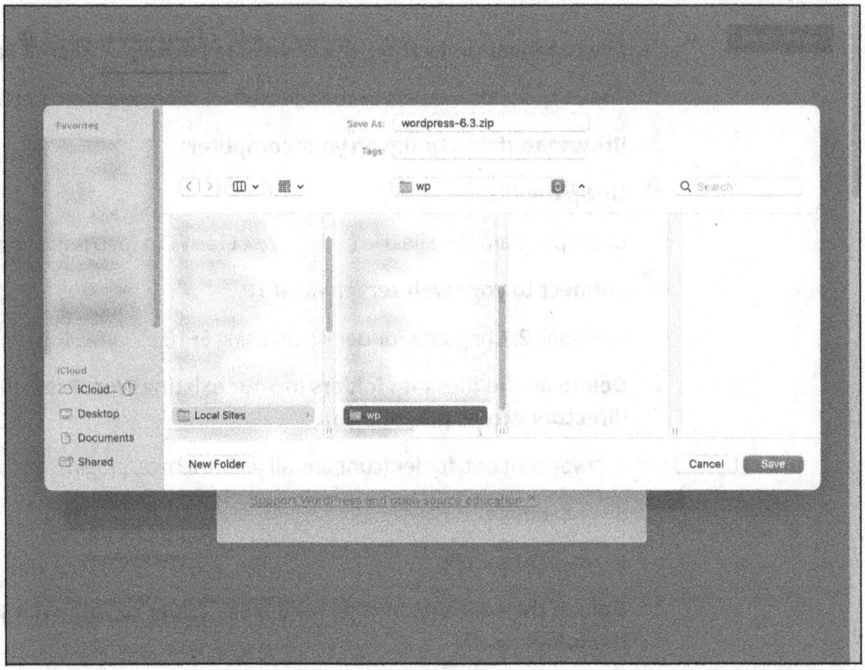

FIGURE 5-6: Downloading the WordPress files to your computer.

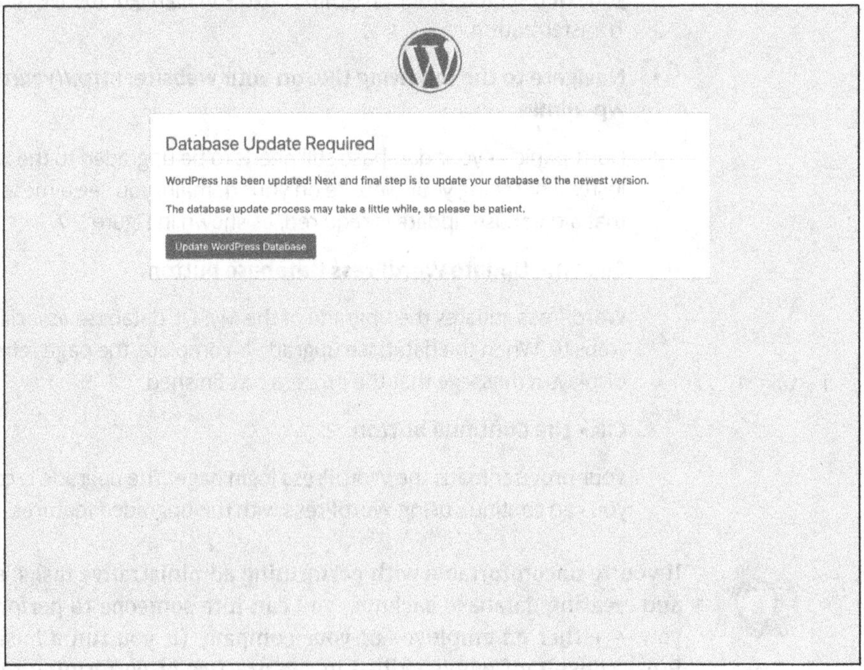

FIGURE 5-7: Click the button to update your WordPress database.

IN THIS CHAPTER

» Moving to WordPress from a different platform

» Handling the database backup management

» Backing up plugins and themes

» Storing images and media files

» Switching from your current hosting provider to a new one

Chapter 6

Backing Up, Packing Up, and Moving to a New Host

As a WordPress website owner, you may need to move your site to a different home on the web, either to a new web host or to a different account on your current hosting account. Or maybe you're an owner who needs to move your site right now.

This chapter covers the best way to migrate a site that exists within a different platform (such as Blogger, Movable Type, or TypePad) to WordPress. This chapter also takes you through how to back up your WordPress files, data, and content and then move them to a new hosting provider or a different domain.

Migrating Your Existing Site to WordPress

So you have a site on a different content management system (CMS) and want to move your site to WordPress? This chapter helps you accomplish just that. WordPress makes it relatively easy to pack up your data and archives from one platform and move to a new WordPress site.

By default, WordPress lets you move your site from such platforms as Blogger, TypePad, and Movable Type. It also gives you a nifty way to migrate from any platform via RSS feeds, as long as the platform you're importing from has an RSS feed available. Some platforms, such as Medium (`https://medium.com`), have some limitations on RSS feed availability, so be sure to check with your platform provider. In this chapter, you discover how to prepare your site for migration and how to move from the specific platforms for which WordPress provides importer plugins.

Movin' on up

TECHNICAL STUFF

For each platform, the `WordPress.org` platform provides a quick and easy way to install plugins so that you can import and use your content right away. The importers are packaged in a plugin format because most people use an importer just once, and some people don't use the importer tools at all. The plugins are there for you to use if you need them. `WordPress.com`, on the other hand, has the importers built into the software. Note the differences for the version you're using.

Website owners have a variety of reasons to migrate from one system to WordPress:

- **Simple curiosity:** WordPress currently powers more than 43.1 percent of all websites on the Internet today, and people are naturally curious to check out software that is popular for generating content.
- **More control of your website:** This reason applies particularly to those who have a site on Blogger, TypePad, or any other hosted service. Hosted programs limit what you can do, create, and mess with. When it comes to plugins, add-ons, and theme creation, hosting a WordPress site on your own web server wins hands down. In addition, you have complete control of your data, archives, and backup capability when you host your site on your own server.
- **Ease of use:** Many people find the WordPress interface easier to use, more understandable, and a great deal more user-friendly than many of the other publishing platforms available today.

REMEMBER

In the WordPress software, the importers are added to the installation as plugins. The importer plugins included in this chapter are the plugins packaged within the WordPress software; you can also find them by searching the Plugins page at `https://wordpress.org/plugins/tags/importer`. You can import content from several other platforms by installing other plugins that aren't available from the official WordPress Plugin page, but you may have to do an Internet search to find them.

Preparing for the big move

Depending on the size of your site (that is, how many posts and comments you have), the migration process can take as little as 5 minutes in some cases or more than 30 minutes in others — and it could take even longer if you have a large site. As with any major change or update you make, no matter where your site is hosted, the very first thing you need to do is create a backup of your site. You should back up the following:

- **Archives:** Posts, comments, and trackbacks
- **Template:** Template and image files
- **Plugins:** Plugin files (do this by transferring the `/wp-content/plugins` folder from your hosting server to your local computer via SFTP)
- **Links:** Any links, banners, badges, and elements you have on your current site
- **Media:** Any media files (images, video, audio, or documents) you use on your site

Table 6-1 gives you a few tips on creating the export data for your site in a few major publishing platforms. (This table assumes that you're logged in to your site software.)

TIP

The WordPress import script allows for a maximum file size of 128MB as defined by most web hosts. If you get an "out of memory" error, try dividing the import file into pieces and uploading them separately. The import script is smart enough to ignore duplicate entries, so if you need to run the script a few times to get it to take everything, you can do so without worrying about duplicating your content. (You could also attempt to temporarily increase your PHP memory limit by making a quick edit of the `wp-config.php` file; for more information on this technique, see Book 2, Chapter 3.)

TABLE 6-1 Backing Up Your Website Data on Major Platforms

Publishing Platform	Backup Information
Movable Type	Click the Import/Export button on the menu of your Movable Type Dashboard and then click the Export Entries From link. When the page stops loading, save it on your computer as a `.txt` file.
TypePad	Click the name of the site you want to export and then click the Import/Export link on the Overview menu. Click the Export link at the bottom of the Import/Export page. When the page stops loading, save it on your computer as a `.txt` file.
Blogger	Back up your template by copying the text of your template to a text editor, such as Notepad. Save it on your computer as a `.txt` file.
LiveJournal	Make sure you are logged into your Live Journal account, then browse to `https://livejournal.com/export.bml` and enter your information. Choose XML as the format. Save this file on your computer.
Tumblr	Log in to your Tumblr account, then browse to `https://www.tumblr.com/oauth/apps` and follow the directions there to create a Tumblr app. When you're done, copy the OAuth Consumer Key and Secret Key, and paste them into a text file on your computer. Use these keys to connect your WordPress site to your Tumblr account.
WordPress	Choose Tools➪ Export on the Dashboard, choose your options on the Export page, and then click the Download Export File button. Save this file on your computer.
RSS feed	Point your browser to the URL of the RSS feed you want to import. Wait until it loads fully. (You may need to set your feed to display all posts.) View the source code of the page, copy and paste that source code into a `.txt` file, and save the file on your computer.

Converting templates

Every program has a unique way of delivering content and data to your site. Template tags vary from program to program; no two tags are the same. Also, each template file requires conversion if you want to use *your* template with your new WordPress site. In such a case, you have two options:

- **Convert the template yourself.** To accomplish this task, you need to know WordPress template tags and HTML. If you have a template that you're using on another platform and want to convert it for use with WordPress, you need to swap the original platform tags for WordPress tags.
- **Hire an experienced WordPress consultant to do the conversion for you.** See Book 1, Chapter 4 for a list of WordPress consultants.

To use your own template, make sure that you've saved *all* the template files, the images, and the stylesheet from your previous site setup. You need them to convert the template(s) for use in WordPress.

REMEMBER

Thousands of free themes are available for use with WordPress, so it may be a lot easier to abandon the template you're currently working with and find a free WordPress template that you like. If you paid to have a custom design done for your site, contact the designer of your theme, and hire them to perform the template conversion for you. Alternatively, you can hire several WordPress consultants to perform the conversion for you — including yours truly.

Moving your site to WordPress

You've packed all your stuff, and you have your new place prepared. Moving day has arrived!

This section takes you through the steps for moving your site from one platform to WordPress. This section assumes that you already have the WordPress software installed and configured on your own domain.

Find the import function that you need by following these steps:

1. **On the Dashboard, choose Tools⇨ Import.**

   The Import page appears, listing blogging platforms such as Blogger and Movable Type from which you can import content. (See Figure 6-1.)

2. **Find the publishing platform you're working with.**
3. **Click the Install Now link to install the importer plugin and begin using it.**

The following sections provide some import directions for some of the most popular platforms (other than WordPress, that is). Each platform has its own content export methods, so be sure to check the documentation for the platform you're using.

Importing from Blogger

Blogger is the blogging application owned by Google.

To begin the import process, first complete the steps in the previous section, "Moving your site to WordPress." Then follow these steps:

1. **Click the Install Now link below the Blogger heading on the Import page, and install the plugin for importing from Blogger.**
2. **Click the Run Importer link.**

   The Import Blogger page loads, with instructions for importing your file, as shown in Figure 6-2.

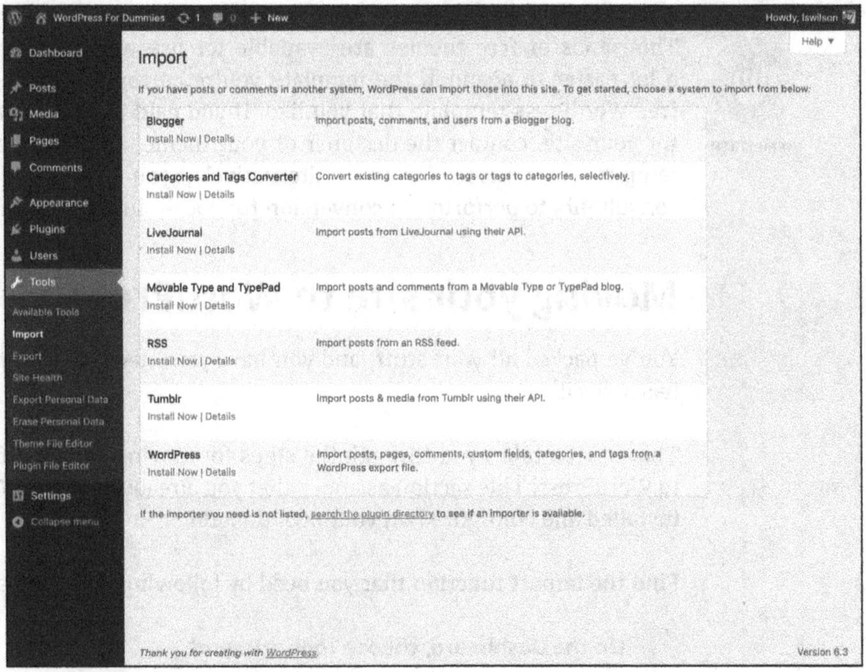

FIGURE 6-1: The Import page of the (self-hosted) `WordPress.org` Dashboard.

3. **Log in to your Blogger account.**
4. **In your Blogger account, click the blog you'd like to import.**
5. **In your Blogger account, choose Settings⇨ Other.**

   This link is on the left menu.
6. **In your Blogger account, choose Back Up Content⇨ Save to Your Computer.**

   Save the `.xml` file to your computer.
7. **On your WordPress Dashboard, on the Import Blogger page, click the Choose File button to upload the Blogger XML file.**
8. **Click the Upload and Import button.**

   This step uploads the file. The screen refreshes to the Import Blogger → Assign Authors screen.
9. **Click the Set Authors button to assign the authors to the posts.**

   The Blogger username appears on the left side of the page; a drop-down menu on the right side of the page displays the WordPress login name.

10. **Assign authors by choosing them from the drop-down menu.**

    If you have only one author on each blog, the process is especially easy: Use the drop-down menu on the right to assign the WordPress login to your Blogger username. If you have multiple authors on both blogs, each Blogger username is listed on the left side with a drop-down menu to the right of each username. Choose a WordPress login for each Blogger username to make the author assignments.

11. **Click Save Changes.**

    You're done!

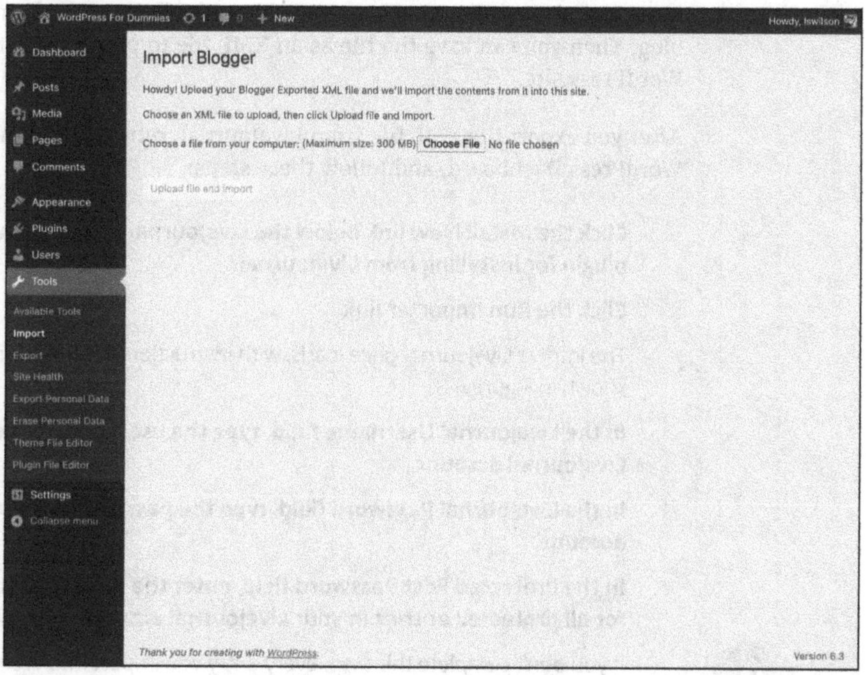

FIGURE 6-2: The Import Blogger page on the WordPress Dashboard.

Importing from LiveJournal

Both WordPress.com and WordPress.org offer an import script for LiveJournal users, and the process of importing from LiveJournal to WordPress is the same for each platform.

To export your site content from LiveJournal, log in to your LiveJournal site and then type `https://www.livejournal.com/export.bml` in your browser's address bar.

LiveJournal lets you export the XML files by month, so if you have a site with several months' worth of posts, be prepared to be at this process for a while. First, you have to export the entries one month at a time; then you have to import them into WordPress — yep, you guessed it — one month at a time.

TIP

To speed the process a little, you can save all the exported XML LiveJournal files in one text document by copying and pasting each month's XML file into one plain-text file (created in a text editor such as Notepad, for PC, or TextEdit on a Mac), thereby creating one long XML file with all the posts from your LiveJournal blog. Then you can save the file as an XML file to prepare it for import into your WordPress site.

After you export the XML file from LiveJournal, return to the Import page of your WordPress Dashboard, and follow these steps:

1. **Click the Install Now link below the LiveJournal heading, and install the plugin for installing from LiveJournal.**
2. **Click the Run Importer link.**

   The Import LiveJournal page loads, with instructions for importing your file, as shown in Figure 6-3.
3. **In the LiveJournal Username field, type the username for your LiveJournal account.**
4. **In the LiveJournal Password field, type the password for your LiveJournal account.**
5. **In the Protected Post Password field, enter the password you want to use for all protected entries in your LiveJournal account.**

   WARNING

   If you don't complete this step, every entry you import into WordPress will be viewable by anyone. Be sure to complete this step if any of your entries in your LiveJournal account are password-protected (or private).
6. **Click the Connect to LiveJournal and Import button.**

   This step connects your WordPress site to your LiveJournal account and automatically imports all entries from your LiveJournal into your WordPress installation. If your LiveJournal site has a lot of entries, this process could take a long time, so be patient.

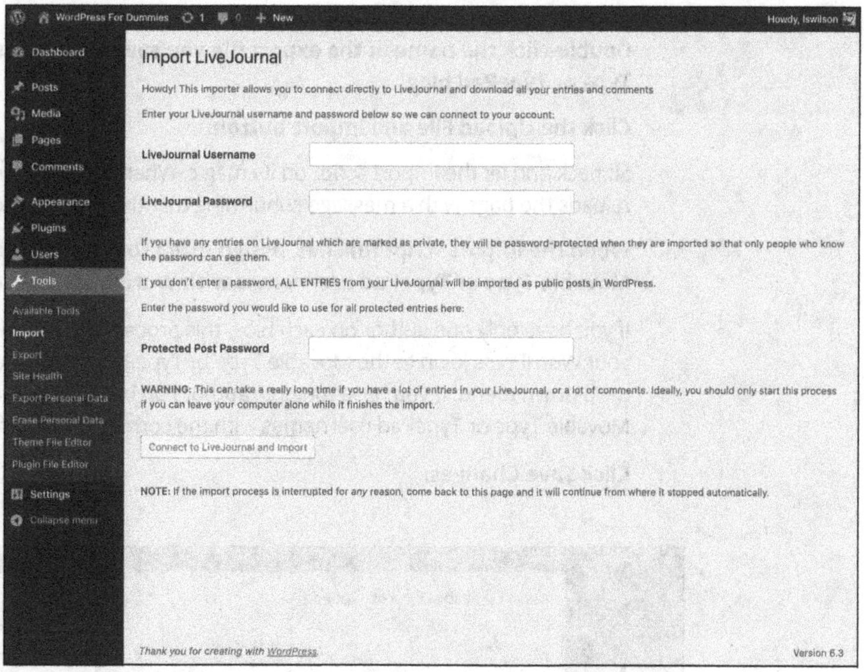

FIGURE 6-3: The Import LiveJournal page on the WordPress Dashboard.

Importing from Movable Type and TypePad

Six Apart created both Movable Type and TypePad. These two platforms run on essentially the same code base, so the import/export procedure is the same for both. Refer to Table 6-1, earlier in this chapter, for details on how to run the export process in both Movable Type and TypePad. This import script moves all your site posts, comments, and trackbacks to your WordPress website.

Go to the Import page of your WordPress Dashboard by following steps 1 and 2 in the "Moving your site to WordPress" section, earlier in this chapter. Then follow these steps:

1. **Click the Install Now link below the Movable Type and TypePad heading, and install the plugin for importing from Movable Type and TypePad.**
2. **Click the Run Importer link.**

   The Import Movable Type or TypePad page loads, with instructions for importing your file, as shown in Figure 6-4.
3. **Click the Choose File button.**

   A window opens, listing your files.

4. **Double-click the name of the export file you saved from your Movable Type or TypePad blog.**
5. **Click the Upload File and Import button.**

   Sit back and let the import script do its magic. When the script finishes, it reloads the page with a message confirming that the process is complete.
6. **When the import script finishes, assign users to the posts, matching the Movable Type or TypePad usernames with WordPress usernames.**

   If you have only one author on each blog, this process is easy; you simply assign your WordPress login to the Movable Type or TypePad username by using the drop-down menu. If you have multiple authors on both blogs, match the Movable Type or TypePad usernames with the correct WordPress login names.
7. **Click Save Changes.**

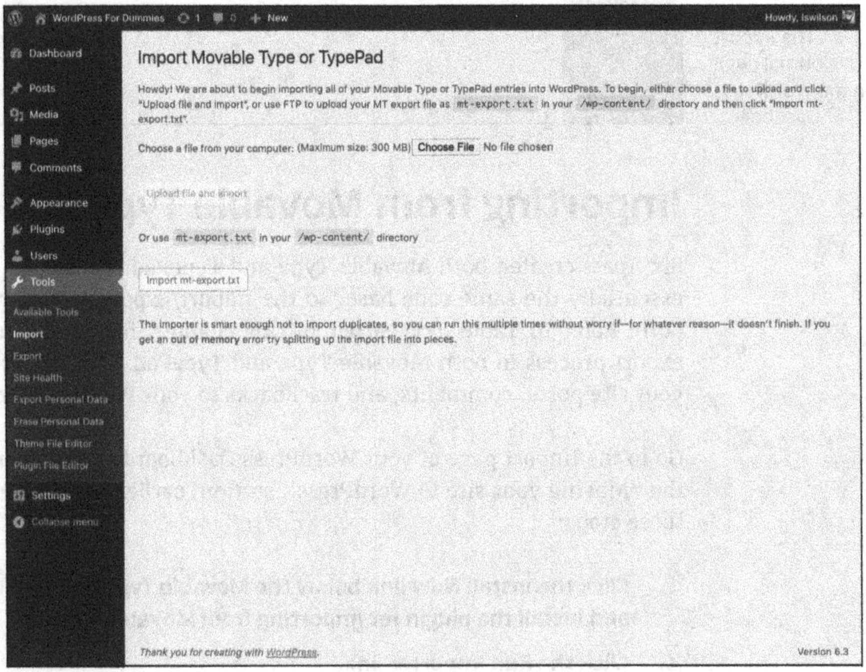

FIGURE 6-4: The Import Movable Type or TypePad page on the WordPress Dashboard.

Importing from Tumblr

With the Tumblr import script for WordPress, it's easy to import the content from your Tumblr account to your WordPress blog. To complete the import, follow these steps:

1. **Go to** `https://www.tumblr.com/oauth/apps`**.**

   The Tumblr login page appears.

2. **Enter your email address and password to log in to your Tumblr account.**

   The Register Your Application page appears.

3. **Complete the Register Your Application form by filling in the following fields:**
   - *Application Name:* Type the name of your WordPress website in the text box.
   - *Application Website:* Type the URL of your WordPress website in the text box.
   - *Default Callback URL:* Type the URL of your WordPress website in the text box.

   Seven text fields are in this form, but you have to fill in these only these three fields; you can leave the rest blank.

4. **Click the Register button.**

   Make sure to select the check box that says `I'm not a robot` to prove that you're human and not a spammer.

   The Applications page refreshes and displays your registered app information at the top.

5. **Copy the OAuth Consumer Key, and paste it into a text file on your computer.**

6. **Copy the Secret Key, and paste it into the same text file where you placed the OAuth Consumer Key in Step 5.**

7. **On your Dashboard, choose Tools⇨ Import and then click the Tumblr link.**

   The Import Tumblr page of your Dashboard opens.

8. **Insert the OAuth Consumer Key into the indicated text box.**

   Use the OAuth Consumer Key you saved to a text file in Step 5.

9. **Insert the Secret Key in the indicated text box.**

   Use the Secret Key you saved to a text file in Step 6.

10. **Click the Connect to Tumblr button.**

    The Import Tumblr page appears, with a message instructing you to authorize Tumblr.

11. **Click the Authorize the Application link.**

    The Authorization page on the Tumblr website asks you to authorize your WordPress site access to your Tumblr account.

12. **Click the Allow button.**

    The Import Tumblr page opens on your WordPress Dashboard and displays a list of your sites from Tumblr.

13. **Click the Import This Blog button in the Action/Status section.**

    The content of your Tumblr account is imported into WordPress. Depending on how much content you have on your Tumblr site, this process may take several minutes to complete. Then the Import Tumblr page refreshes with a message telling you that the import is complete.

Importing from WordPress

With the WordPress import script, you can import one WordPress site into another; this is true for both the hosted and self-hosted versions of WordPress. WordPress imports all your posts, comments, custom fields, and categories into your site. Refer to Table 6-1, earlier in this chapter, to find out how to use the export feature to obtain your site data.

When you complete the export, follow these steps:

1. **Click the Install Now link below the WordPress title on the Import page, and install the plugin to import from WordPress.**
2. **Click the Run Importer link.**

   The Import WordPress page loads, with instructions for importing your file, as shown in Figure 6-5.

3. **Click the Choose File button.**

   A window opens, listing the files on your computer.

4. **Double-click the export file you saved earlier from your WordPress blog.**
5. **Click the Upload File and Import button.**

   The import script gets to work, and when it finishes, it reloads the page with a message confirming that the process is complete.

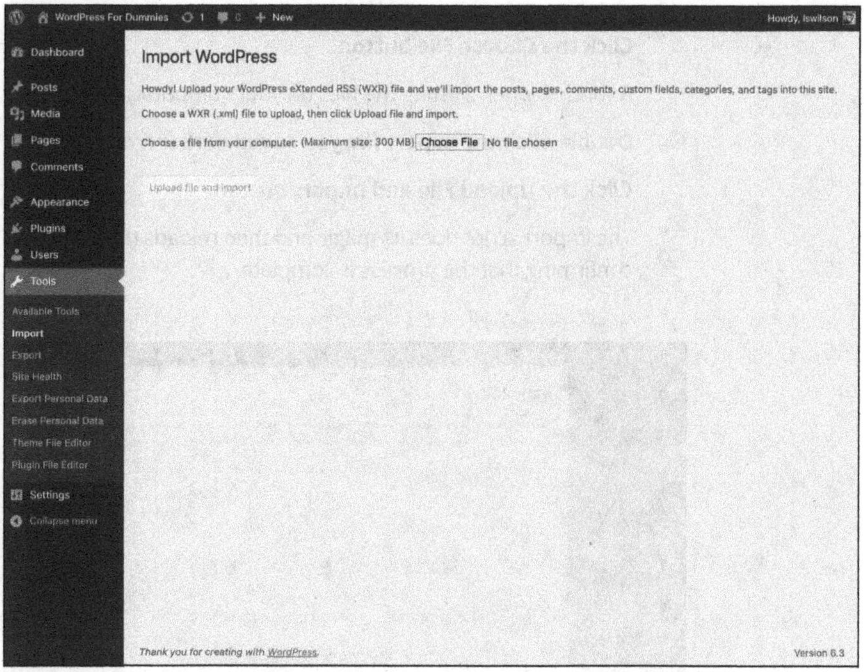

FIGURE 6-5: The Import WordPress page on the WordPress Dashboard.

Importing from an RSS feed

If all else fails, or if WordPress doesn't provide an import script that you need for your current site platform, you can import your site data via the RSS feed for the site you want to import. With the RSS import method, you can import posts only; you can't use this method to import comments, trackbacks, categories, or users.

REMEMBER

`WordPress.com` currently doesn't let you import site data via an RSS feed; this function works only with the self-hosted `WordPress.org` platform.

Refer to Table 6-1, earlier in this chapter, for the steps to create the file you need to import via RSS. Then follow these steps:

1. **On the Import page of the WordPress Dashboard, click the Install Now link below the RSS heading, and install the plugin to import from an RSS feed.**
2. **Click the Run Importer link.**

   The Import RSS page loads, with instructions for importing your RSS file, as shown in Figure 6-6.

3. **Click the Choose File button.**

   A window opens, listing the files on your computer.

4. **Double-click the export file you saved earlier from your RSS feed.**
5. **Click the Upload File and Import button.**

   The import script does its magic and then reloads the page with a message confirming that the process is complete.

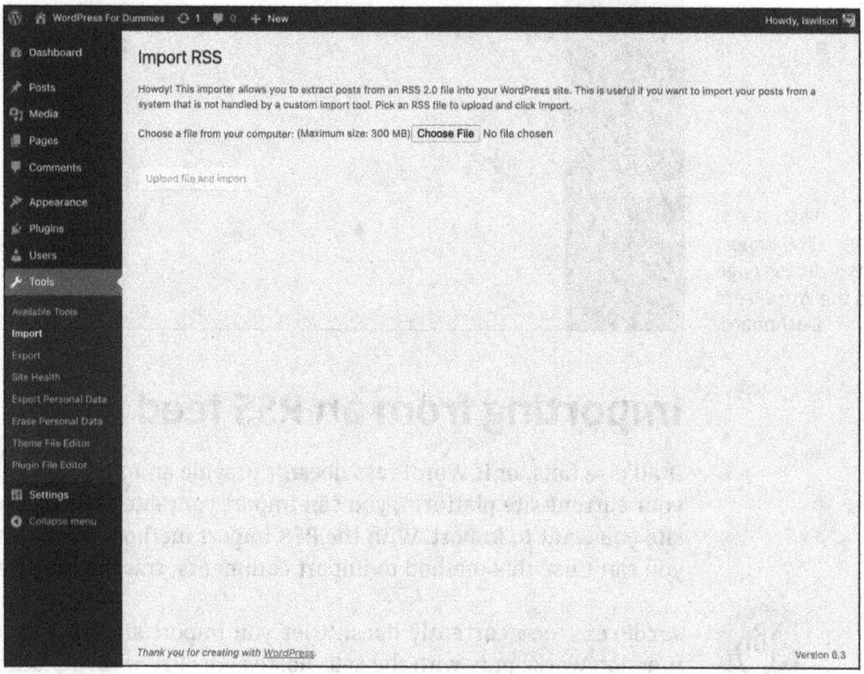

FIGURE 6-6: The Import RSS page of the WordPress Dashboard.

Finding other import resources

WordPress documentation has a long list of other available scripts, plugins, workarounds, and outright hacks for importing from other platforms. You can find that information at `https://wordpress.org/documentation/article/importing-content/`.

REMEMBER

Volunteers contribute to the documentation for WordPress. When you refer to it, be aware that not everything listed in it is necessarily up to date or accurate, including import information (or any other information about running your WordPress site).

Moving Your Website to a Different Host

There may come a time when you decide that you need to switch from your current hosting provider to a new one. There are numerous reasons why you'd have to do this. Perhaps you're unhappy with your current provider and want to move to a new one, or your current provider is going out of business and you're forced to move. Transferring an existing website — with all its content, files, and data — from one host to another can seem like a daunting task. This section should make it easier for you.

You can go about it in two ways:

- Backing up your database and downloading essential files manually
- Using a plugin to automate as much of the process as possible

Obviously, using a tool to automate the process for you is the more desirable way to go, but just in case you need to do it manually, in the next section I provide the instructions for both methods.

Creating a backup and moving manually

Book 2, Chapter 5 provides step-by-step instructions for making a backup of your database by using phpMyAdmin. Follow the steps in that chapter, and you'll have a backup of your database with all the recent content you've published to your site — *content* being what you (or someone else) wrote or typed on your site via the WordPress Dashboard, including

- Blog posts, pages, and custom post types
- Categories, taxonomies, and tags
- Post and page options, such as excerpts, time and date, custom fields, post categories, post tags, and passwords
- WordPress settings you configured on the Settings menu of the Dashboard
- All widgets that you created and configured
- All plugin options that you configured for the plugins you installed

Other elements of your website aren't stored in the database, so you need to download those elements, via SFTP, from your web server. Following is a list of those elements, with instructions on where to find them and how to download them to your computer:

- **Media files:** Media files are the files you uploaded by using the WordPress media upload feature, including images, videos, audio files, and documents. Media files are located in the `/wp-content/uploads` folder. Connect to your web server via SFTP, and download that folder to your computer.
- **Plugin files:** Although all the plugin settings are stored in the database, the plugin *files* are not. The plugin files are located in the `/wp-content/plugins` folder. Connect to your web server via SFTP, and download that folder to your computer.
- **Theme files:** Widgets and options you've set for your current theme are stored in the database, but the physical theme template files, images, and stylesheets are not. They're stored in the `/wp-content/themes` folder. Connect to your web server via SFTP, and download that folder to your computer.

Moving the database and files to the new host

When you have your database and WordPress files stored safely on your computer, moving them to a new host just involves reversing the process. Follow these steps:

1. **Create a new database in your new hosting account.**

   The steps for creating a database are in Book 2, Chapter 3.
2. **Import your database backup into the new database you just created:**
   (a) *Log in to the cPanel for your hosting account.*

   (b) *Click the phpMyAdmin icon, and click the name of your new database on the left menu.*

   (c) *Click the Import tab at the top.*

   (d) *Click the Browse button and select the database backup from your computer.*

   (e) *Click the Go button. The old database imports into the new.*
3. **Install WordPress in your new hosting account.**

   The steps for installing WordPress are in Book 2, Chapter 3.

4. **Edit the `wp-config.php` file to include your new database name, username, password, prefix, and database host.**

   Information on editing the information in the `wp-config.php` file is in Book 2, Chapter 3.

5. **Upload all that you downloaded from the `/wp-content` folder to your new hosting account.**

   Be sure that you upload these files into the `/wp-content` folder in your new hosting account.

6. **Browse to your domain in your web browser.**

   Your website should work, and you can log in to the WordPress Dashboard by using the same username and password as before because that information is stored in the database you imported.

BACKING UP AND MOVING WITH A PLUGIN

The aptly named Solid Backups plugin is regularly used by a lot of freelancers to move a WordPress website from one hosting environment to another. This plugin isn't free or available in the WordPress Plugin Directory; you need to pay for it. But it's worth every penny, because it takes the entire backup and migration process and makes mincemeat out of it. In other words, it's very easy to use, and you can do the job in minutes instead of hours.

You can purchase the Solid Backups plugin from SolidWP at `https://solidwp.com/backups/`; as of this writing, pricing starts at $99 per year. After you've purchased the plugin, you can download and install it (see plugin installation instructions in Book 7). Then follow the instructions the plugin gives you on the WordPress Dashboard to make a backup copy of your website and move it to another server.

3 Exploring the WordPress Dashboard

Contents at a Glance

IN THIS CHAPTER

» Logging in to your WordPress Dashboard

» Finding your way around the Dashboard

» Configuring Dashboard modules

» Getting some help

Chapter 1

Logging in and Taking a Look Around

With WordPress successfully installed, you can explore your new publishing software. This chapter guides you through the preliminary setup of your new WordPress website by using the Dashboard. When you publish with WordPress, you spend a lot of time on the Dashboard, which is where you make all the exciting behind-the-scenes stuff happen. On this Dashboard, you can find all the settings and options that enable you to set up your site just the way you want it. (If you still need to install and configure WordPress, check out Book 2, Chapter 3.)

Feeling comfortable with the Dashboard sets you up for successful entrance into the WordPress publishing world. You'll tweak your WordPress settings several times throughout the life of your site. In this chapter, as you go through the various sections, settings, options, and configurations available to you, understand that nothing is set in stone. You can set options today and change them at any time.

Logging in to the Dashboard

I find that the direct approach (also known as *jumping in*) works best when I want to get familiar with a new software tool. To that end, follow these steps to log in to WordPress and take a look at the guts of the Dashboard:

1. **Open your web browser, and type the WordPress login-page address (or URL) in the address box.**

   The login-page address looks something like this:

   `https://www.yourdomain.com/wp-login.php`

   TIP

   If you installed WordPress in its own folder, include that folder name in the login URL. If you installed WordPress in a folder ingeniously named `wordpress`, the login URL becomes

   `https://www.yourdomain.com/wordpress/wp-login.php`

2. **Type your username or email address in the Username or Email Address text box and your password in the Password text box.**

   REMEMBER

   In case you forget your password, WordPress has you covered. Click the Lost Your Password link (located near the bottom of the page), enter your username or email address, and then click the Get New Password button. WordPress resets your password and emails the new password to you.

   After you request a password, you receive two emails from your WordPress site. The first email contains a link that you click to verify that you requested the password. After you verify your intentions, you receive a second email containing your new password.

3. **Select the Remember Me check box if you want WordPress to place a cookie in your browser.**

   The cookie tells WordPress to remember your login credentials the next time you show up. The cookie set by WordPress is harmless and stores your WordPress login on your computer. Because of the cookie, WordPress remembers you the next time you visit. Because this option tells the browser to remember your login, don't select Remember Me when you're using your work computer, other devices (such as a tablet or mobile phone), or a computer at an Internet café.

   REMEMBER

   Before you set this option, make sure that your browser is configured to allow cookies. (If you aren't sure how, check the help documentation of the Internet browser you're using.)

4. **Click the Log In button.**

After you log in to WordPress, you see the Dashboard page.

Navigating the Dashboard

You can consider the Dashboard to be a control panel of sorts because it offers several quick links and areas that provide information about your site, starting with the actual Dashboard page shown in Figure 1-1. When you view your Dashboard for the very first time, all the modules appear in the expanded (open) position by default.

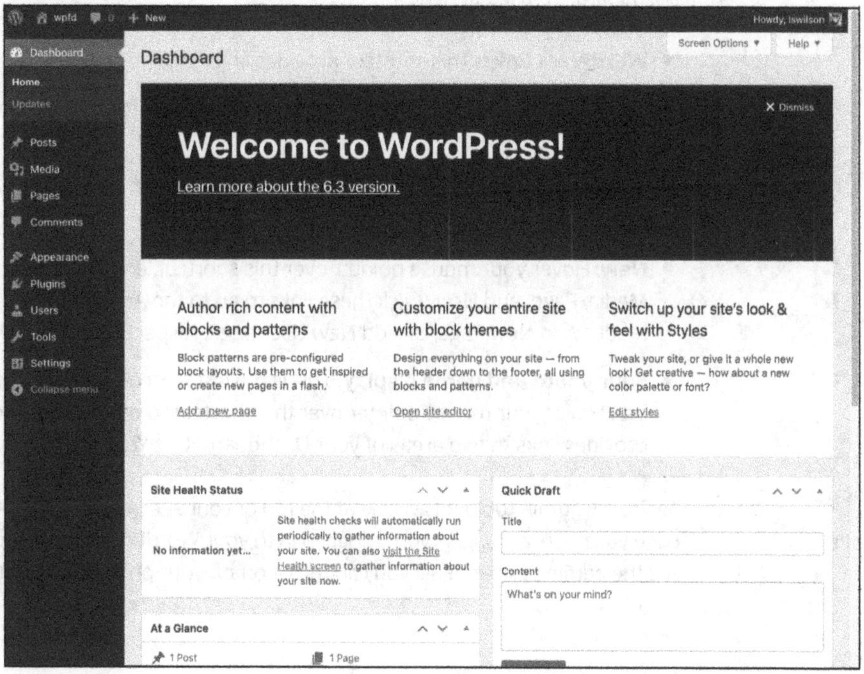

FIGURE 1-1: The WordPress Dashboard.

You can change how the WordPress Dashboard looks by modifying the order in which the modules (such as At a Glance and Activity) appear in it. You can expand (open) and collapse (close) the individual modules by clicking anywhere within the title bar of the module. This feature is really nice because it lets you use the Dashboard for just those modules that you use regularly. The concept is easy: Keep the modules you use all the time open, and close the ones that you use only occasionally; open the latter modules only when you really need them. You save screen space by customizing your Dashboard to suit your needs.

TIP

The navigation menu of the WordPress Dashboard appears on the left side of your browser window. When you need to get back to the main Dashboard page, click the Dashboard link at the top of the navigation menu on any of the screens on your WordPress Dashboard.

DISCOVERING THE ADMIN TOOLBAR

The admin toolbar is the menu you see at the top of the Dashboard (refer to Figure 1-1). The admin toolbar appears at the top of every page on your site by default, and it appears at the top of every page of the Dashboard if you set it to do so in your profile settings (see Book 3, Chapter 3). The nice thing is that the only person who can see the admin toolbar is you, because it displays only for the user who is logged in. The admin toolbar contains shortcuts that take you to the most frequently viewed areas of your WordPress Dashboard, from left to right:

- **WordPress links:** This shortcut provides links to various `WordPress.org` sites.
- **The name of your website:** This shortcut takes you to the front page of your website.
- **Comments page:** The next link is a comment-balloon icon; click it to visit the Comments page of your Dashboard.
- **New:** Hover your mouse pointer over this shortcut, and you find links titled Post, Media, Page, and User. Click these links to go to the Add New Post, Upload New Media, Add New Page, or Add New User page, respectively.
- **Your photo and name display:** This is the last item on the far right side of the toolbar. Hover your mouse pointer over this shortcut to open a drop-down menu that provides links to two areas of your Dashboard: Edit Your Profile and Log Out.

Again, the admin toolbar is visible at the top of your site only to you, no matter what page you're on, as long as you're logged in to your WordPress site. If you prefer not to see the admin toolbar at all, you can turn it off on your profile page on the Dashboard.

In the following sections, I cover the Dashboard page as it appears when you log in to your WordPress Dashboard for the first time. Later in this chapter, in the "Arranging the Dashboard to Your Tastes" section, I show you how to configure the appearance of your Dashboard so that it best suits how you use the available modules.

Welcome to WordPress! module

This module, shown in Figure 1-2, appears at the top of your Dashboard screen the first time you log in to your new WordPress installation. It can stay there, if you want it to. Also notice a small link on the right side of that module labeled Dismiss. That link allows you to remove this module if you'd rather not have it there.

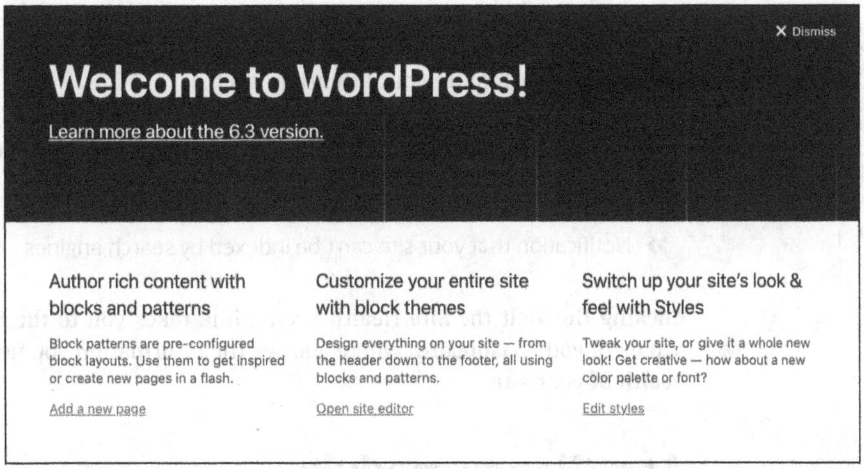

FIGURE 1-2: The Welcome to WordPress! module provides helpful links to get you started.

The makers of the WordPress software have done extensive user testing to discover what items users want to use immediately when they log in to a new WordPress site. The result of that user testing is a group of links presented in the Welcome to WordPress! module, including

- **Add a New Page:** Clicking this link takes you to the Add New Page screen on the WordPress Dashboard. This takes you directly to a new page editor, where you can immediately create a new page on your WordPress website using the block editor, which I cover in Book 4, Chapter 1.
- **Open Site Editor:** Clicking this link opens the Site editor screen on the WordPress Dashboard, where you are able to configure the settings for your website header and footer using blocks and patterns. I cover the block editor in Book 4, Chapter 1 and the site editor in Book 6, Chapter 2.
- **Edit Styles:** Clicking this link opens the Styles screen in the site editor where you are able to choose from a set of predefined styles for the theme you are using. These styles make adjustments to the visual look and feel of your website by changing the color scheme, font family, font styles, and more. I cover how to customize the look of your website using WordPress themes in Book 6.

Site Health Status module

The Site Health Status module of the Dashboard gives you details about the status of your WordPress and server configurations and settings. If you have a brand-new installation, you won't see anything listed in this module at all (refer to

Figure 1-1). As time goes on, however, you may see notices about settings or configurations that require your attention, such as

- Inactive or outdated plugins that should be removed or updated
- Inactive or outdated themes that should be removed or updated
- Notification that your site can't be indexed by search engines

Clicking the Visit the Site Health Screen link takes you to the Site Health Status screen of your Dashboard, where you see the information you need to improve the health of your site.

At a Glance module

The At a Glance module of the Dashboard shows what's going on in your website right now — this very second! Figure 1-3 shows the expanded At a Glance module in a brand-spanking-new WordPress site.

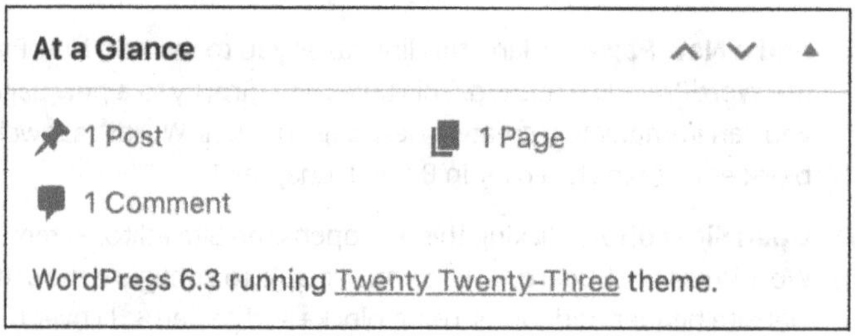

FIGURE 1-3: The At a Glance module of the Dashboard, expanded so that you can see the available features.

The At a Glance module shows the following default information:

- **The number of posts you have:** This number reflects the total number of posts you currently have in your WordPress site. The site in Figure 1-3, for example, has one post. The link is blue, which means that it's clickable. When you click the link, you go to the Posts screen, where you can view and manage the posts in your site. (Book 4, Chapter 2 covers managing posts.)
- **The number of pages:** The number of pages in your site, which changes when you add or delete pages. (*Pages,* in this context, refers to the static pages you create in your blog.) Figure 1-3 shows that the site has one page. Clicking this link takes you to the Pages screen, where you can view, edit, and delete your current pages. (Learn the difference between WordPress posts and pages in Book 4, Chapter 3.)

- **The number of comments:** The number of comments on your site. Figure 1-3 shows that this blog has one comment. Clicking the Comments link takes you to the Comments screen, where you can manage the comments on your site. (Book 3, Chapter 4 covers comments.)
- **Which WordPress theme you're using:** Figure 1-3 shows that the website is using the theme called Twenty Twenty-Three. The theme name is a link that, when clicked, takes you to the Themes page, where you can view and activate themes on your website.
- **The version of WordPress you're using:** Figure 1-3 shows that this site is using WordPress version 6.3. This version announcement changes if you're using an earlier version of WordPress. When WordPress software is upgraded, this statement tells you that you're using an outdated version of WordPress and encourages you to upgrade to the latest version.

Activity module

The module below the At a Glance module is Activity, shown in Figure 1-4. Within this module, you find

- **Recently Published:** WordPress displays a maximum of five of the most recently published posts in this area. Each one is clickable and takes you to the Edit Post screen, where you can view and edit the post.
- **Recent Comments:** WordPress displays a maximum of five of the most recent comments on your site.
- **The author of each comment:** The name of the person who left the comment appears below it. This section also displays the author's picture (or avatar), if they have one.
- **A link to the post the comment was left on:** The post title appears to the right of the commenter's name. Click the link to go to that post on the Dashboard.
- **An excerpt of the comment:** This excerpt is a snippet of the comment this person wrote.
- **Comment management links:** When you hover your mouse pointer over the comment, six links appear below it. These links give you the opportunity to manage those comments right from your Dashboard: The first link is Unapprove, which appears only if you have comment moderation turned on. The other five links are Reply, Edit, Spam, Trash, and View. (These links don't appear in Figure 1-4 because they appear only after you've hovered your mouse pointer over the comment.)

» **View links:** These links — All, Mine, Pending, Approved, Spam, and Trash — appear at the bottom of the Activity module and allow you to click and view specific types of comments on your site.

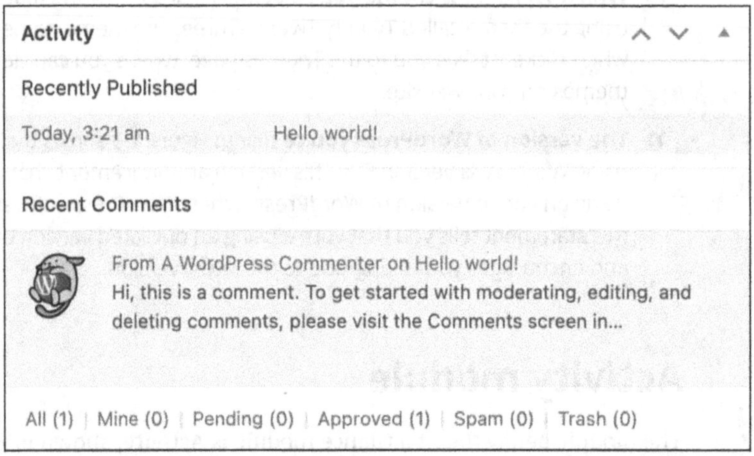

FIGURE 1-4: The Activity module of the Dashboard.

TIP

You'll find more information on managing your comments in Book 3, Chapter 4.

Quick Draft module

The Quick Draft module, shown in Figure 1-5, is a handy form that allows you to write and save a post from your WordPress Dashboard. Using this module saves your new post as a draft only; it doesn't publish the post to your live site. When you've typed a title in the Title text field and written the content in the What's On Your Mind? text box, click the Save Draft button to save the post. A link appears; you can click it to go to the Edit Post page to further edit the post and configure the post settings, including publishing. I cover the options for posts in Book 4, Chapter 2.

If you're using a new WordPress blog and a new installation of WordPress, the Drafts list doesn't appear in the Quick Draft module, because you haven't written any posts that are set to Draft status. After you've written a few posts, you may save some of those posts as Drafts, to be edited and published at a later date. Those drafts show up in the Drafts sections of the Quick Draft module.

WordPress displays up to five drafts and displays the title of the post and the date it was last saved. Click the post title to go to the Edit Post page, where you can view, edit, and manage the draft post.

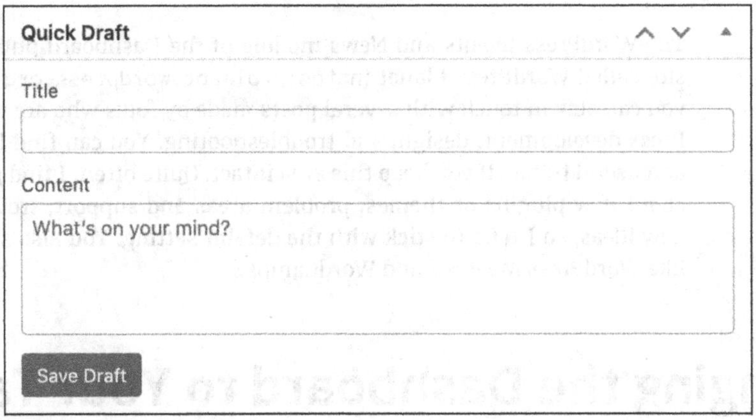

FIGURE 1-5: The Quick Draft module of the Dashboard.

WordPress Events and News module

The WordPress Events and News module of the Dashboard (see Figure 1-6) gives you details about WordPress events in your area. (I discuss various WordPress events, such as Meetups and WordCamps, in Book 1, Chapter 4.) In this module, click the small pin icon next to the Attend an Upcoming Event Near link to enter your location. The WordPress Events and News module then displays events that are local to you.

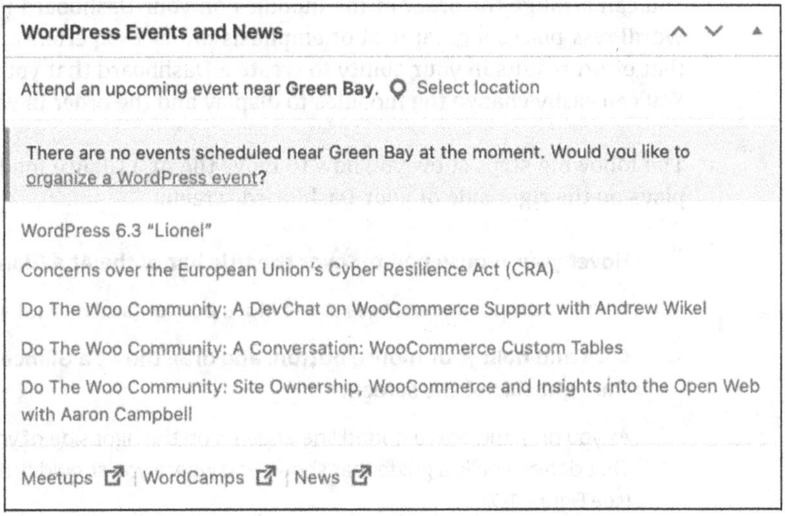

FIGURE 1-6: The WordPress Events and News module.

The WordPress Events and News module of the Dashboard pulls in posts from a site called WordPress Planet (`https://planet.wordpress.org`). In this module, you can stay in touch with several posts made by folks who are involved in WordPress development, design, and troubleshooting. You can find lots of interesting and useful tidbits if you keep this area intact. Quite often, I find great information about new plugins or themes, problem areas and support, troubleshooting, and new ideas, so I tend to stick with the default setting. You also see links to events like WordPress Meetups and WordCamps.

Arranging the Dashboard to Your Tastes

One handy feature of WordPress allows you to create your own workspace on the Dashboard. In the following sections, you find out how to customize your WordPress Dashboard to fit your needs, including modifying the layout, changing links and RSS feed information, and even rearranging the modules on different pages of the Dashboard. Armed with this information, you can open your Dashboard and customize your workspace.

Changing the order of modules

You can arrange the order of the modules on your Dashboard to suit your tastes. WordPress places a great deal of emphasis on user experience, and a big part of that effort results in your ability to create a Dashboard that you find most useful. You can easily change the modules to display and the order in which they display.

The following steps show you how to move the At a Glance module so that it displays on the right side of your Dashboard screen:

1. **Hover your mouse pointer over the title bar of the At a Glance module.**

   Your mouse pointer changes to the Move pointer (a cross with arrows).

2. **Click and hold your mouse button, and drag the At a Glance module to the right side of the screen.**

   As you drag the box, a dotted line appears on the right side of your screen. That dotted line is a guide that shows you where you should drop the module (see Figure 1-7).

3. **Release the mouse button when you have the At a Glance module in place.**

   The At a Glance module is now positioned on the right side of your Dashboard screen, at the top. The other modules on the right side of the Dashboard have shifted down, and the Activity module is the module in the top-left corner of the Dashboard screen.

4. **(Optional) Click the gray arrow to the right of the At a Glance title.**

   The module collapses. Click the arrow again, and the module expands. You can keep that module opened or closed, based on your preference.

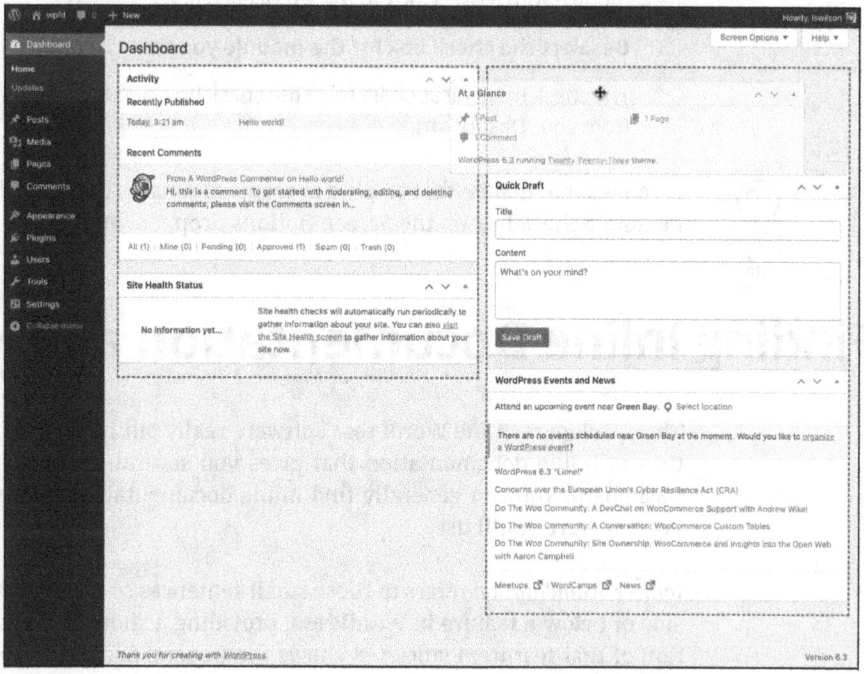

FIGURE 1-7: A dotted line appears as a guide when you drag and drop modules on the WordPress Dashboard.

Repeat these steps with each module that you want to move on the Dashboard by dragging and dropping them so that they appear in the order you prefer.

REMEMBER

When you navigate away from the Dashboard, WordPress remembers the changes you made. When you return, you still see your customized Dashboard, and you don't need to redo these changes in the future. The changes you make in the layout of your Dashboard are unique to you. Even if you have a WordPress site with multiple user accounts, WordPress remembers the changes you make on your Dashboard but doesn't apply those changes to any other users on your site. That feature makes this experience unique to your needs and preferences.

Removing Dashboard modules

If you find that your Dashboard contains a few modules that you never use, you can get rid of them by following these steps:

1. **Click the Screen Options button at the top of the Dashboard.**

   The Screen Options drop-down menu opens, displaying the title of each module with a check box to the left of each title.

2. **Deselect the check box for the module you want to hide.**

   The check mark disappears from the check box, and the module disappears from your Dashboard.

TIP

If you want a module that you hid to reappear, enable that module by selecting the module's check box on the Screen Options drop-down menu.

Finding Inline Documentation and Help

The developers of the WordPress software really put in time and effort to provide tons of inline documentation that gives you several tips and hints right on the Dashboard. You can generally find inline documentation for nearly every WordPress feature you'll use.

Inline documentation refers to those small sentences or phrases that you see alongside or below a feature in WordPress, providing a short but very helpful explanation of that feature. Figure 1-8 shows the General Settings screen, where a lot of inline documentation and guiding tips correspond with each feature. These tips can clue you into what the features are, how to use those features, and what recommended settings to use for those features.

In addition to the inline documentation that you find scattered throughout the Dashboard, a useful Help tab is located in the top-right corner of your Dashboard. Click this tab to open a panel containing help text that's relevant to the screen you're currently viewing on your Dashboard. If you're viewing the General Settings screen, for example, the Help tab displays documentation relevant to the General Settings screen. Likewise, if you're viewing the Add New Post screen, the Help tab displays documentation with topics relevant to the settings and features you find on the Add New Post page of your Dashboard.

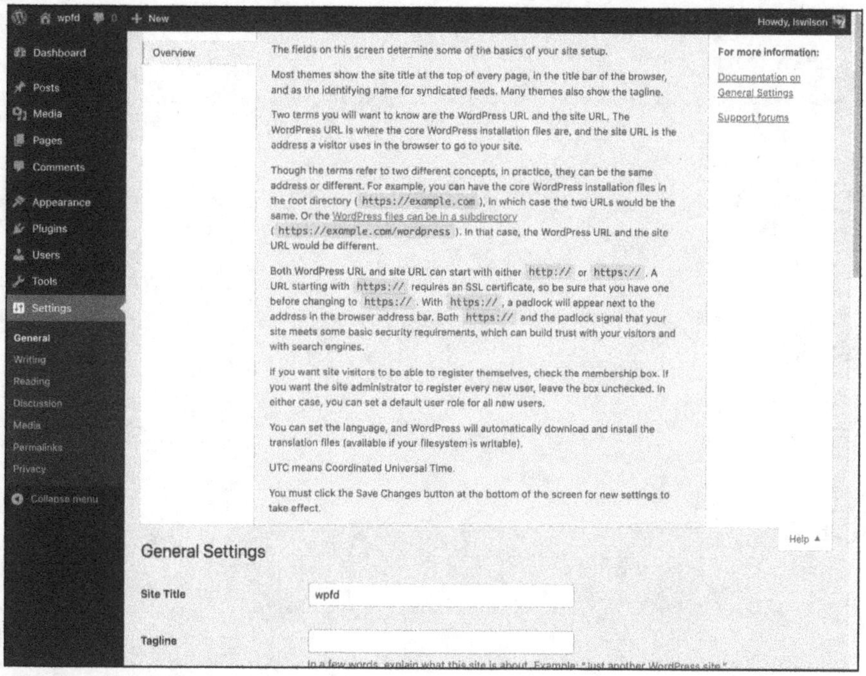

FIGURE 1-8: Inline documentation on the General Settings page on the WordPress Dashboard.

TIP

The inline documentation and the topics and text you find in the Help tab are there to assist you while you work with the WordPress platform, making the experience as easy to understand as possible. Another place you can visit to find help and useful support for WordPress is the WordPress Forums support page at `https://wordpress.org/support/forums/`.

IN THIS CHAPTER

» Configuring your WordPress general settings

» Putting together your personal profile

» Formatting your website

Chapter 2

Exploring Tools and Settings

As exciting as it is to dig in and start publishing right away, you should attend to a few housekeeping items first, including adjusting the settings that allow you to personalize your website. I cover these settings first in this chapter because they create your readers' experience with your website.

The navigation menu is located on the left side of every screen of the WordPress Dashboard. You find it there everywhere you go; like a loyal friend, it's always there for you when you need it!

The navigation menu is divided into nine menus (not counting the Dashboard menu, which I discuss in Book 3, Chapter 1). Hover your mouse pointer over a menu, and another menu flies out to the right to reveal a submenu of items. The submenu items take you to areas on your Dashboard that allow you to perform such tasks as publishing a new post, configuring your site settings, and managing your comments.

The settings that allow you to personalize your site are the first ones that I cover in the next part of this chapter. Sections with additional information contain a cross-reference telling you where you can find more in-depth information on that topic in this book.

Configuring the Settings

At the very bottom of the navigation menu, you find the Settings option. Hover your mouse pointer over the Settings link. A menu appears that contains the following links, which I discuss in the sections that follow:

- General
- Writing
- Reading
- Discussion
- Media
- Permalinks
- Privacy

General

After you install the WordPress software and log in, you can put a personal stamp on your site by giving it a title and description, setting your contact email address, and identifying yourself as the author of the site. You take care of these and other settings on the General Settings screen.

To begin personalizing your site, start with your general settings by following these steps:

1. **Choose Settings ⇨ General.**

   The General Settings screen appears, as shown in Figure 2-1.

2. **Enter the name of your site in the Site Title text box.**

   The title you enter here is the one that you give your site to identify it as your own. In Figure 2-1, I gave the new site the title *WordPress All-In-One For Dummies,* which appears on my website, as well as in the title bar of the viewer's web browser.

   TIP

   Give your website an interesting and identifiable name. You can use *Fried Green Tomatoes,* for example, if you're writing about the topic, the book, the movie, or even anything remotely related to the lovely Southern dish.

3. **In the Tagline text box, enter a five- to ten-word phrase that describes your site.**

   Figure 2-1 shows that the tagline is *by Lisa Sabin-Wilson*. Therefore, this site displays the site title, followed by the tagline: *WordPress All-in-One For Dummies by Lisa Sabin-Wilson.*

   REMEMBER

   The general Internet-surfing public can view your site title and tagline, which various search engines (such as Google, Yahoo!, and Bing) grab for indexing, so choose your words with this fact in mind. (You can find more information about search engine optimization, or SEO, in Book 5.)

4. **In the WordPress Address (URL) text box, enter the location where you installed the WordPress software.**

   Be sure to include the `https://` portion of the URL and the entire path to your WordPress installation, such as `https://yourdomain.com`. If you installed WordPress in a folder in your directory — in a folder called `wordpress`, for example — you need to make sure to include it here. If you installed WordPress in a folder called `wordpress`, the WordPress address would be `https://yourdomain.com/wordpress` (where *`yourdomain.com`* is your domain name).

5. **In the Site Address (URL) text box, enter the web address where people can find your site by using their web browsers.**

   Typically, what you enter here is the same as your domain name (`https://yourdomain.com`). If you install WordPress in a subdirectory of your site, the WordPress installation URL is different from the Site Address (URL). If you install WordPress at `https://yourdomain.com/wordpress/` (WordPress Address [URL]), you need to tell WordPress that you want the site to appear at `https://yourdomain.com` (the Site Address [URL]).

6. **Enter your email address in the Administration Email Address text box.**

   WordPress sends messages about the details of your site to this email address. When a new user registers for your site, for example, WordPress sends you an email alert.

7. **Select a Membership option.**

   Select the Anyone Can Register check box if you want to keep registration on your site open to anyone. Leave the check box deselected if you'd rather not have open registration on your site.

8. **From the New User Default Role drop-down menu, choose the role that you want new users to have when they register for user accounts in your site.**

Each user role is assigned a different level of access to your site:

- *Subscriber:* The default role. You may want to maintain this role as the one assigned to new users, particularly if you don't know who's registering. Subscribers have access to the Dashboard screen, and they can view and change the options in their profiles in the Profile screen. (They don't have access to your account settings, however — only to their own.) Each user can change their username, email address, password, bio, and other descriptors in their user profile. Subscribers' profile information is stored in the WordPress database, and your site remembers them each time they visit, so they don't have to complete the profile information each time they leave comments on your site.
- *Contributor:* In addition to the access subscribers have, contributors can upload files and write, edit, and manage their own posts. Contributors can write posts, but they can't publish the posts; the administrator reviews all contributor posts and decides whether to publish them. This setting is a good way to moderate content written by new authors.
- *Author:* In addition to the access contributors have, authors can publish and edit their own posts.
- *Editor:* In addition to the access authors have, editors can moderate comments, manage categories, manage links, edit pages, and edit other authors' posts.
- *Administrator:* Administrators can edit all the options and settings in the WordPress site.

9. **From the Site Language drop-down menu, choose your preferred language.**

   The default language for WordPress is English.

10. **From the Timezone drop-down menu, choose your UTC time.**

    This setting refers to the number of hours that your local time differs from Coordinated Universal Time (UTC). This setting ensures that all the posts and comments left on your site are time-stamped with the correct time. If you're lucky enough, as I am, to live on the frozen tundra of Wisconsin, which is in the Central Standard Time (CST) zone, you choose **−5** from the drop-down menu because that time zone is 5 hours off UTC.

TIP

If you're unsure what your UTC time is, you can find it at the Greenwich Mean Time website (`https://greenwichmeantime.com`). GMT is essentially the same thing as UTC. WordPress also lists some major cities in the Timezone drop-down menu so that you can more easily choose your time zone if you don't know it.

REMEMBER

If you live in a state in the United States that recognizes Daylight Savings Time (DST), your GMT will change by an hour during different times of the year. In the spring and summer months, my GMT is –5 until early November, when I turn my clocks back an hour; then it's –6. If you choose the city nearest to you from the Timezone drop-down menu, WordPress automatically makes those GMT changes for you, so you don't have to remember to do it when your state is under DST.

11. **For the Date Format option, select the format in which you want the date to appear in your site.**

    This setting determines the style of the date display. The default format displays time like this: April 1, 2024.

    Select a different format by selecting the radio button to the left of the option you want. You can also customize the date display by selecting the Custom option and entering your preferred format in the text box. You can find out how to customize the date format at `https://wordpress.org/documentation/article/customize-date-and-time-format`.

12. **For the Time Format option, select how you want time to display on your site.**

    This setting is the style of the time display. The default format displays time like this: 12:00 a.m.

    Select a different format by selecting the radio button to the left of the option you want. You can also customize the date display by selecting the Custom option and entering your preferred format in the text box. Find out how at `https://wordpress.org/documentation/article/customize-date-and-time-format`.

    TIP

    You can format the time and date in several ways. Go to `http://php.net/manual/en/function.date.php` to find potential formats at the PHP website.

13. **From the Week Starts On drop-down menu, choose the day on which the week starts in your calendar.**

    Displaying the calendar in the sidebar of your site is optional. If you choose to display the calendar, you can select the day of the week on which you want your calendar to start.

REMEMBER

Click the Save Changes button at the bottom of any page where you set new options. If you don't click Save Changes, your settings aren't saved, and WordPress reverts to the preceding options. Each time you click the Save Changes button, WordPress reloads the current screen, displaying the new options that you just set.

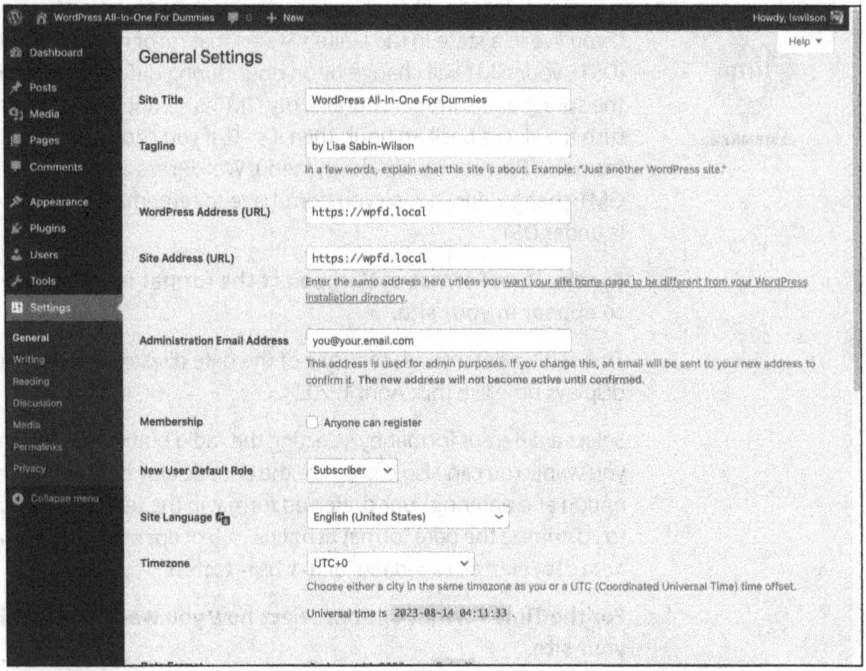

FIGURE 2-1: Personalize the settings of your WordPress site on the General Settings screen.

Writing

Choose Settings ⇨ Writing, and the Writing Settings screen opens. (See Figure 2-2.)

This screen of the Dashboard lets you set some basic options for writing your content. Table 2-1 gives you some information on choosing how your content looks and how WordPress handles some specific conditions.

REMEMBER

After you set your options, be sure to click the Save Changes button; otherwise, the changes won't take effect.

TIP

Go to `https://wordpress.org/documentation/article/update-services` for comprehensive information on update services.

Reading

The third item in the Settings menu is Reading. Choose Settings ⇨ Reading to open the Reading Settings screen. (See Figure 2-3.)

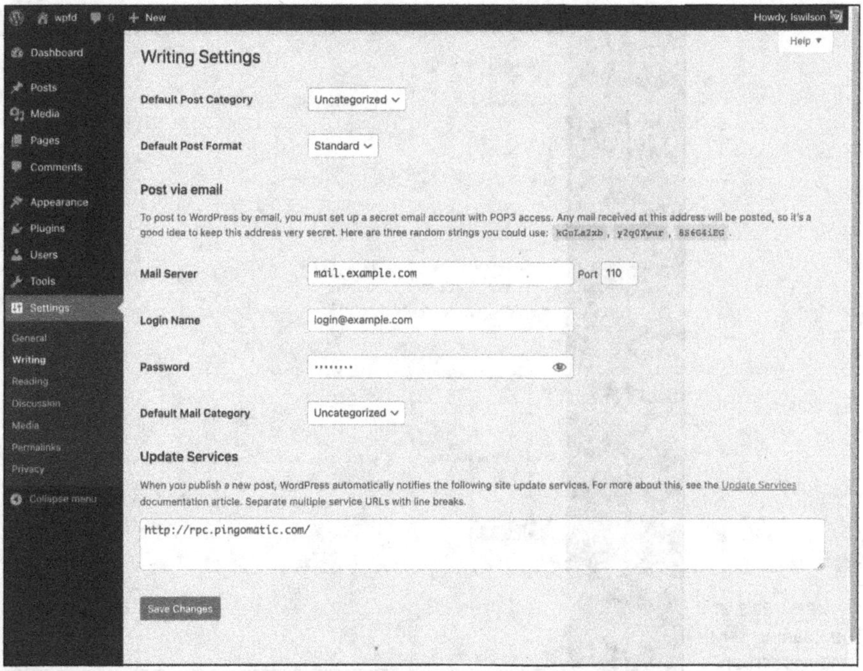

FIGURE 2-2: The Writing Settings screen.

TABLE 2-1 Writing Settings Options

Option	Function	Default
Default Post Category	Choose the category that WordPress defaults to any time you forget to choose a category when you publish a post.	Uncategorized
Default Post Format	Choose the format that WordPress defaults to any time you create a post and don't assign a post format.	Standard
Post via Email	Publish content from your email account by entering the mail server, port, login name, and password for the account you'll be using to send posts to your WordPress site.	N/A
Default Mail Category	Set the category that posts made via email are submitted to when these types of posts are published.	Uncategorized
Update Services ***Note:*** This option is available only if you allow your site to be indexed by search engines (covered in the following "Reading" section).	Indicate which ping service you want to use to notify the world that you've made updates, or new posts. The default, XML-RPC, updates all the popular services simultaneously.	`rpc.pingomatic.com`

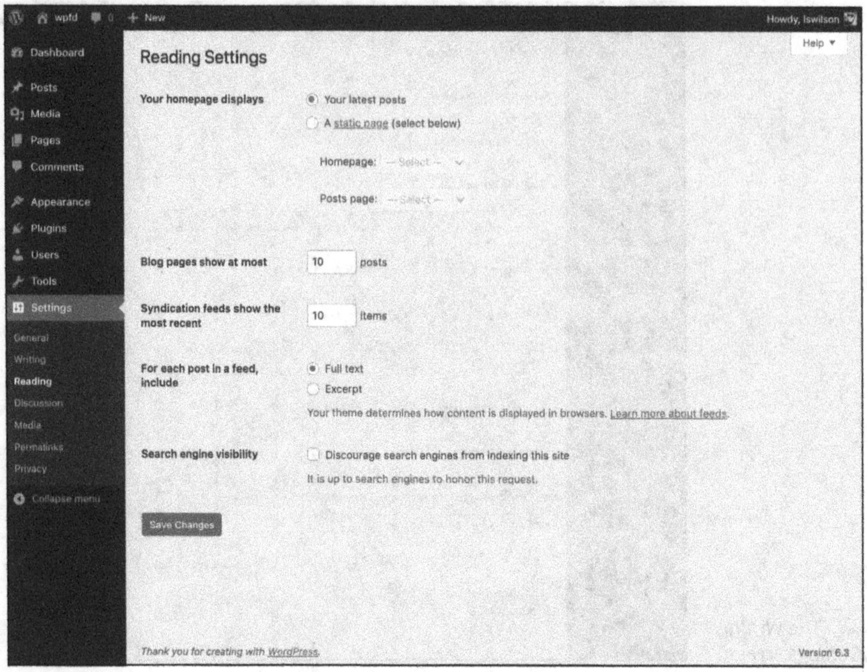

FIGURE 2-3: The Reading Settings screen.

You can set the following options on the Reading Settings screen:

- **Your Homepage Displays:** Select the radio button to show a page instead of your latest posts on the front page of your site. You can find detailed information about using a static page for your front page in Book 4, Chapter 3, including information on how to set it up by using the fields in this section that appear after you select the radio button.
- **Blog Pages Show at Most:** In the text box, enter the maximum number of posts you want to appear on each site page (default: 10).
- **Syndication Feeds Show the Most Recent:** In the text box, enter the maximum number of posts that you want to appear in your RSS feed at any time (default: 10).
- **For Each Post in a Feed, Include:** Select the Full Text or Excerpt radio button. Full Text publishes the entire post to your RSS feed, whereas Excerpt publishes a portion of the text. (Check out Book 1, Chapter 1 for more information on WordPress RSS feeds.)
- **Search Engine Visibility:** By default, your website is visible to all search engines, such as Google and Yahoo!. If you don't want your site to be visible to search engines, select the Discourage Search Engines from Indexing This Site check box.

TIP

Generally, you want search engines to be able to find your site. If you have special circumstances, however, you may want to enforce privacy on your site. A friend of mine has a family site, for example, and she blocks search engine access to it because she doesn't want search engines to find it. When you have privacy enabled, search engines and other content bots can't find your website or list it in their search engines.

REMEMBER

Be sure to click the Save Changes button after you set all your options on the Reading Settings screen to make the changes take effect.

Discussion

Discussion is the fourth item on the Settings menu; choose Settings⇨Discussion to open the Discussion Settings screen. (See Figure 2-4.) The sections of this screen let you set options for handling comments and publishing posts to your site.

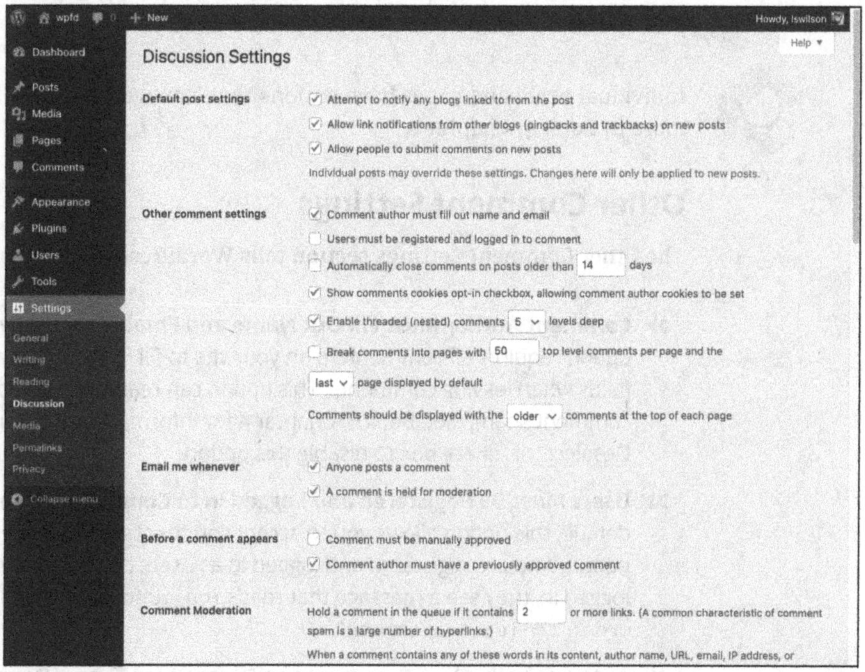

FIGURE 2-4: The Discussion Settings screen.

The following sections cover the options available to you on the Discussion Settings screen, which deals mainly with how comments and trackbacks are handled on your site.

Default Post Settings

With the Default Post Settings options, you can tell WordPress how to handle post notifications. Here are your options:

- **Attempt to Notify Any Blogs Linked to from the Post:** If you select this check box, your site sends a notification (or *ping*) to any site you've linked to in your posts. This notification is also commonly referred to as a *trackback*. (Find out more about trackbacks in Book 3, Chapter 4.) Deselect this check box if you don't want these notifications sent.
- **Allow Link Notifications from Other Blogs (Pingbacks and Trackbacks) on New Posts:** By default, this check box is selected, and your site accepts notifications via pings or trackbacks from other sites that have linked to yours. Any trackbacks or pings sent to your site appear on your site in the Comments section of the post. If you deselect this check box, your site doesn't accept pingbacks or trackbacks from other sites.
- **Allow People to Submit Comments on New Posts:** By default, this check box is selected, and people can leave comments on your posts. If you deselect this check box, no one can leave comments on your content.

TIP

Individual posts and pages have options that can override these settings. Find out more in Book 4, Chapter 2.

Other Comment Settings

The Other Comment Settings section tells WordPress how to handle comments:

- **Comment Author Must Fill Out Name and Email:** Enabled by default, this option requires all commenters on your site to fill in the Name and Email fields when leaving comments. This option can really help you combat comment spam. (See Book 3, Chapter 4 for information on comment spam.) Deselect this check box to disable this option.
- **Users Must Be Registered and Logged in to Comment:** Not enabled by default, this option allows you to accept comments on your site only from people who are registered and logged in as users on your site. If the user isn't logged in, they see a message that reads `You must be logged in in order to leave a comment.`
- **Automatically Close Comments on Posts Older Than *X* Days:** Select the check box next to this option to tell WordPress you want comments on older posts to be closed automatically. Fill in the text box with the number of days you want to wait before WordPress closes comments on posts (default: 14).

REMEMBER

Many people use this very effective antispam technique to keep comment and trackback spam down on their sites.

» **Show Comments Cookies Opt-In Checkbox, Allowing Comment Author Cookies to Be Set:** If you select the check box next to this option, which is unchecked by default, WordPress places a check box underneath the comments form on your website and a notice that says `Save my name, email, and website in this browser for the next time I comment.` When the user selects this box, WordPress remembers to set a cookie in the user's browser that remembers their information the next time they visit your site.

» **Enable Threaded (Nested) Comments *X* Levels Deep:** From the drop-down menu, you can choose the level of threaded comments you want to have on your site. The default is 5; you can choose up to 10 levels. Instead of displaying all comments on your site in chronological order, nesting them allows you and your readers to reply to comments within a comment.

» **Break Comments into Pages with *X* Top Level Comments per Page and the Last/First Page Displayed by Default:** Fill in the text box with the number of comments you want to appear on one page (default: 50). This setting can really help sites that receive a large number of comments. It allows you to break a long string of comments into several pages, which makes the comments easier to read and helps speed the load time of your site because the page isn't loading such a large number of comments at the same time. If you want the last (most recent) or first page of comments to display, choose Last or First from the drop-down menu.

» **Comments Should Be Displayed with the *X* Comments at the Top of Each Page:** From the drop-down menu, choose Older or Newer. Older displays the comments on your site from oldest to newest. Newer displays the comments on your site from newest to oldest.

Email Me Whenever

The two options in the Email Me Whenever section are enabled by default:

» **Anyone Posts a Comment:** Enabling this option means that you receive an email notification whenever anyone leaves a comment on your site. Deselect the check box if you don't want to be notified by email about every new comment.

» **A Comment Is Held for Moderation:** This option lets you receive an email notification whenever a comment is awaiting your approval in the comment moderation queue. Deselect this option if you don't want to receive this notification.

Before a Comment Appears

The two options in the Before a Comment Appears section tell WordPress how you want WordPress to handle comments before they appear in your site:

- **Comment Must Be Manually Approved:** Disabled by default, this option keeps every single comment left on your site in the comment moderation queue until you, as the administrator, log in and approve it. Select this check box to enable this option.
- **Comment Author Must Have a Previously Approved Comment:** Enabled by default, this option requires comments posted by all first-time commenters to be sent to the comment moderation queue for approval by the administrator of the site. After comment authors have been approved for the first time, they remain approved for every comment thereafter (and this setting can't be changed). WordPress stores each comment author's email address in the database, and any future comments that match any stored emails are approved automatically. This feature is another measure that WordPress has built in to combat comment spam.

Comment Moderation

In the Comment Moderation section, you can set options to specify what types of comments are held in the comment moderation queue to await your approval.

To prevent spammers from spamming your site with a *ton* of links, enter a number in the Hold a Comment in the Queue If It Contains *X* or More Links text box. The default number of links allowed is 2. Try that setting, and if you find that you're getting a lot of spam comments that contain links, consider dropping that number to 1, or even 0, to prevent those comments from being published on your site. Sometimes, legitimate commenters include a link or two in the body of their comments; after a commenter is marked as approved, they're no longer affected by this method of spam protection.

The large text box in the Comment Moderation section (not shown in Figure 2-4 because it's at the bottom of the page) lets you type keywords, URLs, email addresses, and IP addresses so that if they appear in comments, you want to hold those comments in the comment moderation queue for your approval.

Disallowed Comment Keys

In this section (not shown in Figure 2-4), type a list of words, URLs, email addresses, and/or IP addresses that you want to flat-out ban from your site. Items placed here don't even make it into your comment moderation queue; the WordPress system filters them as spam. I'd give examples of disallowed words, but the words I have in my disallowed list aren't family-friendly and have no place in a nice book like this one.

WHAT ARE AVATARS, AND HOW DO THEY RELATE TO WORDPRESS?

An *avatar* is an online graphical representation of a person. It's a small icon that people use to represent themselves on the web in areas where they participate in conversations, such as discussion forums and site comments.

Gravatars are globally recognized avatars; they're avatars that you can take with you wherever you go. They appear alongside comments, posts, and discussion forums as long as the site you're interacting with is Gravatar-enabled.

Gravatars aren't automatic; you need to sign up for an account with Gravatar so that you can receive an avatar via your email address. Find out more about Gravatar by visiting `https://gravatar.com`.

Avatars

The final section of the Discussion Settings screen is Avatars. (See the nearby sidebar "What are avatars, and how do they relate to WordPress?" for more information about avatars.) In this section (see Figure 2-5), you can select settings for the use and display of avatars on your site, as follows:

1. **In the Avatar Display section, select the Show Avatars option if you want your site to display avatars next to comment authors' names.**
2. **In the Maximum Rating section, set the rating for the avatars that do display on your site.**

   This feature works similarly to the movie rating system you're used to. You can select G, PG, R, and X ratings for the avatars that appear on your site. If your site is family-friendly, you probably don't want it to display R- or X-rated avatars.
3. **Choose a default avatar in the Default Avatar:**
   - Mystery Person
   - Blank
   - Gravatar Logo
   - Identicon (Generated)
   - Wavatar (Generated)
   - MonsterID (Generated)

- Retro (Generated)
- RoboHash (Generated)

4. **Click the Save Changes button.**

   Avatars appear in a couple of places:

   - *The Comments screen of the Dashboard:* In Figure 2-6, the comment displays the commenter's avatar next to it.
   - *The comments on individual posts to your site:* Figure 2-6 shows a comment on my personal blog.

To enable the display of avatars in comments on your site, the Comments template (`comments.php`) in your active theme has to contain the code to display them. Hop on over to Book 6 for information about blocks and templates, including blocks that allow you to display avatars in your comment list.

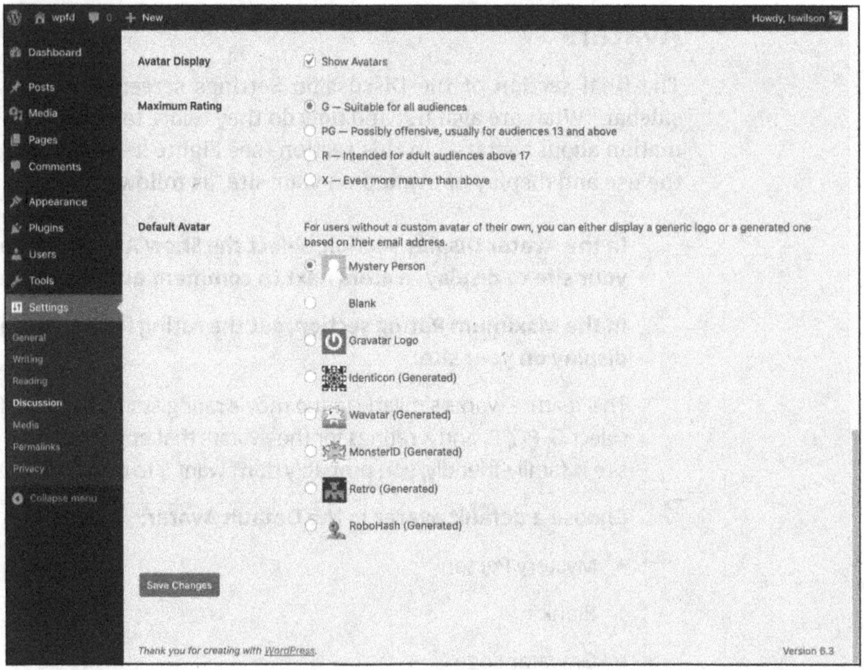

FIGURE 2-5: Default avatars that you can display.

REMEMBER

Click the Save Changes button after you set all your options on the Discussion Settings screen to make the changes take effect.

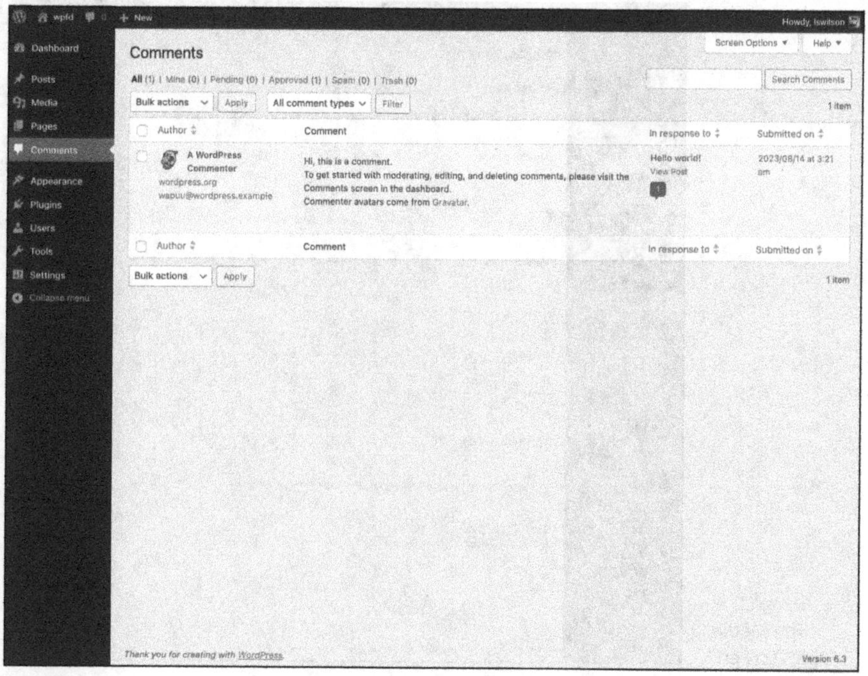

FIGURE 2-6: Comment authors' avatars appear in the Comments screen of the WordPress Dashboard.

Media

The next item on the Settings menu is Media. Choose Settings⇨Media to open the Media Settings screen. (See Figure 2-7.)

On the Media Settings screen, you can configure the options for how your image files (graphics and photos) are resized for use in your site.

The first set of options on the Media Settings screen deals with images. WordPress automatically resizes your images for you in three sizes. The dimensions are referenced in pixels, first by width and then by height. (The setting 150 × 150, for example, means 150 pixels wide by 150 pixels high.)

- **Thumbnail Size:** The default is 150 × 150; enter the width and height numbers of your choice. Select the Crop Thumbnail to Exact Dimensions check box to resize the thumbnail to the exact width and height you specify. Deselect this check box to make WordPress resize the image proportionally.
- **Medium Size:** The default is 300 × 300; enter the width and height numbers of your choice.
- **Large Size:** The default is 1024 × 1024; enter the width and height numbers of your choice.

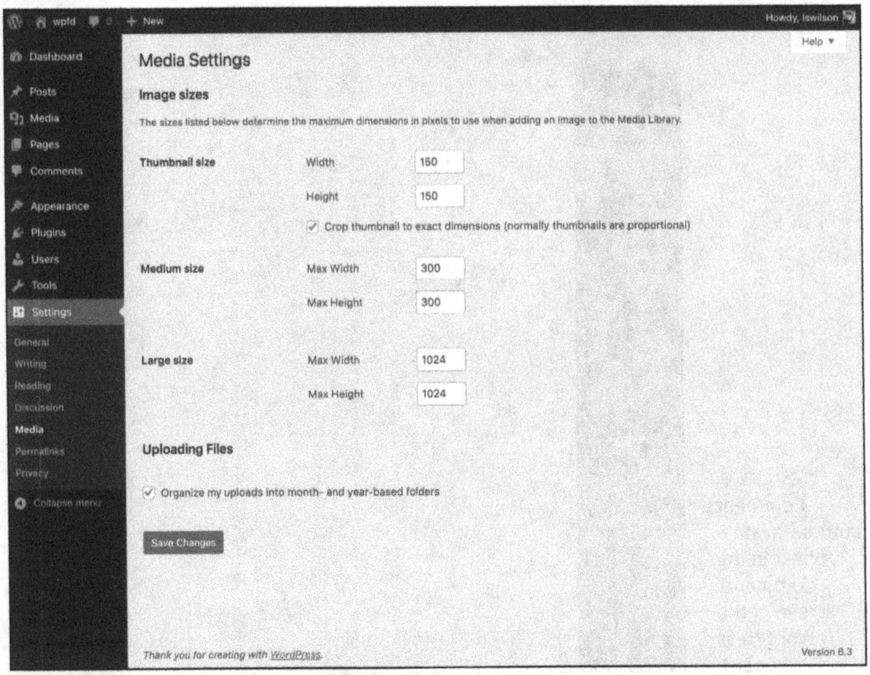

FIGURE 2-7: The Media Settings screen.

TIP

Book 6 goes into detail about using blocks, block patterns, and the site editor, including how you can edit image sizes other than the three listed above. You can use these additional image sizes in and around your website. There's also a feature called Featured Image, which you can use in posts that display on archive and search results pages.

The last option on the Media Settings page is in the Uploading Files section. By default, the Organize My Uploads into Month- and Year-Based Folders check box is selected, directing WordPress to organize your uploaded files in folders by month and by year. Files that you upload in October 2023, for example, would be in the following folder: `/wp-content/uploads/2023/10/`. Deselect this check box if you don't want WordPress to organize your files by month and year.

REMEMBER

Be sure to click the Save Changes button to save your configurations.

Book 4, Chapter 5 details how to insert images into your WordPress posts and pages.

Permalinks

The next link on the Settings menu is Permalinks. Choose Settings⇨Permalinks to view the Permalink Settings screen, shown in Figure 2-8.

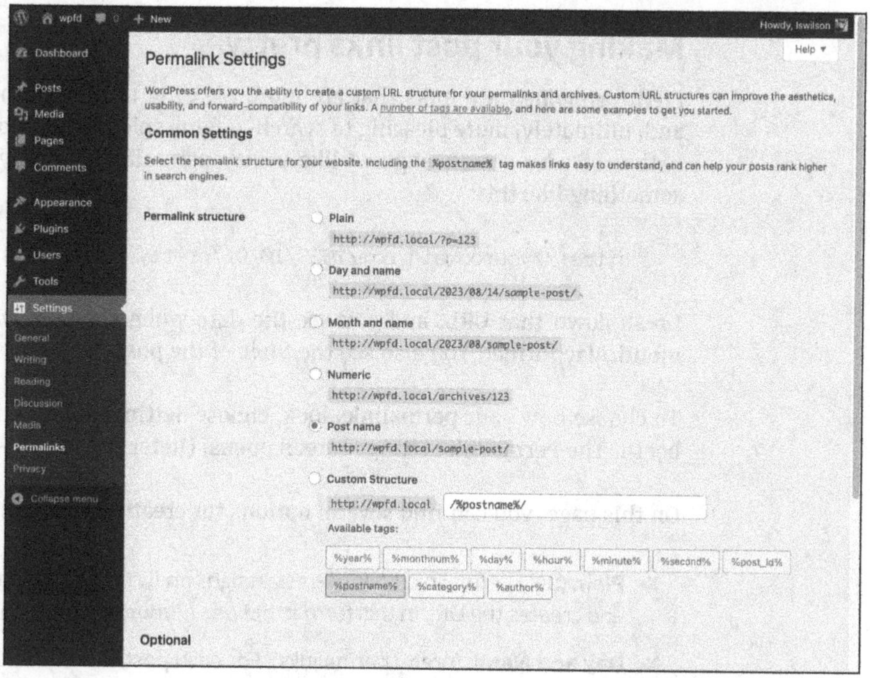

FIGURE 2-8: The Permalink Settings screen.

Each post you create on your site has a unique URL called a *permalink*, which is a permanent URL for all your website posts, pages, and archives.

Permalinks are meant to be permanent links to your posts (which is where the *perma* part of that word comes from, in case you're wondering). Ideally, the permalink of a post never changes. WordPress creates the permalink automatically when you publish a new post.

A plain post permalink in WordPress looks like this:

```
https://yourdomain.com/?p=100
```

The p stands for *post*, and 100 is the ID assigned to the individual post. You can leave the permalinks in this format if you don't mind letting WordPress associate each post with an ID number. WordPress, however, lets you take your permalinks to the beauty salon for a bit of a makeover so that you can create pretty permalinks. (You probably didn't know that permalinks could be pretty, did you?)

WARNING

Changing the structure of your permalinks in the future affects the permalinks for all the posts on your site . . . new and old. Keep this fact in mind if you ever decide to change the permalink structure. An especially important reason: Search engines such as Google and Bing index the posts on your site by their permalinks, so changing the permalink structure makes all those indexed links obsolete.

Making your post links pretty

Pretty permalinks are links that are more pleasing to the eye than standard links and, ultimately, more pleasing to search-engine spiders. (See Book 5 for an explanation of why search engines like pretty permalinks.) Pretty permalinks look something like this:

```
https://yourdomain.com/2023/10/01/pretty-permalinks
```

Break down that URL, and you see the date when the post was made, in year/month/day format. You also see the topic of the post.

To choose how your permalinks look, choose Settings⇨Permalinks on the Dashboard. The Permalink Settings screen opens. (Refer to Figure 2-8.)

On this page, you can find several options for creating permalinks:

- **Plain** (ugly permalinks): WordPress assigns an ID number to each site post and creates the URL in this format: `https://yourdomain.com/?p=100`.
- **Day and Name** (pretty permalinks): For each post, WordPress generates a permalink URL that includes the year, month, day, and post slug/title: `https://yourdomain.com/2023/10/01/sample-post/`.
- **Month and Name** (also pretty permalinks): For each post, WordPress generates a permalink URL that includes the year, month, and post slug/title: `https://yourdomain.com/2023/10/sample-post/`.
- **Numeric** (not so pretty): WordPress assigns a numerical value to the permalink. The URL is created in this format: `https://yourdomain.com/archives/123`.
- **Post Name** (my preferred): WordPress takes the title of your post or page and generates the permalink URL from those words. If I were to create a page that contains my bibliography of books and give it the title *Books*, with the Post Name permalink structure, WordPress would create the permalink URL `https://webdevstudios.com/books`. Likewise, a post titled "WordPress Is Awesome" would get a permalink URL like this `https://webdevstudios.com/wordpress-is-awesome`.
- **Custom Structure:** WordPress creates permalinks in the format you choose. You can create a custom permalink structure by using tags or variables, as I discuss in the next section.

To create the pretty-permalink structure, select the Day and Name radio button, then scroll down to click the Save Changes button at the bottom of the page.

Customizing your permalinks

A *custom permalink structure* is one that lets you define which variables you want to see in your permalinks by using the tags in Table 2-2.

TABLE 2-2 Custom Permalinks

Permalink Tag	Results
%year%	Four-digit year (such as 2024)
%monthnum%	Two-digit month (such as 01 for January)
%day%	Two-digit day (such as 30)
%hour%	Two-digit hour of the day (such as 15 for 3 p.m.)
%minute%	Two-digit minute (such as 45)
%second%	Two-digit second (such as 10)
%post_id%	The unique numerical ID of the post (such as 344)
%postname%	Text — usually, the post name — separated by hyphens (such as making-pretty-permalinks)
%category%	The text of the category name in which you filed the post (such as books-i-read)
%author%	The text of the post author's name (such as lisa-sabin-wilson)

If you want your permalink to show the year, month, day, category, and post name, select the Custom Structure radio button in the Customize Permalink Structure page of your WordPress Dashboard, and type the following tags in the Custom Structure text box:

```
/%year%/%monthnum%/%day%/%category%/%postname%/
```

If you use this permalink format, a link for a post made on October 1, 2023, called "WordPress All-in-One For Dummies" and filed in the Books I Read category, would look like this:

```
https://yourdomain.com/2023/10/01/books-i-read/
wordpress-all-in-one-for-dummies
```

REMEMBER

Be sure to include the slashes before tags, between tags, and at the end of the string of tags. This format ensures that WordPress creates correct, working permalinks by using the correct rewrite rules located in the `.htaccess` file for your site. (See the following section for more information on rewrite rules and `.htaccess` files.)

REMEMBER

Don't forget to click the Save Changes button at the bottom of the Customize Permalink Structure screen; otherwise, your permalink changes aren't saved.

Making sure that your permalinks work with your server

After you set the format for the permalinks for your site by using any options other than the default, WordPress writes specific rules, or directives, to the `.htaccess` file on your web server. The `.htaccess` file in turn communicates to your web server how it should serve up the permalinks, according to the permalink structure you chose to use.

To use an `.htaccess` file, you need to know the answers to two questions:

- Does your web server configuration use and give you access to the `.htaccess` file?
- Does your web server run Apache with the `mod_rewrite` module?

If you don't know the answers, contact your hosting provider to find out.

If the answer to both questions is yes, proceed to the following section. If the answer is no, contact your hosting provider to find out how to make sure WordPress permalinks work with your hosting server.

Creating .htaccess files

You and WordPress work together in glorious harmony to create the `.htaccess` file that lets you use a pretty-permalink structure in your site. To create the `.htaccess` file, you need to be comfortable uploading files via SFTP and changing permissions. Turn to Book 2, Chapter 2 if you're unfamiliar with either of those tasks.

TIP

If `.htaccess` already exists, you can find it in the root of your directory on your web server — that is, the same directory where you find your `wp-config.php` file. If you don't see it in the root directory, try changing the options of your SFTP client to show hidden files. (Because the `.htaccess` file starts with a period [`.`], it may not be visible until you configure your SFTP client to show hidden files.)

If you don't already have an `.htaccess` file on your web server, follow these steps to create an `.htaccess` file on your web server and create a new permalink structure:

1. **Using a plain-text editor (such as Notepad for Windows or TextEdit for a Mac), create a blank file; name it `htaccess.txt` and upload it to your web server via SFTP.**
2. **After the file is uploaded to your web server, rename the file `.htaccess` (notice the period at the beginning), and make sure that it's writable by the server by changing permissions to 755 or 777.**
3. **Create the permalink structure on the Customize Permalink Structure page of your WordPress Dashboard.**
4. **Click the Save Changes button at the bottom of the Customize Permalink Structure page.**

   WordPress inserts into the `.htaccess` file the specific rules necessary for making the permalink structure functional on your site.

If you follow the preceding steps correctly, you have an `.htaccess` file on your web server with the correct permissions set so that WordPress can write the correct rules to it. Your pretty-permalink structure works flawlessly. Kudos!

If you open the `.htaccess` file and look at it now, you see that it's no longer blank. It should have a set of code in it called *rewrite rules*, which looks something like this:

```
# BEGIN WordPress
<IfModule mod_rewrite.c>
RewriteEngine On
RewriteBase /
RewriteCond %{REQUEST_FILENAME} !-f
RewriteCond %{REQUEST_FILENAME} !-d
RewriteRule . /index.php [L]
</IfModule>
# END WordPress
```

TECHNICAL STUFF

I could delve deeply into `.htaccess` and all the things you can do with this file, but I'm restricting this chapter to how it applies to WordPress permalink structures. If you want to unlock more mysteries about `.htaccess`, check out "Comprehensive Guide to .htaccess" at `www.javascriptkit.com/howto/htaccess.shtml`.

Privacy

The next link on the Settings menu is Privacy. Choose Settings ⇨ Privacy to view the Privacy Settings screen, shown in Figure 2-9.

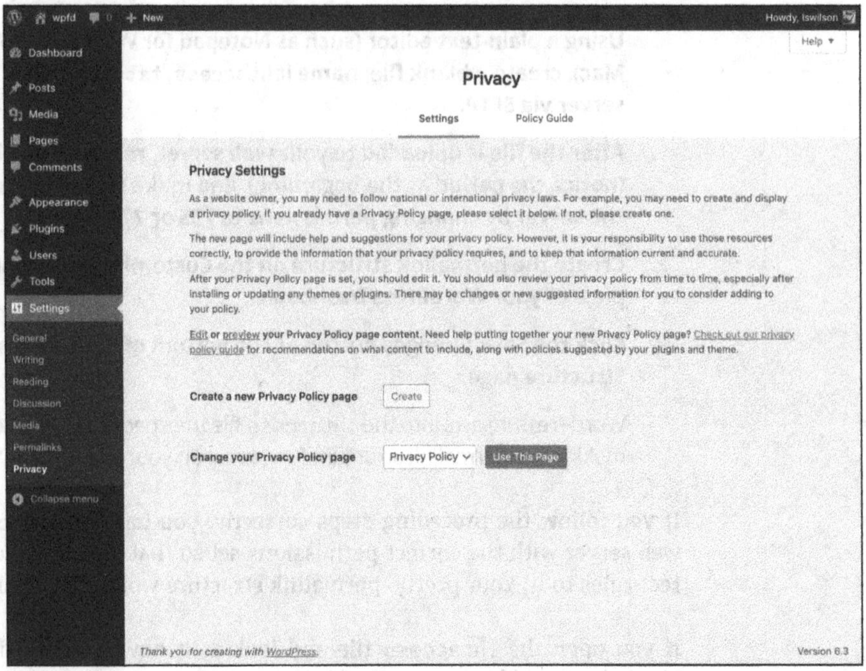

FIGURE 2-9: The Privacy Settings screen.

On May 25, 2018, the European Union (EU) enacted a law called General Data Protection Regulation, or GDPR for short. The GDPR is a set of rules designed to give European citizens more control of their personal data that's stored on websites they browse on the Internet. As an owner of a website, you may be required to follow these laws to protect the privacy of your visitors' and users' data on your website. Part of this law requires you to publish a privacy page on your website that lays out your privacy policy, which helps your website remain in compliance with GDPR rules.

TIP

Even though the GDPR was written to pertain to citizens of the EU, there are international implications, as well, particularly if visitors to your website are located in the EU. Because you can't know whether an EU citizen is going to visit your site, it's a good rule of thumb for your website to have a basic privacy policy. You can read more about the GDPR at `https://gdpr-info.eu`.

To help you, every new WordPress installation comes with a Privacy Policy page in draft form. The Privacy Settings screen displays this draft page in the Change Your Privacy Policy Page drop-down menu. Click the Use This Page button to use the default page that WordPress provided, or click the Add New Page link in the Pages menu to create your own.

This is where I tell you that I'm not a lawyer and am not equipped to give you any legal advice on what your Privacy Policy page should contain to make your website compliant with the GDPR, but WordPress offers a handy guide. Click the Check Out Our Privacy Policy Guide link on the Privacy Settings screen to view the Privacy Policy Guide screen on your Dashboard (see Figure 2-10). In addition to tips, the screen offers a template for a good Privacy Policy page.

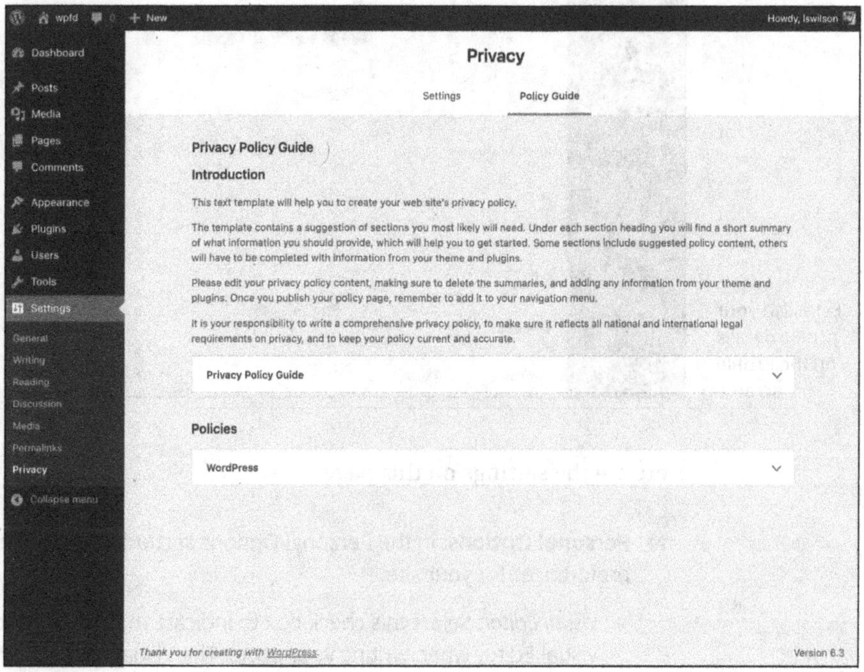

FIGURE 2-10: The Privacy Policy Guide screen.

Creating Your Personal Profile

To personalize your site, visit the Profile screen of your WordPress Dashboard.

To access the Profile screen, hover your mouse pointer over the Users link on the Dashboard navigation menu, and click the Your Profile link. The Profile screen appears, as shown in Figure 2-11.

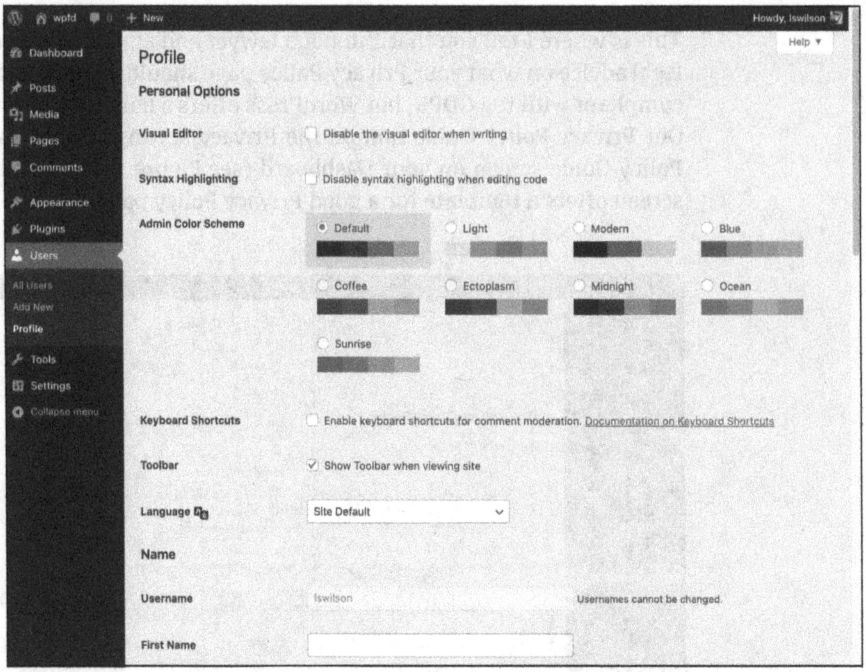

FIGURE 2-11: Establish your profile details on the Profile screen.

Here are the settings on this page:

- **Personal Options:** In the Personal Options section, you can set these preferences for your site:
  - *Visual Editor:* Select this check box to indicate that you want to use the Visual Editor when writing your posts. The Visual Editor refers to the formatting options you find on the Write Post screen (discussed in detail in Book 4, Chapter 2). By default, the check box is deselected, which means that the Visual Editor is off. To turn it on, select the check box.
  - *Syntax Highlighting:* Select this check box to disable syntax highlighting. This option disables the feature on the Dashboard theme and plugin code editors that displays code in different colors and fonts, according to the type of code being used (HTML, PHP, CSS, and so on). I cover theme and plugin code in Book 6 and Book 7, respectively.
  - *Admin Color Scheme:* These options set the colors for your Dashboard. The Default color scheme is automatically selected for you in a new installation, but you have other color options, including Light, Blue, Coffee, Ectoplasm, Midnight, Ocean, and Sunrise.

- *Keyboard Shortcuts:* This check box enables you to use keyboard shortcuts for comment moderation. To find out more about keyboard shortcuts, click the Documentation on Keyboard Shortcuts link; you're taken to the Keyboard Shortcuts page (`https://wordpress.org/documentation/article/keyboard-shortcuts-classic-editor/ - keyboard-shortcuts-for-comments`) of the WordPress Support Guides, which offers helpful information.
- *Toolbar:* This setting allows you to control the location of the admin toolbar (see Book 3, Chapter 1) on your site. By default, the admin toolbar appears at the top of every page of your site when you're viewing the site in your browser. It's important to understand that the admin toolbar appears only to users who are logged in, however. Regular visitors who aren't logged in to your site can't see the admin toolbar.
- *Language:* Back in Book 2, Chapter 3, you installed WordPress on your web server and selected a language preference for your website. In this setting, you can keep the Site Default language or select your preferred language from a drop-down menu.

» **Name:** Input personal information (such as your first name, last name, and nickname), and specify how you want your name to appear publicly. Fill in the text boxes with the requested information.

The rest of the options aren't shown in Figure 2-11; you have to scroll down to see them.

» **Contact Info:** In this section, provide your email address and other contact information to tell your visitors who you are and where they can contact you. Your email address is the only required entry in this section. This address is the one WordPress uses to notify you when you have new comments or new user registrations on your site. Make sure to use a real email address so that you get these notifications. You can also insert your website URL into the website text field.

» **About Yourself:** Provide a brief bio for yourself, and change the password for your site, if you want:

- *Biographical Info:* Type a short bio in the Biographical Info text box. This information can appear publicly if you're using a theme that displays your bio, so be creative!

WARNING

When your profile is published to your website, anyone can view it, and search engines, such as Google and Yahoo!, can pick it up. Always be careful with the information in your profile. Think hard about the information you want to share with the rest of the world!

- *Profile Picture:* Display the current photo that you've set in your Gravatar account. You can set up a profile picture or change your existing one within your Gravatar account at `https://gravatar.com`.

» **Account Management:** Manage your password and user sessions, as follows:

- *New Password:* When you want to change the password for your site, click the Generate Password button in the New Password section. You can use the password that WordPress generates for you or type your own password in the text field that appears.

TIP

Directly below the New Password text field is a password helper, where WordPress helps you create a secure password. It alerts you if the password you chose is too short or not secure enough by telling you that it's Weak or Very Weak. When creating a new password, use a combination of letters, numbers, and symbols to make it hard for anyone to guess (such as *b@Fmn2quDtnSLQblhml%jexA*). When you create a password that WordPress thinks is a good one, it lets you know by saying that the password is Strong.

TIP

A strong password is hard for someone to guess, but it can also be hard for you to remember. Password management tools like 1Password (`https://1password.com`) or LastPass (`https://www.lastpass.com`) help make it easier because you don't have to remember the password.

WARNING

Change your password frequently. Some people on the Internet make it their business to attempt to hijack sites for their own malicious purposes. If you change your password monthly, you lower your risk by keeping hackers guessing.

- *Sessions:* If you're logged in to your site on several devices, you can log yourself out of those locations by clicking the Log Out Everywhere Else button. This option keeps you logged in at your current location but logs you out of any other location where you may be logged in. If you're not logged in anywhere else, the button is inactive, and a message appears that says `You are only logged in at this location.`

REMEMBER

When you finish setting all the options on the Profile screen, don't forget to click the Update Profile button to save your changes.

Setting Your Site's Format

In addition to setting your personal settings on the Dashboard, you can manage the day-to-day maintenance of your site. The following sections take you through the links to these pages on the Dashboard navigation menus.

Posts

Hover your mouse pointer over the Posts link on the navigation menu to reveal a submenu with four links: All Posts, Add New, Categories, and Tags. Each link gives you the tools you need to publish content to your site:

- **All Posts:** Opens the Posts screen, where a list of all the saved posts you've written on your site appears. On this screen, you can search for posts by date, category, or keyword. You can view all posts, only posts that have been published, or only posts that you've saved but haven't published (drafts). You can also edit and delete posts from this page. Check out Book 4, Chapter 2 for more information on editing posts on your site.
- **Add New:** Opens the Add New Post screen, where you can compose your posts, set the options for each post (such as assigning a post to a category, or making it a private or public post), and publish the post to your site. You can find more information on posts, post options, and publishing in Book 4, Chapter 2.

  TIP

  You can also get to the Add New Post screen by clicking the Add New button on the Posts screen or by clicking the +New link on the admin toolbar and choosing Post.
- **Categories:** Opens the Categories screen, where you can view, edit, add, and delete categories on your site. Find more information on creating categories in Book 3, Chapter 5.
- **Tags:** Opens the Tags screen on your WordPress Dashboard, where you can view, add, edit, and delete tags on your site. Book 3, Chapter 5 provides more information about tags and using them on your site.

Media

Hover your mouse pointer over the Media link on the navigation menu to reveal a submenu with two links:

- **Library:** Opens the Media Library screen. On this screen, you can view, search, and manage all the media files you've ever uploaded to your WordPress site.
- **Add New:** Opens the Upload New Media screen, where you can use the built-in uploader to transfer media files from your computer to the media directory in WordPress. Book 4, Chapter 5 takes you through the details of uploading images, videos, audio, and documents by using the WordPress upload feature.

TIP

You can also get to the Upload New Media screen by clicking the Add New button on the Media Library screen or by clicking the +New link on the admin toolbar and choosing Media.

Pages

People use this feature to create pages on their sites such as About Me or Contact Me. Turn to Book 4, Chapter 3 for more information on pages. Hover your mouse pointer over the Pages link on the navigation menu to reveal a submenu list with two links:

- **All Pages:** Opens the Pages screen, where you can search, view, edit, and delete pages on your WordPress site.
- **Add New:** Opens the Add New Page screen, where you can compose, save, and publish a new page on your site. Book 4, Chapter 3 describes the difference between a post and a page. The difference is subtle, but posts and pages are very different!

TIP

You can also get to the Add New Page screen by clicking the Add New button on the Pages screen or by clicking the +New link on the admin toolbar and choosing Page.

Comments

Comments on the navigation menu don't have a submenu list of links. You simply click Comments to open the Comments screen, where WordPress gives you these options:

- **All:** Shows all comments that currently exist on your site, including approved, pending, and spam comments
- **Mine:** Shows all the comments you have created on your own website
- **Pending:** Shows comments that you haven't yet approved and are pending in the comment moderation queue
- **Approved:** Shows all comments that you've approved
- **Spam:** Shows all the comments that are marked as spam
- **Trash:** Shows comments that you've marked as Trash but not yet deleted from your blog

Book 3, Chapter 4 gives you details on how to use the Comments section of your WordPress Dashboard.

Appearance

When you hover your mouse pointer over the Appearance link on the Dashboard navigation menu, a submenu appears, displaying the following links:

- **Themes:** Opens the Themes screen, where you can manage the themes available on your site. Check out Book 6, Chapter 1 to find out about using themes on your WordPress site and managing themes on this page.
- **Editor:** Opens the Site Editor screen, where you can customize the visual appearance of your website using the block editor.

Book 6 provides information about WordPress themes and the site editor options.

Plugins

The next item on the navigation menu is Plugins. Hover your mouse pointer over the Plugins link to view the submenu links:

- **Installed Plugins:** This link opens the Plugins screen, where you can view all the plugins installed on your website. On this page, you can activate, deactivate, and delete plugins.
- **Add New:** This link opens the Add Plugins screen, where you can search for plugins in the official WordPress Plugins page (`https://wordpress.org/plugins`) by keyword, author, or tag. You can also install plugins directly to your site from the Plugins page.

Users

The Users submenu has three links:

- **All Users:** Opens the Users screen, where you can view, edit, and delete users of your WordPress site. Each user has a unique login name and password, as well as an email address assigned to their account. You can view and edit a user's information on the Users page.

» **Add New:** Opens the Add New User screen, where you can add new users to your WordPress site. Simply type the user's username, first name, last name, email (required), website, and a password in the fields provided, and click the Add User button. You can also specify whether you want WordPress to send login information to a new user by email. If you want, you can also assign a new role for the new user. Turn to the "Configuring the Settings" section at the beginning of this chapter for more info about user roles.

» **Your Profile:** Turn to the "Creating Your Personal Profile" section earlier in this chapter for more information about creating a profile page.

Tools

The last item on the navigation menu (and subsequently in this chapter!) is Tools. Hover your mouse pointer over the Tools link to view the submenu:

» **Available Tools:** Opens the Tools screen on your Dashboard. WordPress comes packaged with two extra features that you can use on your site, if needed: Press This and Category/Tag Converter.

» **Import:** Opens the Import screen of your Dashboard. WordPress allows you to import from a different publishing platform. This feature is covered in depth in Book 2, Chapter 6.

» **Export:** Opens the Export screen of your Dashboard. WordPress allows you to export your content from WordPress so that you can import it into a different platform or to another WordPress-powered site.

» **Export Personal Data:** Opens the Export Personal Data screen. This screen gives you the opportunity to input the username or email address of a registered user on your site and obtain an authorization from the user to verify and approve the request to download personal data. When verification is complete, the user receives an email with a link to download their personal data in `.zip` format.

» **Erase Personal Data:** Opens the Erase Personal Data screen on the Dashboard. This screen gives you the ability to input the username or email address of a registered user to obtain verification from that user to erase their personal data from the site. After verification from the user has been completed, the user receives an email confirming that their personal data has been erased from the site.

- **Theme File Editor:** Opens the Edit Themes screen on the Dashboard, but not before initiating a pop-up window that warns you that using this editor to make changes to your active theme is not recommended and should be limited only to users who know what they are doing in the code. If you would rather not proceed after reading the warning, click the Go Back button to exit the screen; otherwise, click the I Understand button to proceed with editing files.
- **Plugin File Editor:** Opens the Edit Plugins page and is the same experience as the Theme File Editor. Proceed with caution.

REMEMBER

The Theme File Editor link and Plugin File Editor link appear in the Tools menu unless you are using a Block Theme (see Book 6); if that's the case, the Theme File Editor link appears in the Appearance menu, and the Plugin File Editor link appears in the Plugins menu (see Book 7).

IN THIS CHAPTER

» Deciding what roles to assign users

» Allowing new users to register

» Adding a new user

» Making changes to user profiles

» Using tools to manage multiauthor sites

Chapter 3
Managing Users and Multiple Authors

A *multiauthor site* involves inviting others to coauthor, or contribute posts, pages, or other content to your site. You can expand the offerings on your website by using multiauthor publishing because you can have several people writing on different topics or offering different perspectives on the same topic. Many people use this type of site to create a collaborative writing space on the web, and WordPress doesn't limit the number of authors you can add to your site.

Additionally, you can invite other people to register as *subscribers*, who don't contribute content but are registered members of the site, which can have benefits, too. (You could make some content available to registered users only, for example.)

This chapter takes you through the process of adding users to your site, takes the mystery out of the different user roles and capabilities, and gives you some tools for managing a multiauthor website.

Understanding User Roles and Capabilities

Before you start adding new users to your site (see Book 3, Chapter 2), you need to understand the differences among the user roles, because each user role is assigned a different level of access and grouping of capabilities to your site, as follows:

- **Subscriber:** Subscriber is the default role. Assign this role to new users, particularly if you don't know who's registering. Subscribers get access to the Dashboard page, and they can view and change the options in their profiles on the Profile screen. (They don't have access to your account settings, however — only to their own.) Each user can change their username, email address, password, bio, and other descriptors in their user profile. The WordPress database stores subscribers' profile information, and your site remembers them each time they visit, so they don't have to complete the profile information each time they leave comments on your site.
- **Contributor:** In addition to the access subscribers have, contributors can upload files and write, edit, and delete their own posts. Contributors can write posts, but they can't publish the posts; the administrator reviews all contributor posts and decides whether to publish them. This setting is a good way to moderate content written by new authors.
- **Author:** In addition to the access contributors have, authors can publish and edit their own posts.
- **Editor:** In addition to the access authors have, editors can moderate comments, manage categories, manage links, edit pages, and edit other authors' posts.
- **Administrator:** Administrators can manage all the options and settings in a WordPress installation.
- **Super Admin:** This role exists only when you have the multisite feature activated in WordPress. See Book 8 for more about the multisite feature.

TIP

For a full list of user roles and capabilities, check out the WordPress documentation at `https://wordpress.org/documentation/article/roles-and-capabilities/`.

Allowing New User Registration

Each user level has a different set of capabilities. Book 3, Chapter 2 discusses the General Settings of the WordPress Dashboard, in which you set the default role for users who register on your website. Keep the default role set to Subscriber because when you open registration to the public, you don't always know who's registering until after they register — and you don't want to arbitrarily hand out higher levels of access to the settings of your website unless you know and trust the user.

When users register on your website, you, as the administrator, get an email notification (sent to the email address you set on the General Settings screen) so you always know when a new user registers; then you can go to your Dashboard and edit the user to set their role any way you see fit.

REMEMBER

New users can register on your site only after you enable the Anyone Can Register option on the General Settings screen on your Dashboard (see Book 3, Chapter 2). If you don't have this option enabled, users see a message on the registration page telling them that registration isn't allowed, as shown in Figure 3-1.

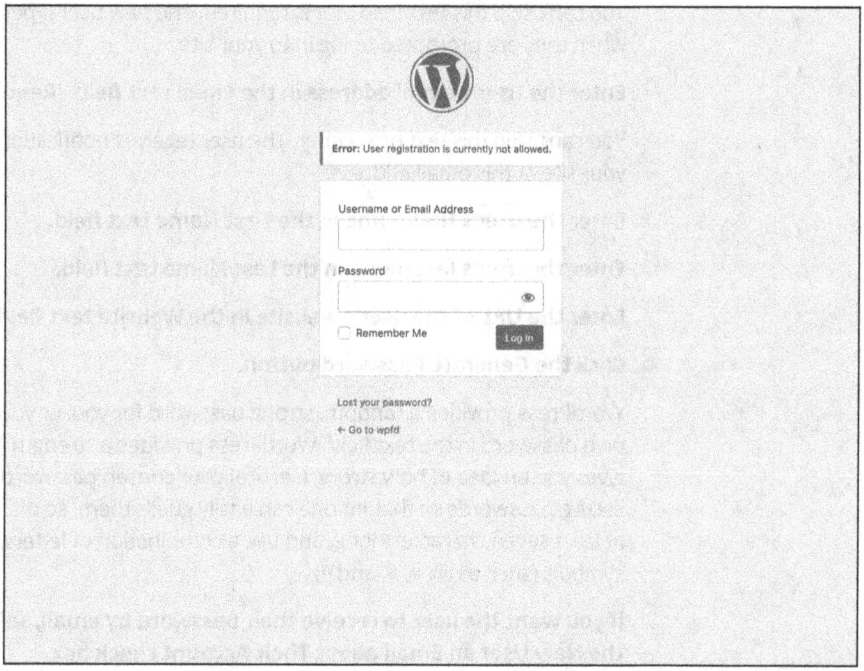

FIGURE 3-1: The message to users that registration isn't allowed.

By the way, the direct URL for registration on a blog that has registration enabled is `https://yourdomain.com/wp-login.php?action=register`. With registration enabled (in General Settings), a user sees a form inviting them to input their desired username and email address. After they do, they get a confirmation notice in their Inbox including an authorization link that they must click to authenticate their registration.

After a user has registered, you, as the site administrator, can manage their user account and assign a user role.

Adding New Users Manually

Allowing new users to register by using the WordPress registration interface is just one way to add users to your site. As the site administrator, you can also add new users manually by following these steps:

1. **Log in to your WordPress Dashboard by inputting your username and password in the form at `https://yourdomain.com/wp-login.php`.**
2. **Click the Add New link in the Users submenu of the Dashboard.**

   The Add New User screen loads, as shown in Figure 3-2.
3. **Enter the username in the Username text field. (Required)**

   You can't skip this text field as it is required. The new user types this username when they are prompted to log in to your site.
4. **Enter the user's email address in the Email text field. (Required)**

   You can't skip this text box, either. The user receives notifications from you and your site at this email address.
5. **Enter the user's first name in the First Name text field.**
6. **Enter the user's last name in the Last Name text field.**
7. **Enter the URL of the user's website in the Website text field.**
8. **Click the Generate Password button.**

   WordPress provides a random, strong password for you, or you can type your own password in the text field. WordPress provides a strength indicator that gives you an idea of how strong (secure) your chosen password is. You want secure passwords so that no one can easily guess them, so make the password at least seven characters long, and use a combination of letters, numbers, and symbols (such as @, #, $, and ^).
9. **If you want the user to receive their password by email, select the Send the New User an Email about Their Account check box.**
10. **From the Role drop-down menu, choose Subscriber, Contributor, Author, Editor, or Administrator.**
11. **Click the Add New User button.**

    The Add New User screen loads, and the email notification is sent to the user you just added. When the screen loads, all the fields are cleared, allowing you to add another new user if you want.

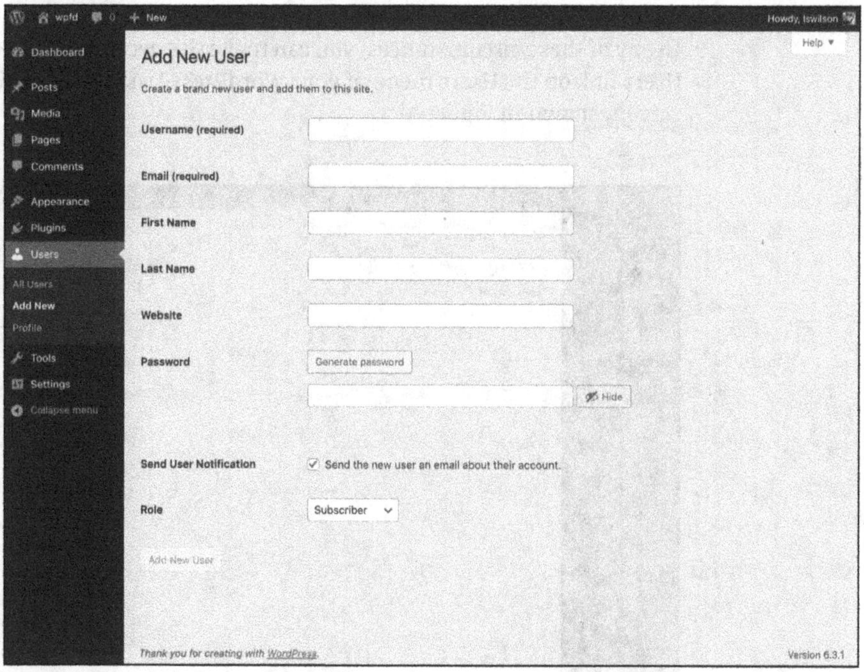

FIGURE 3-2: The Add New User screen of the WordPress Dashboard.

Editing User Details

After users register and settle into their accounts on your site, you, as the site administrator, have the ability to edit their accounts. You may never have to edit user accounts at all, but you have the option to do so if you need to. Most often, users can access the details of their own accounts and change their email addresses, names, passwords, and so on. Following are some circumstances under which you may need to edit user accounts:

- **Edit user roles.** When a user registers, you may want to increase their role, or level of access, on your site; promote an existing user to administrator; or demote an existing administrator or editor a notch or two.
- **Edit user emails.** If a user loses access to the email account that they registered with, they may ask you to change their account email address so that they can access their account notifications again.
- **Edit user passwords.** If a user loses access to the email account with which they registered, they can't use WordPress's Lost Password feature, which allows users to gain access to their account password through email recovery. In that case, a user may ask you to reset their password for them so that they can log in and access their account again.

In any of these circumstances, you can make the necessary changes by clicking the Users link on the Users menu of your WordPress Dashboard, which loads the Users screen, shown in Figure 3-3.

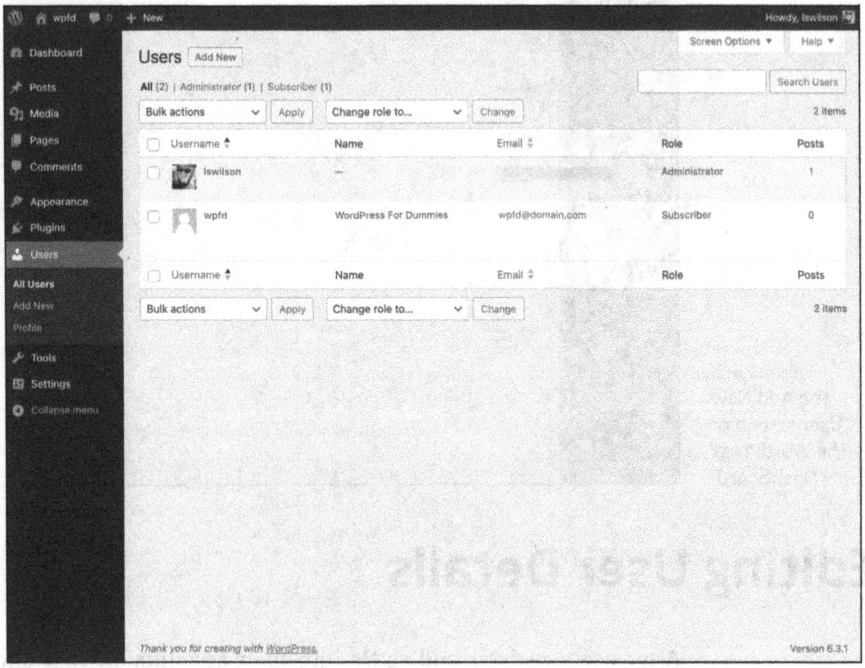

FIGURE 3-3: The Users screen lets you manage all the users on your site.

Figure 3-3 shows the Users screen for a site that has multiple users with different levels of access, or roles. When you hover your mouse pointer over the name of a user, an Edit link appears below the user listing. Click that Edit link to access the Edit User screen, where you can edit different pieces of information for that user, including

- **Personal Options:** These options include Visual Editor, Color Scheme, Keyboard Shortcuts, and Toolbar preferences.
- **Name:** Specify a user's role, first and last names, nickname, and display name.
- **Contact Info:** These options include the user's email address and website.
- **Biographical Info:** This section provides a few lines of biographical info for the user (optional, but some WordPress themes display authors' biographies). This section also displays the user's profile picture.
- **Account Management:** Here, you can set a new password for the user, or send them a password reset link to their email. This action does not change the user's password.

The Edit User screen looks the same, and has the same features, as the Profile screen that you deal with in Book 3, Chapter 2. Feel free to visit that chapter to get the lowdown on the options and settings on this screen.

Managing a Multiauthor Site

You may love running a multiauthor site, but the job has its challenges. The minute you become the owner of a multiauthor site, you immediately assume the role of manager for the authors you invite into your space. At times, those authors look to you for support and guidance, not only on their content management, but also for tips and advice about how to use the WordPress interface. It's a good thing you have this book at the ready so that you can offer up the gems of information you're finding within these pages!

You can find many tools to assist you in managing a multiauthor site, as well as making your site more interactive by adding some features, which can make it a more rewarding and satisfying experience not only for you and your readers, but for your authors as well.

The tools listed in the following sections come by way of plugins, which are add-ons that extend the scope of WordPress by adding different functionality and features. You can find information on the use and installation of plugins in Book 7.

Tools that help authors communicate

When you're running a multiauthor site, communication is crucial for sharing information, giving and receiving inspiration, and making certain that no two authors are writing the same post (or similar posts) on your site. Use the following tools to manage the flow of communication among everyone involved:

- **Post Status Notifications:** In the "Understanding User Roles and Capabilities" section, earlier in this chapter, I mention that the role of contributor can write and save posts to your site, but those posts don't get published to the site until an administrator approves them. This plugin notifies the administrator, via email, when a new post is submitted for review. Additionally, the contributing author gets an email notification when an administrator has published the post to the site.

  `https://wordpress.org/plugins/wpsite-post-status-notifications`
- **Editorial Calendar:** This plugin gives you an overview of scheduled posts, post authors, and the dates when you scheduled the posts to publish to your

site. This plugin can help you prevent multiple author posts from publishing too close together or, in some cases, right on top of one another; you simply reschedule posts by using a drag-and-drop interface.

https://wordpress.org/plugins/editorial-calendar

» **Send Users Email:** This plugin allows you to send emails in bulk to users who are currently registered on your website. It allows you to send to individual users, all users, or filter users by role and send emails only to authors, for example. You can personalize the message and even do a little styling of the email before you send it.

https://wordpress.org/plugins/send-users-email

» **User Notes:** When you run a website that has multiple authors, you may find it useful to leave notes on an user profile that are visible to site administrators only. These notes can be helpful and can serve as a tool for reminders.

https://wordpress.org/plugins/user-notes

Tools to promote author profiles

One way to operate a successful multiauthor site involves taking every opportunity to promote your authors and their information. Authors often get involved in posting content on websites in addition to yours, for exposure. The plugins in this list give you tools to promote authors' bios, links, social network feeds, and more:

» **Simple Author Box:** This plugin gives you an author box at the end of every post on your site that displays the author's photo, name, and description, as well as social media profiles like Facebook, Twitter, LinkedIn, and more. (See Figure 3-4.)

https://wordpress.org/plugins/simple-author-box

» **Author Avatars List/Block:** This plugin gives you a widget to display a list of authors on your website. It enables the display of author avatars, names, and short bios.

https://wordpress.org/plugins/author-avatars

» **Authors List:** This plugin provides a shortcode that you can place within your content using the shortcode block, or within a text widget in a sidebar, that displays a list of authors on your site. Each author is linked to their archive page, which displays a full listing of posts they've authored.

https://wordpress.org/plugins/authors-list

- **Author Signature:** This plugin adds a Signature section to the user profile that allows users to add their signature so it appears beneath every post they are the author of.

  https://wordpress.org/plugins/author-signature

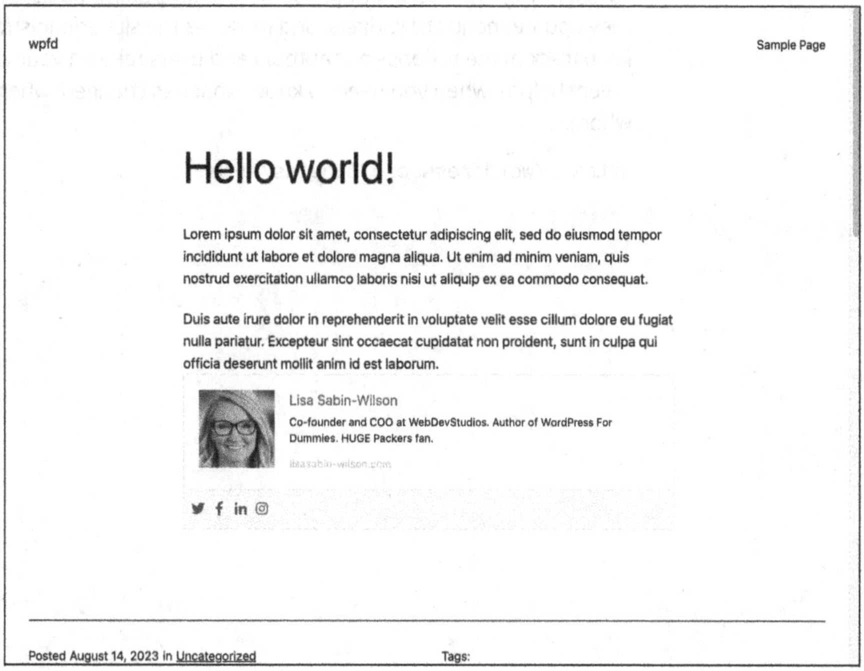

FIGURE 3-4: The Simple Author Box displayed at the end of a post.

Tools to manage multiauthor blog posts

The plugins listed in this section can help you, the site administrator, manage your group of authors and registered users by giving you some tools to track users' activity, list their posts, and stay up to date and notified when your authors publish new content:

- **Co-Authors Plus:** This plugin allows you to assign multiple authors to one post, which you may find especially helpful when you have several authors collaborating on one post, allowing those authors to share the byline and credit.

  https://wordpress.org/plugins/co-authors-plus

» **Authors Posts Widget:** This plugin provides a very easy way to show a list of authors on a site with a count of the number of posts each author has published.

`https://wordpress.org/plugins/authors-posts-widget/`

» **Stream:** This plugin records the actions of the registered users on your site, such as when they log in or log out, when they publish posts and pages, when they update menus or widgets, and more. As the site administrator, you can keep track of the actions your authors and users take on your website, which is very helpful when you need to know what has changed, when, and by whom.

`https://wordpress.org/plugins/stream/`

IN THIS CHAPTER

» Making the decision to allow comments

» Using comments to interact with readers

» Understanding trackbacks

» Working with comments and trackbacks

» Using Akismet to help combat spam

Chapter 4
Dealing with Comments and Spam

One exciting aspect of publishing with WordPress is getting feedback from your readers on posts you publish to your site. Feedback, also known as *comments,* is akin to having a guestbook on your site.

People leave comments for you that are published to your site, and through these comments, you can respond to and engage your readers in conversation about the topic. Having this function on your site allows you to expand the thoughts and ideas you present in your posts by giving readers the opportunity to add their two cents' worth.

In this chapter, you can decide whether to allow comments on your site, figure out how to manage those comments, use trackbacks, and find out how to deal with the negative aspects of allowing comments (such as spam).

Deciding to Allow Comments on Your Site

Some publishers say that a blog without comments isn't a blog at all, because the point of having a blog on your website, in some minds, is to foster communication and interaction between the site authors and the readers. This belief is common in the publishing community because experiencing visitor feedback via comments is part of what's made Internet publishing so popular. Allowing comments is a personal choice, however, and you don't have to allow them if you don't want to.

Positive aspects of allowing comments

Allowing comments on your site lets audience members actively involve themselves in your site by creating a discussion and dialogue about your content. Mostly, readers find commenting to be a satisfying experience when they visit sites because comments enable them to be part of the discussion.

Depending on the topic you write about, allowing comments sends the message that you, as the author/owner of the site, are open to the views and opinions of your readers. Having a comment form on your site that readers can use to leave their feedback on your posts (such as the one shown in Figure 4-1) is like having a great big Welcome to My Home sign on your site; it invites users in to share thoughts and participate in discussions.

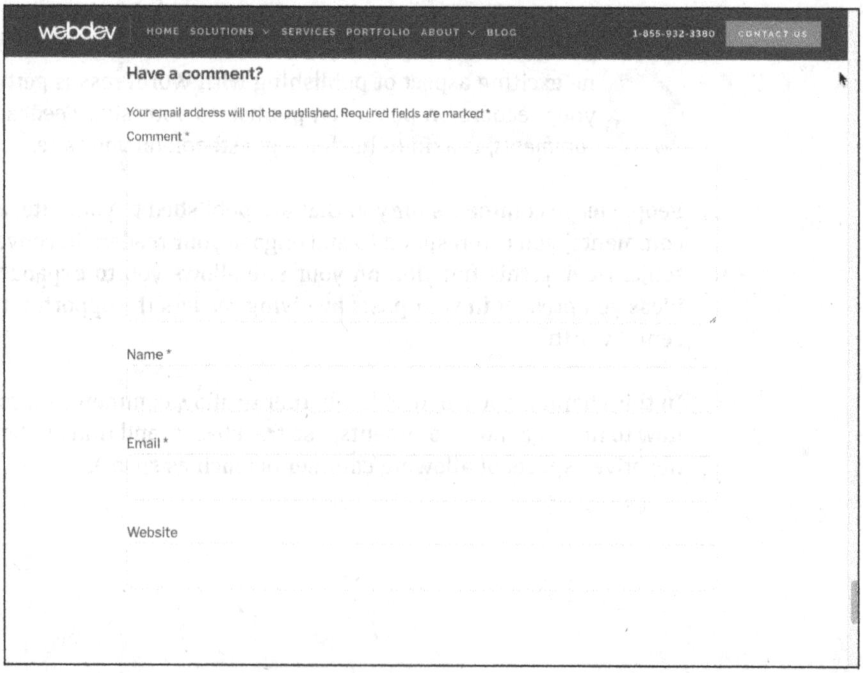

FIGURE 4-1: Readers use the Have a Comment? form to share their comments.

If you want to build a community of people who come back to your site frequently, respond to as many comments that your readers leave on your posts as possible. When people take the time to leave you a comment on your content, they like to know that you're reading it, and they appreciate hearing your feedback. Also, open comments keep discussions lively and active on your site. Figure 4-2 illustrates what comments look like after they're published to your site. (*Note:* The actual design and layout of the comments on sites varies from theme to theme; you can find information on theme design in Book 6.)

FIGURE 4-2: A visitor's comment on a post.

Reasons to disallow comments

Under certain circumstances, you may not want to allow readers to leave comments freely on your site. If you wrote a post on a topic that's considered very controversial, for example, you may not want to invite comments, because the topic may incite flame wars or comments that are insulting to you or your readers. If you're not interested in your readers' point of view or feedback, or if your content doesn't really lend itself to reader feedback, you may decide to disallow comments.

REMEMBER

In making the decision to have comments, you have to be prepared for the fact that not everyone is going to agree with what you write — especially if you're writing on a topic that invites a wide array of opinions, such as politics or religion. As a site owner, you make the decision ahead of time about whether you want readers dropping in and leaving their own views, or even disagreeing with you about yours (sometimes vehemently!).

If you're on the fence about whether to allow comments, the WordPress platform allows you to toggle that decision on a per-post basis. Therefore, each time you publish a post on your website, you can indicate in Post Options (on the Add New Post screen of your Dashboard) whether this particular post should allow discussion. You may choose to disallow all comments on your site (a setting that you can configure in Discussion Settings) or disallow them for only certain posts (a setting that you can configure on the Edit Post screen, which I talk about in Book 4, Chapter 1).

Interacting with Readers through Comments

People can leave comments for you that are published to your site, and you can respond to and engage your readers in conversation about the topic at hand. (Refer to Figures 4-1 and 4-2.) Having this function on your site creates the opportunity to expand the thoughts and ideas that you present in your post by giving your readers the opportunity to share their own thoughts.

The WordPress Dashboard gives you full administrative control of who can and can't leave comments. In addition, if someone leaves a comment that has questionable content, you can edit the comment or delete it. You're also free to disallow comments on your blog. The Discussion Settings screen of your Dashboard contains all the settings for allowing or disallowing comments on your site. See Book 3, Chapter 2 to dig into those settings, what they mean, and how you can use them to configure the exact interactive environment that you want for your site.

Tracking Back

The best way to understand trackbacks is to think of them as comments except for one thing: *Trackbacks* are comments left on your blog by other blogs, not by actual people. Although this process may sound mysterious, it's actually perfectly reasonable.

A trackback happens when you make a post on your site and, within that post, you provide a link to a post made by another author on a different site. When you publish that post, your site sends a sort of electronic memo to the site you linked to. That site receives the memo and posts an acknowledgment of receipt in a comment within the post that you linked to on that site. Trackbacks work between most publishing platforms — between WordPress and Blogger, for example, as well as between WordPress and Drupal.

That memo is sent via a *network ping* (a tool used to test, or verify, whether a link is reachable across the Internet) from your site to the site you link to. This process works as long as both sites support trackback protocol. Trackbacks can also come to your site by way of a *pingback* — which really is the same thing as a trackback, but the terminology varies from platform to platform.

Sending a trackback to a site is a nice way of telling the author that you like the information they presented in their post. Every author appreciates the receipt of trackbacks to their posts from other authors.

Managing Comments and Trackbacks

When you invite readers to comment on your site, you, as the site administrator, have full access to manage and edit those comments through the Comments page, which you can access on your WordPress Dashboard.

To find your comments, click the Comments link on the Dashboard navigation menu; the Comments screen opens. (See Figure 4-3.)

When you hover your mouse pointer over a comment, several links appear that give you the opportunity to manage the comment:

- **Unapprove:** This link appears only if you have comment moderation turned on, and only for approved comments. The comment is placed in the moderation queue, which you get to by clicking the Awaiting Moderation link that appears below the Manage Comments header. The moderation queue is a kind of holding area for comments that haven't yet been published to your blog.
- **Reply:** Click this link, and a text box drops down. In this text box, you can type and submit your reply to the person who commented. This feature eliminates the need to load your live site to reply to a comment.

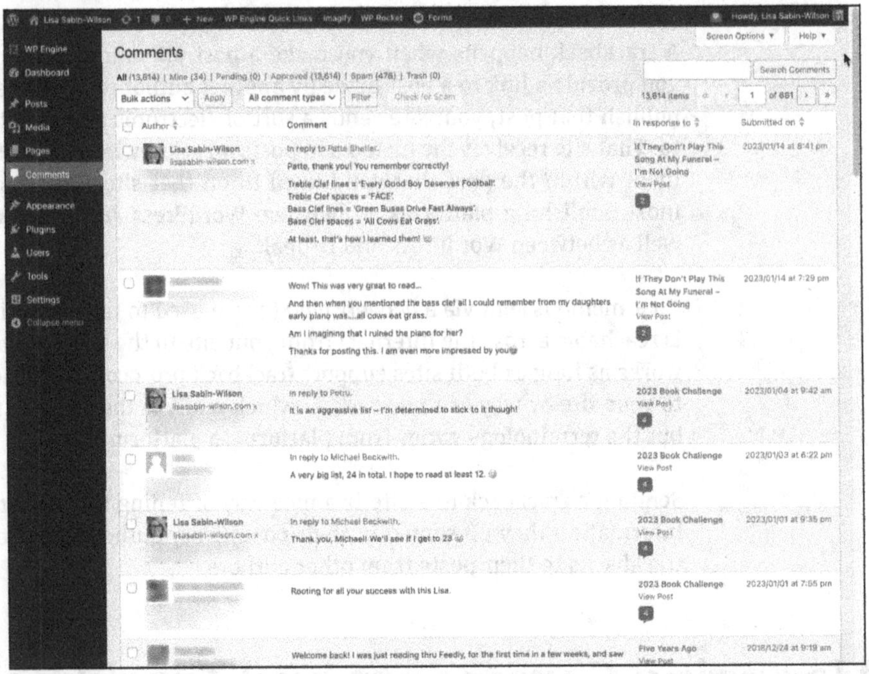

FIGURE 4-3: The Comments screen contains all the comments and trackbacks on your site.

- **Quick Edit:** Click this link to open the comment options without leaving the Comments page. You can configure post options such as name, email, URL, and comment content. Click the Save button to save your changes.
- **Edit:** Click this link to open the Edit Comment page, where you can edit fields such as name, email, URL, and comment content (see Figure 4-4).
- **Spam:** Click this link to mark the comment as spam and toss it into the spam bin, where it will never be heard from again. Spam is automatically deleted every 15 days if you use the Akismet plugin, which is discussed in the next section, "Tackling Spam with Akismet."
- **Trash:** This link does exactly what it says: sends the comment to the Trash and deletes it from your blog.

TIP

If you have a lot of comments listed in the Comments page and want to bulk-manage them, select the boxes to the left of all the comments you want to manage. Then choose one of the following from the Bulk Actions drop-down menu in the top-left corner: Approve, Mark As Spam, Unapprove, or Delete.

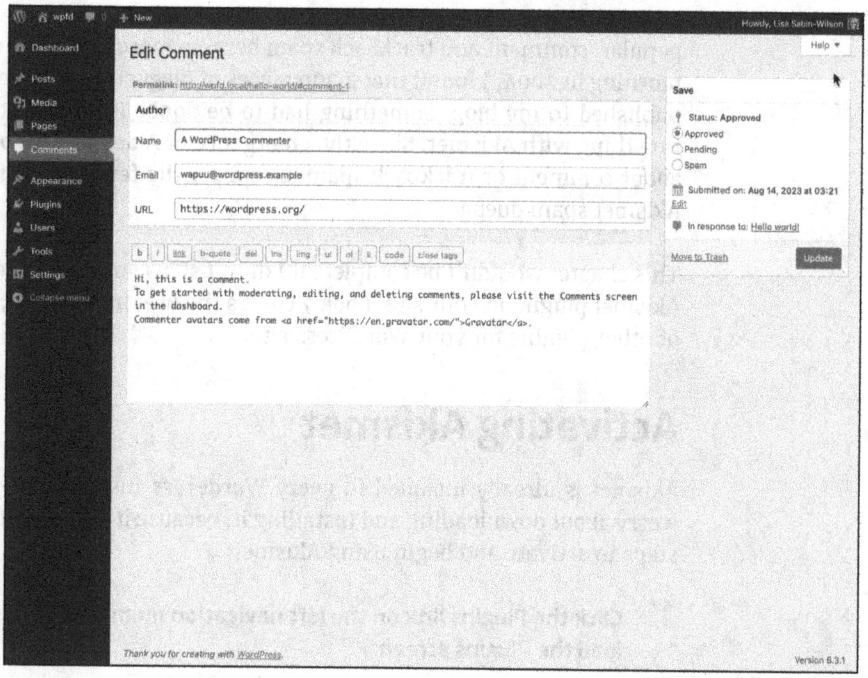

FIGURE 4-4: Edit a user's comment on the Edit Comment page.

If you have your options set so that comments aren't published to your site until you approve them, you can approve comments from the Comments screen as well. Just click the Pending link to list the comments that are pending moderation. If you have comments and/or trackbacks awaiting moderation, they appear on this page, and you can approve them, mark them as spam, or delete them.

WordPress immediately notifies you of any comments sitting in the moderation queue, awaiting your action. This notification, which appears on every single page, is a small circle, or bubble, on the left navigation menu, to the right of Comments.

Tackling Spam with Akismet

I touch on Akismet a few times throughout this book because it's my humble opinion that Akismet is the mother of all plugins, and that no WordPress site is complete without a fully activated version of Akismet running on it. Apparently, WordPress agrees, because the plugin has been packaged in every WordPress software release beginning with version 2.0. Akismet was created by the folks at Automattic.

I've been blogging since 2002, when I started with the Movable Type blogging platform. I moved to WordPress in 2003. As blogging became more and more popular, comment and trackback spam became more and more of a nuisance. One morning in 2004, I found that 2,300 pieces of disgusting comment spam had been published to my blog. Something had to be done! The folks at Automattic did a fine thing with Akismet. Since the emergence of Akismet, I've barely had to think about comment or trackback spam except for the few times a month I check my Akismet spam queue.

This chapter wouldn't be complete if I didn't show you how to activate and use the Akismet plugin on your site. Book 7 covers the use, installation, and management of other plugins for your WordPress site.

Activating Akismet

Akismet is already included in every WordPress installation; you don't have to worry about downloading and installing it, because it's already there. Follow these steps to activate and begin using Akismet:

1. **Click the Plugins link on the left navigation menu of the Dashboard to load the Plugins screen.**
2. **Click the Activate link below the Akismet plugin name and description.**

   The Akismet Configuration screen appears, with a green Set Up Your Akismet Account button (see Figure 4-5).
3. **If you already have an API key, click the Manually Enter an API Key link.**

   This takes you to the Akismet screen on your WordPress Dashboard.

   An *API key* is a string of numbers and letters that functions like a unique password given to you by Akismet; it's the key that allows your `WordPress.org` application to communicate with your Akismet account. Enter your API key in the text field on the Akismet screen and click the Connect with API Key button to complete your setup.

   You can stop here if you already have a key, but if you don't have an Akismet key, continue with the following steps.
4. **Click the Set Up Your Akismet Account button on the Akismet Configuration screen.**

   The Pricing page of the Akismet website opens (`https://akismet.com/pricing`).
5. **Choose among these options for obtaining an Akismet key:**
   - *Enterprise:* Custom pricing for people who own a large business, or a corporate site, and who want additional priority support and an unlimited number of sites.

- *Business:* $59 per year for people who run large websites or multisite installations.
- *Pro:* $9.95 per month for people who own a small commercial or professional website.
- *Personal:* Name your price. Type the amount you're willing to pay for the Personal plan. This option is for people who own one small, personal WordPress-powered site. You can choose to pay nothing ($0), but if you'd like to contribute a little cash toward the cause of combating spam, you can opt to spend up to $120 per year for your Akismet key subscription.

6. **Select and pay for (if needed) your Akismet key.**

   After you've gone through the sign-up process, Akismet provides you an API key. Copy that key by selecting it with your mouse pointer, right-clicking, and choosing Copy from the shortcut menu.

7. **Go to the Akismet screen by clicking the Akismet Anti-Spam link on the Settings menu on your WordPress Dashboard.**
8. **Enter the API key in the API Key text box, and click the Save Changes button to fully activate the Akismet plugin (as shown in Figure 4-6).**

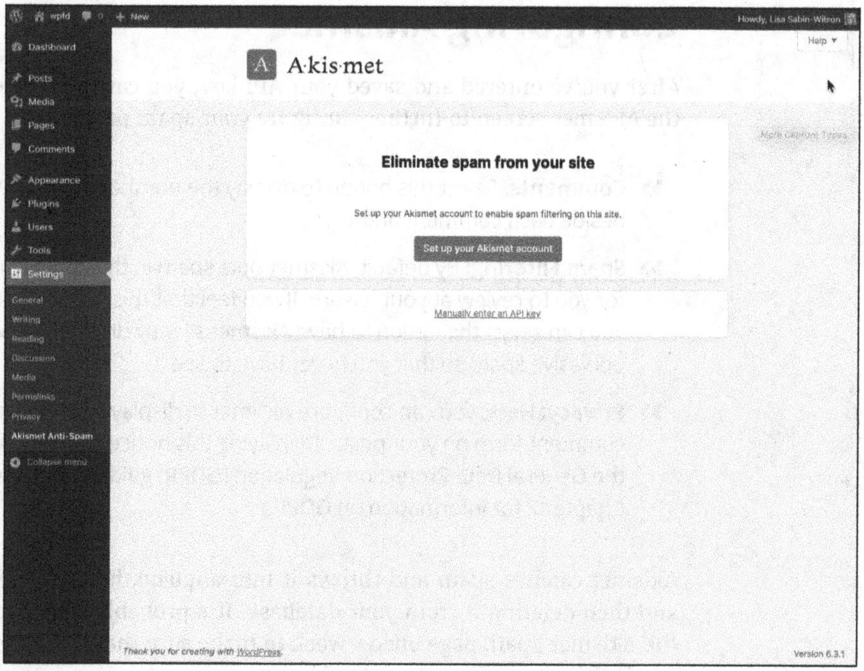

FIGURE 4-5: After you activate Akismet, WordPress tells you to set up your Akismet account.

Dealing with Comments and Spam

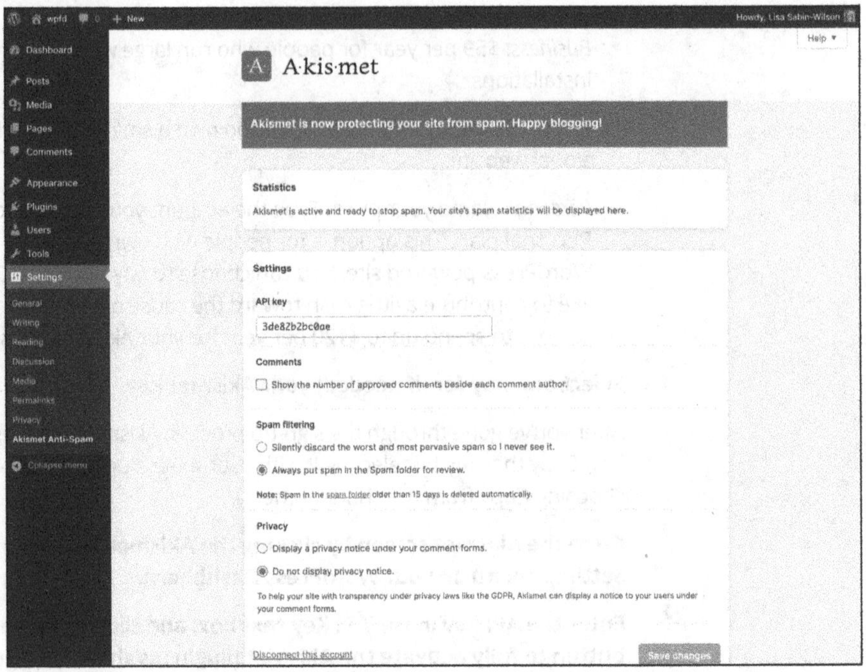

FIGURE 4-6: The Akismet verification confirmation message on the Akismet screen.

Configuring Akismet

After you've entered and saved your API key, you can configure three options on the Akismet screen to further configure your spam protection:

- **Comments:** Select this option to display the number of approved comments beside each comment author.
- **Spam Filtering:** By default, Akismet puts spam in the Spam comment folder for you to review at your leisure. If you feel that this setting isn't strict enough, you can select the option to have Akismet silently discard the worst and most pervasive spam so that you never have to see it.
- **Privacy:** Here, you can configure Aksimet to display a privacy notice below the comment form on your posts. Displaying this notice can help you adhere to the General Data Protection Regulation (GDPR) guidelines. (See Book 3, Chapter 2 for information on GDPR.)

Akismet catches spam and throws it into a queue, holding the spam for 15 days and then deleting it from your database. It's probably worth your while to check the Akismet Spam page once a week to make sure that the plugin hasn't captured any legitimate comments or trackbacks.

IN THIS CHAPTER

» Exploring content archive options in WordPress

» Creating and editing categories

» Creating tags and editing them

Chapter 5 Creating Categories and Tags

WordPress provides you many ways to organize, categorize, and archive content on your website. Packaged within the WordPress software is the capability to automatically maintain chronological, categorized archives of your publishing history, which provides your website visitors different ways to find your content. WordPress uses PHP and MySQL technology to sort and organize everything you publish in an order that you and your readers can access by date and category. This archiving process occurs automatically with every post you publish to your site.

In this chapter, you find out all about WordPress archiving, from categories to tags and more; how to distinguish between categories and tags; and how to use categories and tags to create topical archives of your site content.

Archiving Content with WordPress

When you create a post on your WordPress site, you can file that post in a category that you specify. This feature makes for a nifty archiving system in which you and your readers can find posts that you've placed within a specific category. Articles you post are also sorted and organized by date (day/month/year) so that you can easily locate posts that you published at a certain time. A plugin called Archive Page allows you to easily create a nicely formatted site map that displays the archives of a site on a page.

Visit `https://lisasabin-wilson.com/archives` to see an example of an archive page. The example page contains chronological sections by month. It also contains the latest posts and the different categories and tags found within that site. If you click a date, tag, or category on that page, you're taken to a page with a full listing of posts from that date, tag, or category, and each post title is linked to that post. (See Figure 5-1.)

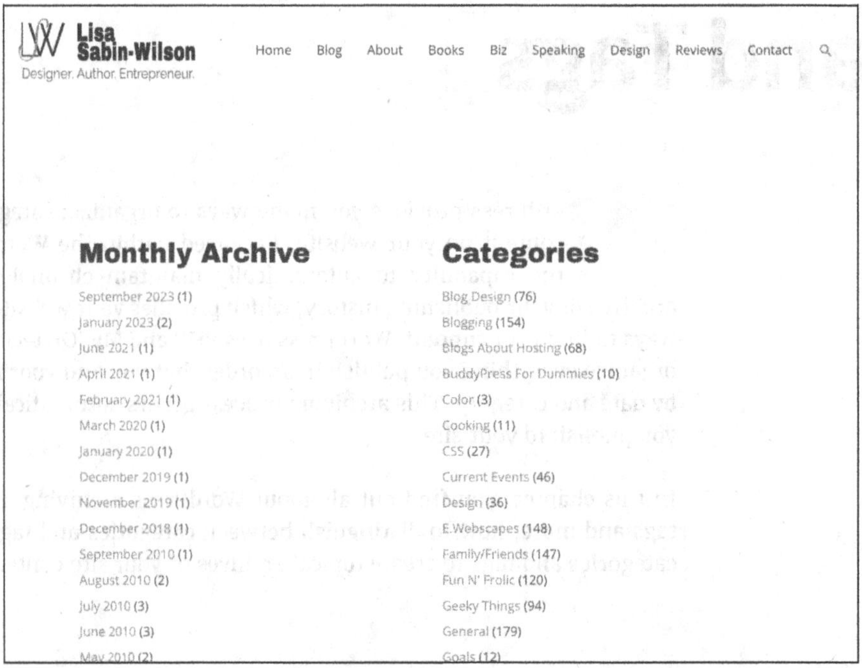

FIGURE 5-1: An archive listing of published posts by date, tag, or category.

TIP

You can easily create an archive listing like the one shown in Figure 5-1 by using a WordPress plugin called Archivist – Custom Archive Templates, which you can find on the WordPress Plugins page at `https://wordpress.org/plugins/archivist-custom-archive-templates`. This plugin is easy to install and to use.

You just need to create a page and add any of the shortcodes provided by the plugin to automatically build an archives page that links to all the content you've published on your site. Easy archives!

WordPress archives and organizes your content for you in more ways than by date and category, such as the following:

- **Categories:** Create categories of topics in which you can file your posts so that you can easily archive relevant topics. Many websites display content by category; all content is displayed by topic rather than in a simple chronological listing.
- **Tags:** Tagging your posts with micro keywords, called *tags,* further defines related content within your site, which can improve your site for SEO purposes by helping the search engines find related and relevant content, as well as provide additional navigation to help your readers find relevant content on your site.
- **Date Based:** Your content is automatically archived by date based on the day, month, year, and time of day you publish it.
- **Author:** Content is automatically archived by author based on the author of the post and/or page. You can create an author archive if your site has multiple content contributors.
- **Keyword (or Search):** WordPress has a built-in search function that allows you and your readers to search for keywords, which presents an archive listing of content that's relevant to your chosen keywords.
- **Custom Post Types:** You can build custom post types based on the kind of content your site offers.
- **Attachments:** WordPress has a built-in media library where you can upload different media files, such as photos, images, documents, videos, and audio files (to name a few). You can build an archive of those files to create things such as photo galleries, eBook archives (PDFs), and video galleries.

Building categories

In WordPress, a *category* is what you determine to be the main topic of an individual piece of content on your site. Through the use of categories, you can file your posts into topics by subject. To improve your readers' experiences in navigating your site, WordPress organizes posts by the categories you assign to them. Visitors can click the categories they're interested in to see the posts you've written on those particular topics.

The list of categories you set up is displayed on your site in a few places, including the following:

- **Body of the post:** In most WordPress themes, you see the title followed by a statement such as `Filed In:` *`Category 1`*, *`Category 2`*. The reader can click the category name to go to a page that lists all the posts you've made in that particular category. You can assign a single post to more than one category.
- **Navigation menu:** Almost all sites have a navigation menu that visitors can use to navigate your site. You can place links to categories on the navigation menu, particularly if you want to draw attention to particular categories.
- **Sidebar of your theme:** You can place a full list of category titles in the sidebar. A reader can click any category and arrive at a page on your site that lists the posts you've made within that particular category.

Subcategories (also known as *category children*) can further refine the main category topic by listing specific topics related to the main (*parent*) category. On your WordPress Dashboard, on the Manage Categories page, subcategories appear directly below the main category. Here's an example:

Books I Enjoy (main category)

Fiction (subcategory)

Nonfiction (subcategory)

Trashy romance (subcategory)

Biographies (subcategory)

For Dummies (subcategory)

You can create as many levels of categories as you like. Biographies and *For Dummies* could be subcategories of Nonfiction, for example, which is a subcategory of the Books I Enjoy category. You aren't limited to the number of category levels you can create.

Changing the name of a category

Upon installation, WordPress gives you one default category to get you started: Uncategorized. (See the Categories screen shown in Figure 5-2.) That category name is pretty generic, so you'll definitely want to change it to one that's more specific to you. (On my site, I changed it to Life in General. Although that name's still a bit on the generic side, it doesn't sound quite so . . . well, uncategorized.)

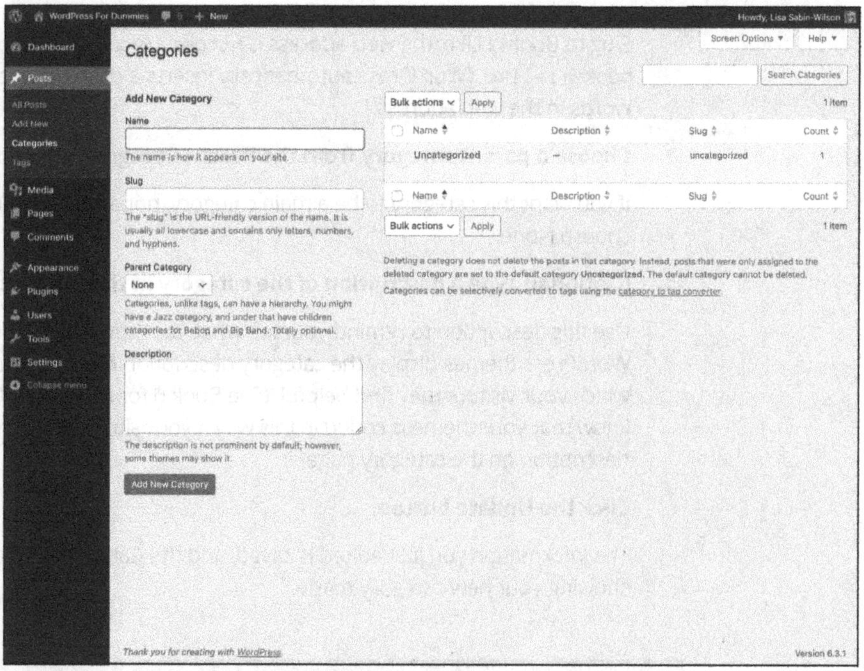

FIGURE 5-2: The Categories screen on the Dashboard of a brand-new WordPress site shows the default Uncategorized category.

REMEMBER

The default category also serves as kind of a fail-safe. If you publish a post to your site and don't assign that post to a category, the post is assigned to the default category automatically, no matter what you name the category.

So how do you change the name of that default category? When you're logged in to your WordPress Dashboard, just follow these steps:

1. **Click the Categories link on the Posts submenu of the Dashboard navigation menu.**

   The Categories screen opens, containing all the tools you need to set up and edit category titles for your site.

2. **Click the title of the category that you want to edit.**

   If you want to change the Uncategorized category, click the word *Uncategorized* to open the Edit Category screen. (See Figure 5-3.)

3. **Type the new name for the category in the Name text field.**

4. **Type the new slug in the Slug text field.**

   The term *slug* refers to the lowercased word(s) used in the web address for the specific category. The category Books, for example, has a web address of `https://yourdomain.com/category/books`; if you change the Category

Slug to Books I Like, the web address is `https://yourdomain.com/category/books-i-like`. (WordPress automatically inserts a dash between the slug words in the web address.)

5. **Choose a parent category from the Parent Category drop-down menu.**

   If you want this category to be a main category, not a subcategory, choose None.

6. **(Optional) Type a description of the category in the Description text box.**

   Use this description to remind yourself what your category is about. Some WordPress themes display the category description right on your site, too, which your visitors may find helpful. (See Book 6 for more about themes.) You know that your theme is coded in this way if your site displays the category description on the category page(s).

7. **Click the Update button.**

   The information you just edited is saved, and the Categories screen reloads, showing your new category name.

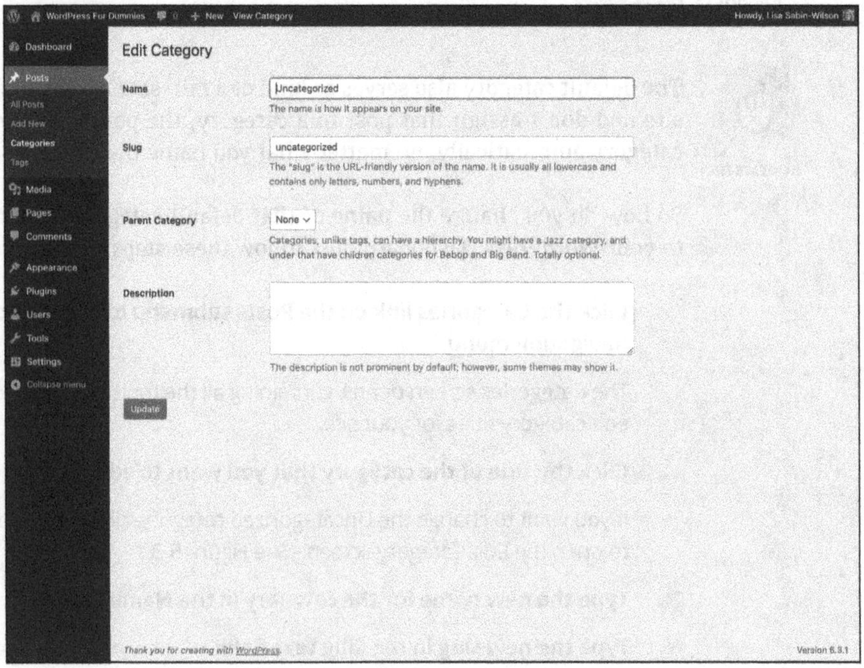

WordPress For Dummies
New
View Category
Howdy, Lisa Sabin-Wilson
Dashboard
Posts
All Posts
Add New
Categories
Tags
Media
Pages
Comments
Appearance
Plugins
Users
Tools
Settings
Collapse menu
Edit Category
Name
Uncategorized
The name is how it appears on your site.
Slug
uncategorized
The "slug" is the URL-friendly version of the name. It is usually all lowercase and contains only letters, numbers, and hyphens.
Parent Category
None
Categories, unlike tags, can have a hierarchy. You might have a Jazz category, and under that have children categories for Bebop and Big Band. Totally optional.
Description
The description is not prominent by default; however, some themes may show it.
Update
Thank you for creating with WordPress.
Version 6.3.1

FIGURE 5-3: Editing a category in WordPress on the Edit Category screen.

Creating new categories

Today, tomorrow, next month, next year — while your site grows in size and age, continuing to add new categories further defines and archives the history of your posts. You aren't limited in the number of categories and subcategories you can create for your site.

Creating a new category is as easy as following these steps:

1. **Click the Categories link on the Posts submenu of the Dashboard navigation menu.**

   The Categories screen opens, displaying the Add New Category section on the left side (see Figure 5-4).

2. **Type the name of your new category in the Name text field.**

   If you want to create a category in which you file all your posts about the books you read, for example, you might type **Books I Enjoy**.

3. **Type a name in the Slug text field.**

   The slug creates the link to the category page that lists all the posts you've made in this category. If you leave this field blank, WordPress automatically creates a slug based on the category name. If the category is Books I Enjoy, WordPress automatically creates a category slug like this: `http://`*`yourdomain.com`*`/category/books-i-enjoy`. If you want to shorten it, you can. Type **books** in the category Slug text box, and the link to the category becomes `http://`*`yourdomain.com`*`/category/books`.

4. **Choose the category's parent from the Parent Category drop-down menu.**

   Choose None if you want this new category to be a parent (or top-level) category. If you'd like this category to be a subcategory of another category, choose the category you want to be the parent of this one.

5. **(Optional) Type a description of the category in the Description text box.**

   Some WordPress templates are set up to display the category description directly below the category. Providing a description helps you further define the category intent for your readers. The description can be as short or as long as you like.

6. **Click the Add New Category button.**

   That's it! You've added a new category to your blog. Armed with this information, you can add an unlimited number of categories to your new site.

You can delete a category by hovering your mouse pointer on the title of the category you want to delete and then clicking the Delete link that appears below the category title.

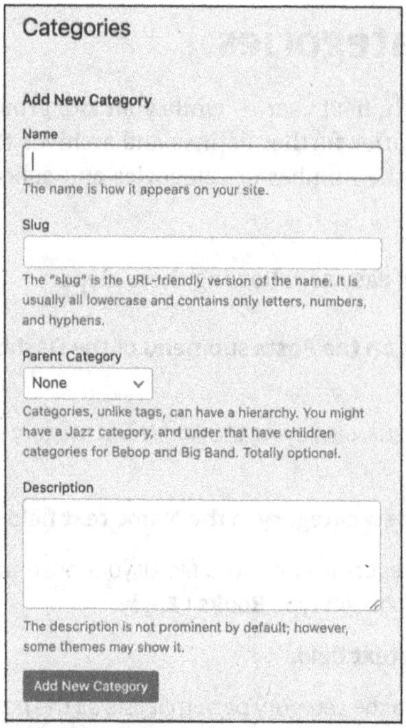
Categories
Add New Category
Name
The name is how it appears on your site.
Slug
The "slug" is the URL-friendly version of the name. It is usually all lowercase and contains only letters, numbers, and hyphens.
Parent Category
None
Categories, unlike tags, can have a hierarchy. You might have a Jazz category, and under that have children categories for Bebop and Big Band. Totally optional.
Description
The description is not prominent by default; however, some themes may show it.
Add New Category

FIGURE 5-4: Create a new category on your site.

WHAT ARE TAGS, AND HOW/WHY DO I USE THEM?

Don't confuse tags with categories. *Tags* are clickable, comma-separated keywords that help you microcategorize a post by defining the topics in it. Unlike WordPress categories, tags don't have a hierarchy; there are no parent tags and child tags. If you write a post about your dog, for example, you can put that post in the Pets category — but you can add some specific tags that let you get a whole lot more specific, such as `poodle` or `small dogs`. If someone clicks your `poodle` tag, they find all the posts you've ever made that contain the `poodle` tag.

Another reason to use tags: Search-engine spiders harvest tags when they crawl your site, so tags help other people find your site when they search for specific words.

You can manage your tags on the WordPress Dashboard by clicking the Tags link on the Posts menu. The Tags screen opens, allowing you to view, edit, delete, and add new tags.

WARNING

Deleting a category doesn't delete the posts and links in that category. Instead, posts in the deleted category are reassigned to the Uncategorized category (or whatever you named the default category).

TECHNICAL STUFF

If you have an established WordPress site that has categories already created, you can convert some or all of your categories to tags. To do so, look for the Category to Tag Converter link in the bottom-right corner of the Category page of your WordPress Dashboard. Click that link to convert your categories to tags. (See the nearby sidebar "What are tags, and how/why do I use them?" for more information on tags.)

Creating and Editing Tags

In Book 4, Chapter 2, you find out all about publishing your posts in WordPress and assigning tags to your content. This section takes you through the steps of managing tags, which is similar to the way you manage categories. To create a new tag, follow these steps:

1. **Click the Tags link on the Posts submenu, which is on the Dashboard's navigation menu.**

   The Tags screen opens, as shown in Figure 5-5. The left side of the screen displays the Add New Tag section.

   TIP

   Unlike what it does for categories and links, WordPress doesn't create a default tag for you, so when you visit the Tags page for the first time, no tags are listed on the right side of the page.

2. **Type the name of your new tag in the Name text field.**

   Suppose you want to create a tag in which you file all your posts about the books you read. In the Name text box, type something like **Fiction Books**.

3. **Type a name in the Slug text field.**

   The *slug* is the permalink of the tag and can help identify tag archives on your site by giving them their own URL, such as `https://yourdomain.com/tag/fictional-books`. By default, the tag slug adopts the words from the tag name.

4. **(Optional) Type a description of the tag in the Description text box.**

   Some WordPress templates are set up to display the tag description directly below the tag name. Providing a description further defines the category intent for your readers. The description can be as short or as long as you want.

5. **Click the Add New Tag button.**

   That's it! You've added a new tag to your site. The Add New Tag screen refreshes in your browser window with blank fields, ready for you to add another tag to your site.

6. **Repeat steps 1–5 to add an unlimited number of tags to your site.**

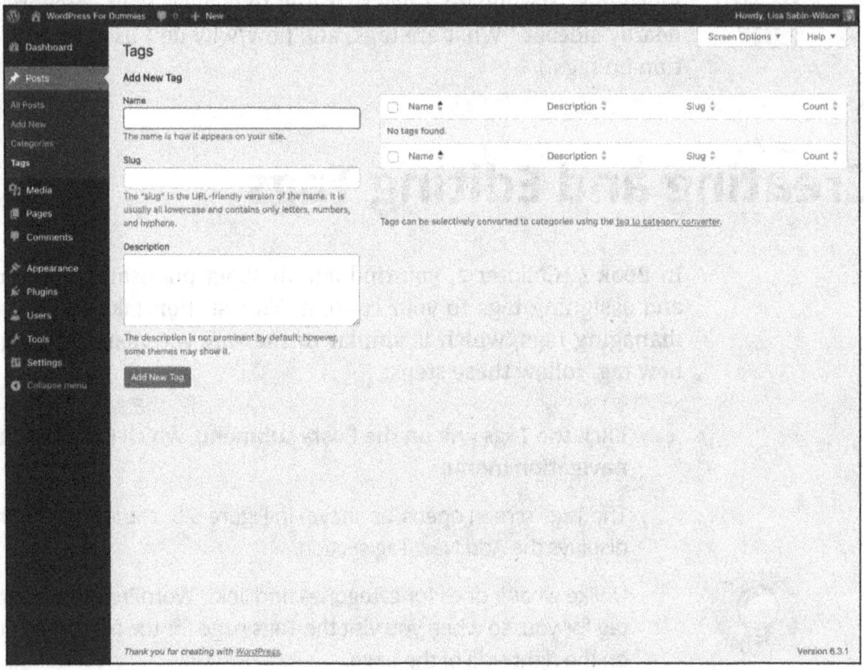

FIGURE 5-5: The Tags screen of the Dashboard.

Once you have several tags on your website, you can delete them on the Tags screen by clicking the Delete link underneath each tag when you hover your mouse pointer over it. Alternatively, you can delete multiple tags at once by selecting the check mark to the left of each tag you want to edit, select Delete from the Bulk Actions drop-down menu at the top of the Tags screen, and then click the Apply button. The Bulk Actions menu gives you the ability to delete several tags with just one action, rather than having to delete them all individually — very helpful if you have hundreds of tags!

TIP

You use the Tags and Categories pages of your Dashboard to manage, edit, and create new tags and categories to which you assign your posts when you publish them. Book 4, Chapter 2 contains a lot of information about how to assign tags and categories to your posts, and offers a few good tips on how you can create new categories and tags right on the Edit Post screen.

4
Publishing Your Site with WordPress

Contents at a Glance

IN THIS CHAPTER

» Using the block editor

» Discovering the available blocks for your content

» Configuring block options and settings

Chapter 1
Exploring the WordPress Block Editor

The idea behind the block editor is to give users a variety of blocks with which to create posts and pages on their WordPress sites. Compare WordPress blocks to the blocks you played with as a child; you were able to take one block and stack it on top of the next block and the next to build a tower of blocks to the moon. Each block within the WordPress editor gets filled with content (text, images, video, and so on) and is stacked atop another block with more content, and so on, until you have a full page of content created with blocks that you can configure with options to control formatting and display and move around on the page to create the experience you want for your readers.

This chapter takes you through the new block editor in WordPress.

TIP

WordPress named the new block editor Gutenberg after Johannes Gutenberg, the inventor of the printing press. Generically, everyone refers to it as the block editor, but if you hear or see the term *Gutenberg* tossed around in the WordPress support forums or at a WordPress meetup or WordCamp, you'll know that people are talking about the editor in WordPress.

Using the Block Editor

The purpose of the block editing experience is to put more publishing control and formatting options in the hands of the users in a way that doesn't require any specialized knowledge or training in the technology that makes it happen, such as PHP, JavaScript, HTML, or CSS. Now editors can create and format posts and pages more easily than ever before. You can insert images, change font sizes and color, and create tables and columns — and you don't even have to know how to code.

Discovering available blocks

By default, when you first load the Edit Post screen on your Dashboard (see Figure 1-1), the area where you type the text of your post consists of a single, standard paragraph block; you see it in the area that says *Type / to choose a block*. Click into this area with your mouse, and you see that block settings for the paragraph block displays on the right side of the screen in the settings panel, within the Block section. Every block available in the editor has unique options and settings associated with it, and you will always find the settings on the right side of your screen, as shown in Figure 1-1. You will also find the options for a block in the block toolbar once you start adding text to it, directly above the block within the editor, as shown in Figure 1-2. I take you through both the block options and block settings in detail for the paragraph block in the "Configuring block settings" section, later in this chapter.

TIP

The settings panel has two sections: Post and Block. The Post section contains the global settings that I cover in "Refining Your Post Options" in Book 4, Chapter 2. The Block section of the settings panel contains additional settings that you can configure for each block. Notice that as you switch to editing a different kind of block, the Block section of the settings panel changes to display the unique settings for the block you're currently using. By default, when you visit the Add Post screen for the first time, you will not see the settings panel on the right side of your screen. You can toggle it on and off by clicking the interface icon at the very top right of your screen — the icon looks like a square with a right column, which you can see in its open state next to the Publish button on the top right of Figure 1-1. The block options toolbar for the paragraph block is shown in Figure 1-2.

You can use the standard paragraph blocks to write your posts and leave it at that. But the block editor has several blocks available that give you a variety of layout and formatting options for your content.

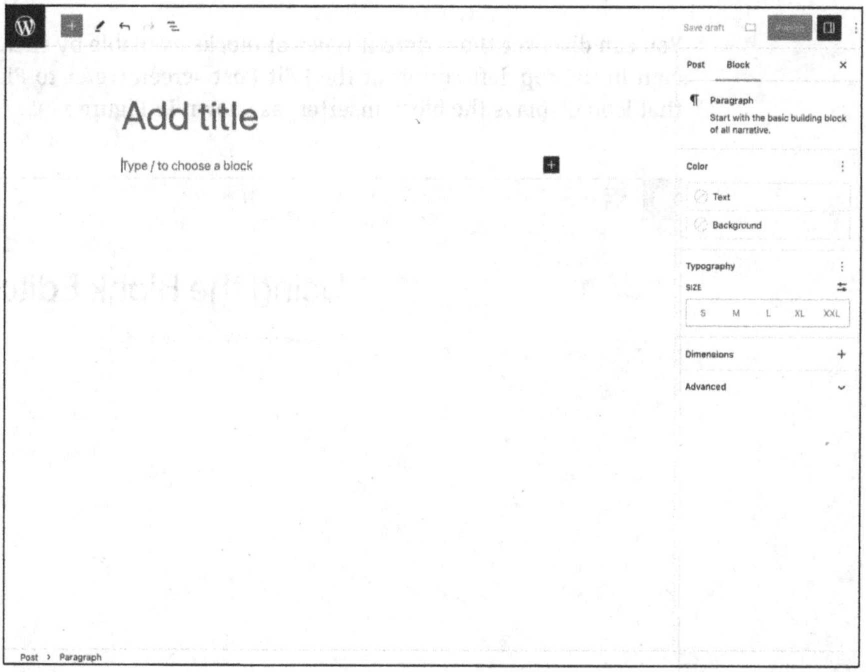

FIGURE 1-1: The Add New Post screen showing the paragraph block and block settings panel.

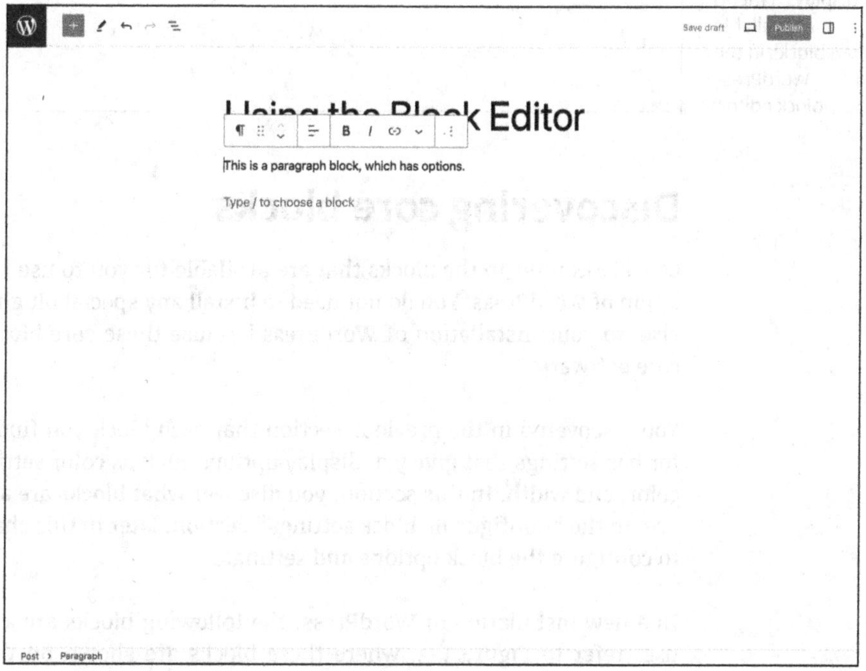

FIGURE 1-2: The block options toolbar for the paragraph block.

You can discover the different types of blocks available by clicking the small plus sign in the top-left corner of the Edit Post screen (refer to Figure 1-1). Clicking that icon displays the block inserter, as shown in Figure 1-3.

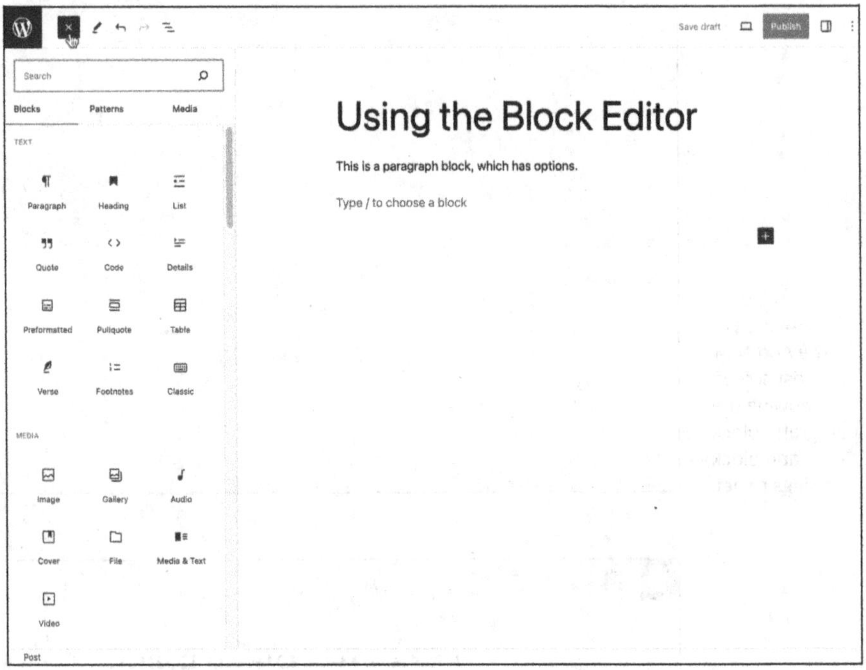

FIGURE 1-3: The block inserter displays a menu of available blocks in the WordPress block editor.

Discovering core blocks

Core blocks refer to the blocks that are available for you to use in a default installation of WordPress. You do not need to install any special plugin, or add anything else, to your installation of WordPress because these core blocks are part of the core software.

You discovered in the previous section that each block you find in the block editor has settings that give you display options such as color settings, font size and color, and width. In this section, you discover what blocks are available for you to use. In the "Configuring block settings" section, later in this chapter, you see how to configure the block options and settings.

In a new installation of WordPress, the following blocks are available for you to use (refer to Figure 1-3, where these blocks are shown on the left side of the screen):

- **Text:** The blocks in this section provide formatting and placement options for text within your content. These blocks include:
  - *Paragraph:* This inserts a block that allows you to create a standard paragraph of text.
  - *Heading:* This inserts a block that allows you to insert header text with H1, H2, H3, H4, H5, and H6 tags to help your visitors (and search engines) understand the structure of your content. (See Book 5, Chapter 3 for search engine optimization tips.)
  - *List:* This inserts a block that allows you to create a bulleted or numbered list.
  - *Quote:* This inserts a block that allows you to enter a quote with a citation that's stylized for visual emphasis.
  - *Code:* This inserts a block that allows you to insert and display code snippets that respect standard code-formatting rules and prevent the application from executing the code you've written.
  - *Details:* This block functions like an accordion, which is simply a heading that, when clicked, expands a block of text nested underneath. When you click on it again, the block of text closes, or gets hidden.
  - *Preformatted:* This inserts a block that allows you to add text that gets displayed exactly as is intended in code or HTML format. The text is typically displayed in a monospace font (such as Courier New), and the Preformatted editor respects your spacing and tabs, keeping them in place. (Preformatted text is helpful for people who include code samples within their posts or pages. Also, this option prevents the application from executing the code.)
  - *Pullquote:* This inserts a block that allows you to enter a quote, with citation, that gives special visual emphasis to the text.
  - *Table:* This inserts a table editor that allows you to include a table of rows and columns, much as you would do in a standard word processing program such as Microsoft Word.
  - *Verse:* This inserts a verse editor that allows you to enter a verse of poetry or song lyrics or to quote a small number of lyrics or lines of poetry. The text gets special formatting and spacing to give it visual emphasis.
  - *Footnotes:* Using this block gives you the ability to add footnotes to your content so you can provide citations or source references within your content. Footnotes are displayed as superscript text that corresponds to a matching reference at the bottom of a page.
  - *Classic:* This inserts a block with the old, classic editor that users of earlier WordPress versions are used to and may be more comfortable with.

- **Media:** The blocks in this section deal with the insertion, presentation, and formatting of media files such as images, video, and audio files. These blocks include:
  - *Image:* This inserts a block that allows you to insert an image into your post or page.
  - *Gallery:* This inserts a block that allows you to upload and display multiple images in your post or page. (I discuss the use of the gallery block in detail in Book 4, Chapter 5.)
  - *Audio:* This inserts a block that allows you to upload an audio file and embed it in an audio player in your post or page. (I discuss the use of the audio block in detail in Book 4, Chapter 5.)
  - *Cover:* This inserts a block that allows you to upload an image and add it to your post or page with text overlaid on it. (I discuss the use of the cover block in detail in Book 4, Chapter 5.)
  - *File:* This inserts a block that allows you to upload a file (such as .doc or .pdf) and add it to your post or page for your visitors to download.
  - *Media & Text:* This inserts a two-column block that allows you to display media (image or video) and text side by side. The options for this block allow you to align the media to the right or to the left of the text block. You also can define the width of the block, making it the width of the reader's computer screen or the width of the rest of the content on your page.
  - *Video:* Clicking this block inserts a block that allows you to upload a video file and embed it in a video player in your post or page. (I discuss the use of the video block in detail in Book 4, Chapter 5.)
- **Design:** The blocks in this section allow you to create different layouts for your content on every post or page. The layout elements include tables, columns, and buttons. These elements enable you to create pages and posts that look different or the same, allowing you to be as creative as you want to be. In the block inserter, scroll down to the Design section to see a listing of available blocks in this section heading. Figure 1-4 shows the Design blocks:
  - *Buttons:* This inserts a clickable button within your page or post. People usually use a button to link to a section of their site that they feel is important, such as a contact form or an online shop.
  - *Columns:* This inserts a column editor that allows you to create a section of text in side-by-side columns. The options for this block allow you to define the number of columns as well as the colors of the columns and text. (I discuss the use of the columns block for adding images in a post in Book 4, Chapter 5.)

- *Group:* This block allows you to gather multiple blocks inside one container so that you are able to set design and layout options and have those settings apply to all of the blocks within the container.
- *Row:* Allows you to arrange a grouping, or a nesting, of blocks in a horizontal fashion, like columns in a table.
- *Stack:* Allows you to arrange a grouping, or a nesting, of blocks in a vertical fashion, like rows in a table.
- *More:* This inserts a block that serves as a marker point for your post or page excerpt. The content that appears above this block is shown as the excerpt on pages such as an archive or search results page.
- *Page Break:* This inserts a block that serves as a marker point for a page break, allowing you to create a post or a page that has a multipage experience. The content that appears above this block is displayed on the page with navigation links, prompting the reader to navigate to page 2 of your post or page to read the rest.
- *Separator:* This inserts a block that creates a break between sections of content by using a horizontal separator or line. Options for this block allow you to determine the style of the separator line: Short Line, Wide Line, or Dots.
- *Spacer:* This inserts a block that creates white space within your post or page. This block doesn't get filled with any kind of content; rather, it exists to allow you to create a space between content blocks at a height that you can define in the block options.

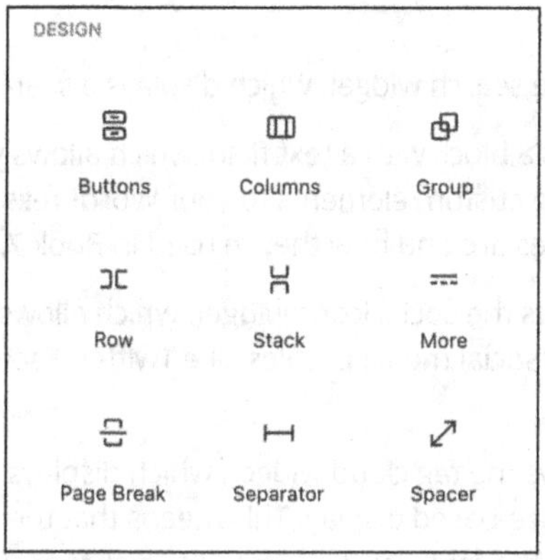

FIGURE 1-4: The blocks available in the Design section of the Block Inserter panel.

* **Widgets:** These blocks are available in the block editor to allow you to insert blocks with predefined content. Scroll to the Widgets section to find the full list of available blocks in this section. Figure 1-5 shows the Widgets blocks:
  * *Archives:* This inserts the archives widget, which displays a list of monthly archives of your posts.
  * *Calendar:* This inserts the calendar widget, which displays a listing of posts in calendar format.
  * *Categories List:* This inserts the category widget, which displays a list of categories on your site.
  * *Custom HTML:* This inserts a block with an HTML editor that allows you to write HTML code and preview it as you type and edit.
  * *Latest Comments:* This inserts the latest comments widget into your post or page. This widget displays a list of the most recent comments left on your site. Options for this block allow you to define the number of comments you want to display and to toggle the display of the comment avatar, date, and excerpt.
  * *Latest Posts:* This inserts the latest posts widget into your post or page. This widget displays a list of the most recent posts you've published to your site. Options for this block allow you to sort the post list by newest to oldest, oldest to newest, and ascending or descending in alphabetical order.
  * *Page List*: This inserts the page list widget, which displays all of the published pages, by title, in list format.
  * *RSS:* This inserts the RSS widget, which can display content from any website's RSS feed. See Book 1 for further information about RSS technology.
  * *Search:* This inserts the search widget, which displays a search form.
  * *Shortcode:* This inserts a block with a text field, which allows you to include a shortcode for adding custom elements to your WordPress page or post. I cover what shortcodes are and how they're used in Book 7, Chapter 3.
  * *Social Icons:* This inserts the social icons widget, which allows you to display icons that link to your social media profiles, like Twitter, Facebook, YouTube, and more.
  * *Tag Cloud:* This displays the tag cloud widget, which displays every tag on your site with a font size-based display. This means that the more often a tag is used, the larger the font size. Likewise for small font sizes for tags that are not used as often.

FIGURE 1-5: The blocks available in the Widgets section of the Block Inserter panel.

» **Theme:** The blocks available in this section get used most often in the Site Editor feature, particularly when you are creating templates, which I talk about more in Book 6, Chapter 3. Figure 1-6 displays most of the blocks available in the Theme section; you will need to scroll down in the Block Inserter panel to see the rest of them. All of the blocks listed here allow you to insert various items from the content on your website, such as:

- *Navigation:* This inserts a block that displays a navigation menu. If you have more than one navigation menu, it provides a drop-down menu that allows you to select the menu you want.
- *Site Logo:* This inserts a block that displays your site logo by providing an image upload field: You to click it to select an image from your Media Library or an image from your computer to upload.
- *Site Title:* This inserts the title of your site, as set in the General Settings page on your Dashboard (see Book 2, Chapter 2).
- *Site Tagline:* This inserts the tagline of your site, as set in the General Settings page on your Dashboard (see Book 2, Chapter 2).
- *Query Loop:* This block allows you to display posts from different post types and other query parameters available for you to set up within the block options.
- *Posts List:* This inserts a list of posts and displays them based on the various settings available in the block options.

- *Avatar:* This inserts a block that displays a user's profile photo. The user must have an avatar defined at the Gravatar website (`https://gravatar.com`). Read more about Gravatars in Book 3, Chapter 2.
- *Title:* This inserts a block that displays the title of the post or page you are currently editing on the Dashboard.
- *Excerpt:* This inserts a block that displays the excerpt of the post or page you are currently editing on the Dashboard.
- *Featured Image:* This inserts a block that displays the Featured Image of the post or page you are currently editing on the Dashboard.
- *Author:* This inserts a block that displays the Post Author name, biography, and avatar from the post or page you are currently editing on the Dashboard.
- *Author Name:* This inserts a block that displays the post author's name from the post or page you are currently editing on the Dashboard.
- *Date:* This inserts a block that displays the date of the post or page you are currently editing on the Dashboard.
- *Modified Date:* This inserts a block that displays the date the last time the post you are currently editing on the Dashboard was changed.
- *Categories:* This inserts a block that displays the assigned categories of the post or page you are currently editing on the Dashboard.
- *Tags:* This inserts a block that displays the assigned tags of the post or page you are currently editing on the Dashboard.
- *Next Post:* This inserts a block that displays the linked title of the post or page that follows the one you are currently editing on the Dashboard.
- *Previous Post:* This inserts a block that displays the linked title of the post or page that precedes the one you are currently editing on the Dashboard.
- *Read More:* This inserts a block that displays the text "Read More," which is linked to the post or page you are currently editing on the Dashboard.
- *Comments:* This inserts a block that displays the comments for the post you or page you are currently editing on the Dashboard.
- *Comments Form:* This inserts a block that displays the title and number of comments for the post or page you are currently editing on the Dashboard.
- *Login/out:* This inserts a block that displays login and logout links for WordPress.

- *Term Description:* This inserts a block that displays the description of a category, tag, or custom taxonomy term.
- *Archive Title:* This inserts a block that displays the title of an archive.
- *Search Results Title:* This inserts a block that displays the search results title based on the keyword being searched for.
- *Author Biography:* This inserts a block that displays the post author description that is set in the post author's profile in the Description field. (See Book 3, Chapter 2.)

FIGURE 1-6: The blocks available in the Theme section of the Block Inserter panel.

» **Embeds:** This block allows you to embed content from various services on the web, such as a video from YouTube, a specific tweet from Twitter, or a photo from Instagram. Currently, the WordPress block editor allows you to embed content from 34 services. The services in this embed list are likely to change over time, with new ones being added and old ones removed, as services on the web continue to evolve; thus, I have not listed them here. Figure 1-7 shows many of the blocks in the Embeds section; scroll down the Embeds heading in the block inserter to display all of the available blocks in this section.

FIGURE 1-7: The blocks available in the Embeds section of the Block Inserter panel.

Inserting new blocks

WordPress gives you a variety of ways to add a new block to your post or page. As you work with the block editor more and more, you'll develop a favorite method of adding new blocks based on your preferences and writing style. Pretty soon, muscle memory will take over and you'll be inserting new blocks with your eyes closed.

In a brand-new post, the Edit Post screen gives you the title field to type your post title in and a paragraph block to write the content of your page. From there, you can add new blocks to add different types of content to your page. You can insert a new block into your page by using any of the following methods:

- **Use the block inserter:** This method is covered in the "Discovering available blocks" section, earlier in this chapter, and illustrated in Figure 1-3.
- **Add Block:** When you have added some content to a post, you'll see an icon within the content that looks like a plus sign. Click that icon to display a list of the six most commonly used blocks that you can add to your page (see Figure 1-8). Choosing a block from that list inserts the block directly below the existing one. You can also click the Browse All link at the bottom of the block list to open the Block Inserter panel on the left (refer to Figure 1-3).

- **Options:** Every block has a small toolbar of styling options for that block (discussed in the following section, "Configuring block settings"). The three vertical dots on the right side of the toolbar menu are labeled Options when you hover your mouse pointer over the three dots; click it to display a drop-down menu of additional settings (see Figure 1-9). Two of those options are labeled Add Before and Add After. Click either option to insert a standard paragraph block before or after the block you're currently working in.
- **Press Enter (or Return on a Mac):** Press the Enter key on your keyboard when you're in a standard paragraph block to insert a new paragraph block into your page. Then you can continue using the paragraph block or add a different block from the available blocks list in the Block Inserter panel.
- **Use slash commands:** When you click inside a standard paragraph block and press the slash (/) key on your keyboard, a list of frequently used blocks appears, shown in Figure 1-10. You can navigate to the block you need by pressing the down-arrow key and then pressing Enter to select it, or you can start typing the name of the block you want to use in the text box and then press the Enter key when you find it to insert it into your page. This editing experience is intended to be mouseless; you can keep typing away and adding blocks from your keyboard.

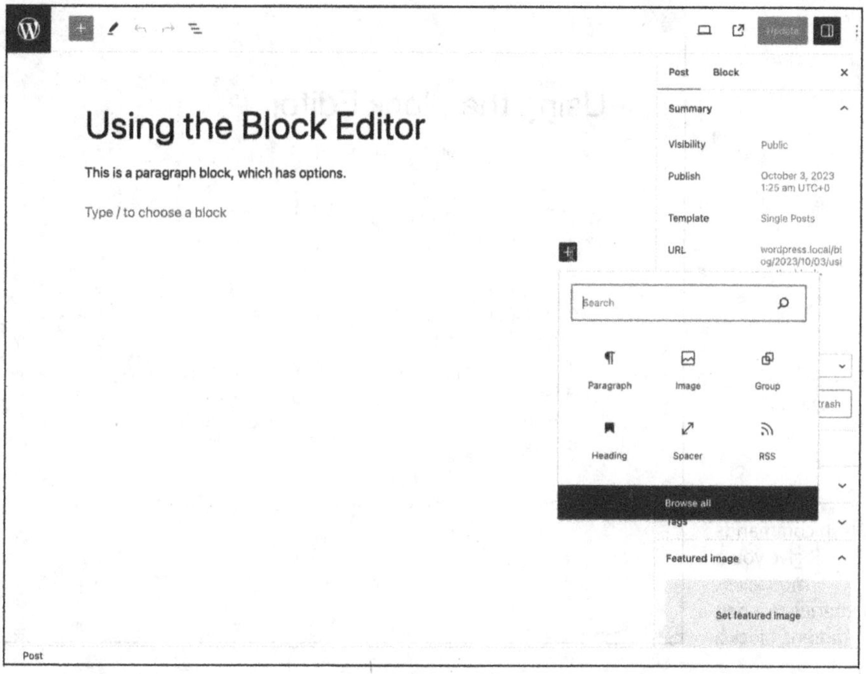

FIGURE 1-8: Add a new block to your page by using the Add Block feature within the editor.

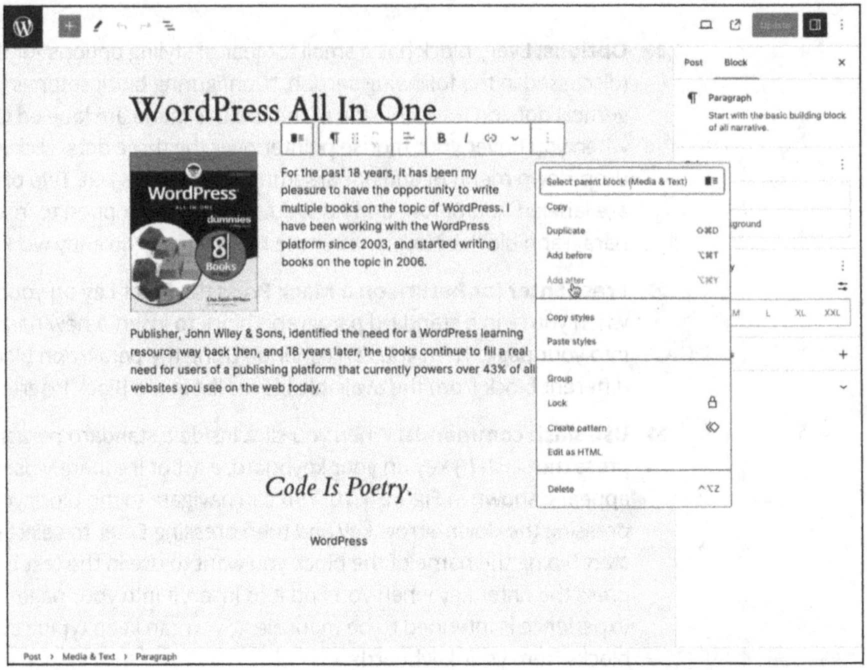

FIGURE 1-9: Add a new block before or after an existing block from the Options menu in the block toolbar.

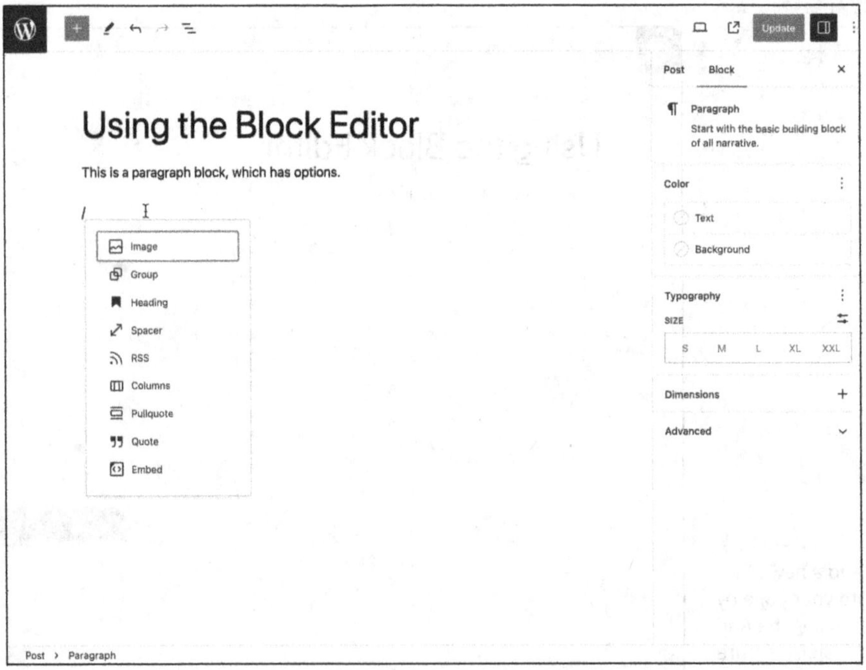

FIGURE 1-10: Slash commands give you a mouseless experience when adding blocks.

Configuring block settings

Each individual block has a toolbar of options you can use to configure display settings for your content, such as font size, font color, background color, and block width and/or height. In the "Discovering available blocks" section, earlier in this chapter, I discuss the different ways you can use the block options toolbar and the block settings panel shown in Figures 1-1 and 1-2 in that section.

In this section, you discover how to work with the block settings in the block toolbar, and block settings in settings panel for two of the most commonly used blocks: Paragraph and Image.

Paragraph block settings

You use the paragraph block to create a basic block of text. Add the block to your post or page and then add the text inside the box provided. When you're working within this block, options toolbar displays the paragraph block options, as shown in Figure 1-11.

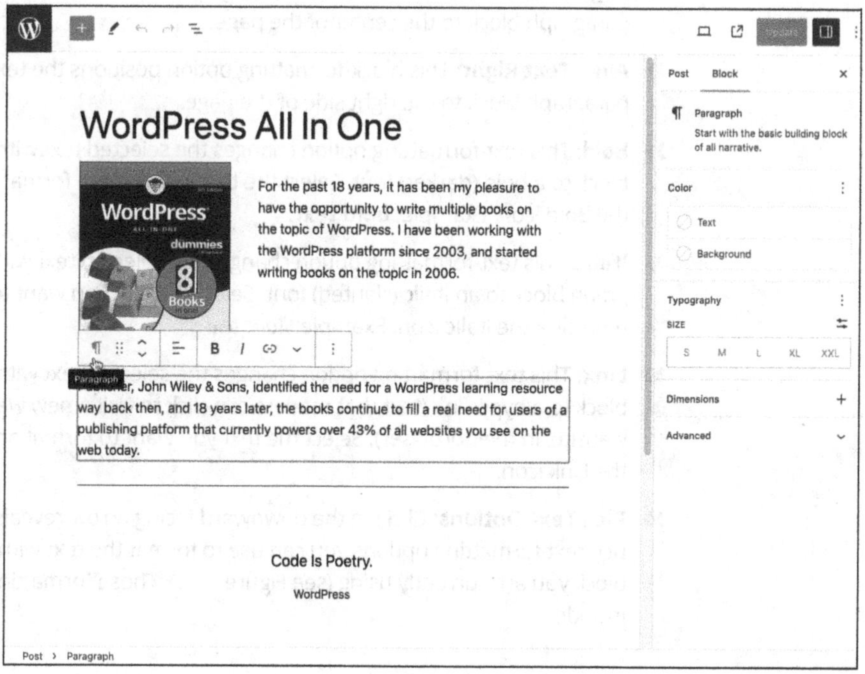
WordPress All In One
For the past 18 years, it has been my pleasure to have the opportunity to write multiple books on the topic of WordPress. I have been working with the WordPress platform since 2003, and started writing books on the topic in 2006.
Paragraph
r, John Wiley & Sons, identified the need for a WordPress learning resource way back then, and 18 years later, the books continue to fill a real need for users of a publishing platform that currently powers over 43% of all websites you see on the web today.
Code Is Poetry.
WordPress
Post
Block
Paragraph
Start with the basic building block of all narrative.
Color
Text
Background
Typography
SIZE
S M L XL XXL
Dimensions
Advanced
Post › Paragraph

FIGURE 1-11: The paragraph block options toolbar.

This toolbar provides a variety of options, including the following (from left to right):

- **Transform To:** This option allows you to change the type of block you're using. If you want to change from a paragraph to a quote block, for example, click the Transform To icon and then click the quote block to transform it. The block types you can change to from a paragraph block include heading, list, quote, columns, pullquote, code, group, preformatted, and verse.
- **Move Block Tools:** Use this option to move the paragraph block to a different location within your content. Click and hold the icon that looks like six dots with your mouse and drag the block to the location you want and then release the icon. You can also move the block by using the up and down arrows that appear to the right of the six dots icon. Selecting the up arrow will move the block one spot above and the down arrow will move the block one spot below the next block in your content.
- **Align Text Left:** This block-formatting option positions the text within a paragraph block to the left side of the page.
- **Align Text Center:** This block-formatting option positions the text within a paragraph block to the center of the page.
- **Align Text Right:** This block-formatting option positions the text within a paragraph block to the right side of the page.
- **Bold:** This text-formatting option changes the selected text within a paragraph block to a bold (darker) font. Select the text you want to format and then click the Bold icon. Example: **bold text**.
- **Italic:** This text-formatting option changes the selected text within a paragraph block to an italic (slanted) font. Select the text you want to format and then click the Italic icon. Example: *italic text*.
- **Link:** This text-formatting option changes the selected text within a paragraph block to a hyperlink (text that readers can click to visit a new web pages or website, in their browser). Select the text you want to format and then click the Link icon.
- **Rich Text Options:** Clicking the downward facing arrow reveals a list of rich text formatting options you can use to format the text within the block you are currently using (see Figure 1-12). Those formatting options include:

- *Footnote:* Clicking this option inserts the footnote block at the bottom of your post that is linked to the paragraph block associated to it. The footnote block allows you to add content to that corresponds with the content the note is attached to.
- *Highlight:* This option changes the color of the background of the text you've selected. It's very much like using a highlighter marker to highlight text in a book. You are able to choose the color of the highlight in the block settings sidebar using the color picker provided.
- *Inline Code:* This text-formatting option changes the formatting within the paragraph block to display as code, rather than regular text. Select the text you want to format as code and then click the Inline Code option.
- *Inline Image:* This text-formatting option allows you to insert an image in line with the paragraph text around it. Place your mouse pointer in the area in the paragraph you'd like to insert the image and then click the Inline Image option.
- *Keyboard input:* This option applies the `<kbd>` tag to the text you've selected from the content within the block you are using. The `<kbd>` tag is HTML that stands for Keyboard Input Element and is used wherever you have a need to display text that is intended to be entered by a user via the keyboard.
- *Language:* This option allows you to specify the language that should be used for the text you have selected within the block you are using. This option provides you with a text field in which you would type the two letter language abbreviation, such as *es* for *Spanish*, or *fr* for *French*.
- *Strikethrough:* This text-formatting option changes the selected text within a paragraph block to display with a line through it. Select the text you want to format and then click the Strikethrough icon. Example: ~~`strikethrough text`~~.
- *Subscript:* This option allows you to format text you've added to the block you are using as a subscript, which is usually a number that is placed a bit lower, and is sized a bit smaller, than the rest of the text in the paragraph; for example, $H_2 0$.
- *Superscript:* This option allows you to format text you've added to the block you are using as superscript, which is usually placed a bit higher, and sized a bit smaller, than the rest of the text in the paragraph; for example, `Trademark™`.

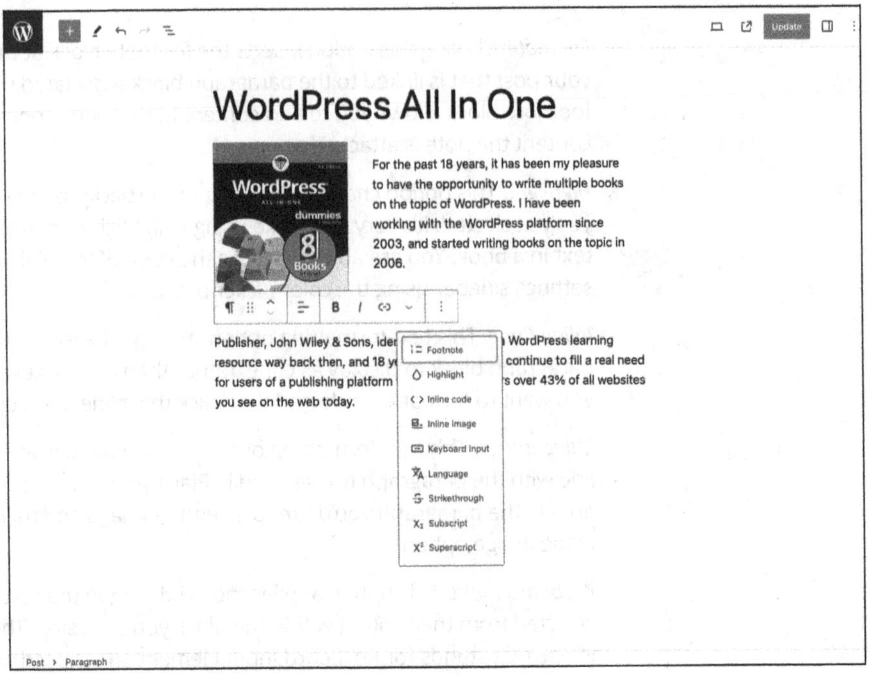
WordPress All In One
For the past 18 years, it has been my pleasure to have the opportunity to write multiple books on the topic of WordPress. I have been working with the WordPress platform since 2003, and started writing books on the topic in 2006.
Footnote
Highlight
Inline code
Inline image
Keyboard input
Language
Strikethrough
Subscript
Superscript
Post › Paragraph

FIGURE 1-12: The block toolbar for the paragraph block showing the rich text options.

» **Options:** Clicking this icon reveals a drop-down menu of options for the entire block, not just the content within the block, as shown in Figure 1-13. (This option exists on every block toolbar, so I'll cover it here and you can refer to this list for other blocks later in this section.) Click the Options icon on the block toolbar to reveal a drop-down menu of options:

- *Copy:* This option allows you to select a block and then click Copy to copy it to your clipboard so that you can paste it within your content elsewhere on your post or page.
- *Duplicate:* This duplicates the block you're currently using and inserts it below the current block.
- *Add Before:* This inserts a blank default block directly above the block you're currently using.
- *Add After:* This inserts a blank default block directly below the block you're currently using.
- *Copy Styles*: This copies the style, or the CSS/HTML, you've used for the block you are currently using. You can then apply the same styles to another block by using the Paste Styles option in the Options menu on the block toolbar.

- *Paste Styles:* This pastes the style, or the CSS/HTML or style options, you've previously copied using the Copy Styles option in the Options menu on the block toolbar in order to apply the styles to the current block you are using.
- *Group:* This option allows you to select multiple blocks and create a group block, which you can customize with settings such as font color, background color, and hover color.
- *Lock:* This option prevents a block from being deleted or moved.
- *Create Pattern:* This option allows you to create a reusable block or a block pattern from the block you are currently using. Block patterns are covered in Book 6, Chapter 3.
- *Move To:* This option creates a blue line between all of the existing blocks within your post. With your mouse, select the text you want to move and then click the Move To option. Use the arrows on your keyboard to position the blue line wherever you want your selected content to appear, and then click Enter key on your keyboard to move the selected text to that position.
- *Edit as HTML:* This changes the block editor to an HTML editor so you can view and create content in HTML code.
- *Delete:* This removes the block from the Edit Post screen. Use this feature carefully, because when you remove a block, it's gone for good.

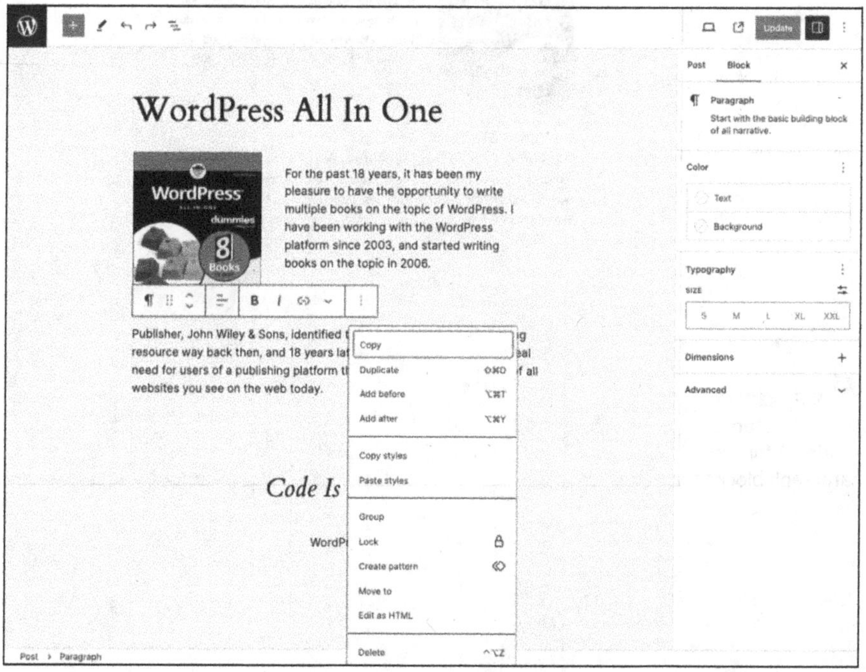

FIGURE 1-13: The block toolbar for the paragraph block showing the Options menu.

USING KEYBOARD SHORTCUTS

Some people like the ability to use keyboard shortcuts to accomplish things that normally take a mouse click to do. Keyboard shortcuts can make quick work of common editing actions by reducing dependence on the computer mouse, which can also benefit those who have carpal tunnel syndrome or other ailments associated with joint or muscle pain and strain. WordPress provides a variety of keyboard shortcuts to accomplish things like making text bold or italic, saving a post, and undoing changes. In the top-right corner of the Edit Post screen is an icon that looks like three dots stacked on top of one another. Hover your mouse pointer over this icon, and then click the Keyboard Shortcuts link to open a small window that shows you all of the available the shortcuts you can use when editing and creating posts and pages in WordPress.

Additional options for the paragraph block are available in the settings sidebar on the right side of the Edit Post screen, as shown in Figure 1-14.

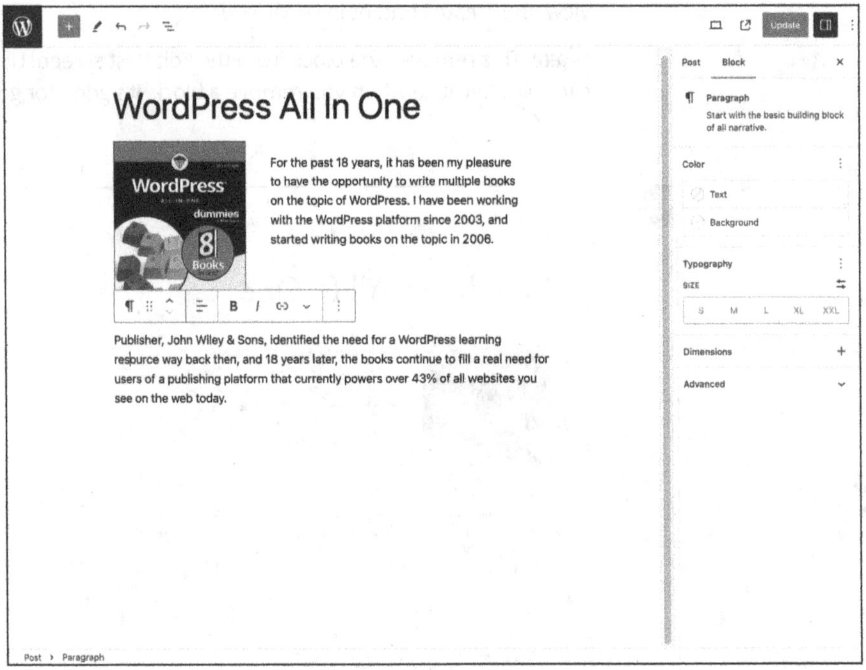

Update
Post
Block
WordPress All In One
For the past 18 years, it has been my pleasure to have the opportunity to write multiple books on the topic of WordPress. I have been working with the WordPress platform since 2003, and started writing books on the topic in 2006.
Publisher, John Wiley & Sons, identified the need for a WordPress learning resource way back then, and 18 years later, the books continue to fill a real need for users of a publishing platform that currently powers over 43% of all websites you see on the web today.
Paragraph
Start with the basic building block of all narrative.
Color
Text
Background
Typography
SIZE
S
M
L
XL
XXL
Dimensions
Advanced
Post › Paragraph

FIGURE 1-14: Settings sidebar for the paragraph block.

Those options include:

- **Color:** This section allows you to set the text color and background color of the paragraph block with the following options:
  - *Text:* Here, you can change the color of the text used in the paragraph block you're currently using. Since I am using the Twenty Twenty-Three theme, I can choose from one of five preselected colors or click the blank box above the "No color selected" label to display the color picker to select another color. Figure 1-15 shows the Text Color options with the preselected colors and the color picker for the paragraph block.
  - *Background:* Here, you can select a background color for the paragraph block you're currently using. Choose one of five preselected colors or click the custom color picker icon to select another color. You can choose between using a solid color or a gradient color that combines two different colors. The gradient options are located in the Gradient section of the background color option panel.

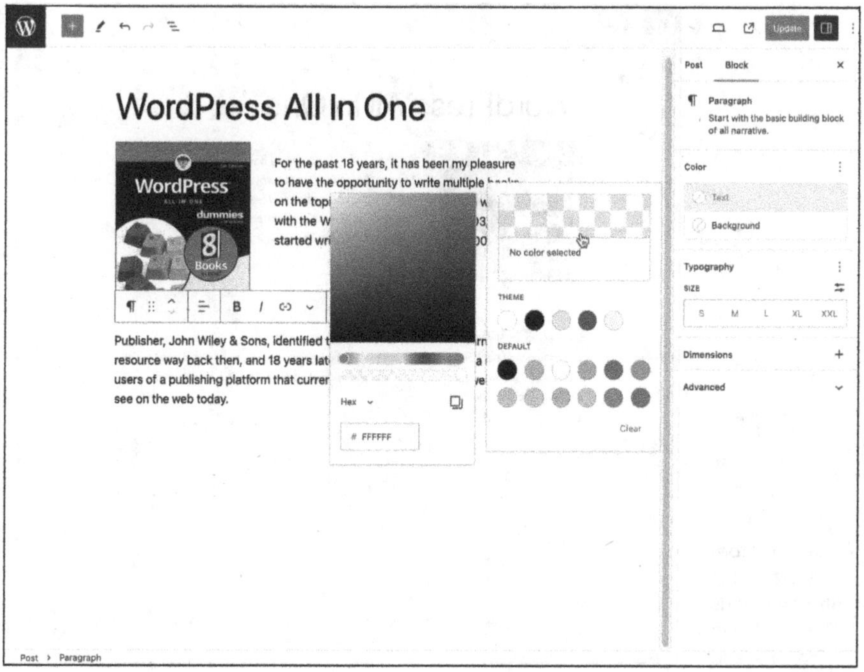

FIGURE 1-15: Text color options for the paragraph block.

- **Typography:** This section allows you to set the font size and other options for the paragraph block.
  - *Size:* By default, you can configure the text size options by clicking S (Small), M (Medium), L (Large), XL (Extra-Large), or XXL (Extra-Extra-Large) and you're able to see the effect of those changes on your screen so you can decide on which one you'd like to use. Additionally, you can click the Set Custom Size icon on the right side of the Size section that gives you two additional ways to set the font size: a text field into which you can type a numeric value, or a slider that you can use your mouse to slide to the left for a smaller font or to the right for a larger size font (see Figure 1-16).
  - *Typography:* Clicking the icon that looks like three dots stacked on top of one another to the right of the Typography heading reveals a list of other font options you can change, including Font Family, Appearance, Line Height, Letter Spacing, Text Decoration, and Letter Case (see Figure 1-17). Clicking the Reset All link at the bottom of the options list restores all of the font styling options back to their default state.

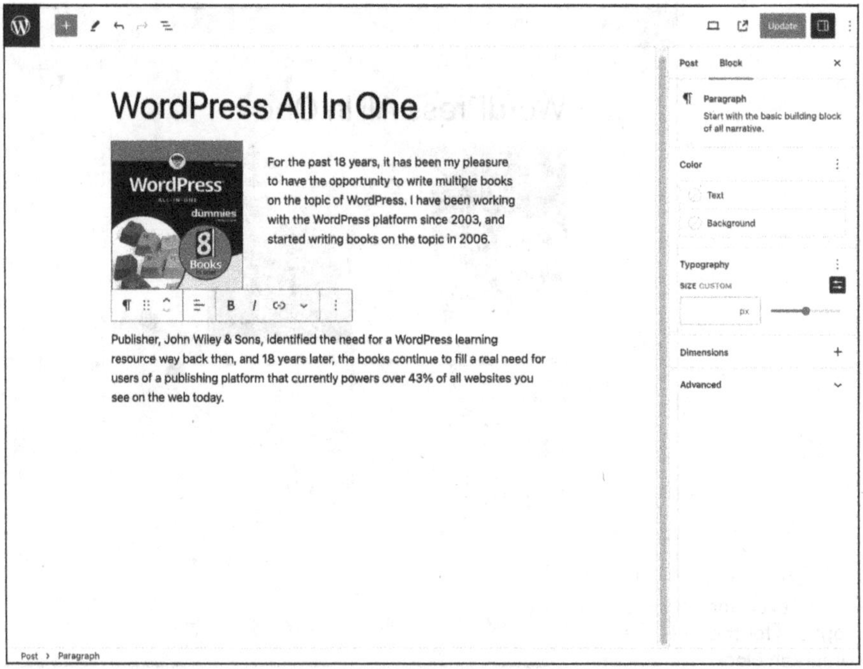

Update
Post
Block
WordPress All In One
Paragraph
Start with the basic building block of all narrative.
For the past 18 years, it has been my pleasure to have the opportunity to write multiple books on the topic of WordPress. I have been working with the WordPress platform since 2003, and started writing books on the topic in 2006.
Color
Text
Background
Typography
SIZE CUSTOM
px
Publisher, John Wiley & Sons, identified the need for a WordPress learning resource way back then, and 18 years later, the books continue to fill a real need for users of a publishing platform that currently powers over 43% of all websites you see on the web today.
Dimensions
Advanced
Post › Paragraph

FIGURE 1-16: Set a custom text size using other methods like a text field or slider.

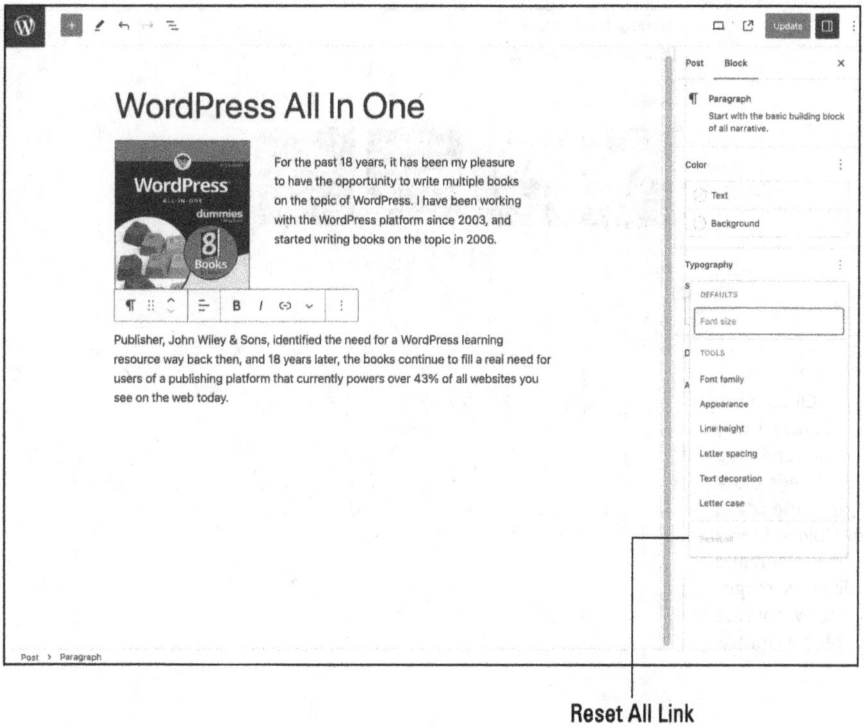
Update
Post
Block
WordPress All In One
For the past 18 years, it has been my pleasure to have the opportunity to write multiple books on the topic of WordPress. I have been working with the WordPress platform since 2003, and started writing books on the topic in 2006.
Publisher, John Wiley & Sons, identified the need for a WordPress learning resource way back then, and 18 years later, the books continue to fill a real need for users of a publishing platform that currently powers over 43% of all websites you see on the web today.
Paragraph
Start with the basic building block of all narrative.
Color
Text
Background
Typography
DEFAULTS
Font size
TOOLS
Font family
Appearance
Line height
Letter spacing
Text decoration
Letter case
Post › Paragraph
Reset All Link

FIGURE 1-17: Typography options available in the paragraph block.

Image block settings

You use the image block to add a single image to your post. Add the block to your post or page and then use one of these options:

- **Upload:** Click the Upload button to select an image from your computer. This action uploads the image from your computer to your website and inserts the image into your post via an image block. WordPress also adds this image to your Media Library so you can reuse this image in the future.
- **Media Library:** Click the Media Library button to choose an image from the WordPress Media Library. When the Select or Upload Media screen opens (see Figure 1-18), select an image in the Media Library section and then click the Select button to add the image to your post.
- **Insert from URL:** Click the Insert from URL button to display a small text box where you can paste or type the URL (or link) for the image you want to use. Press the Enter key on your keyboard or click the Apply button to insert the image into the image block you're using.

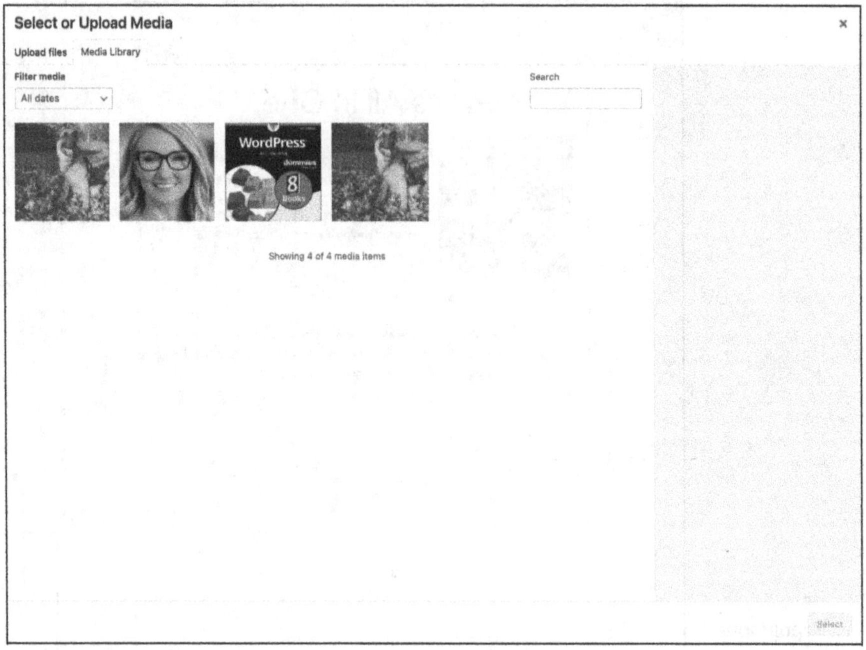

FIGURE 1-18: Clicking the Media Library button in the image block opens the Select or Upload Media screen and displays images in the WordPress Media Library.

- **Drag an Image:** This cool option allows you to select an image from your computer and drag it into the WordPress block editor to add it to a block. The dragged image also gets added to the Media Library for future use.
- **Write Caption:** When you've added an image to an image block, you see an optional field directly below it labeled Write Caption. This field is optional; if you do nothing with it, nothing displays on your site. If you type words in this field, however, those words appear below the image as a caption.

When you're working within this block, notice the small toolbar of options that appears at the top of the block. This toolbar provides a variety of options for the image block, including the following (from left to right):

- **Transform To:** Click this option to change the type of block you're using. If you want to change from an image block to a cover block, for example, click the Change Block Type icon and then select the cover block to swap it. The block types you can change from an image block include columns, media & text, gallery, cover, file, and group. In this menu you also find the Styles section, where you can select Default or Rounded, which sets the style for the corners of the image you've inserted into your post.

- **Move Block Tools:** The settings here are the same as those discussed in the previous section, "Paragraph block settings."
- **Apply Duotone Filter:** Click this option to open the Duotone menu, with options allowing you to select a combination of two colors that add a two-tone filter to your image.
- **Align:** Click this icon to open a menu of alignment options:
  - *None:* This is autoselected as the default alignment option for the heading.
  - *Wide Width:* Click this option to set the width of the header to the width of the content on the page.
  - *Full Width:* Click this option to increase the width of the heading to the width of the screen you're viewing the content on. The left edge of the heading extends all the way to the viewing screen.
  - *Align Left, Align Center, Align Right*: These alignment options are discussed in the previous section, "Paragraph block settings."
- **Add Caption:** Click this icon to type a caption underneath the image.
- **Link:** This option allows you to set a URL for the image, which makes the image clickable. When a visitor to your site clicks the image, they're taken to the URL you specified.
- **Crop:** Click this icon to crop the image you've added to your content. The options are Zoom, Aspect Ratio, and Rotate.
- **Add Text Over Image:** Click this icon to type text over the image.
- **Replace:** This option allows you to replace the image and opens the Media Library when you click it.
- **More Options:** The settings here are the same as the ones discussed in the previous section, "Paragraph block settings."

Additional options are available for the image block in the Settings panel on the right side of the Edit Post screen, as shown in Figure 1-19.

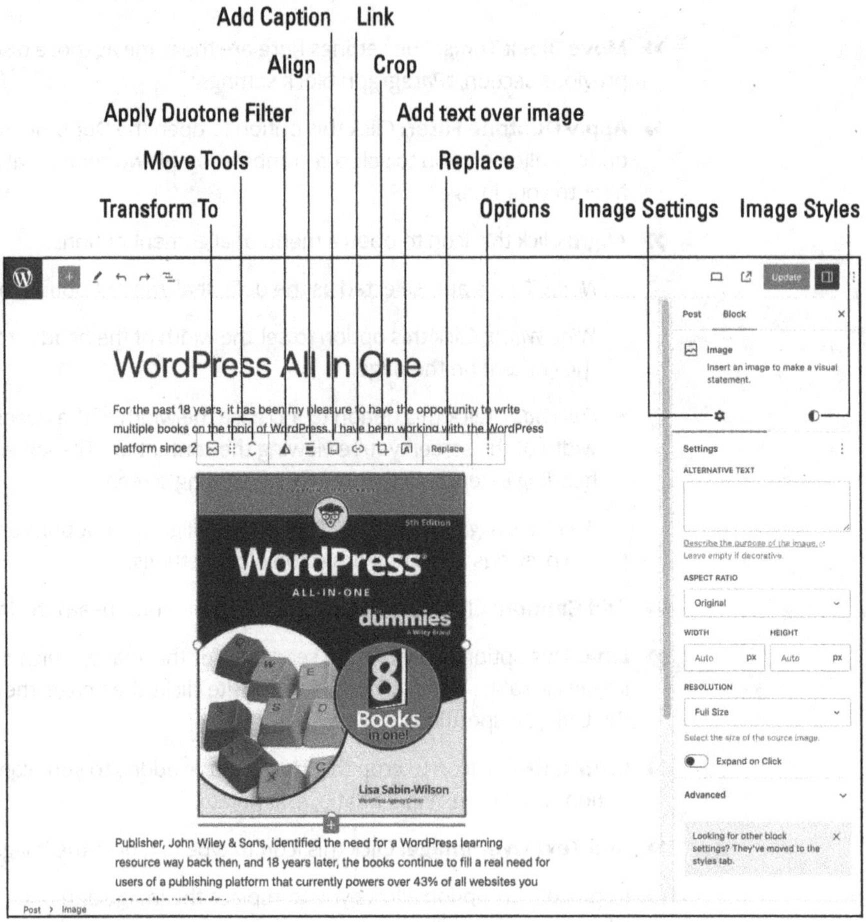

FIGURE 1-19: Options in the Settings panel for the image block.

Some of the most used options for the image block include:

- **Image Settings:** Clicking the gear icon gives you access to the Settings panel for the image block (refer to Figure 1-19). The options in this section allow you to set the alternative text, size, and dimensions of the image in the image block.
  - *Alternative Text:* Enter descriptive text in the Alt Text field to describe the image you're using in the image block. Also referred to as *alternative text*, this description helps people who can't see the image on your site; when the image doesn't load on your site, the alternative text is displayed, providing context for the missing image. This option is also an accessibility feature that helps those who use screen readers to browse the web. (Screen readers allow visually impaired users to understand the text that's displayed on the website with a speech synthesizer or Braille display.) Additionally, alternative text descriptions assist in search engine optimization (SEO).

- *Aspect Ratio*: This setting deals with the proportional relationship between the image width and the image height. There are several options for you to choose from here, including Original, Square, Standard, and Portrait.
- *Width and Height:* To set a specific width and height for the image used in the image block, enter numbers in the Width and Height fields in the image block Settings panel.
- *Resolution:* To set the resolution of the image used in the image block, choose a predefined size from the Resolution drop-down menu in the image block Settings panel. The available options are Thumbnail, Medium, Large, and Full Size. The dimensions for these options are defined in the WordPress settings on your Dashboard; to see them, choose Settings ➪ Media.
- *Expand on Click*: Enable this toggle to allow your readers to click your image and view it in a pop-up window, with a larger size.

» **Image Styles:** Click the icon that looks like a half-white, half-dark moon to access the Styles for the image block. Here, you can set options like filters, borders, and border radius.

The WordPress block editor does not stop here. In Book 6, Chapter 3, you learn about how you can create block patterns for content or layouts that you use frequently, but don't want to have to re-create each time you want to use them. In the next two chapters, you will use blocks to create posts and pages.

IN THIS CHAPTER

» Navigating the Edit Post screen

» Refining your post options

» Publishing your post

» Editing your post

Chapter 2

Writing Your First Post

It's finally time to write your first post on your new WordPress site! The topic you choose to write about and the writing techniques you use to get your message across are all on you; I have my hands full writing this book! I *can* tell you, however, how to write the wonderful passages that can bring you blog fame. Ready?

Composing a post is a lot like typing an email: You give it a title, you write the message, and you click a button to send your words into the world. By using the different options that WordPress provides — content blocks, discussion options, categories, and tags, for example — you can configure each post the way you like. This section covers the minimal steps you take to compose and publish a post on your site.

Composing Your Post

When you're writing (or editing) a blog post, the editor window adopts the visual look and feel of the WordPress theme you're using — this is what WordPress refers to as *full site editing* (more about this in Book 6, Chapter 2). In this chapter, I'm using the default Twenty Twenty-Three theme, which is considered a block theme. Thus, the post editor adopts the same visual look a live website does, so I know how it will look on my website when I publish the post.

Follow these steps to write a basic post:

1. **Click the Add New Post link on the Posts menu of the Dashboard.**

   The Edit Post screen opens, as shown in Figure 2-1.

2. **Type the title of your post in the Add Title text field at the top of the Edit Post screen.**

3. **Type the content of your post in the area below the Add Title field.**

   The first time you visit the Edit Post screen, this area displays a message that says `Type / to choose a block`. I cover blocks in Book 4, Chapter 1.

4. **Click the Save Draft link, located in the top-right corner of the Edit Post screen.**

   The Save Draft link changes to a message that says Saved.

   WordPress has a built-in autosave feature to make sure that your content is saved and protected from being lost. Imagine spending an hour writing a long post and then the power goes out due to a storm in your area! You don't need to worry about all your work being lost, because WordPress thoughtfully saves it for you. The default interval is 10 seconds, so if you don't click the Save Draft link, WordPress saves your post for you automatically. When the storm is over, you'll find a draft of the post you were working on before lightning struck.

In Figure 2-2, you can see the post that I created, titled "WordPress All In One," uses three blocks from the block editor. In order, the post uses the media & text block, the paragraph block, and the pullquote block. You can see the same post in Figure 2-3, but this time the figure is of the front page of my website. That is a result of the Site Editor feature in WordPress, where your content looks and is formatted the same while you are creating it as it does when you are viewing it on the front end of the website.

At this point, you can skip to the "Publishing Your Post" section, later in this chapter, for information on publishing your post to your site, or you can continue with the following sections to discover how to refine the options for your post.

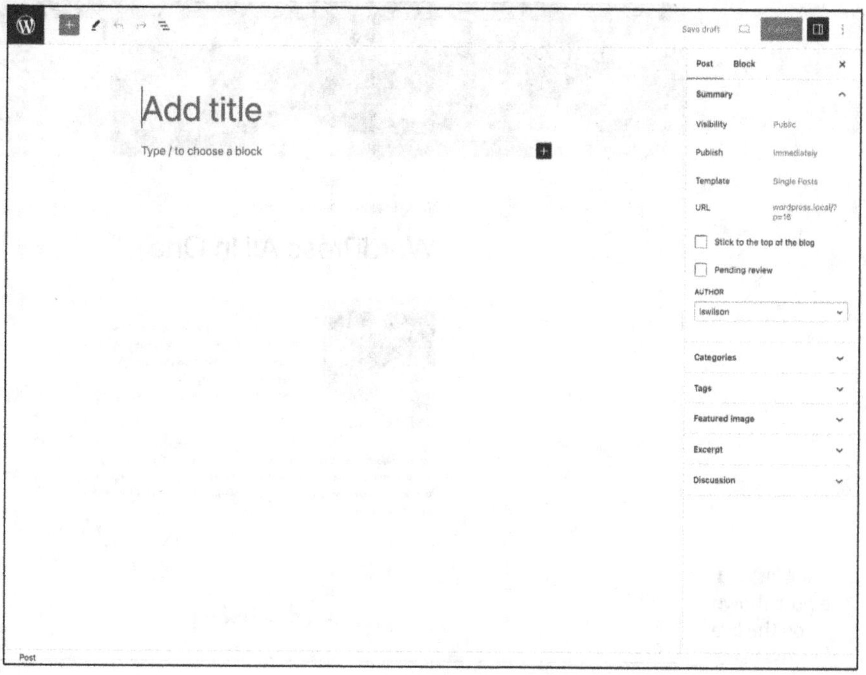
Save draft
Add title
Type / to choose a block
Post
Block
Summary
Visibility
Public
Publish
Immediately
Template
Single Posts
URL
wordpress.local/?p=16
Stick to the top of the blog
Pending review
AUTHOR
lswilson
Categories
Tags
Featured image
Excerpt
Discussion
Post

FIGURE 2-1: The Edit Post screen on the Dashboard.

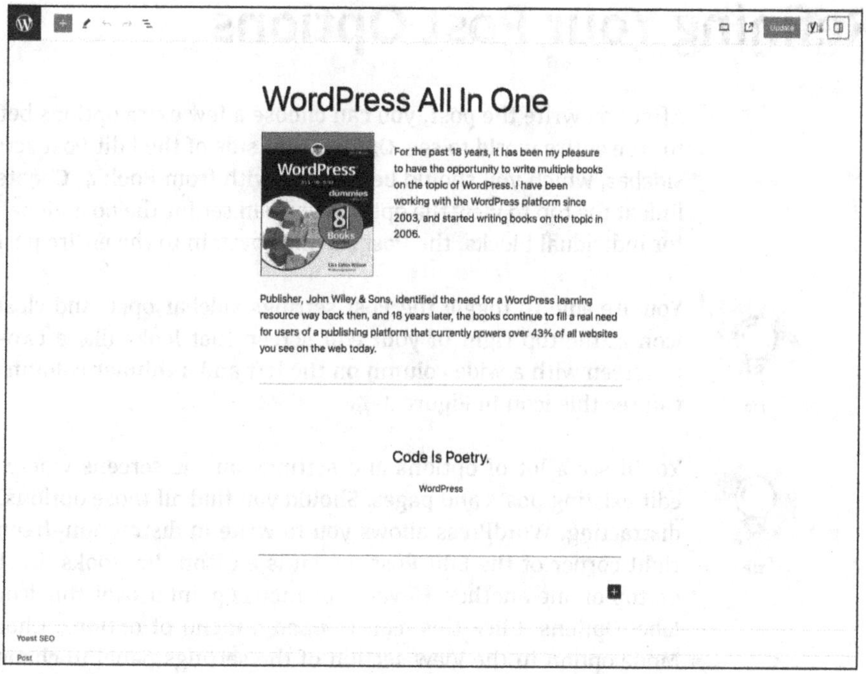
Update
WordPress All In One
WordPress
dummies
8
Books
For the past 18 years, it has been my pleasure to have the opportunity to write multiple books on the topic of WordPress. I have been working with the WordPress platform since 2003, and started writing books on the topic in 2006.
Publisher, John Wiley & Sons, identified the need for a WordPress learning resource way back then, and 18 years later, the books continue to fill a real need for users of a publishing platform that currently powers over 43% of all websites you see on the web today.
Code Is Poetry.
WordPress
Yoast SEO
Post

FIGURE 2-2: A post titled "WordPress All In One" created using three blocks from the block editor.

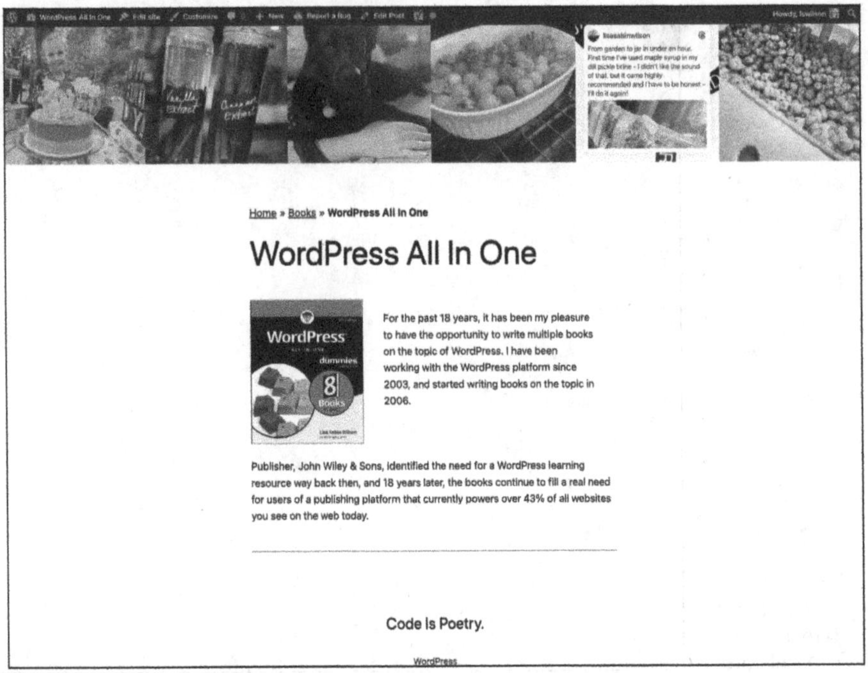
Home » Books » WordPress All In One
WordPress All In One
For the past 18 years, it has been my pleasure to have the opportunity to write multiple books on the topic of WordPress. I have been working with the WordPress platform since 2003, and started writing books on the topic in 2006.
Publisher, John Wiley & Sons, identified the need for a WordPress learning resource way back then, and 18 years later, the books continue to fill a real need for users of a publishing platform that currently powers over 43% of all websites you see on the web today.
Code Is Poetry.
WordPress

FIGURE 2-3: The post shown on the live website.

Refining Your Post Options

After you write the post, you can choose a few extra options before you publish it for the entire world to see. On the right side of the Edit Post screen is the settings sidebar, which you should be familiar with from Book 4, Chapter 1. Click the Post link at the top to view the options you can set for the post globally. Unlike settings for individual blocks, the Post settings pertain to the entire post.

TIP

You are able to toggle the Post settings sidebar open and closed by clicking the icon at the top right of your edit screen that looks like a two-column interface (a screen with a wide column on the left and a thinner column on the right). You can see this icon in Figure 2-4.

TIP

You'll see a lot of options and settings on the screens where you add new and edit existing posts and pages. Should you find all those options, links, and menus distracting, WordPress allows you to write in distraction-free mode. In the top-right corner of the Edit Post screen is an icon that looks like three dots stacked on top of one another. Hover your mouse pointer over this icon, and you see the label Options. Click this icon to open a menu of options. Choose the Fullscreen Mode option in the View section of the settings panel to change the screen view to full screen, which removes all the distractions of those pesky links, menus, and settings. You can restore the screen to normal by performing the same action and deselecting Fullscreen Mode.

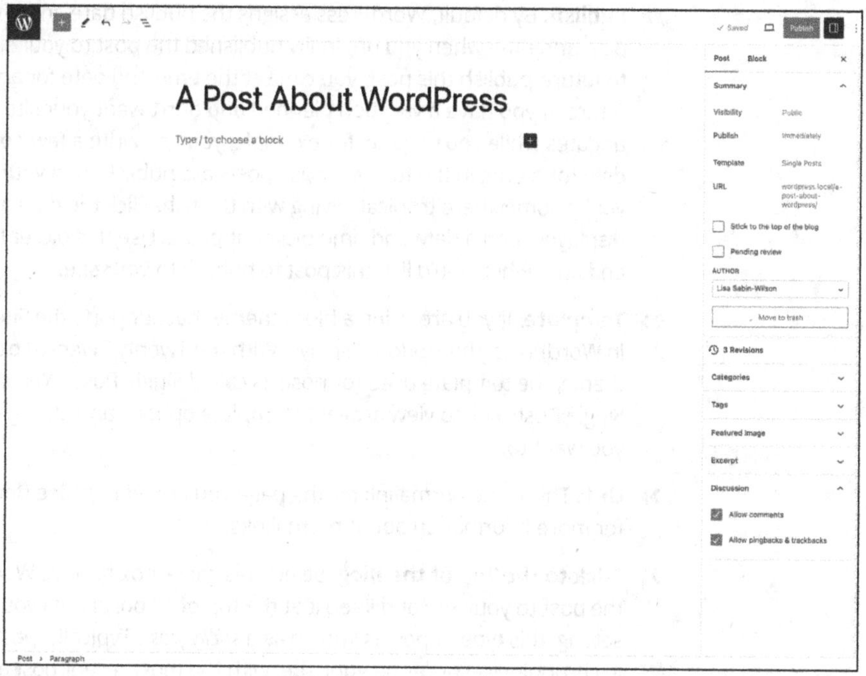

FIGURE 2-4: The Post settings sidebar on the Edit Post screen.

The Post settings include the following under the Summary heading:

- **Visibility:** By default, the visibility status of your post is set to Public. You can select three status options by clicking the Public link in the post settings panel:
  - *Public:* Select this option to make the post viewable by everyone who visits your site.
  - *Private:* Select this option to make the post viewable only by site administrators and editors. Saving a post with this status prevents anyone else from viewing the post on your site.
  - *Password Protected:* Select this option to create a password for your post. By assigning a password to a post, you can publish a post that only you can see. You also can share the post password with a friend who can see the content of the post after they enter the password. But why would anyone want to password-protect a post? Suppose that you just ate dinner at your

mother-in-law's house, and she made the worst pot roast you've ever eaten. You can write all about it! Protect it with a password and give the password to your trusted friends so that they can read about it without offending your mother-in-law.

- **Publish:** By default, WordPress assigns the publish date and time as the exact date and time when you originally published the post to your site. If you want to future-publish this post, you can set the time and date for any time in the future. If you have a vacation planned and don't want your site to go without updates while you're gone, for example, you can write a few posts and set the date for a time in the future. Those posts are published to your site while you're somewhere tropical, diving with the fish. Click the date and time displayed, and a date and time picker appears. Use this picker to set the date and time when you'd like this post to publish to your site.
- **Template:** If you are using a block theme that supports the Site Editor feature in WordPress, this option displays. With the Twenty Twenty-Four default theme, the template used for posts is called Single Posts. You can click the Single Posts link to view available template options and change the template if you want to.
- **URL:** This is the permalink for the page you are editing. See Book 3, Chapter 2 for more information about permalinks.
- **Stick to the Top of the Blog:** Select this check box to have WordPress publish the post to your site and keep it at the top of all posts until you change this setting; this type of post is known as a *sticky post*. Typically, posts are displayed in chronological order on your site, with the most recent post at the top. If you make a post sticky, it remains at the top no matter how many other posts you make after it. When you want to unstick the post, deselect the check box. Don't forget to click the Update button that appears at the top of the screen to save your changes.
- **Pending Review:** Select this check box to save the post as a draft with the status of Pending Review. This option alerts the administrator of the site that a contributor created a post that's waiting for administrator review and approval. (This feature is helpful for sites that have multiple authors.) Generally, only contributors use the Pending Review option. Note that this option is available only for new posts. You won't see it in the settings panel of posts that have already been published.
- **Author:** If you're running a multiauthor blog, you can choose the name of the author you want to assign to the post you're editing. By default, your own author name is selected in the Author drop-down menu.
- **Move to Trash:** Click this button to delete the post you've been working on. This action doesn't permanently delete the post, however. You can find and

restore that post by visiting the Posts screen on your Dashboard (choose Posts ⇨ All Posts) and clicking the Trash link.

- **Revisions:** In the previous section, "Composing Your Post," I mention the autosave feature. Its function is to automatically save the work you've done on posts you're creating so that you don't lose any of it. Each time you edit a post, WordPress automatically saves the old version of your post and stores it as a revision, making it available for you to access later. This section gives you an indication of how many revisions a post has. When you click the Revisions link, you see the Compare Revisions screen, where you can review and restore revisions of your post.
- **URL:** A URL is the direct link, also known as a permalink, to the post you're about to publish. Although you can't change the domain portion of this URL (`https://`*`domain.com`*), you can adjust the part of the URL that appears in the link after the final slash at the end of your domain. For a post titled "WordPress Tips," WordPress automatically creates a URL from that title, such as `http://`*`domain.com`*`/wordpress-tips`. Click the URL, and the permalink field appears, in which you can change the URL for your post (or page) from the one that WordPress automatically created for you. For example, you could shorten the slug for the post title "WordPress Tips" to simply "wordpress," so that the URL for the post is `http://`*`domain.com`*`/wordpress`.
- **Categories:** Click the Categories section in the post settings panel to file your posts in different categories and to organize them by subject. (See more about organizing your posts by category in Book 3, Chapter 5.) Select the check box to the left of the category you want to use.

  TIP

  Don't see the category you need in the Categories section? Click the Add New Category link in the Categories section of the post settings panel to add a new category right there on the page you're using to create or edit your post.
- **Tags:** Click the Tags section in the post settings panel and type your desired tags in the Add New Tag text box. Be sure to separate tags with commas so that WordPress knows where each tag begins and ends. Cats, Kittens, Feline represents three different tags, for example, but without the commas, WordPress would consider those three words to be one tag. See Book 3, Chapter 5 for more information on tags and how to use them.
- **Featured Image:** Some WordPress themes are configured to use an image (photo) to represent each post on your site. The image can appear on the home/front page, blog page, archives page, search results page, or anywhere within the content displayed on your website. If you're using a theme that has this option, you can easily define it by clicking the Featured Image section in the post settings panel and then clicking Set Featured Image. This action opens a window that allows you to upload a new image or select an existing image from the Media Library.

» **Excerpt:** Excerpts are short summaries of your posts. Many authors use these snippets to show teasers of their posts on their website, thereby encouraging readers to click the Read More links to read the posts in their entirety. By default, WordPress automatically creates an excerpt based on the text contained in the first paragraph of your post. But if you want to control what text is displayed for the excerpt of your post, click the Excerpt section of the post setting panel and then type your desired text in the Write an Excerpt box, which is displayed when you click the Excerpt section in the setting panel. Excerpts can be any length in terms of words, but the point is to keep them short and sweet to tease your readers into clicking the Read More link.

» **Discussion:** Decide whether to let readers submit comments through the comment system by clicking the Discussion section of the post settings panel and then selecting the Allow comments check box. Additionally, you can enable pingbacks and trackbacks by selecting the Allow pingbacks & trackbacks check box. By default, both options are selected for posts you create on your site. For more on trackbacks, see Book 3, Chapter 4.

Publishing Your Post

You've given your new post a title and written the content of the post by assembling all the content blocks you need to create the post you want. Maybe you've even added an image or other type of media file to the post (see Book 4, Chapter 5), and you've configured the tags, categories, and other options in the settings panel. Now the question is: To publish or not to publish (yet)?

WordPress gives you three options for saving or publishing your post when you're done writing it. These options are located in the top-right corner of the Edit Post screen (refer to Figure 2-1). The options for saving or publishing your post include:

» **Save Draft:** Click this link to save your post as a draft. The Save Draft link refreshes with a message that says Saved, indicating that your post has been successfully saved as a draft. The action of saving as a draft also saves all the post options you've set for the post, including blocks, categories, tags, and featured images. You can continue editing; the post is saved as a draft until you decide to publish it or delete it. Posts saved as drafts can't be seen by visitors to your site. To access your draft posts on your Dashboard, visit the Posts screen (choose Posts ⇨ All Posts), and click the Drafts link on the top menu.

» **Preview:** Click the Preview icon (next to Save Draft; it looks like a laptop computer) to view your post in a new window, as it would appear on your live site if you'd published it. Previewing the post doesn't publish it to your site yet. Previewing simply gives you the opportunity to view the post on your site and check it for any formatting or content changes you want to make.

TIP

Clicking the Preview icon gives you three options in which to view your content: Desktop, Tablet, and Mobile. This is handy for when you want to check and see how your content will look on a smartphone or on a tablet before you publish it to your site. Responsive Design is what theme designers do to make sure your content looks good on all devices, because sometimes, content on a mobile phone or a tablet can look different than the content on your desktop computer, so it's good to check your content by clicking the Preview icon before you publish.

- **Publish:** Click the Publish button when you're ready to publish your post or page to your website and allow your visitors to view it when they visit. WordPress puts a small fail-safe feature in place to make sure that you want to publish the post live: When you click the Publish button, the settings sidebar changes to a panel with the heading `Are you ready to publish?` (see Figure 2-5). This panel even provides the option to double-check some of your settings, such as visibility and publish date. Additionally, this panel reminds you if you've forgotten to select a category and/or a tag for this post. Click the Publish button at the top a second time to publish the post to your website.

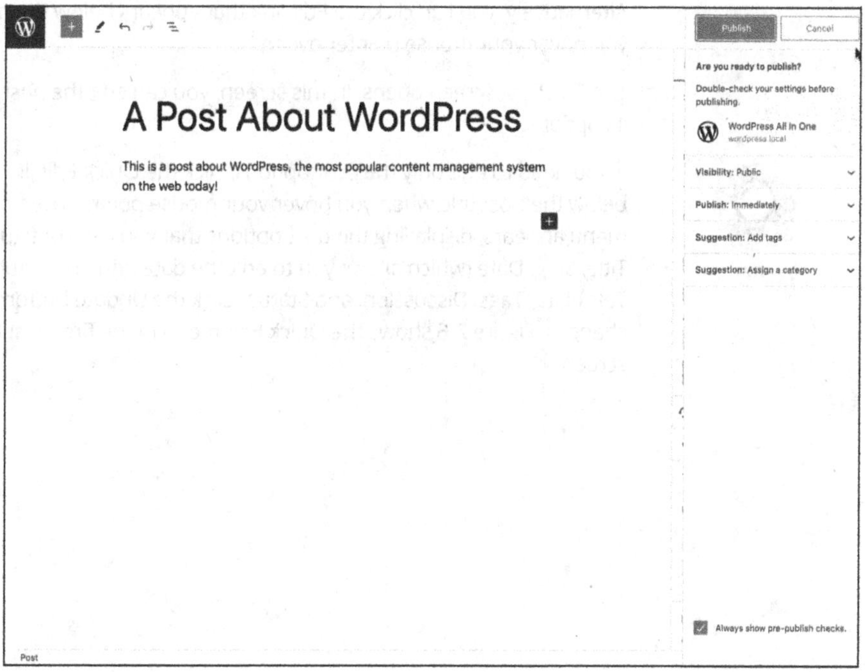

FIGURE 2-5: Double-check your settings before publishing.

Being Your Own Editor

While I write this book, I have copy editors, technical editors, and proofreaders looking over my shoulder, making recommendations, correcting typos and grammatical errors, and telling me when I get too long-winded. You, on the other hand, probably aren't so lucky! You are your own editor and have full control of what you write, when you write it, and how you write it.

You can always go back to edit previous posts to correct typos, grammatical errors, and other mistakes by following these steps:

1. **Find the post that you want to edit by clicking the All Posts link on the Posts menu of the Dashboard.**

   The Posts screen opens, listing the 20 most recent posts you've created.

   TIP

   To filter that listing of posts by date, choose a date from the All Dates drop-down menu at the top of the Posts screen (choose Dashboard ⇨ Posts). For example, if you choose January 2024, the Posts page reloads, displaying only those posts that were published in January 2024.

   You also can filter the post listing by category. Choose your desired category from the All Categories drop-down menu.

2. **When you find the post you need, click its title.**

   Alternatively, you can click the Edit link that appears below the post title when you hover your mouse pointer over it.

   The Edit Post screen opens. In this screen, you can edit the post and/or any of its options.

   TIP

   If you need to edit only the post options, click the Quick Edit link that appears below the post title when you hover your mouse pointer over it. A Quick Edit menu appears, displaying the post options that you can configure, such as Title, Slug, Date (which allows you to edit the date and time), Author, Password, Template, Tags, Discussion, and Status. Click the Update button to save your changes. Figure 2-6 shows the Quick Edit menu in the first post listed on the screen.

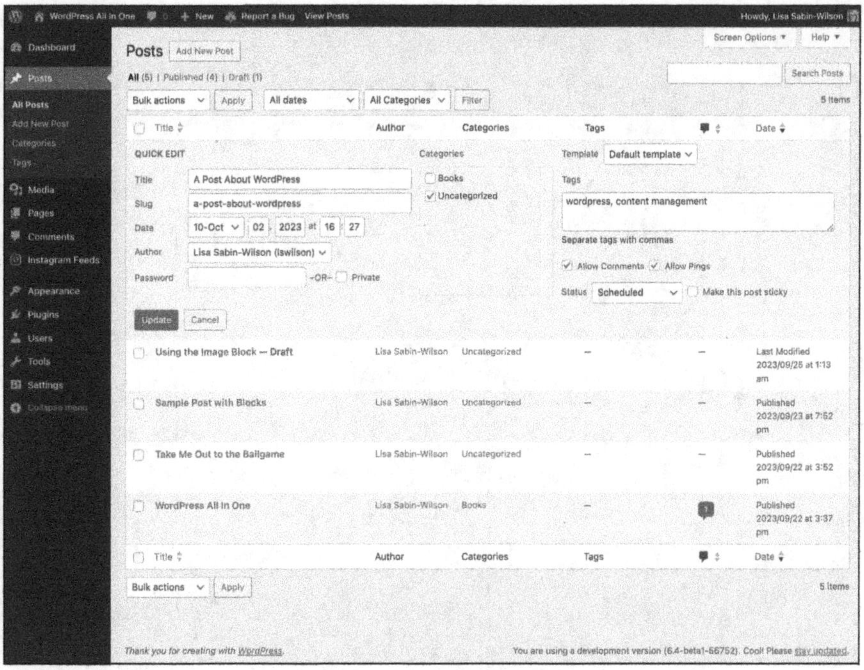

FIGURE 2-6: The Quick Edit menu on the Posts screen on the Dashboard.

3. **Edit your post; then click the Update button.**

   The Edit Post screen displays a message that the post has been updated.

Congratulations on publishing your first post on your site!

IN THIS CHAPTER

» Differentiating between posts and pages

» Creating a new static page on your website

» Adding a blog to your site

Chapter 3
Creating a Static Page

In Book 3, Chapter 5, I discuss the different ways that content gets archived by WordPress, and in Book 3, Chapter 1, I give you a brief introduction to the concept of pages and where to find them on the WordPress Dashboard.

This chapter takes you through the full concept of pages in WordPress, including how to write and publish them, and how you can add a blog to your website. We start by fully explaining the difference between posts and pages in WordPress so that you know which to publish for different situations.

Understanding the Difference between Pages and Posts

Pages, in WordPress, are different from posts because they don't get archived the way your posts do. Pages aren't categorized or tagged, they don't appear in your listing of recent posts or in date archives, and they aren't syndicated in the RSS feeds available on your site — because content within pages generally never, or very rarely, changes. (Book 3, Chapter 5 gives you all the details on how the WordPress archives work.)

REMEMBER

Use pages for static or stand-alone content that exists separately from the archived post content on your site, such as an About or Contact page.

With the page feature, you can create an unlimited number of static pages separate from your posts. People commonly use this feature to create About Me or Contact Me pages, among other things. Table 3-1 illustrates the differences between posts and pages by showing you the different ways the WordPress platform handles them.

TABLE 3-1 Differences between a Post and a Page

WordPress Options	Page	Post
Appears in blog post listings	No	Yes
Appears as a static page	Yes	No
Appears in category archives	No	Yes
Appears in monthly archives	No	Yes
Appears in Recent Posts listings	No	Yes
Appears in site RSS feed	No	Yes
Appears in search results	Yes	Yes
Uses tags and/or categories	No	Yes

Creating the Front Page of Your Website

For the most part, when you visit a site powered by WordPress, the blog can appear on the main page or as a separate page of the site. I keep a personal blog at `https://lisasabin-wilson.com/blog`, powered by WordPress (of course). My personal website shows my latest blog posts on the front page. This setup is typical of a site run by WordPress. (See Figure 3-1.)

On the other hand, the front page of my personal site at `https://lisasabin-wilson.com` (see Figure 3-2) displays the contents of a static page that I created in WordPress. This static page serves as a portal that displays pieces of content from other sections of my website. My site includes a blog but also serves as a full website with all the sections I need to provide my clients and readers of my books the information they need.

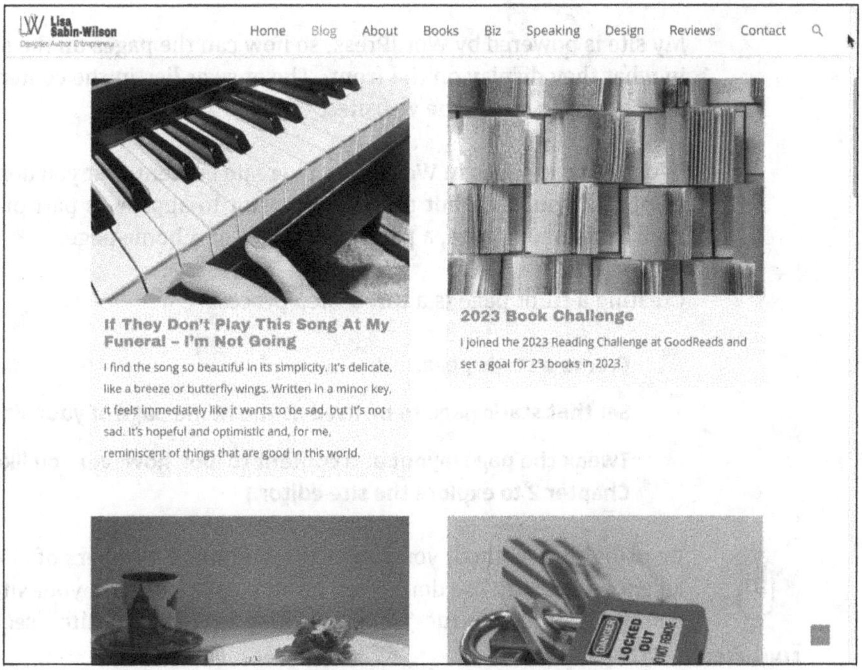

FIGURE 3-1: My personal blog at `lisasabin-wilson.com/blog`.

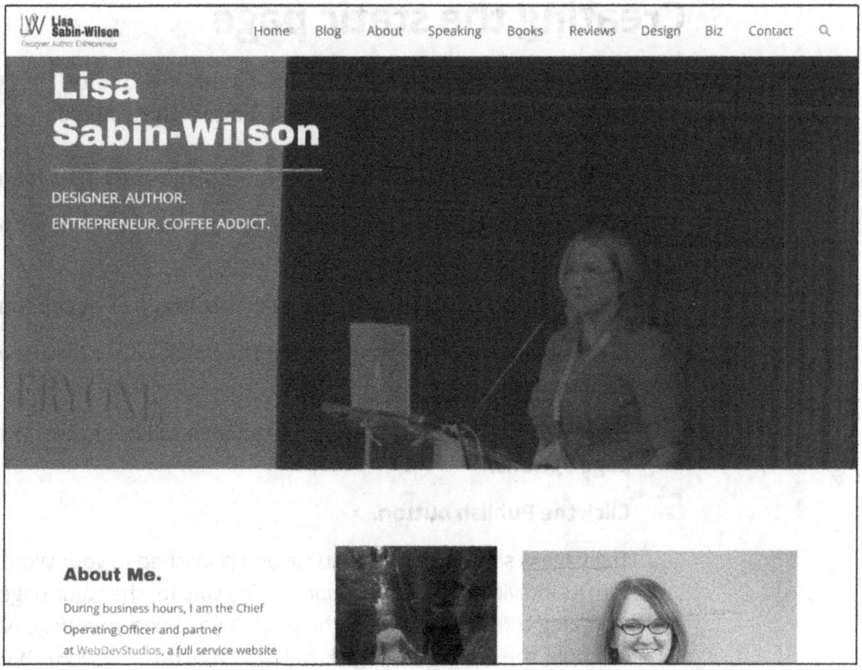

FIGURE 3-2: The front page of my website built with a static page in WordPress.

My site is powered by WordPress, so how can the pages on the site differ so much in what they display on the front? The answer lies in the content types and templates used to create the websites.

You use static pages in WordPress to create content that you don't want to appear as part of your blog but that you do want to appear as part of your overall site, such as an About page, a page of services, or a home page.

Creating a front page is a three-step process:

1. **Create a static page.**
2. **Set that static page to be used as the home page of your site.**
3. **Tweak the page layout and content to look however you like. (See Book 6, Chapter 2 to explore the site editor.)**

REMEMBER

By using this method, you can create unlimited numbers of static pages to build an entire website. You don't even need to have a blog on your site unless you want one. (If you do, see the "Adding a Blog to Your Website" section, later in this chapter.)

Creating the static page

To have a static page appear on the home page of your site, first you need to create that page on the WordPress Dashboard. Follow these steps:

1. **On the Dashboard, click the Add New link on the Pages menu.**

   The Edit Page screen opens, allowing you to create a new page for your WordPress site, as shown in Figure 3-3.

2. **Type a title for your page in the Add Title text box at the top.**
3. **Create content for this page, using the block editor (see Book 4, Chapter 1).**
4. **Set the options for this page as detailed in following section, "Setting page options."**
5. **Click the Publish button.**

   The page is saved to your database and published to your WordPress site with its individual URL (or *permalink*). The URL for the static page consists of your blog URL and the title of the page. If you titled your page About Me, for example, the URL of the page is `http://yourdomain.com/about-me`. (See Book 3, Chapter 2 for more information about permalinks.)

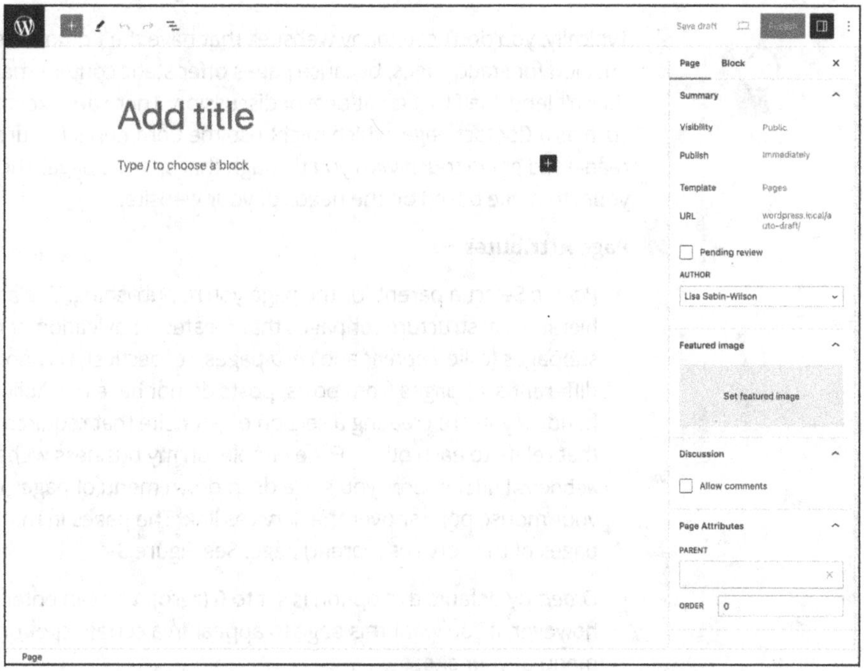

FIGURE 3-3: Create the static page that you want to use as your home page.

Setting page options

Before you publish a new page to your site, you can change options to use different features in WordPress. These features are similar to those available for publishing posts, which you can read about in Book 4, Chapter 2. For a static page, however, you don't find as many options. Those options appear in the settings panel on the right side of the Edit Page screen (refer to Figure 3-3).

The page options include the following (all covered in Book 4, Chapter 2):

- **Visibility** (Public, Private, or Password Protected)
- **Publish**
- **Template**
- **URL**
- **Pending Review**
- **Author**
- **Featured Image**
- **Discussion**

TIP

Typically, you don't see many websites that have the Comments feature enabled for static pages, because pages offer static content that generally doesn't lend itself to a great deal of discussion. There are exceptions, however, such as a Contact page, which might use the Comments feature as a way for readers to get in touch with you through that specific page. The choice is yours to make based on the needs of your website.

- **Page Attributes**
  - *Parent:* Select a parent for the page you're publishing. The ability to have a hierarchical structure for pages that creates a navigation of main pages and subpages (called *parent* and *child* pages, respectively) is another feature that differentiates pages from posts; posts do not have this ability. This comes in handy if you are creating a section of your site that requires multiple pages that relate to each other. For example, on my business website at `https://webdevstudios.com`, you see a drop-down menu of pages when you hover your mouse pointer over the Services link. The pages in that menu are child pages of the Services (parent) page. See Figure 3-4.
  - *Order:* By default, this option is set to 0 (zero). You can enter a number, however, if you want this page to appear in a certain spot on the page menu of your site.

    A page with the page order of 1 appears first on your navigation menu, a page with the page order of 2 appears second, and so on. You don't have to use the Order option, however, because you can define the order of pages and how they appear on your menu by using the WordPress navigation menu feature (see Book 6, Chapter 2).

Assigning a static page as the home page

After you create the page that you want to use for the home page of your website, you need to let WordPress know your intentions. Follow these steps to set a static page as the home page:

1. **On the Dashboard, click the Reading link on the Settings menu.**

   The Reading Settings screen displays.

2. **In the Your Homepage Displays section, select the A Static Page option.**
3. **From the Homepage drop-down menu, choose the page you want to use as the home page (see Figure 3-5).**
4. **Click the Save Changes button at the bottom of the Reading Settings screen.**

   WordPress displays the page you selected in Step 3 as the front page of your site. Figure 3-6 shows my site displaying a static page as the home page.

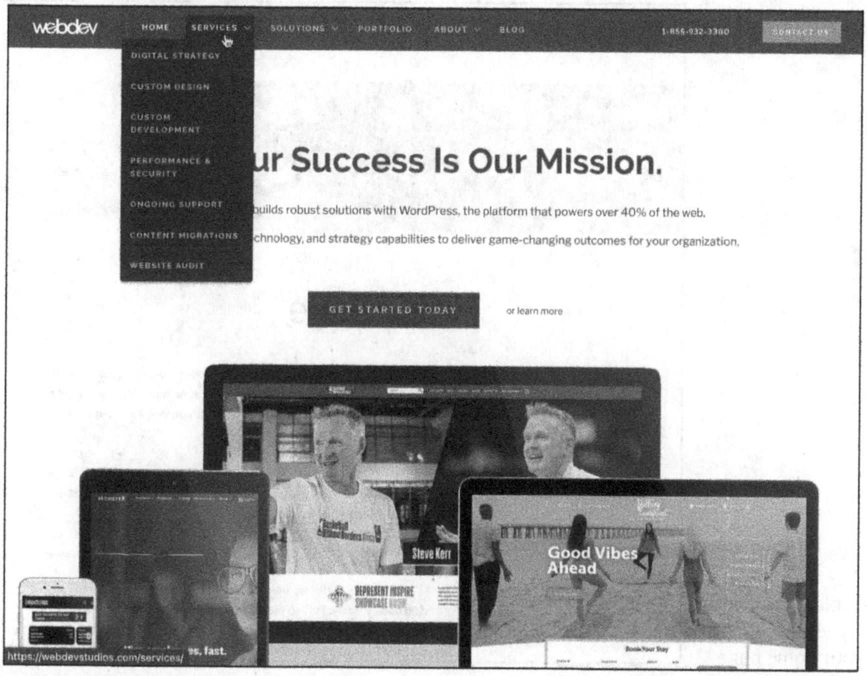

FIGURE 3-4: A drop-down menu created with parent and child pages.

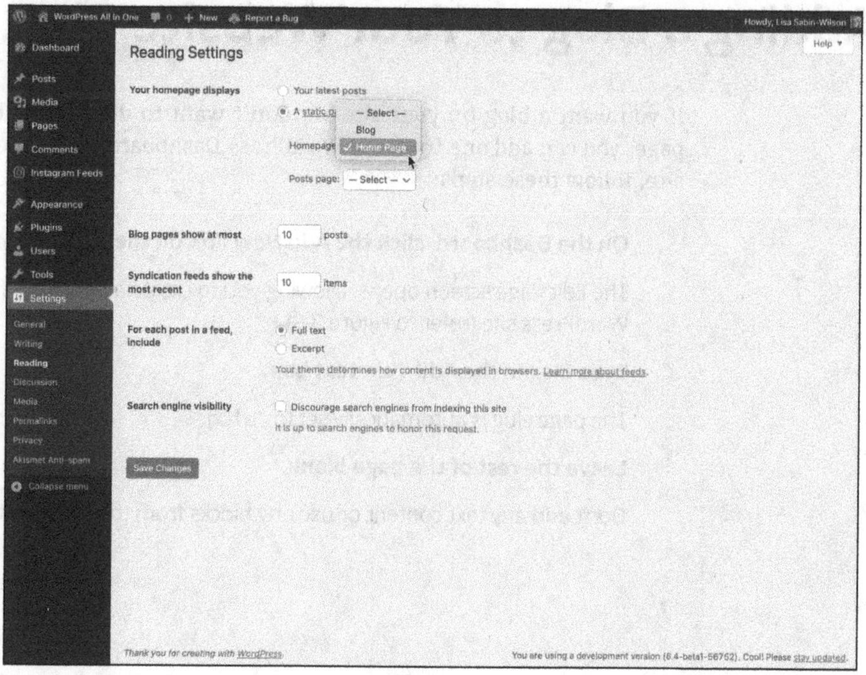

FIGURE 3-5: Choosing which page to display as the home page.

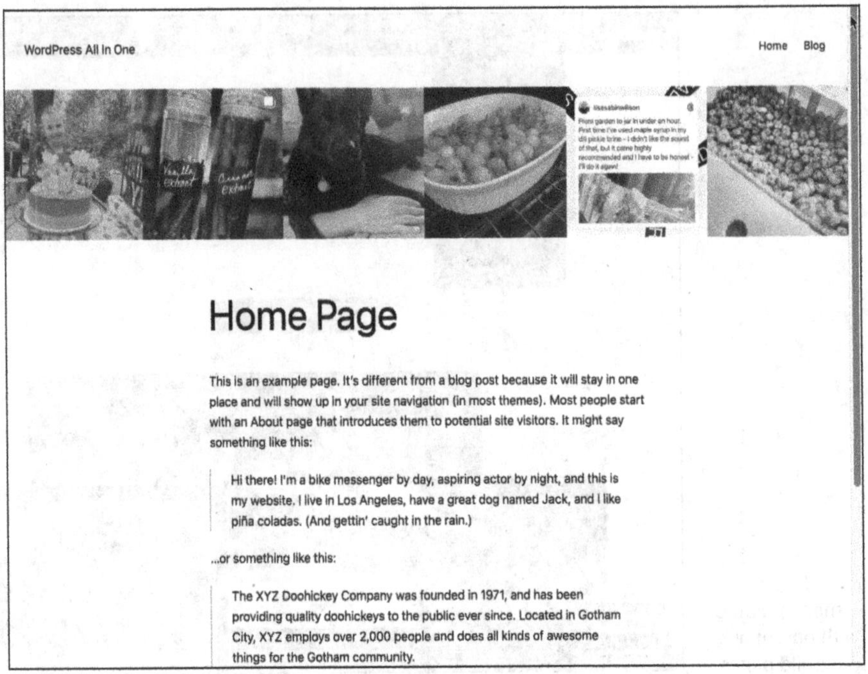

FIGURE 3-6: WordPress displays the page you selected as your home page.

Adding a Blog to Your Website

If you want a blog on your site but don't want to display the blog on the home page, you can add one from the WordPress Dashboard. To create the blog for your site, follow these steps:

1. **On the Dashboard, click the Add New link on the Pages menu.**

   The Edit Page screen opens, allowing you to create a new page for your WordPress site (refer to Figure 3-3).

2. **Type** Blog **in the Add Title text box.**

   The page slug is automatically set to `/blog`.

3. **Leave the rest of the page blank.**

   Don't add any text content or use any blocks from the block editor on this page.

4. **Click the Publish button.**

   WordPress asks whether you're sure you want to publish this page. Click the Publish button a second time, and the blog page you created is saved to your database and published to your WordPress site. Now you have a blank page that redirects to `http://`*`yourdomain.com`*`/blog`.

   Next, you need to assign the page you created as your blog page.

5. **On the Dashboard, click the Reading link on the Settings menu.**

   The Reading Settings screen displays.

6. **From the Posts Page drop-down menu, select the page you created in steps 1 through 4: Blog (see Figure 3-7).**

7. **Click the Save Changes button at the bottom of the Reading Settings screen.**

   The options you set are saved, and your blog is at `http://`*`yourdomain.com`*`/blog` (where *`yourdomain.com`* is the actual domain name of your site). When you navigate to `http://`*`yourdomain.com`*`/blog`, your blog appears. Figure 3-8 shows the blog page created in these steps.

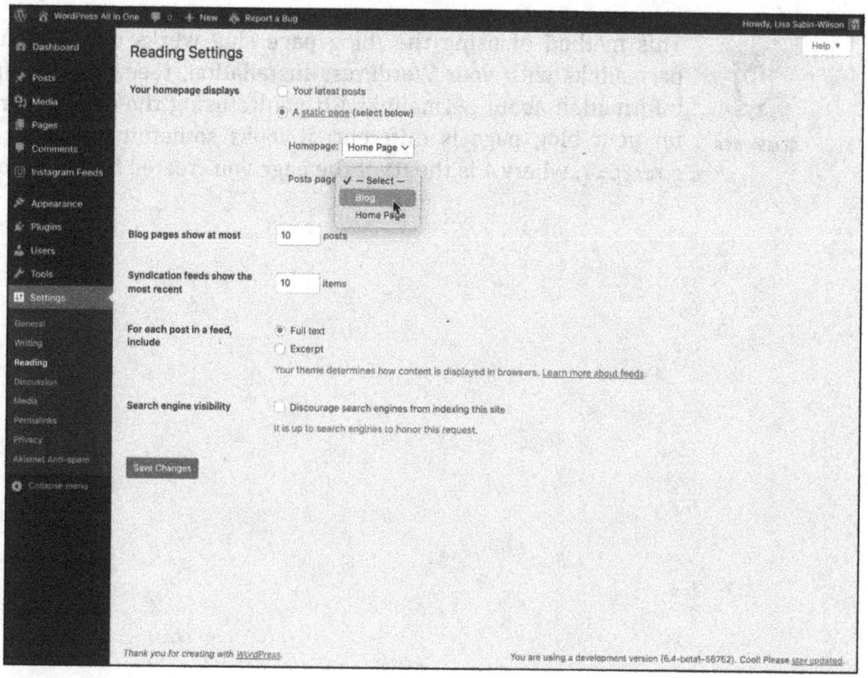

FIGURE 3-7: Choosing which page will display the blog.

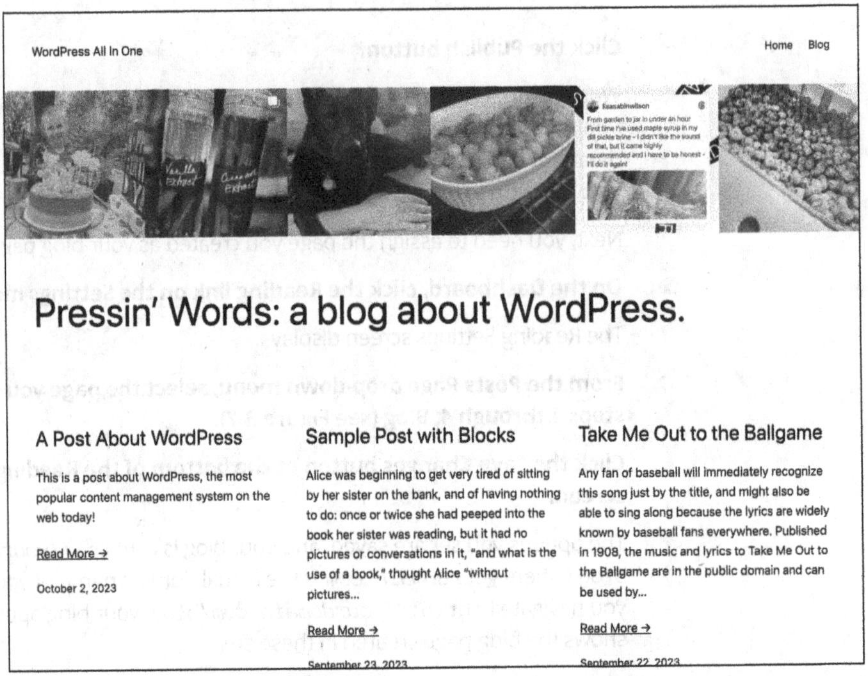

FIGURE 3-8: WordPress displays the blog on the page selected on the Reading Settings screen.

REMEMBER

This method of using the /blog page slug works only if you're using custom permalinks with your WordPress installation. (See Book 3, Chapter 2 for more information about permalinks.) If you're using the default permalinks, the URL for your blog page is different; it looks something like `http://yourdomain.com/?p=4`, where 4 is the ID of the page you created for your blog.

IN THIS CHAPTER

» Working with files in the Media Library

» Navigating the Media Library page

» Viewing and editing media files

» Exploring great plugins to manage media

Chapter 4 Managing Media

In Book 3, Chapter 2, I discussed the Media Settings page on your Dashboard, where you are able to set a few options on how media files are handled, including image sizes and media file organization.

This chapter takes you through how to work with media files in the Media Library located on your Dashboard navigation menu, labeled Media. In this chapter, you discover what the different options on the Media Library page can do for you, as well as how to upload and delete media files and how that can affect the traffic and display of your posts.

Finally, you discover how you can edit media files, in particular the image editing features available from within the Media Library section of the Dashboard. Book 4, Chapter 5 takes you through how to add different media files to your pages and posts, but first, this chapter gets you started on managing those media files, because the older and larger your website gets, the more overwhelming the Media Library can seem if you have thousands of media files to deal with!

Adding New Files to the Media Library

Throughout this book, you discover several ways of adding new media to your WordPress website. Book 4, Chapter 1 introduced you to the block editor and the image block, where you can add an image to a post or page on your site. Book 4, Chapter 5 covers all of the different ways you can use blocks to add media files to your pages, including image galleries, documents, videos, and audio. All image or file-related blocks in the block editor interact with the Media Library, because that's where all of your media files are organized and stored.

TIP

What exactly is media? *Media* consists of files like images, videos, audio recordings, and documents, such as Microsoft Word (`.doc`) or Adobe PDF (`.pdf`).

Getting to know allowed media file types

Before you begin uploading files to the Media Library, you'll want to understand the types of files that you are able to add:

- **Images:** You can upload images that have the following extensions: `.png`, `.jpg` / `.jpeg`, `.gif`, `.webp`, and `.ico`.
- **Video:** You can upload videos that have the following file extensions: `.mp4`, `.m4v`, `.mov`, `.wmv`, `.avi`, `.mpg`, `.ogv`, `.3gp`, and `.3g2`.
- **Audio:** You can upload audio recordings that have the following file extensions: `.mp3`, `.m4a`, `.ogg`, and `.wav`.
- **Documents:** You can upload documents that have the following file extensions: `.pdf`, `.doc`, `.docx` `.ppt`, `.pptx`, `.pps`, `.ppsx`, `.odt`, `.xls`, and `.xlsx`.

WARNING

You may find that there are plugins available for you to allow additional file types. However, certain file types may be misused by hackers on the Internet and can be a big security risk for your website. To protect you, WordPress disables these file types by default. Some of those extensions include `.svg`, `.bmp`, `.psd`, `.ai`, `.pages`, `.css`, `.js`, `.json`, `.flv`, `.f4l`, and `.qt`.

Uploading a new file to the Media Library

First things first: Before uploading new media files, you need to locate the Media Library, which you can do by clicking the Media link on the Dashboard navigation. Figure 4-1 displays the Media Library on a brand-new site, so it's completely empty.

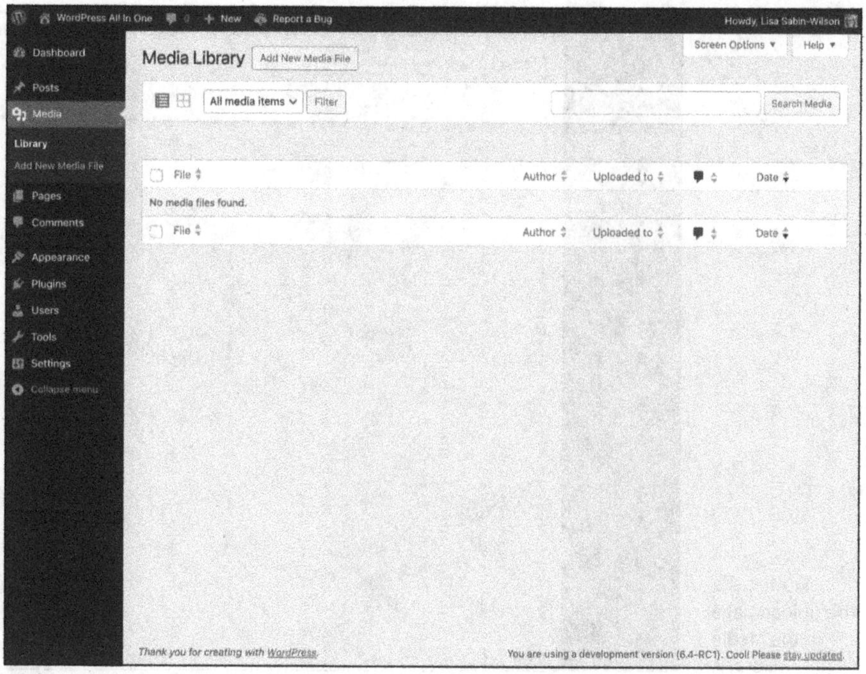

FIGURE 4-1: The Media Library on the Dashboard.

Since there is no media to manage in an empty Media Library, adding some files to the library will give you the opportunity to understand some of the media management options in the "Understanding Media Library Features" section, later in this chapter. The following steps are the same steps you will take to upload any kind of file type; in this list, I am uploading an image file with the `.jpg` extension:

1. **On the Media Library page (refer to Figure 4-1), click the Add New Media File button at the top of the page.**

   The upload page opens in your browser window, as shown in Figure 4-2. This page gives you two options for uploading files: Drop Files to Upload and Select Files. This list covers one option. The second option is covered later in the next section, "Uploading multiple files at once." Choose whichever method works best for you.

2. **Click the Select Files button.**

   A dialog window from your computer opens, where you can select a file from your computer to upload into the Media Library, shown in Figure 4-3.

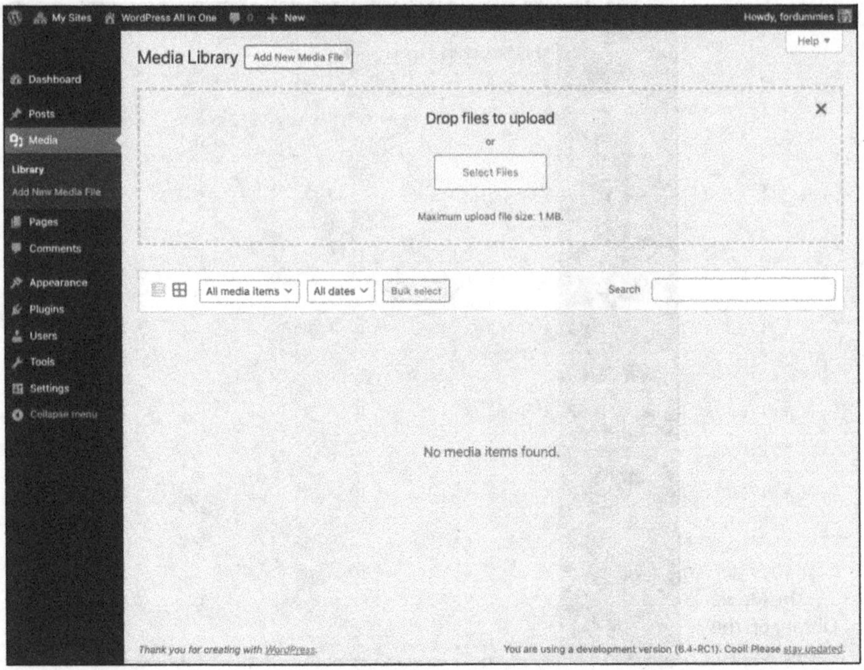

FIGURE 4-2: The upload page in the Media Library.

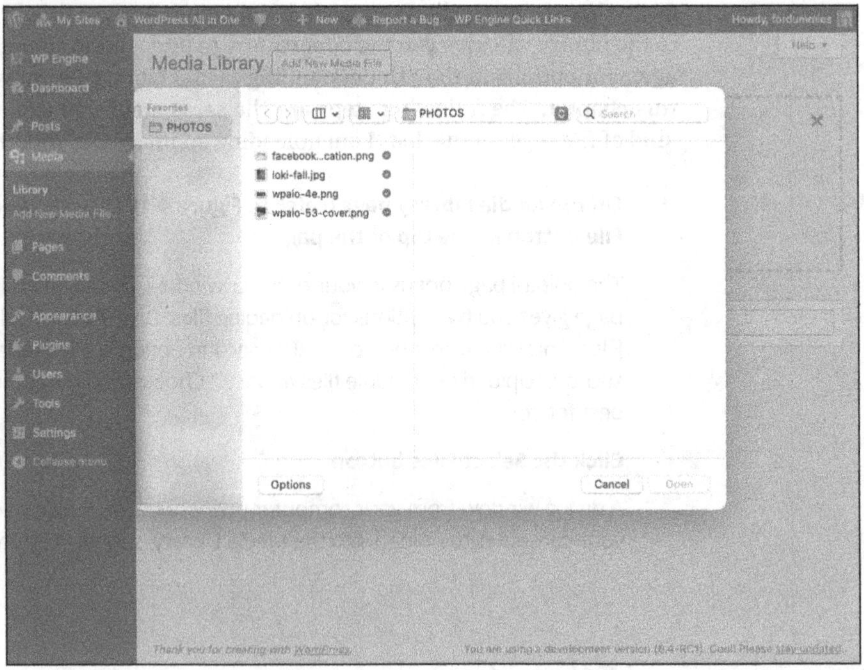

FIGURE 4-3: A dialog window allows you to select a file from your computer.

3. **Select the file you want to upload and press Enter or Return on a PC, or click the Open button.**

   You see the progress bar grow as your file is uploaded, and when it is finished, a thumbnail version of your file displays on your Media Library page (see Figure 4-4).

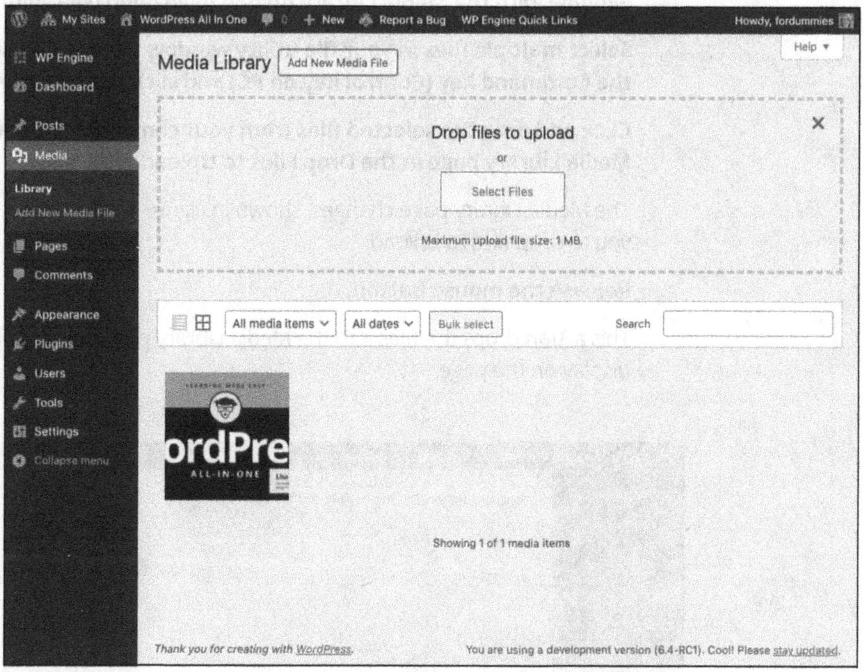

FIGURE 4-4: A thumbnail version of the file displays on the page after uploading.

Uploading multiple files at once

In the previous section, you uploaded one file to the Media Library by clicking the Select Files button. However, you are able to upload multiple files at once using the same steps, and the only difference in Step 3 is that you select more than one file to upload. WordPress allows that!

The Media Library gives you another way of uploading files from your computer by dragging and dropping them. Follow these steps:

1. **Locate the files you want to upload on your computer in the file utility Finder (Mac) or File Explorer (PC).**
2. **Position the file utility window on top of, or to the side, of your browser window with the Media Library upload page open (see Figure 4-5).**
3. **Select multiple files in your file utility window by pressing and holding the Command key (Control key on PC) and clicking the individual files.**
4. **Click and drag the selected files from your computer window to the Media Library page in the Drop Files to Upload area, shown in Figure 4-6.**

   The Media Library page changes, shown in Figure 4-6, with a message telling you to drop files to upload.
5. **Release the mouse button.**

   This action drops the files into the Media Library page, and the files upload and display on the page.

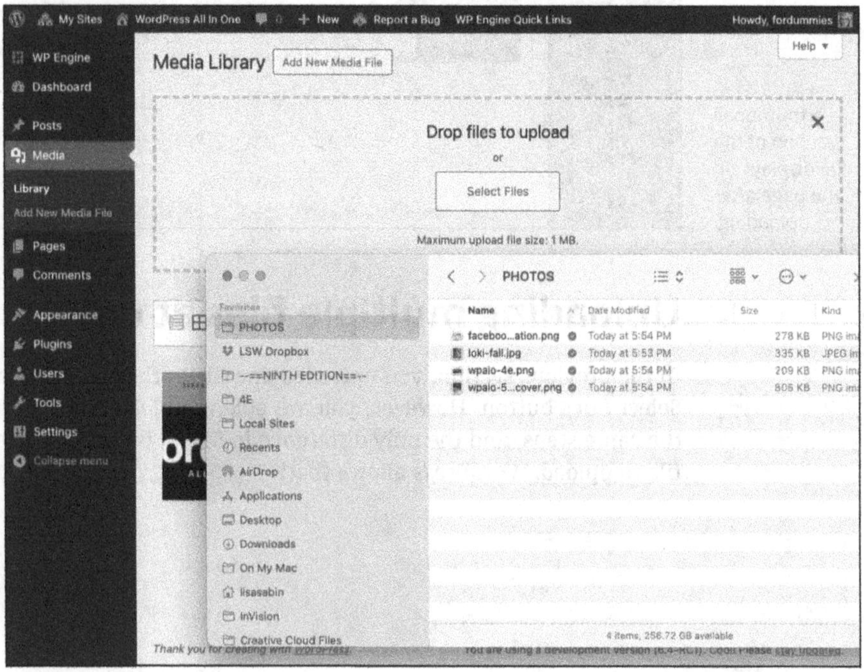

FIGURE 4-5: The Finder window is positioned on top of the browser window with the Media Library open.

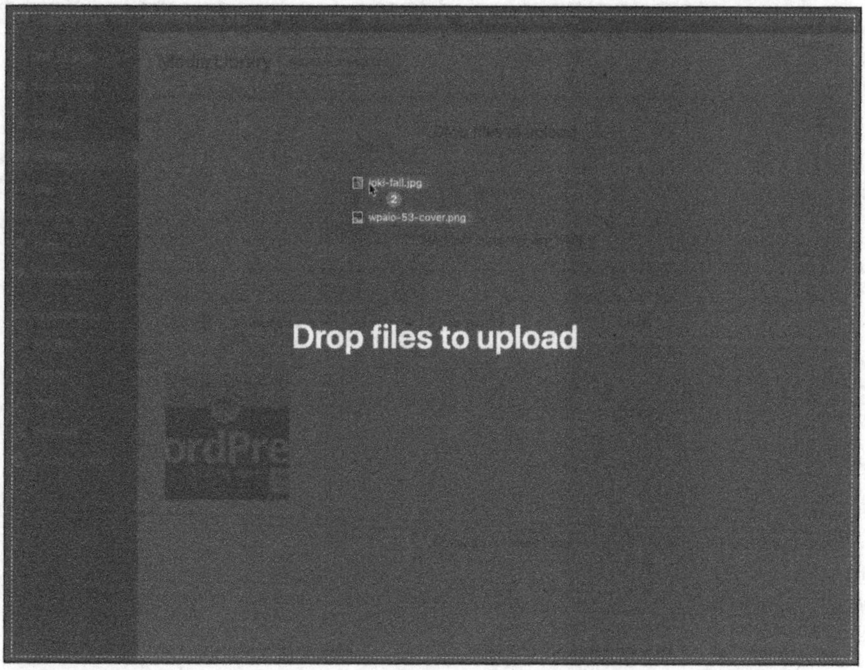

FIGURE 4-6: Drag images from your computer to the Media Library on your Dashboard.

Understanding Media Library Features

In Figure 4-1, you saw a brand-new Media Library page with no files included in it yet. Figure 4-7 shows the same page with 12 files added to the Media Library, with a variety of different file types, including images, video, audio, and documents.

Filtering options in the Media Library

Once you have some files added to your Media Library, there are two filtering options for viewing the files you have uploaded: Grid View and List View. The List View filter has more options for you than the Grid View, but let's look at both of them, starting with the Grid View shown in Figure 4-7.

There are two icons on the page underneath the Media Library page title that you can see in Figure 4-7. The List View icon looks like a task list, and the Grid View icon looks like a window.

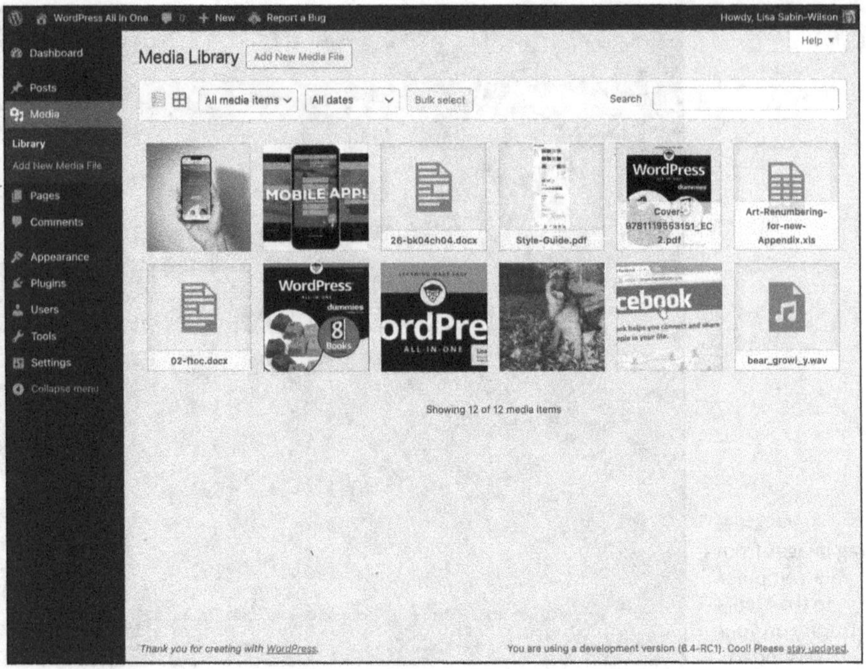

FIGURE 4-7: The Media Library page is populated with different file types.

Managing files in Grid View

Click the Grid View icon, and the files in the Media Library will display in a grid format on your screen (refer to Figure 4-7). In the Grid View format, you have some options for managing files in your Media Library.

To the right of the Grid View and List View icons is the All Media Items drop-down menu, which allows you to filter the files by type (see Figure 4-8). If you want to view only the images on your site, for example, you can click Images from the menu.

The following is a list of all file types you can use this filter for:

- **Images:** All photos and images with the image file type extension, such as `.png`.
- **Audio:** All audio files with the audio file type extension, such as `.mp3`.
- **Video:** All video files with the video file type extension, such as `.mp4`.
- **Documents:** All documents with the document file type extension, such as `.doc`.
- **Spreadsheets:** All spreadsheet documents with the spreadsheet extension, such as `.xls`.

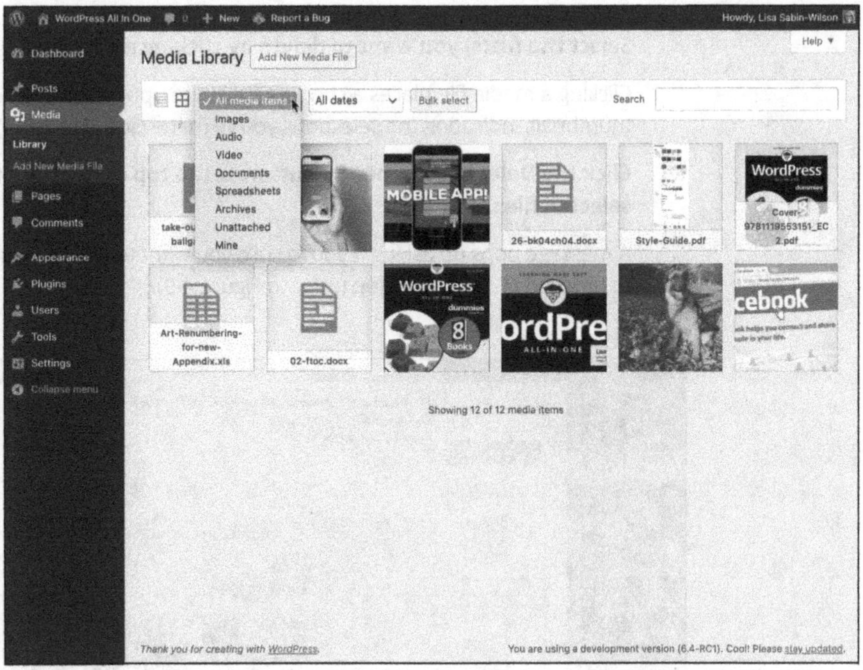

FIGURE 4-8: The All Media Items drop-down menu lets you filter the files by type.

- **Archives:** All archive files with the archive file type extension, such as `.zip`.
- **Unattached:** All media files that are not associated or attached to a post or page.
- **Mine:** All media files that you've uploaded. If there are multiple users on your website, it's helpful to be able to filter out only the images you've added and filter out everyone else's.

To the right of the All Media Items menu is the All Dates drop-down menu. When you click it, it displays a menu of dates by month and year, which allows you to filter all the files in your Media Library accordingly.

Next to the All Dates menu is the Bulk Select button, which allows you to select files for deletion. The following steps show you how to delete one or more media files:

1. **Click the Bulk Select button.**

   This changes the Grid View to an interactive screen, where you can click one or more files.

2. **Select the file(s) you want to delete by clicking each one.**

   Clicking a media file places a check mark in the upper-right corner of the file thumbnail, indicating the selections you've made (see Figure 4-9).

3. **Click the Delete Permanently button at the top of the page to remove the selected files.**

   A message pops up asking if you're sure you want to delete these files; click OK to proceed or Cancel to stop (refer to Figure 4-9).

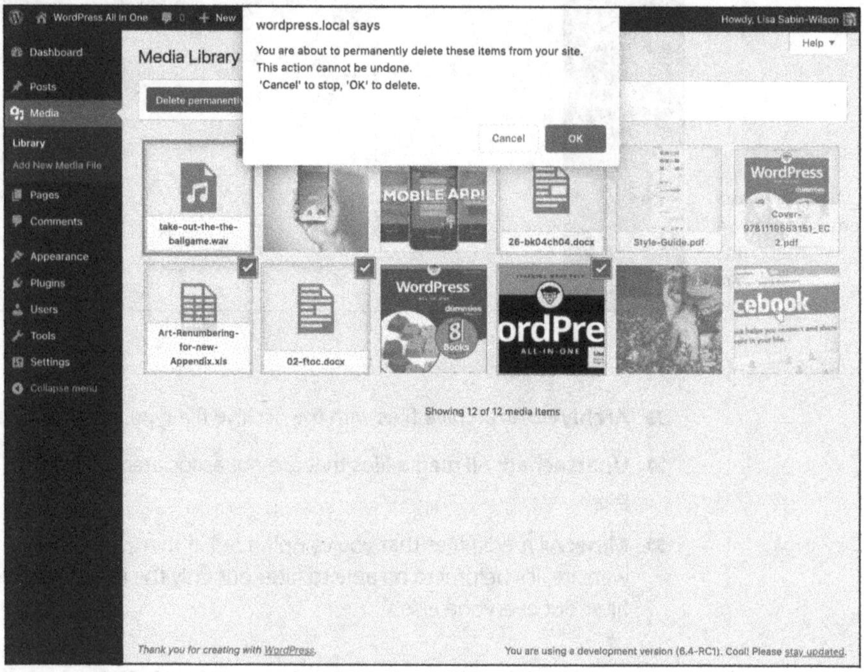

FIGURE 4-9: Deleting files from the Media Library in Grid View.

The final option covered in this section for the Grid View is the media file search, which is a form field located above the media file grid on the top right (refer to Figure 4-8). Simply type your search term in the form field and press Enter or Return on a PC, and the grid populates with media files that are relevant to the search term you entered. The Media Library search isn't a very robust search, and it's limited to returning only those media files that contain the exact words you search for in its filename. For example, if I search for "dog," I will not get any files returned in my search, even though I have photos of dogs in my Media Library. That's because the search isn't smart enough to detect *image* content, so it's currently limited to filenames that include the word "dog" in its search results. With the emergence of Artificial Intelligence (AI), however, it's possible we will see a more robust and intelligent search in the Media Library in the future — one can dream!

Managing files in List View

Click the List View icon, and the files in the Media Library will display in a list format on your screen (see Figure 4-10). Some of the options in List View are the same as those in Grid View, including filtering media files by file type, filtering media files by month and year, and the Media Library search feature. See the previous section for details.

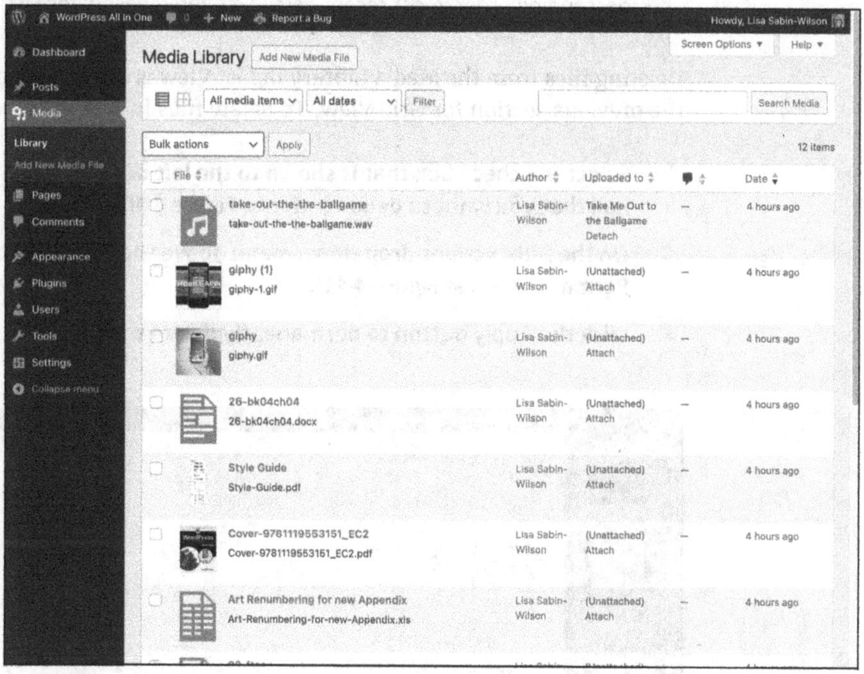

FIGURE 4-10: Files in the Media Library organized in List View.

Right away, you can see that List View offers a lot more information about the individual media files than Grid View does. The files are organized in rows on the page in order of the most recent, and you can sort those rows in different ways by clicking the headings of the columns, such as:

- **File:** Refers to the filename. Clicking File sorts the list alphabetically in ascending (A-Z) or descending (Z-A) order.
- **Author:** Refers to the user who added the image to the Media Library. Clicking Author sorts the authors alphabetically in ascending (A-Z) or descending (Z-A) order by the author's username.
- **Uploaded To:** Refers to a post or page that an image is currently used in. This is referred to as Attached, and files that have not been added to a post or a

page are referred to as Unattached. Clicking Uploaded To sorts the list by Unattached and Attached files.

- **Comments:** Refers to images that have received comments from your website readers. Clicking the Comments icon sorts the list by the number of comments, ordered from most to least.
- **Date:** Refers to the date the image was uploaded. Clicking Date sorts the list by date in ascending order (oldest dates first and most recent dates last) or descending order (most recent dates first and oldest dates last).

Deleting files from the Media Library in List View is different than what you did in the previous section for Grid View. To delete files in List View, follow these steps:

1. **Select the check box that is shown to the left of each image file thumbnail that you want to delete (refer to Figure 4-10).**
2. **On the Bulk Actions drop-down menu above the file list, click Delete Permanently (see Figure 4-11).**
3. **Click the Apply button to permanently delete the files.**

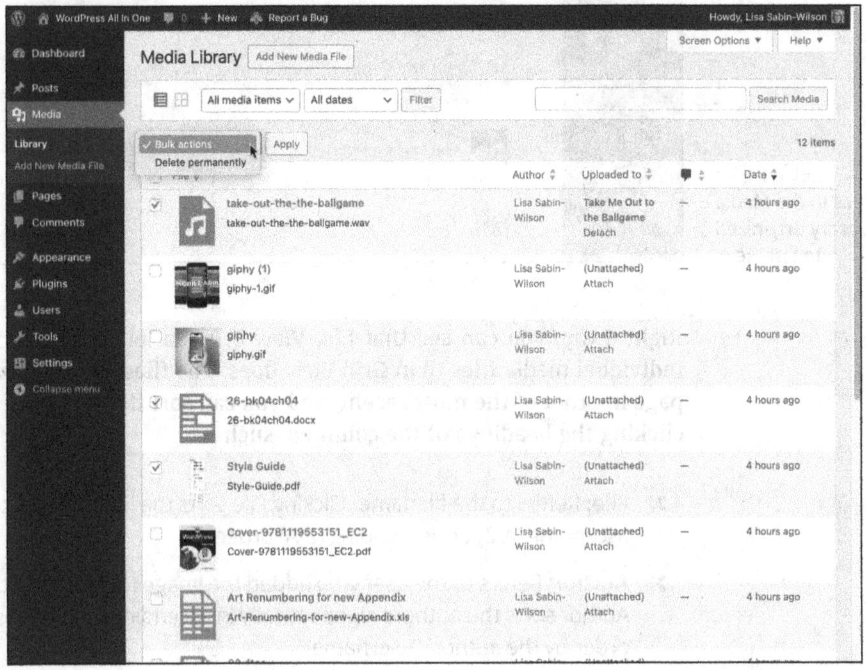

FIGURE 4-11: Deleting files from the Media Library in List View.

Other Media Library view settings

The different views and layouts of the Media Library covered so far have been the default views. You can change those default views in the Screen Options section of the Media Library page. You will find the link for the Screen Options at the top-right corner of the Media Library page (visible in Figure 4-11); click it to open the Screen Options panel, shown in Figure 4-12.

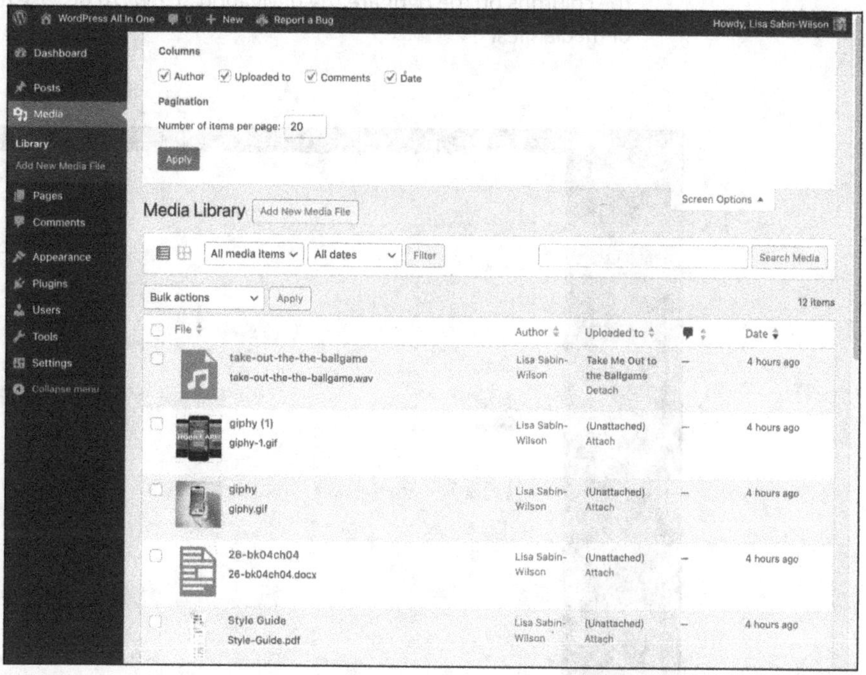

FIGURE 4-12: The Screen Options panel on the Media Library page.

The Screen Options panel shows the default settings for the Media Library page, and there are several settings you can change, including:

» **Columns:** This section of the Screen Options panel has four boxes selected; they are selected by default. You can deselect them to remove them as column headings from the List View (and come back and re-add them if you need to later):

- Author
- Uploaded To
- Comments
- Date

» **Number of items per page:** By default, this is set to display 20 files per page before you have to click to the next page to load more files. You can change this to whatever number you want; just keep in mind that the larger the number, the more time it will take this page to load because media tends to be some of the largest files in your WordPress installation. If you set this number to 1,000, for example, you will have to wait a longer time for all of the media files to load on this page. Figure 4-13 shows the Media Library in List View with only five files showing on the page; you can see above and below the columns on the right are the navigation arrows to browse to the next page of media files.

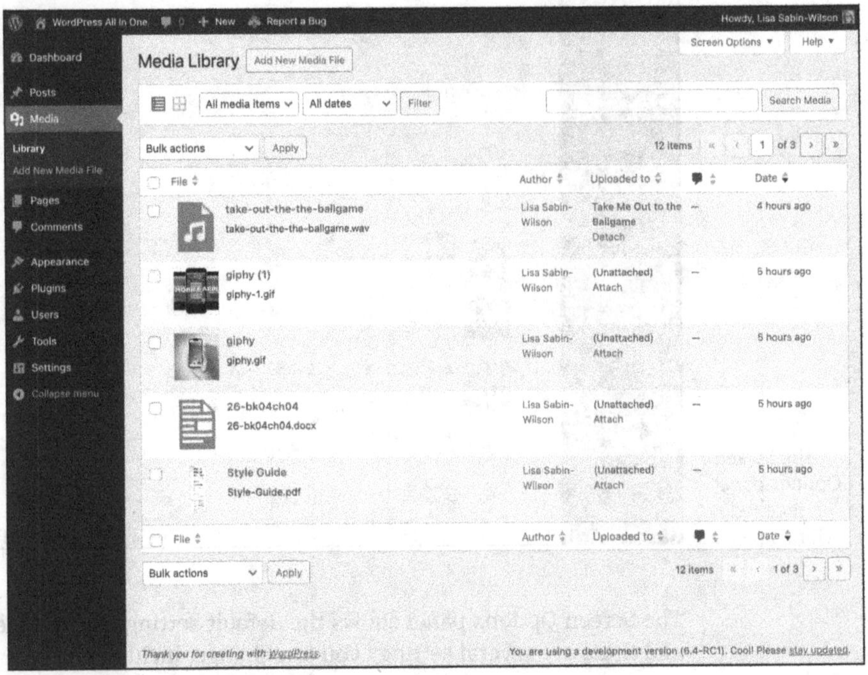

FIGURE 4-13: Media Library in List View with five files on the page.

Viewing and Editing Media File Details

What happens if you click an actual file? The Edit Media page opens on your Dashboard, where you can view and edit the details of the media file (see Figure 4-14). All media files have the same options that you can edit and information that you can view, with the exception of image files. There's a button under images that links to a basic image editor you can use to edit image file types.

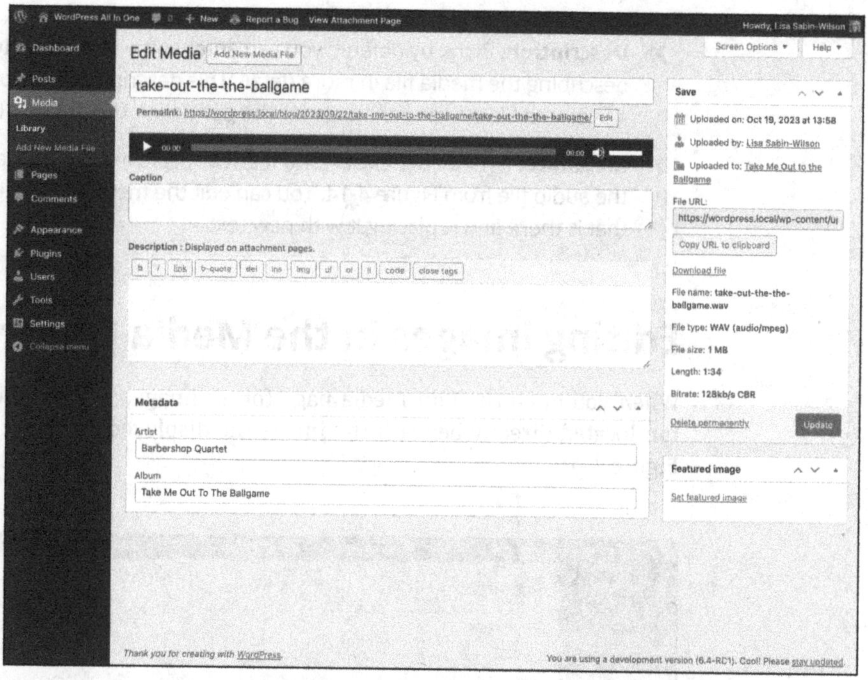

FIGURE 4-14: Edit Media page on the Dashboard.

Editing file details on the Edit Media page

The Edit Media page varies depending on which media file type you upload to your site. In Figure 4-14, you see an audio media file I uploaded on the Edit Media page, and on the right sidebar in the Save module, you see the length and bitrate of the audio file listed. On the other hand, the Edit Media page for a document, like a `.pdf` or `.doc`, will not list length and bitrate, because that does not apply to the file you are editing.

In the main body of the Edit Media page, you can change, add, or delete the following information for a file:

- **Title:** Change the title of the media file to make it more descriptive.
- **Permalink:** Book 5, Chapter 3 covers information about why you might want to change permalinks for SEO purposes for your posts and pages. You are able to change the permalink for images for the same reasons under the title on the Edit Media page.
- **Caption:** Blank by default; you can enter short text relevant to the media file in this text box. The text you include displays on the live website for your visitors. This is an excellent spot to include things like photographer credits or artist acknowledgments.

» **Description:** Blank by default; you can enter some text in this text box describing the media file in more detail. This description is visible on the live site on the file attachment page (or the permalink URL for the file).

» **Metadata:** If metadata exists for a file, it appears in the metadata fields, like the audio file from Figure 4-14. You can edit the metadata by deleting the text that is there and replacing it with new text.

Editing images in the Media Library

When you open the Edit Media page for an image, you see the Edit Image button located directly beneath the image file displayed on the screen, as shown in Figure 4-15.

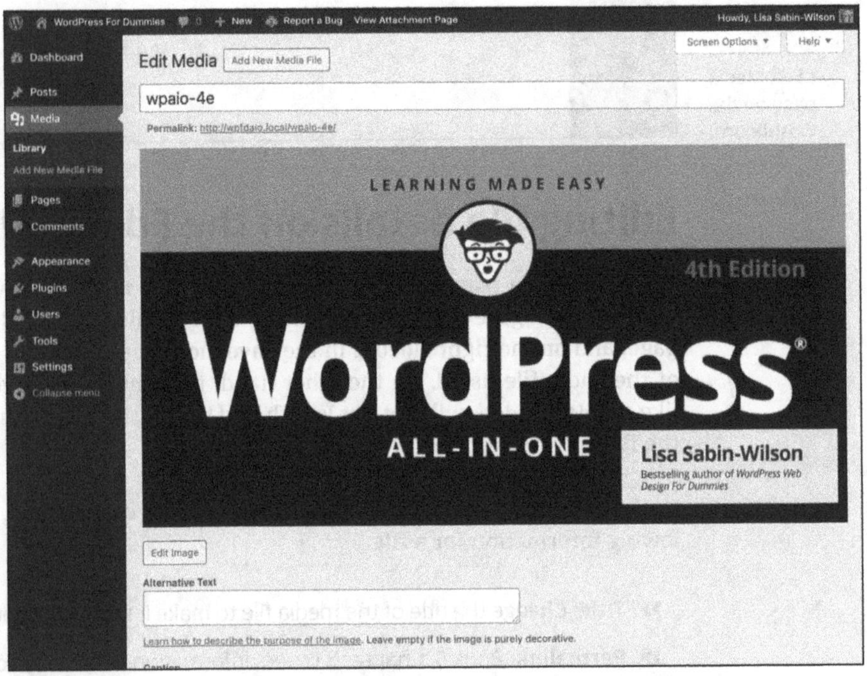

FIGURE 4-15: Edit Media page for an image showing the Edit Image button.

Click the Edit Image button, and the Edit Media page opens with some of the same media settings discussed in the previous section: editing file details on the Edit Media page, including Title, Permalink, Caption, and Description. However, since this is an image, you see some other editing options directly above the image, as shown in Figure 4-16:

- **Crop:** Cropping an image means trimming the edges of the image to your desired size or proportions. Click the image and drag your mouse pointer to select the area you want to crop, then release the mouse button to set the selection. You can also use the Aspect Ratio, Selection, and Starting Coordinates settings to the right of the image to refine your crop selection before you click the Apply Crop button to crop your image. Click the Clear Crop button to clear your choice if you want to start over.
- **Scale:** Images can only be scaled down, not scaled up. Click the Scale button, enter the desired dimensions in the text fields provided, and then click the small Scale button that appears to the right of the text fields when you've made changes. If you dislike the results and want to change something back, click the Restore Original Image link that appears only if you've made changes.
- **Image Rotation:** Click this button for a drop-down menu of options for image rotation, including Rotate 90° Left, Rotate 90° Right, Rotate 180°, Flip Vertical, and Flip Horizontal.
- **Undo/Redo:** Remove or restore the changes you've made to your image. You can click these buttons as many times as you want to cycle through your edit history with the image you are editing.
- **Cancel Editing:** Click this button anytime to cancel image editing and return to the Edit Media page.
- **Save Edits:** Click this button to save any changes you've made to the image and return to the Edit Media page.

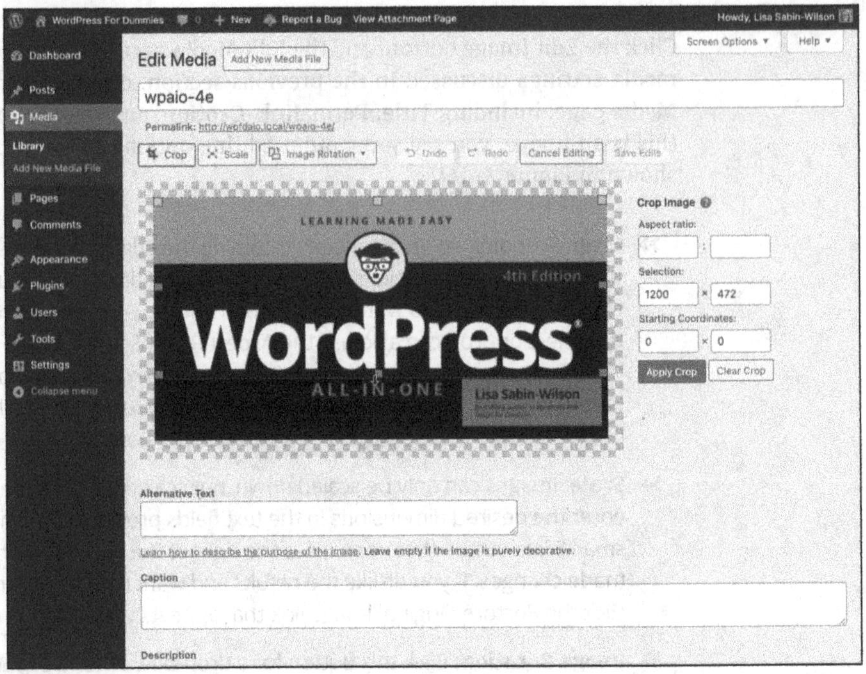

FIGURE 4-16: Cropping an image on the Edit Media page.

Discover Some Great Plugins to Manage Media

The WordPress Media Library has some good tools for managing media. Still, some plugins are available that provide great features that extend the already fantastic features in WordPress. Here are three great plugins for managing media:

- **FileBird (`https://wordpress.org/plugins/filebird`):** This plugin adds categorization to the Media Library, allowing you to locate your files quickly. It's ideal for sites that have an extensive Media Library, because it takes managing them to the next level.
- **Media Library Assistant (`https://wordpress.org/plugins/media-library-assistant`):** This plugin provides several enhancements to the Media Library, with some great features such as enhanced search media that includes the name/slug of a file and captions.
- **Real Media Library (`https://wordpress.org/plugins/real-media-library-lite`):** This plugin allows you to organize your media files in folders and provides you with a file manager right on your WordPress Dashboard.

IN THIS CHAPTER

» Inserting photos and other images into your post

» Adding multiple images displayed side by side

» Adding a cover photo to your post

» Creating photo galleries in WordPress

» Inserting video and audio files

» Podcasting with WordPress

Chapter 5

Embedding Video, Audio, and Other Media

Adding images and photos to your posts and pages can really dress up the content. By using images and photos, you give your content a dimension that you can't express in plain text. Through visual imagery, you can call attention to your content and improve the delivery of the message by adding depth to it.

The same goes for adding video and audio files to your posts and pages. Video lets you provide entertainment through moving, talking (or singing!), and streaming video. Audio files let you talk to your visitors and add a personal touch. Many website owners use video and audio to report news and to broadcast Internet radio and television shows. The possibilities are endless!

In this chapter, you discover how to enhance your website by adding images, video, and audio to your content. You even find out how to run a full-fledged photo gallery on your site, all through the `WordPress.org` software and its integrated Media Library.

REMEMBER

You add these extras to your site in the Upload/Insert area of the Add New Post page. You can add them as you're writing your post or come back and add them later. The choice is yours!

Inserting Images into Your Content

Adding an image to a post is easy with the WordPress image uploader. Jump right in and give it a go. From the Dashboard, click the Add New link on the Posts menu, and the Edit Post screen loads in your browser. On the Edit Post screen, click the Add Block icon to open the block selector, and click the Image icon to add an image block to your post, as shown in Figure 5-1.

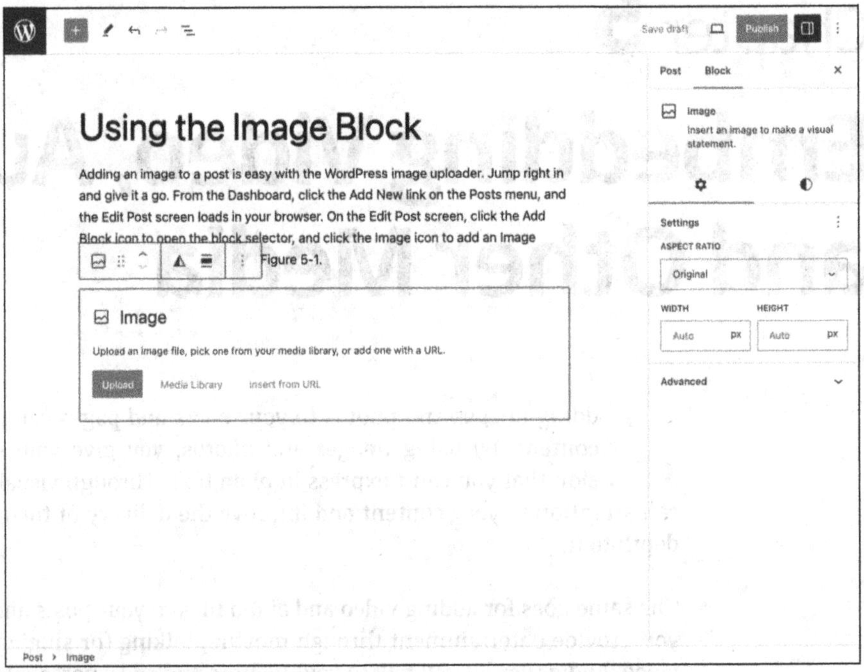

FIGURE 5-1: An image block in the WordPress block editor.

The image block gives you four ways to add an image to your post, which are described in detail in the following sections of this chapter:

» **Upload:** Click the Upload button to select an image from your computer. This action uploads the image from your computer to your website and inserts the image into your post via an image block. WordPress also adds this image to your Media Library so you can reuse the image in the future.

- **Media Library:** Click the Media Library button to choose an image from the WordPress Media Library (see Book 4, Chapter 4). When the Select or Upload Media screen opens, select an image from the Media Library and then click the Select button to add the image to your post.
- **Insert from URL:** Click the Insert from URL button to display a small text box where you can paste or type the URL (or link) for the image you want to use. Press the Enter key on your keyboard or click the Apply button to insert the image into the image block you're using.
- **Drag an Image:** While this block doesn't explicitly say so, it behaves like many other image upload areas in WordPress. You can select an image from your computer and drag it into the WordPress block editor to add it to a block. The dragged image also gets added to the Media Library for future use.

Uploading an image from your computer

After you've added the image block to your post, you can add an image from your computer's hard drive by following these steps:

1. **Click the Upload button in the image block.**

   A dialog box opens, allowing you to select an image (or multiple images) from your computer's hard drive. (See Figure 5-2.)

2. **Select your image(s) from your hard drive and click the Open button.**

   The image is uploaded from your computer to your website, and the Edit Post screen displays your uploaded image ready for editing if needed.

3. **Edit the details for the image in the Image Settings section of the settings panel on the right side of the Edit Post screen (see Figure 5-3).**

   The Image Settings section provides several image options, which are covered Chapter 4, Book 1:

   - Alternative Text
   - Aspect Ratio
   - Width and Height
   - Resolution

TIP

WordPress automatically creates small- and medium-size versions of the original images you upload through the built-in image uploader. A thumbnail is a smaller version of the original file. You can edit the thumbnail size by clicking the Settings link and then clicking the Media menu link. In the Image Sizes section of the Media Settings page, designate the desired height and width of the small and medium thumbnail images generated by WordPress.

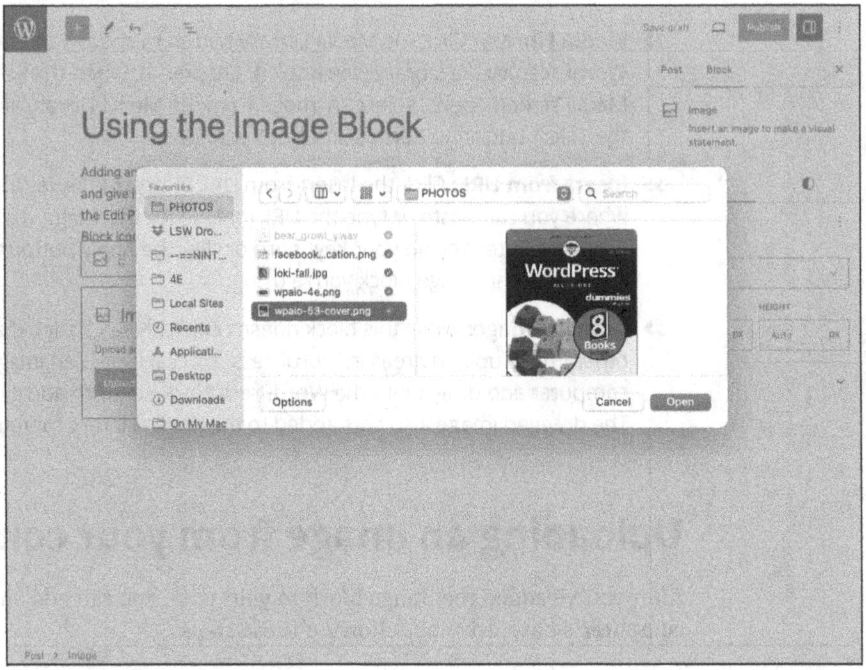

FIGURE 5-2: Uploading an image from your computer.

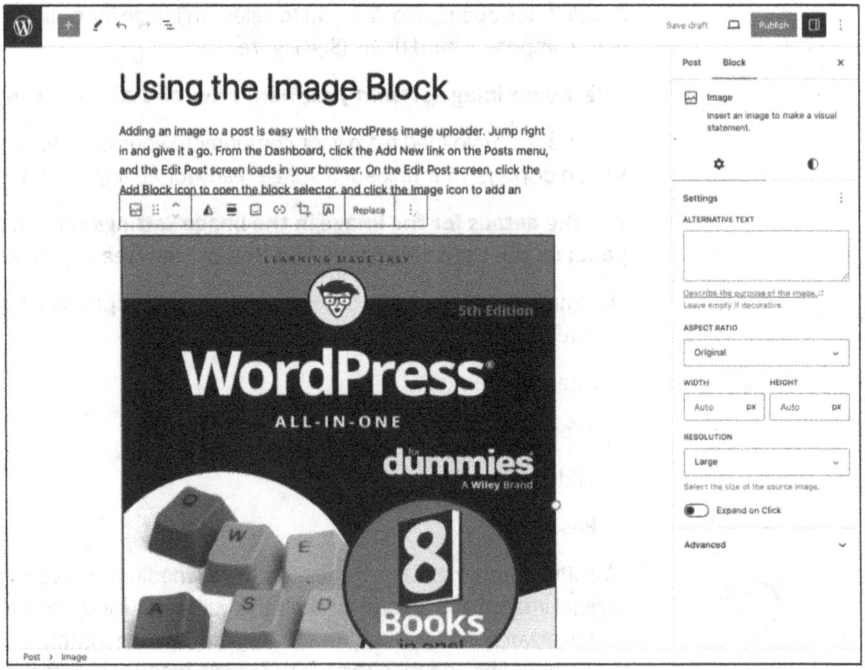

FIGURE 5-3: You can set several options for your image after you add it to your post.

4. **Use the image block toolbar to set the display options for the image.**

   Figure 5-3 shows the toolbar for the image block at the top of the image. In Book 4, Chapter 1, I cover how to use the toolbar options for the image block at length.

5. **Continue adding content to your post or publish it.**

Inserting an image from the Media Library

The WordPress Media Library contains all the images you've ever uploaded to your website, making those images available for use in any post or page you create on your site. After you've added an image block to your post, you can add an image from the Media Library by following these steps:

1. **Click the Media Library button in the image block (refer to Figure 5-1).**

   The Select or Upload Media screen opens, with the Media Library section displayed (see Figure 5-4).

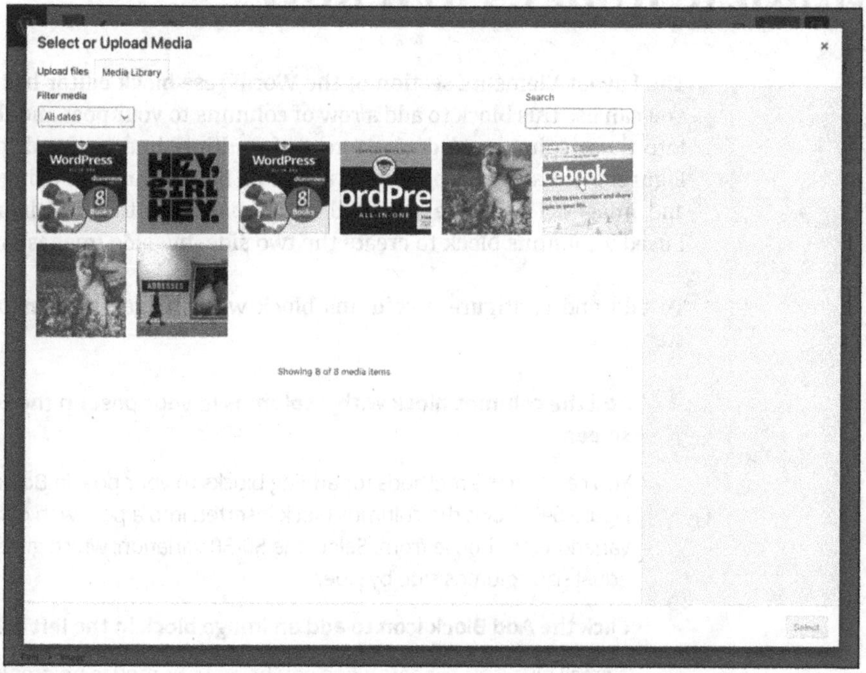

FIGURE 5-4: The Select or Upload Media screen.

2. **Select the image you want to use by clicking it.**

3. **Click the Select button.**

   The Select or Upload Media screen closes, and the Edit Post screen reappears. WordPress inserts the image you've chosen into the post you're creating.

4. **Set the options for the image.**

   Complete steps 3 and 4 of the previous section, "Uploading an image from your computer."

5. **Continue adding content to your post or publish it.**

TIP

You can also insert an image into your post using a URL or dragging an image from your computer to your WordPress website. These techniques are covered in Book 4, Chapter 4.

Using the Columns Block to Insert Multiple Images in a Row

The Layout Elements section of the WordPress block editor has a columns block. You can use this block to add a row of columns to your post and then insert images into those columns to create a row of multiple images for display in your post. Figure 5-5 displays a post with a grid of images created using various columns and images. I used the standard image block for the first image you see; then I used a columns block to create the two side-by-side images on the page.

To add and configure a columns block with images in your post, follow these steps:

1. **Add the columns block with 2 columns in your post on the Edit Post screen.**

   You can find the methods for adding blocks to your post in Book 4, Chapter 1. Figure 5-6 shows the columns block inserted into a post with different variations to choose from. Select the 50/50 variation, which gives you two equal size columns side by side.

2. **Click the Add Block icon to add an image block in the left column.**

   A small plus icon appears when you hover your mouse pointer in the first (left) column. When you click that icon, the WordPress block-selector window appears, and you can select the image block and insert it into the first column, as shown in Figure 5-7.

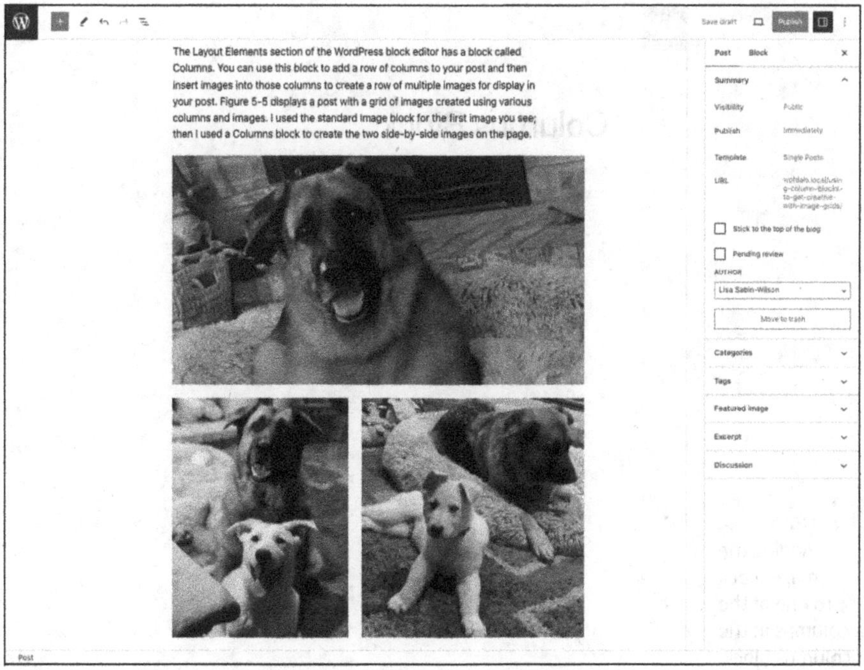

FIGURE 5-5: A grid of images in a blog post using the columns and image blocks.

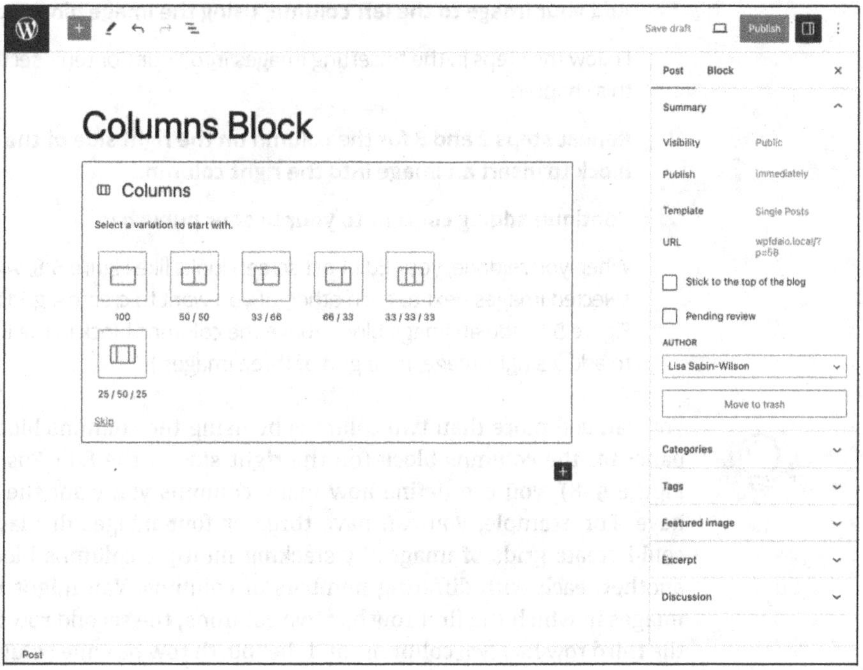

FIGURE 5-6: The columns block in the WordPress block editor.

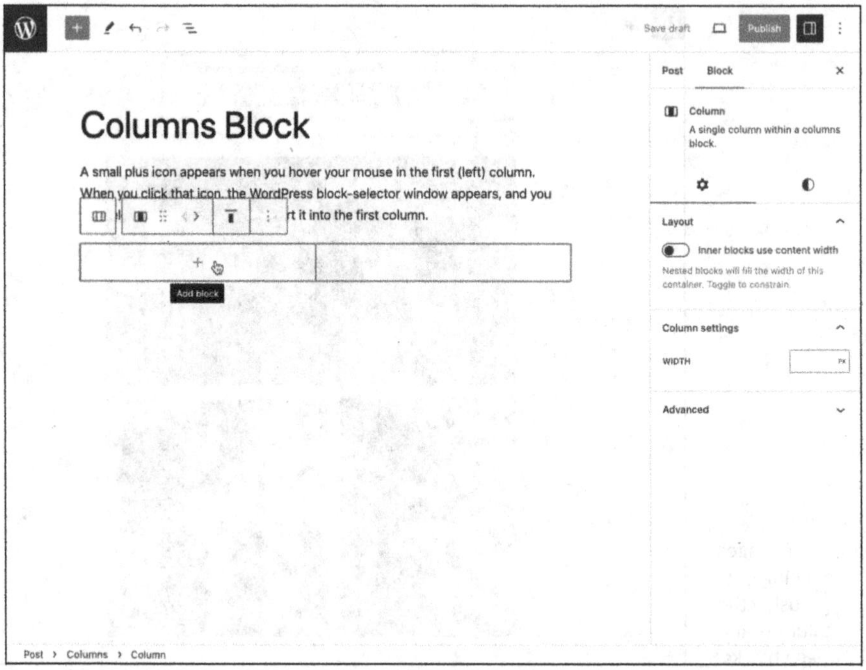

FIGURE 5-7: Adding the image block to one of the columns in the columns block.

3. **Add your image to the left column, using the image block options.**

   Follow the steps in the "Inserting Images into Your Content" section, earlier in this chapter.

4. **Repeat steps 2 and 3 for the column on the right side of the columns block to insert an image into the right column.**

5. **Continue adding content to your post or publish it.**

   When you're done, your Edit Post screen looks like Figure 5-8, with your two selected images next to each other. (If you want to create a grid like the one in Figure 5-5, add an image block above the columns block in the Edit Post screen to add a single image, for a grid of three images.)

TIP

You can add more than two columns by using the columns block. In the settings panel for the columns block (on the right side of the Edit Post screen shown in Figure 5-8), you can define how many columns you want the columns block to have. For example, you can have three or four images displayed in a row. You could create grids of images by stacking multiple columns blocks on top of one another, each with differing numbers of columns. You might have four rows of images in which the first row has two columns, the second row has four columns, the third row has two columns, and the fourth row has one column. That arrangement would create an interesting image grid.

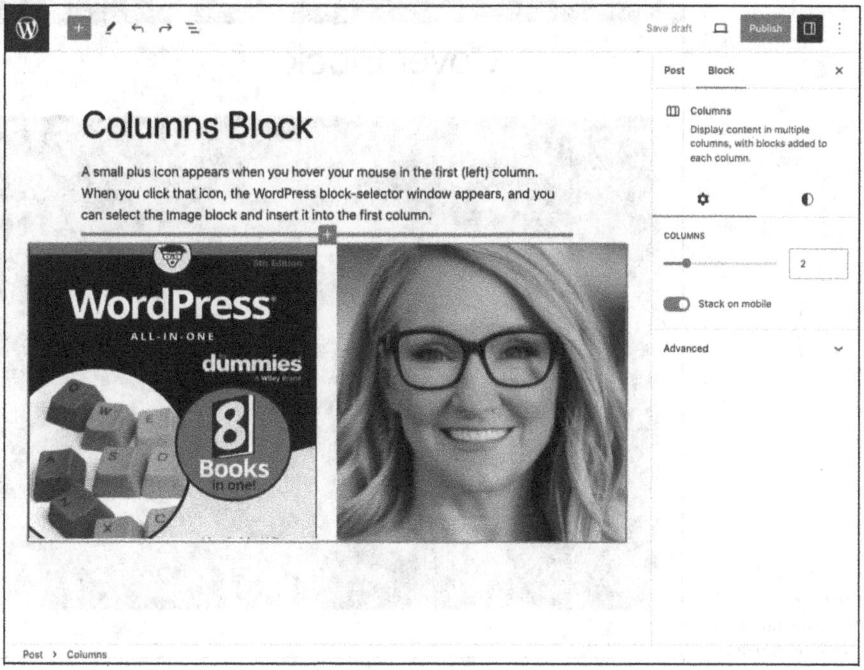

FIGURE 5-8: The columns block on the Edit Post screen.

Inserting a Cover Image into a Post

The WordPress block editor has a cover block, which you can use in place of a heading to add emphasis to a section of your site. The cover block allows you to display a short line of text on top of an image of your choice. Figure 5-9 displays a cover block with a photo of my adorable dogs.

Using the cover block is a nice way to separate different sections of your post content. For example, you can use it in place of a regular heading to add more visual emphasis and appeal to your content.

To add and configure a cover block in your post, follow these steps:

1. **Add the cover block to your Edit Post screen.**

   You can find the methods for adding blocks to your post in Book 4, Chapter 1. Figure 5-10 shows the cover block inserted into a post.

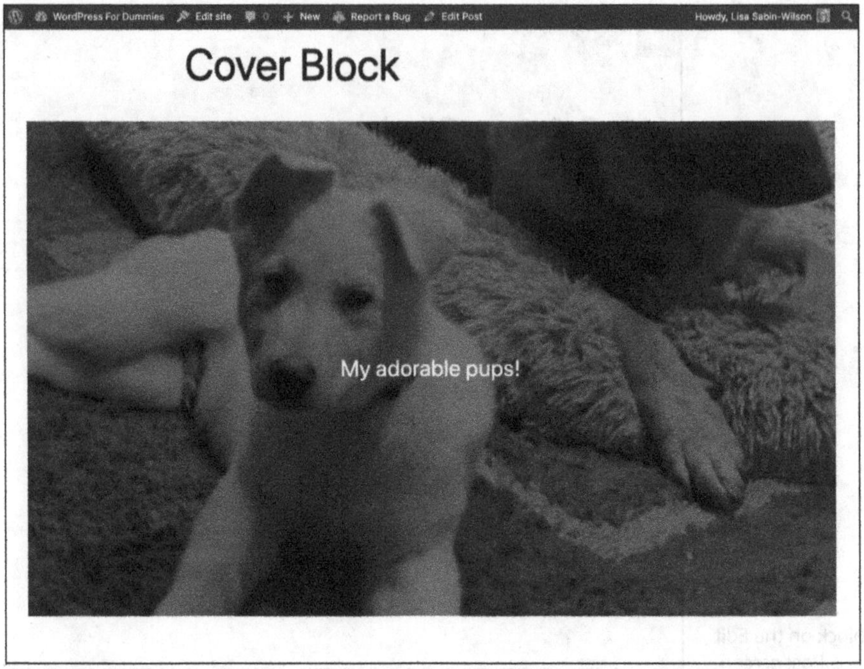

FIGURE 5-9: An example of the cover block in use on my site.

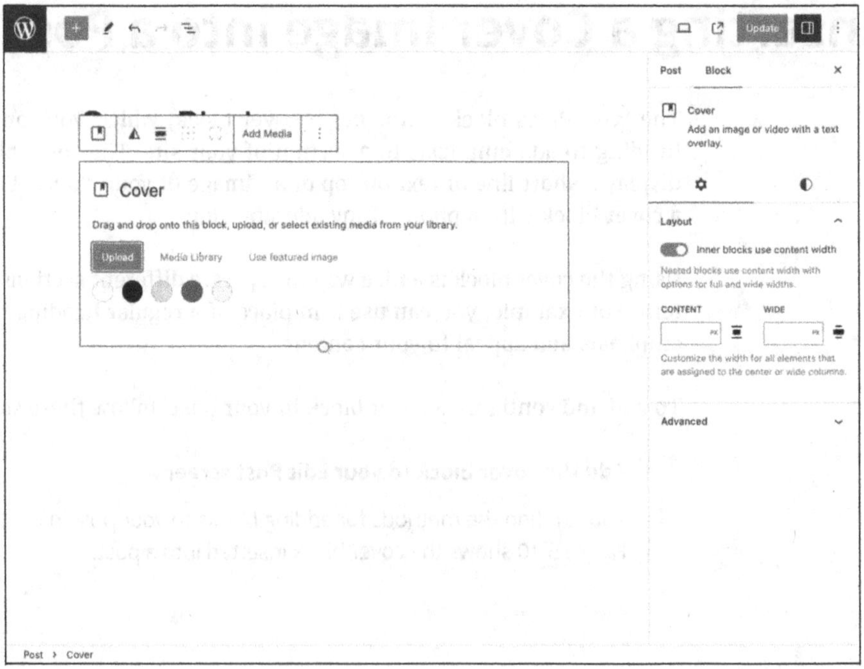

FIGURE 5-10: The cover block in the WordPress block editor.

2. **Click the Upload button to select an image from your computer, or click the Media Library button to select an image from the Media Library.**

   The steps for these two methods are listed in the sections "Uploading an image from your computer" and "Inserting an image from the Media Library," both earlier in this chapter. When you're done, the image appears on the Edit Post screen in your content.

3. **Add your desired text in the cover block.**

   Click the text `Write title` in the cover block, and type your own text over it. In Figure 5-11, I added text that displays on top of the image I added in the cover block.

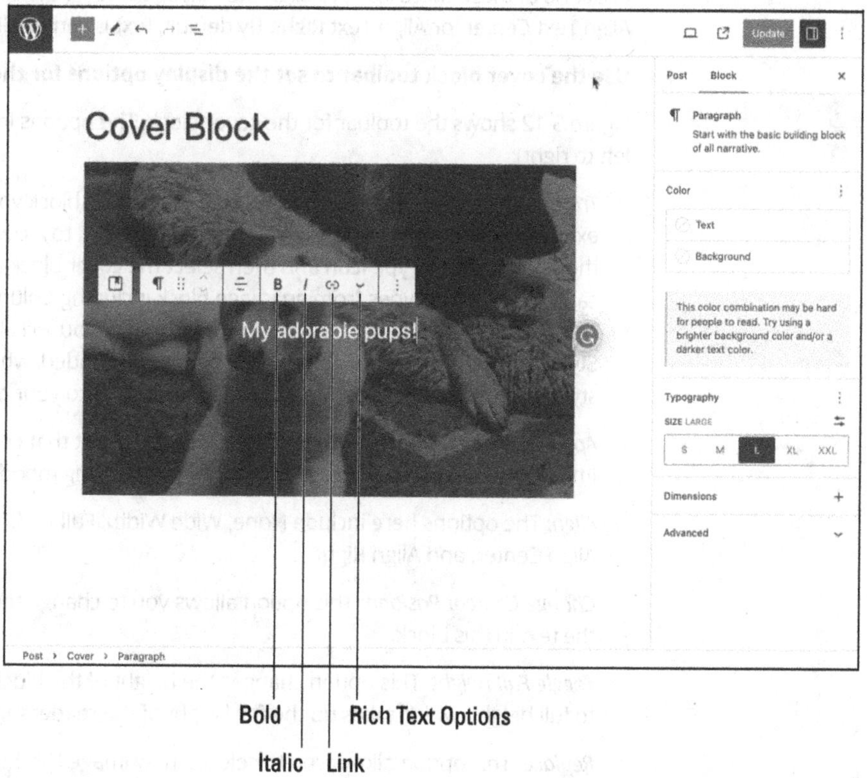

FIGURE 5-11: Adding text in the cover block.

4. **(Optional) Edit the display of the text you added in Step 3.**

   Figure 5-11 shows the text added to the cover block. You can use the small toolbar above the text to adjust the format of the text added to the image:

   - *Bold:* Click this icon to make the text bold (darker). Example: **bold text.**
   - *Italic:* Click this icon to make the text italic (slanted). Example: *italic text.*
   - *Link:* Click this icon to create a hyperlink by adding a URL to the text.
   - *Rich text options:* Click this drop-down menu for several text format options (this is covered in Book 4, Chapter 1).

5. **(Optional) Adjust text alignment by using the cover block toolbar.**

   Click one of these three icons to align the text in the cover block: Align Text Left, Align Text Center, or Align Text Right. By default, text is center-aligned.

6. **Use the cover block toolbar to set the display options for the image.**

   Figure 5-12 shows the toolbar for the cover block. The options include (from left to right):

   - *Transform To:* Click this option to change the type of block you're using. For example, if you want to change from an image block to a cover block, click the Change Block Type icon and then select the cover block to swap it. You can change block types from an image block including Columns, Media and Text, Gallery, Cover, File, and Group. In this menu, you will also find the Styles section, where you can select Default or Rounded, which sets the style for the corners of the image you've inserted into your post.
   - *Apply Duotone Filter:* A duotone filter is a digital effect that converts an image into two contrasting colors, typically enhancing mood and simplicity.
   - *Align:* The options here include None, Wide Width, Full Width, Align Left, Align Center, and Align Right.
   - *Change Content Position:* This option allows you to change the position of the text in this block.
   - *Toggle Full Height:* This option changes the height of the block from regular to full height, which takes up the full height of the readers' screen.
   - *Replace:* This option allows you to select a new image for the block by either uploading or selecting an existing image from the media library.
   - *More Options:* The options menu has several selections, which are covered in detail in Book 4, Chapter 1.

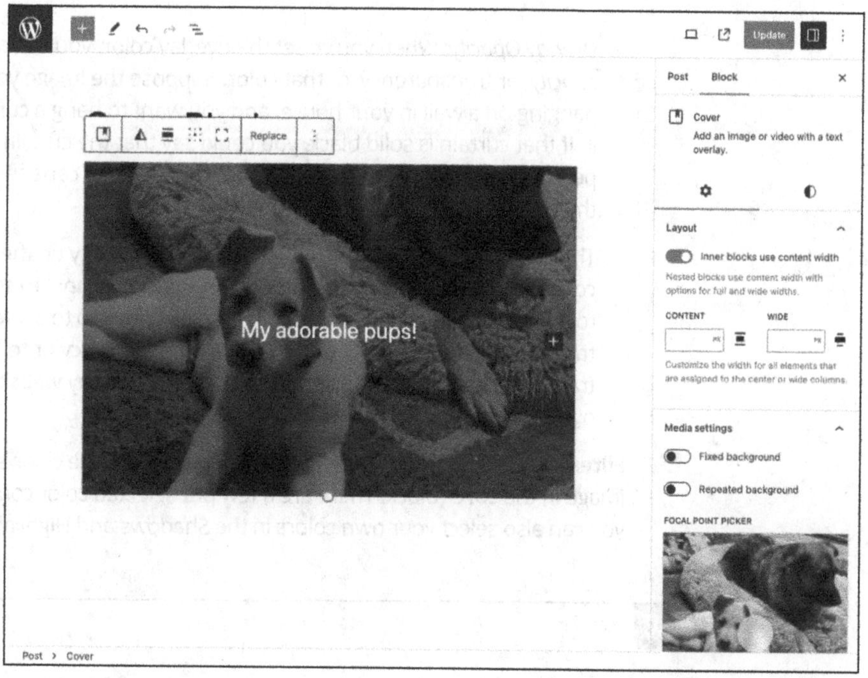

FIGURE 5-12: The toolbar for the cover block.

7. **(Optional) Set the cover block settings to a fixed background.**

   You see settings for the cover block in the settings panel on the right of the Edit Post screen. In the Cover Settings section is a toggle setting called Fixed Background. By default, this setting is set to off. Click the toggle button to set the background image to fixed. A fixed background means that the image is locked in place and doesn't move as your visitors scroll down the page of your website. It's a neat effect; give it a try! If you don't like the effect, toggle the Fixed Background option off.

8. **(Optional) Set a color overlay for the image in the cover block.**

   In the settings panel, click the Styles icon, where you can set options for the following:

   - *Text:* Click in the Text area to change the color of the text in the cover block.
   - *Heading:* Click in the Heading area to change the color of the Heading text, if added.
   - *Overlay Color:* Click in the Overlay area to set the color for the image's background as one of the predefined colors in the settings panel, or click in the color picker area above the predefined colors to choose a custom color. The color you choose is overlaid on the image.

- *Overlay Opacity:* When you've set the overlay color, you can also set the *opacity,* or transparency, of that color. Suppose the image you're using is hanging on a wall in your house, and you want to hang a curtain in front of it. If that curtain is solid black, you could say that the curtain has 100 percent opacity (or zero transparency) because you can't see the image on the wall through the curtain.

  The same concept applies to the background opacity on the image in the cover block. You can use the slider in the settings panel to set the opacity to any point between 0 and 100. Set the opacity to 0 to achieve full transparency; set it to 50 to achieve half transparency or to 100 for no transparency. Figure 5-13 shows a cover block on my website with the overlay color of dark gray and 20 percent opacity.

9. **Filters:** Click in the Duotone section to create a two-tone color effect for the image in the cover block. There are a few pre-selected color combinations, but you can also select your own colors in the Shadows and Highlights section.

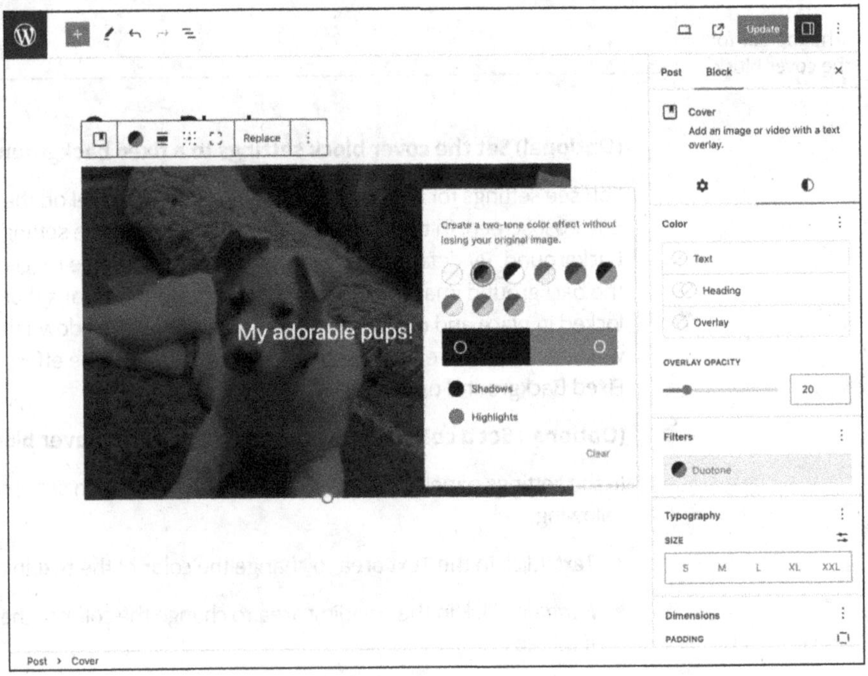

FIGURE 5-13: The cover block used on a site with the predefined Dark Greyscale Duotone Filter with the Overlay Opacity set to 20.

Inserting a Photo Gallery

You can use the WordPress block editor to insert a full photo gallery into your posts. Upload all your images; instead of adding an image block, use the gallery block.

Follow these steps to insert a photo gallery into a blog post:

1. **Add the gallery block to your post on the Edit Post screen.**

   You can find the methods for adding blocks to your post in Book 4, Chapter 1. Figure 5-14 shows the gallery block inserted into a post.

2. **Click the Upload button to select an image from your computer, or click the Media Library button to select an image from the Media Library.**

   The Create Gallery screen opens. The steps for these two methods appear in the sections "Uploading an image from your computer" and "Inserting an image from the Media Library," both earlier in this chapter. The only difference is that you can select multiple images to include in the gallery block; when selected, the images appear at the bottom of the Create Gallery screen.

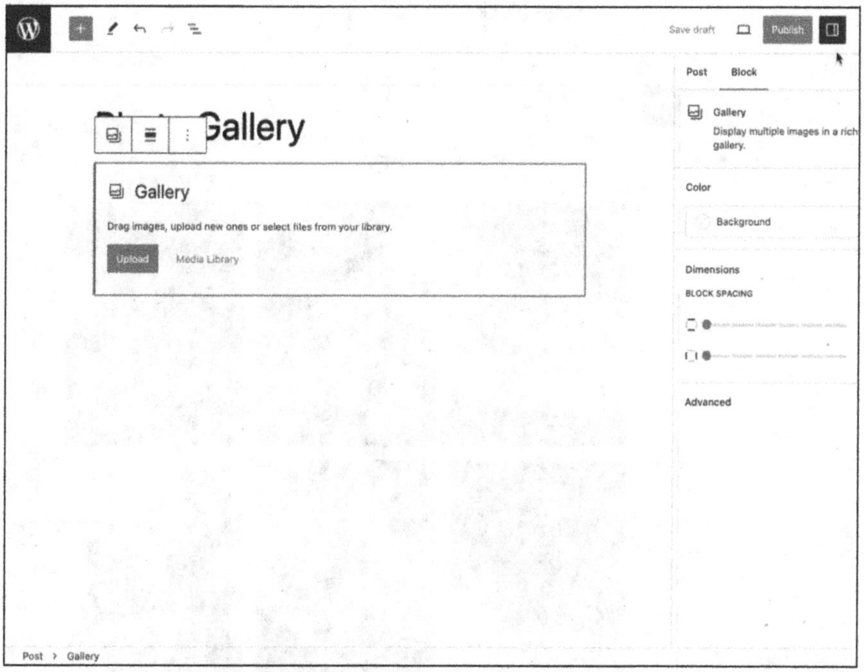

FIGURE 5-14: The gallery block in the WordPress block editor.

3. **Click the Create a New Gallery button.**

   The Edit Gallery screen opens, displaying all the images you selected in Step 2.

4. **(Optional) Add a caption for each image by clicking the Caption This Image area and typing a caption or short description.**

5. **(Optional) Set the order in which the images appear in the gallery using the drag-and-drop option on the Edit Gallery page.**

   Drag and drop images to change their order.

6. **Click the Insert Gallery button.**

   WordPress inserts the selected images into your post in the gallery block (see Figure 5-15).

7. **Use the gallery block toolbar to set the display options for the gallery.**

   Figure 5-15 shows the toolbar for the gallery block. The options include (from left to right):

   - *Transform To:* Click this option to change the type of block you're currently using. For example, if you want to change from a gallery block to an image block, click the Transform to Type icon and then select the image block to swap it. The only block type you can change to from a gallery block is an image block.

FIGURE 5-15: The gallery block populated with selected images.

- *Align*: The options here include None, Wide Width, Full Width, Align Left, Align Center, and Align Right.
- *Add Caption:* Add text for a caption, if desired.
- *Add:* This opens a drop-down menu with options to select more images from the media library or upload new images from your computer.
- *Options:* These settings are discussed in Book 4, Chapter 1.

8. **Use the gallery block options in the settings panel on the right side of the Edit Post page to configure options for your gallery:**
   - *Columns:* Select how many columns of images you want to appear in your gallery.
   - *Crop Images:* By default, this option creates image thumbnails that are cropped to the same size to align evenly. If you prefer different-size thumbnails in your gallery, you can turn this setting off.
   - *Link To:* Select Attachment Page, Media File, or None to tell WordPress what you'd like the images in the gallery to link to.
   - *Resolution:* Select Thumbnail, Medium, or Full size to tell WordPress what size images you want to use in your gallery.

WORDPRESS IMAGE AND GALLERY PLUGINS

Here are a few great WordPress plugins for handling images and galleries:

- **NextGEN Gallery Plugin (`https://wordpress.org/plugins/nextgen-gallery`):** Gives you a complete WordPress gallery management system with options for batch-uploading photos, importing photo metadata, and sorting photos, group galleries, and photo albums
- **Smart Slider 3 (`https://wordpress.org/plugins/smart-slider-3`):** Gives you options to create beautiful image sliders that are responsive on mobile and are search-engine-optimized, as well as a slide library with several premade slides to get you started
- **FooGallery (`https://wordpress.org/plugins/foogallery`):** Quick and easy-to-use image gallery creator with multiple options for photo galleries and photo albums

Some great WordPress plugins work in tandem with the WordPress gallery feature. Check out Book 7, Chapter 2 for information on installing and using WordPress plugins on your website.

Check out the nearby "WordPress image and gallery plugins" sidebar for a few interesting and helpful plugins to help you create beautiful image galleries and photo albums on your website.

TIP

Matt Mullenweg, co-founder of WordPress, created a blog that uses only photos and images in a grid format. You can see his photo blog at `https://matt.blog`.

Inserting Video Files into Your Posts

Many website owners want to go beyond offering just written content for the consumption of their visitors by including different types of media, such as audio and video files. WordPress makes it easy to include these different types of media files in your posts and pages by using the built-in file-upload feature.

You can include videos in posts or pages by embedding code offered by popular third-party video providers such as YouTube (`https://www.youtube.com`) and Vimeo (`https://vimeo.com`). Website owners can also produce and upload their own video shows, an activity known as *vlogging* (video blogging).

TIP

Check out a good example of a video blog at `https://www.tmz.com/videos`. TMZ is a popular celebrity news website that produces and displays videos for the web and for mobile devices.

WARNING

When dealing with video and audio files on your site, remember to upload and use only media that you own or have permission to use. Copyright violation is a very serious offense, especially on the Internet, and using media that you don't have permission to use can have serious consequences; results can include having your website taken down, facing heavy fines, and even going to jail. I'd hate to see that happen to you, so play it safe and use only those media files you own or have permission to use.

Whether you're producing your own videos for publication or embedding other people's videos, placing a video file in a post or page has never been easier with WordPress.

Several video services on the web allow you to add videos to your website by embedding them in your posts and pages. Google's YouTube service (`https://www.youtube.com`) is a good example of a third-party video service that allows you to share its videos.

Adding a link to a video from the web

In these steps, adding a video from the web adds a hyperlink to the video. Use these steps if all you want to do is provide a text link to a page with the video, rather than embed the video itself in your post or page (covered in the "Adding video using the embed block" section later in this chapter).

To add a link to a video from the web, follow these steps:

1. **Add a paragraph block to your post, and type your content in it.**
2. **Select the text you'd like to link.**

   The Insert from URL page appears.
3. **Click the Link icon on the paragraph block toolbar.**

   A small text box opens.
4. **Type the video's URL (Internet address) in the text box.**

   Type the full URL, including the `http://` and www portions of the address, as shown in Figure 5-16. Video providers, such as YouTube, usually list the direct links for the video files on their sites; you can copy and paste one of those links into the text box.

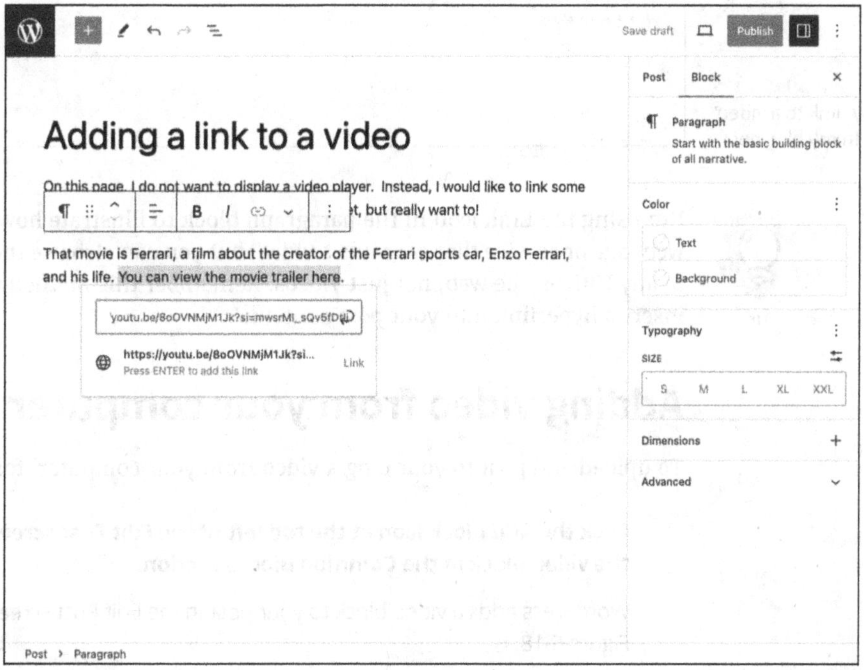

FIGURE 5-16: Add a video by linking to a URL.

5. **Press Enter.**

   A link to the video is inserted into your post, as shown in Figure 5-17. WordPress doesn't embed the actual video in the post; it inserts only a link to the video. Your site visitors click the link to load another page on which the video plays.

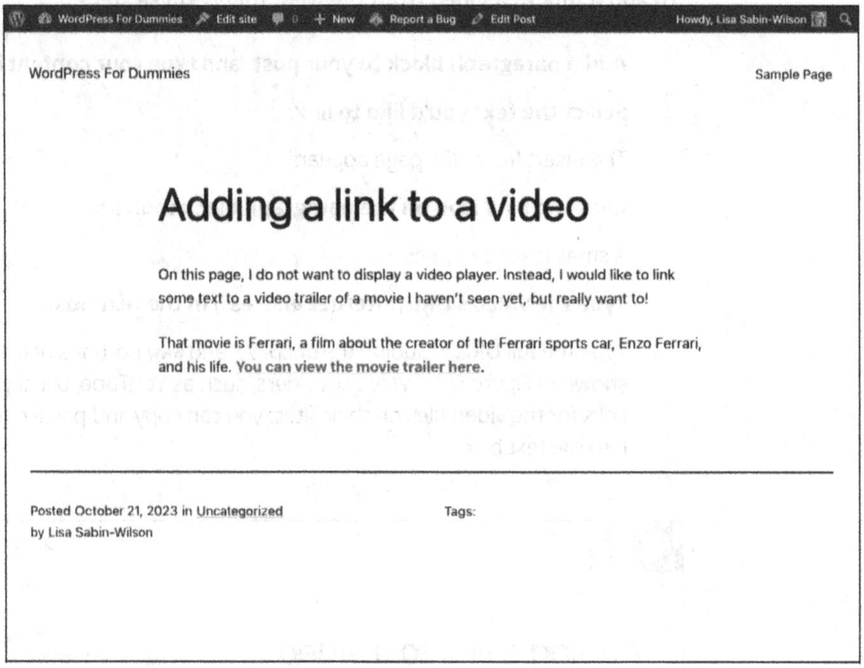

WordPress For Dummies
Edit site
New
Report a Bug
Edit Post
Howdy, Lisa Sabin-Wilson
WordPress For Dummies
Sample Page
Adding a link to a video
On this page, I do not want to display a video player. Instead, I would like to link some text to a video trailer of a movie I haven't seen yet, but really want to!
That movie is Ferrari, a film about the creator of the Ferrari sports car, Enzo Ferrari, and his life. You can view the movie trailer here.
Posted October 21, 2023 in Uncategorized
by Lisa Sabin-Wilson
Tags:

FIGURE 5-17: A link to a video in my blog post.

TIP

I'm using the Link icon in the paragraph block to illustrate how you can link to a webpage or service that contains a video, but you can also use the Link icon to link to any URL on the web, not just videos. Remember this method when you want to insert a hyperlink into your post content.

Adding video from your computer

To upload and post to your blog a video from your computer, follow these steps:

1. **Click the Add Block icon at the top left of the Edit Post screen, and select the video block in the Common Blocks section.**

   WordPress adds a video block to your post in the Edit Post screen, as shown in Figure 5-18.

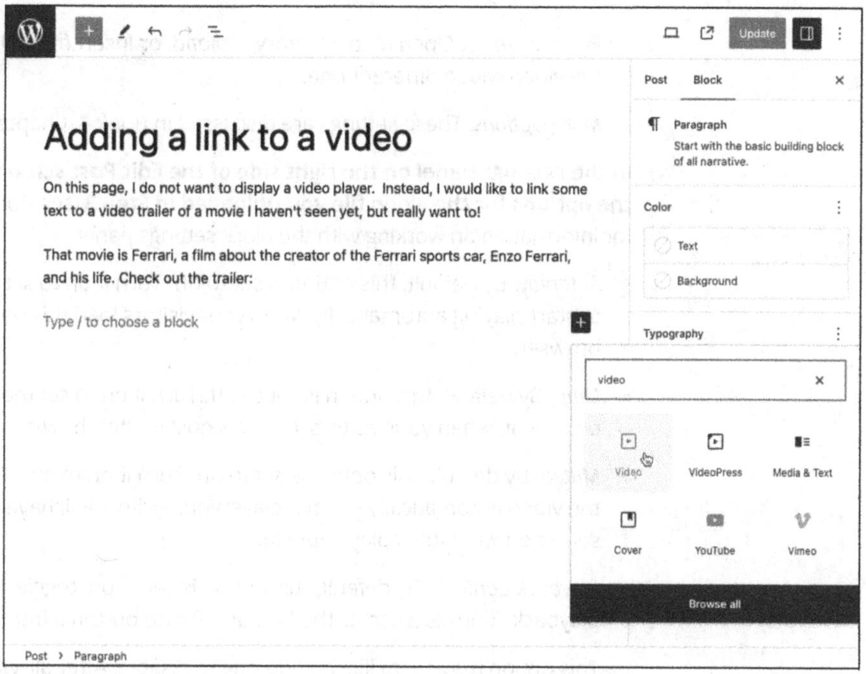
Update
Post
Block
Adding a link to a video
On this page, I do not want to display a video player. Instead, I would like to link some text to a video trailer of a movie I haven't seen yet, but really want to!
That movie is Ferrari, a film about the creator of the Ferrari sports car, Enzo Ferrari, and his life. Check out the trailer:
Type / to choose a block
Paragraph
Start with the basic building block of all narrative.
Color
Text
Background
Typography
video
Video
VideoPress
Media & Text
Cover
YouTube
Vimeo
Browse all
Post › Paragraph

FIGURE 5-18: Adding a video block to a post in the Edit Post screen.

2. **Click the Upload button that appears once you add the video block.**

   A window opens, displaying the video files on your computer.

3. **Select the video file you want to upload from your computer and click Open.**

   The video is uploaded from your computer to your web server and is inserted into the video block on the Edit Post screen.

4. **(Optional) Add a caption in the text field below the video player.**
5. **Use the video block's toolbar to set display options for the video.**

   The video block toolbar provides the following options (see Book 4, Chapter 1 for information on using block toolbars):

   - *Transform, Drag and Move:* These options are covered in detail in Book 4, Chapter 1.
   - *Align:* The options here include None, Wide Width, Full Width, Align Left, Align Center, and Align Right.
   - *Caption:* Add text for a caption, if desired.
   - *Text Tracks:* This option allows you to upload files formatted as WebVTT (.vtt) that display as subtitles, or captions, when the video is played.

- *Replace:* Select Open Media Library, Upload, or Insert from URL to replace the video with a different one.
- *More Options:* These settings are discussed in Book 4, Chapter 1.

6. **In the settings panel on the right side of the Edit Post screen, configure the options for the video file you uploaded in Step 3** (see Book 4, Chapter 1 for information on working with the block settings panel):
   - *Autoplay:* By default, this option is set to off. Turn it on to set the video to start playing automatically when your visitors load this post in their browser.
   - *Loop:* By default, this option is set to off. Turn it on to set the video to play, on repeat, when your visitors load this post in their browser.
   - *Muted:* By default, this option is set to off. Turn it on to mute the sound of the video automatically when it plays; your visitors will have to toggle the sound on when they play your video.
   - *Playback Controls:* By default, this option is set to on; toggle it off to remove playback controls (such as the Play and Pause buttons) from your video.

     This option may seem like an odd one to disable. After all, why put a video on your page if no one can click the Play button to view it? Well, if you use this in conjunction with the Autoplay option, you can set a video to automatically play for your visitors without giving them a way to pause or mute the video. However, please don't do this — it is a horrible experience for visitors on your site because it autoplays the video and your visitors may not be expecting it. Always allow your visitors to pause, play, and mute videos. People of the Internet will thank you.
   - *Play Inline:* By default, this option is set to off; turn it on to ensure that the video doesn't automatically enter full-screen mode when playing on smartphones.
   - *Preload:* Preload is an HTML5 attribute that tells the web browser how much video data it should fetch and cache (or store) when a webpage with a video is visited. Preload can reduce the lag time it could take to load a video, especially if the video file is very large. This attribute is used when a video is served from the same server that hosts the website — not to embed third-party videos. The options are Auto (fetches the entire video); Metadata (fetches only the metadata, such as video dimensions and length); and None (fetches none of the video data). The default attribute for the video block is Metadata; to change it, choose a different option on the Preload drop-down menu.

- *Poster Image:* When you embed a video in a post, by default, the first thing your visitor sees is the first frame of that video. Click the Select Poster Image button to upload an image, or select an image from the Media Library, to use as the video poster image on your site.

  Figure 5-19 shows a video of a Ferrari sports car that I uploaded to a post. You see that the video displays a random screen grab of the video before visitors click the Play button. Using the Poster Image, I uploaded an image of a Ferrari that replaces the first frame and gives the video a nicer appearance. Figure 5-20 shows the video on my site after I applied the Poster Image to the video.

7. **Save and publish your post, or add more content and publish the post later.**

TIP

I don't recommend uploading your own videos directly to your WordPress site if you can help it. Many video service providers, such as YouTube and Vimeo, give you free video storage. Embedding videos in a WordPress page or post from one of those services is easy, and by using those services, you're not using your own storage space or bandwidth limitations. Additionally, if many people visit your site and view your video simultaneously, loading it from a third-party site such as YouTube will make visitors' experience much faster.

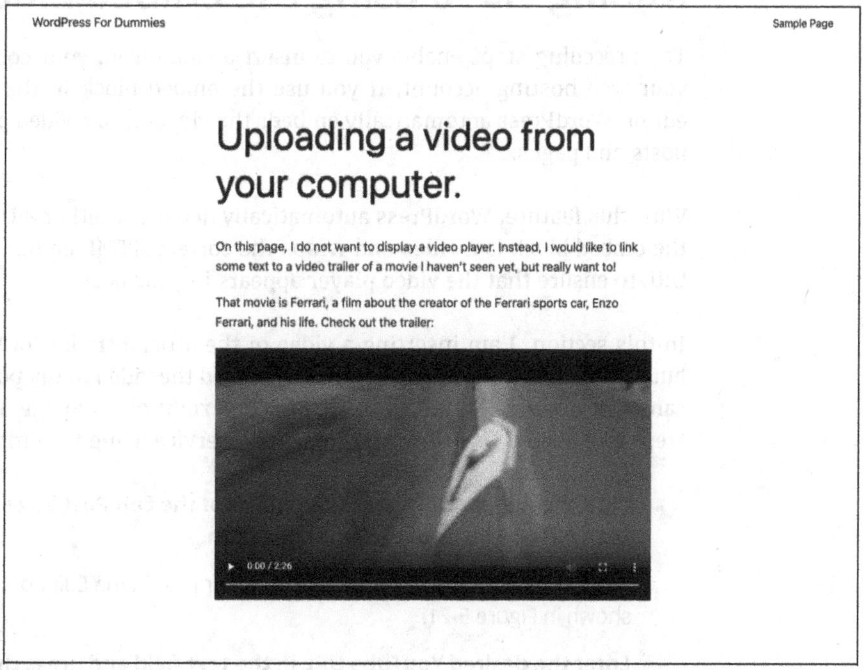
WordPress For Dummies
Sample Page
Uploading a video from your computer.
On this page, I do not want to display a video player. Instead, I would like to link some text to a video trailer of a movie I haven't seen yet, but really want to!
That movie is Ferrari, a film about the creator of the Ferrari sports car, Enzo Ferrari, and his life. Check out the trailer:
0:00 / 2:26

FIGURE 5-19: A video displayed without a poster image defined.

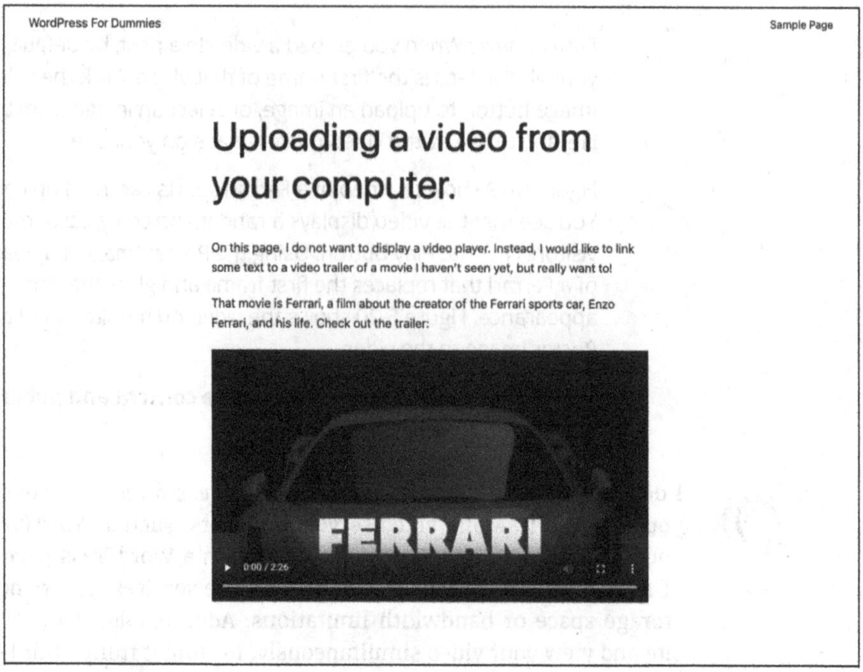
WordPress For Dummies
Sample Page
Uploading a video from your computer.
On this page, I do not want to display a video player. Instead, I would like to link some text to a video trailer of a movie I haven't seen yet, but really want to!
That movie is Ferrari, a film about the creator of the Ferrari sports car, Enzo Ferrari, and his life. Check out the trailer:
FERRARI
0:00 / 2:26

FIGURE 5-20: A video displayed with a poster image defined.

Adding video using the embed block

The preceding steps enable you to insert a video from your computer hosted on your web hosting account. If you use the embed block in the WordPress block editor, WordPress automatically embeds the video(s) in a video player within your posts and pages.

With this feature, WordPress automatically detects whether a URL you include in the embed block is a video and wraps the correct HTML embed code around that URL to ensure that the video player appears in your post.

In this section, I am inserting a video of the official trailer for the movie *Ferrari*, but instead of a link to the video, I will embed the video in my post so that readers can click the Play button to view the video right on my page. Follow these next steps to embed a video from a third-party service using the embed block:

1. **Click the Add Block icon at the top left of the Edit Post screen, and select the YouTube block in the Embed section.**

   WordPress adds the YouTube block to your post in the Edit Post screen, as shown in Figure 5-21.

2. **Enter the desired YouTube URL in the text field and press the Enter key.**

   WordPress embeds the video in your post, as shown in Figure 5-22.

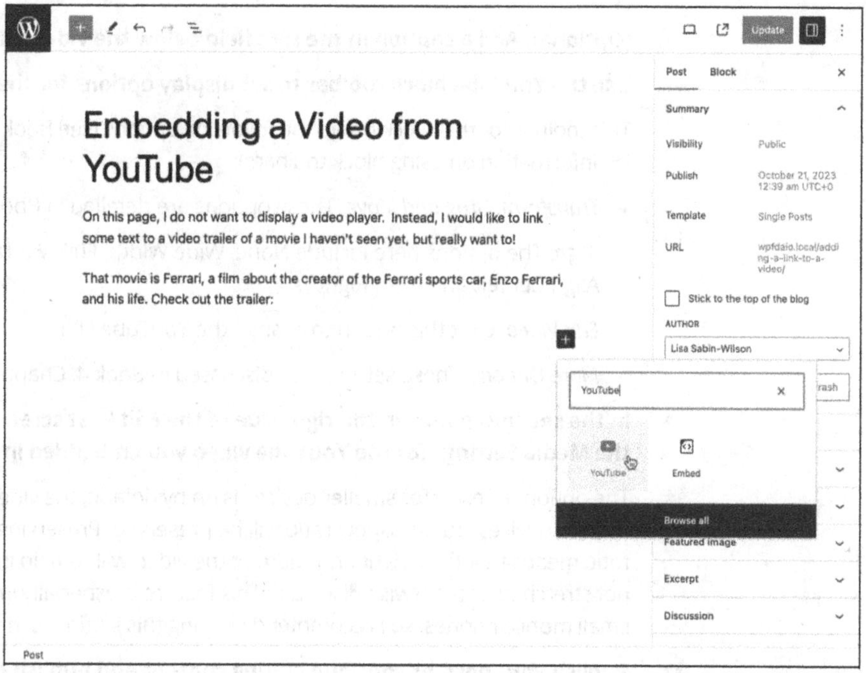

FIGURE 5-21: Adding the YouTube block to a post.

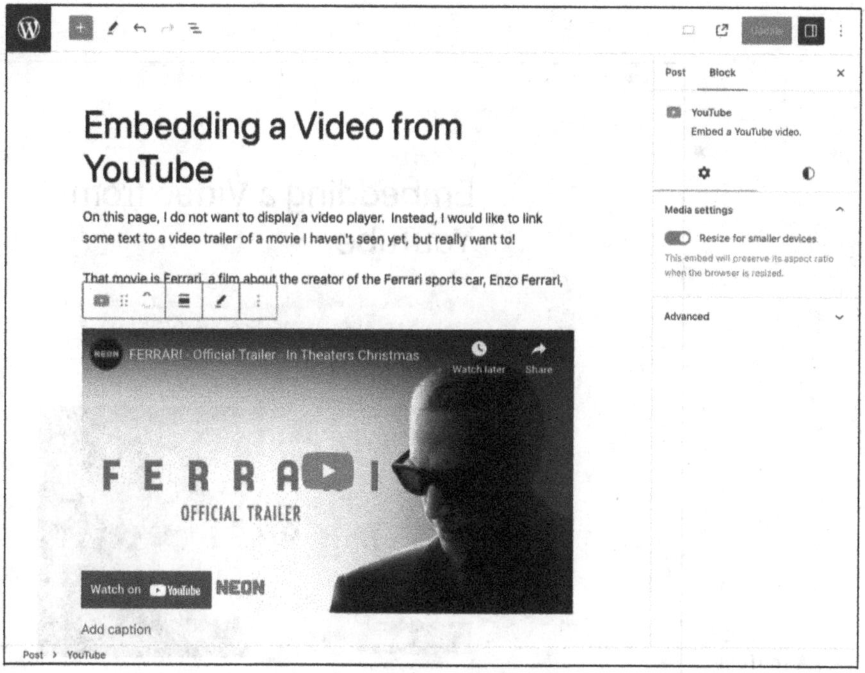

FIGURE 5-22: A block added to the Edit Post screen.

3. **(Optional) Add a caption in the text field below the video player.**
4. **Use the YouTube block toolbar to set display options for the video.**

   This toolbar for this block offers the following options (see Book 4, Chapter 1 for information on using block toolbars):

   - *Transform, Drag and Move:* These options are detailed in Book 4, Chapter 1.
   - *Align:* The options here include None, Wide Width, Full Width, Align Left, Align Center, and Align Right.
   - *Edit Video:* Click this option to change the YouTube URL.
   - *More Options:* These settings are discussed in Book 4, Chapter 1.

5. **In the settings panel on the right side of the Edit Post screen, configure the Media Settings for the YouTube video you embedded in Step 2.**

   The option to resize for smaller devices is on by default; the video will shrink on smaller devices, but its aspect ratio will be preserved. Preserving the aspect ratio means that the height and width of the video will remain in proportion, not stretched or otherwise distorted. This feature is especially important on small mobile phones, so I recommend keeping this setting turned on.

6. **Publish your post, or continue editing content and publish the post later.**

   Figure 5-23 shows the post on a live website with the YouTube video displayed.

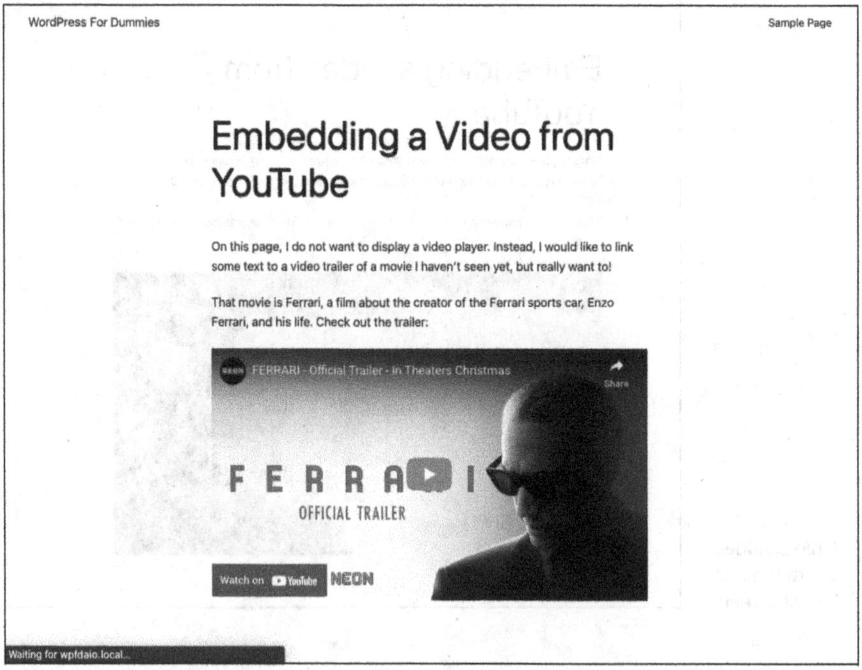

FIGURE 5-23: A YouTube video embedded in a post.

TECHNICAL STUFF

I'm using the embed block in this example to illustrate how you can embed a video from YouTube, but several embed blocks allow you to embed all kinds of data from different services on the web. Book 4, Chapter 1 covers the blocks available in the Embeds section of the Block Inserter panel in greater detail.

Inserting Audio Files into Your Blog Posts

Audio files can be music or voice recordings, such as recordings of you speaking to your readers. These files add a nice personal touch to your site. You can easily share audio files on your blog using the audio block in the WordPress block editor. After you insert an audio file into a post, your readers can listen to it on their computers or download it to an MP3 player and listen to it while driving to work, if they want.

The audio files you add to your site can include music or voice in formats such as `.mp3`, `.midi`, or `.wav` (to name just a few). Some website owners produce their own audio files in regular episodes, called *podcasts*, to create an Internet radio show. Often, you can find these audio files available for syndication on a variety of streaming services, such as iTunes and Spotify. (See the "Podcasting with WordPress" section, later in this chapter, for more information.)

To insert an audio file into your site, follow these steps:

1. **Click the Add Block icon at the top left of the Edit Post screen, and select the audio block in the Common Blocks section.**

   WordPress adds the audio block to your post in the Edit Post screen, as shown in Figure 5-24.

2. **Click the Upload button that appears once you add the audio block to your post.**

   A window opens, displaying the files that exist on your computer.

3. **Select the audio file you want to upload from your computer and click Open.**

   The audio is uploaded from your computer to your web server and is inserted into the audio block on the Edit Post screen.

4. **(Optional) Add a caption in the text field below the audio player.**

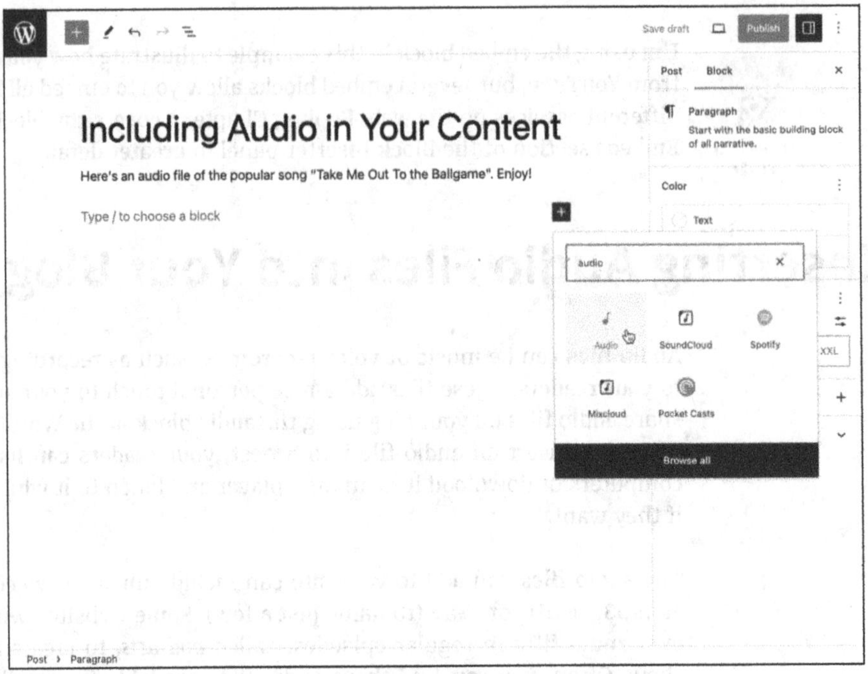

FIGURE 5-24: Adding the audio block to a post in the Edit Post screen.

5. **Use the audio block toolbar to set display options for the audio file.**

   The toolbar offers the following options (see Book 4, Chapter 1 for information on using block toolbars):

   - *Transform, Drag, and Move:* These options are detailed in Book 4, Chapter 1.
   - *Align:* The options here include None, Wide Width, Full Width, Align Left, Align Center, and Align Right.
   - *Replace:* Select Open Media Library, Upload, or Insert from URL to replace the audio file with a different one.
   - *More Options:* These settings are discussed in Book 4, Chapter 1.

6. **In the settings panel on the right side of the Edit Post screen, configure the options for the audio file you uploaded in Step 3:**

   - *Autoplay:* By default, this option is set to off. Turn it on to set the audio to play automatically when visitors load this post in their browser.
   - *Loop:* By default, this option is set to off. Turn it on to set the audio to play, on repeat, when your visitors load this post in their browser.
   - *Preload:* The default attribute for the audio block is None; to change it, choose a different option on the Preload drop-down menu. See the "Adding video from your computer" section, earlier in this chapter, for details on the Preload attribute.

7. Save and publish your post, or add more content and publish the post later.

Figure 5-25 displays a post with an embedded audio player for an uploaded audio file.

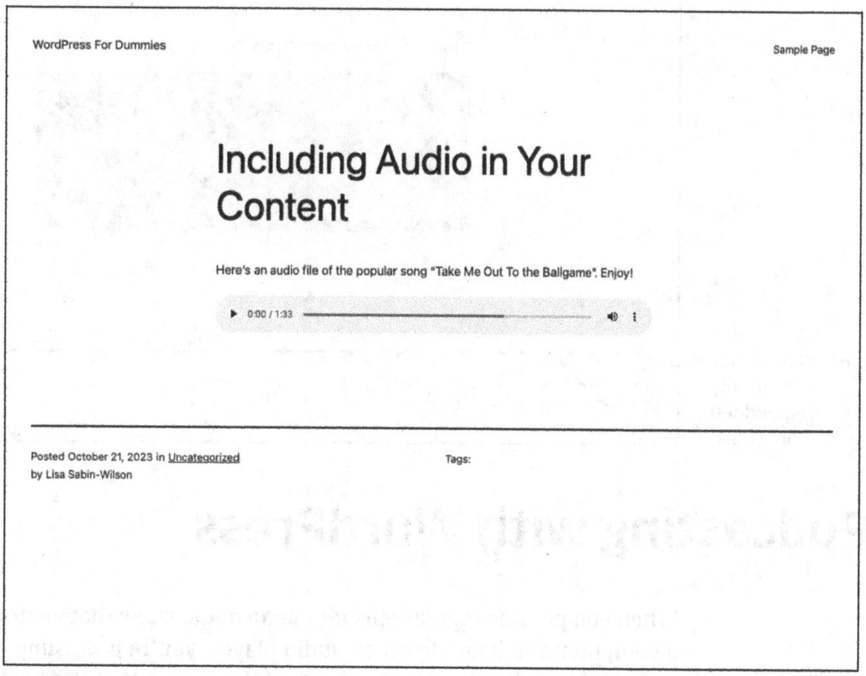

WordPress For Dummies
Sample Page
Including Audio in Your Content
Here's an audio file of the popular song "Take Me Out To the Ballgame". Enjoy!
0:00 / 1:33
Posted October 21, 2023 in Uncategorized
by Lisa Sabin-Wilson
Tags:

FIGURE 5-25: An audio player embedded in a post.

Inserting Audio Using the Embed Block

In this chapter I mention the services that you can embed by using the embed block in the WordPress block editor. Some of those services allow you to embed audio files from sources such as Spotify, Soundcloud, Mixcloud, and ReverbNation, to name a few. To embed audio from any of these sources, follow the same steps you took in the previous section, "Inserting Audio Files into Your Blog Posts." You only need the direct URL for the audio you want to embed. Figure 5-26 shows a post with an embedded audio file from Spotify.

REMEMBER

Embedded songs and other audio files from third-party services obey the licensing rules of those services. Suppose you embed an audio file from Spotify. In that case, you embed a random 25- to 30-second sample of the song, with a message telling your readers to log into their Spotify account to listen to the full version.

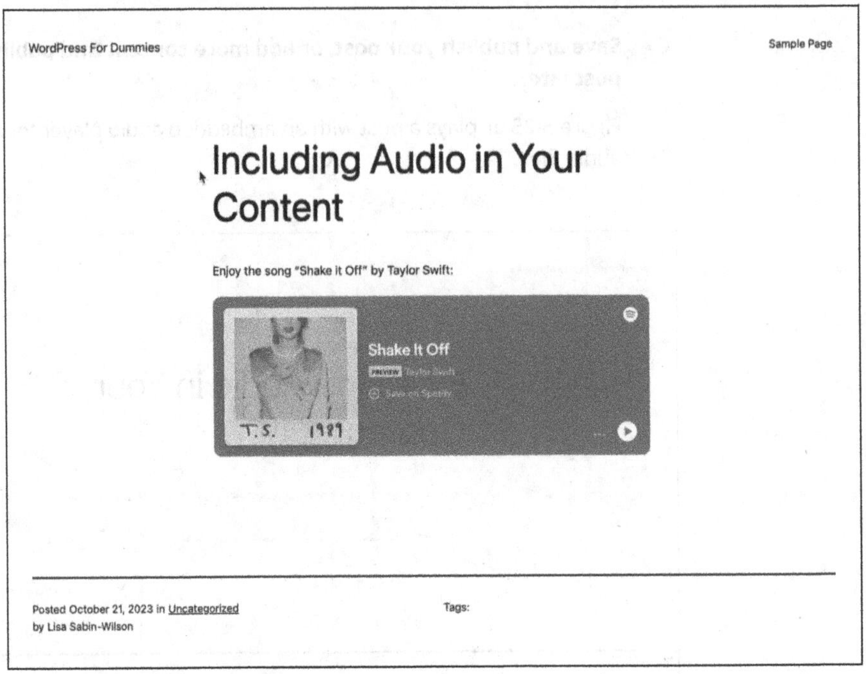

FIGURE 5-26: An audio player from Spotify embedded in a post.

Podcasting with WordPress

When you provide regular episodes of an audio show that visitors can download to a computer and listen to on an audio player, you're *podcasting.* Think of a podcast as a weekly radio show that you tune into, except that it's hosted on the Internet rather than on a radio station.

Several plugins are available in WordPress for podcasting that allow you to easily insert audio files into your WordPress posts and pages. The plugins that are dedicated to podcasting provide features that go beyond embedding audio files in a website. Some of the most important of these features include the following:

- **Archives:** You can create an archive of your audio podcast files so that your listeners can catch up on your show by listening to past episodes.
- **RSS feed:** An RSS feed of your podcast show allows visitors to subscribe to your syndicated content so that they can be notified when you publish future episodes.
- **Promotion:** A podcast isn't successful without listeners, right? You can upload your podcast to services such as Apple Podcasts (`https://apps.apple.com/us/app/apple-podcasts/id525463029`), so that when people search for podcasts by subject, they find your podcast.

The following plugins go beyond audio file management. They're also dedicated to podcasting and have all the features you need:

- **Simple Podcasting (`https://wordpress.org/plugins/simple-podcasting`):** Simple Podcasting, which includes full Apple Podcasts support, allows you to upload audio files using the usual WordPress methods (audio blocks). The plugin also includes a Podcast block in the new WordPress block editor for easy publishing of podcasts on your website.
- **Seriously Simple Podcasting (`https://wordpress.org/plugins/seriously-simple-podcasting`):** This plugin uses the native WordPress interface with minimal settings to make podcasting with WordPress as easy as possible. You can run multiple podcasts, obtain stats on who's listening, do audio and videocasting, and publish to popular services such as iTunes, Google Play, and Stitcher.

TIP

I discuss web hosting requirements in Book 2, Chapter 1. If you're a podcaster who intends to store audio files in your web hosting account, you may need to increase the storage and bandwidth for your account so that you don't run out of space or incur higher fees from your web hosting provider. Discuss these issues with your web hosting provider to determine what you have to pay for increased disk space and bandwidth.

5
Examining Social Media and SEO

Contents at a Glance

IN THIS CHAPTER

» Understanding what analytics can tell you about your site

» Choosing an analytics-tracking option

» Deciphering analytics terminology

» Working with Google Analytics

Chapter 1
Understanding Analytics

Every business on the face of the Earth needs to figure out what works and what doesn't if it wants to succeed. Site owners often know basic statistics about their sites, such as the current number on their hit counters or how many people visit their site daily or weekly. These stats may give you the big picture, but they don't really address why something is or isn't working.

You need to get at least a basic understanding of analytics if you want to make the most of your site. The data provided by free programs such as Google Analytics can really help you grow as a content publisher. In this chapter, you discover how to incorporate various data-measuring tools into your WordPress installation, decipher what the data is telling you, and determine how to act on it.

Google Analytics provides you with a tremendous amount of information about your content. The goal of this chapter is to help you interpret the data, understand where your traffic is coming from, understand which of your content is the most popular among your visitors, know how to draw correlations between various data sets, and then use all of that information to shape the content you write. This process may sound very geeky and accountant-like, but in reality, it gives you a road map that helps you improve your business.

Understanding the Importance of Analytics

Personally, I avoid math like my nephew avoids vegetables. Most people's eyes glaze over when they hear the word *analytics* followed by *stats*, any type of *percentages*, and anything that sounds very mathematical.

You should view analytics not as a bunch of numbers, but as a tool set that tells a story. It can tell you how people are finding your content, what content is most popular, and where users are sharing that content. Knowing what type of content is popular, where your site is popular (in which time zones, countries, and states, for example), and even what time of day your posts get more readers is all valuable information. Understanding your audience's interest in your content, as well as their preferences on when and how they read your content, is important.

At one point in my life, I had a pretty popular political blog. Through studying analytics and reactions to my content, I figured out that if I posted my blog between 9:30 a.m. and 10 a.m. EST, my posts garnered the most comments and got the most traffic throughout the day. When I posted after noon, my posts got about half as many comments and half as much traffic over a 24-hour period. Additionally, I saw that my site was getting shared and voted for on the social news site Reddit (`https://www.reddit.com`) more often than on Facebook (`https://www.facebook.com`), so I prioritized the Reddit share button over the Facebook share button. This change increased the amount of traffic I received from Reddit because people had the visual reminder to share the post with their friends and vote for posts as favorites.

I was able to continue to drill down from there. Not only did I have the information on where my content was being shared, but I was also able to garner more information for analytics. Posts that had a picture included with the first three paragraphs often had a lower *bounce rate* (the interval of time it takes for a visitor to visit a site and then bounce away to a different site) than posts that had no picture at all. If I wrote the post while elevating my left leg and wearing a tinfoil helmet, I saw a 25 percent bump in traffic. (Okay, maybe that last one isn't true.)

Exploring the Options for Tracking Data

You have a lot of options when it comes to tracking data on your site. Google Analytics (detailed in the following list) is the most popular tool, but several options are available. Analytics is popular because of its widespread use, the amount of content written on how to maximize it, and the fact that it's free.

Here are three popular tools:

- **StatCounter (`https://statcounter.com`):** StatCounter has both a free and a paid service. The paid service doesn't kick in until you get to 250k pageviews a month.

  StatCounter (shown in Figure 1-1) uses the log generated by your server and gives you the ability to configure the reports to fit your needs. If you want to use a log file, you need to have a self-hosted blog and know where your log file is stored. StatCounter requires a little more technical knowledge than your average analytics app because you have to deal with your log file instead of cutting and pasting a line of code into your site. The main advantage of StatCounter is that it reports in real time, whereas Google Analytics always has a little bit of lag in its reporting.

- **Jetpack (`https://wordpress.org/plugins/jetpack`):** The Jetpack plugin provides a pretty good stat package for its hosted-blog users. Shortly after launching, `WordPress.com` provided a WordPress Stats plugin that self-hosted users can use. (See Figure 1-2.) If you use this package, your stats appear on the WordPress Dashboard, but to drill down deeper into them, you need to access the stats on `WordPress.com`. The advantages of WordPress stats are that they're pretty easy to install and present a very simplified overview of your data. The downside is they don't drill as deep as Google Analytics, and the reporting isn't as in-depth. Neither can you customize reports.

- **Google Analytics (`https://marketingplatform.google.com/about/analytics`):** Google Analytics can seem overwhelming when you sit in front of it for the first time, but it has the most robust stats features this side of Omniture. (Omniture is an enterprise-level stats package, which is overkill if you're a personal or small-business site owner.)

  WordPress plugins (covered in the "Adding Google Analytics to Your WordPress Site" section, later in this chapter) bring a simplified version of Google Analytics (see Figure 1-3) to your WordPress Dashboard, much like the `WordPress.com` Stats plugin. If you feel overwhelmed by Google Analytics and prefer to have your stats broken down in a much more digestible fashion, this plugin is for you: It provides a good overview of analytics information, including goals that you can set up. Although the plugin doesn't offer everything that Google Analytics brings to the table, it provides more than enough so that you can see the overall health of your website and monitor where your traffic is coming from, what posts are popular, and how people are finding your website. Besides the Dashboard Stats Overview, this plugin gives you a breakdown of traffic to each post, which is a nice bonus.

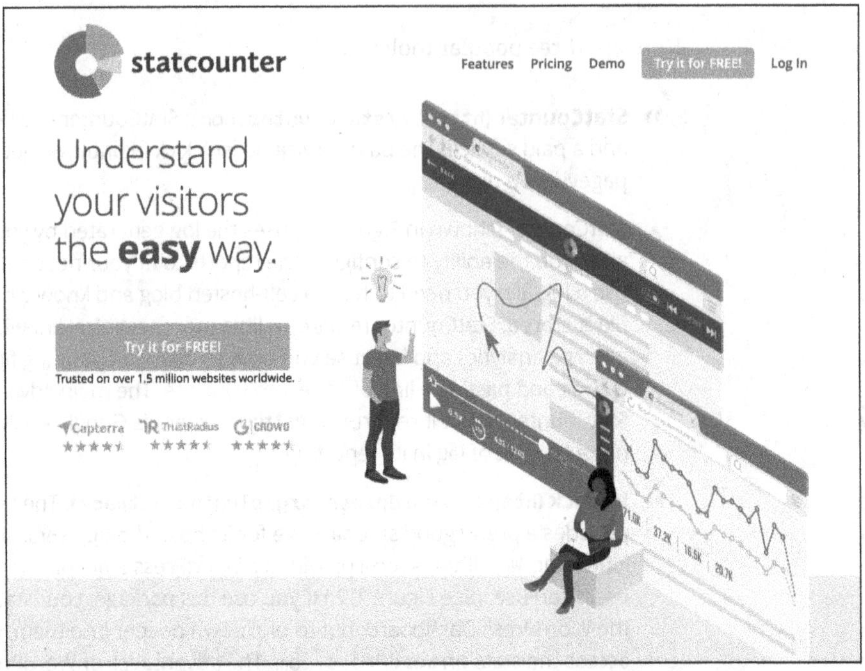

FIGURE 1-1: StatCounter offers real-time stats.

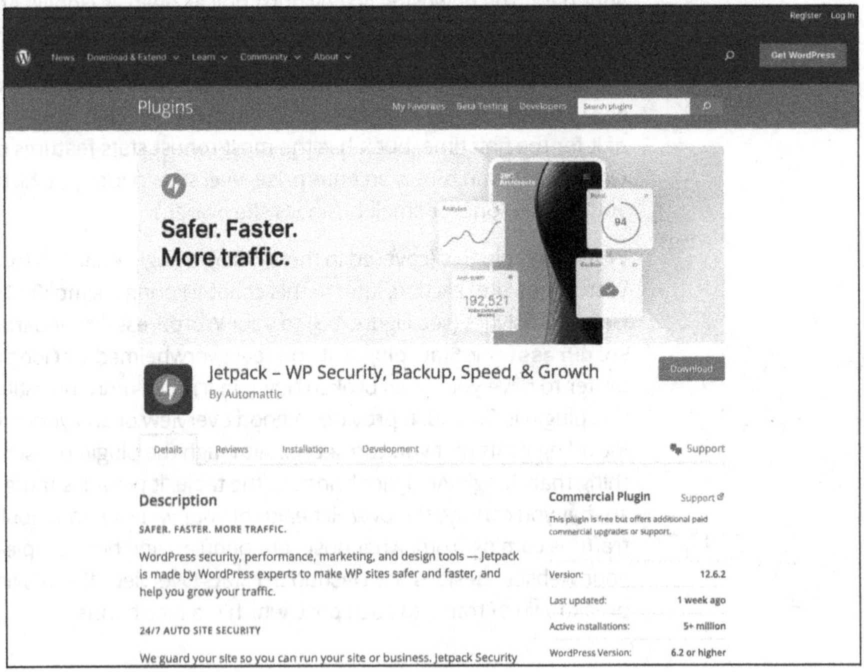

FIGURE 1-2: The JetPack plugin offers a Stats feature for tracking your website traffic.

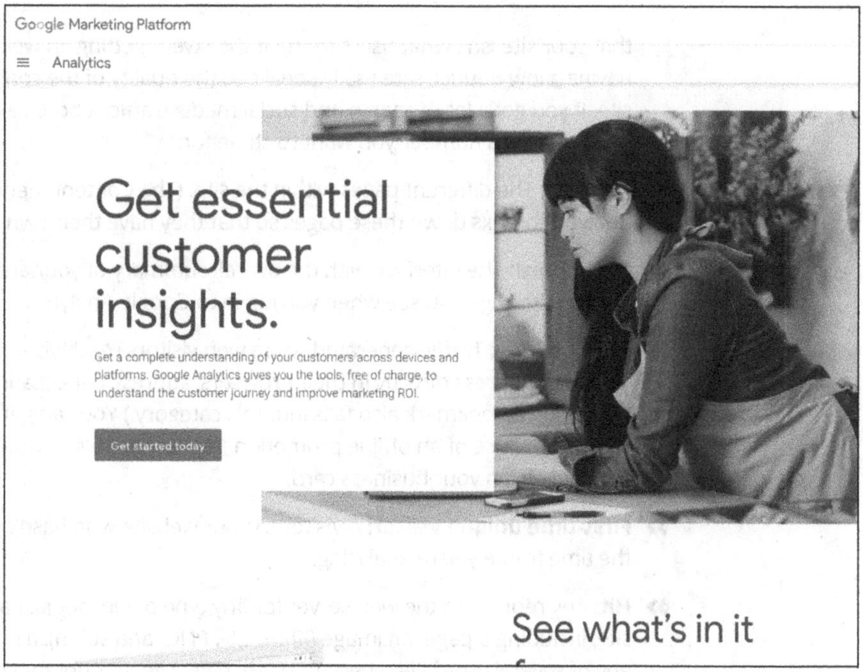

FIGURE 1-3: The Google Analytics website.

Understanding Key Analytics Terminology

One of the reasons why people find analytics programs so overwhelming is that they use obscure terminology and jargon. Here, I've defined some of the most popular terms, listed in alphabetical order:

- **Bounce rate:** The percentage of single-page visits or visits in which the person leaves your site from the entrance page. This metric measures visit quality. A high bounce rate generally indicates that visitors don't find your site entrance pages relevant to them.

  The more compelling your pages are, the more visitors stay on your site and convert to purchasers or subscribers, or complete whatever action you want them to complete. You can minimize bounce rates by tailoring landing pages to each ad that you run (in the case of businesses) or to the audience based on the referring site (a special bio page for your Twitter profile, for example). Landing pages should provide the information and services that the ad promises.

  When it comes to site content, a high bounce rate from a social media source (such as a social news site like Reddit) can tell you that users didn't find the content interesting, and a high bounce rate from search engines can mean that your site isn't what users thought they were getting. In web publishing, having a low bounce rate really speaks to the quality of the content on your site. If you get a lot of search and social media traffic, a bounce rate of below 50 percent is a number you want to strive for.

- **Content:** The different pages within the site. (The Content menu of Google Analytics breaks down these pages so that they have their own statistics.)
- **Dashboard:** The interface with the overall summary of your analytics data. It's the first page you see when you log in to Google Analytics.
- **Direct traffic:** Traffic generated when web visitors reach your site by typing your web address directly in their browsers' address bars. (Launching a site by clicking a bookmark also falls into this category.) You can get direct-traffic visitors because of an offline promotion, repeat readers or word of mouth, or simply from your business card.
- **First-time unique visitor:** A visitor to your website who hasn't visited before the time frame you're analyzing.
- **Hit:** Any request to the web server for any type of file, not just a post on your site, including a page, an image (JPEG, GIF, PNG, and so on), a sound clip, or any of several other file types. An HTML page can account for several hits: the page itself, each image on the page, and any embedded sound or video clips. Therefore, the number of hits a website receives doesn't give you a valid gauge of its popularity, but indicates server use and how many files have been loaded.
- **Keyword:** A database index entry that identifies a specific record or document. (That definition sounds way fancier than a keyword actually is.) Keyword searching is the most common form of text search on the web. Most search engines do text query and retrieval by using keywords. Unless the author of the web document specifies the keywords for their document (which you can do by using meta tags), the search engine has to determine them. (So you can't guarantee how Google indexes the page.) Essentially, search engines pull out and index words that it determines are significant. A search engine is more likely to deem words important if those words appear toward the beginning of a document and are repeated several times throughout the document.
- **Meta tag:** A special HTML tag that provides information about a webpage. Unlike normal HTML tags, meta tags don't affect how the page appears in a user's browser. Instead, meta tags provide information such as who created the page, how often it's updated, the title of the page, a description of the page's content, and keywords that represent the page's content. Many search engines use this information when they build their indexes, although most

major search engines rarely index the `keywords` meta tag anymore because it has been abused by people trying to fool search results.

- **Pageview:** Refers to the number of unique views a web page has received. A *page* is defined as any file or content delivered by a webserver that generally would be considered to be a web document, which includes HTML pages (`.html`, `.htm`, `.shtml`), posts or pages within a WordPress installation, script-generated pages (`.cgi`, `.asp`, `.cfm`), and plain-text pages. It also includes sound files (`.wav`, `.aiff`, and so on), video files (`.mov`, `.mpeg`, and so on), and other nondocument files. Only image files (`.jpeg`, `.gif`, `.png`), JavaScript (`.js`), and Cascading Style Sheets (`.css`) are excluded from this definition. Each time a file defined as a page is served or viewed in a visitor's web browser, a *pageview* is registered by Google Analytics. The pageview statistic is more important and accurate than a hit statistic because it doesn't include images or other items that may register hits on your site.
- **Path:** A series of clicks that results in distinct pageviews. A path can't contain nonpages, such as image files.
- **Referral:** Event that occurs when a user clicks any hyperlink that takes them to a page or file in another website, which could be text, an image, or any other type of link. When a user arrives at your site from another site, the server records the referral information in the hit log for every file requested by that user. If the user found the link by using a search engine, the server records the search engine's name and any keywords used as well. Referrals give you an indication of what social media sites, as well as links from other websites, are directing traffic to your site.
- **Referrer:** The URL of an HTML page that refers visitors to a site.
- **Traffic sources:** A metric that tells you how visitors found your website, such as via direct traffic, referring sites, or search engines.
- **Unique visitors:** The number of unduplicated (counted only once) visitors to your website over the course of a specified time period. The server determines a unique visitor by using *cookies,* which are small tracking files stored in your visitors' browsers that keep track of the number of times they visit your site.
- **Visitor:** A stat designed to come as close as possible to defining the number of distinct people who visit a website. The website, of course, can't really determine whether any one "visitor" is really two people sharing a computer, but a good visitor-tracking system can come close to the actual number. The most accurate visitor-tracking systems generally employ cookies to maintain tallies of distinct visitors.

Adding Google Analytics to Your WordPress Site

In the following sections, you sign up for Google Analytics, install it on your blog, and add the WordPress plugin to your site.

Signing up for Google Analytics

To sign up for Google Analytics, follow these steps:

1. **Go to `https://marketingplatform.google.com/about/analytics` and click the Get Started Today button, which is located in the top-right corner of the page.**

   A page where you can sign up for a Google account or sign in via an existing Google account appears. If you don't have a Google account, follow the link to sign up for one.

2. **Sign in via your Google account by entering your email address and password in the text boxes and then clicking Sign In.**

   The first of a series of walk-through pages appears.

3. **Click the button labeled Get Started Today as shown in Figure 1-3.**

   The Create an Account page appears in your browser window.

4. **Type your desired account name in the Account Name field.**

   This is the name to identify your account.

5. **Click the Next button.**

   The Create a Property page appears in your browser window. Typically, this will be the name of the website you want to track using Google Analytics.

6. **Fill in the rest of the fields on this page.**

   Location, Time Zone, and Currency appear as drop-down menus in which you can select the options that apply to you and your website property. You can edit these details later in your Google Analytics Admin panel.

7. **Click the Next button.**

   The Describe Your Business page appears in your browser window with fields to fill in for Industry and Business size.

8. **Click the Next button.**

The Choose Your Business Objectives page loads in your browser window, where you can select the topics that are most important to you and your business. Those topics currently include:

- *Generate Leads:* Analyze your visitor metrics and attract new visitors.
- *Drive Online Sales:* Analyze purchase behavior and get more sales.
- *Raise Brand Awareness:* Spread the word about your site.
- *Examine User Behavior:* Learn how people use your website.
- *Get Baseline Reports:* Access a variety of different types of reports.

9. Click the Create button.

The Google Analytics Terms of Service Agreement window appears. Select your region and read the terms of service, and select the check boxes that state that you accept the terms.

10. Click the I Accept button.

The Start Collecting Data screen appears. Select the Web option under the Choose a Platform heading. The Installation Instructions screen loads in your browser window, and you can see and copy your Google tag ID (see Figure 1-4). You are now finished creating your new Google Analytics account and ready to install it on your website.

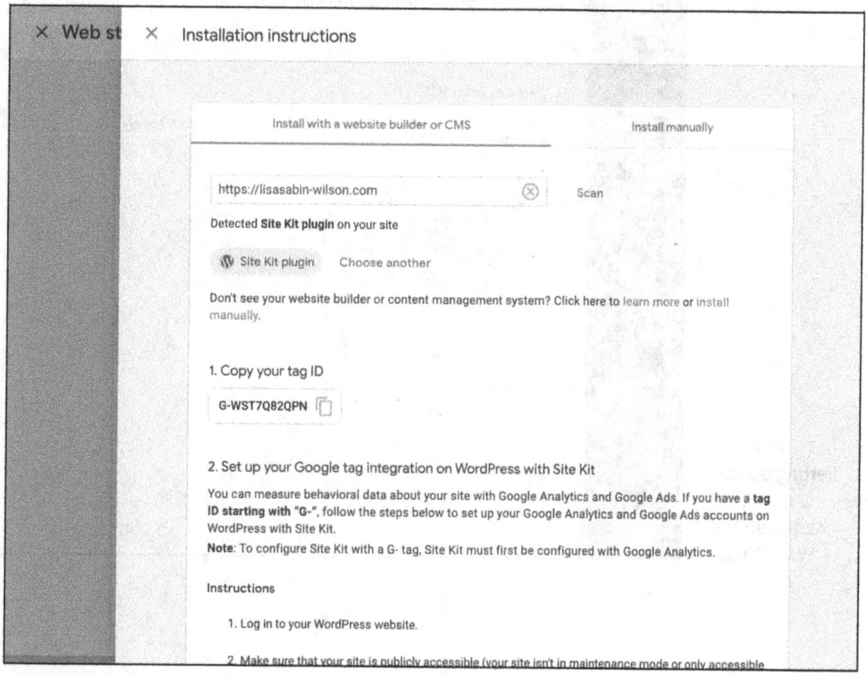

FIGURE 1-4: Installation Instructions page in Google Analytics.

Installing the tracking code

After you set up your Google Analytics account and obtain the tracking ID to install in your WordPress site, you're ready for the installation. The easiest way to accomplish this task is to use the SiteKit by Google plugin for WordPress (`https://wordpress.org/plugins/google-site-kit`). Follow these steps:

1. **Log in to your WordPress Dashboard.**
2. **Click the Add New link on the Plugins menu.**

   The Add Plugins screen appears.
3. **Search for the Google Site Kit, and install and activate it.**
4. **Click the Dashboard link in the new Site Kit menu.**

   The Set Up Site Kit screen appears.
5. **Select the Connect Google Analytics check box as part of your setup, and click the Sign In with Google button.**

   See Figure 1-5.

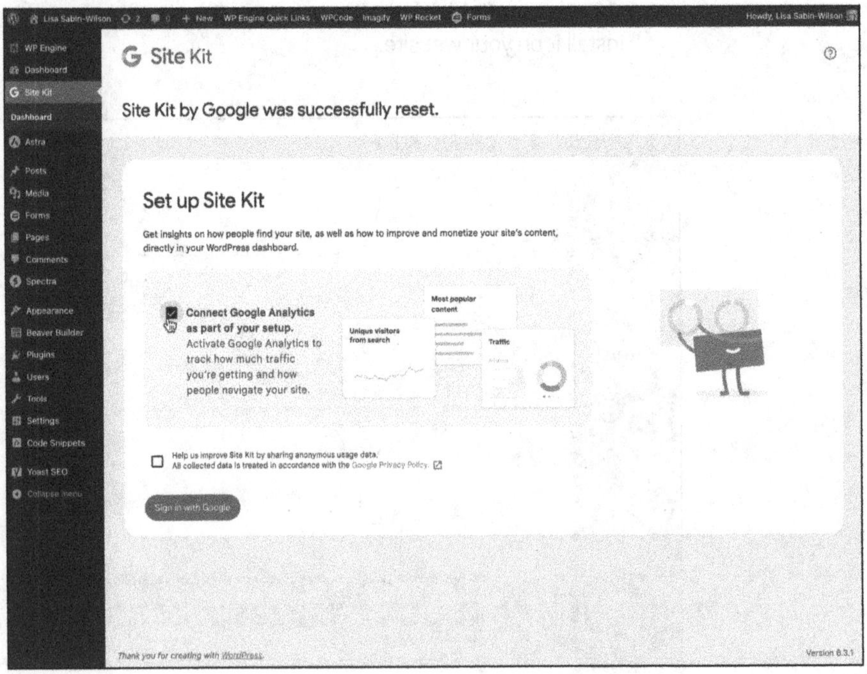

FIGURE 1-5: Setting up the Google Site Kit plugin for WordPress.

6. **Authenticate with your Google account by clicking the link on this page.**

   When you've authenticated with your Google account, Google gives you an access code that you need to copy and paste into the Access Code text field in the resulting window.

7. **Click the Save Changes button.**

   This step saves your access code and reloads the settings screen.

8. **Choose the website property you want to add from the Google Analytics Account drop-down menu.**

   If you have more than one Google Analytics property in your account, all these properties appear in this drop-down menu. Choose the one that you want to associate with the site you're currently on.

9. **Click the Save Changes button at the bottom of the settings screen.**

   This action saves the configuration settings you made, and also inserts the correct JavaScript code into your website so that Google Analytics can start tracking your website stats.

Verifying that you installed the code properly

After you install your code, check whether you installed it correctly. When you log back in to Google Analytics, click the Data Streams link in the property you just set up. The Data Streams page reports back that Google is receiving data from your website, which means that the installation of your tracking ID was a success. (See Figure 1-6.)

Using the data from the plugin

After you install Google Site Kit plugin, you see a Site Kit Summary widget on your Dashboard when you visit the main Dashboard page (see Figure 1-7). On this widget you see a short summary of your visitor stats, including Total Impressions, Average Time on Page, Total Unique Visitors, and Total Clicks.

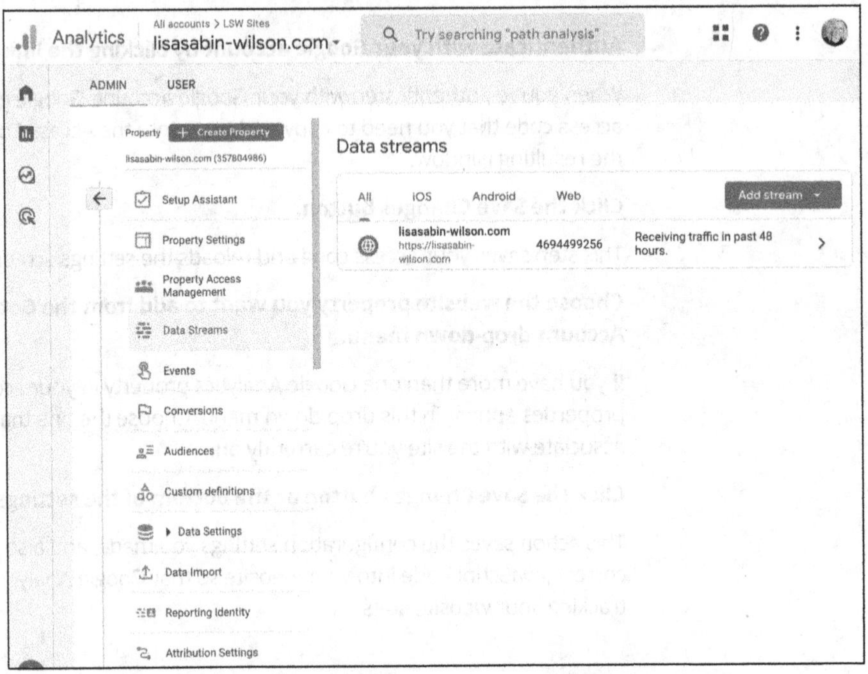

FIGURE 1-6: Tracking code is in place and collecting data.

FIGURE 1-7: The Google Site Kit Summary Dashboard widget.

When you click the Visit Your Site Kit Dashboard link, you are taken to the Site Kit page on your Dashboard, shown in Figure 1-8. This page shows a great deal more detail about the user statistics and analytics for your site, including:

- **Find Out How Your Audience Is Growing:** This section includes numbers and graphics that show you data on all users on your site, including where they come from (search, social media, and so on), their location, and the devices they are using (desktop, mobile, and so on).
- **Search Traffic Over the Last 28 Days:** This section includes traffic for the past 28 days and includes information like Total Impressions, Total Clicks, and Unique Visitors From Search engines.
- **See how your content is doing:** This section gives you information on the top search queries for your site — what your users are searching for when they found your website. This section also includes how well individual posts are doing and what your top posts are for the past 28 days, including reports on pageviews, sessions, engagement rate, and session duration. This section is not seen in Figure 1-8; you need to scroll down to see it in your browser.

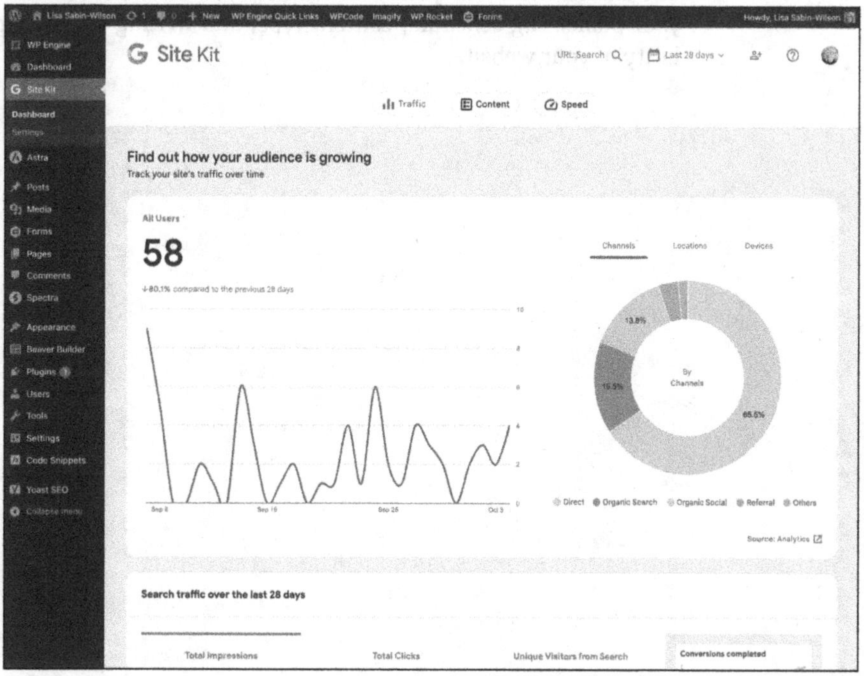

FIGURE 1-8: The Google Site Kit page on the WordPress Dashboard.

- **How visitors are experiencing your site:** This section of the Site Kit page helps you keep track of how fast your visitor is able to open your site, and gives you helpful recommendations for improving the overall performance of your website in terms of page speed. This section is not seen in Figure 1-8; you need to scroll down to see it in your browser.

By examining all of these data sets, you can get a handle on the traffic that's coming to your blog. Pay attention to the data, and use it to answer the following questions:

- What posts are most popular?
- Do the popular posts have a unique theme or type?
- Do long posts or short posts help increase traffic?
- Are you getting more traffic on desktop or mobile devices?
- Do videos, lists, or any other specific types of posts give you more traffic than the rest?

The answers to these questions can help you draw various conclusions and adapt your publishing schedule, content type, and writing style to optimize the popularity of your website.

IN THIS CHAPTER

» Understanding why you need to monitor your brand

» Finding out which monitoring tools are right for you

» Cleaning and aggregating your monitoring data

» Turning your WordPress Dashboard into a listening post

Chapter 2
Monitoring Your Brand on the WordPress Dashboard

This chapter focuses on the importance of listening to social media, using the free monitoring services available to you, and integrating these sources into your WordPress installation so that you can turn your run-of-the-mill WordPress installation into a social media listening hub.

A *social media listening hub* is a collection of information from several sources, including mentions of your site, keywords, topics that you write about, and even information about competitors. You can sign up for paid services that monitor these topics, such as Brand24 (`https://brand24.com`) and Hootsuite (`https://www.hootsuite.com`). But most of these services cost money and give you another place to log in to, and you may not use these kinds of services to their full capacity. For a small business or an independent site owner, the investment (both time and financial) doesn't always make sense. By leveraging the power of the WordPress platform, you can easily cut down on both the time and financial commitment of monitoring platforms.

In this chapter, I walk you through determining what sources you should pull your data from, determining and searching for the keywords you deem important, and integrating your search results into your WordPress Dashboard. Additionally, I look at some other tools that can help you expand your monitoring practices.

Exploring Reasons for a Social Media Listening Hub

When you begin to engage in the world of social media, one of the most important things you can do is monitor what Internet users are saying about your company, your site, you, or your products. By investigating what Internet users are saying, you can find and participate in discussions about your site or company and come to an understanding about the way your community views your site (or brand). With this information, you can participate by responding to comments on other sites, like Twitter or Facebook Groups, or by creating targeted content on your own site.

The conversations happening about your area of interest or niche amount to really great intelligence. For a business, regardless of whether you participate in social media, social media users are talking about your company, so you need to be aware of what they're saying. If you're blogging about a particular topic, you can evolve your content by tracking what members of your niche are saying about it.

Eavesdropping on yourself

By monitoring your niche, or your industry, you can eavesdrop on thousands of conversations daily and then choose those in which you want to participate. The social media listening hub you create allows you to follow various conversations going on through microblogging services such as Twitter, Facebook, blogs, news sites, Reddit, and even comments on YouTube. If someone says something negative about you, you can respond quickly to fix the situation. You can attempt to step in and make sure that people are informed about what you're doing.

Keeping tabs on your brand

Think about what keywords or phrases you want to monitor. You want to monitor your name and your blog/company name, of course, as well as other keywords that are directly associated with you.

TIP

Monitor common misspellings and permutations of the name of your brand. The Microsoft Keyword Planner tool (`https://about.ads.microsoft.com/en-us/solutions/tools/keyword-planner`) can help you determine all the common spellings and uses of the keywords you're monitoring. You can also find common misspellings for your brand by examining some of the terms people used to find your page with Google Analytics (`https://marketingplatform.google.com/about/analytics`; see Book 5, Chapter 1) or a paid tool such as Trellian Keyword Discovery Tool (`https://www.keyworddiscovery.com/search.html`).

If New York Jets quarterback Aaron Rodgers wanted to set up a monitoring service, for example, he might use the keywords *Aaron Rodgers, Arron Rodgers, Aaron Rogers, Former Green Bay Packers Quarterback, New York Jets Quarterback*, and perhaps even the phrase associated with his touchdown celebration: *discount double check.* If he wanted to expand this service past direct mentions of him or his team, he could also include more general terms such as *NFL Football* or even *NFC Teams.* The general term *NFL Football* may be *too* general, though, producing too many results to monitor.

Additionally, you may want to view your site or company through the lens of your customers. What terms do they associate with your company? Looking at your site from other points of view can provide good ideas for keywords, but not always. Although you don't always want your company to be known for these terms and may not see yourself that way, getting the perspective of other people can open your eyes to how users view your website.

Don't think of this process as just pulling in keywords, either. You can pull in multiple feeds, just as you do with an RSS reader, which allows you to monitor specific sites. So if you concentrate on an industry, and a website deals specifically with your industry and has an active news flow pushed through an RSS feed, you may want to consider adding specific websites to the mix of feeds you run through WordPress.

The setup in WordPress that I describe in this chapter gives you the convenience of having everything in one place and can help you monitor your brand, company, or website. If you own a restaurant, hotel, or bar and want to pick up review sites such as Yelp and TripAdvisor, these tools can't do the job. Most social media monitoring tools don't count review sites as social media.

REMEMBER

When your content changes, be sure to change what keywords and content you're monitoring to match the evolution of what you're writing about.

Exploring Different Listening Tools

You can find tons of monitoring and listening tools that oversee the social media space. If you work for a large company, you can use large, paid tools such as Alterian (`https://www.alterian.com`), and Khoros (`https://khoros.com`). Pricing for these tools runs from a few hundred dollars to tens of thousands per month. Most individuals and small businesses can't make that investment. If you're one of the smaller guys, you can create your own monitoring service right in WordPress by importing free monitoring tools onto your Dashboard to create a social media listening hub.

Some monitoring tools pick up site coverage, Twitter remarks, and forum comments. Other tools pick up content created with video and pictures. Try the monitoring services mentioned in the following sections, and determine which give you the best results and which make you feel the most comfortable. Then choose the best tools to create a good monitoring mix. One solution probably can't cover everything, so experiment with different combinations of tools.

TIP

Most, but not all, of these tools use Boolean search methods, so you need to understand how to narrow your searches. If you want to combine terms, put AND between two items (*cake AND pie*). If you use OR, you can broaden your search, such as to track common misspellings (*MacDonalds OR McDonalds*). Finally, if you want to exclude terms, you can use the NOT operator to exclude items from your search. Use NOT if you want to search for a term that could have an alternative meaning that's irrelevant to what you're actually looking for (*Afghan NOT blanket*, for example, if you're writing about Afghanistan).

Although some of the monitoring tools in the following sections don't apply to every type of website, I'd include them in most monitoring setups.

For each search that you do on a monitoring service, you need to log the feed address. To make recording these addresses easy, open a spreadsheet or a document into which you can paste the various feeds. You can collect them in one place before you begin to splice them together (which you do in the "Creating Your Own Personal Monitoring Mix" section, later in this chapter). Think of this document as a holding area.

Monitoring with Google Alerts

Most social media experts consider Google Alerts (`https://www.google.com/alerts`) to be a must-use monitoring source for anyone dabbling in social media. Google Alerts allows you to set up monitoring on news sites, blogs, pictures, videos, and groups. You can toggle the number of results you see, from 20 to 50, and you can choose how often they come in (in real time, daily, or weekly). You can also have Google deliver your alerts to your email or via RSS.

Google Alerts isn't perfect, but it doesn't have many drawbacks. Some of the specialized searches (such as Boardreader, which targets message boards; see the "Searching communities with Boardreader" section, later in this chapter) pick up more in their areas of expertise than Google Alerts does, but in general and compared with other tools, Google Alerts covers the widest range of content.

You can easily set up Google Alerts by following these steps:

1. **Navigate to `https://www.google.com/alerts` in your web browser.**

   The Alerts page loads, welcoming you to the Google Alerts website.

2. **In the search text box, type the keyword or phrase that you want to monitor.**

   If you enter a phrase in which the words have to go in that particular order, put the phrase in quotation marks. For example, I would type "WordPress For Dummies" if I wanted to monitor mentions of my book.

3. **From the Show Options drop-down menu, choose the type of monitoring that you want to use.**

   The options send you different kinds of alerts:

   - *How Often:* Determine how often you'll receive these notices. Because you'll receive the updates via RSS and not email (which you set up in Step 4), you want the highest frequency possible, so choose the As-It-Happens option. Other options include a daily, weekly, and monthly digest.
   - *Sources:* Select the type of sources you want Google Alerts to search in (for example, news, blogs, video, the web, or books).
   - *Language:* Select the language you want Google Alerts to search.
   - *Region:* Select the region you want Google Alerts to search.
   - *How Many:* Select how many results you want to receive. If you choose As-It-Happens for How Often, for example, you receive items in real time, so you don't need to specify the number of items; choose Only the Best Results or All Results.

4. **Choose your delivery type from the Deliver To drop-down menu.**

   To make the delivery source an RSS feed, as opposed to an email, choose RSS Feed.

Monitoring Your Brand on the WordPress Dashboard

5. **Click the Create Alert button.**

   You see your Google Alert Management screen, where you can get the RSS feeds for all your Google Alerts.

6. **To get the URL of the RSS feed, right-click the RSS Feed icon to the right of the alert you created, and choose Copy Link Address from the shortcut menu that appears.**

7. **Paste the copied link location into a document in which you list all the feeds that you plan to aggregate later.**

8. **Repeat steps 2–7 for all the alerts you want to monitor.**

TIP

Before you start importing the feed into your WordPress Dashboard, you may want to receive the update via email for a few days to test the quality of the results you're getting. If your results aren't quite right, you can always narrow your search criteria. Doing this saves you the time of parsing all your RSS feeds, blending them, and then having to go back and edit everything because your RSS feeds are set up wrong. Using email as a test is a massive time-saver.

Tracking conversations on Twitter with RSS

Tracking mentions on Twitter (now known as X) via RSS is relatively simple. You just need to know what you're looking for and how to build the RSS links so you can monitor them. You can look for several items to monitor your brand and reputation via the Twitter social network, including the following:

- **Username:** Monitor when your Twitter name is mentioned and by whom.
- **Hashtags:** Monitor specific Twitter hashtags (such as #wordpress).
- **Keywords:** Monitor Twitter for a specific word.

The Twitter service itself doesn't make RSS feeds available for public consumption on the web, but a service called RSS.app will turn your Twitter links into RSS feeds. You can find this service by visiting RSS.app (`https://rss.app`), which offers a 7-day free trial and costs $8.32 per month thereafter, and allows you to create RSS feeds for a specific user or search term on Twitter. You can create those links on the RSS.app Dashboard. (See Figure 2-1.)

Following are examples of Twitter links that I created and was able to add to my RSS.app account and save as RSS links:

- Twitter RSS URL for the search for my Twitter username: `https://rssviewer.app/https%3A%2F%2Frss.app%2Ffeeds%2FIxdhJU4i7HfgEXLE.xml`

» Twitter RSS URL for the keywords *WordPress For Dummies*: `https://rssviewer.app/https%3A%2F%2Frss.app%2Ffeeds%2FBQCutgwp5gBwKNS5.xml`

» Twitter RSS URL for the hashtag #WordPress: `https://rssviewer.app/https%3A%2F%2Frss.app%2Ffeeds%2FejCkIc4nxJ7zZT3w.xml`

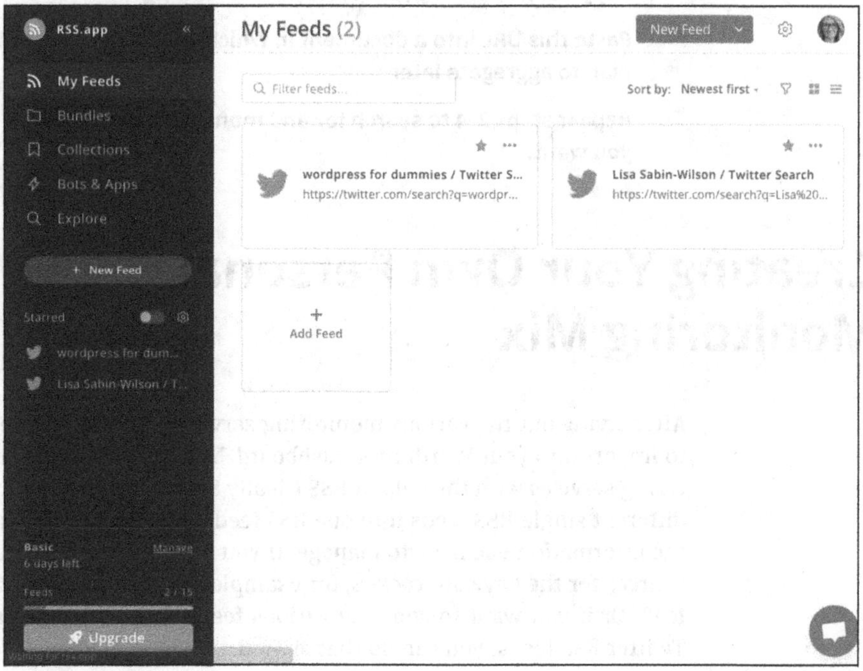

FIGURE 2-1: Feeds created in the RSS.app search service.

Build the Twitter RSS URLs that you want to monitor by copying the link provided by RSS.app (displayed in your browser's address bar) and including it in the document where you're listing all the RSS feeds you want to aggregate later.

Searching communities with Boardreader

Boardreader (`http://boardreader.com`) is a must-add tool because it focuses on groups and message boards, where conversations have been happening much longer than on Facebook and Twitter. Many other monitoring tools overlook these areas when talking about monitoring the web, but you can find many vibrant communities that are worth being part of, in addition to monitoring what's being said about your blog or company.

To set up your Boardreader tracking, follow these steps:

1. **Navigate to `http://boardreader.com`.**
2. **In the text box, type the search term that you want to monitor; then click the Search button.**
3. **Copy the URL from your browser's address bar.**
4. **Paste this URL into a document in which you list all the feeds that you plan to aggregate later.**
5. **Repeat steps 2-4 to search for and monitor as many search terms as you want.**

Creating Your Own Personal Monitoring Mix

After trying out the various monitoring services, you can create a mix of services to import into your WordPress Dashboard. You import the results of these monitoring services with the help of RSS (Really Simple Syndication). You can combine different single RSS feeds into one RSS feed and create an organized setup for all the information you have to manage. If you have various RSS feeds from different sources for the keyword *cookies*, for example, you can combine them into one RSS feed. Or if you want to combine various feeds based on sources such as all your Twitter RSS feeds, you can do that as well.

After you copy the locations for all your RSS feeds in one document, you need to group those RSS feeds. Grouping your RSS feeds keeps your monitoring system nice and tidy, and allows you to set up the WordPress Dashboard easily. After you group these feeds, you splice them together to make one master feed per grouping (see the following section). If you're tracking a variety of keywords, you may want to put your feeds into groups. Wendy's Restaurants, for example, could make these keyword groupings:

- **Grouping 1:** Your brand, products, and other information about your company
  - Wendy's (the company name)
  - Frosty (a prominent product name)
  - Wendy Thomas (a prominent person in the company)

- **Grouping 2:** Competitors
  - McDonald's
  - Burger King
  - In-N-Out Burger
- **Grouping 3:** Keyword-based searches (Burgers)
  - Hamburgers
  - Cheeseburgers
- **Grouping 4:** Keyword-based searches (Fast Food)
  - Fast food
  - Drive-through
- **Grouping 5:** Keyword-based searches (Chicken)
  - Chicken sandwiches
  - Chicken salad
  - Chicken nuggets

In each of these groups, you place your Google Alerts feed, RSS.app feed, and whatever other feeds you feel will provide information about that subject area. You can blend each group of feeds into one master feed for that group and bring them into WordPress.

REMEMBER

WordPress limits you to five groups of RSS feeds on the Dashboard. Any more than five groups slows the Dashboard and is more than WordPress can handle.

Grouping all your various feeds gives you the most complete monitoring solution by covering multiple monitoring tools and blending them. You get more coverage of your brand or blog than you would by using Google Alerts alone. On the downside, you may see some duplicates because of overlaps between the services.

If you feel overwhelmed by duplicate search results, you can blend one feed that covers only your brand, or you can simplify setting up your monitoring even more by keeping one feed for each item, as follows:

- **General overview:** Google Alerts or social mention
- **Message boards:** Boardreader
- **Microblogging:** Twitter search

Editing the Dashboard to Create a Listening Post

After you choose your data sources, clean up your feeds, and put them all in individual RSS feeds, you can finally bring them into WordPress and set up your social media listening hub.

You can bring these RSS feeds onto your Dashboard through a plugin called Dashboard Widgets Suite, which you can find in the WordPress Plugins page at `https://wordpress.org/plugins/dashboard-widgets-suite`.

Follow these steps to set up the Dashboard Widgets Suite plugin and configure it to create a social-listening Dashboard in WordPress:

1. **From the Plugins menu on the left side of your WordPress installation, choose Add New.**

   This step takes you to the form where you can search for new plugins.

2. **In the search text box, type Dashboard Widgets Suite; then click the Search Plugins button.**

   The search results page appears.

3. **Search for the Dashboard Widgets Suite plugin, and click the Install Now link, which installs the plugin on your site.**
4. **When the installation is complete, activate the plugin by clicking the Activate button on the Add Plugins screen that appears to the right of the Dashboard Widgets Suite plugin name.**
5. **Choose Dashboard Widgets from the Dashboard settings menu.**

   The Dashboard Widgets screen appears.

6. **Ensure that the Enable the Control Panel Widget check box is selected (as it should be by default).**
7. **Leave all the rest of the default settings in place, and click the Save Changes button.**
8. **Click the Widgets link on the Appearance menu.**

   The Widget settings page appears.

9. **Use the block inserter to add the blocks you want to show on your Dashboard.**

   In Figure 2-2, within the Widgets block on the top right of my Dashboard, you see that I added two RSS feed sections using the RSS block, each with their own title using the Header block.

10. **Configure the RSS widget to display information from your selected RSS.**

11. **Repeat steps 8-10 for the other widgets on your Dashboard by using your other selected feeds.**

    After you have your feeds set up, you can configure the appearance of your WordPress Dashboard.

12. **Drag and drop the new widget boxes where you want them on your Dashboard.**

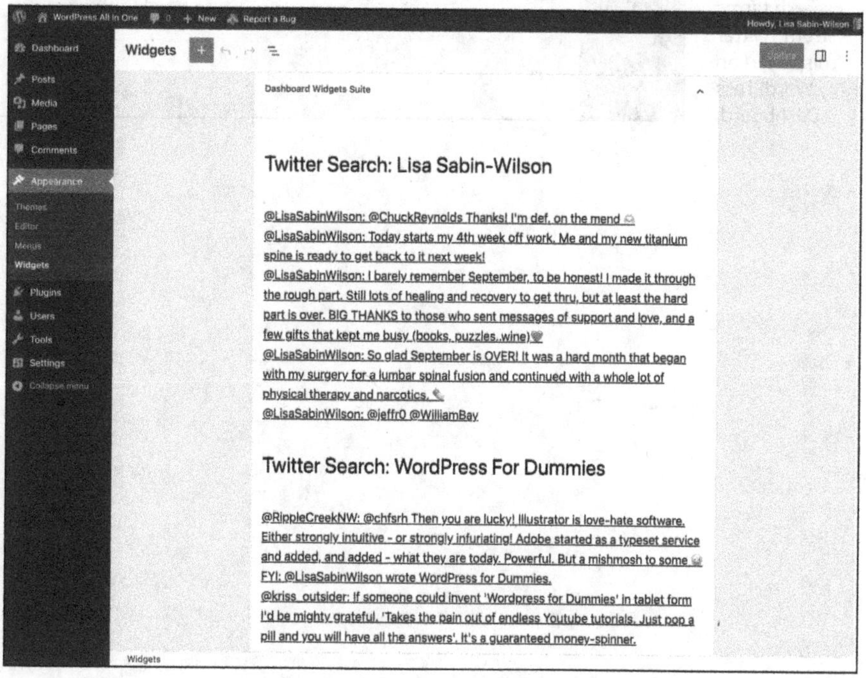

FIGURE 2-2: Configuring the Dashboard widget box.

Figure 2-3 displays my Dashboard with the RSS feeds from the search I found on RSS.app for my name: Lisa Sabin-Wilson, and for the term *WordPress For Dummies*. Now, whenever I log in to my WordPress site, I can see what's being said on Twitter about me or my book in real time.

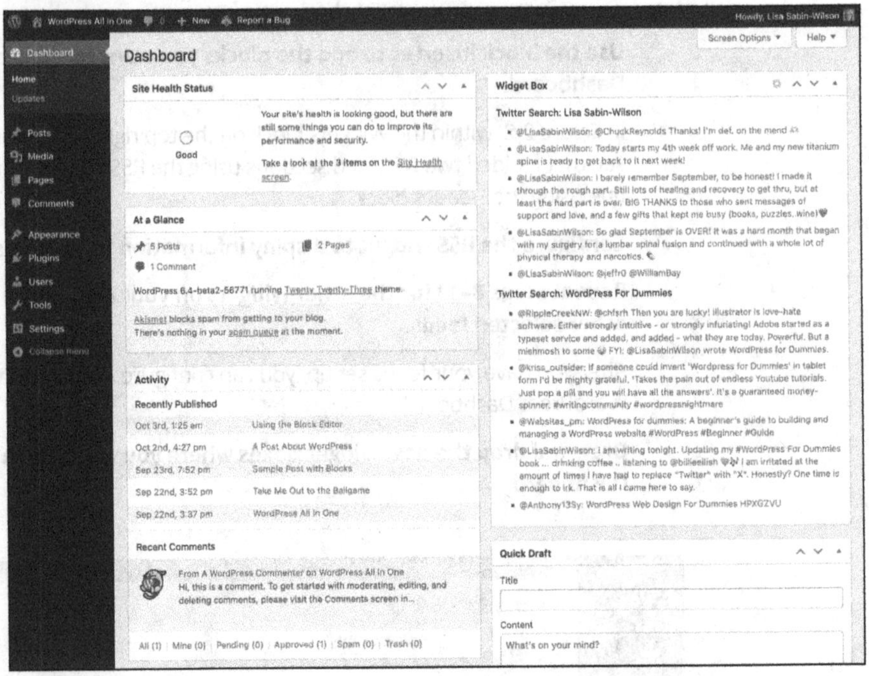

FIGURE 2-3: *Lisa Sabin-Wilson* and *WordPress For Dummies* search terms from Twitter displayed on my WordPress Dashboard.

IN THIS CHAPTER

» Understanding why SEO is important for your website

» Appreciating the advantages of using SEO with WordPress

» Getting your site into good SEO shape

» Finding information about your niche

» Creating SEO-improvement strategies

Chapter 3 Maximizing Your Site with Search Engine Optimization

Google, Yahoo!, Bing, and other search engines have a massive impact on a website. Search engines can easily refer the largest amount of traffic to your site and, if dealt with properly, can help you grow a large audience over time. Often, bloggers don't discover the importance of search engine optimization (SEO) until their sites have been around for a while. By taking the time to make sure that you're following SEO best practices from the get-go, you can reap the rewards of a consistent flow of search engine traffic.

If you've been publishing content on the web for a while and haven't been following the practices in this chapter, roll up your sleeves and dive back into your site to fix some of the SEO practices that you may have overlooked (or just didn't know about) over the history of your website. If you've been publishing content on your website for only a few months, this process doesn't take long. If you have a large backlog of content . . . well, pull up a chair; this fix is going to take a while. But don't worry; you're in safe hands. This chapter helps you through the difficult task of optimizing your site for search engines.

Understanding the Importance of Search Engine Optimization

Talk about SEO usually puts most people to sleep. I'm not going to lie: Hardcore SEO is a time-consuming job that requires a strong analytical mind. Casual bloggers and even most small-business owners don't need to understand all the minute details that go into SEO. Everyone with a website who desires traffic, however, needs to become familiar with some of the basic concepts and best practices. Why, you ask?

One thousand pageviews. That's why.

You're not going to get a thousand pageviews right off the bat by changing your SEO, of course. SEO deals with following best practices when it comes to writing content on the web. By following these simple guidelines and using WordPress, you can increase search engine traffic to your site. Period. To be honest, you probably won't rank number one in really tough categories just by following SEO best practices. But you definitely can increase your traffic significantly and improve your rank for some long-tail keywords. *Long-tail keywords* are keywords that aren't searched for often, but when you amass ranking for a lot of them over a period of time, the traffic adds up.

REMEMBER

You want as many search results as possible on the first two pages of Google and other search engines to be from your site(s). (Most search engine visitors don't go past the first two pages of Google.) This search-results aim is a more reasonable goal than trying to rank number one for a highly competitive keyword.

TIP

If you really do want to rank number one in a competitive space, check out sites such as SEOBook (`www.seobook.com`) and Moz (`https://moz.com`), which can help you achieve that difficult goal.

Outlining the Advantages That WordPress Presents for SEO

Using WordPress as your content management system comes with some advantages, including the fact that WordPress is designed to function well with search engines. Search engines can crawl the source code of a WordPress site pretty easily, which eliminates issues that a lot of web programmers face when optimizing a site. The following list outlines some of WordPress's SEO advantages:

- **Permalinks:** These are URLs where your content is permanently housed. As your site grows and you add more content, the items on your front page get pushed and replaced by more recent content. Visitors can easily bookmark and share permalinks so that they can return to a specific post on your site, so these old posts can live on. One of the technical benefits of WordPress is that it uses the Apache `mod_rewrite` module to establish the permalink system, which allows you to create and customize your permalink structure. (See Book 3, Chapter 2 for more information on custom permalinks.)
- **Pinging:** When you post new content, WordPress has a built-in pinging system that notifies major indexes automatically so that they can come crawl your site again. This system helps speed the indexing process and keeps your search results current and relevant.
- **Plugins:** The fact that WordPress is so developer-friendly allows you to use the latest SEO plugins. Do you want to submit a site map to Google? There's a plugin for that. Do you want to edit the metadata of a post? There's a plugin for that. As of this writing, more than 59,000 plugins are available in the WordPress Plugins repository, which means that you can use an advanced plugin ecosystem to help power your website. Book 5, Chapter 4 covers a few key plugins that can help you with SEO.
- **Theme construction:** SEO, social media, and design all work together. You can push a ton of people to your webpage by using proper SEO and robust social media profiles, but if your site has a confusing or poorly done design, visitors aren't going to stay. Likewise, a poorly designed site prevents a lot of search engines from reading your content.

  In this situation, *poorly designed* doesn't refer to aesthetics — how your site looks to the eye. Search engines ignore the style of your site and your CSS, for the most part. But the structure — the coding — of your site can affect search engines that are attempting to crawl your site. WordPress is designed to accommodate search engines: It doesn't overload pages with code, so that search engines can easily access the site. Most WordPress themes have *valid* code, which is code that's up to standards based on the recommendations of the World Wide Web Consortium, or W3C (`https://www.w3.org`). Right from the start, having valid code allows search engines to access your site much more easily.

REMEMBER

When you start changing your code or adding a lot of plugins to your site, check to see whether your code validates. *Validated* code means that the code on your website fits a minimum standard for browsers. Otherwise, you could be preventing search engines from easily crawling your site.

TIP

If you want to check out whether your site validates, use the free validator tool at `http://validator.w3.org`. (See Figure 3-1.)

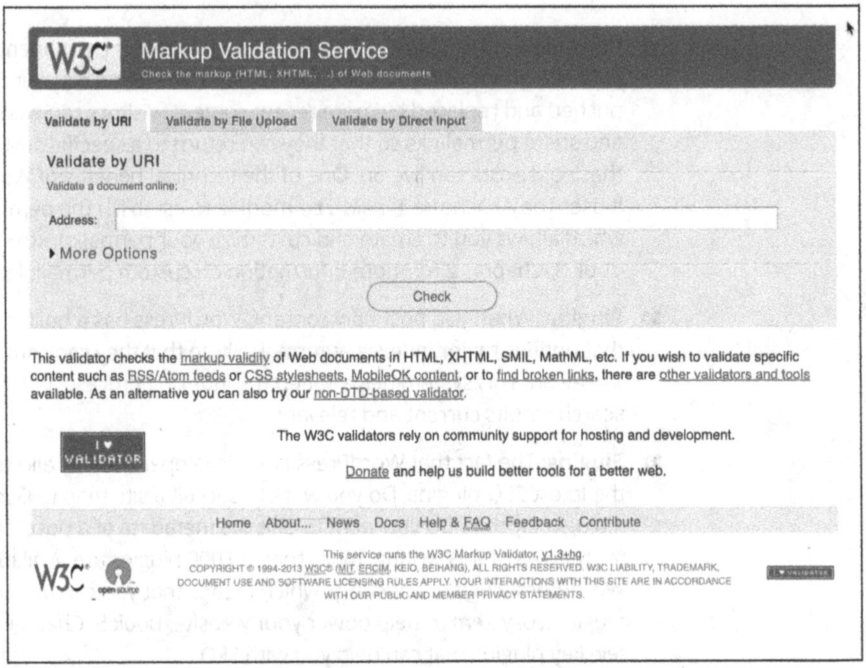

FIGURE 3-1: The W3C Markup Validation Service.

Understanding How Search Engines See Your Content

Search engines don't care what your site looks like because they can't see what your site looks like; their crawlers care only about the content. The crawlers care about the material on your site, the way it's titled, the words you use, and the way you structure those words.

You need to keep this focus in mind when you create the content of your site. Your URL structure and the keywords, post titles, and images you use in posts all have an effect on how your website ranks. Having a basic understanding of how search engines view your content can help you write content that's more attractive to search engines. Here are a few key areas to think about when you craft your content:

- **Keywords in content:** Search engines take a close look at the keywords or combination of keywords you use. Keywords are often compared with the words within links that guide people to the post and in the title of the post itself to see whether they match. The better these keywords align, the better ranking you get from the search engine.

» **Post title:** Search engines analyze the title of your post or page for keyword content. If you're targeting a specific keyword in your content, and that keyword is mentioned throughout the post, mention it in the post title as well. Also, both people and search engines place a lot of value on the early words of a title.

» **URL structure:** One of the coolest things about WordPress is the way it allows you to edit permalinks for a post or page. (See Figure 3-2.) You can always edit the URL to be slightly different from the automated post title so that it contains relevant keywords for search terms, especially if you write a cute title for the post.

  Suppose that you write a post about reviewing Facebook applications and title it "So Many Facebook Applications, So Little Time." You can change the URL structure to something much more keyword-based — perhaps something like `facebook-applications-review`. This reworking removes a lot of the fluff words from the URL and goes right after the keywords you want to target.

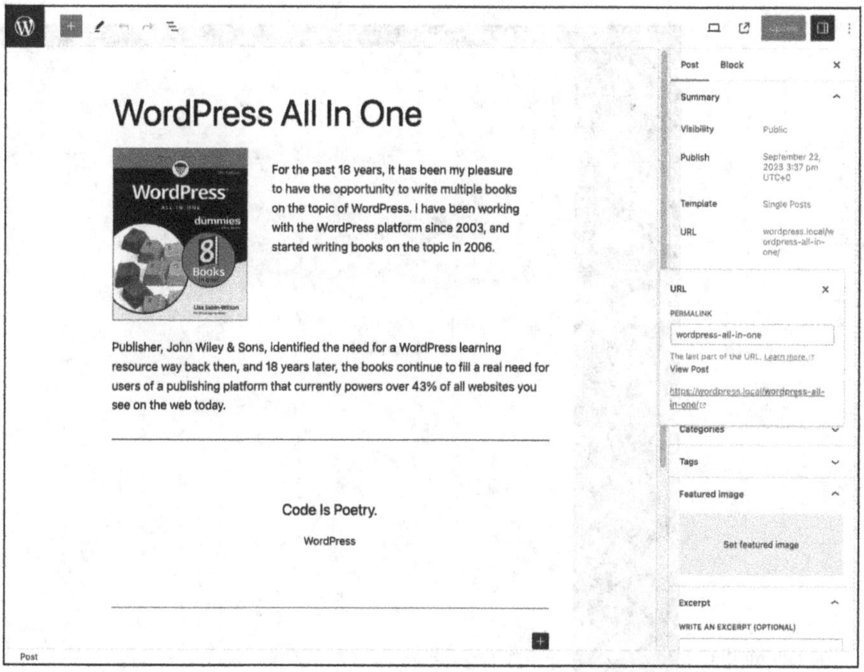

Post
Block
Summary
Visibility
Public
Publish
September 22, 2023 3:37 pm UTC+0
Template
Single Posts
URL
wordpress.local/wordpress-all-in-one/
WordPress All In One
For the past 18 years, it has been my pleasure to have the opportunity to write multiple books on the topic of WordPress. I have been working with the WordPress platform since 2003, and started writing books on the topic in 2006.
Publisher, John Wiley & Sons, identified the need for a WordPress learning resource way back then, and 18 years later, the books continue to fill a real need for users of a publishing platform that currently powers over 43% of all websites you see on the web today.
URL
PERMALINK
wordpress-all-in-one
The last part of the URL. Learn more.
View Post
https://wordpress.local/wordpress-all-in-one/
Categories
Tags
Featured image
Set featured image
Excerpt
WRITE AN EXCERPT (OPTIONAL)
Code Is Poetry.
WordPress
Post

FIGURE 3-2: The URL section of the Post settings panel allows you to edit the permalink of a post or page.

» **Image titles and other image information:** This item is probably the most-missed item when it comes to SEO. You need to fill out the image information for your posts in the Edit Media screen (see Figure 3-3), or in the settings panel for the Image block, if you are inserting an image using the block editor. This information is a powerful way for people to discover your content and is an additional piece of content that can tie keywords to your posts. This information includes the filename of your image. Saving an image file to your site as `DS-039`.jpg, for example, offers nothing for readers or search engines and thus has no value to search engines or for you because it doesn't contain a real keyword.

  For a picture with Facebook, for example, you can give it a title of `Facebook-application`.jpg to make it more understandable to search engines. Leverage the keyword title and *alt tags* (alternative text added to the image within the HTML markup that tells search engines what the picture is) because they provide extra content for the search engines to see, and using them can help you get a little more keyword saturation within your posts.

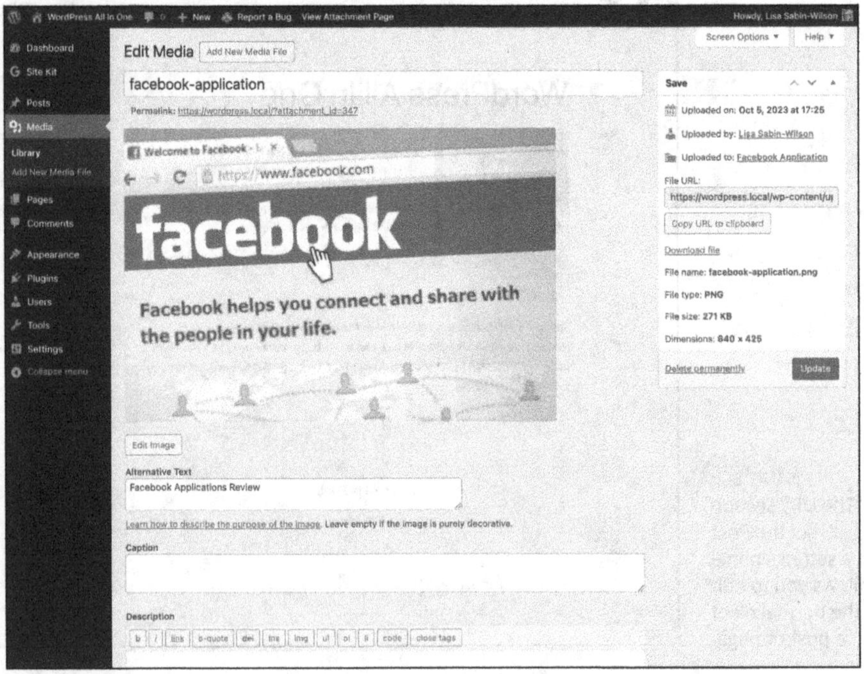

FIGURE 3-3: The Edit Media screen.

Using links as currency

If content is king, links are the currency that keeps the king in power. No matter how good a site you have, how great your content is, and how well you optimize that content, you need links. Search engines assess the links flowing into your site for number and quality, and they evaluate your website accordingly.

If a high-quality site that has high Google search rankings features a link to your page, search engines take notice and assume that you have some authority on a subject. Search engines consider these high-quality links to be more important than low-quality links. Having a good number of mid-quality links, however, can help as well. (This tactic, like many well-known approaches to improving site rank, is based only on trial and error. Google keeps its algorithm a secret, so no one knows for sure.)

Being included in a listing of links on a site, having a pingback or trackback when other authors mention your content in their posts, or even leaving a comment on someone's site can provide links back to your site. If you want to check out how many links you currently have coming to your site, go to Google, type **link:** `www.`*`yoursite`*`.com` in the search text box, and click Google Search. You can also search for competitors' sites to see where they're listed and to what sites they're linked.

Although you do need to try to get other sites to link to your site (called *outside links*) because outside links factor into search engine algorithms, you can help your own ranking by adding internal links. If you have an authoritative post or page on a particular subject, you should link internally to it within your site. Take `ESPN.com` (`http://www.espn.com`), for example. The first time this site mentions an athlete in a post, it links to the profile of that athlete on the site. It essentially tells the search engines each time they visit `ESPN.com` that the player profile has relevancy, and the search engine indexes it. If you repeatedly link some of your internal pages that are gaining page rank to a profile page over a period of time, that profile page is going to garner a higher search engine ranking (especially if external sites are linking to it, too).

This internal and external linking strategy uses the concept of pillar posts (authoritative or popular), in which you have a few pages of content that you consider to have high value and try to build external and internal links to that content so that you can get these posts ranked highly in search results.

Submitting to search engines and directories

After you get some content on your website (ten posts or so), submit your website to some search engines. Plenty of sites out there charge you to submit your site to search engines, but honestly, you can easily submit your site yourself. Also, with the help of some plugins (described in Book 5, Chapter 4), you can get your information to search engines even more easily than you may think.

After you submit your website or site map, a search engine reviews it for search engine crawling errors; if everything checks out, you're on your way to having your site crawled and indexed. This process — from the submission of your site through its first appearance in search engine results — can easily take 4 to 6 weeks, so be patient. Don't resubmit, and don't freak out that search engines are never going to list your site. Give the process time.

Not to be confused with search engines are website and blog directories. Directories can lead to a small amount of traffic, and some directories, such as Best of the Web (`https://botw.org`) or About Us (`https://aboutus.com`), actually supply information to search engines and other directories. The main benefit of getting listed in directories isn't really traffic, but the number of *backlinks* (links to your site from other websites) that you can build into your site. Another real benefit from being listed in directories is reputation and trust — so make sure the directories you are listing your website on are reputable and legitimate.

TIP

Although submitting your site to directories may not be as important as submitting to search engines, you may still want to do it. Because filling out 40 or more forms is pretty monotonous, create a single document in which you prewrite all the necessary information: site title, URL, description, contact information, and your registration information. This template helps speed the submission process to multiple sites.

Optimizing Your Site under the Hood

Some optimization concepts happen "under the hood": You can't readily see these adjustments on your page, but they have an effect on how search engines deal with your content.

Metadata

The metadata on a website contains the information that describes to search engines what your site is about. Additionally, the information often contained in the metadata shows up as the actual search engine results in Google. The search engine pulls the page title and page description that appear in search results from the header of your site. If you do nothing to control this information, Google and other search engines often pull their description from the page title and the first few sentences of a post or page.

Although the title and the first few sentences sound good in principle, they may not represent what your site is actually about. You probably don't sum up your topic in the first two sentences of a post or page. Those first few lines likely aren't the best ad copy or the most enticing information. Fortunately, some plugins (such as the Yoast SEO plugin, which is on the WordPress Plugins page at `https://wordpress.org/plugins/wordpress-seo`), allow you to control these details on a post and page level. (See Book 5, Chapter 4 for more about the Yoast plugin.)

Include descriptive page titles, descriptions, and targeted keywords for each post via these plugins or frameworks. This information has an effect on your results and often helps people decide whether to click the link to your website.

The `robots.txt` file

When a search engine goes to your website, it first looks at your `robots.txt` file to get the information about what it should and shouldn't be looking for and where to look.

You can alter your `robots.txt` file to direct search engines to the information that they should crawl and to give specific content priority over other content. Several plugins allow you to configure your `robots.txt` file.

TIP

For easy way to view and edit the contents of the `robots.txt` file for your WordPress website, check out the WP Robots Txt plugin (`https://wordpress.org/plugins/wp-robots-txt`). This plugin adds additional fields in the Reading Settings page on your Dashboard that enable you to edit the content of the file.

Researching Your Niche

When you're working to improve your SEO, you can use a lot of publicly available data. This data can help you determine where you should try to get links and what type of content you may want to target. These two sites can help you get a general picture of the niche you're working in:

- **Google (`https://www.google.com`):** You can find what types of links are flowing into a website by typing **link:** `www.yoursite.com` in the Google search text box and clicking Google Search. (Replace *yoursite.com* with the domain you want to target.) Google gives you a list of the sites linking to your site. By doing this search for other websites in your niche, you can find out the sources of their links — industry-specific directories you may not know about, places where they've guest-authored, and other resource sites that you may be able to get listed on.

This data gives you information about what to target for a link-building campaign.

- **Semrush (`https://www.semrush.com`):** Semrush (see Figure 3-4) offers both paid and free versions, and spending a few dollars for a month's access to the light version of the product can be a good investment. (The free version lets you look up only ten results at a time.) Semrush allows you to see the terms for which other websites rank. Use this information to judge the health of the competitor's domain, the number of terms for which it ranks in Google's top 20, and the terms themselves.

  You can use this information in a lot of ways. You can see what terms you may want to work into your content, for example. Semrush provides not only information about what terms search engines use to rank these sites, but also information about how competitive your site's keywords are with the same keywords on other websites.

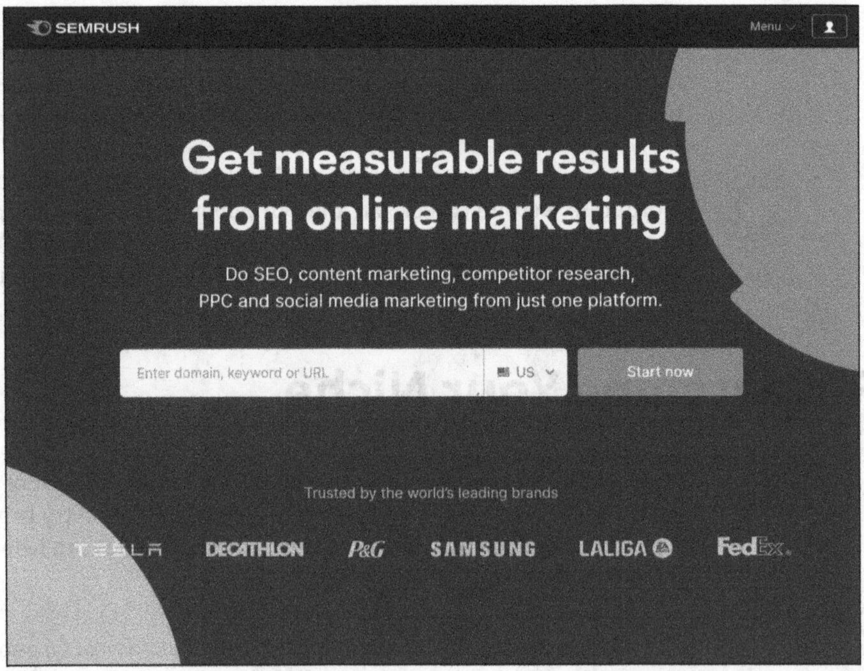

FIGURE 3-4: Semrush helps you evaluate your competition.

Creating Search Engine Strategies

You can use the techniques discussed in previous sections of this chapter when you set up your site, write strategic content, and begin to build links into your website. The next section deals with setting up your website so that it's optimized for search engines.

Setting up your site

When setting up your site, you're going to want to follow some best practices to make sure that your site is optimized for search engines. Following are some of these best practices:

» **Permalinks:** First, set up your permalink structure. Log in to your WordPress account, and on the sidebar, select Permalinks in the Settings section. The Permalink Settings page appears. (See Figure 3-5.) Select the Post Name radio button.

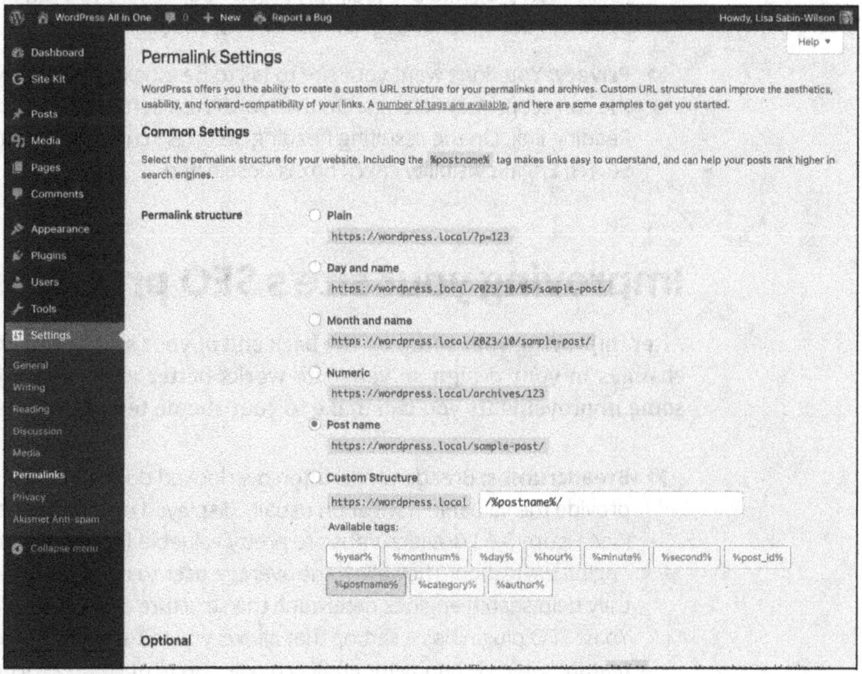

FIGURE 3-5: The WordPress Permalink Settings page.

Making this change gives you a URL that contains just your domain and the title of your post. If you use a focused category structure in which you've carefully picked out keywords, you may want to add the category to the URL. In that case, you enter ***/%category%/%postname%/*** in the text box.

WARNING

Avoid using the default URL structure, which includes just the number of your post, and don't use dates in the URL. These numbers have no real value when doing SEO. WordPress by default numbers all your posts and pages with specific ID numbers. If you haven't set up a custom permalink structure in WordPress, permalinks for your posts end up looking something like this: `http://`*`yourdomain`*`.com/?p=12` (where 12 is the specific post ID number). Although these numbers are used for many WordPress features, including exclusions of data and customized RSS feeds, you don't want these numbers in your URLs because they don't contain any keywords that describe the post.

Also, if you already have an established site and are just now setting up these permalinks, you must take the time to install a redirection plugin. You can find several of these plugins available in the Plugin Directory on `WordPress.org` (`https://wordpress.org/plugins/`). You must establish redirection for your older content so that you don't lose the links that search engines, such as Google and Yahoo!, have already indexed for your site. One good redirection plugin to use is simply called Redirection; you can find it at `https://wordpress.org/plugins/redirection`.

- **Privacy:** You don't want your site to fail to be indexed because you didn't set the correct privacy settings. On the WordPress Settings menu, click the Reading link. On the resulting Reading Settings screen, make sure that the Search Engine Visibility check box is deselected.

Improving your site's SEO practices

After improving your setup on the back end of your site, you'll want to make some changes in your design so your site works better with search engines. Here are some improvements you can make to your theme templates:

- **Breadcrumbs:** Breadcrumbs, often overlooked during website creation, provide the valuable navigation usually displayed on a page above the title. (See Figure 3-6.) Breadcrumbs are pretty valuable for usability and search engine navigation. They allow the average user to navigate the site easily, and they help search engines determine the structure and layout of your site. The Yoast SEO plugin has a setting that allows you to turn on the breadcrumbs feature, which is handy for an SEO plugin. Go to `https://wordpress.org/plugins/wordpress-seo`.

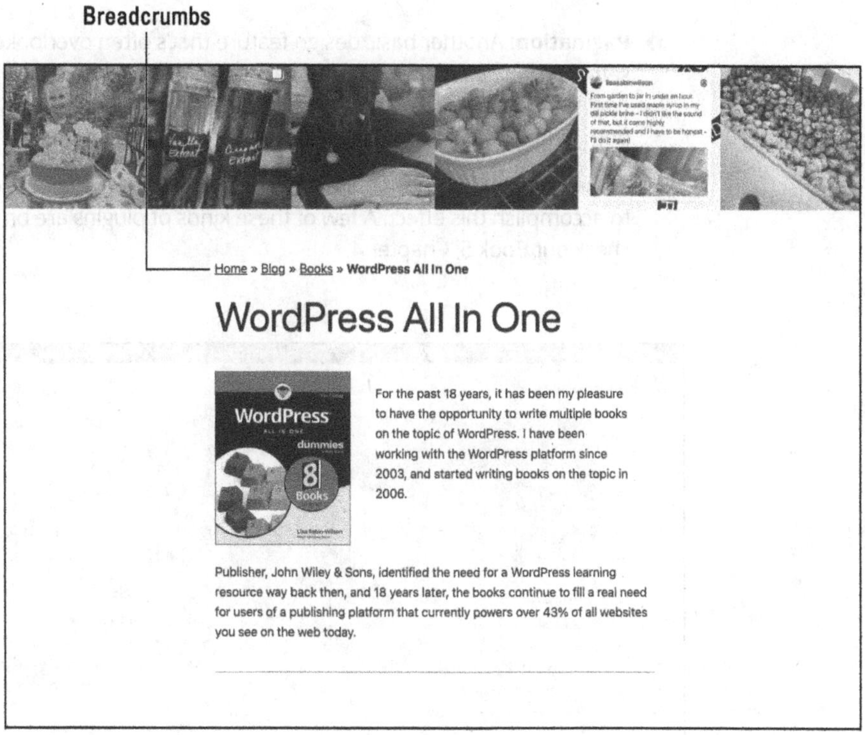
Breadcrumbs
Home » Blog » Books » WordPress All In One
WordPress All In One
For the past 18 years, it has been my pleasure to have the opportunity to write multiple books on the topic of WordPress. I have been working with the WordPress platform since 2003, and started writing books on the topic in 2006.
Publisher, John Wiley & Sons, identified the need for a WordPress learning resource way back then, and 18 years later, the books continue to fill a real need for users of a publishing platform that currently powers over 43% of all websites you see on the web today.

FIGURE 3-6: Users and search engines can follow the breadcrumbs.

- **Validated code and speed:** If you're not a professional web designer, you probably don't do a lot of coding on your site. But if you make some small edits to your WordPress installation or add a lot of code through widgets, do it properly by putting it directly in your CSS rather than coding into your site. Coding these features properly helps improve the speed of your site and the way search engines crawl it. Check out Book 6 for more information about coding the templates in your theme.

  When it comes to improving site speed, proper code has a lot to do with performance. You can take other steps to help improve the speed of your site, such as installing caching plugins, including the W3 Total Cache plugin (`https://wordpress.org/plugins/w3-total-cache`). The quality of your hosting (see Book 2, Chapter 1), the size of your image files (make sure that you set image-file quality to web standards), the number of images you're using, and third-party widgets or scripts (such as installing a widget provided by Twitter or Facebook) can all affect the speed and performance of your site.

- **Pagination:** Another basic design feature that's often overlooked during site setup, *pagination* creates bottom navigation that allows people and search engines to navigate to other pages. (See Figure 3-7.) Pagination can really help both people and search engines navigate your category pages.

  Some themes don't have built-in pagination, so you may need to add a plugin to accomplish this effect. A few of these kinds of plugins are on the market; check out Book 5, Chapter 4.

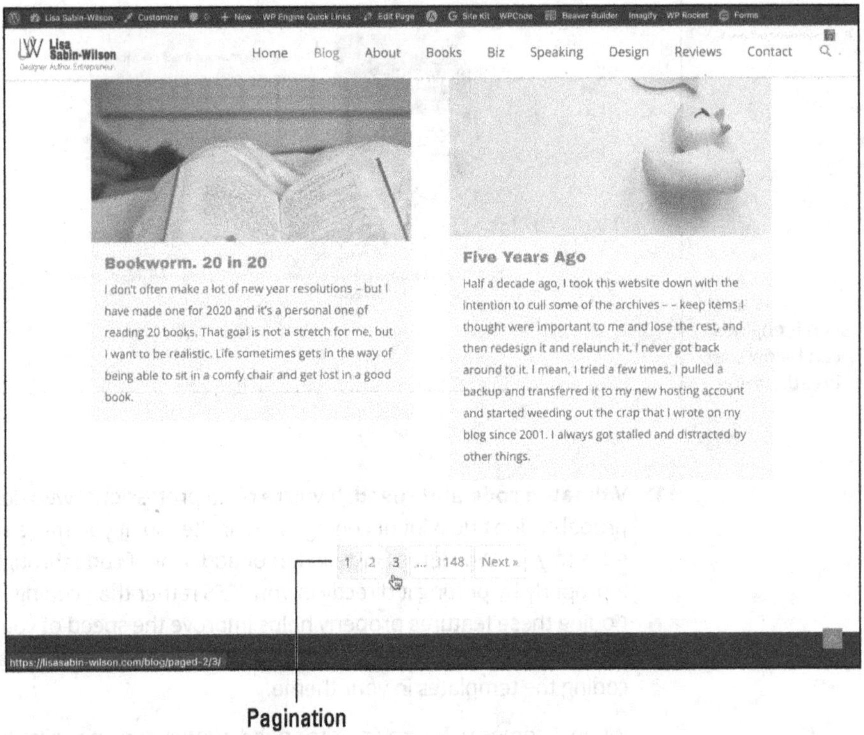

FIGURE 3-7: Pagination in action.

REMEMBER

Links pass on authority. When you link to a site or a site links to you, the link is saying that your site has value for the keyword in the link. So evaluate the links that you have, and think about whether you really want to link to those websites.

Dealing with duplicate content

WordPress does have one major problem when it comes to SEO: It creates so many places for your content to live that duplicate content can confuse search engines. Fortunately, plugins and some basic editing easily take care of these issues. Here's what to do:

- **Take care of your archive page on your site.** This page displays archives such as category, date-based archives, and so on. You don't want your archive page to present full posts — only truncated versions (short excerpts) of your posts. Check your theme to see how your archive is presented. If your archive shows complete posts, see whether your theme has instructions about how to change your archive presentation. (Each theme is unique, but check out the information in Book 6; it's full of great information on using the site editor to create unique layouts for archive pages.)
- **Make sure that search engines aren't indexing all your archives by using a robots plugin.** You want robots going through only your category archive, not the author index and other archives.

Creating an editorial SEO list/calendar

Planning your posts from now until the end of time can take some of the fun out of publishing. Still, it doesn't hurt to create a list of keywords that your competitors rank for importance and some of the content they've discussed. Take that list and apply it to new posts, or write *evergreen content* (topics that aren't time-sensitive) centered on what you want to say. Planning your content can really help in figuring out what keywords you want to target when you want to write content to improve the ranking of targeted keywords.

TIP

If you feel that your site content is more oriented toward news or current events, create a reference list of keywords to incorporate into your newer posts so that you can rank for these targeted terms.

Establishing a routine for publishing on your site

Although you can't really call this high strategy, getting into the habit of posting content regularly on your site helps you get the basics down. Here are some things to keep in mind:

- **Properly title your post.** Make sure that your post includes the keyword or phrase for which you're trying to rank.
- **Fix your URL.** Remove stop words or useless words from your URL, and make sure that the keywords you want to target appear in the URL of your post. *Stop words* are filler words such as *a*, *so*, *in*, and *an*. For a comprehensive list of stop words, check out `https://www.link-assistant.com/seo-stop-words.html`.

» **Choose a category.** Make sure that you have your categories set up and that you place your posts in the proper categories. Whatever you do, don't use the uncategorized category; it brings no SEO value to the table.

» **Fill out metadata.** If you're using a theme framework, the form for metadata often appears right below the post box. If you aren't using a theme framework, you can use the Yoast SEO plugin (`https://wordpress.org/plugins/wordpress-seo`); see Figure 3-8. When activated, this plugin usually appears toward the bottom of your posting page. Make sure that you completely fill out the title, description, keywords, and other information that the plugin or theme framework asks for.

» **Tag posts properly.** You may want to get into the habit of taking the keywords from the Yoast SEO plugin and pasting them into the tags section of the post.

» **Fill out image info.** Take the time to completely fill out your image info whenever you upload pictures to your posts. Every time you upload an image to WordPress, you see a screen in which you can fill in the URL slug, description, and alt text for the image you've uploaded.

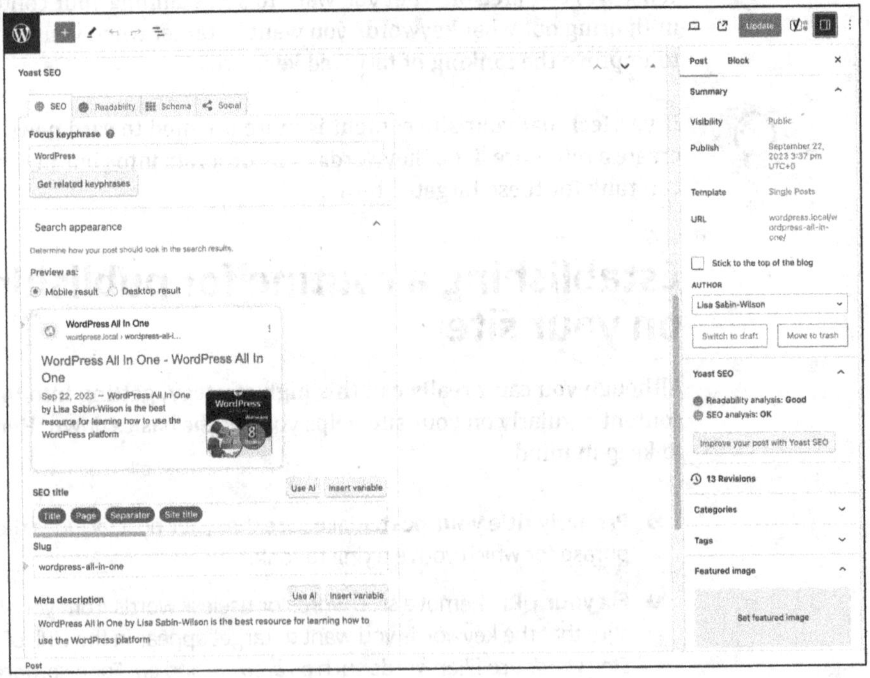

FIGURE 3-8: The Yoast SEO metadata form.

Creating a link-building strategy

In previous sections of this chapter, I tackle most of the onsite SEO strategy and concepts. In this section, I explain how you can start working on your off-page strategy. Here are some things to keep in mind:

- **Fill out your social media profiles.** As I discuss in Book 5, Chapter 2, a lot of social media sites pass on page rank through their profiles. Take the time to fill out your social media profile properly, and list your site in these profiles.

  Social media sites allow you to link to your site with a descriptive word. Industry professionals say that this link has value to search engines, which is debatable, but adding it can never hurt.
- **Use forum signatures.** If you participate in forums, you can easily generate traffic and earn some links to your website from other websites by including your site URL in your forum signature.
- **Examine your competitor's links.** See where your competitors or other people in your niche are getting links — such as directories, lists, guest blogs, and friends' sites — and then try to get links on those sites. Try to determine the relationships, and figure out whether you can establish a relationship with those sites as well.
- **Guest-author.** Find some of the top sites in your niche and then ask them whether you can guest-author. Guest-authoring gives you a link from a respected source and builds a relationship with other content creators. Also, guest-authoring can't hurt your subscriber numbers; often, you see a bump after you guest-author on a large site.
- **Use website directory registration.** Directory registration, albeit a time-consuming affair, can often provide a large number of backlinks to your site from respected sources.
- **Comment on other sites.** A lot of sites pass on page rank because the links in their comment section are live. Make sure that when you engage other people, you properly fill out your information before you post, including the URL to your site. Don't start posting inane comments on random sites to get links. Doing so is considered rude and can lead to your site being marked as spam in various commenting systems.
- **Participate in social sharing.** Getting involved in Reddit, Facebook, Twitter, and other social communities allows you to participate in social media with people who have similar interests. You can build links to your site by submitting content to social news and community sites.

IN THIS CHAPTER

» Using plugins for SEO best practices

» Automating SEO tasks with the Yoast SEO plugin

» Generating site maps with the XML Sitemap Generator for Google plugin

» Redirecting traffic to your site with the Redirection plugin

» Optimizing page performance with the WP-Optimize plugin

Chapter 4
Exploring Popular SEO Plugins

When you have the concepts of search engine optimization (SEO) down and the beginnings of your strategy properly mapped out, you can install the tools you need. In this chapter, I go through some of the most popular SEO-related plugins. All of these plugins have good developers behind them and good track records.

Several plugins in the WordPress Plugins page (`https://wordpress.org/plugins/`) assist with SEO, so it's hard to decide which ones to use. In Book 7, I cover plugins in detail, but in this chapter, I discuss the most common plugins, as well as the ones that I use myself, because they're solid, reliable plugins that deliver good SEO results.

Exploring Must-Use Plugins for SEO Best Practices

Here are the plugins that I cover in this chapter:

- **Yoast SEO:** Gives you complete control of the search engine optimization of your site.
- **XML Sitemap Generator for Google:** Generates an XML site map that's sent to Google, Yahoo!, Bing, and `Ask.com`. When your site has a site map, site crawlers can more efficiently crawl your site. One of the bonuses of the site map is that it notifies search engines every time you post.
- **Redirection:** Helps when you move from an old site to WordPress or when you want to change the URL structure of an established site. It allows you to manage 301 redirections (when the web address of a page has changed, a 301 redirect tells search engines where they can find the new web address of the page); track any 404 errors (errors that are displayed when you try to load a page that doesn't exist) that occur on the site; and manage any possible incorrect web address (URL) issues with your website.
- **WP-Optimize:** Helps you improve the performance of your website by optimizing your website for size, speed, and performance.

TIP

Check out Book 7, Chapter 2 for information on plugin installation.

Yoast SEO

The Yoast SEO plugin (`https://wordpress.org/plugins/wordpress-seo`) makes your life much easier because it automates many SEO tasks for you. Of all the plugins I cover, this one is an absolute must for your site. It gives you a lot of control of your SEO, and it's very flexible.

The Yoast SEO plugin breaks down each option on the configuration page, which allows you to preselect options right off the bat or make some changes to the plugin.

After you install this plugin, click the SEO link on the Dashboard to open the General - Yoast SEO page. (See Figure 4-1.)

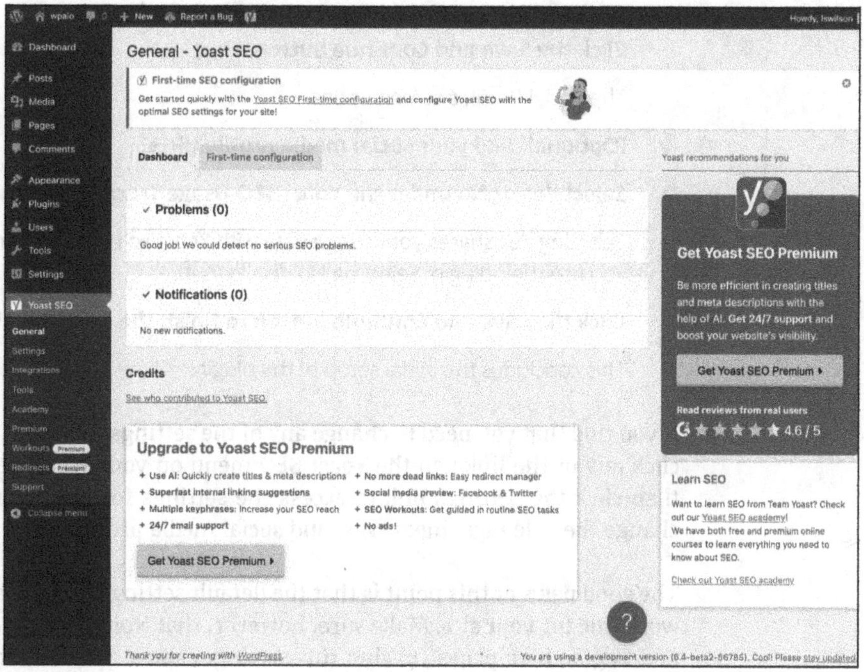

FIGURE 4-1: The General - Yoast SEO page on the WordPress Dashboard.

Click the General tab and follow these steps:

1. **Click the Yoast First-Time Configuration tab.**

   This step opens the First-Time Configuration section and starts the configuration process.

2. **Click the Continue button in the SEO Data Optimization section.**

   This step takes you to the next section of the Yoast SEO for WordPress configuration and opens the Site Representation screen, where you fill out the following:

   - *Does your site represent an Organization or a Person?* Select either Organization or Person from the drop-down menu provided. This data is shown as metadata on your site and is intended to appear in Google's Knowledge Graph, a knowledge base that Google uses to enhance its search results. Your site can be a company or a person.
   - *Website name:* Type the name of your website in the field provided.
   - *Name:* Type your name in the field provided.
   - *Personal logo or avatar:* Upload an image to use as your personal avatar or logo for your website.

3. **Click the Save and Continue button.**

   The Social Profiles screen opens.

4. **(Optional) Add your social media profile URLs.**

5. **Select Yes or No under the Yoast SEO Usage Tracking heading.**

   Selecting Yes shares your usage data with Yoast so they can learn about how you use their plugin. Selecting No disallows it.

6. **Click the Save and Continue button to finish the configuration.**

   This concludes the initial setup of the plugin.

If you find that you need to change any of the settings in the configuration wizard, click any of the links on the Yoast SEO menu on your WordPress Dashboard and then click the Settings link to access the settings for the plugin, where you can change the title tags, meta tags, and social media profile URLs.

The good news at this point is that the default settings that are selected by default work fine for your site. Make sure, however, that Noindex is selected for Category and Tag archive pages (to find this setting, choose SEO ⇨ Settings ⇨ Categories & Tags). This ensures that that the search engines aren't indexing your archive pages by deselecting the Show Categories in Search Results feature on the Categories page, and again on the Tags page. Indexing archive pages would provide the search engines duplicate content — one of the top ways of getting penalized by Google, which means that you run the risk of having your site removed from Google's search engine results.

REMEMBER

If you change any of the settings, remember to click the Save Changes button at the bottom of any of the Yoast SEO settings pages to save any changes.

TIP

You can use the Yoast SEO plugin without changing any of the default options. If you aren't confident about fine-tuning it, you don't have to. But don't forget to put in the proper information for your home page, including title, description, and keywords.

The Yoast SEO plugin also gives you full control of SEO settings for each individual page and post on your site by allowing you to configure the following for pages, posts, and any custom post types:

- Facebook and Twitter share title, description, and image
- Title
- Slug (or permalink)

- Meta description (the short snippet of text that appears in search engine listings)
- Preferred focus keywords

Another nice feature of the Yoast SEO plugin is that it gives you real-time analysis of your content by rating its readability and keyword analysis. It also makes recommendations for improving both before you publish your content.

Yoast SEO creates Google XML site maps for you, which you can configure by choosing Dashboard ⇨ Yoast SEO ⇨ Settings ⇨ Site Features ⇨ APIs ⇨ XML Sitemaps. You can view your sitemap at `https://yourdomain.com/sitemap_index.xml` Don't worry, though — if you decide not to use the Yoast SEO plugin, the next section has you covered with a plugin that creates XML site maps for you as well.

XML Sitemap Generator for Google

You can use XML Sitemap Generator for Google (`https://wordpress.org/plugins/google-sitemap-generator`) right out of the box with very little configuration. If you use the Yoast SEO plugin mentioned in the previous section, you don't need this plugin because Yoast SEO generates site maps the same way this plugin does. After you install it, you need to tell the plugin to create your site map for the first time. You can accomplish this easy task by following these steps:

1. **Click the XML-Site Map link on the Settings menu on your Dashboard.**

   The XML Sitemap Generator for Google options page appears in your browser window. (See Figure 4-2.)

2. **In the top module, titled Search Engines Haven't Been Notified Yet, click the Your Sitemap link in the option that begins with the words *Notify Search Engines*.**

   The XML Sitemap Generator for Google page refreshes, and the Search Engines Haven't Been Notified Yet module is replaced by the Result of the Last Ping module, showing the date when your site map was last generated.

3. **(Optional) View your site map in your browser.**

   Click the first site map link in the top module or visit `http://yourdomain.com/sitemap.xml` (where *`yourdomain`*`.com` is your actual domain).

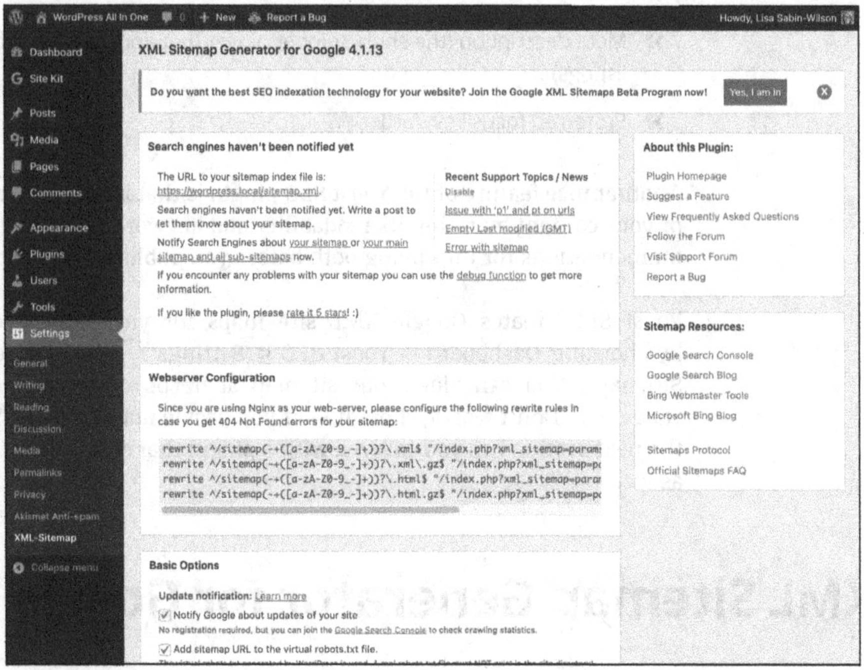

FIGURE 4-2: XML Sitemap Generator for Google settings.

You never need to visit your site map or maintain it. The XML Sitemap Generator for Google maintains the file for you. Every time you publish a new post or page on your website, the plugin automatically updates your site map with the information and notifies Google that you've updated your site with new content. Basically, the plugin sends an invitation to Google to come to your site and index your new content in their search engines.

TIP

Having a Google Search Console account can help Google find and index new content on your site. If you don't already have one of these accounts, visit `https://search.google.com/search-console/about`, click the Start Now button on that page, log in with your existing Google account, and follow the onscreen steps to create a new Google account. After you sign in to the account, you can set up the Add Your Site Map to Google to your Google Console. In the Basic Options section at the bottom of the XML Sitemap Generator for Google page (refer to Figure 4-2), select every check box you see (scroll down the page to see more options not shown in the figure).

All the other default settings are fine for you to use, so leave those as they are. In the Sitemap Content section (not shown in Figure 4-2; scroll down to see it), which is in the middle of the XML Sitemap Generator for Google page, select the following check boxes: Include Home Page, Include Posts, Include Static Pages, and Include the Last Modification Time. Making these selections allows search engines to crawl your site in the most efficient way.

REMEMBER

Be sure to click the Save Changes button at the bottom of the page to make sure any changes you've made get saved.

Redirection

If you're redoing the URL (permalink) structure of your site or moving a site to WordPress from another blogging platform, such as Drupal or Joomla, you really need to use the Redirection plugin (`https://wordpress.org/plugins/redirection`). Redirection allows you to maintain the links that are currently coming into your site by rerouting (or redirecting) people coming in through search engines and other existing links going to the new permalink. If you change URLs, you need to reroute/redirect old links to maintain the integrity of incoming traffic from websites and search engines that are still using the old URL.

Using Redirection is a pretty simple process. After you install the Redirection plugin, click the Redirection link on the Tools menu, and the Welcome to Redirection opens in your browser with some basic details on how to use the plugin. Read through that information, and then follow these steps to set up the plugin:

1. **Click the Start Setup button on the Welcome to Redirection page.**

   The Basic Setup page loads in your browser window.

2. **The settings on the Basic Setup page can remain deselected.**

   You will be able to change these settings at a later date, if you want to. They include:

   - *Monitor Permalink Changes in WordPress Posts and Pages*
   - *Keep a Log of All Redirects and 404 Errors*
   - *Store IP Information for Redirects and 404 Errors*

3. **Click the Continue button.**

   The Import Existing Redirects page loads in your browser window.

4. **(Optional) Check the posts that display on this page to import the redirects into your site.**

   The Redirection plugin automatically creates redirects when you change a post (or page) permalink. However, if you have done that before installing this plugin, you will find those posts listed on this page where you have the ability to import them so they are included in the posts that the Redirection plugin monitors.

5. **Click the Continue button.**

   The REST API page loads in your browser window. This is an informational page for you to read without any settings that you need to configure.

6. **Click the Finish Setup button.**

   The Setting Up Redirection page displays with a progress bar that auto-fills up to 100 percent once complete.

7. **Click the Continue button.**

   The Installation Complete page displays.

8. **Click the Ready to Begin! button.**

   The Redirections page appears in your browser window (see Figure 4-3). This is the page where you can add, edit, and manage your redirects.

To add a new redirection on the Redirections page on the Dashboard (see Figure 4-3), add the old URL in the Source URL text box, enter the new URL in the Target URL text box, and then click the Add Redirect button, which reloads the Redirections page with your new settings displayed.

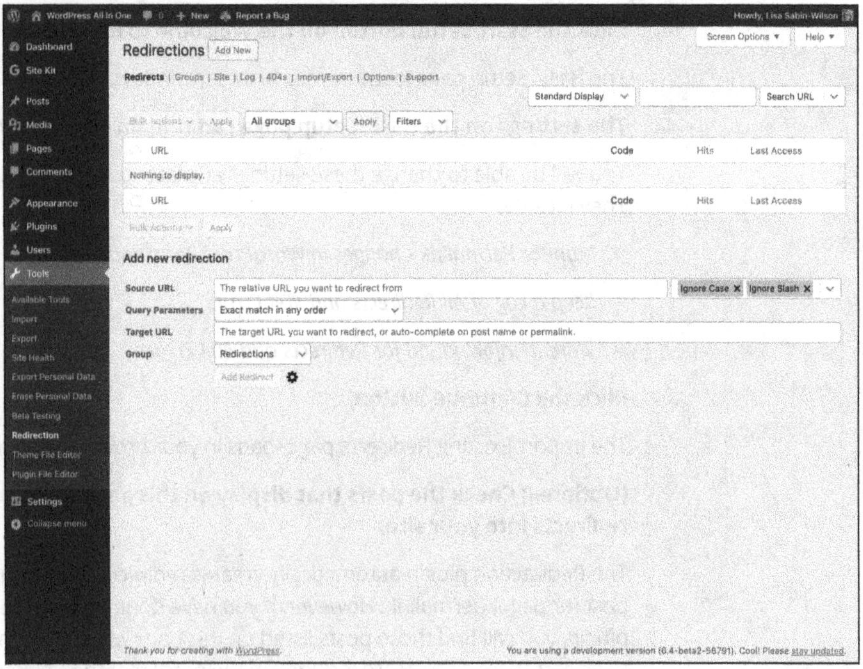

FIGURE 4-3: The Redirection plugin allows you to redirect traffic from your old URL.

WP-Optimize — Cache, Clean, Compress

You might be wondering why a plugin created for optimization would be included in a chapter about SEO and search engine performance. That's because Google has made it very clear to website owners that websites with good performance scores, on both desktop and mobile, will be prioritized for higher rankings than websites that score lower in performance. Knowing that, you can see why website optimization is important if you want good SEO results — if your website does not perform well, it's not going to rank well.

The WP-Optimize plugin (`https://wordpress.org/plugins/wp-optimize`) is a great plugin for making sure your WordPress site scores high on page speed and performance. It also offers cache, clean, and compress features. By caching your website's content, the plugin reduces the load time for returning visitors and improves the overall user experience. WP-Optimize's cleaning feature helps remove unnecessary data from your database, further enhancing your site's performance. By reducing the size of image files, the plugin's compression feature helps improve the loading speed and functionality of websites.

Once installed and activated, you see a new menu item on your Dashboard labeled WP-Optimize. Click that link to open the WP-Optimize settings page, shown in Figure 4-4.

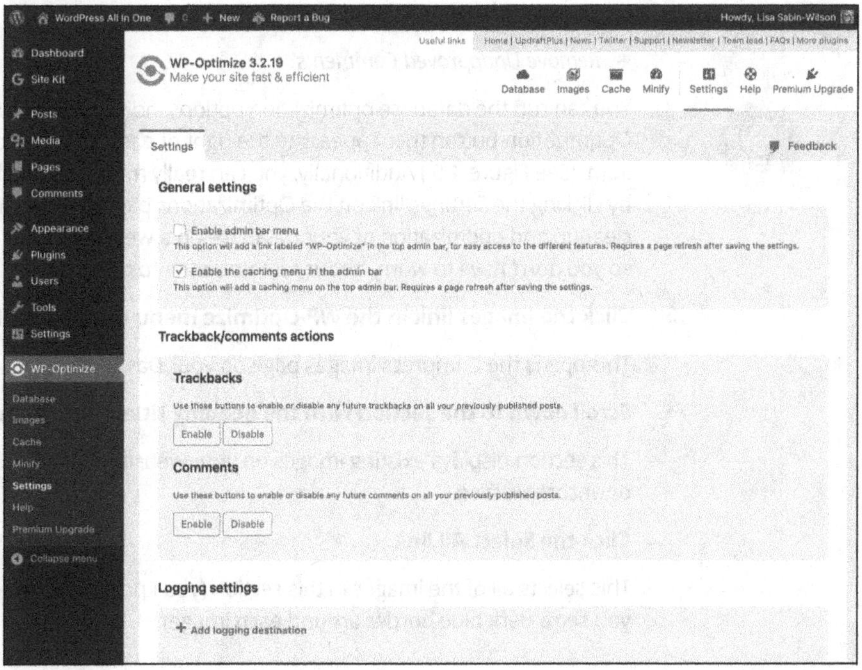

FIGURE 4-4: The WP-Optimize settings page.

WARNING

I recommend running a backup of your database before running this plugin just to make sure you have a good backup available in case you notice anything wrong after running the plugin on your site. That really goes for any plugin that makes changes to your database. Check out Book 2, Chapter 6 for information about backing up your website.

To begin immediately enhancing your website's performance, activate the plugin and follow these steps to go over a few options:

1. **Click the Database link in the WP-Optimize menu on the Dashboard.**

   The Optimizations screen opens in your browser window.

2. **Click the Run All Selected Optimizations button.**

   This runs all of the optimizations that are checked by default. These options deal with database optimization and size. A very large database that is filled with unnecessary data can negatively affect the performance of your site. The optimization options here include:

   - *Optimize Database Tables*
   - *Clean All Post Revisions*
   - *Clean All Auto-Draft Posts*
   - *Clean All Trashed Posts*
   - *Remove Spam and Trashed Comments*
   - *Remove Unapproved Comments*

   TIP

   You can run the database optimization options individually by clicking the Run Optimization button that appears to the right of each database optimization item. (See Figure 4-5.) Additionally, you can really make this plugin work for you by clicking the Settings link on the Optimizations page and enabling scheduled cleanup and optimization of your database on a weekly or monthly schedule so you don't have to worry about remembering to do it.

3. **Click the Images link in the WP-Optimize menu on the Dashboard.**

   This opens the Compress images page on your Dashboard.

4. **Scroll down to the section with the heading titled Uncompressed Images.**

   This section displays existing images on your website that are large in size, or uncompressed.

5. **Click the Select All link.**

   This selects all of the images in this section (you know they are selected when you see a dark blue border around each image).

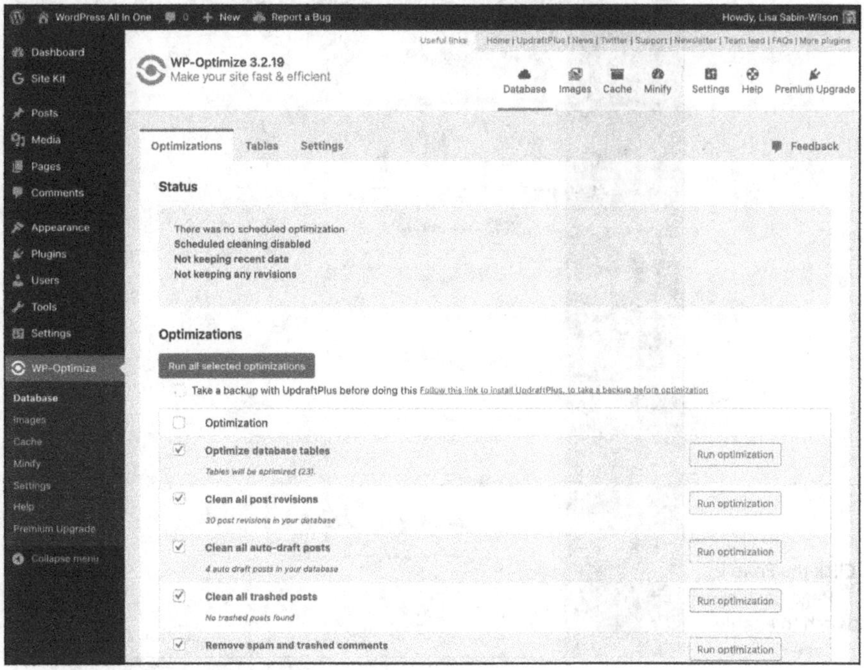

FIGURE 4-5: Click the Run Optimization button to the right of each database item.

6. **Click the Compress the Selected Images button.**

   The more images you have, the longer this will take. A window pops up showing you the progress of the image compression. When it's done, the message in the window changes to a message telling you the images were successfully compressed. Click the Close button to close this window.

   TIP

   Once you have used the WP-Optimize plugin to run image compression on your existing image, you can tell the plugin to automatically compress new images as you add them by turning that option on in the Compress Images page on your Dashboard. There are other options in that section that you can set as well, but the default settings work well for this first run.

7. **Click the Cache link in the WP-Optimize menu on the Dashboard.**

   The Page Cache page loads in your browser window.

8. **Click the Enable Page Caching switch. (See Figure 4-6.)**

   This enables page caching on your website. This action is all that is needed to cache your website pages with this plugin. At this point, the plugin will detect and configure itself with the best caching optimization for your website. There are several other settings in this section of the plugin that you can also set, but the default settings work well for this first run.

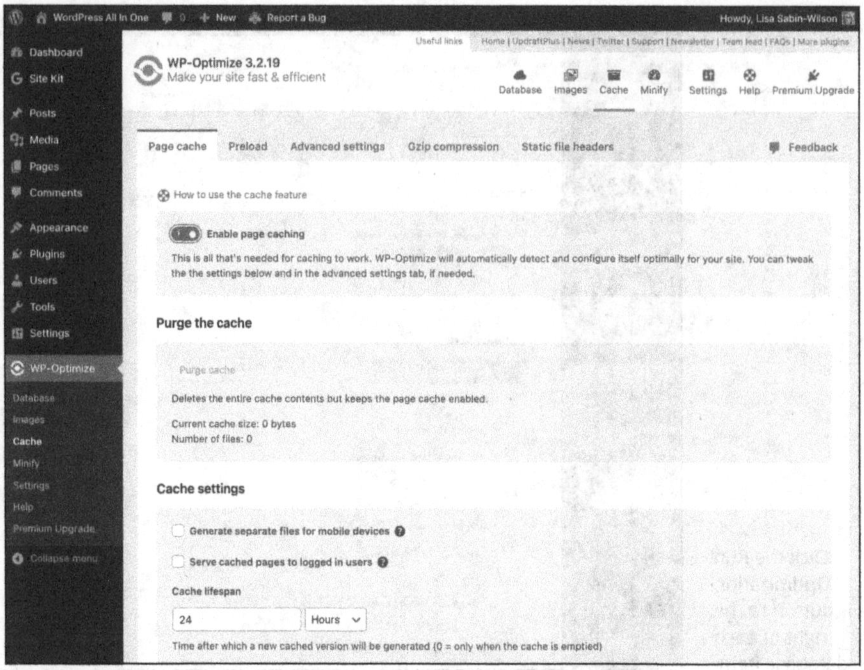

FIGURE 4-6: Click the Enable Page Caching switch to enable page caching.

TIP

You are able to monitor and test your page speed progress and score by visiting Google's PageSpeed Insights website at `https://pagespeed.web.dev`. Enter your website's domain in the text box at the top and it will run your website through its tests and give you the results. If you're wondering what a good Google page speed score is to aim for, you should aim for mobile scores of 60+ and desktop scores of 90+. The nice thing about using this tool is that it will give you suggestions for what you can do to improve your score if it is on the lower side.

6

Customizing the Look of Your Site

Contents at a Glance

IN THIS CHAPTER

» Understanding free theme options

» Exploring things to avoid with free themes

» Previewing a theme on the Themes page

» Installing your new theme

» Discovering premium (for purchase) theme options

Chapter 1 Finding and Installing WordPress Themes

WordPress themes are groups of files, called *templates*, bundled together. When activated in WordPress, themes determine the look and basic function of your site.

Because themes set the design style of your site, including how content displays on it, they're the first and most basic way of customizing your site to fit your unique needs. Some of the most amazing things about the WordPress community are the thousands of free themes that are available — and the new ones that are released each week.

Although finding one WordPress theme among thousands of options can be challenging, it's a fun adventure, and you can explore the various designs and features to ultimately find the right theme for you and your site. In this chapter, you discover the options for finding and installing free themes on your WordPress site. I also discuss premium theme options and tell you a few things to avoid.

Getting Started with Free Themes

WordPress comes packaged with one very useful default theme called Twenty Twenty-Four (named after the year 2024 and released in version 6.4 of WordPress). Most bloggers who use WordPress usually don't waste any time at all in finding a theme that they like better than the default theme. The Twenty Twenty-Four theme is meant to get you started. Although you're not limited to the default theme, it's a very functional theme that can be used right away. Feel free to use it to get started.

Free WordPress themes are popular because of their appealing designs and their ease of installation and use. They're great tools to use when you launch your new site, and if you dabble a bit in graphic design and CSS (Cascading Style Sheets), you can customize one of the free WordPress themes to fit your needs.

With thousands of free WordPress themes available and new ones appearing all the time, your challenge is to find the right one for your site. Here are a few things to remember while you explore. (Also see the nearby "Are all WordPress themes free? sidebar" for information about free versus commercial themes.)

- **Free themes are excellent starting places.** Find a couple of free themes, and use them as starting points for understanding how themes work and what you can do with them. Testing free themes, their layouts, and their options helps you identify what you want in a theme.
- **You'll switch themes frequently.** Typically, you'll find a WordPress theme that you adore and then, a week or two later, find another theme that fits you or your site better. Don't expect to stay with your initial choice. Something new will pop up on your radar screen. Eventually, though, you'll want to stick with a theme that fits your needs best and doesn't aggravate visitors because of continual changes.
- **You get what you pay for.** Although there are many free WordPress themes, largely, you receive limited or no support for them. Free themes are often a labor of love. The designers have full-time jobs and responsibilities; they often release these free projects for fun, passion, and a desire to contribute to the WordPress community. Therefore, you shouldn't expect (or demand) support for these themes. Some designers maintain very active and helpful forums to help users, but those forums are rare. Just be aware that with most free themes, you're on your own.

» **Download themes from reputable sources.** Themes are essentially pieces of software. Therefore, they can contain things that could be scammy, spammy, or potentially harmful to your site or computer. It's vital that you do your homework by reading online reviews and downloading themes from credible, trusted sources. The best place to find free WordPress themes is the theme directory of the WordPress website (see Figure 1-1) at `https://wordpress.org/themes`.

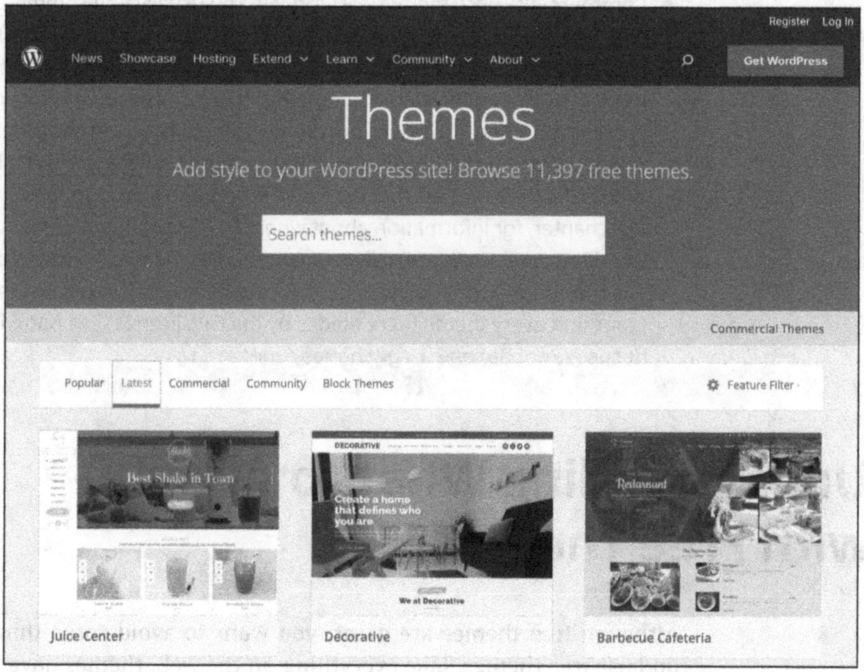

FIGURE 1-1: The WordPress theme directory is the most trusted resource for free themes.

By using free themes, you can have your site up and running with a new design — without the help of a professional — pretty fast. And with thousands of themes available, you can change your theme as often as you want.

ARE ALL WORDPRESS THEMES FREE?

Not all WordPress themes are created equal, and it's important for you, the user, to know the difference between free and premium themes:

- **Free:** These themes are free, period. You can download and use them on your website at absolutely no cost. It's a courtesy to include a link to the designer in the footer of your site, but you can remove that link if you want to.
- **Commercial:** These themes cost money. You usually find commercial themes available for download only after you've paid anywhere from $10 to $500. The designer feels that these themes are a cut above the rest and, therefore, are worth the money you spend for them. Commercial themes also come with a mechanism to obtain support for the use of the theme. Generally, you aren't allowed to remove any designer credits that appear in these themes, and you aren't allowed to redistribute the themes. (See the "Exploring Premium Theme Options" section, later in this chapter, for information about where to find premium themes.) The official WordPress website has a gallery of commercial themes for you to choose from. The commercial themes listed on their site have been vetted by the WordPress team, and every theme there abides by the GPL license (See Book 1, Chapter 2): `https://wordpress.org/themes/commercial/`.

Understanding What to Avoid with Free Themes

Although free themes are great, you want to avoid some things when you find and use free themes. Like everything on the web, themes have the potential to be abused. Although free themes were conceived to allow people (namely, designers and developers) to contribute work to the WordPress community, they've also been used to wreak havoc for users. As a result, you need to understand what to watch out for and what to avoid when searching for free themes:

- **Spam links:** Many free themes available outside the WordPress website include links in the footer or sidebars, and these links can be good or bad. The good uses of these links are designed to credit the original designer and possibly link to their website or portfolio. You should maintain these links as a show of appreciation to the designer, because the links help increase their traffic and clients. Spam links, however, aren't links to the designer's site; they're links to sites you may not ordinarily associate with or endorse on your site. The best example is a link in the footer that links to odd, off-topic, and uncharacteristic keywords or phrases, such as *weight loss supplement* or *best flower deals.* Mostly, this spam technique is used to increase the advertised site's search engine ranking for that particular keyword by adding another link from your site, or worse, to take the site visitor who clicks it to a site that is unrelated to the linked phrase.

- **Hidden malicious code:** Unfortunately, the WordPress community has received reports of hidden malicious code within a theme. This hidden code can produce spam links, security exploits, and abuses on your WordPress site. Hackers install code in various places that run this type of malware. Unscrupulous theme designers can, and do, place code in theme files that inserts hidden malware, virus links, and spam. You may see a line or two of encrypted code that looks like it's just part of the theme code. Unless you have a great deal of knowledge of PHP or JavaScript, you may not know that the theme is infected with dangerous code. That's why is so important to download themes from reputable sources.
- **Themes that lack continued development:** WordPress software continues to improve with each new update. Two or three times a year, WordPress releases new software versions, adding new features, security patches, and numerous other updates. Sometimes, a code function is superseded or replaced, causing a theme to break because it hasn't been updated for the new WordPress version. Additionally, to use new features added to WordPress (because the software updates add features), the theme needs to be updated accordingly. Because free themes typically come without any warranty or support, one thing you should look for — especially if a theme has many advanced back-end options — is whether the developer is actively maintaining the theme for current versions of WordPress. Active maintenance typically occurs more with plugins than with themes, but it's worth noting.
- **Endless searches for free themes:** Avoid searching endlessly for the perfect theme. Trust me — you won't find it. You may find a great theme and then see another with a feature or design style you wish that the other theme had, but the new theme may lack certain other features. Infinite options can hinder you from making a final decision. Peruse the most popular themes on the WordPress Themes page, choose five that fit your criteria, and then move on. You always have the option to change a theme later, especially if you find the vast amount of choices in the directory to be overwhelming.

The results of unsafe theme elements can range from simply annoying to downright dangerous, affecting the integrity and security of your computer and/or hosting account. For this reason, the WordPress Themes page is considered to be the safest place from which to download free themes. WordPress designers develop these themes and upload them to the theme directory, and the folks behind the WordPress platform vet each theme. On the official WordPress Themes page, themes that contain unsafe elements simply aren't allowed.

REMEMBER

The WordPress Themes page isn't the only place to find free WordPress themes, but it's the place to find the most functional and *safest* themes available. Safe themes contain clean code and basic WordPress functions that are considered to be fundamental requirements in a theme to ensure that your website functions with the minimum requirements. The `WordPress.org` website lists the basic requirements that theme developers have to meet before their themes are accepted into the theme directory; you can find that list of requirements at `https://wordpress.org/themes/getting-started`. I highly recommend that you stick to the WordPress Themes page for themes to use on your site; you can be certain that those themes don't contain any unsafe elements or malicious code.

TIP

If you suspect or worry that you have malicious code on your site — either through a theme you're using or a plugin you've activated — a good place to get your site checked is the Sucuri website (`https://sitecheck.sucuri.net`), which offers a free website malware scanner. Sucuri provides expertise in the field of web security for WordPress users in particular, and it even has a free plugin you can install to check your WordPress site for malware and/or malicious code. You can find that plugin at `https://wordpress.org/plugins/sucuri-scanner`.

Previewing Themes on the Themes Page

While you're visiting the WordPress theme directory, you can easily browse the various themes by using the following features (refer to Figure 1-1):

- **Search:** Type a keyword in the search box near the top of the page, and press the Enter (or Return on a Mac) key. A new page opens, displaying themes related to the keyword you searched for.
- **Popular:** Click the Popular link to view the themes that have been downloaded most often.
- **Latest:** Click the Latest link to view themes recently added to the directory.
- **Commercial:** Click the Commercial link to view commercial themes in the directory.
- **Community:** Click the Community link to view themes that are supported by a community of developers.

» **Block Themes:** Click the Block Themes link to view themes that support the site editor feature (read more about the site editor in Book 6, Chapter 2).

» **Feature Filter:** Click the Feature Filter to view choices available by which to filter your theme search, such as layout, features, and subject. Figure 1-2 shows the Feature Filter menu.

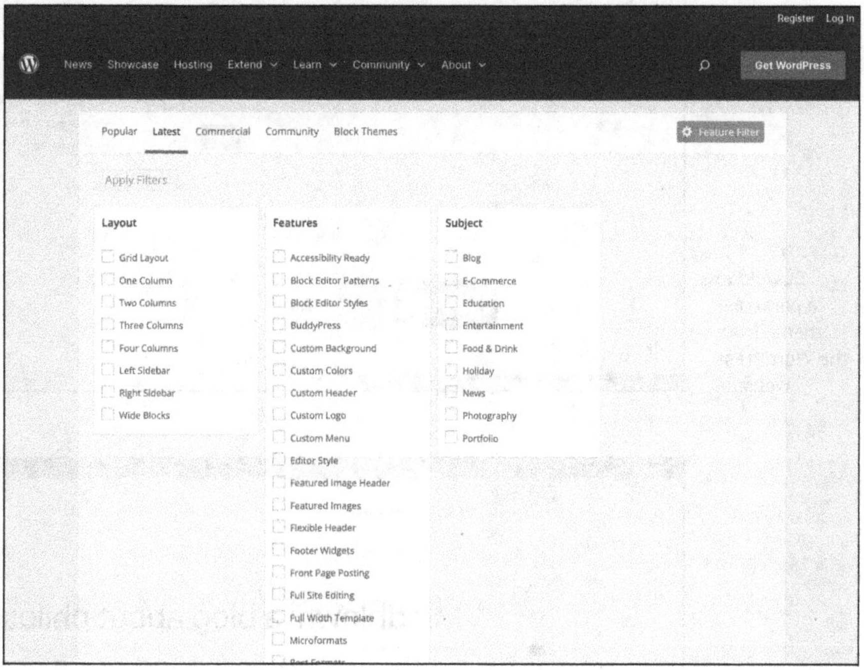

FIGURE 1-2: The Feature Filter menu on the WordPress Themes page.

When you find a theme in the directory that you want to examine more closely, click the More Info button that appears when you hover your mouse pointer over the theme, and then do one of the following:

» **Download:** Click this button (see Figure 1-3) to download the theme to your computer.

» **Preview:** Click the Preview button on the Themes page (shown in Figure 1-3) to open a preview window, which gives you a preview of how the theme looks on a website (see Figure 1-4).

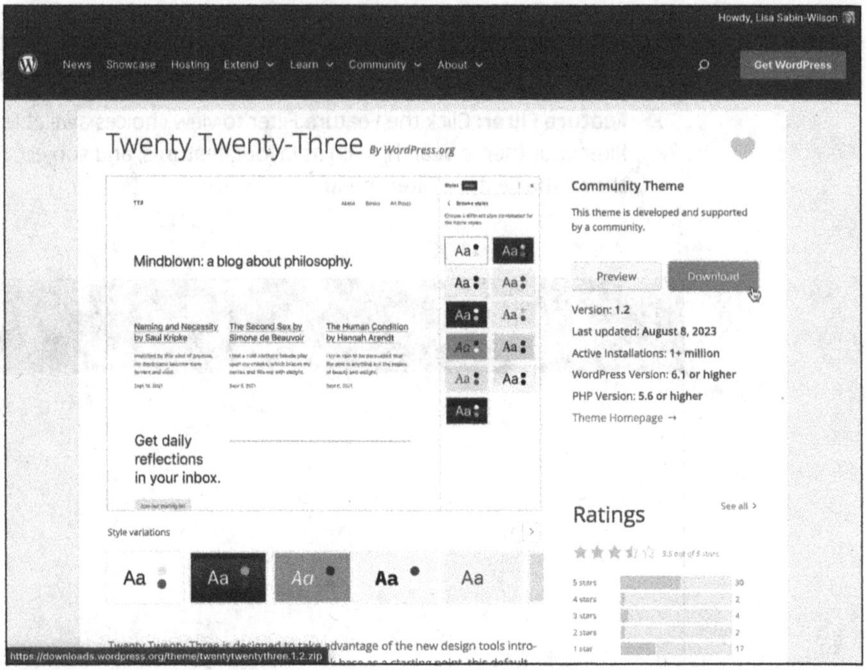

FIGURE 1-3: Download a particular theme from the WordPress website.

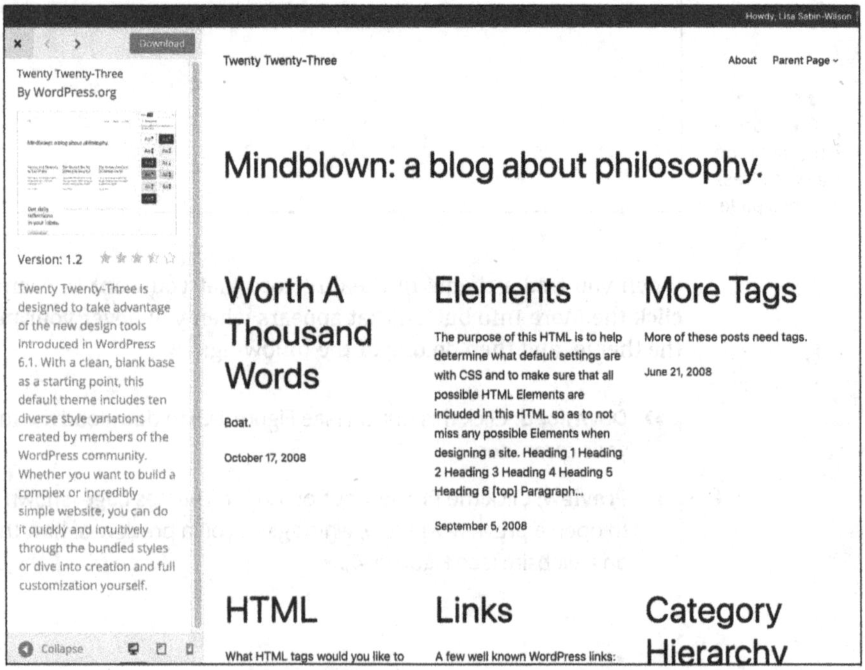

FIGURE 1-4: Previewing a theme from the WordPress Themes page.

Installing a Theme

After you find a WordPress theme you like, you can install the theme on your WordPress site via SFTP (Secure File Transfer Protocol, covered in Book 2, Chapter 2) or via the WordPress Dashboard's theme installer.

To install a theme via SFTP, follow these steps:

1. **Download the theme file from the Themes page.**

   Theme files are provided in compressed format (`.zip` file).

2. **Unzip or extract the theme's `.zip` file.**

   You see a new folder on your desktop, typically labeled with the corresponding theme name.

3. **Upload the theme folder to your web server.**

   Connect to your hosting server via SFTP, and upload the extracted theme folder to the `/wp-content/themes` folder on your server (see Figure 1-5).

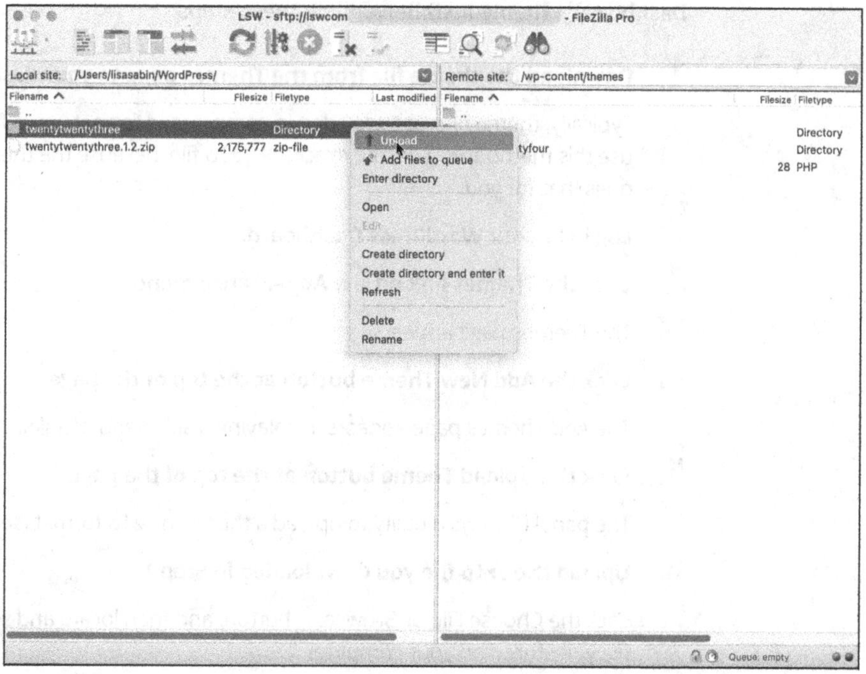

FIGURE 1-5: Uploading the theme folder to a web server via SFTP.

REMEMBER

After you extract the theme's `.zip` file, it's the resulting folder that you need to upload to your web server, not the `.zip` file.

To install a theme via the Dashboard's theme installer, follow these steps:

1. **Download the theme file from the WordPress website to your local computer.**

   Typically, theme files are provided in compressed format (`.zip` file). When you use this method, you don't extract the `.zip` file, because the theme installer does that for you.

2. **Unzip or extract the theme's `.zip` file.**

   You see a new folder on your desktop, typically labeled with the corresponding theme name.

3. **Upload the theme folder to your web server.**

   Connect to your hosting server via SFTP, and upload the extracted theme folder to the `/wp-content/themes` folder on your server.

To install a theme you've downloaded from the WordPress themes page via the Dashboard's theme installer, follow these steps:

1. **Download the theme file from the Themes page to your desktop.**

   Typically, theme files are provided in compressed format (`.zip` file). When you use this method, you don't extract the `.zip` file, because the theme installer does that for you.

2. **Log in to your WordPress Dashboard.**
3. **Click the Themes link on the Appearance menu.**

   The Themes page appears.

4. **Click the Add New Theme button at the top of the page.**

   The Add Themes page appears, displaying a submenu of links.

5. **Click the Upload Theme button at the top of the page.**

   The panel displays a utility to upload a theme in `.zip` format (see Figure 1-6).

6. **Upload the `.zip` file you downloaded in Step 1.**

   Click the Choose File or Browse. . . button, and then locate and select the `.zip` file you stored on your computer.

7. **Click the Install Now button.**

   WordPress unpacks and installs the theme in the appropriate directory for you. Figure 1-7 shows the message you see after installing a theme via this method.

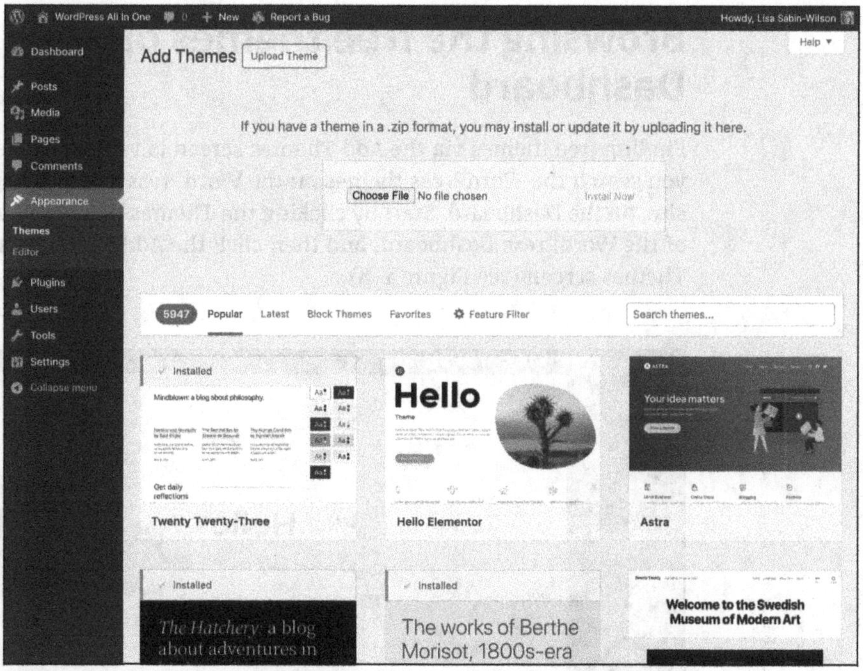

FIGURE 1-6: Installing a theme via the Dashboard's theme installer.

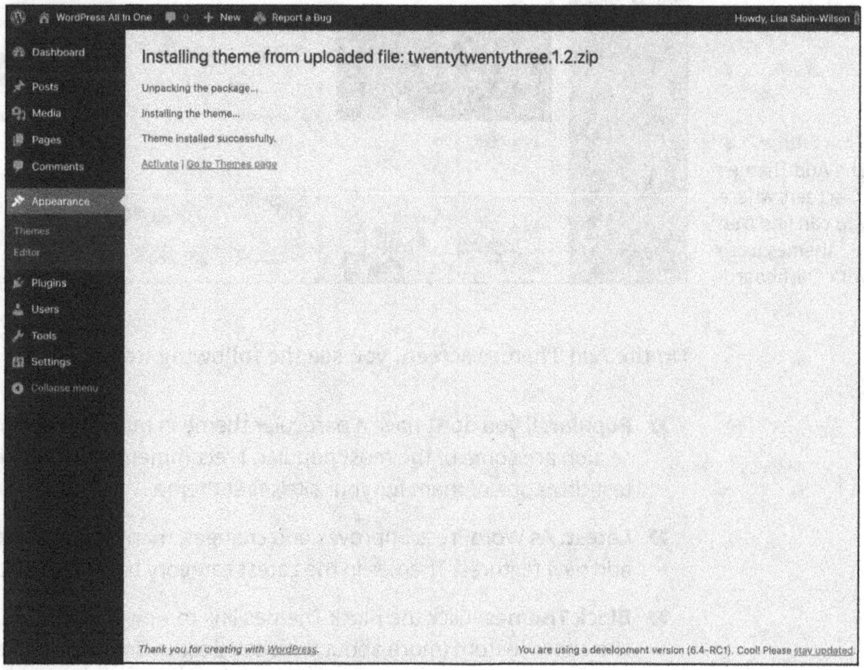

FIGURE 1-7: The message you see when you've installed a theme using the theme uploader.

Browsing the free themes on the Dashboard

Finding free themes via the Add Themes screen is very convenient because it lets you search the WordPress themes on the WordPress Themes page from your own site, on the Dashboard. Start by clicking the Themes link on the Appearance menu of the WordPress Dashboard, and then click the Add New button to open the Add Themes screen (see Figure 1-8).

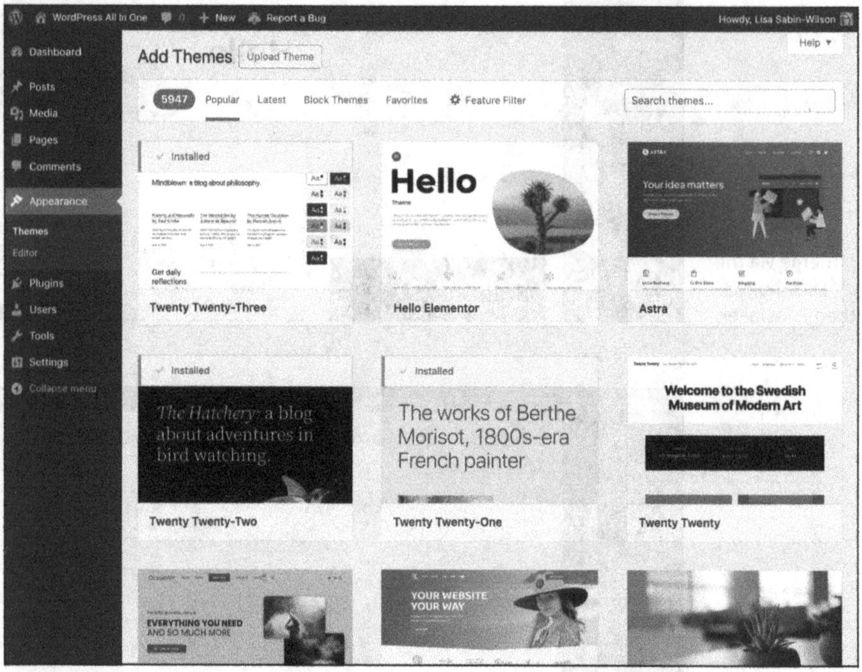

FIGURE 1-8: The Add Themes screen, where you can find free themes from your Dashboard.

On the Add Themes screen, you see the following items:

- **Popular:** If you don't have a particular theme in mind, the themes in this section are some of the most popular. I recommend that you install and test-drive one of them for your site's first theme.
- **Latest:** As WordPress improves and changes, many themes need updating to add new features. Themes in the Latest category have been updated recently.
- **Block Themes:** Click the Block Themes link to view themes that support the site editor feature (more about the site editor in Book 6, Chapter 2).

» **Favorites:** If you marked themes as favorites on the WordPress website, you can find them on the Add Themes screen. After you click the Favorites link, fill in your `WordPress.org` username in the text field and click the Get Favorites button. (Note: This feature only works if you're logged into your `WordPress.org` user account.)

» **Feature Filter:** This link gives you a variety of filters from which to choose to find a theme you're looking for. You can filter by Layout, Features, and Subject. After you select your desired filters, click the Apply Filters button to view the themes that match your set filters.

» **Search themes:** If you know the name of a free theme, you can easily search for it by keyword, author, or tag. You also can refine your search based on specific features of the theme, including color, layout, and subject (such as Holiday).

After you find the theme you want, click the Install button that appears when you hover your mouse pointer over the theme's thumbnail.

Previewing and activating a theme

After you upload a theme via SFTP or install it via the theme installer, you can preview and activate your desired theme.

TIP

The WordPress Theme Preview option allows you to see how the theme would look on your site without actually activating it. If you have a site that's receiving traffic, it's best to preview any new theme before activating it to ensure that you'll be happy with its look and functionality. If you're trying to decide among several new theme options, you can preview them all before changing your live site.

To preview your new theme, follow these steps:

1. **Log in to your WordPress Dashboard.**
2. **Click the Themes link on the Appearance menu.**

   The Themes page appears, displaying your current (activated) theme and any themes that are installed in the `/wp-content/themes` directory on your web server.
3. **Preview the theme you want to use.**

   Click the Live Preview button that appears when you hover your mouse pointer over the theme thumbnail. A preview of your site with the theme appears in your browser, as shown in Figure 1-9. The left side panel displays a thumbnail image and description of the theme.

4. **Choose whether to install the theme.**

   Click the Install button in the top-right corner of the left side panel to install the theme, or close the preview by clicking the Cancel (X) button in the top-left corner of the panel.

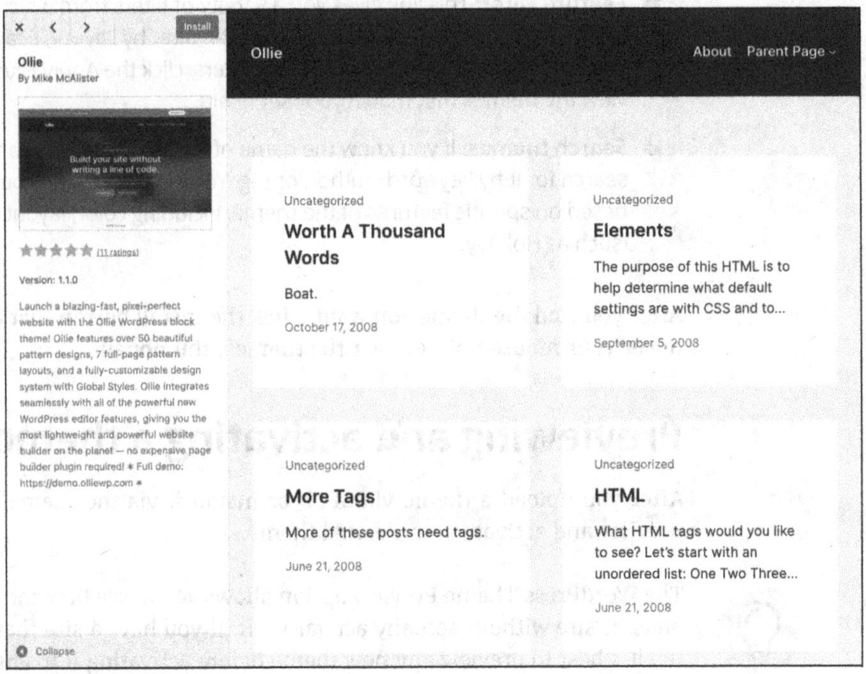

FIGURE 1-9: A WordPress theme preview on the Dashboard.

To activate a new theme without previewing it, follow these steps:

1. **Log in to your WordPress Dashboard.**
2. **Click the Themes link on the Appearance menu.**

   The Themes page appears, displaying your current (activated) theme and any themes that are installed in the /wp-content/ on your web server.

3. **Find the theme you want to activate.**
4. **Click the Activate button that appears when you hover your mouse pointer over the theme thumbnail.**

   The theme immediately becomes live on your site.

Exploring Premium Theme Options

Thousands of free WordPress themes are available, but you may also want to consider premium (for purchase) themes for your site. Remember the adage "You get what you pay for" when considering free services or products, including WordPress and free themes.

Typically, when you download and use something that's free, you get no assistance with the product or service. Requests for help generally go unanswered. Therefore, your expectations should be low because you aren't paying anything. When you pay for something, you usually assume that you will have support or service for your purchase and that the product is of high (or acceptable) quality.

WordPress, for example, is available free. But you have no guarantee of support while using the software, except for the active WordPress support forum. Moreover, you have no right to demand service.

Here are some things to consider when contemplating a premium theme. (I selected the commercial companies listed later in this chapter based on these criteria.)

- **Selection:** Many theme developers offer a rich, diverse selection of themes, including themes designed for specific industries, topics, or uses (such as video, blogging, real estate, or magazines). Generally, you can find a good, solid theme to use for your site from one source.
- **Innovation:** To differentiate them from their free counterparts, premium themes include innovative features such as theme settings or advanced options that extend WordPress to help you do more.
- **Great design with solid code:** Although many beautiful themes are free, premium themes are professionally coded and nicely designed, and require dozens of hours to build, which simply isn't feasible for many developers of free themes.
- **Up to date:** Book 1, Chapter 3 takes you through the WordPress development and release cycle, and with that schedule you can expect that WordPress releases two or three new versions per year (sometimes four!). You want to look for commercial themes that support the latest versions of WordPress and all of the new features that come along with it.
- **Support:** Most commercial companies have full-time support staff to answer questions, troubleshoot issues, and point you to resources beyond their support. Often, premium-theme developers spend more time helping customers troubleshoot issues outside the theme products. Therefore, purchasing a premium theme often gives you access to a dedicated support

community, which you can ask about advanced issues and upcoming WordPress features; otherwise, you're on your own.

- **Stability:** No doubt you've purchased a product or service from a company only to find later that the company has gone out of business. If you choose to use a premium theme, purchase a theme from an established company with a solid business model, a record of accomplishment, and a dedicated team devoted to building and supporting quality products.

REMEMBER

Although some free themes have some or all of the features in the preceding list, for the most part, they don't. Keep in mind that just because a designer calls a theme *premium* doesn't mean that the theme has passed through any kind of quality review. The view of what constitutes a premium theme can, and will, differ from one designer to the next.

TIP

Fully investigate any theme before you spend your money on it. Here are some things to check out before you pay:

- Email the designer who is selling the premium theme and ask about a support policy.
- Contact people who've purchased the theme and ask about their experiences with the theme and the designer.
- Carefully read any terms that the designer has published on their site to find any licensing restrictions that exist.
- If the premium theme designer has a support forum, ask whether you can browse the forum to find out how actively the designer answers questions and provides support. Are users waiting weeks to get their questions answered, for example, or does the designer seem to be on top of support requests?
- Search online for the theme and the designer. Often, users of premium themes post about their experiences with the theme and the designer. You can find both positive and negative information about the theme and the designer before you buy.

The developers in the following list are doing some amazingly innovative things with WordPress themes. Some of them have a library of multiple themes you can choose from, and some have just one theme that they develop with a library of add-ons you can use to enhance the theme. I highly recommend that you explore their offerings:

- **WP Astra (`https://wpastra.com`):** Shown in Figure 1-10, WP Astra emphasizes an experience using popular site-builder plugins such as Beaver Builder (`https://www.wpbeaverbuilder.com`) and Elementor (`https://elementor.com`).

» **Kadence WP (`https://www.kadencewp.com`):** Shown in Figure 1-11, Kadence WP has a great team and WordPress themes that are as much high-quality (from a code standpoint) as they are beautiful. They offer a large library of starter themes, along with a library of add-ons from a design library to build out pages and sections of your website.

» **Creative Market (`https://creativemarket.com/templates-themes/website-app/wordpress/business`):** Shown in Figure 1-12, Creative Market isn't just a commercial theme shop; rather, they offer multiple products for website designers and developers like graphics, fonts, photos, and more. They do have an extensive WordPress theme selection available at pretty reasonable prices.

TIP

You are not able to find, preview, or install premium themes by using the Add Themes feature of your WordPress Dashboard. You can find, purchase, and download premium themes only from third-party websites. After you find a premium theme you like, you need to install it via the SFTP method or by using the Dashboard upload feature. (See the "Installing a Theme" section, earlier in this chapter.) You can find a very nice selection of premium themes on the WordPress website at `https://wordpress.org/themes/commercial`.

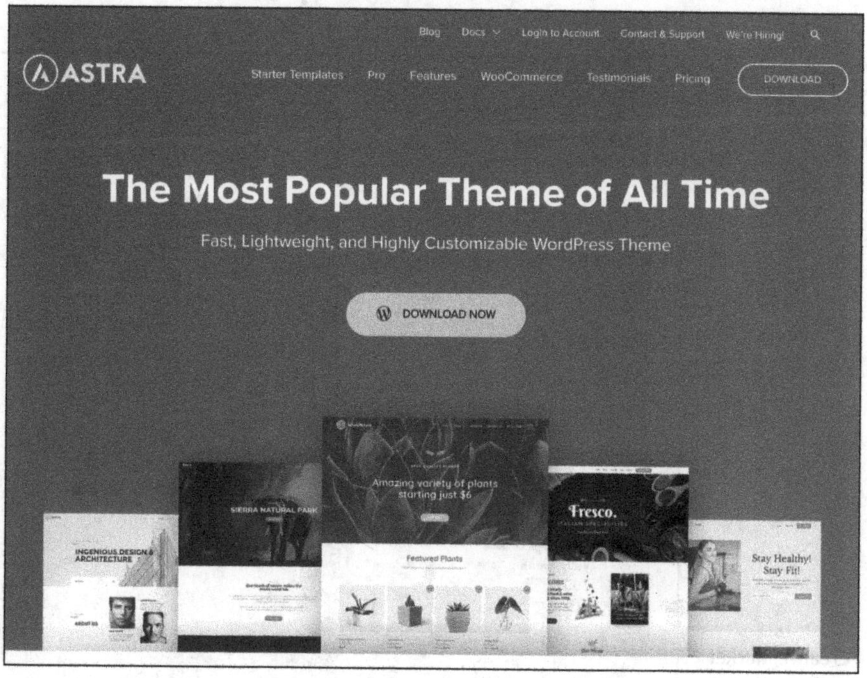

FIGURE 1-10: WP Astra, provider of commercial WordPress themes.

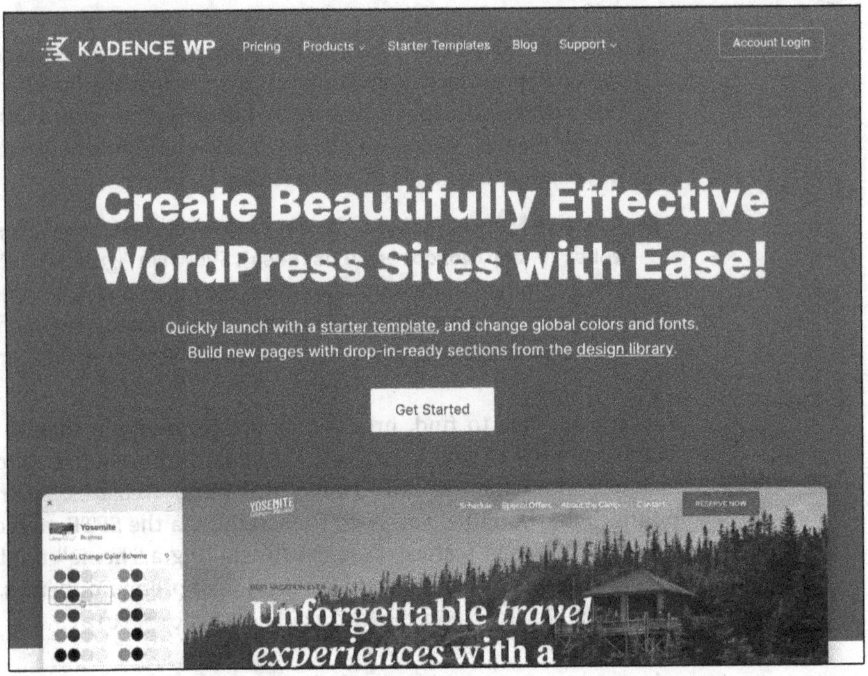

FIGURE 1-11: Kadence WP theme offerings.

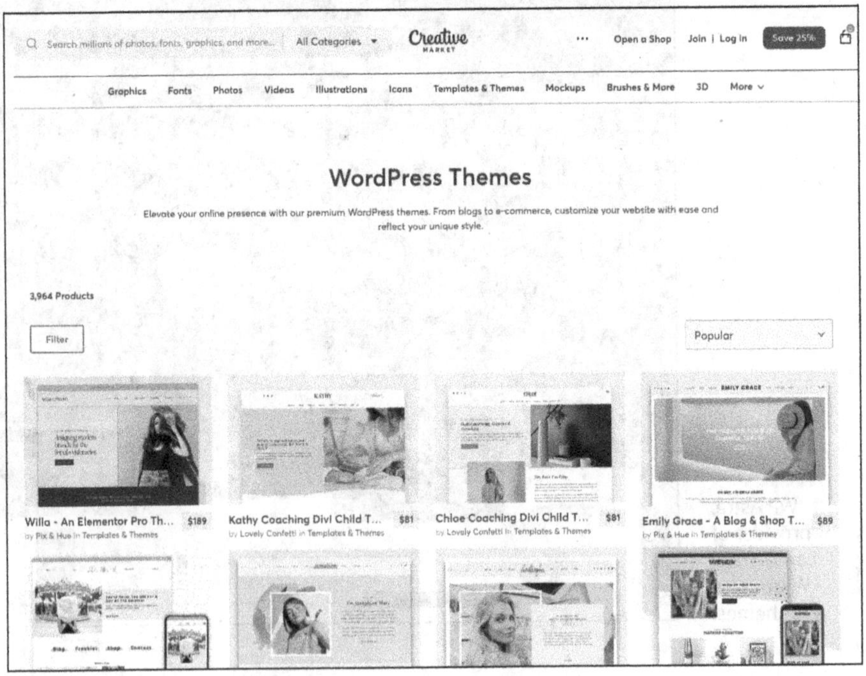

FIGURE 1-12: Creative Market WordPress theme offerings.

IN THIS CHAPTER

» Understanding block themes

» Navigating the site editor

» Using the site editor

» Understanding block patterns

Chapter 2 Exploring the Site Editor and Block Themes

Most of what we do today is on the web, and when you decide to publish a website online, you invite visitors of all types to share the experience. For this reason, creating a visually appealing and functional website is essential. With the introduction of block themes and the site editor, WordPress has taken bold steps forward, offering users greater flexibility and control than ever before.

This chapter helps you understand what sets block themes apart from others, and learn how to use the site editor feature. This chapter also introduces you to block patterns (Book 6, Chapter 3 goes into greater detail on how to use and create them). If this is your first time exploring block themes and the site editor, this chapter will ensure that you can take full advantage of the available features.

Discovering Block Themes

In WordPress, you can think of blocks as a site-building tool kit. With the block editor, content creation is modular, and each piece of content, whether it's a paragraph, image, video, quote, or something else, is an individual block that you can arrange and style independently from one another, giving you a more visual and intuitive way to create posts and pages.

Various blocks are available, including blocks for text, headings, images, galleries, columns, buttons, widgets, and many more, which I cover in Book 4, Chapter 1. Additionally, developers can create custom blocks, allowing for a vast range of possibilities for design and content layout within WordPress.

Why block themes are different

In Book 6, Chapter 1, I discuss how to find, install, and activate WordPress themes of all types. *Block themes* are a unique category of themes that are built with, and specifically for, blocks. Block themes use blocks in WordPress to create all parts of your website, not just posts and pages. In block themes, you can use blocks to create the header, footer, sidebar, and navigation menus without relying on plugins or needing to hire — or be — a developer.

Using a block theme also allows you to create custom templates for pages like About and Contact pages. You can also use blocks to add a custom layout to pages dynamically created by WordPress, like Archive pages, Search Results pages, or the 404 (Page Not Found) pages.

The site editor in WordPress, which I cover in the "Exploring the Site Editor" section, later in this chapter, allows block themes to tap into all of these great features. Themes that are not block themes can still use the block editor for content on posts and pages, but they do not have the extensive capability to be a full site editor like a block theme can.

Finding block themes

The Themes page, which you learned about in Book 6, Chapter 1, is filled with a variety of themes waiting to be discovered. Among them are the block themes — a newer, dynamic facet of WordPress design. You can effortlessly pinpoint these block themes using the Themes page's filtering options. Just set the filtering option to Block Themes, as shown in Figure 2-1, and you're presented with a list of block themes explicitly created for the site editor feature.

TIP

Head over to `https://wordpress.org/themes/tags/full-site-editing`, and you'll find the collection of themes crafted with full site editing in mind, ready for you to add to your tool kit.

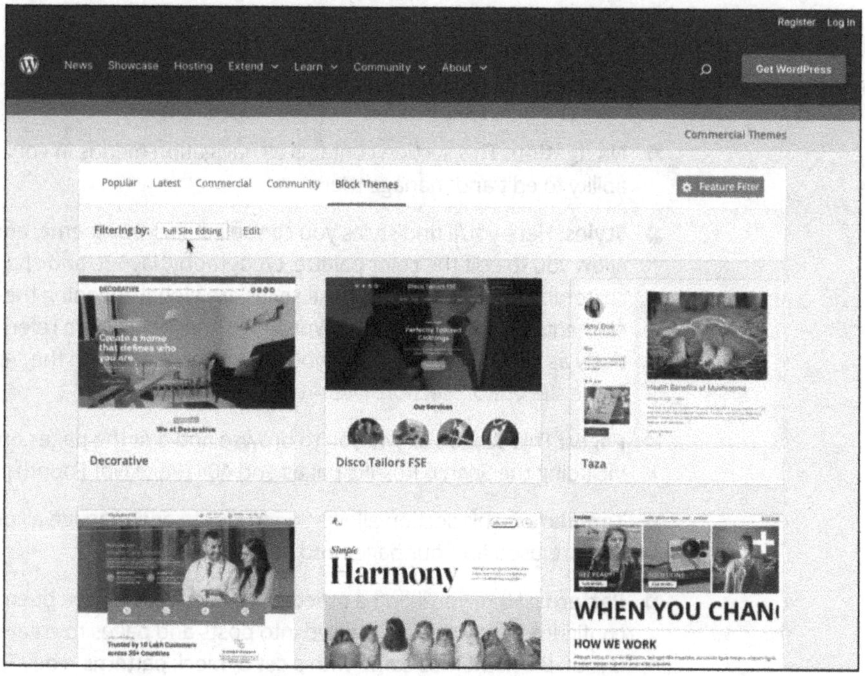

FIGURE 2-1: Filter set to Full Site Editing on the WordPress Themes page.

Finding available options in block themes

With block themes in WordPress, the platform has taken a significant step forward in offering users an even more flexible experience. The themes are designed to work seamlessly with the block editor. The relationship between block themes and the site editor makes customizing your website a lot easier than using a theme that is not compatible with the site editor because you are no longer activating a static design. With a block theme and the site editor, you can mold the theme to fit your tastes.

The options in a block theme are structured to give you granular control over every element on your site. The choices are many: from global styles that determine your website's visual design elements, like typography and color schemes; to specific block settings that allow for detailed customization of individual blocks. Using a block theme means that whether you're setting the tone for your entire website or adjusting the look of a single button, the block theme options have got you covered. Being able to edit your entire site with blocks gives you flexibility and creative freedom without the need for complex coding.

The block theme design options shown in Figure 2-2 in the site editor allow you +to customize the look of your website. They include

- **Navigation:** This section contains all navigation menus in your theme and the ability to edit and manage them.
- **Styles:** Here you'll find styles you can select for your theme, and options that allow you to edit the color palette, typography, layout, and spacing; as well as customize specific blocks. These styles are global, meaning they affect all elements on your website. In WordPress these styles are referred to collectively as the Style Book, which you'll learn more about in the "Applying styles in the site editor" section, later in this chapter.
- **Pages:** This section allows you to browse and edit the pages on your website, including the Search Results pages and 404 (Page Not Found) pages.
- **Templates:** This section allows you to create and manage all of the templates that are used for your pages and posts.
- **Patterns:** Here you'll find a collection of blocks that have been combined and configured; they can be inserted into posts and pages to create a specific layout. Block themes come with a set of block patterns ready for you to use, and you can also create your own patterns. You can find more information in the "Understanding Block Patterns" section, later in this chapter.

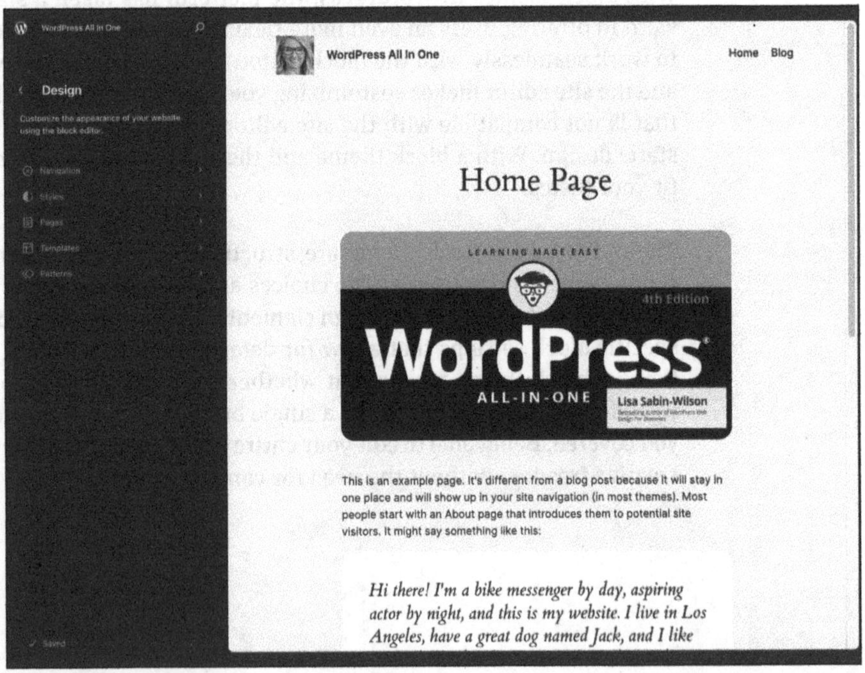

FIGURE 2-2: The Design screen in the site editor.

Exploring the Site Editor

At this point in this chapter, you understand what block themes and the site editor are and what you can do with them. But knowing what they are and knowing where to go to find the areas of your site that you want to work with, and how to work with them, are different matters. By the end of this section, you will know how to do all of that.

The Design screen in the site editor (refer to Figure 2-2) contains navigation links to the areas within the site editor to customize different parts of your site. But how do you get into the site editor? It's easy when you follow these steps:

1. **Log in to your Dashboard.**
2. **Click the Editor link in the Appearances section.**

   The Design screen in the site editor appears in your browser window, as seen in Figure 2-2.
3. **Navigate to the areas you need within the site editor.**

   The next section, "Using the Site Editor," covers these areas.
4. **When you are done using the site editor, click the WordPress logo at the top-left corner of your screen.**

   The main Dashboard page appears in your browser window.

Another simple way to get into the site editor is from the admin toolbar that displays on your live site when logged in as a user, as shown in Figure 2-3. Just click the Edit Site link in the toolbar and the site editor opens, except instead of opening on the main Design screen as described earlier, the site editor opens the page you were visiting in the site editor. For example, if you navigate the About page on your live website and click the Edit Site link in the toolbar, the page template opens in the site editor, allowing you to edit and manage it, as shown in Figure 2-4.

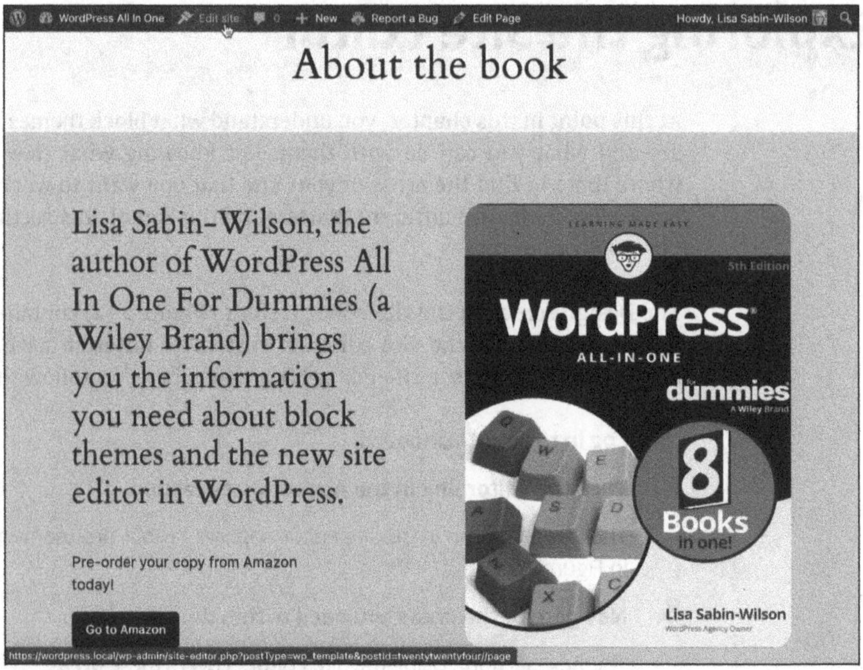

FIGURE 2-3: The Edit Site link in the admin toolbar.

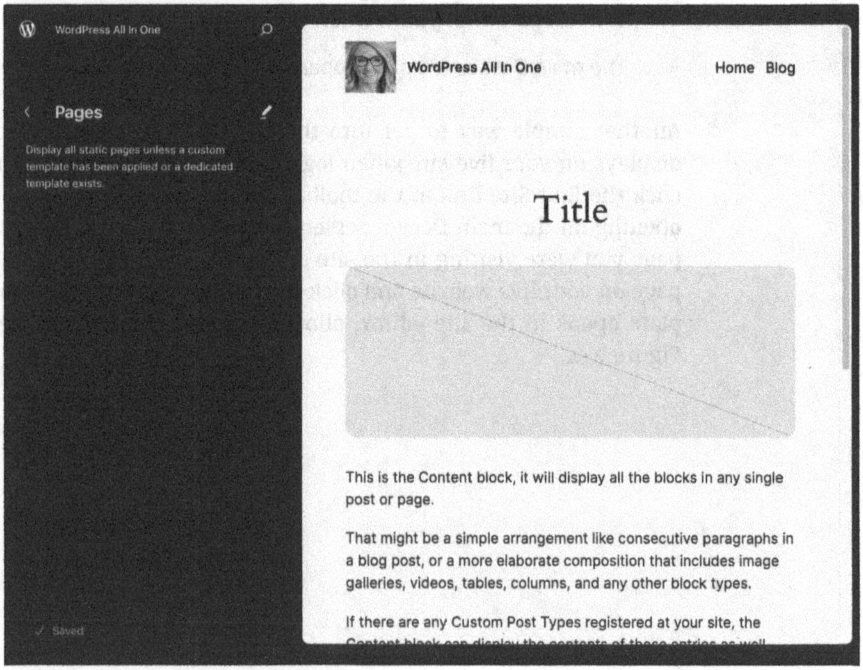

FIGURE 2-4: Editing the page template in the site editor.

Using the Site Editor

In the "Finding available options in block themes" section, earlier in this chapter, I list the five primary options available in the site editor when you have a block theme enabled: Navigation, Styles, Pages, Templates, and Patterns. Within each of these sections of the site editor, you'll make some minor or major changes to create your ideal website.

First, you need to follow the steps in the previous section, "Exploring the Site Editor," to navigate to the Design screen of the site editor (refer to Figure 2-2).

Navigation screen in the site editor

Click the Navigation link on the Design screen to visit the Navigation screen in the site editor to view the navigation menus included on your site. You can easily edit menus, like rearranging, deleting, or adding links to a menu by opening it in edit mode. Follow these steps:

1. **Click the Editor link on the Appearances menu on your Dashboard.**

   The Design screen of the site editor appears in your browser, displaying the Design screen.

2. **Click the Navigation link on the Design screen in the site editor.**

   The Navigation screen appears in your browser.

3. **Click the pencil icon to the right of the Navigation heading.**

   This opens the Navigation menu in edit mode, as shown in Figure 2-5. You'll see the menu you are currently editing in the site editor on the left side of the screen, and the settings panel on the right side. Here you can use blocks to add new items to a menu.

4. **Click the icon that looks like a plus sign to add a new block to the menu.**

   There are two plus sign icons on the shown in Figure 2-5. You can click either one to use the block inserter, which opens and displays several blocks for adding new items to the menu (see Figure 2-6), including:

   - *Page Link:* Allows you to add a link to your created page
   - *Custom Link:* Allows you to add a link to any location on the web
   - *Spacer:* Creates blank space between elements on a page
   - *Buttons:* Allows you to add a button to your menu
   - *Page List:* Adds a complete list of published pages from your website
   - *Search:* Adds a search form

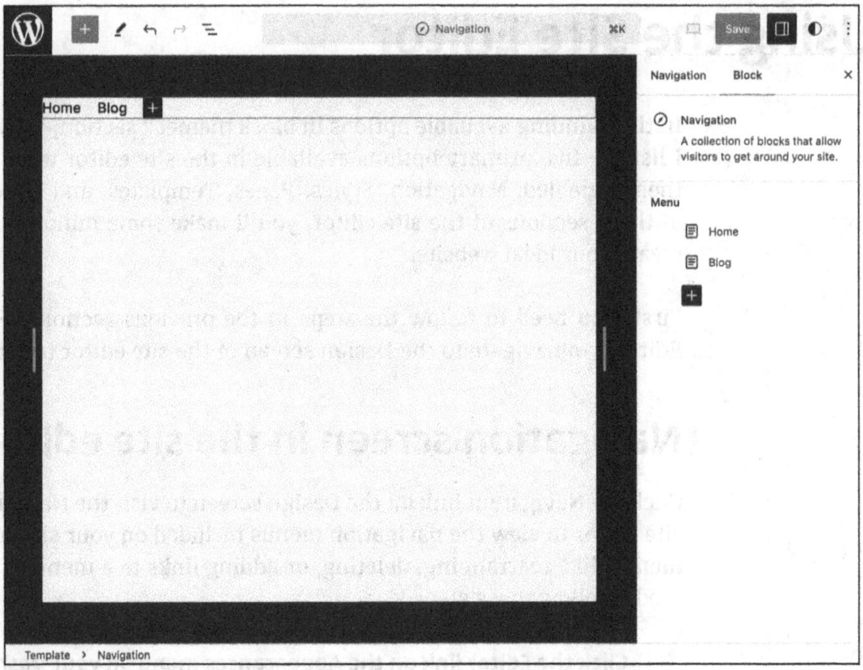

FIGURE 2-5: Editing a navigation menu in the site editor.

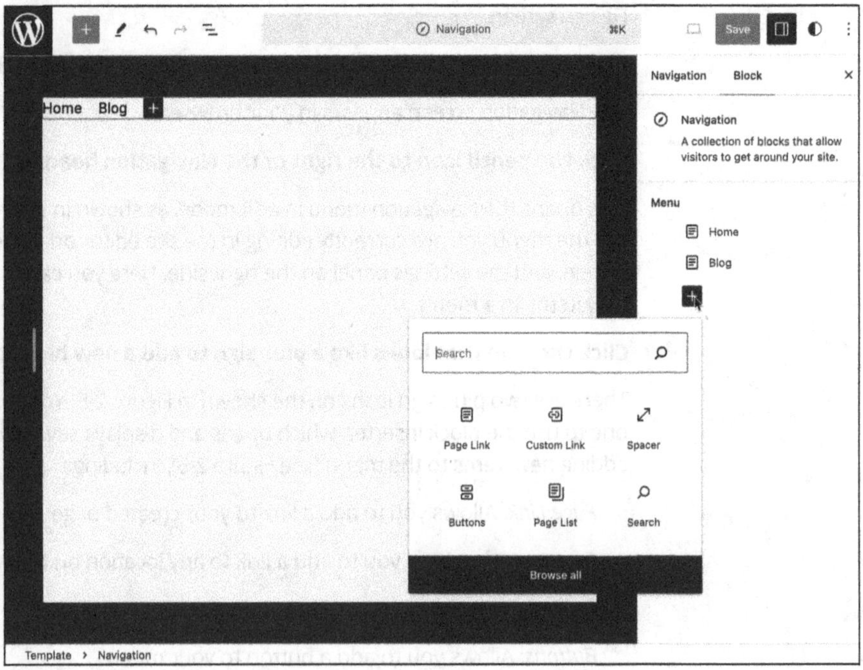

FIGURE 2-6: Selecting blocks to add to the Navigation menu.

Once you add and remove items from the Navigation menu, you may want to edit the items before you save the final changes. Figure 2-6 shows the settings for individual menu items, where you can change the attributes of a page link by following these steps:

1. **Click an individual Page Link in the Navigation settings panel.**

   The Page Link settings panel appears on the right side.

2. **Edit the various fields on the settings panel.**

   You can change the Label, Description, and attributes. There is a URL field on the settings panel; however, I do not recommend changing it because that will break the link on your live site. Edit the page URL (Permalink) within the editor for that page instead.

3. **Click the Styles icon to access style settings for the Page Link block.**

   Options available for the Page Link block include adding an arrow icon to a link and changing the Typography and Dimensions settings.

4. **Click the Save button at the top of the settings panel.**

   A confirmation message appears in the settings panel asking if you are ready to save. Click the Save button again to save your changes. The Page Link settings panel returns, allowing you to either close the panel or continue making edits.

You will go through these steps when adding blocks to the Navigation menu. The settings and style options will differ based on the type of block you are using, but the concept is the same across all of them. In the end, you are using the block editor to revisit the information I covered in Book 4, Chapter 1, which explains in greater detail how to work with blocks and their settings.

Another part of your website's navigation is your site logo, which is the first thing some people want to edit on a new site because it helps personalize the site as yours. Additionally, site logos are images that are usually linked to the home page, so the site logo is displayed on every page on your website. When your visitors click it, they are taken back to your home page, so you can consider the site logo as being like the lighthouse of your website, always giving visitors to your site a way back to your home page.

Follow these steps to add a site logo to your website using the site editor:

1. **Click the Editor link in the Appearances menu on your Dashboard.**

   The site editor appears in your browser, displaying the Design screen.

2. **Click the Patterns link on the Design screen in the site editor.**

   The Patterns screen appears in your browser.

3. **Scroll to the bottom of the left navigation panel on the Patterns screen to find the Template Parts section.**

4. **Click the Header link under the Template Parts heading.**

   This opens the Header screen, which contains the title, logo, and main navigation menus for your website.

5. **Click the Header template.**

   This opens the Header screen in your browser, with the information about the Header template on the left side panel, and the Header template displayed on the right.

6. **Click the site logo.**

   In Figure 2-7, the site logo is my photo, but I want to change it to display my logo. Clicking it opens the Site Logo options toolbar.

7. **Click on the Upload icon, or select Replace on the options toolbar.**

   Select an image from the Media Library or upload a file from your computer.

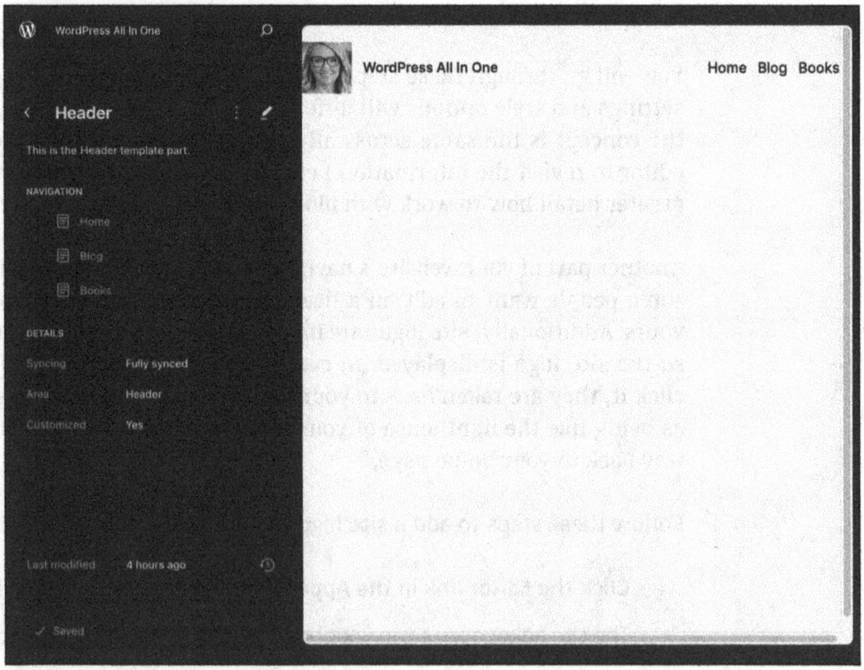

FIGURE 2-7: The site logo block showing my photo.

8. **Edit the Site Logo settings and styles in the settings panel on the right.**

   Figure 2-8 shows the Site Logo edit screen with the site logo toolbar and settings panel. You can edit the site logo image width, among other options.

9. **Click the Save button at the top of the settings panel.**

   A confirmation message in the settings panel asks if you are ready to save. Click the Save button again to save your changes. The Page Link settings panel returns, allowing you to either close the panel or continue making edits to the site logo.

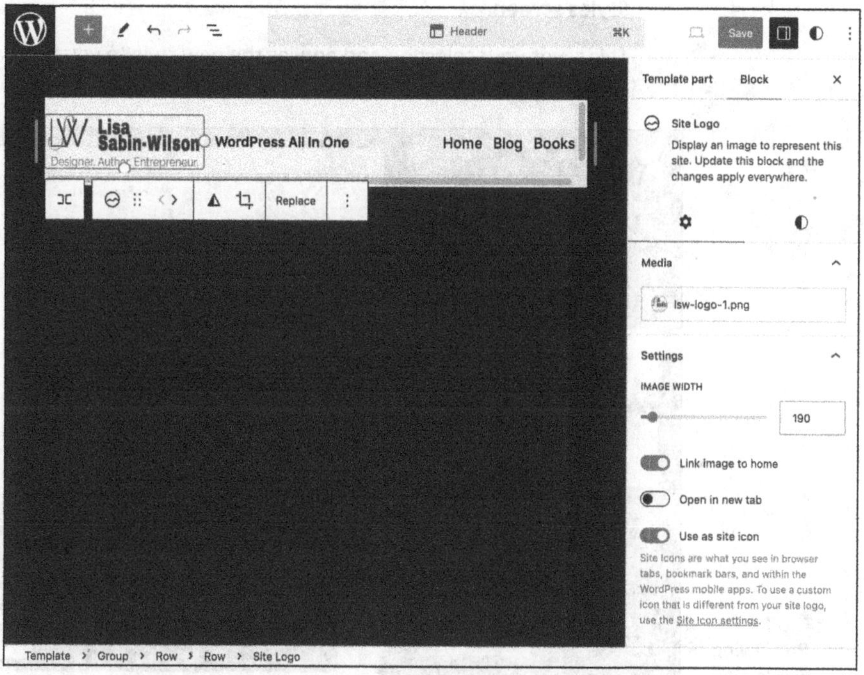

FIGURE 2-8: Editing the site logo block toolbar and settings panel in the site editor.

Applying styles in the site editor

The WordPress site editor allows developers of block themes to tap into various design elements such as color palettes, typography, and layout. The styles that a theme developer chooses to include are the exact ones users can select by browsing the site editor. In the following steps, I am using the default Twenty Twenty-Four block theme to select a predefined style:

1. **Click the Editor link in the Appearances menu on your Dashboard.**

   The site editor appears in your browser, displaying the Design screen.

2. **Click the Styles link on the Design screen in the site editor.**

   The Styles screen appears in your browser with the available styles on the left side panel and the home page of your website on the right side. The default Twenty Twenty-Four theme has eight predefined styles, as shown in Figure 2-9.

3. **Click a style to preview your site with the new style.**

   The right side of your screen changes to display your site with the new style applied. You can click as many of them as you like. New styles will get applied to your site after you complete the next step.

4. **Click the Save button at the bottom of the left side panel on the Styles screen.**

   This saves your selection and applies the new style to your entire site.

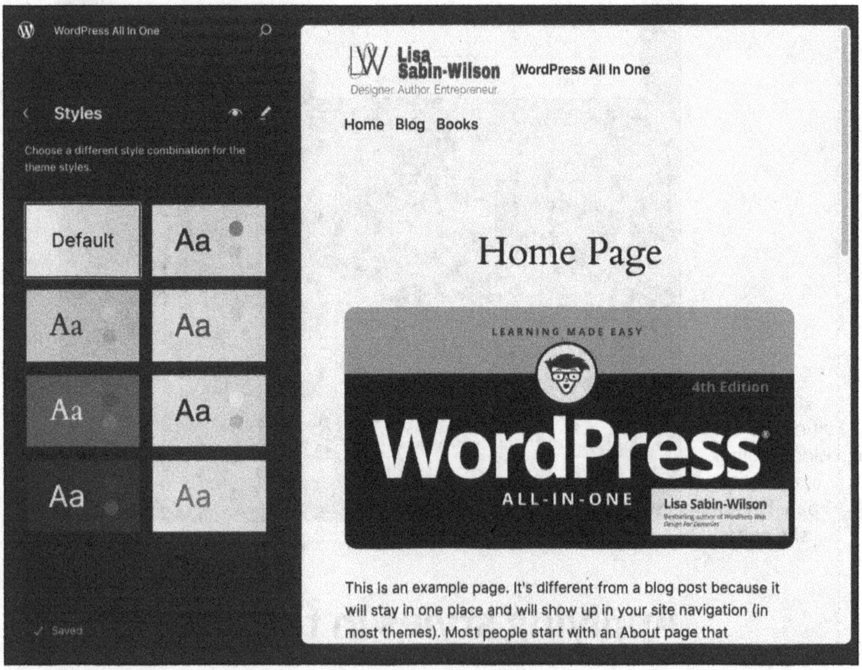

FIGURE 2-9: Previewing and selecting predefined styles on the Styles screen in the site editor.

Global styles can be applied to the entire website instead of just one item. In Book 4, Chapter 1 you discovered that each block in the block editor has a settings panel that contains options for the block settings and style.

When you make and save changes to the style of a block you've added to a page, you've affected the style for just that block, on just that page. I refer to this as editing a *local block*, which is different than editing a *global block*, which is what you do in the Styles section of the site editor, rather than on a single post or page.

TIP

In addition to editing blocks globally in the Styles section of the site editor, you can edit design elements globally, like Typography, Colors, and Layout, by clicking those terms in the right settings panel in the Style Book. See Figure 2-10.

Follow these steps to edit global styles in the site editor using the Style Book feature:

1. **Click the Editor link in the Appearances menu on your Dashboard.**

   The site editor appears in your browser, displaying the Design screen.

2. **Click the Styles link on the Design screen in the site editor.**

   The Styles screen appears in your browser.

3. **Click the icon that looks like an eye to the right of the Styles title.**

   The Styles screen changes on the right side of your browser window, displaying all blocks in the block editor. If you scroll down in that window, you will see all the blocks listed, one after the other.

4. **Click anywhere on the right side of the Styles screen.**

   This opens the Style Book in your browser with the blocks listed on the left side of your screen and the settings panel on the right, as shown in Figure 2-10.

5. **Find the block you want to edit and click it.**

   The block settings panel displays on the right side of your browser, allowing you to edit the settings and styles for your chosen block. See Book 4, Chapter 1 for detailed information on editing blocks.

6. **Click the Save button at the top right of your screen.**

   This saves all of your changes.

REMEMBER

In Book 4, Chapter 1 you discovered how to use blocks from the block editor in your pages and posts. You also discovered how to use the settings panel to configure the settings and style options for the block. If you choose to change the style of a block globally, it will override any of the styles you configured previously for that block.

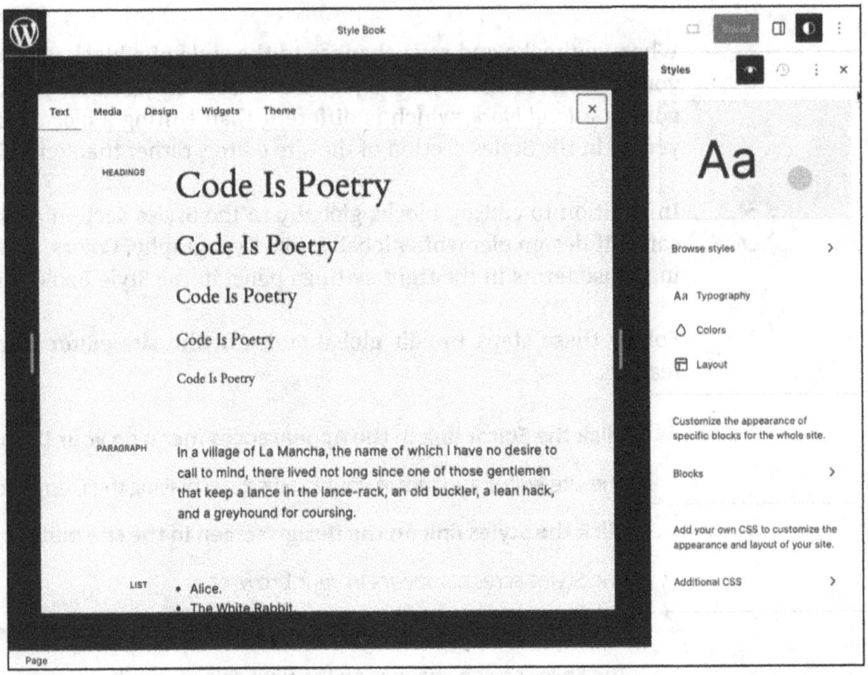

FIGURE 2-10: The Style Book in the site editor for editing global styles.

You may wonder why you would want to edit a block's global style, instead of just setting the styles as you create pages (locally). For some, it's about consistency and branding. For example, if you want all of the buttons on your site to be the same color red, you can edit the button block in the Style Book to set the color to red. Once you've done that, any time you add the button block to a page or post, it will have the same color red as all the rest of your buttons.

Applying global styles in this manner also saves you time so you don't have to worry about setting the button color whenever you add the button block to your content.

Managing pages in the site editor

In the Pages section of the site editor, you can create new pages and manage existing ones. When you click the Pages link on the Design screen in the site editor, the Pages screen opens with a list of all your pages on the left side. Figure 2-11 shows a page from my site titled "About the book" in the site editor.

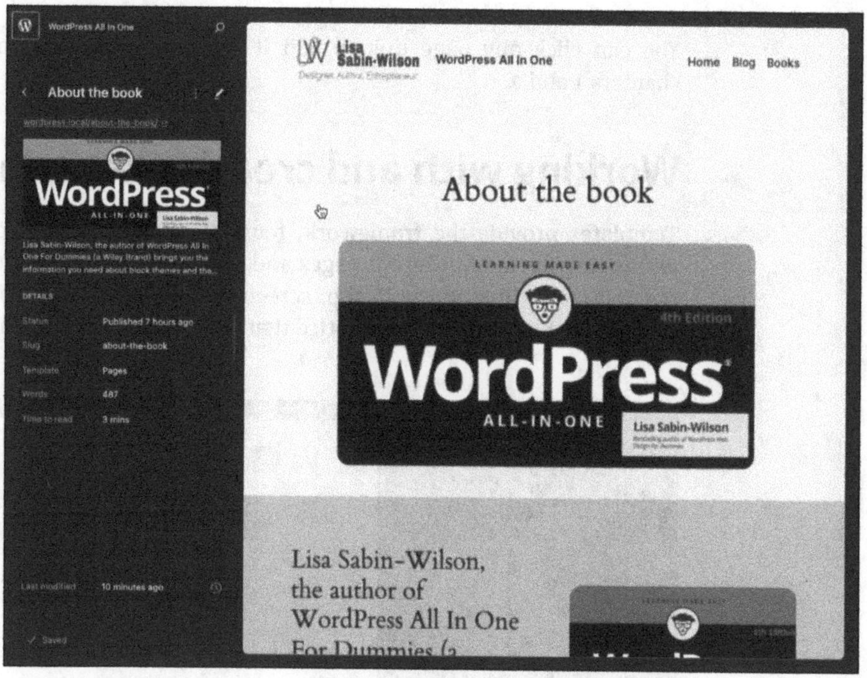

FIGURE 2-11: The Pages section of the site editor.

When you click a page link on the left sidebar, the page is opened in the site editor and you can view the following helpful information about the page:

- **Title:** The title you gave the page when you created it.
- **Permalink:** (URL): The permalink, or URL, of the page.
- **Featured Image:** If you upload an image as the featured image, you see a small version.
- **Excerpt:** The first few lines of the content you added to your page.
- **Status:** This indicates if it's a published page or one that you saved as a draft. Additionally, it displays how long ago you did that (for example, 7 hours ago).
- **Slug:** The slug is used in the page or post permalink.
- **Template:** The layout that is assigned to the page. This is found in the Templates section of the site editor, which is covered in the next section.
- **Words:** The number of words found in your content.
- **Time to read:** An average approximation of how long it will take someone will read the page.
- **Last modified:** An indication of the last time the page was edited and saved (for example, 10 minutes ago).

You can click any page link to edit it using the methods covered in Book 4, chapters 1 and 2.

Working with and creating templates

Templates provide the framework, foundation, and format for how your content is displayed on different pages and sections of your website. When you click the Templates link on the Design screen in the site editor to view the Templates screen (see Figure 2-12), you notice that your theme has various templates.

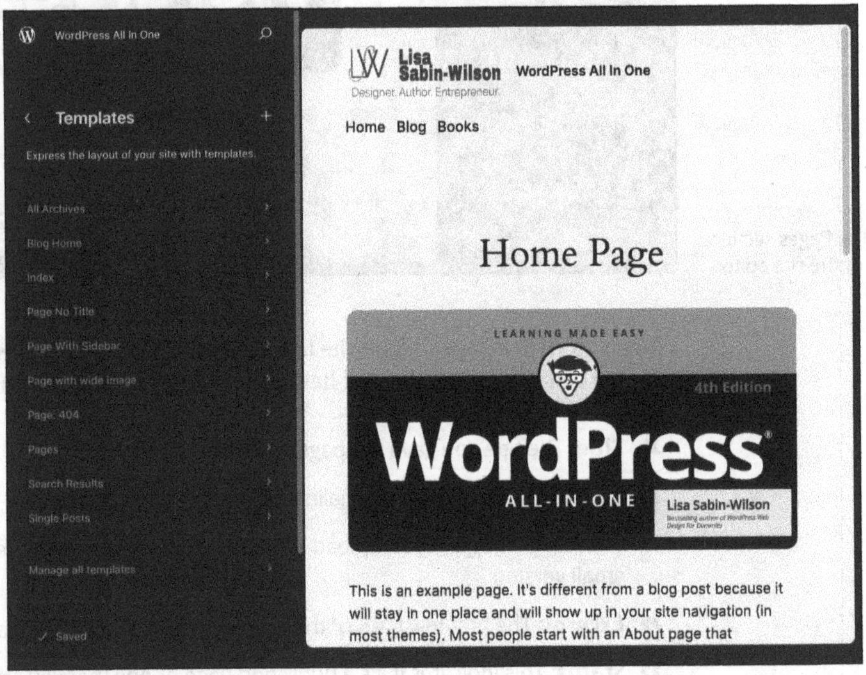

FIGURE 2-12: The Templates screen in the site editor.

The types, names, and number of templates listed on this screen depend on the block theme you are using. Some themes offer a dozen or more templates; some are less prolific and offer fewer than five. The good news is you can add your own once you are familiar and comfortable with how templates are created and used.

In Figure 2-12, you can see the list of templates is many, and that's because the default Twenty Twenty-Four theme has provided the templates on that list. They include:

- **All Archives:** This template is applied to archive listings for posts, authors, categories, tags, dates, and more.

» **Blog Home:** This template is applied to the posts page you set on the Reading Settings screen in Book 3, Chapter 2. You can configure settings such as the title, the number of blog posts per page, and comments setting (open or closed).

» **Index:** This default page serves as a fallback for when a template is not defined for a page or post.

» **Page No Title:** This template is applied to pages where you do not want to display the page title on the live website.

» **Page With Sidebar:** This template is applied to pages where you want to display a sidebar, as shown in Figure 2-13.

» **Page with wide Image:** This template is the same as the Pages template, except the header image is wider and takes up more space, horizontally.

» **Page: 404:** This template is used for the 404 (Page Not Found) page, which is a page your website displays when a visitor requests a page that does not exist. The purpose of a 404 page is to help a visitor get back to the areas on your website that do have content. People get creative with their 404 pages — check out `https://www.canva.com/learn/404-page-design` for some inspiration.

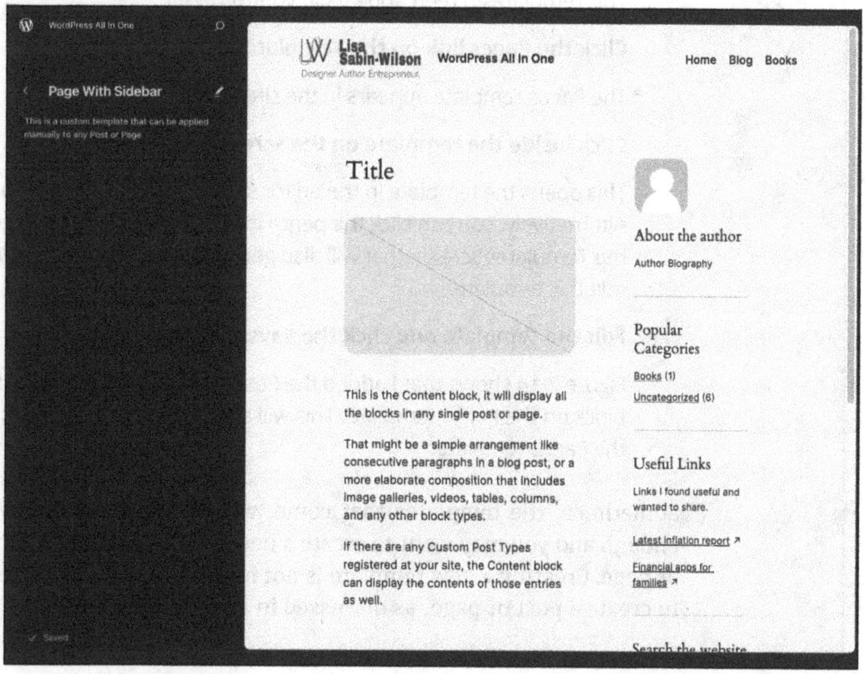

FIGURE 2-13: The Templates section of the site editor shows the Page With Sidebar template.

- **Pages:** This is the default template for all static pages (see Book 4, Chapter 3).
- **Search Results:** When a visitor uses the search form on your website, this template is applied to the search results page.
- **Single Posts:** This is the default template for all single posts on your website.
- **Single Posts with Sidebar (not shown in Figure 2-12):** This is a template to display single posts with a sidebar.

If you are using a different block theme than the default Twenty Twenty-Four, the list of templates you see on the Templates section of the site editor will be different from mine, but the concept is still the same. You can easily change a template by editing the blocks used to create it by adding new blocks, removing existing blocks, or changing the settings and styles of the blocks in the template.

The following steps take you through editing the Pages template in the site editor from the Twenty Twenty-Four theme:

1. **Click the Editor link in the Appearances menu on your Dashboard.**

   The site editor appears in your browser, displaying the Design screen.

2. **Click the Templates link on the Design screen in the site editor.**

   The Templates screen appears in your browser.

3. **Click the Pages link on the Templates screen.**

   The Pages template appears in the site editor.

4. **Click inside the template on the screen's right side.**

   This opens the template in the editor so you can make your changes. Alternatively, you can click the pencil icon to the right of the Pages heading in the Templates screen; that will also get you into the site editor, where you can edit this template.

5. **Edit the template and click the Save button.**

   Figure 2-14 shows that I added the Post Author block underneath the Title block on the Pages template. This will affect every page on my site that uses the Pages template.

Sometimes, the templates that come with the theme you have activated aren't enough and you may want to create a new template that you can apply to any post or page. Creating a new template is not much different than using the block editor to create a post or page, as discussed in Book 4, Chapter 1.

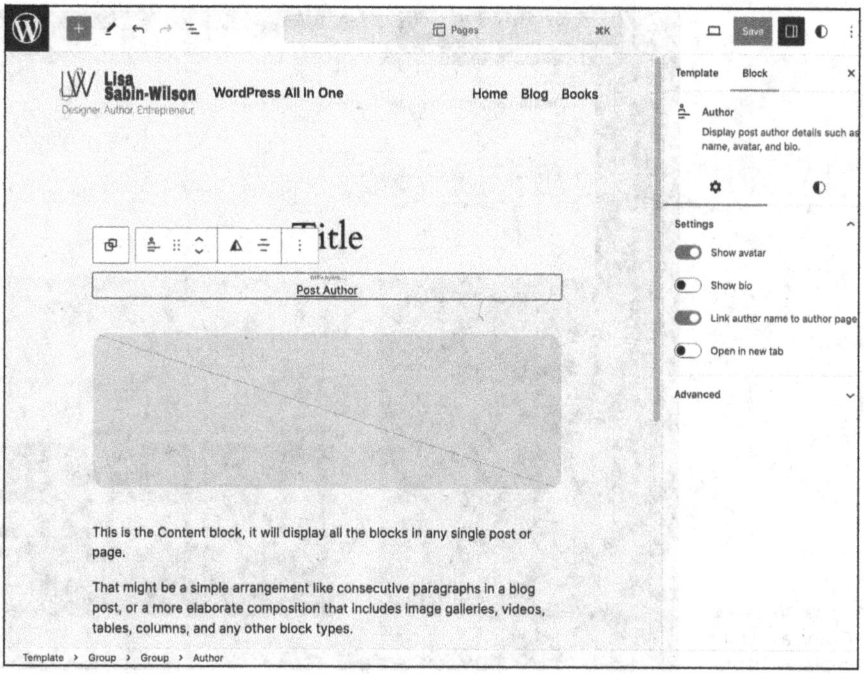

FIGURE 2-14: Modifying a template in the site editor.

Follow these steps to create a new template:

1. **Click the Editor link in the Appearances menu on your Dashboard.**

   The site editor appears in your browser, displaying the Design screen.

2. **Click the Templates link on the Design screen in the site editor.**

   The Templates screen appears in your browser.

3. **Click the icon that looks like a plus sign to the right of the title on the Templates screen.**

   The Add Template window pops up.

4. **Select the Custom Template option on the Add Template window.**

   The Create Custom Template window pops up, with a Name field in which you can type a description of the template you are creating. For practice purposes, I typed in Test Template (see Figure 2-15).

5. **Click the Create button.**

   This loads the new blank Test Template in the site editor window.

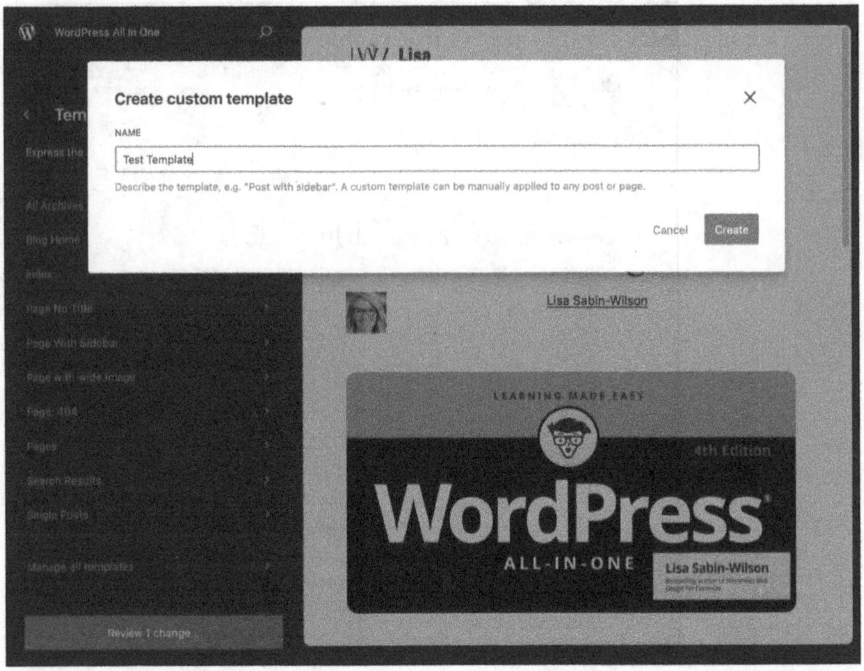

FIGURE 2-15: Giving a custom template a name.

6. **Add blocks to the Test Template.**

   Using the knowledge you've gained so far in this chapter and Book 4 about using the block editor and adding and styling blocks to your preference, build the template you want by adding blocks and content to the Test Template.

7. **Click the Save button at the top right.**

   This saves the Test Template as a new template and lists it on the Templates screen in the site editor, along with all other templates.

You can change the template on any page by editing the page and setting the template in the settings panel on the right side of the editor. Figure 2-16 illustrates how and where I set the new Test Template created in the previous steps to a new page on my website. You find the Template link in the right-side settings panel; click the link to change it. Be sure to save your changes before you leave.

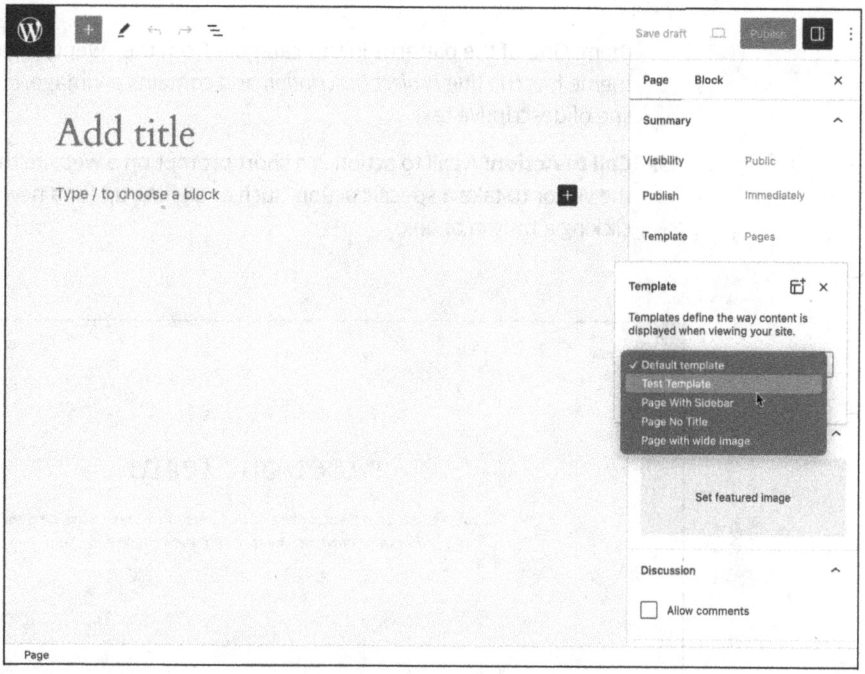

FIGURE 2-16: Applying a template to page.

Understanding Block Patterns

Block patterns are predefined combinations of blocks that allow you to save them and quickly and easily apply them to the overall layout of your website. The developer of the theme you are using may have included some block patterns for you to use, and you can also create your own. Book 6, Chapter 3 discusses block patterns in detail, including how to use and create them in the site editor.

You can view all block patterns included in your theme by clicking the Patterns link on the Design screen in the site editor to load the Patterns page in your browser. You'll find information on how to add them to a post or a page in Book 6, Chapter 3.

Patterns are categorized based on the type of content the pattern was created for. For example, the first three categories in the Twenty Twenty-Four theme, after the catch-all "All Patterns" category, are

- **About:** The patterns in this category were designed to create blocks that allow you to tell your visitor all about yourself. You find patterns like the Meet Our Team pattern shown in Figure 2-17.
- **Banners:** The patterns found in this category can be added to your content when you need to briefly group text and images together to call attention to

them. One of the patterns in this category from the Twenty Twenty-Four theme has the title *Project Description* and contains an image, title, and one line of descriptive text.

» **Call to Action:** A call to action is a short prompt on a website that encourages the visitor to take a specific action, such as signing up for a newsletter or clicking a button or link.

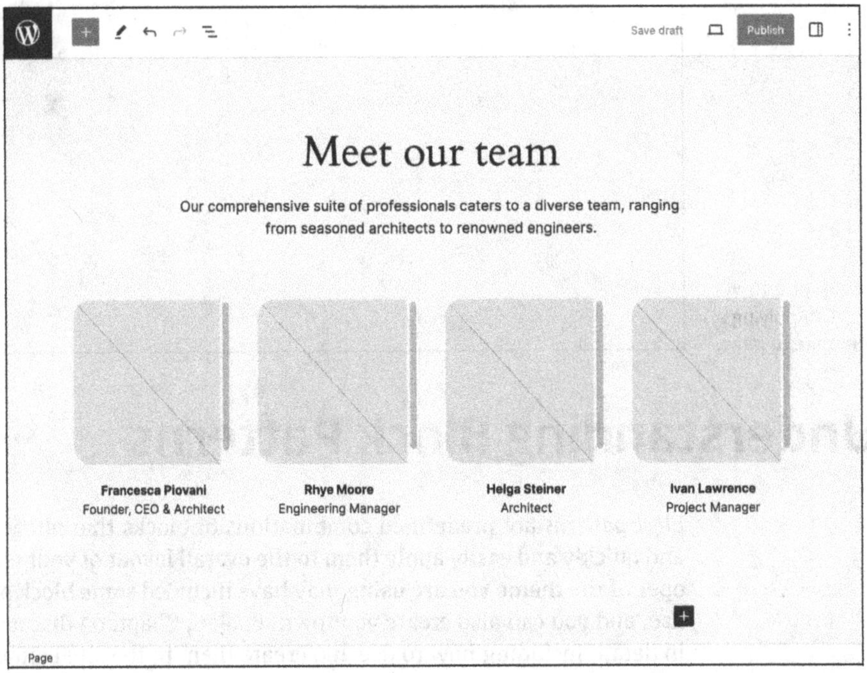

FIGURE 2-17: A pattern found in the About category in the Twenty Twenty-Four theme patterns.

SITE EDITOR COMMAND PALETTE

Navigating the site editor to view all of the available block patterns can get a little crazy if you have a lot of patterns. Luckily, the WordPress development team anticipated such an issue and created the Command Palette feature to give you a method to quickly navigate your site's content, including block patterns.

You can access the Command Palette in the site editor by clicking the title at the top of a page loaded in the editor. When the Command Palette field pops up, you can start typing the block pattern you are looking for. You can also access the Command Palette using the keyboard shortcut ctrl+k on a PC or cmd+k on a Mac.

IN THIS CHAPTER

» Applying block patterns to your website

» Working with existing block patterns

» Creating a simple block pattern

» Finding new block patterns

Chapter 3

Using and Creating Block Patterns

In Book 6, Chapter 2, you learned about block themes and the site editor, and the concept of block patterns came up as well, as a way of creating and managing your content. *Block patterns* are predefined combinations of blocks that allow you to save them, and then quickly and easily apply them to the overall layout of your website. There are several ways to use block patterns to create pages and layouts.

Some default block patterns are included in your WordPress installation, and if you are using a block theme, some block theme developers include a library of block patterns, like the default Twenty Twenty-Four theme. You can download patterns and even create your own. This chapter takes you through discovering how to do all of those things.

Discovering Block Patterns

In Book 4, Chapter 1 you were introduced to using single blocks from the block editor to create content and build out your posts and pages. Then, in Book 6, Chapter 2, you discovered how to use the site editor with block themes to manage your website's look, design, and layout. In block themes, part of the site editor is a library of block patterns, but you don't need a block theme to use block patterns. WordPress, with or without a block theme, has a small library of prebuilt block patterns that you can use.

The best way I have been able to describe block patterns to people is to ask them to imagine layering one block on top of another until they have the layout they want for their content, then saving those layers as one unique pattern that you can use repeatedly.

Synced and unsynced block patterns

Two types of block patterns can be created:

- **Synced patterns:** Once you create a pattern and set it as *synced*, it can be used as many times as you want on different pages, and if you edit or change anything in it, the changes get broadcast to all instances of the block throughout your site. For example, if you use the synced block pattern on your home page, About page, and Contact page, you only need to edit a synced pattern once, and the changes happen everywhere the pattern is being used.
- **Unsynced patterns:** These block patterns are the exact opposite of synced patterns. With *unsynced* patterns, you can create the block pattern and use it anywhere you want on your website, as many times as you want, but if you edit or change anything in the block pattern on one page, the changes do not happen everywhere the pattern is being used.

A perfect synced pattern example is a Call to Action (CTA). Often buttons or links, CTAs prompt site visitors to act, like signing up for a newsletter or purchasing a product. For a consistent look across the site, you can create a CTA block pattern and set it as a synced pattern. Edit once, and it updates everywhere it's used, ensuring a uniform CTA for users to engage with. Figure 3-1 shows a standard CTA format on my site, added above the footer area that displays my logo and three columns of links.

Figure 3-2 shows a good example of the use of an unsynced pattern, which displays a block pattern that uses the following blocks added to the group block to make the pattern:

- Image block
- Heading block
- Paragraph block
- Button block

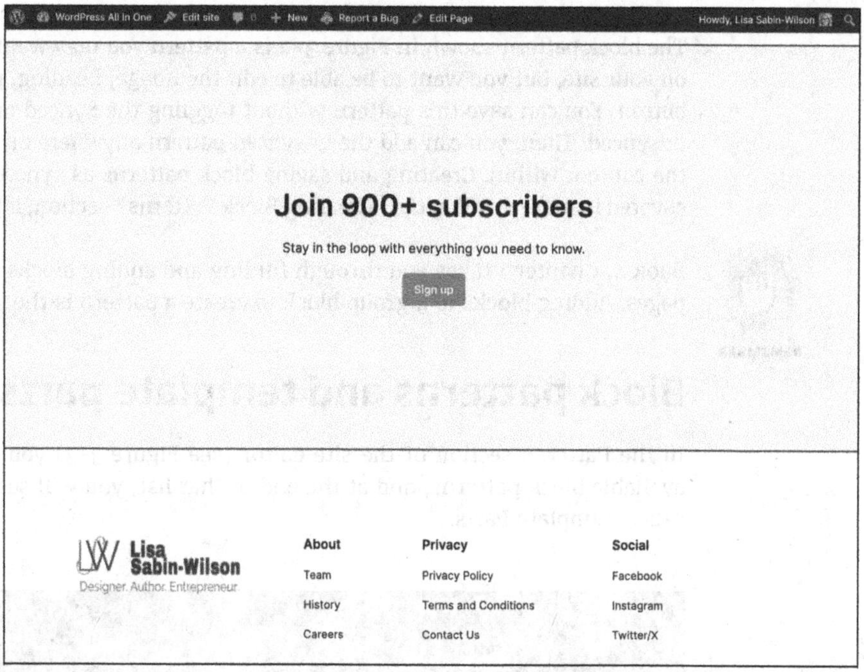

FIGURE 3-1: A Call to Action (CTA) synced block pattern.

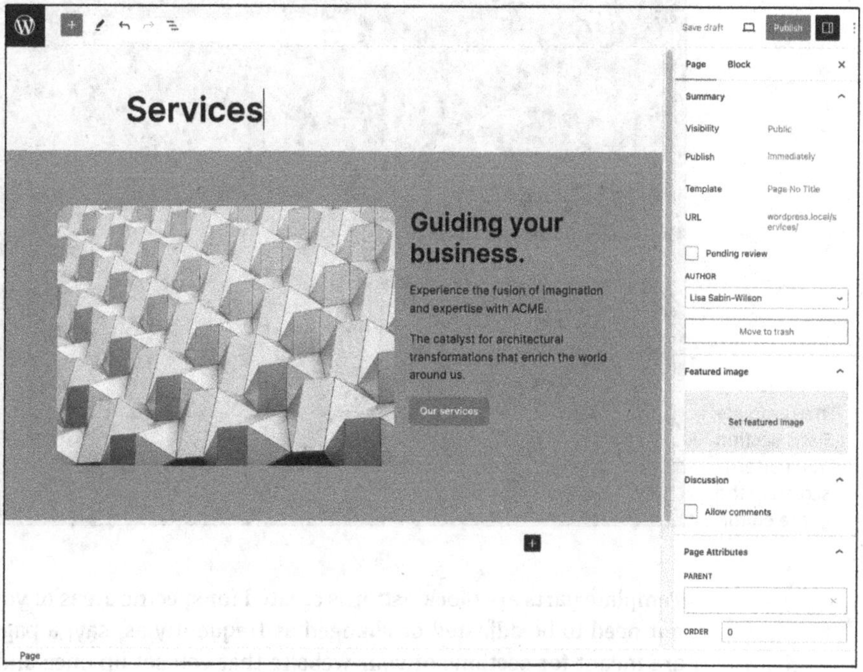

FIGURE 3-2: An unsynced block pattern can be added to any page and allows you to edit the content.

The block pattern shown in Figure 3-2 is a pattern you may want to use elsewhere on your site, but you want to be able to edit the image, heading, paragraph text, or button. You can save this pattern without toggling the Synced option to save it as unsynced. Then, you can add the unsynced pattern anywhere on your site and edit the content within. Creating and saving block patterns as synced or unsynced are covered in more detail in the "Creating Block Patterns" section, later in this chapter.

REMEMBER

Book 4, Chapter 1 takes you through finding and adding blocks to your posts and pages. Adding blocks to a group block to create a pattern is the same.

Block patterns and template parts

In the Patterns section of the site editor (see Figure 3-3) you will find a list of available block patterns, and at the end of that list, you will see another heading called Template Parts.

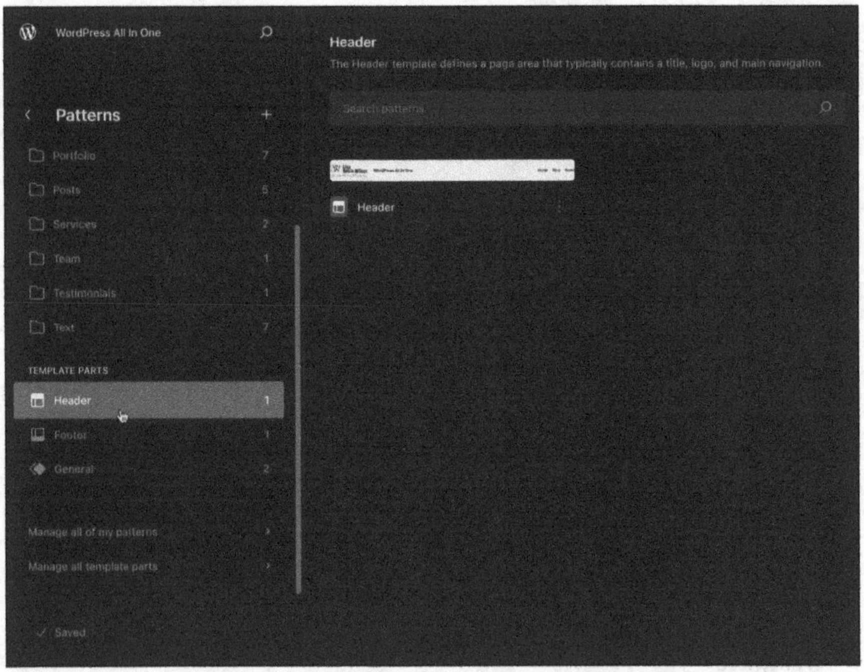

FIGURE 3-3: The Template Parts section of the Patterns screen in the site editor.

Template parts are block patterns created for specific areas of your website that do not need to be adjusted or changed as frequently as, say, a page. Template parts are meant for sections of your website that you set up once and then see all over your site. Think of the headers and footers of your website — these are perfect examples of template parts crafted with WordPress blocks.

There is little difference between a template part and a synced block pattern. Both are synced block patterns used several times throughout the site, and both are meant to look the same and contain the same elements, no matter where they are used. The point for both is that you only have to edit them once, and your edits get applied automatically to every instance of them on your site.

REMEMBER

A template part is best used to create blocks for use on global areas of your website, such as the header, footer, and sidebar. These areas are not part of your content for pages or posts, and are typically used on every site page.

Using Existing Block Patterns

Adding block patterns to a page is similar to adding a single block from the block editor, which you did in Book 4, Chapter 1. Follow these steps to find block patterns and add them to a page:

1. **Click Add New in the Pages menu on your Dashboard.**

   This opens the WordPress edit page screen.

2. **Type a title in the Add Title section.**
3. **Press the Enter (or Return on a Mac) key.**
4. **Click the Block Inserter icon (plus sign) at the top-left side of the page.**

   This opens the Block Inserter panel.

5. **Click the Patterns tab.**

   This displays all the pattern categories in the Block Inserter panel, as shown in Figure 3-4.

6. **Click a pattern category.**

   In Figure 3-5, I've selected the Banners category because I want to add a banner at the top of my About Me page. Using the default Twenty Twenty-Four theme, the available pattern categories include

   - *All Patterns:* Displays all available patterns in the Pattern panel
   - *About:* Patterns that use blocks that work well for an About page
   - *Banners:* Patterns that use blocks that work well as a display banner
   - *Call to Action:* Patterns that use a combination of heading, paragraph, and buttons blocks
   - *Featured:* Patterns that the theme developer decided to categorize as featured

Using and Creating Block Patterns

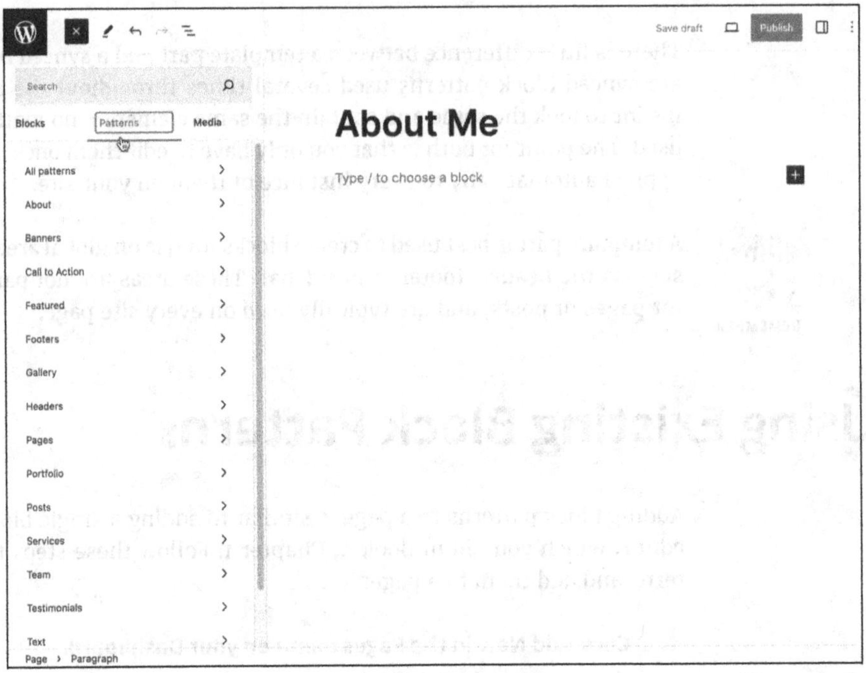

FIGURE 3-4: The Patterns section of the block inserter.

- *Footers:* Patterns that use blocks that work well as a site footer
- *Gallery:* Patterns that use blocks that include galleries for photos and images
- *Headers:* Patterns that use blocks that work well as a site header
- *Pages:* Multiple patterns put together to create an entire page or a layout for the whole page
- *Portfolio:* Patterns that use images or galleries to display a body of work
- *Posts:* Patterns that use blocks to creatively display blog posts
- *Services:* Patterns that use blocks that work well to provide a list of services
- *Team:* Patterns that use blocks to display a team or group of people
- *Testimonials:* Patterns that use blocks to display testimonials, like a quote, photo, or citation
- *Text:* Patterns that use blocks to display text or content differently

7. **Click the pattern you want to use.**

   This adds the selected pattern to your page. In Figure 3-5, you see that I selected the Text with Alternating Images block pattern, and Figure 3-6 displays that pattern added to my page in the site editor.

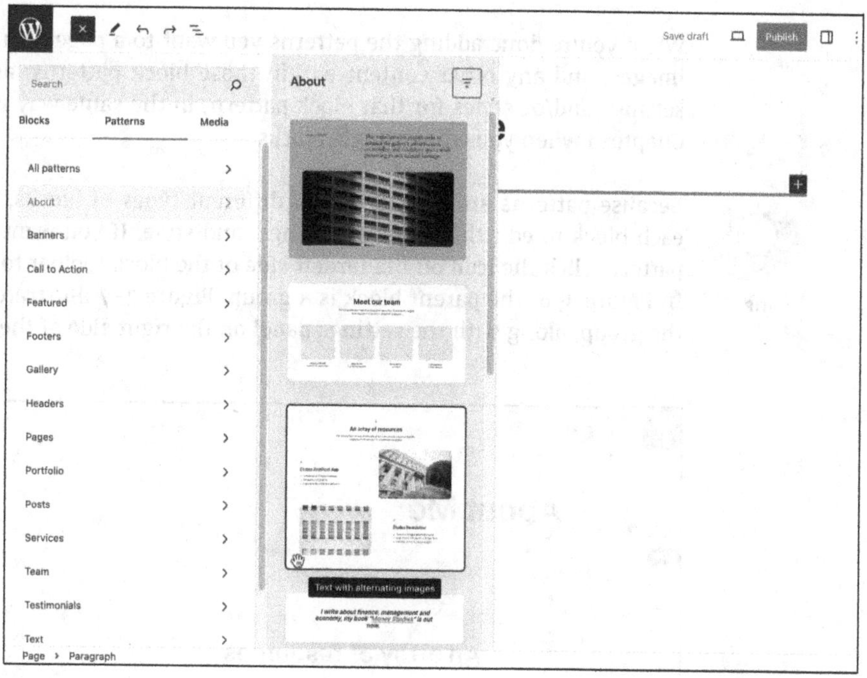

FIGURE 3-5: Block patterns in the About category.

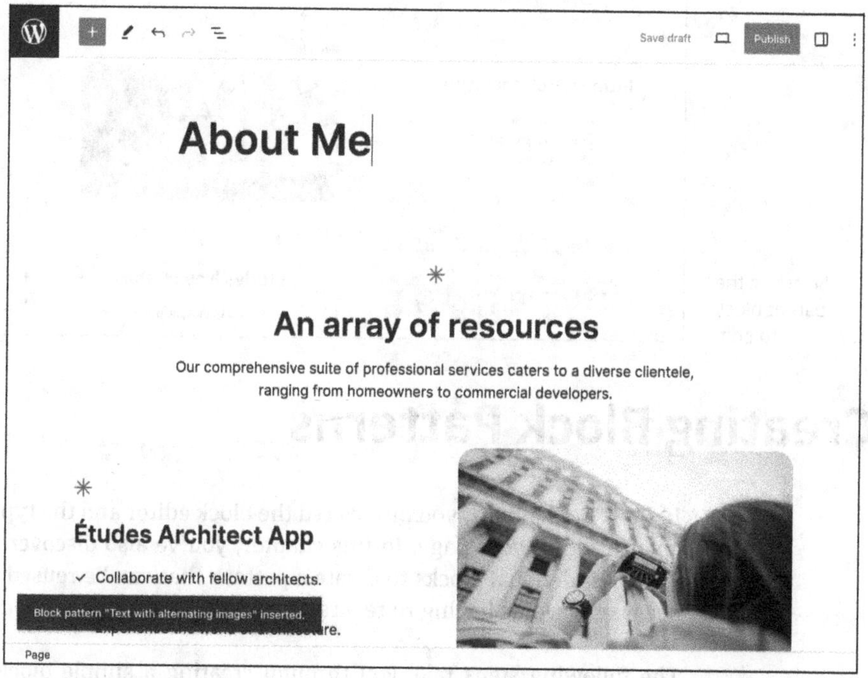

FIGURE 3-6: A page with the Text with Alternating Images block pattern added.

When you're done adding the patterns you want to a page, you can edit the text, images, and any other content within those block patterns, as well as edit the settings and/or styles for that block pattern, in the same way you did in Book 4, Chapter 1 when you edited single blocks.

TIP

Because patterns are a collection of different types of blocks, you need to click each block to edit the content, settings, and style. If you want to edit the entire pattern, click the icon on the far left side of the block toolbar to select the parent. In Figure 3-6, the parent block is a group. Figure 3-7 illustrates the selection of the group, along with the settings panel on the right side of the screen.

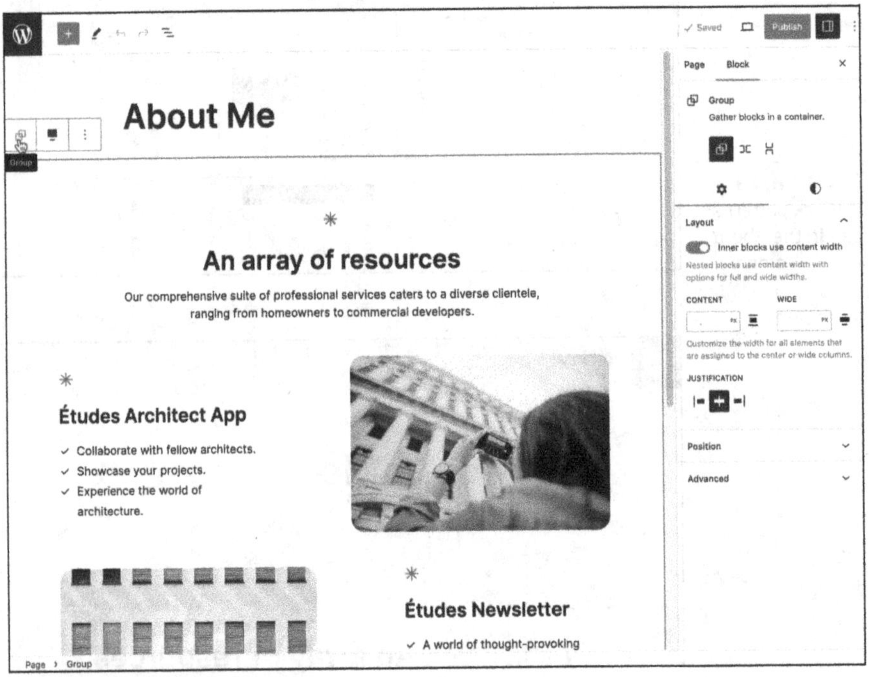

FIGURE 3-7: Selecting the parent block to edit.

Creating Block Patterns

In Book 4, Chapter 1, you discovered the block editor and the types of blocks available to add to your page. In this chapter, you've also discovered how combining a set of individual blocks to create a pattern that can be reused can save you time because it avoids having to re-create a similar pattern repeatedly.

The following steps take you through creating a simple block pattern that has an image on the left side and a heading, paragraph text, and a button on the right side:

1. **Click Add New in the Pages menu on your Dashboard.**

   This opens the WordPress edit page screen.

2. **Type a title in the Add Title section.**
3. **Press the Enter (or Return on a Mac) key.**
4. **Click the Block Inserter icon (plus sign) at the top-left side of the page.**

   This opens the Block Inserter panel.

5. **Type the word "Columns" in the search form in the block inserter.**

   The block inserter displays blocks that are relevant to the term.

6. **Click the columns block.**

   This inserts the columns block into your page, and the Block Inserter panel closes.

7. **Select the 50/50 layout, as shown in Figure 3-8.**

   There are several choices for the columns; selecting the 50/50 layout inserts a block with two columns on your page.

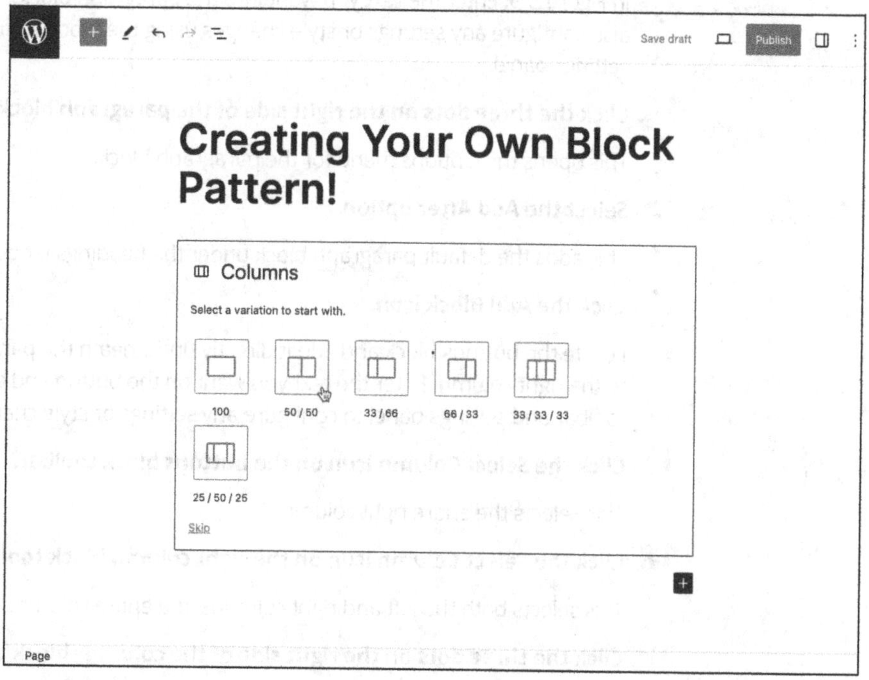

FIGURE 3-8: Selecting your preferred layout in the columns block.

8. **In the left column of the columns block, click the plus sign to open the block inserter inline.**

9. **Use the search form to search for the image block.**

10. **Click the image block to add it to the left side of the columns block.**

    With the image block added, you can add an image by uploading one from your computer or selecting one from the Media Library. You can also configure any settings or style changes using the block toolbar and settings panel.

11. **In the right column of the columns block, click the plus sign to open the block inserter inline.**

    Locate the headings block and add it to the right column, then enter the text you want displayed in the headings block. You can also configure any settings or style changes using the block toolbar and settings panel.

12. **Click the three dots on the right side of the headings block toolbar.**

    This opens the Options menu for the headings block.

13. **Select the Add After option.**

    This adds the default paragraph block under the headings block, as shown in Figure 3-9. Enter the text you want into the paragraph block. You can also configure any settings or style changes using the block toolbar and settings panel.

14. **Click the three dots on the right side of the paragraph block toolbar.**

    This opens the Options menu for the paragraph block.

15. **Select the Add After option.**

    This adds the default paragraph block under the headings block.

16. **Click the Add Block icon.**

    Locate the buttons block and add it directly underneath the paragraph block to the right column. Enter the text you want on the button and use the block toolbar and settings panel to configure any settings or style changes.

17. **Click the Select Column icon on the buttons block toolbar.**

    This selects the entire right column.

18. **Click the Select Column icon on the right column block toolbar.**

    This selects both the left and right columns, the entire columns block.

19. **Click the three dots on the right side of the columns block toolbar.**

    This opens the Options menu for the columns block.

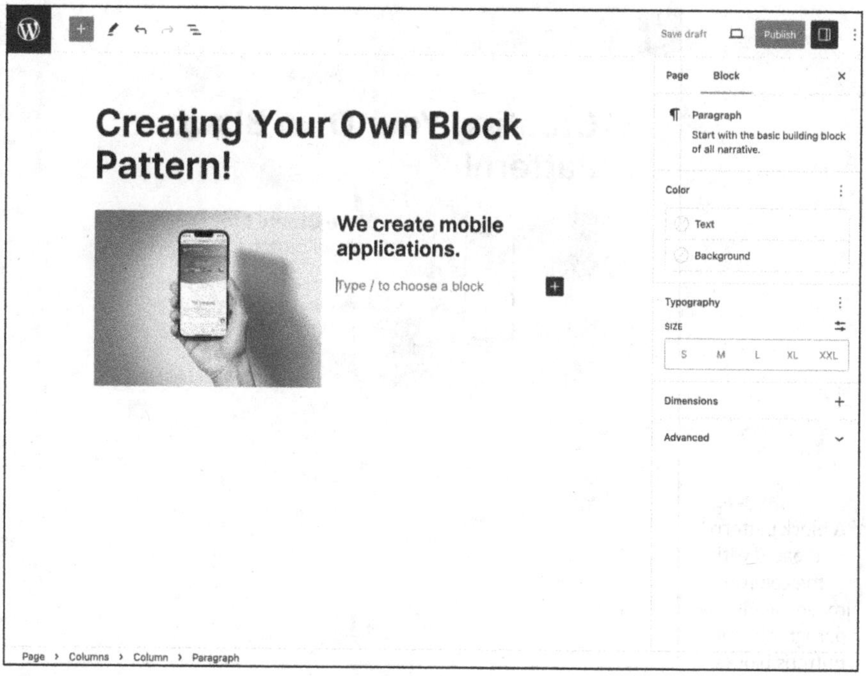

FIGURE 3-9: The paragraph block underneath the headings block.

20. **Select the Create Pattern option.**

    This pops up a Create Pattern window.

21. **Type a title for your pattern in the Name field.**

22. **Click the Categories field to view a drop-down menu of available categories to select.**

23. **Select the desired category for your new block pattern.**

24. **Deselect the Synced toggle.**

    Selected by default, deselecting this toggle ensures that you can use this block with edits later on. See the "Synced and unsynced block patterns" section, earlier in this chapter.

25. **Click the Create button.**

    This saves the block pattern to the existing block pattern library. Figure 3-10 displays the block pattern completed in these steps.

It's easy to see how useful it is to create your block patterns because they save so much time, especially if you regularly manage a great deal of content on your website.

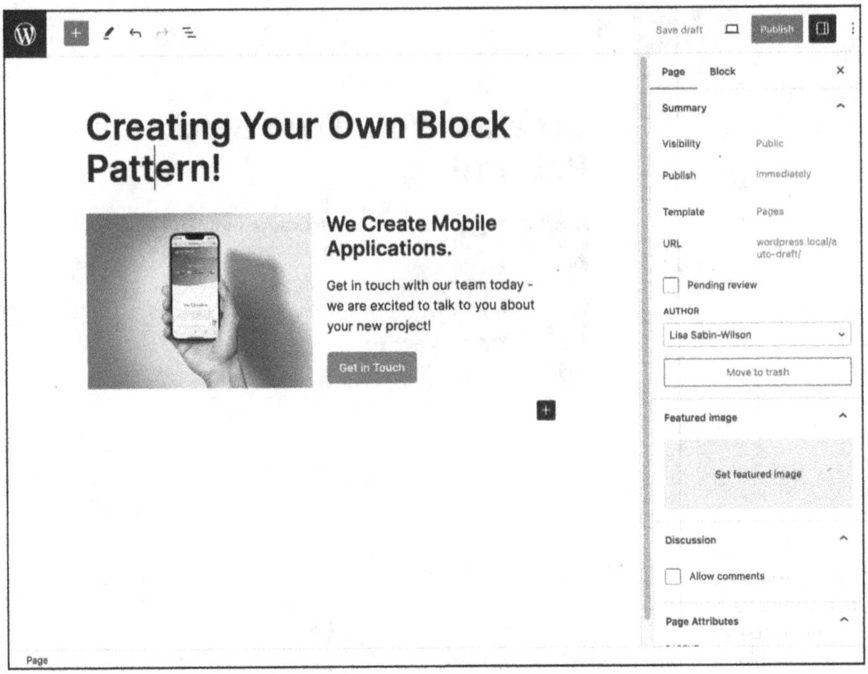

FIGURE 3-10: A block pattern created with the columns, image, heading, paragraph, and buttons blocks.

It is possible to create full-page layouts by adding several blocks and block patterns on a page, adding those collections of blocks and patterns to a group block, and saving it as a pattern. The Twenty Twenty-Four theme has a few of these in the site editor; they are called *full-page layouts* and you can find them in the Pages section of the Patterns screen in the site editor. You can also find them in the block inserter in the Pages category.

Finding New Block Patterns

When it comes to block patterns, you can use the ones that WordPress and your existing theme give you. Here are a few ways you can find, install, and experiment with block patterns:

- **WordPress Patterns page (`https://wordpress.org/patterns`):** The official WordPress website has a library of block patterns you can choose from. Browse through the library, find one you like, and click the Copy button to put the pattern details in your Clipboard. Then, you can return to your website and open up a page you want to add it to, right-click in the site editor with your mouse, and select Paste. That's it — the entire pattern, styles and all, appears on your screen. Figure 3-11 shows a page that I am editing where

I pasted this pattern in: `https://wordpress.org/patterns/pattern/sales-banner`.

» **WordPress Plugins page (`https://wordpress.org/plugins/search/block+patterns`):** You can search on the official WordPress Plugins page for block patterns that developers have released full libraries for and packaged them in a plugin that you can install and activate on your site.

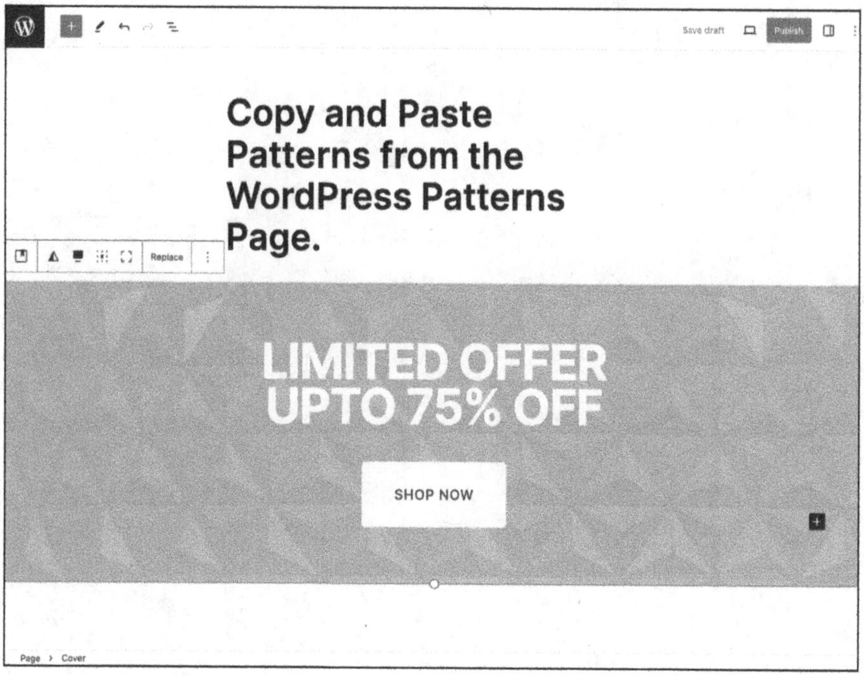

FIGURE 3-11: Copy and paste patterns from the WordPress Patterns page.

7

Using and Developing Plugins

Contents at a Glance

IN THIS CHAPTER

» Extending WordPress with plugins

» Comparing plugins to themes

» Finding plugins both on and outside of the WordPress website

» Evaluating the trustworthiness of plugins

» Comparing free versus commercial plugins

Chapter 1
Introducing WordPress Plugins

Half the fun of running a WordPress-powered website is playing with the hundreds of plugins that you can install to extend your site's functionality and options. WordPress plugins are like those really cool custom rims you put on your car: Although they don't come with the car, they're awesome accessories that make your car better than all the rest.

Plugins can be very simple, such as a plugin that changes the appearance of the Dashboard menu. Or they can be very complex, accomplishing hefty tasks such as providing a complete e-commerce solution with product listings, a shopping cart, and payment processing.

In this chapter, you find out what plugins are, how to find and install them, and how they enhance your site to make it unique. Using plugins can also greatly improve your readers' experiences by providing them various tools they can use to interact and participate — just the way you want them to!

I assume that you already have WordPress installed on your web server. If you're skipping around in the book and haven't yet installed WordPress on your web server, you can find instructions in Book 2, Chapter 3.

REMEMBER

WordPress.com users can't install or configure plugins on their hosted blogs. I don't make the rules, so please don't kill the messenger.

Extending WordPress with Plugins

By itself, WordPress is a powerful program for web publishing, but customizing WordPress with plugins makes WordPress even more powerful. A *plugin* is a small piece of software that, when added to WordPress, interacts with it to provide some extensibility to WordPress, giving it almost limitless ways to handle web content.

Plugin developers are the people who write these gems and share them with the rest of us — sometimes for free. Like WordPress, many plugins are free to anyone who wants to further tailor and customize a site to meet specific needs.

REMEMBER

Plugins aren't part of the core software; neither are they software programs themselves. They typically don't function as stand-alone software. They require the host program (WordPress, in this case) to function.

You can choose any plugins you need to expand your online possibilities. Plugins can turn your WordPress installation into a full-featured gallery for posting images on the web, an online store to sell your products, a user forum, or a social networking site. WordPress plugins can be simple, perhaps adding a few minor features, or complex enough to change your entire WordPress site's functionality.

Here are just a few examples of things that plugins let you add to your WordPress site:

- **Email notification:** Your biggest fans can sign up to have an email notification sent to them every time you update your website.
- **Social media integration:** This plugin allows your readers to submit your content to some of the most popular social networking services, such as Twitter, Facebook, and Reddit.
- **Stats program:** This plugin keeps track of where your traffic is coming from; which posts on your site are most popular; and how much traffic is coming through your website on a daily, monthly, and yearly basis.

There's a popular saying among WordPress users: "There's a plugin for that." The idea is that if you want WordPress to do something new, or if you have an idea for a new feature for your site, you have a good chance of finding an existing plugin that can help you do what you want. Currently, there are more than

59,000 plugins available on the WordPress website (`https://wordpress.org/plugins`), and this number is growing at a rate of a few new plugins each day. In addition, thousands more plugins are available outside the WordPress website for free or for a fee.

Identifying Core Plugins

Some plugins hold a very special place in WordPress in that they're shipped with the WordPress software and are included by default in every WordPress installation. The number of core plugins has changed over the years, but currently, only one plugin holds this special position, and it is called Akismet. The Akismet plugin has the sole purpose of protecting your blog from comment spam. Although other plugins address the issue of comment spam, the fact that Akismet is packaged with WordPress and works quite well means that most WordPress users rely on Akismet for their needs. Book 3, Chapter 4 covers how to activate and configure Akismet on your site.

Figure 1-1 shows the core plugins in a new installation of WordPress.

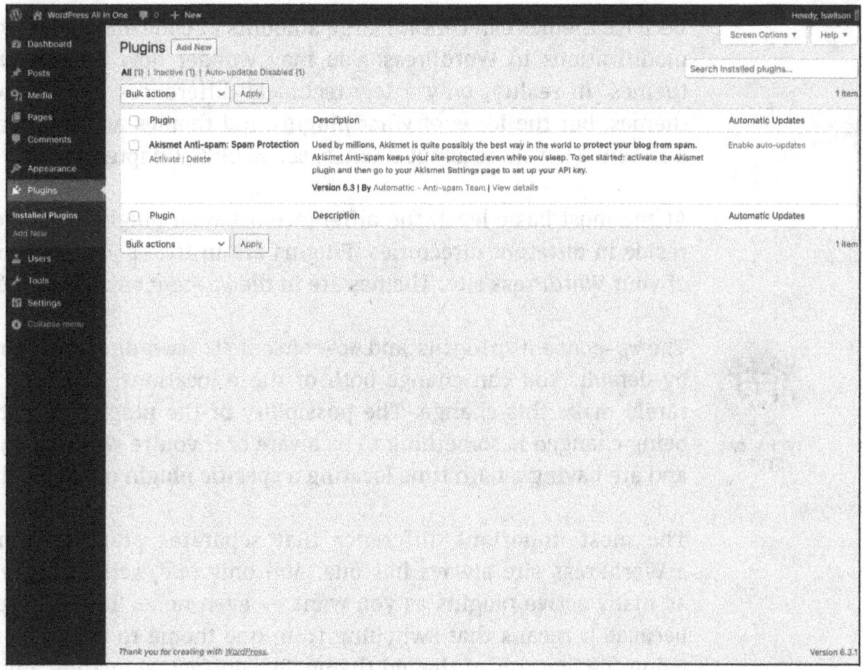

FIGURE 1-1: Akismet is a core plugin in WordPress.

REMEMBER

The idea of core plugins is to offer a base set of plugins to introduce you to the concept of plugins while providing a benefit. The Akismet plugin is useful because comment spam is a very real and very big issue for WordPress sites.

Although WordPress automatically includes this plugin, your site doesn't have to run it. Plugins are disabled by default; you must activate them manually in order to use them. You can delete core plugins, just as you can delete any other plugins, and they won't be replaced when you upgrade WordPress.

Future versions of WordPress may offer different sets of core plugins. It's possible that a current core plugin will cease being a core plugin and that other plugins will be included. Although this topic has been much discussed in WordPress development circles over the past few years, as of this writing, no definitive decisions have been made, so the current set of core plugins is likely to stay for a while longer.

Distinguishing between Plugins and Themes

Because themes can contain large amounts of code and add new features or other modifications to WordPress, you may wonder how plugins are different from themes. In reality, only a few technical differences exist between plugins and themes, but the ideas of what plugins and themes are supposed to be are quite different. (For more about themes, see Book 6, Chapter 1.)

At the most basic level, the difference between plugins and themes is that they reside in different directories. Plugins are in the `wp-content/plugins` directory of your WordPress site. Themes are in the `wp-content/themes` directory.

TECHNICAL STUFF

The `wp-content/plugins` and `wp-content/themes` directories are set up this way by default. You can change both of these locations, although WordPress users rarely make this change. The possibility of the plugins' and themes' locations being changed is something to be aware of if you're working on a WordPress site and are having a hard time locating a specific plugin or theme directory.

The most important difference that separates plugins from themes is that a WordPress site always has one, and only one, active theme, but it can have as many active plugins as you want — even none. This difference is important because it means that switching from one theme to another prevents you from using the features of the old theme. By contrast, activating a new plugin doesn't prevent you from making use of the other active plugins.

Because WordPress can have only one theme but many plugins activated at one time, it's important that the features that modify WordPress be limited to plugins, while the theme remains focused on the appearance of the site. For you, the user, this separation of functionality and appearance is the most important difference between plugins and themes. (See the nearby sidebar, "Other differences between plugins and themes.")

TIP

This separation of plugins for functionality and themes for appearance isn't enforced by WordPress, but it's a good practice to follow. You can build a theme that includes too much functionality, and you may start to rely on those functions to make your site work, which ultimately makes switching to another theme difficult.

The functionality role of plugins doesn't mean that control of the appearance of a WordPress site is limited to its theme. Plugins are just as capable of modifying the site's appearance as a theme is. The WPtouch mobile plugin, for example (available at `https://wordpress.org/plugins/wptouch`), can provide a different version of your site to mobile devices such as smartphones by replacing the functionality of the theme when the user visits the site on a mobile device.

OTHER DIFFERENCES BETWEEN PLUGINS AND THEMES

TECHNICAL STUFF

Other technical differences separate plugins and themes. The differences matter mostly to developers, but it could be important for you to know these differences as a nondeveloper WordPress user:

- Plugins load before the theme, which gives plugins some special privileges over themes; the result can be that one or more plugins prevent the theme from loading. The built-in WordPress functions in the `wp-includes/pluggable.php` file can be overridden with customized functions, and only plugins load early enough to override these functions.
- Themes support a series of structured template files and require a minimum set of files to be valid. By comparison, plugins have no structured set of files and require only a single .php file with a comment block at the top to tell WordPress that the file is a plugin.
- Themes support a concept called *child themes,* wherein one theme can require another theme to be present to function; no such feature is available to plugins.

Finding Plugins on the WordPress Website

The largest and most widely used source of free WordPress plugins is the WordPress Plugins page (`https://wordpress.org/plugins`). As shown in Figure 1-2, this directory is filled with more than 59,000 plugins that cover an extremely broad range of features. Due to the large number of plugins freely available, and the fact that each plugin listing includes ratings and details such as user-reported compatibility with WordPress versions, the Plugins page of the WordPress website should be your first stop when you're looking for a new plugin to fill a specific need.

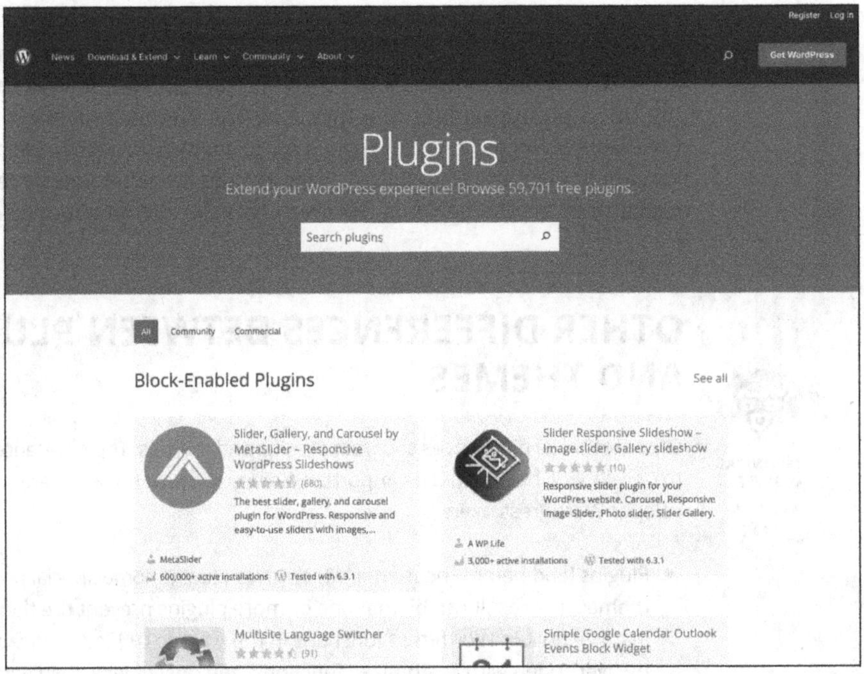

FIGURE 1-2: The Plugins page of the WordPress website.

Although you can search for plugins directly on the WordPress website, WordPress has a built-in feature for searching for plugins on the Add Plugins screen (shown in Figure 1-3 in the following section). This feature even allows you to easily install a plugin from WordPress without having to download it and upload it to your site.

The following sections show you how to find plugins.

Searching for plugins from the Dashboard

Before you start installing plugins on your site, it's important to explore the Plugins page of your WordPress Dashboard and understand how to manage the plugins after you install them. Click the Add New link on the Plugins menu of your WordPress Dashboard to view the Add Plugins screen, shown in Figure 1-3.

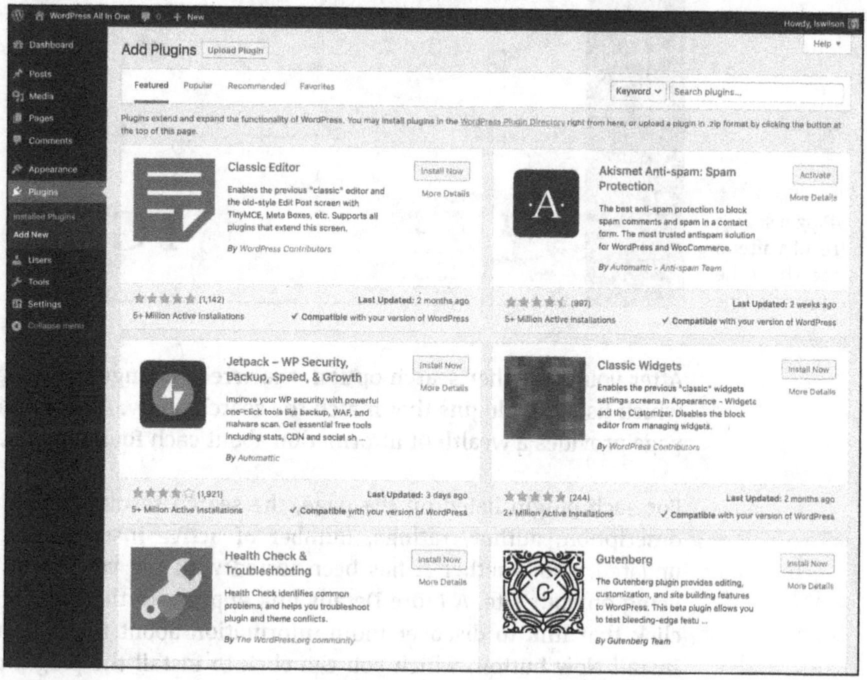

FIGURE 1-3: The Add Plugins screen.

At the top of the Add Plugins screen is a series of links and features that provide several ways to find plugins. (If you're looking to install a plugin, turn to Book 7, Chapter 2.)

Search

Figure 1-4 shows the search results screen. This screen enables you to search for WordPress plugins either by typing a search term in the Search box or by clicking one of the popular tag links to narrow the list of plugins.

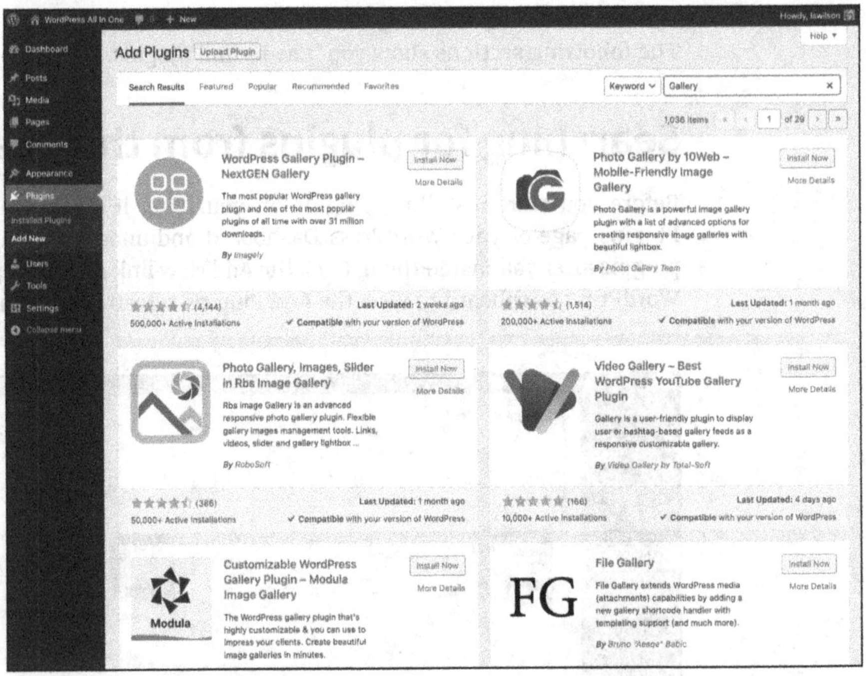

FIGURE 1-4: Plugin search results after a search for the term *Gallery*.

After you use either search option, the screen changes to a Search Results page, which lists the plugins that match the search query. As shown in Figure 1-4, this page provides a wealth of information about each found plugin.

For each plugin listed on the page, the search results show the plugin's name, description, author, ratings, number of active installations, time it was last updated, and whether it has been tested with the version of WordPress you're using on your site. A More Details link appears to the right of the plugin name; click that link to discover more information about the plugin. You also see an Install Now button, which you can click to install the plugin on your site. (I go into detail about these links in the "Evaluating Plugins before Installing" section, later in this chapter.)

Upload Plugin

Click the Upload Plugin button at the top of the Add Plugins screen to display the upload feature, as shown in Figure 1-5. The Upload section allows for easy installation of downloaded plugin Zip files without using SFTP or some other method to upload the files to the server. This feature makes it quick and easy to install downloaded plugin Zip files. Although this feature works with plugins you find on the Plugins page of the WordPress website, it's used mostly to install plugins that aren't available on the WordPress site because they can't be installed by searching for them on the Add Plugins screen.

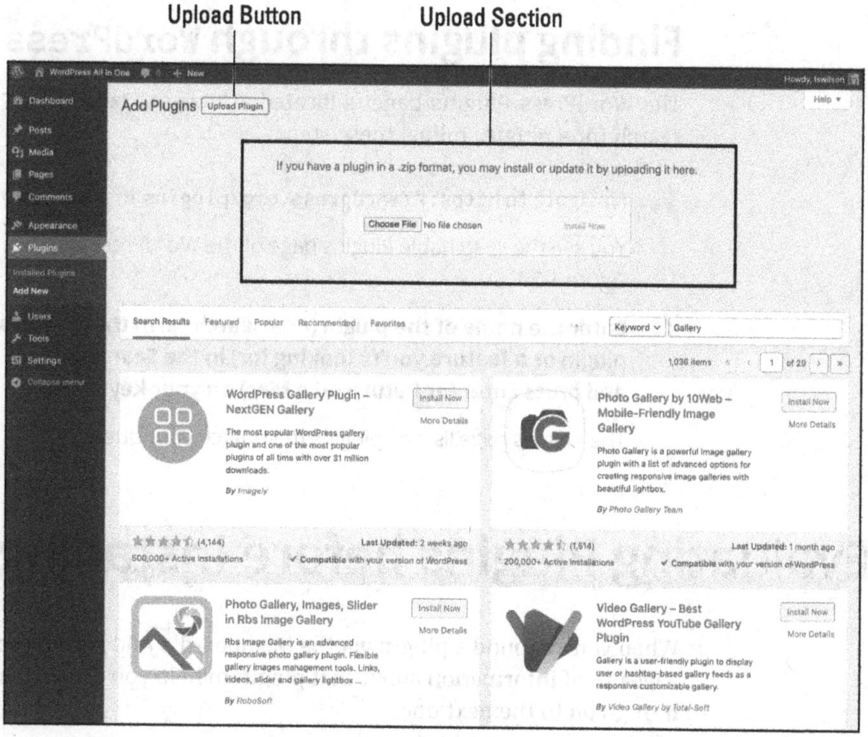

FIGURE 1-5: The upload feature on the Add Plugins screen.

After selecting the file to upload, click the Install Now button. You then have the option to go back to the Add Plugins screen or to activate the newly installed plugin.

Featured, Popular, Recommended, and Favorites

The Featured, Popular, Recommended, and Favorites screens are very similar. The Featured screen shows the plugins from the WordPress website that are listed as Featured. The Popular screen includes a listing of all the plugins sorted by their popularity. The Recommended screen lists plugins that WordPress recommends specifically for you, based on plugins you've already installed on your site. (If you already have a photo-gallery plugin installed, for example, the Recommended screen might recommend a plugin that helps you handle image and photo optimization.) The Favorites screen first asks you to log in to `WordPress.org` if you have an account, and it lists any plugins that you've marked as favorites.

Beyond these differences, each page is identical to the Search Results page. Each listed plugin has options that let you view more details about the plugin and install it.

Finding plugins through WordPress.org

The WordPress Plugins page is located at `https://wordpress.org/plugins`. To search for a plugin, follow these steps:

1. **Navigate to `https://wordpress.org/plugins` in your browser.**

   You see the searchable Plugins page of the WordPress website. (Refer to Figure 1-2.)

2. **Enter the name of the plugin (or a search term that's relevant to the plugin or a feature you're looking for) in the Search Plugins text field, and press Enter (or Return on a Mac) on your keyboard.**

   The Plugins page lists all plugins that match your query.

Evaluating Plugins before Installing

When you've found a plugin via the Dashboard's Add Plugins screen, you can find a wealth of information about that plugin to help you decide whether to download it or go on to the next one.

The methods described here for evaluating plugins are no substitutes for testing plugins thoroughly. Testing a plugin is good practice unless you're familiar enough with the code and the developers to feel comfortable that bugs or security issues are unlikely. To test a plugin, set up a stand-alone site used just for testing, install the plugin, and check for any issues before trusting the plugin on your main site.

TIP

Look at the version number of the plugin. If the number includes the word *Alpha* or *Beta*, the plugin isn't fully ready; it's in the process of being tested and may have bugs that could affect your site. You may want to wait until the plugin has been thoroughly tested and released as a full version. Generally, the higher the version number, the more *mature* (that is, tested and stable) the plugin is.

REMEMBER

As with many things in life, you have no guarantees with plugins. The best you can do is find information about the plugin to determine whether it's trustworthy.

Details

Click the More Details link to the right of the plugin's name to find information taken from the plugin's page on the WordPress site. Figure 1-6 shows an example of what details are available. As on the Plugins page, Description, Installation, FAQ, Changelog, Screenshots, and Reviews tabs are available.

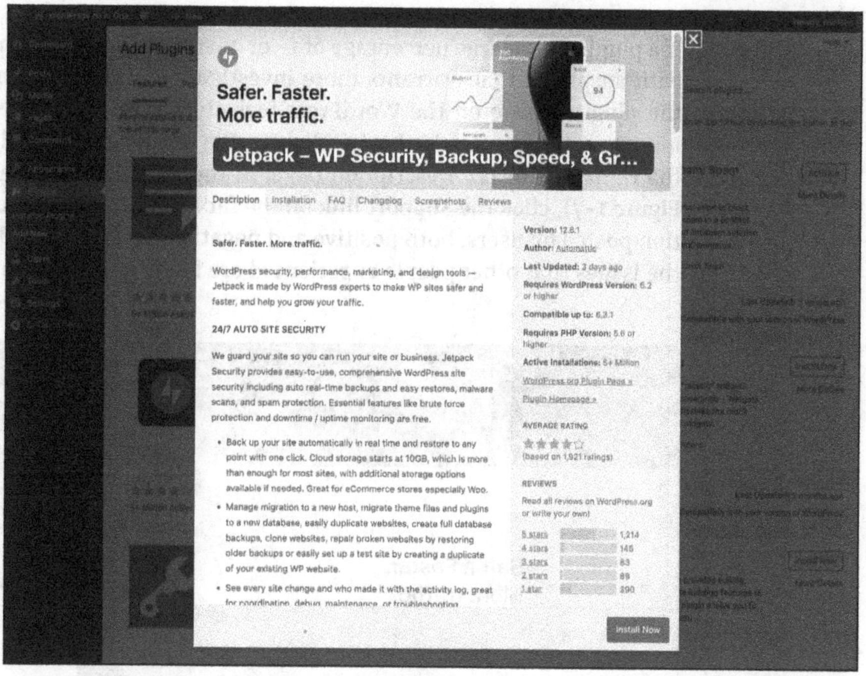

FIGURE 1-6: Details on the Jetpack plugin.

TIP Make sure to check out each plugin's Description page. You could find some very important information that isn't present on the Search Results page. When you're considering a plugin that you don't have experience with, this information can help you determine how reliable and trustworthy that plugin is.

Ratings

Consider the plugin's rating and the number of people who submitted a rating. The more people who rated the plugin, the more you can trust the rating; the fewer people who rated the plugin, the less you can trust the rating. A plugin that has fewer than 20 ratings probably isn't very trustworthy. A plugin that has more than 100 ratings is very trustworthy. Any plugin rated 20 to 100 times is acceptably trustworthy.

TIP Don't use just ratings as your only method of assessing trustworthiness; combine ratings with comments left by users. If the plugin has a 5-star rating given by 1,000 users but has dozens of negative comments and very little positive commentary, don't trust the plugin very much. If the plugin has a 3-star rating given by 10 users but has nothing but positive comments, the plugin may have some issues, yet still work very well for some users.

If a plugin has a large percentage of 1- or 2-star ratings, you can regard the plugin with suspicion that warrants more investigation. Take the extra step of visiting the plugin's page on the WordPress website to see what other people are saying about it. You can do this by clicking the WordPress.org Plugin Page link on the right side of the Description page, in the FYI box. On the plugin's page (see Figure 1-7), click the Support link on the far right of the page to see the information posted by users, both positive and negative. You can then determine whether the issues that other people experienced are likely to hinder you.

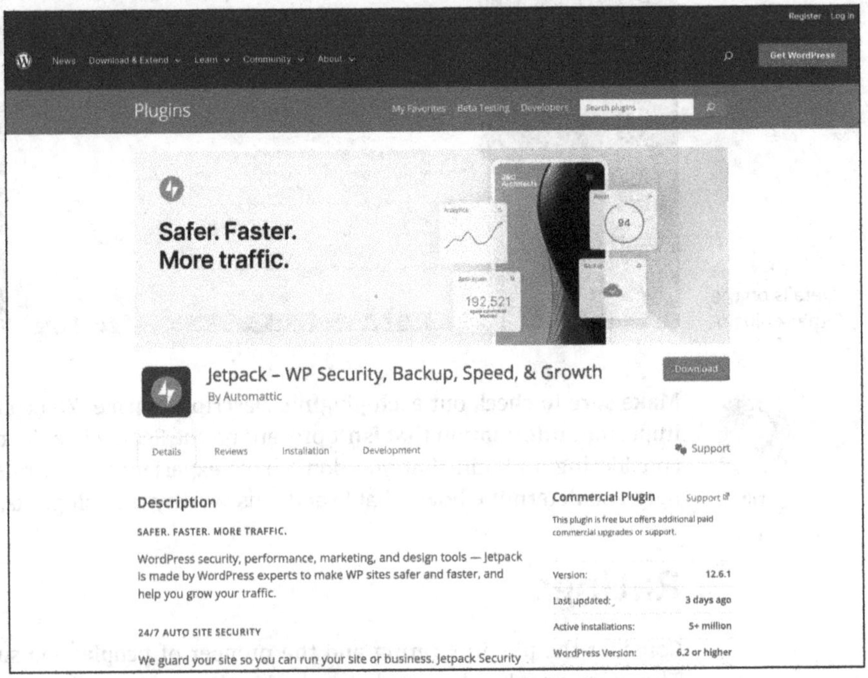

FIGURE 1-7: The Jetpack plugin's page on WordPress.org showing the Support link on the far right of the page.

Active installations

The next detail to consider is the number of active installations. The higher the number of installs, the more likely the plugin is to work well; plugins that don't work very well typically don't pick up enough popularity to get many downloads. If a plugin has hundreds of thousands of installations or more, it's extremely popular.

REMEMBER

A low installation count shouldn't necessarily count against a plugin. Some plugins simply provide a feature that has a limited audience, or is just too new. Thus, the installation count is an indicator, but not proof of quality or lack thereof.

The Tested Up To and the Last Updated information should be taken very lightly. If a plugin indicates that the Tested Up To version is for a very old WordPress version, it may have issues with the latest versions of WordPress. But plenty of plugins work just fine with current versions of WordPress even though they don't explicitly indicate support. Many people see an up-to-date plugin as being a sign of quality and upkeep. This reasoning is sometimes flawed, however, because some plugins are simple and don't require updating as often as others. A plugin that hasn't been updated in a while may be functioning perfectly well without any updates. Check the support forum for that plugin to see whether there are any complaints that the plugin doesn't work with the latest versions of WordPress.

Advanced View

To see Advanced View information (see Figure 1-8), click the Advanced View link on the plugin's page. Active Versions and Downloads Per Day aren't foolproof methods of getting a trusted plugin, but the Active Versions Downloads Per Day count on the graph may indicate that people are using the plugin with some success.

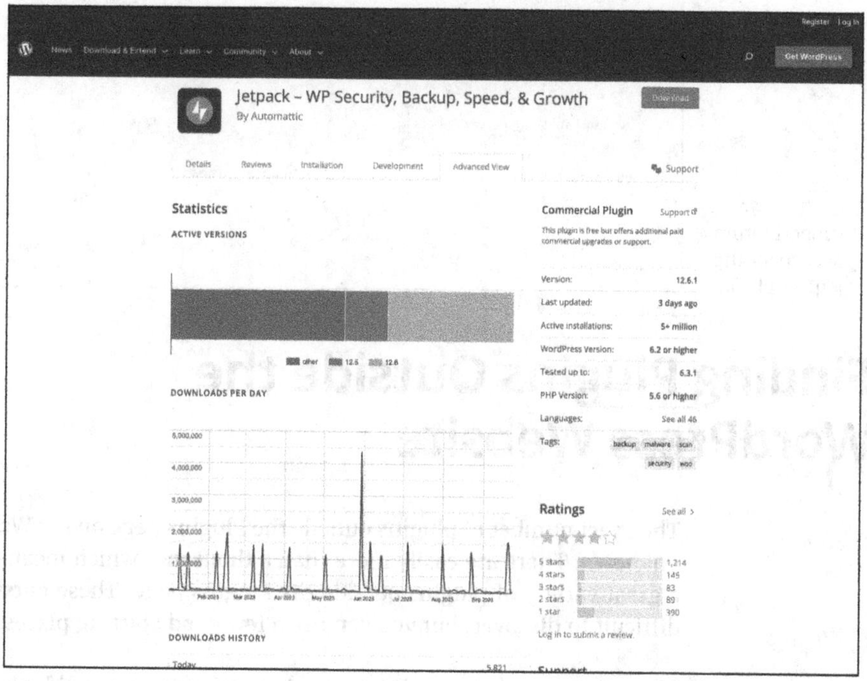

FIGURE 1-8: The download history for the Jetpack plugin on the WordPress website.

Support

Click the Support link below the plugin's banner to view the support forum for that plugin, which is where users of the plugin request help and assistance (see Figure 1-9). By browsing the support forum for the plugin, you can get a good feel for how responsive the plugin's developer is to users, and you can see what types of problems other people are having with the plugin.

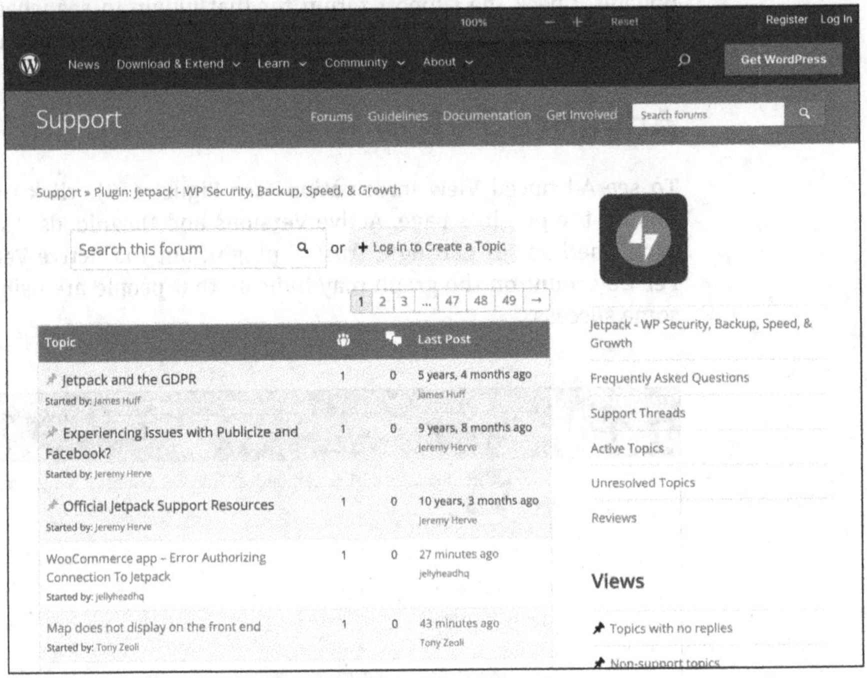

FIGURE 1-9: A support forum section for the Jetpack plugin.

Finding Plugins Outside the WordPress Website

The exact number of plugins outside the Plugins page on the WordPress website is unknown. There are easily more than a thousand, which means that you can find a great variety of plugins outside the Plugins page. These outside plugins can be difficult to discover, but you can use a few good starting places.

Many plugins that aren't on the Plugins page are paid plugins. The official WordPress Plugins page lists only free plugins. If a plugin is for sale (that is, it costs more than a penny), it can't get listed in the Plugin Directory, so the author needs to find other methods of listing and promoting their products.

Over the past few years, the market for commercial plugins has grown tremendously. It isn't possible to list all the companies that currently offer WordPress plugins in this chapter, so the following listing is a sampling to introduce you to the world of plugins outside the Plugin Directory.

The following sites offer WordPress plugins:

- **CodeCanyon (`https://codecanyon.net`):** With thousands of plugins, this online marketplace is the paid-plugins version of the Plugin Directory. Just as the Plugin Directory contains plugins from a large number of developers, CodeCanyon is a collection of plugins from various developers rather than plugins from a single company.
- **Gravity Forms (`www.gravityforms.com`):** For many WordPress users, Gravity Forms is the number-one plugin they are happy to pay for. Typically, it's the first and last recommendation people give someone who wants to create forms in WordPress.
- **WooCommerce (`https://woocommerce.com`):** WooCommerce is a popular plugin with a full-featured e-commerce solution that you can integrate into your WordPress site. Essentially, this plugin turns your WordPress site into an online store. WooCommerce itself is free; however, there are several add-on plugins that extend the feature set of WooCommerce, including different payment gateways, shipping options, and product inventory options, for example.

Although these sites give you a taste of what commercial plugin sites have to offer, other sources of information about new, exciting plugins can be helpful. Many popular WordPress news sites talk about all things WordPress, including reviews and discussions of specific plugins. Check out the following sites if you want to know more about what plugins are being talked about:

- **WPTavern (`https://wptavern.com`):** This standard WordPress news site often publishes articles about what's being talked about in the WordPress community, including plugins.
- **Post Status (`https://poststatus.com`):** Post Status is an all-things-WordPress news site. If there's buzz on a topic in the WordPress world, you're likely to find discussions about it here.

TIP

One great thing about using a community or news site to discover new plugins is that you aren't alone in deciding whether to trust a plugin. You can get some other opinions before you take a chance on a plugin.

If you aren't finding what you want on the Plugins page of the WordPress website, don't know anyone who offers the solution you're looking for, and aren't seeing anything on community sites, it's time to go to a trusty search engine (such as Google) to see what you can find.

A good way to start is to search for the words *wordpress* and *plugin* along with one or a few words that describe the feature you want. If you want a plugin that provides advanced image-gallery features, for example, search for *wordpress plugin image gallery*. As long as your search isn't too specific, you're likely to get many results. The results often contain blog posts that review specific plugins or list recommended plugins.

WARNING

Some developers include malware, viruses, and other unwanted executables in their plugin code. Your best bet is to use plugins from the official WordPress Plugin Directory or to purchase plugins from a reputable seller. Do your research first, and read up on plugin security in Book 2, Chapter 4.

Comparing Free and Commercial Plugins

Thousands of plugins are available for free, and thousands of plugins have a price. What are the benefits of free plugins versus paid plugins? That's a tough question to answer.

It's tempting to think that some plugins are better than others, which is why they cost money. Unfortunately, things aren't that simple. Some amazing plugins that I'd gladly pay for are free, and some terrible plugins that I wouldn't pay for have a cost.

Often, a paid plugin includes support, which means that the company or person selling the plugin is offering assurance that if you have problems, you'll receive support and updates to address bugs and other issues.

Free plugins typically list places to make support requests or to ask questions, but nothing ensures that the developer will respond to your requests within a certain period — or at all. Even though developers have no obligation to help with support requests from users, many developers work hard to help users with reported issues and other problems. Fortunately, because many free plugins are on the WordPress website, and because the Plugins page there includes a built-in support forum and rating score, you can easily see how responsive a plugin author is to support issues. I believe that the commercial plugin model works in an environment of tens of thousands of free plugins because many WordPress users want the assurance that when they have problems, they have a place to ask questions and get help.

So if people can get paid to produce plugins, why are so many plugins free? One reason why so many plugins are available for free is that many WordPress developers are generous people who believe in sharing their plugins with the community. Other developers feel that having their plugins available to the millions of WordPress users via the Plugin Directory is a great way to market their talents, which can lead to contract work and employment. Buzzwords on a résumé are far less valuable than a plugin you wrote that was downloaded thousands or millions of times.

Another reason to release a free plugin is to entice people to pay for upgrades — a model often referred to as *freemium*. Freemium plugins often have paid plugins that add features to the free plugin. Thus, the freemium model is a mix of the free and paid plugin models — the best of both worlds. The free plugin can be listed in the Plugin Directory, giving the plugin a large amount of exposure. You can get a feel for how the plugin functions, and if you want the additional features, you can purchase the paid plugin.

An example of the freemium model is the WooCommerce plugin (`https://woocommerce.com`). The main plugin is available on the WordPress website (`https://wordpress.org/plugins/woocommerce`), yet it supports a large number of paid plugins to add more features. By itself, the WooCommerce plugin turns a site into a shopping cart. To extend this functionality, paid plugins are available to add payment processing for specific credit-card processors, shipping, download managers, and many other features.

The biggest difference between free and paid plugins is that sometimes, you won't find what you need in a free plugin and have to go with a paid plugin. In the end, what you download is up to you. Many great free plugins are available, and so are many great paid plugins. If you want the features offered by a paid plugin and are willing to pay the price, paid plugins can be very good investments for your site.

TIP

Many free plugins have links to donation pages. If you find a free plugin to be valuable, please send a donation to the developer. Most developers of free plugins say that they rarely, if ever, receive donations. Even a few dollars can really encourage the developer to keep updating old plugins and releasing new free plugins. (See the nearby sidebar, "Developing plugins: A community activity.")

DEVELOPING PLUGINS: A COMMUNITY ACTIVITY

Although plugins are written and developed by people who have the skills required to do so, the WordPress user community is also largely responsible for the ongoing development of plugins. Ultimately, end users are the ones who put those plugins to the true test on their own sites. Those same users are also the first to speak up and let developers know when something isn't working right, helping the developers troubleshoot and fine-tune their plugins.

The most popular plugins are created by developers who encourage open communication with the user base. Overall, WordPress is one of those great open-source projects in which the relationship between developers and users fosters a creative environment that keeps the project fresh and exciting every step of the way.

IN THIS CHAPTER

» Installing WordPress plugins from the Dashboard

» Manually installing WordPress plugins

» Updating plugins

» Activating and deactivating plugins

» Deleting plugins

Chapter 2 Installing and Managing Plugins

With more than 59,000 plugins available, you have a huge number of options for customizing your site. Book 7, Chapter 1 details what types of plugins are available and where to find them. In this chapter, you start putting these plugins to use. This chapter is dedicated to helping you install, activate, deactivate, update, and delete plugins.

Installing Plugins from the WordPress Dashboard

When you find a plugin on the WordPress Plugins page (`https://wordpress.org/plugins/`; see Book 7, Chapter 1) that you want to install, you can do so directly from the Dashboard. (If you find a plugin that isn't in the Plugins Directory, you have to install it manually. See the following section, "Manually Installing Plugins.")

WordPress makes it super-easy to find, install, and then activate plugins for use on your blog. Just follow these steps:

1. **Click the Add New link on the Plugins menu.**

   The Add Plugins screen opens, allowing you to browse official WordPress plugins from your WordPress Dashboard.

2. **Search for a plugin to install on your site.**

   Enter a keyword for a plugin you'd like to search for. For this example, you want to install a plugin that integrates your site with YouTube. To find it, select Keyword in the drop-down menu to the left of the search box, enter **YouTube** in the Search text box on the Add Plugins screen, and then click the Enter key (or Return on a Mac).

   Figure 2-1 shows the results page for the YouTube search phrase. The plugin you're looking for is called "Embed Plus YouTube WordPress Plugin With YouTube Gallery, Channel, Playlist, Live Stream," which is a plugin developed by the developers at YouTube. This plugin is the one you want to install.

TIP

You can also discover new plugins by clicking any of the categories at the top of the Add Plugins screen, such as Featured, Popular, and Recommended.

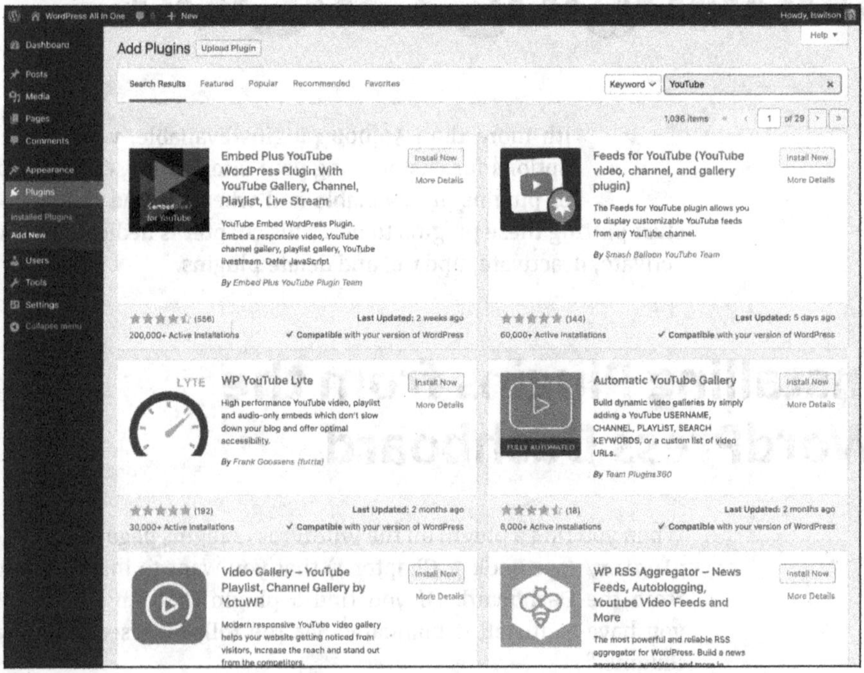

FIGURE 2-1: The Add Plugins screen's search results for the YouTube plugin.

3. **Click the More Details link.**

   A Description window opens, displaying information about the YouTube plugin (including a description, version number, and author name) and an Install Now button.

4. **Click the Install Now button.**

   The Install Now button changes to an Installing button with a spinner icon that spins until it's done installing, then the button text changes to Activate.

5. **Decide whether to activate the plugin now or later.**

   You have two methods of installing the plugin:

   - *Click the Activate button:* Click this button to immediately activate the plugin you just installed on your site.
   - *Return to the Plugins screen:* Click the Plugins link on the Plugins menu to load the Plugins screen on your Dashboard. You see the plugin listed there, but it isn't activated. When you're ready, click the Activate link below the plugin's name.

WARNING

Installation of plugins from the WordPress Dashboard works in most web-hosting configurations. Some web-hosting services, however, don't allow the kind of access that WordPress needs to complete installation. If you get any errors or find that you're unable to use the plugin installation feature, contact your web-hosting provider to find out whether they can assist you.

TIP

If the Dashboard displays any kind of error message after you install the plugin, copy the message and paste it into a support ticket in the `WordPress.org` support forum (`https://wordpress.org/support`) to elicit help from other WordPress users about the source of the problem and the possible solution. When you post about the issue, provide as much information about the issue as possible, including a screenshot or pasted details. Simply saying something like "This plugin doesn't work!" probably won't get you the support you need, and isn't doing you — or the plugin author — any favors in resolving the issue.

Manually Installing Plugins

Installing plugins from the Dashboard is so easy that you'll probably never need to know how to install a plugin manually via SFTP. (Book 2, Chapter 2 explains how to use SFTP.) But the technique is still helpful to know in case the WordPress Plugins page is down or unavailable, or if you are installing a plugin that is not available on the WordPress website.

REMEMBER

Installing the YouTube plugin takes you through the process, but keep in mind that every plugin is different. Be sure to read the description and installation instructions for each plugin you want to install.

Finding and downloading the files

The first step in using plugins is locating the one you want to install. The absolutely best place to find WordPress plugins is the `WordPress.org` website at `https://wordpress.org/plugins`, where, as of this writing, more than 59,000 plugins are available for download.

To find the YouTube plugin, follow these steps:

1. **Go to the official WordPress Plugins page at `https://wordpress.org/plugins`.**
2. **In the search box at the top of the page, enter the keyword YouTube and then click the Search Plugins button.**
3. **Locate the YouTube plugin on the search results page (see Figure 2-2), and click the plugin's name: Embed Plus YouTube WordPress Plugin With YouTube Gallery, Channel, Playlist, Live Stream.**

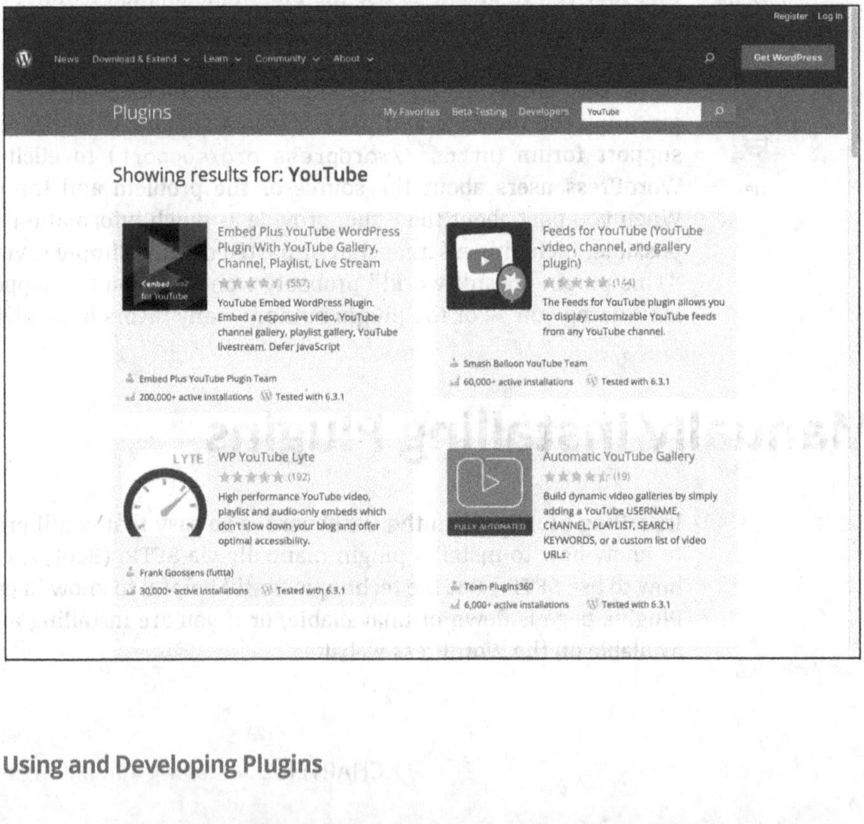

FIGURE 2-2: Use the search feature on the Plugins page to find the plugin you need.

The YouTube plugin page of the WordPress website opens, displaying a description of the plugin as well as other information about the plugin. In Figure 2-3, take note of the important information on the right side of the page:

- *Version:* The number shown in this area is the most recent version of the plugin.
- *Last Updated:* This date is when the author last updated the plugin.
- *Active Installations:* This number tells you how many times this plugin has been downloaded and installed by other WordPress users.
- *WordPress Version:* Figure 2-3 shows that the YouTube plugin is compatible up to WordPress version 4.5 or higher.
- *Tested Up To:* This section tells you what version of WordPress this plugin is compatible up to. If it tells you that the plugin is compatible up to version 5.0, for example, you usually can't use the plugin with versions later than 5.0. I say *usually,* because the plugin developer may not update the information in this section — especially if the plugin files themselves haven't changed. The best way to check is to download the plugin, install it, and see whether it works! As shown in Figure 2-3, the YouTube plugin has been tested up to WordPress version 6.3.1.
- *Tags:* This is a list of keywords that describe the plugin type. Clicking any of these words will take you to a page on the WordPress website that displays plugins that are associated with, or related to, the keyword you clicked on. (Tags are not shown in Figure 2-3; you'll need to scroll down to see them in your browser.)
- *Ratings:* With a rating system of 1 to 5 stars, with 1 being the lowest and 5 being the highest, you can see how other WordPress users rated this plugin. (Ratings are not shown in Figure 2-3; you'll need to scroll down to see them in your browser.)
- *Support:* The Support button is linked to the support forum, and shows the number of issues that have been opened and resolved in the support forum for this plugin. (The Support button is not shown in Figure 2-3; you'll need to scroll down to see it in your browser.)

4. **Click the Download button on the plugin's page.**

   A dialog box opens, asking what Firefox should do with the file. Select the Save File radio button and then click OK to save the file to your hard drive. *Remember where you saved it.*

5. **Locate the file on your hard drive, and open it with your favorite decompression program.**

If you're unsure how to use your decompression program, refer to the documentation available with the program.

6. **Unpack (decompress) the plugin files you downloaded for the YouTube plugin.**

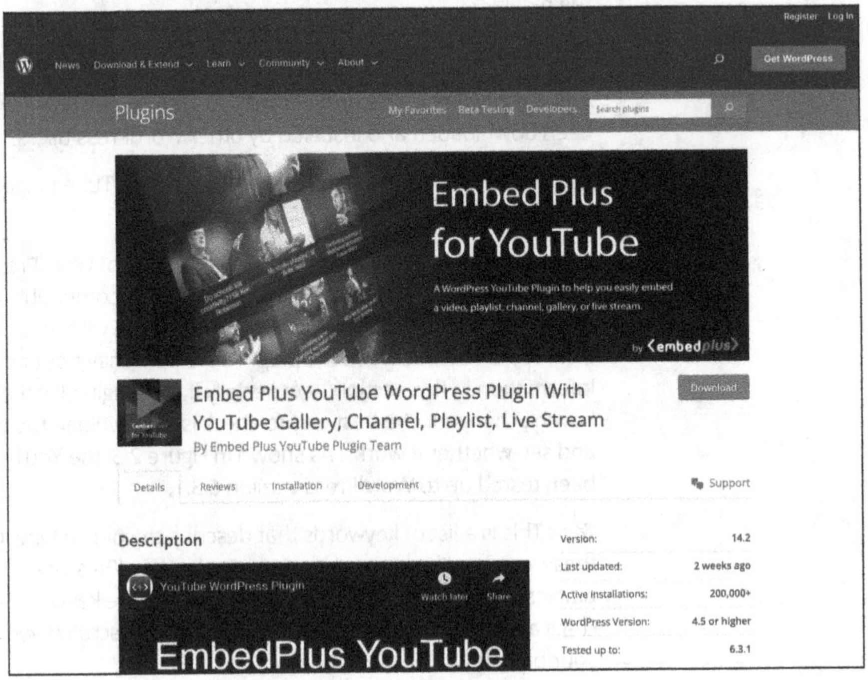

FIGURE 2-3: The download page for the YouTube plugin.

Reading the instructions

Frequently, the plugin developer includes a `readme` file inside the `.zip` file. Do what the title of the file says: Read it. Often, it contains the same documentation and instructions that are on the plugin developer's website.

Make sure that you read the instructions carefully and follow them correctly. Ninety-nine percent of WordPress plugins have great documentation and instructions from the developer. If you don't follow the instructions correctly, the best scenario is that the plugin just won't work on your site. At worst, the plugin will create all sorts of ugly errors, requiring you to start the plugin installation over.

TIP

You can open `readme.txt` files in any text-editor program, such as Notepad or WordPad on a PC or TextEdit on a Mac.

In the case of the YouTube plugin, the `readme.txt` file contains information about the requirements of the plugin and how to use it on your site.

REMEMBER

Every plugin is different in terms of where the plugin files are uploaded and what configurations are necessary to make the plugin work on your site. Read the installation instructions carefully, and follow those instructions to the letter to install the plugin correctly on your site.

Upgrading Plugins

Plugins receive updates that fix bugs, add new features, and update existing features. Some plugins are updated multiple times a week. Other plugins may never be updated. Fortunately, WordPress makes it easy to know when a new plugin version is available and also makes it very easy to update your local Plugins page from the Dashboard.

One of the easiest ways to know that plugin updates are available is to check the version number displayed on the Plugins screen on your Dashboard, directly below the plugin's description. Figure 2-4 shows that the Akismet plugin has an available update, as evidenced by the phrase below the Akismet description `There is a new version of Akismet Anti-Spam available`. Figure 2-4 also shows that the Dashboard page provides alerts about upgrades (the small circle shown next to the word *Plugins* on the left).

You have three ways to update a plugin: from the Plugins page, from the Updates submenu accessible on the Dashboard menu, and updating manually via SFTP.

Updating on the Plugins screen

Updating a plugin on the Plugins screen is easy. You can update plugins one at a time or update all the plugins that need updating in one fell swoop. To update an individual plugin, click the Update Now link at the bottom of the plugin's row (refer to Figure 2-4). WordPress automatically updates the plugin with the files from the new release, displays the message `Updated`, and removes the small icon next to the Plugins-menu link (see Figure 2-5).

TIP

If an error is indicated, take a screenshot or copy the error details and create a support request on the `WordPress.org` community support forum (`https://wordpress.org/support`). The helpful people there can help you figure out the source of your issue and the solution.

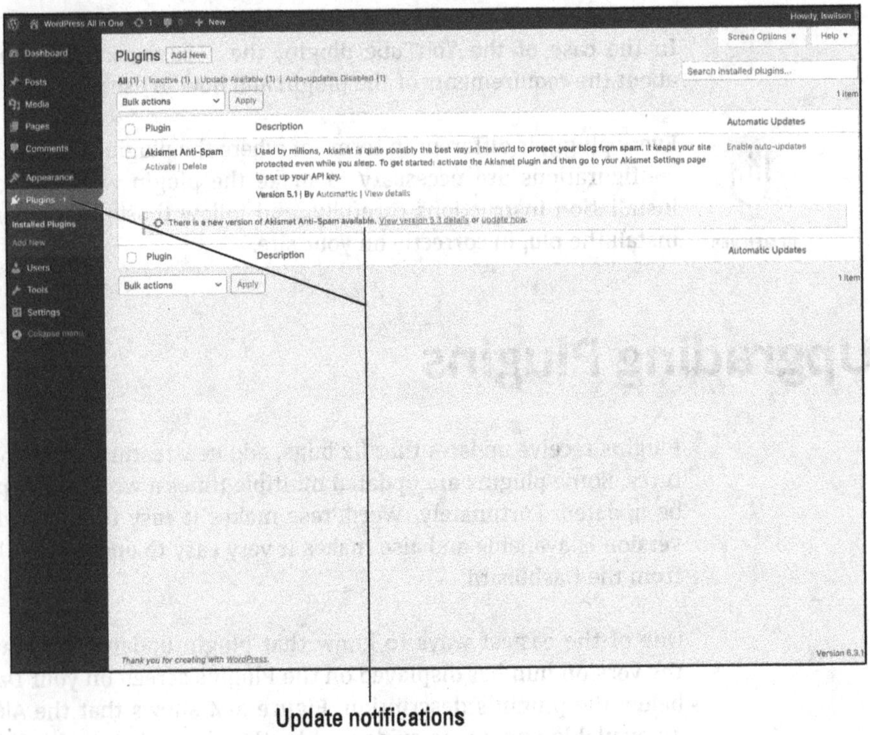

FIGURE 2-4: A WordPress plugin with an available update.

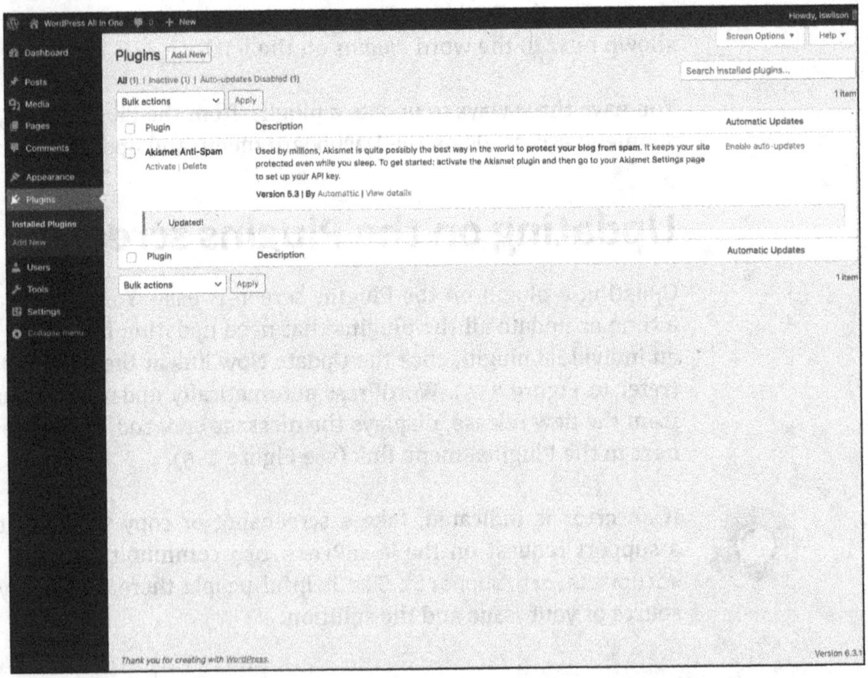

FIGURE 2-5: The result of updating a single plugin from the Plugins screen.

TIP

If updates inside the Dashboard continuously fail, contact your hosting provider to see whether any server-specific issues are preventing WordPress from updating its plugins.

Although clicking the Update Now link is simple and quick, this process can get tedious if you have a large number of plugins. To update all your plugins at the same time, select the check box to the left of each plugin, choose Update from the Bulk Actions drop-down menu, and click the Apply button. All your plugins are updated. Figure 2-6 shows a message at the top of the screen stating that two plugins have been updated.

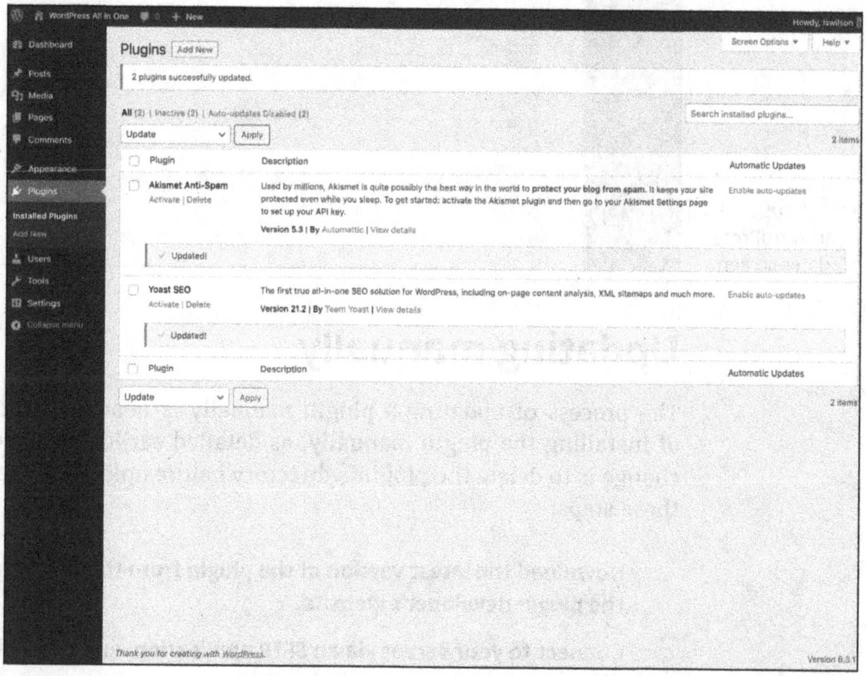

FIGURE 2-6: The results of updating multiple plugins from the Plugins screen.

Updating on the WordPress Updates screen

The WordPress Updates screen (see Figure 2-7), accessible from a submenu of the Dashboard menu, provides a quick way to update WordPress, plugins, and themes in one place. This screen is a one-stop shop for all the updates across your site.

To update all the plugins, in the Plugins section, select the check box next to the Select All header (refer to Figure 2-7) and then click the Update Plugins button. All of your selected plugins are updated.

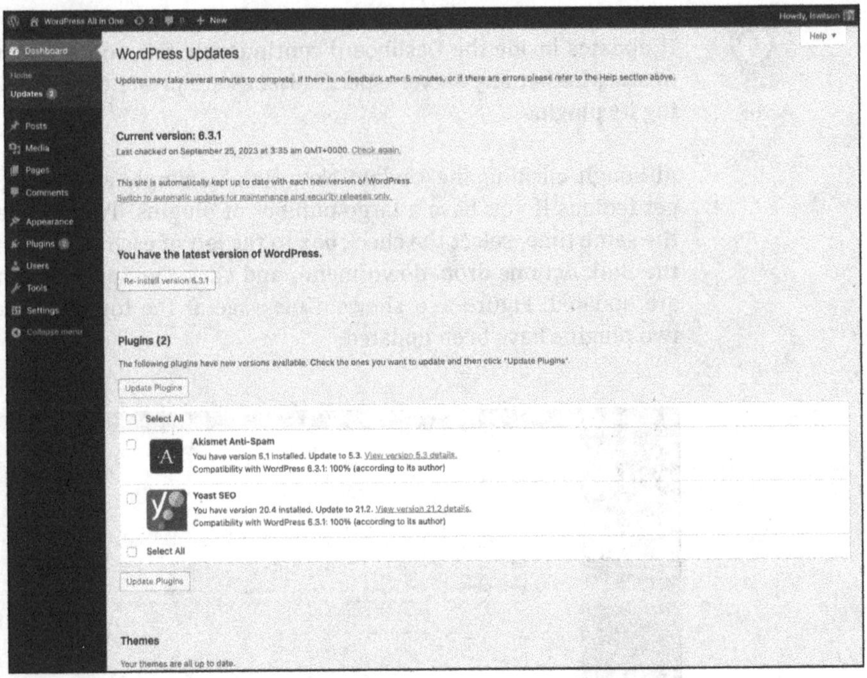

FIGURE 2-7: The WordPress Updates screen.

Updating manually

The process of updating a plugin manually is nearly identical to the process of installing the plugin manually, as detailed earlier in this chapter. The only change is to delete the plugin's directory before uploading the new files. Follow these steps:

1. **Download the latest version of the plugin from the WordPress website or the plugin developer's website.**
2. **Connect to your server via an SFTP application, and go to the `plugins` directory in the `wp-content` directory.**

   You should see a folder with the same name as the plugin you want to upgrade.
3. **Rename this folder so that you have a backup if you need it.**

   Any memorable name, such as `plugin-old`, should suffice.
4. **Upload the new version of your plugin via SFTP to your server so that it's in the `wp-content/plugins` folder.**
5. **Log in to the WordPress Dashboard and activate the upgraded plugin.**

REMEMBER

If you made any changes in the plugin's configuration files before your upgrade, make those changes again after the upgrade. If you need to back out of the upgrade, you can delete the new Plugins page and rename the folder (`plugin-old` to `plugin`, for example).

Activating and Deactivating Plugins

After a plugin is on your site, activating it is simple:

1. **Log in to the WordPress Dashboard.**
2. **Navigate to the Plugins screen by clicking the Plugins menu link.**
3. **Find the plugin you want to activate on the Plugins screen.**
4. **Click the Activate link just below the plugin's name in the listing.**

If everything goes well, you see `Plugin activated` at the top of the screen, which means that the plugin has been activated successfully. (See Figure 2-8.) If a long error message appears in the activation notice, the plugin has an issue that's preventing it from activating. Copy the message that appears in the notice and send the details to the plugin author for help fixing the issue.

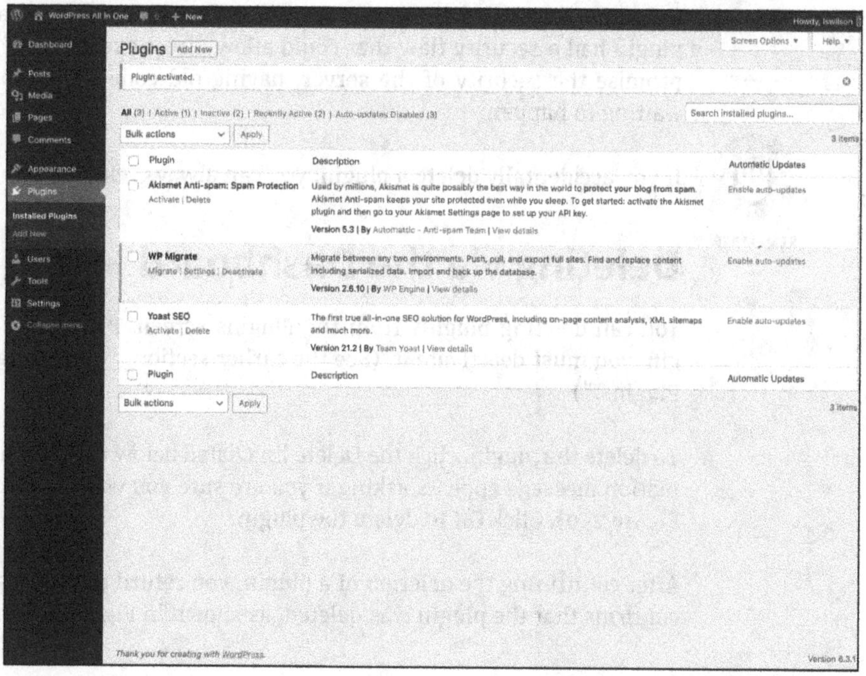

FIGURE 2-8: The Plugins screen when a plugin is activated.

The process of deactivating a plugin is nearly the same as the process of activating a plugin. Follow the same steps, but click the Deactivate link for the plugin that should be deactivated. A message at the top of your Dashboard tells you the plugin has been successfully deactivated.

Deleting Plugins

Sometimes, it's simply time to let go of a plugin and remove it from the site. You could have many reasons for deleting a plugin:

- You no longer need the feature offered by the plugin.
- You want to replace the plugin with a different one.
- You're retiring the plugin because its functionality has been replaced with features built into a new version of WordPress.
- You're removing it due to performance issues (such as the plugin required too many resources to run).

It may be tempting to deactivate undesired plugins and leave them sitting in your `plugins` directory, but take the extra step of deleting plugins that you no longer need. The PHP files of the plugin can still be run manually if someone (or some automated computer program) directly requests that PHP file. If the plugin had a security flaw that could allow direct execution of the code to compromise the security of the server, having old code lying around is a problem waiting to happen.

REMEMBER

If you accidentally delete a plugin, you can always reinstall it.

Deleting via the Dashboard

You can deleting plugins from the Plugins screen. Before you can delete a plugin, you must deactivate it. (See the earlier section, "Activating and Deactivating Plugins.")

To delete the plugin, click the Delete link listed below the plugin's name. A confirmation message appears asking if you are sure you want to delete the plugin (see Figure 2-9). Click OK to delete the plugin.

After confirming the deletion of a plugin, you return to the Plugins screen, which confirms that the plugin was deleted, as shown in Figure 2-10.

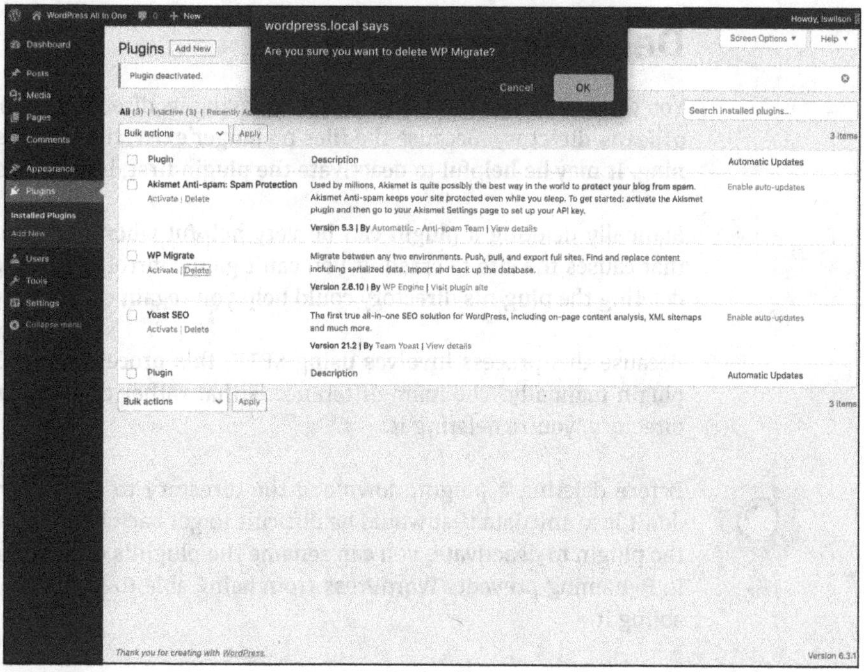

FIGURE 2-9: The confirmation message for deleting a plugin.

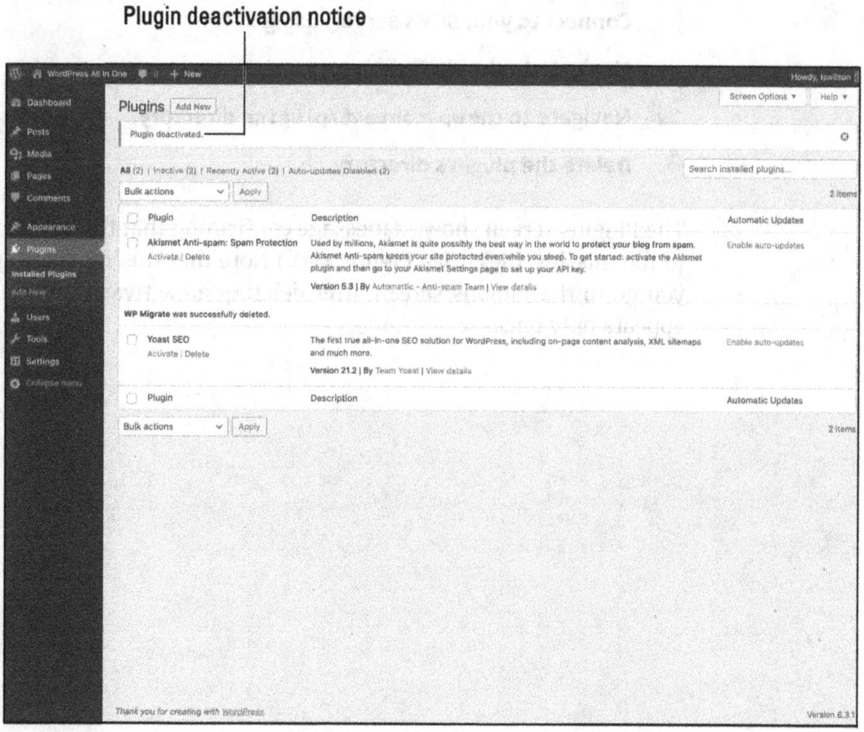

FIGURE 2-10: A notice confirming the deletion of a plugin.

Deleting manually

You can delete a plugin manually by removing its directory from the `wp-content/plugins` directory. Because the files no longer exist, the plugin simply stops running. It may be helpful to deactivate the plugin first, but doing so isn't required.

Manually deleting a plugin can be very helpful when a plugin has a fatal error that causes the site to crash. If you can't gain control of the site again, manually deleting the plugin's directory could help you regain control of your site quickly.

Because this process involves using SFTP, this process is similar to installing a plugin manually. The main difference is that rather than uploading the plugin's directory, you're deleting it.

TIP

Before deleting a plugin, download the directory to a local system so that you don't lose any data that would be difficult to get back later. If your goal is to force the plugin to deactivate, you can rename the plugin's directory rather than delete it. Renaming prevents WordPress from being able to locate the plugin, thus disabling it.

The process works as follows:

1. **Connect to your site's server, using SFTP.**
2. **Navigate to the site's directory.**
3. **Navigate to the `wp-content/plugins` directory.**
4. **Delete the plugin's directory.**

The Plugins screen shows a message confirming that the plugin is deactivated due to the missing files. (See Figure 2-11.) Note that this message appears only when you go to the Plugins screen after deleting an activated plugin manually, and it appears only once.

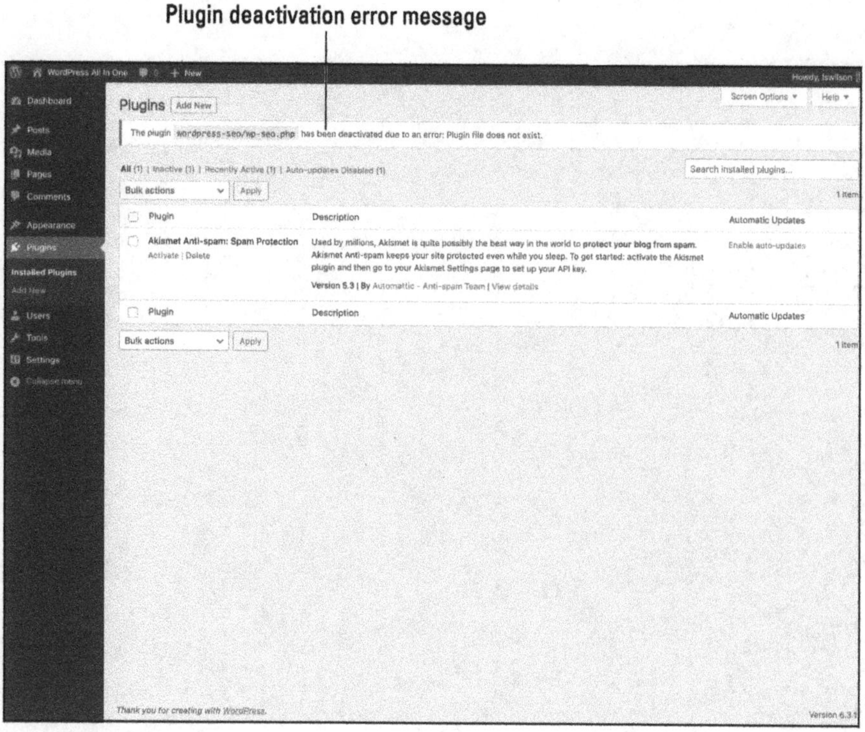

FIGURE 2-11: The error message shown after an active plugin is deleted manually.

IN THIS CHAPTER

- » Exploring activate-and-go plugins
- » Discovering settings screens
- » Using widgets
- » Enhancing your content with shortcodes

Chapter 3 Configuring and Using Plugins

The types of features offered by WordPress plugins are diverse. Similarly, the ways of interacting with plugins are also diverse. Some plugins don't have an interface and can be activated or deactivated only; some provide one or more settings screens to control how the plugins behaves. Other plugins offer widgets and *shortcodes* (short, easy-to-remember codes used to execute PHP functions) used to add new features to sidebars and content.

This chapter digs into the topic of how to interact with plugins. Although this topic is a big one, the examples in this chapter prepare you for different ways of interacting with plugins.

Exploring Activate-and-Go Plugins

Certain plugins are easy to use because they don't have any settings or features to interact with. I call them *activate-and-go* plugins. You simply activate them, and they do what they're intended to do.

Like WordPress plugins as a whole, activate-and-go plugins offer a wide variety of features. The following list offers a sampling of activate-and-go plugins that you'll find useful on your website:

- **Classic Editor (`https://wordpress.org/plugins/classic-editor/`):** This plugin replaces the block editor with the classic editor for WordPress. Using this plugin might be helpful if you are used to using the classic editor, or if you prefer using the classic editor over the block editor. Although there are other settings available to refine your experience with this plugin, just installing and activating this plugin will do the job of replacing the block editor with the classic editor.
- **BBQ: Block Bad Queries (`https://wordpress.org/plugins/block-bad-queries`):** The BBQ plugin helps protect your site against attackers who are trying to exploit specific security vulnerabilities. This plugin doesn't require any configuration; it automatically scans all requests coming to the site and protects against bad ones.
- **Disable All WordPress Updates (`https://wordpress.org/plugins/disable-wordpress-updates`):** WordPress's capability to update itself automatically has been a tremendous help to WordPress users. Keeping WordPress updated not only offers new features and enhancements, but also helps keep your site safe from attackers. For some users, though, the notification to update WordPress can become a distraction, especially if the site is run by many people but a single person is responsible for handling site updates. The Disable All WordPress Updates plugin disables automatic checks for new WordPress versions and also disables any notifications that a new version is available. You still can update WordPress from the Dashboard (as described in Book 2, Chapter 5), but the notifications no longer appear.

To use any of these plugins, simply install and activate them as discussed in Book 7, Chapter 2. When the plugin is activated, it starts doing its job.

REMEMBER

For some plugins, such as BBQ or Disable All WordPress Updates, the results of activating the plugin may be underwhelming. The plugins do their work behind the scenes and don't change anything that's visible to you. Just because you don't see an immediate change, however, doesn't mean that the plugins aren't doing their jobs.

Discovering Settings Screens

Many popular plugins have settings screens that allow you to tweak the functionality of the plugin and tailor it to the specific needs of your site. Often, these settings need to be configured once and updated only when the plugin changes.

The following sections explore a selection of the most popular WordPress plugins, show you how to access settings screens, and describe what you can expect from them.

Typically, you access settings screens from submenus of the Dashboard's Settings page. Another common place to access plugin settings screens (especially for plugins that provide advanced features such as site caching) is the Dashboard's Tools menu.

TIP

If you have a hard time finding the settings screen for a plugin, check the Plugins page for details on how to access the settings screen. For plugins listed on the WordPress website's Plugins page, check the Installation and FAQ tabs. If the Plugins page has a Screenshots tab, one of the screenshots usually shows the settings page.

Akismet

Akismet is bundled in with WordPress and likely is already installed on your WordPress site. Akismet is the answer to comment and trackback spam. Book 3, Chapter 4 covers comment spam and takes you through the steps of installing Akismet on your WordPress website.

Akismet has settings that you can configure after you've installed and activated the plugin. Click the Akismet Anti-Spam link in the Settings menu on your Dashboard to view the Akismet settings page, as shown in Figure 3-1. On this page, you see the following settings:

- **API Key:** This item displays your Akismet API key in a form field. You should never edit this unless you are changing the API key from your original.
- **Comments:** Select this option to display the number of approved comments beside each comment author.
- **Spam Filtering:** By default, Akismet puts spam in the Spam comment folder for you to review at your leisure. If you feel that this setting isn't strict enough, you can have Akismet silently delete the worst and most pervasive spam so that you never have to see it.
- **Privacy:** Here you can select whether you do or don't want to display a privacy notice that gets displayed on your website underneath your comments form. The option not to display the privacy notice is selected by default.
- **Account:** You are able to see information about your current subscription and there is a button labeled Upgrade that you can click in order to upgrade your Akismet account, if desired.

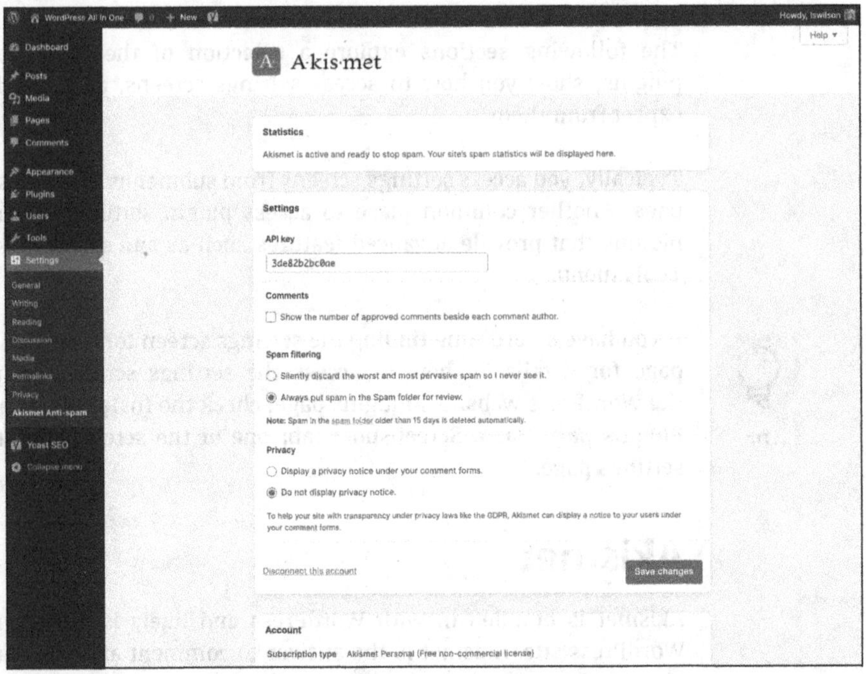

FIGURE 3-1: The Akismet settings page on the Dashboard.

REMEMBER

Akismet catches spam and throws it into a queue, holding the spam for 15 days and then deleting it from your database. It's probably worth your while to check the Akismet spam page once a week to make sure that the plugin hasn't captured any legitimate comments or trackbacks.

XML Sitemap Generator for Google

The XML Sitemap Generator for Google plugin is a good next step for diving into plugin settings pages. This plugin has several options and shows just how intricate settings pages can get.

XML Sitemap Generator for Google is one of WordPress's most popular plugins, with more than 36 million downloads. You can find it on the WordPress website at `https://wordpress.org/plugins/google-sitemap-generator/`.

XML Sitemap Generator for Google makes it easy to automatically add support for sitemaps to your WordPress site. Although most WordPress sites can be scanned easily by search engines, adding sitemaps adds a level of safety to ensure that all the content on the site can be found.

With default settings, the plugin automatically generates sitemaps as content is added or modified on the site. In addition, it notifies Google and Bing of these updates so that it can update the search engine cache with this new data.

The XML Sitemap Generator for Google plugin settings screen is available by clicking the XML-Sitemap link in the Settings menu on your Dashboard. A portion of the XML Sitemap Generator for Google plugin's settings screen is shown in Figure 3-2.

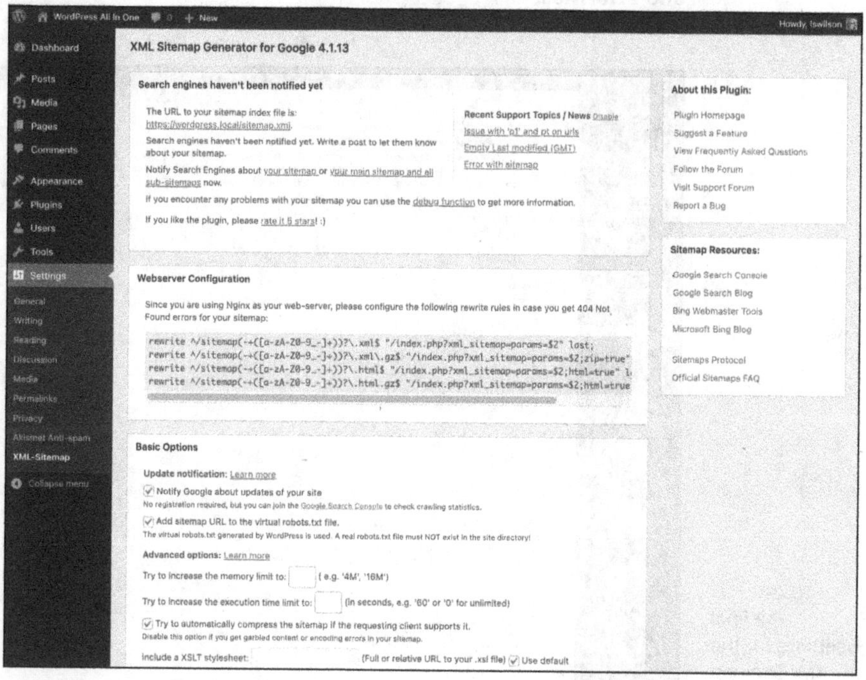

FIGURE 3-2: The settings screen for XML Sitemap Generator for Google.

REMEMBER

Submenu names are limited in length, which means that longer plugin names are shortened to fit properly.

Like the Akismet plugin, Sitemap Generator for Google requires an additional step to be fully functional. Unlike Akismet, Sitemap Generator for Google is very quiet about how to get set up; it doesn't provide that Dashboard-wide notification message. For this reason, it's important to read settings pages and plugin documentation carefully. It can be easy to miss something that's extremely important.

Below the information box used to generate and regenerate sitemaps are the settings for the plugin. Along the right side are links to information about the plugin and sitemaps. This format is common on plugin settings screens.

Scrolling through the Sitemap Generator for Google screen reveals just how exhaustive the available settings are. The settings range from basic options (such as enabling or disabling automatic sitemap generation when the site's content changes), to options that control the information in the generated sitemap, to advanced options that control how many server resources the plugin can consume when generating the sitemap. Nearly every aspect of the plugin's functionality is represented as an option on the settings screen, offering a large amount of flexibility in the way that the plugin functions on the site. For example, Figure 3-3 shows the last two sets of configurations on the settings page, Change Frequencies and Priorities.

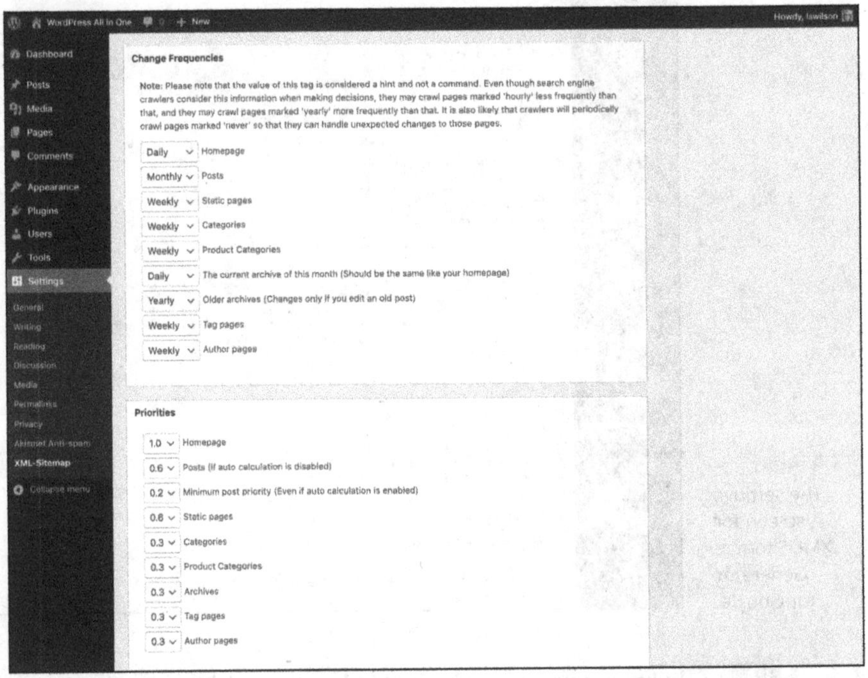

FIGURE 3-3: The final settings for the XML Sitemap Generator for Google.

This type of plugin settings setup is present in many popular plugins. Although the settings can be excessive for some users, most users can get good results by using the default settings. In plugins such as the XML Sitemap Generator for Google, the settings are available for people who want extra control of the plugin's functionality. I recommend reading the settings to get an idea of what options are available.

TIP

If you don't understand a setting, leave it in its default state.

Yoast SEO

Yoast SEO focuses on improving the search engine optimization (SEO) of your WordPress site. (If you're unfamiliar with SEO, see Book 5, Chapter 3.) With more than 500 million downloads, Yoast SEO is easily one of the most-downloaded plugins in the WordPress Plugins page. You can find it on the WordPress website at `https://wordpress.org/plugins/wordpress-seo/`.

Like the plugins in the preceding sections, Yoast SEO requires some additional configuration to function. After it's activated, the plugin creates its own menu on the Dashboard navigation menu on the left side. Click the Settings link on the new Yoast SEO menu to load the Site Features screen, shown in Figure 3-4.

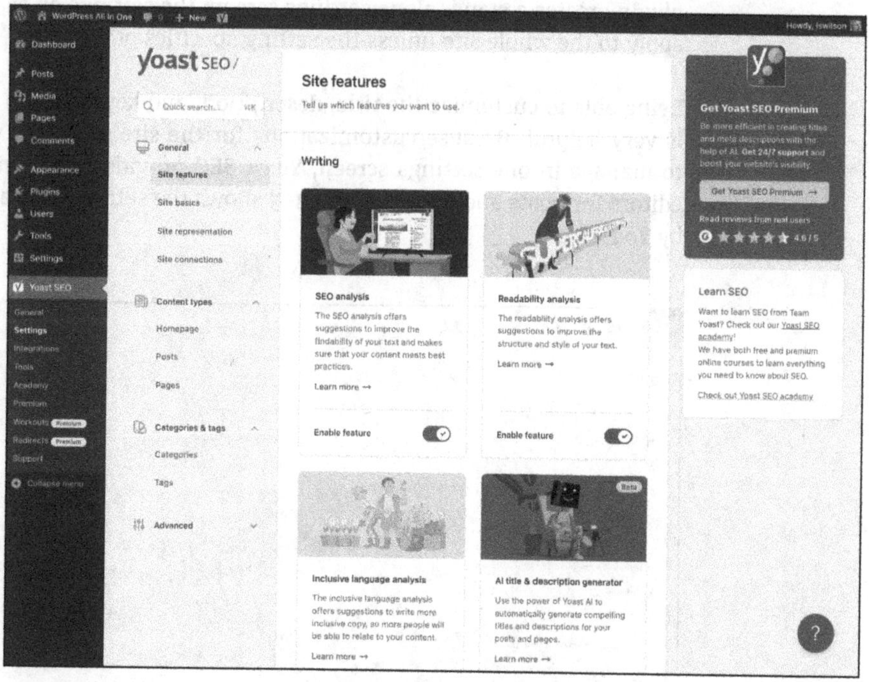

FIGURE 3-4: The Site Features screen for Yoast SEO.

This screen has a variety of settings that control many features of the plugin. In Figure 3-4 you see a navigation menu on the left side of the Site Features page that allows you to configure the settings for different areas of your website. The left navigation menu includes sections for General, Content Types, Categories & Tags, and Advanced. The primary focus of the settings in Yoast SEO is to define the search engine appearance for the different content types within your website. Typically, titles are controlled by the code within the theme files and are modifiable only through code changes. The ability to control titles without making code modifications is one of the primary reasons why SEO plugins such Yoast SEO are so popular. (See Book 5, Chapter 4 for more on the Yoast SEO plugin.)

Many other settings go beyond control of titles. Some of the most commonly used settings on this screen include automatic generation of keywords and description metadata, social media integrations for the title, a description, the image used when someone shares your content on social media sites, and a setting to determine what content is marked as `noindex`.

TECHNICAL STUFF

When you mark a specific page with `noindex`, search engines ignore the content of the page and won't return search results that link to it.

Like the settings for Akismet and the XML Sitemap Generator for Google, the settings for the Yoast SEO plugin affect the site as a whole. Although some of the settings apply only to specific parts of the site, the settings screen as a whole focuses on the entire site, which is true of most plugin settings screens. If the plugin creates a stand-alone settings screen, the settings on that screen typically apply to the whole site unless the setting specifies otherwise.

Being able to customize the title, description, and keywords on each page or post is very helpful. Because customizations for the site's content would be difficult to manage in one settings screen, Yoast SEO provides additional settings in the editors for posts and pages. Figure 3-5 shows the settings box added to the editor by Yoast SEO.

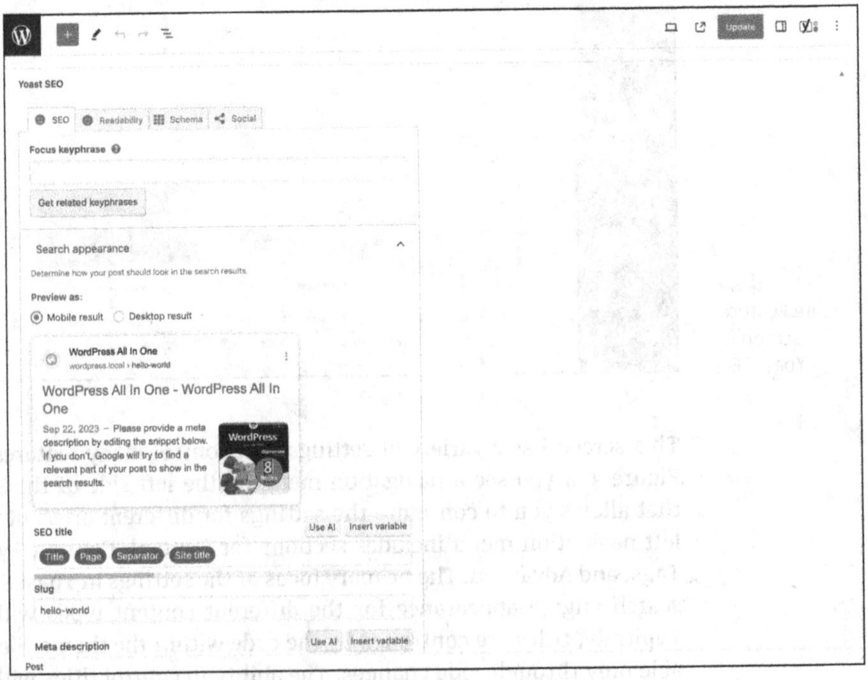

FIGURE 3-5: Yoast SEO settings to control SEO features for a specific post.

Using Widget Blocks

Widgets are powerful and flexible features for adding specific kinds of content to certain areas of your website, such as sidebars or footers, and even within a post or a page. WordPress comes with several built-in widgets, such as a calendar, a listing of pages on the site, a listing of recent comments, and a search tool. Plugins can expand this set of default widget blocks, which are always found in the Widgets section of the block inserter (see Book 4, Chapter 1). The following sections visit plugins that add their own widgets to show you how plugin-provided widgets offer options that enhance your site.

TIP

You can use widgets within posts and pages by finding the widget you want to use in the block inserter. You can use widgets in your header, footer, or sidebar by adding them as blocks in the site editor, covered in Book 6, Chapter 2.

Yoast SEO Breadcrumbs

After activating and setting up Yoast SEO, you can configure it to insert *breadcrumbs* on your pages that provide your users with a trail of links taking them back to where they came from after clicking around your site. You can set up breadcrumbs on the Yoast SEO Breadcrumbs page by clicking the Settings link in the Yoast SEO menu on the Dashboard, and then clicking the Breadcrumbs link under the Advanced menu on the Site Features page, as shown in Figure 3-6.

Once you have the Yoast SEO breadcrumbs set up the way you want them, you can display the Yoast SEO breadcrumbs on any archive page to provide your visitors with that navigation. For example, if you add the breadcrumbs to a category archive page for the category named *Books*, then when you are visiting a post filed in the Books category on the site, the breadcrumbs would look like this: *Home > Books > WordPress All In One.*

Spotlight Social Feeds

The Spotlight Social Feeds plugin serves a single purpose: It makes it easy to add feeds from your Instagram feed. This feature takes the form of a widget block, meaning that you can add the Instagram feed to any area on your site that accepts blocks from the block editor, such as the header or footer, content areas like pages and posts, and sidebars. The Spotlight Social Feeds plugin is available on the WordPress website at `https://wordpress.org/plugins/spotlight-social-photo-feeds/`.

This plugin has its own settings page on the Dashboard labeled Instagram Feeds. Figure 3-7 shows the Feeds settings page, where you can create several different feeds using this plugin.

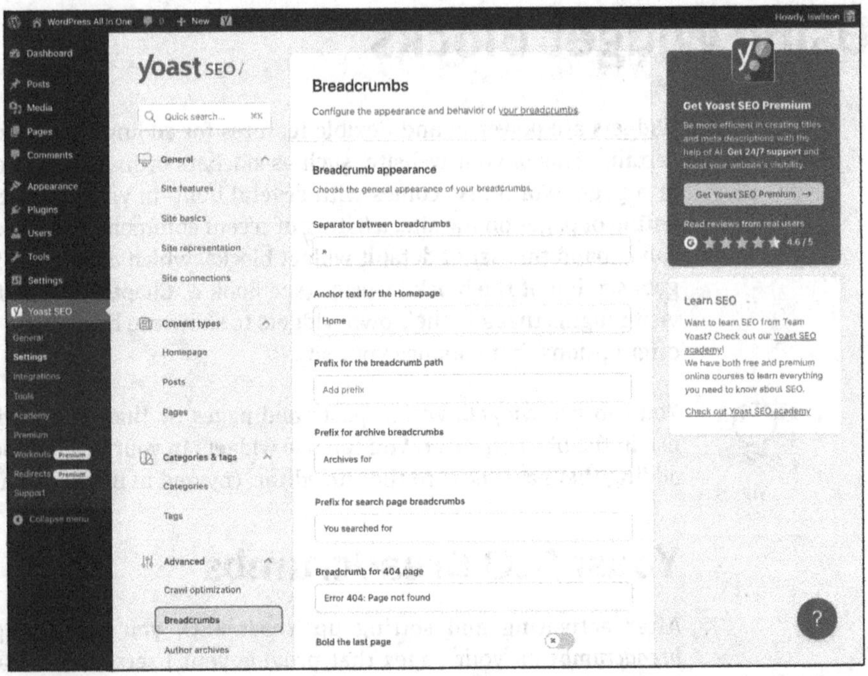

FIGURE 3-6: The Breadcrumbs page in the Yoast SEO settings page.

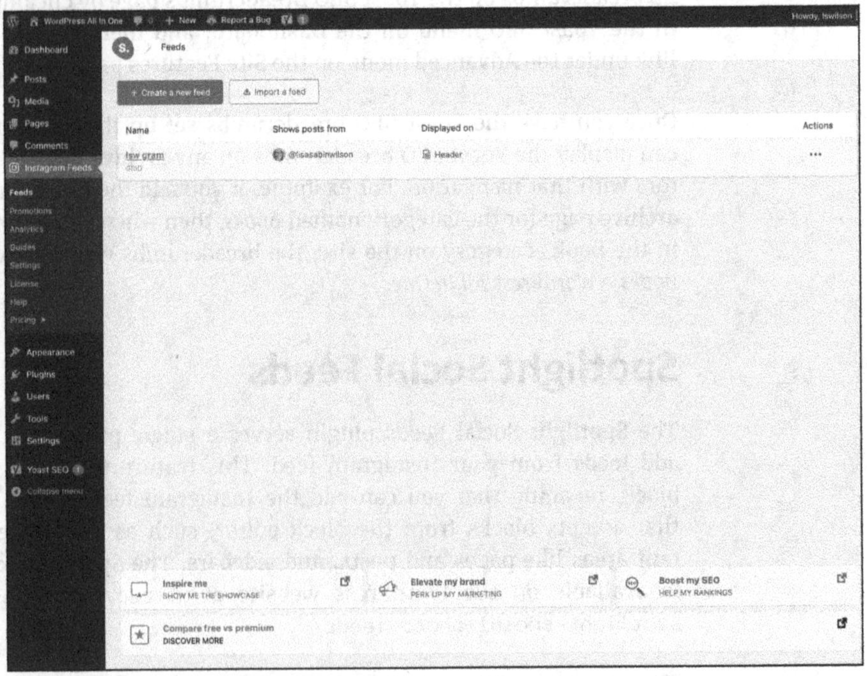

FIGURE 3-7: The Feeds settings page on the WordPress Dashboard.

My Instagram feed is shown in Figure 3-8 using the Spotlight Social Feeds. I've chosen to display it in the header of my website so it will display at the top of every page on my site.

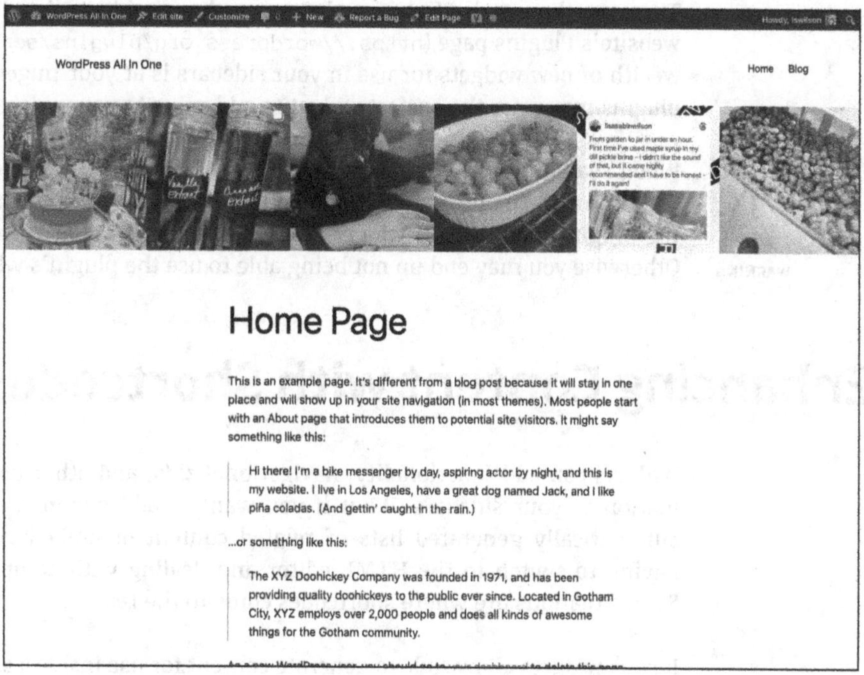

FIGURE 3-8: My Instagram feed created using the Spotlight Social Feeds plugin displayed on my website.

REMEMBER

If you're active on Instagram, using the Spotlight Social Feeds plugin is an easy way to inform or remind your visitors that you can be found on Instagram.

Additional widgets to try

Akismet and Spotlight Social Feeds plugins just scratch the surface of what's possible with widgets offered by plugins. The following list shows additional plugin examples that help fill in your sidebars:

- **Widget for Social Page Feeds (`https://wordpress.org/plugins/facebook-pagelike-widget`):** The Facebook Widget plugin provides a simple way to display your Facebook page likes in the sidebar of your website.
- **Image Widget:** Sometimes, you just want to add an image to a sidebar. Although the built-in Text widget and some HTML can provide this functionality, as well as the Custom HTML widget, some users don't know how to create

the HTML for the image or want a simpler solution for adding images. Luckily, WordPress ships with an Image Block that allows you to upload an image to the site without writing, copying, or pasting HTML markup.

There are thousands of plugins that are, or have, widgets listed on the WordPress website's Plugins page (`https://wordpress.org/plugins/search/widget`), so a wealth of new widgets for use in your sidebars is at your fingertips. One of those plugins may offer the perfect widget to add value to your sidebars.

WARNING

When searching for plugins that have widgets that you can use, be sure to dig a little through the documentation about the plugin to make sure that the widget the plugin provides is a widget block that is compatible with the block editor. Otherwise you may end up not being able to use the plugin's widget.

Enhancing Content with Shortcodes

Widgets can add functionality, navigational aids, and other useful bits of information to your sidebars. What if you want to add dynamic elements (such as automatically generated lists of related content or embedded videos) without having to switch to the HTML editor and dealing with complex embed codes? Such situations are where shortcodes come to the rescue.

Just as widgets allow code to generate content for use inside a sidebar, shortcodes allow code to generate additional content inside a post, page, or other content type. In the following sections, you find out about a few useful shortcodes.

Gallery shortcode

One of the shortcodes built into WordPress is `gallery`. The most basic gallery shortcode is `[gallery]`. In this format, all the default arguments are used. (Shortcodes can also support optional arguments that allow for customization.) By default, a gallery is arranged in three columns and uses thumbnail-size images. The following shortcode displays the gallery in two columns and use medium-size images:

```
[gallery columns="2" size="medium"]
```

In many ways, shortcodes are similar to HTML tags. The `gallery` shortcode looks like an opening HTML tag that swapped the < and > characters for [and].

REMEMBER

WordPress does ship with a gallery block available to use; however, you can also use the shortcode discussed in this section by including it in a text widget block.

Embed shortcode

Shortcodes give you the capability to surround simple WordPress functions in an opening and closing bracket in order to execute features on your site. The embed shortcode provided by WordPress is one such shortcode.

WordPress can automatically embed a video player on your site by using the embed shortcode with a link to a supported video, like one from YouTube. (See Book 4, Chapter 5 for details on which sites are supported.) Although this happens when supported video links are left on a line on their own, supported video links can be surrounded by the embed shortcode to explicitly indicate that the link is to be changed to an embedded video, as follows:

```
[embed]https://videopress.com/v/DK5mLrbr[/embed]
```

By adding the embed shortcode to a post or page using a Custom HTML block, I've embedded a video player that displays Matt Mullenweg's 2017 State of the Word video displays in place of the shortcode, as shown in Figure 3-9.

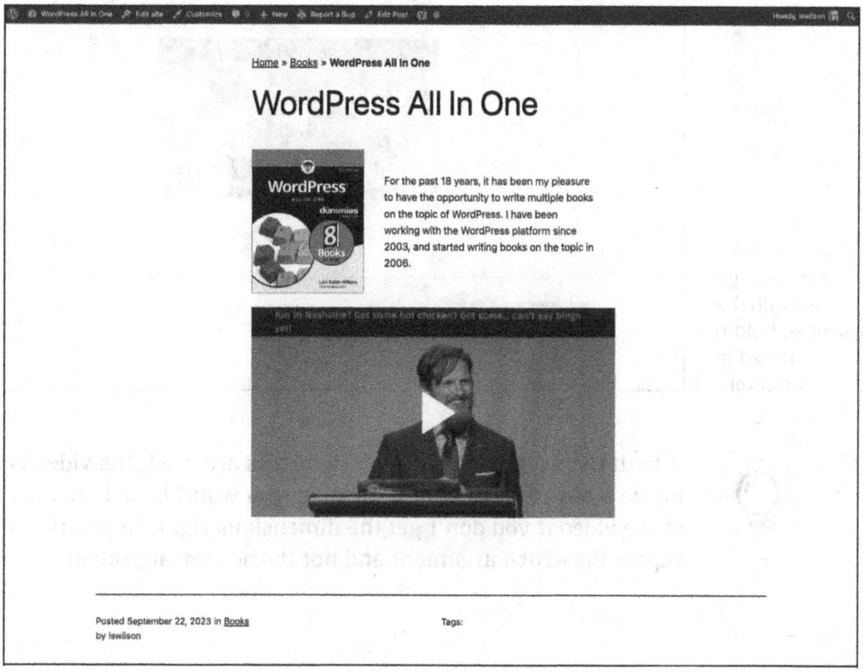
Home » Books » WordPress All In One
WordPress All In One
For the past 18 years, it has been my pleasure to have the opportunity to write multiple books on the topic of WordPress. I have been working with the WordPress platform since 2003, and started writing books on the topic in 2006.
Posted September 22, 2023 in Books by lswilson
Tags:

FIGURE 3-9: The embedded video replacing the embed shortcode.

You may wonder why you'd want to use the embed shortcode instead of putting the link on its own line. The reason is that like the gallery shortcode, the embed shortcode supports arguments that allow you to customize the display of the video. The supported arguments are width and height. The following shortcode modifies the embedded video to have a width of 800 pixels and height of 500 pixels:

```
[embed width="800" height="500"]https://videopress.com/v/
   DK5mLrbr[/embed]
```

(I don't think you'd want a video at a width of 200 pixels; I'm doing this to show how the arguments work.) Figure 3-10 shows the result of this change. Notice that the entire video is smaller.

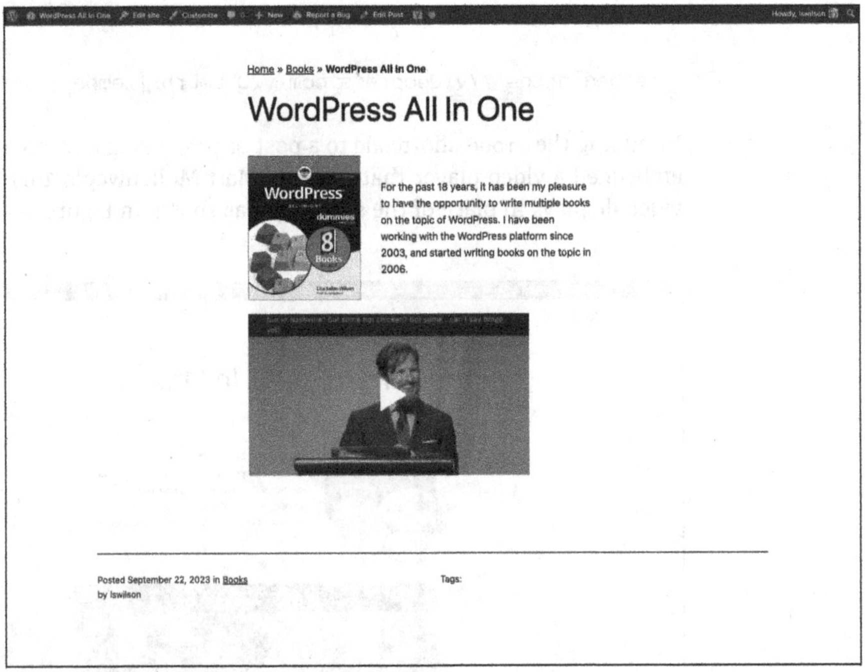
Home » Books » WordPress All In One
WordPress All In One
For the past 18 years, it has been my pleasure to have the opportunity to write multiple books on the topic of WordPress. I have been working with the WordPress platform since 2003, and started writing books on the topic in 2006.
Posted September 22, 2023 in Books
by lswilson
Tags:

FIGURE 3-10: The embedded video with the height and width reduced to 500 pixels.

TIP

If both the width and height arguments are used, the video is scaled down to fit inside a box of those dimensions, so you won't be able to distort the aspect ratio of the video if you don't get the dimensions right. In practice, it's often easiest to supply the width argument and not the height argument.

Embed Twitter links

By default, WordPress has a feature called *oEmbed*, in which a link from a particular service or social media site automatically gets embedded in your post or page and adopts the formatting and style of the site of origin. If you paste a URL from YouTube in a WordPress post, for example, WordPress automatically embeds the video in the YouTube player. The same thing happens with links from Twitter. If you paste a Twitter link in a post, WordPress automatically formats the tweet and embeds it in your post. WordPress also provides us with a Twitter embed block that allows you to add an embedded tweet anywhere that accepts blocks from the block editor.

For the purposes of showing off the use of the embed shortcode, following is an example of using the shortcode to embed a Twitter link. Using the shortcode block in the Add New Post screen, I added the following embed shortcode and Twitter link in order to display the tweet in my post:

```
[embed]https://twitter.com/LisaSabinWilson/
  status/1066037791249874944[/embed]
```

Figure 3-11 displays the output of this shortcode.

FIGURE 3-11: Using a Twitter link inside the embed shortcode.

8

Running Multiple Sites with WordPress

Contents at a Glance

IN THIS CHAPTER

» Deciding whether multiple sites are for you

» Learning the difference between a site and a blog

» Configuring your web server

Chapter 1

Using the Multisite Feature

In this chapter, I introduce you to the network feature that's built into the WordPress software. The Multisite feature allows you, the site owner, to add and maintain multiple sites within one installation of WordPress. In this chapter, you discover how to set up the Multisite feature, explore settings and configurations, gain an understanding of the network administrator role, determine which configuration is right for you (do you want subdirectories or subdomains?), and find some great resources to help you along the way.

When the Multisite feature is enabled, users of your network can run their own sites within your installation of WordPress. They also have access to their own Dashboards with the same options and features covered in the chapters in Book 3. Heck, it probably would be a great idea to buy a copy of this book for every member of your network so that everyone can become familiar with the WordPress Dashboard and its features, too. At least have a copy on hand so that people can borrow yours!

Deciding When to Use the Multisite Feature

Usually, for multiple users to post to one site, the default WordPress setup is sufficient. The *Multi* part of the WordPress Multisite feature's name doesn't refer to how many users have been added to your WordPress website; it refers to the ability to run multiple sites in one installation of the WordPress software. *Multisite* is a bit of a misnomer and an inaccurate depiction of what the software does. *Network of sites* is a much closer description.

Determining whether to use the Multisite feature depends on user access and publishing activity. Each site on the network shares a code base and users but is a self-contained unit. Users still have to access the back end of each site to manage options or post to that site. A limited number of general options are available network-wide, and posting isn't one of those options.

You can use multiple sites on a network to create the appearance that only one site exists. Put the same theme on each site, and the visitor doesn't realize that the sites are separate. This technique is a good way to separate sections of a magazine site, using editors for complete sections (sites) but not letting them access other parts of the network or the back ends of other sites.

Another factor to consider is how comfortable you are with editing files directly on the server. Setting up the network involves accessing the server directly, and ongoing maintenance and support for your users often leads to the network owner's doing the necessary maintenance, which is not for the faint of heart.

Generally, you should use a network of sites in the following cases:

- **You want multiple sites and one installation.** You're a blogger or site owner who wants to maintain another site, possibly with a subdomain or a separate domain, with both sites on one web host. You're comfortable with editing files; you want to work with one code base to make site maintenance easier; and most of your plugins and themes are accessible to all the sites. You can have one login across the sites and manage each site individually.
- **You want to host blogs or sites for others.** This process is a little more involved. You want to set up a network in which users sign up for their own sites or blogs below (or on) your main site and you maintain the technical aspects.

Because all files are shared, some aspects are locked down for security purposes. One of the most puzzling security measures for new users is suppression of errors. Most PHP errors (such as those that occur when you install a faulty plugin or incorrectly edit a file) don't output messages to the screen. Instead, WordPress displays what I like to call the White Screen of Death.

Finding and using error logs and doing general debugging are necessary skills for managing your own network. Even if your web host sets up the ongoing daily or weekly tasks for you, managing a network can involve a steep learning curve.

REMEMBER

When you enable the Multisite feature, the existing WordPress site becomes the main site in the installation.

Although WordPress can be quite powerful, in the following situations the management of multiple sites has its limitations:

- One web hosting account is used for the installation. You can't use multiple hosting accounts.
- You want to post content to multiple sites at one time. WordPress doesn't allow this practice by default.
- If you choose subdirectory sites, the main site regenerates permalinks with `/blog/` in them to prevent collisions with subsites. Plugins, or custom code, are available to prevent this regeneration.

The best example of a large blog network with millions of blogs and users is the hosted service at `WordPress.com` (`https://wordpress.com`). At `WordPress.com`, people are invited to sign up for an account and start a site by using the Multisite feature within the WordPress platform on the WordPress server. When you enable this feature on your own domain and enable the user registration feature, you're inviting users to do the following:

- Create an account.
- Create a blog on your WordPress installation (on your domain).
- Create content by publishing posts and/or pages.
- Upload media files such as photos, audio, and video.
- Invite friends to view the site or sign up for their own accounts.

Understanding the Difference between Sites and Blogs

Each additional blog in a WordPress Multisite network is a *site* instead of a *blog*. What's the difference?

Largely, the difference is one of perception. Everything functions the same way, but people see greater possibilities when they no longer think of each site as being "just" a blog. WordPress can be much more:

- With the addition of the WordPress MU Domain Mapping plugin (`https://wordpress.org/plugins/wordpress-mu-domain-mapping`), you can manage multiple sites that have unique domain names. None of these sites even has to be a blog. The sites can have blog elements, or they can be static sites that use only pages.
- The built-in options let you choose between subdomains or subdirectory sites when you install the network, also discussed later in this chapter in the "Exploring subdomains versus subdirectories" section. If you install WordPress in the root of your web space, you get `subdomain.`*`yourdomain`*`.com` (if you choose subdomains) or *`yourdomain.com`*`/subdirectory` (if you choose subdirectory). Book 8, Chapter 2 discusses the differences and advantages.

REMEMBER

After you choose the kind of sites you want to host and then create those sites, you can't change them. These sites are served virtually, meaning that they don't exist as files or folders anywhere on the server; they exist only in the database. The correct location is served to the browser by using rewrite rules in the `.htaccess` file. (See Book 2, Chapter 4.)

- The main, or parent, site of the network also can be a landing page of the entire network of sites, showcasing content from other sites in the network and drawing in visitors further.

Setting Up the Optimal Hosting Environment

This chapter assumes that you already have the WordPress software installed and running correctly on your web server and that your web server meets the minimum requirements to run WordPress.

Before you enable the WordPress Multisite feature, you need to determine how you're going to use the feature. You have a couple of options:

- Manage a few of your own WordPress blogs or websites.
- Run a full-blown blogging network with several hundred blogs and multiple users.

If you're planning to run a few of your own sites with the WordPress network feature, your current hosting situation probably is appropriate. If, however, you plan to host a large network with hundreds of blogs and multiple users, you should consider contacting your host and increasing your bandwidth, as well as consider the disk-space limitations on your account.

WARNING

Beyond the necessary security measures, time, and administrative tasks that go into running a community of sites, you have a few more things to worry about. Creating a community increases resource use, bandwidth use, and disk space on your web server. In many cases, if you go over the limits assigned to you by your web host, you'll incur great cost. Make sure that you anticipate your bandwidth and disk-space needs before running a large network on your website. (Don't say I didn't warn you!)

Checking out shared versus dedicated hosting

Many WordPress network communities start with grand dreams of developing a large and active community. Be realistic about how your community will operate to make the right hosting choice for yourself and your community.

Small multisite communities can be handled easily by a shared-server solution, whereas larger, more active communities may require a dedicated-server solution. The difference lies in the names:

- **Shared-server solution:** You have one account on one server that has several other accounts on it. Think of this solution as apartment living. One apartment building has several apartments in which multiple people live, all under one roof.
- **Dedicated-server solution:** You have one account and you have one server. That server is dedicated to your account, and your account is dedicated to the server. Think of this solution as living in a private home where you don't share living space with anyone else.

A dedicated-server solution is a more expensive investment for your blog community, whereas a shared-server solution is more economical. Your decision about which solution to go with for your WordPress network blogging community should be based on your realistic estimates of how big and how active your community will be. You can move from a shared-server solution to a dedicated-server solution if your community gets larger than you expected, but it's easier to start with the right solution for your community from day one, if possible.

Exploring subdomains versus subdirectories

The WordPress Multisite feature gives you two ways to run a network of sites on your domain: the subdomain option and the subdirectory option. When you first set up the Multisite feature, it is automatically set to the subdirectory option.

The most popular option (and recommended structure) sets up subdirectories for the sites created within a WordPress network. Subdirectories are more beneficial to SEO (search engine optimization) than subdomains. Subdirectories focus keywords on a single domain, which helps improve the authority for the primary domain. Search engines crawl and track subdomains independently. This means that SEO efforts for the main site will not instantly benefit subdomains.

With the subdirectory option, the username of the site appears first, followed by your domain name. With the subdirectory option, your domain name appears first, followed by the username of the site. Which one should you choose? You can see the difference in the URLs of these two options by comparing the following examples:

- A **subdomain** looks like this: `http://`*`username.yourdomain.com`*
- A **subdirectory** looks like this: `http://`*`yourdomain.com/username`*

While the network is being set up, tables that contain information about the network, including the main site URL, are added to the database. If you're developing a site or want to change the domain later, you need to change every reference to the domain name in the database.

Choosing Linux, Apache, MySQL, and PHP server environments

A network of sites works best on a LAMP (Linux, Apache, MySQL, and PHP) server with the `mod_rewrite` Apache module enabled. `mod_rewrite` is an Apache module that builds URLs that are easy to read. (See the nearby "Apache mod_rewrite" sidebar for more information.) In WordPress, this Apache module is used for permalinks. If your installation uses any permalink other than the default, `?p=123`, you're okay. Your web host can help you determine whether your web server allows this practice; most servers do, and `mod_rewrite` is a requirement for setting up the WordPress Multisite feature. (You can find more information on permalink structures in Book 3, Chapter 2.)

For the purposes of this chapter, I stick to the LAMP server setup because it's most similar to the average web host and is most widely used.

WARNING

Remember that the Apache `mod_rewrite` module is required for WordPress multisites. Today, almost all web hosts have this module enabled; however, if you don't know whether your current hosting environment has this module in place, drop an email to your hosting provider and ask. The provider can answer that question for you (in addition to installing the module for you in the event that your server doesn't have it).

TECHNICAL STUFF

Networks also work well on Nginx and Lightspeed servers, but many users have reported having much difficulty on IIS (Windows) servers. Therefore, I don't recommend setting up WordPress with Multisite features in a Windows server environment without the help of a WordPress developer with experience with IIS servers.

APACHE MOD_REWRITE

Apache (`http://httpd.apache.org`) is software that's loaded and running on your web server. Usually, the only person who has access to Apache files is the web server administrator (probably your web host). Depending on your own web-server account and configuration, you may have access to the Apache software files.

The Apache module that's necessary for the WordPress network to create nice permalink URLs is called `mod_rewrite`. This module must be configured to be active and installed on your server.

You or your web host administrator can make sure that the Apache `mod_rewrite` is activated on your server by opening the `httpd.conf` file and verifying that the following line is included:

```
LoadModule rewrite_module /libexec/mod_rewrite.so
```

If it isn't, type that line on its own line and save the file. You probably need to restart Apache before the change takes effect.

Subdomain sites work by way of a virtual host entry in Apache, also known as a *wildcard* subdomain. On shared hosts, your web hosting provider's support team has to enable this entry for you (or may already have done so for all accounts). It's best to ask your hosting provider before you begin. In these situations, the domain you use for your install must be the default domain in your account. Otherwise, the URLs of your subsites will fail to work properly or won't have a folder name in the URL.

WARNING

Some hosts may require you to have a dedicated IP address, but this requirement isn't a specific software requirement for a WordPress network to function.

Before proceeding with the steps to enable the WordPress Multisite feature, you need to get a few items in order on your web server. You also need to decide how the multiple sites within your network will be handled. You need to have these configurations in place to run the WordPress network successfully. The next section takes you through some of these configurations and items, including virtual host and PHP considerations.

Adding a virtual host to the Apache configuration

You need to add a hostname record pointing at your web server in the Domain Name System (DNS) configuration tool available in your web server's administration software, such as WebHost Manager (WHM), a popular web host administration tool.

WARNING

In this section, you edit and configure Apache server files. If you can perform the configurations in this section yourself (and if you have access to the Apache configuration files), this section is for you. If you don't know how, are uncomfortable with adjusting these settings, or don't have access to configurations in your web-server software, ask your hosting provider for help or hire a consultant to perform the configurations for you. I can't stress enough that you shouldn't edit the Apache server files yourself if you aren't comfortable with it or don't fully understand what you're doing. Web hosting providers have support staff to help you with these things if you need it; take advantage!

The hostname record looks like this: `*.`*`yourdomain.com`* (where *`yourdomain.com`* is replaced by your actual domain name).

In the `httpd.conf` file, you need to make some adjustments in the `<VirtualHost>` section of that file. If you can't find it, you can search for: VirtualHost in your editor. Follow these steps:

1. **Find the `<VirtualHost>` section in the `httpd.conf` file.**

   This line of the `httpd.conf` file provides directives, or configurations, that apply to your website.

2. **Find a line in the `<VirtualHost>` section of the `httpd.conf` that looks like this:**

   ```
   AllowOverride None
   ```

3. **Replace that line with this line:**

   ```
   AllowOverride FileInfo Options
   ```

4. **On a new line, type ServerAlias *.*yourdomain*.com.**

   Replace *yourdomain*.com with whatever your domain is. This line defines the host name for your network site and is essential for the virtual host to work correctly.

5. **Save and close the `httpd.conf` file.**

You also need to add a wildcard subdomain DNS record. Depending on how your domain is set up, you can do this at your registrar or your web host. If you simply pointed to your web host's nameservers, you can add more DNS records at your web host in the web server administration interface, such as WHM (WebHost Manager).

You also should add a `CNAME` record with a value of $*$. CNAME stands for Canonical Name and is a record stored in the DNS settings of your Apache web server that tells Apache you want to associate a new subdomain with the main-account domain. Applying the value of $*$ tells Apache to send any subdomain requests to your main domain. From there, WordPress looks up that subdomain in the database to see whether it exists.

Networks require a great deal more server memory (RAM) than typical WordPress sites (those that don't use the Multisite feature) because multisites generally are bigger, have a lot more traffic, and use more database space and resources because multiple sites are running (as opposed to one with regular WordPress). You aren't simply adding instances of WordPress. You're multiplying the processing and resource use of the server when you run the WordPress Multisite feature. Although smaller instances of a network run fine on most web hosts, you may find that when your network grows, you need more memory. I generally recommend that you start with a hosting account with access to at least 256MB of RAM (memory).

For each site created, nine tables are added to the single database. Each table has a prefix similar to wp_BLOG-ID_tablename (where BLOG-ID is a unique ID assigned to the site).

The only exception is the main site: Its tables remain untouched and remain the same. With WordPress multisites, all new installations leave the main blog tables untouched and number additional site tables sequentially when every new site is added to the network.

Configuring PHP

In this section, you edit the PHP configuration on your web server. PHP needs to have the following configurations in place in the php.ini file on your web server to run WordPress Multisite on your server:

- Set your PHP to *not* display any error messages in the visitor's browser window. (Usually, this setting is turned off by default; double-check to be sure.)
- Find out whether your PHP is compiled with memory-limit checks. You can find out by looking for the text memory_limit in the php.ini file. Usually, the default limit is 8MB. Increase the memory limit to at least 32MB, or even 64MB, to prevent PHP memory errors while running WordPress Multisite.

TIP

The default memory limit for WordPress is 32MB or 64MB for a Multisite setup. As an alternative to editing the php.ini file on your web server to increase the PHP memory limit, you can add this line to the wp-config.php file of your WordPress installation:

```
define( 'WP_MEMORY_LIMIT', '64M' );
```

The 64M portion of that line of code defines the memory limit in megabytes, and you can set it to any value that doesn't exceed 512MB.

IN THIS CHAPTER

» Enabling the network feature

» Differentiating between subdirectories and subdomains

» Configuring the network installation

» Disabling the network

Chapter 2

Setting Up and Configuring Network Features

This chapter covers how to find the files you need to edit the network, how to enable multiple sites in the network, and how to remove the network should you no longer want to have multiple sites in your WordPress install.

By default, access to network settings is disabled to ensure that users don't set up their network without researching all that the setup entails. Setting up a network involves more than configuring options on the Dashboard or turning on a feature, so before enabling and setting up a network, be sure that you read Book 8, Chapter 1.

Here's what you need:

- Backups of your site (explained in Book 2, Chapter 6)
- Ability to edit the `wp-config.php` via SFTP (Book 2, Chapter 2)
- Enabled wildcard subdomains (covered in Book 8, Chapter 1) if you're using subdomains

Enabling the Network Feature

You need to enable access to the Network menu so you can set up the network and allow the creation of multiple sites.

TIP

It's a good idea to download a copy of the original wp-config.php file from your web server and store it on your computer to keep it safe. That way, if you make any mistakes or experience any errors after altering it, you can easily upload the original and start over.

WARNING

If you have any plugins installed and activated on your WordPress installation, deactivate them before you proceed with the network setup. WordPress won't allow you to continue until you deactivate all your plugins.

WordPress makes it pretty easy to enable the network feature, but doing so does require opening a file on your web server called wp-config.php and making a small alteration. Follow these steps to get the process started:

1. **Download the file called `wp-config.php` from the WordPress installation on your web server.**

   It's easiest to use an SFTP program to download a copy of this file from your web server to your computer. If you need a refresher on SFTP, refer to Book 2, Chapter 2.

2. **Using your preferred text editor, open the `wp-config.php` file.**

   Windows users can use Notepad to edit the file; Mac users can use TextEdit.

3. **Click at the end of the line that reads `define( 'DB_COLLATE', '' );` and then press Enter (or Return on a Mac) to create a new blank line.**

4. **Type the following on the new blank line:**

```
define( 'WP_ALLOW_MULTISITE', true );
```

5. **Save the file to your computer as `wp-config.php`.**

6. **Upload the new file to your web server in your WordPress installation directory.**

7. **Go to your WordPress Dashboard in your browser.**

   You see a new item in the Tools menu labeled Network Setup.

8. **Click the Network Setup link on the Tools menu.**

   The Create a Network of WordPress Sites screen displays. (It's covered in the next section and shown in Figure 2-1.) You also see a reminder to deactivate all your plugins before continuing with network setup.

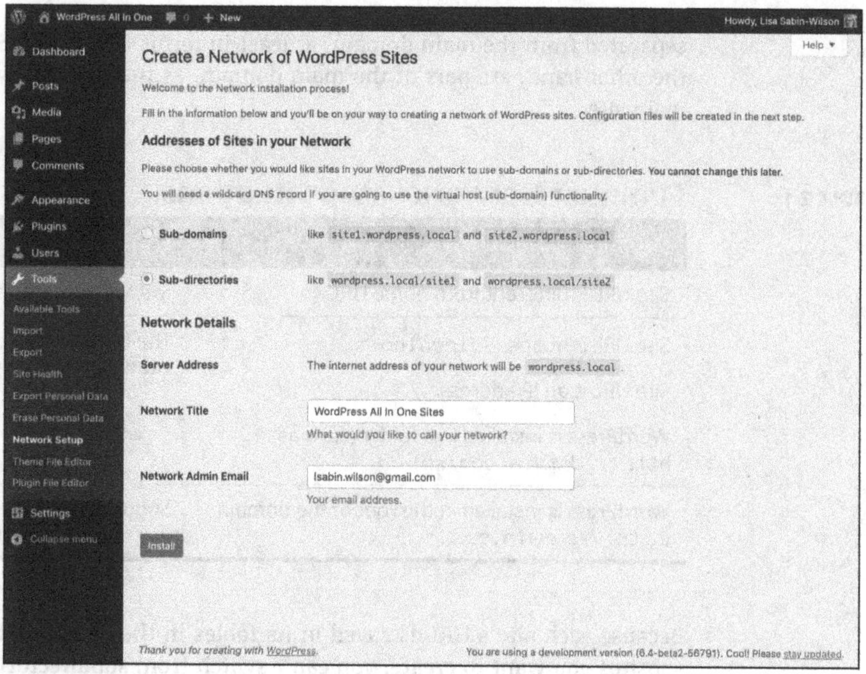

FIGURE 2-1: The Create a Network of WordPress Sites screen on your WordPress Dashboard.

Exploring the Difference between Subdirectories and Subdomains

The choice between subdomains and subdirectories is yours if you're activating Multisite on a fresh WordPress installation. However, if your website is already place and older than a month, you do not have a choice; WordPress enforces the use of subdomains.

REMEMBER

In some cases, depending on your setup, your choice may be limited. WordPress does some autodetection with information about your installation and may prevent you from choosing an option that won't work with your setup.

Table 2-1 explains some of the limitations you may encounter as you try to enable a subdomain or subdirectory format.

Site addresses generate in a similar way; they're virtual. They don't physically exist in your file directory on your web server, and you won't see them in the directory structure on your web server because they're served to the browser *virtually* when that site is requested. From a technical standpoint, subdomains require an extra step in server setup for the wildcards. (Book 8, Chapter 1 covers setting up wildcard subdomains on the server side.) Subdomains are somewhat separated from the main domain, at least in terms of content. Subdirectories, on the other hand, are part of the main domain, as though they were pages off the main site.

TABLE 2-1 **Common Network Setup Situations**

Situation	Format
Site URL is different from home URL.	Network can't be enabled.
Site URL is `https://localhost`. Site URL is an IP address. WordPress is installed in a folder (such as `http://`*`domain`*`.com/wp`).	The Network can use subdirectories only.
WordPress is installed in the root of the domain (`http://`*`domain`*`.com`).	Subdirectories are the default, but you can choose either.

Because each site's URL is saved in its tables in the database, after you pick the subsites you want to create, you can't switch from subdirectories to subdomains (or vice versa) without reinstalling the network.

TIP

If you want your extra sites to have separate domain names, you still need to pick one of these options. Book 8, Chapter 6 covers top-level domains.

Installing the Network on Your Site

The Network Details section of the Create a Network of WordPress Sites page (refer to Figure 2-1) has options that are filled in automatically. The server address, for example, is pulled from your installation and can't be edited. The network title and administrator's email address are pulled from your installation database, too, because your initial WordPress site is the main site of the network.

Follow these steps to complete the installation (and be sure to have your preferred text-editor program handy):

1. **Click the Install button at the bottom of the Create a Network of WordPress Sites screen of your WordPress Dashboard.**

   The Enabling the Network screen opens, as shown in Figure 2-2.

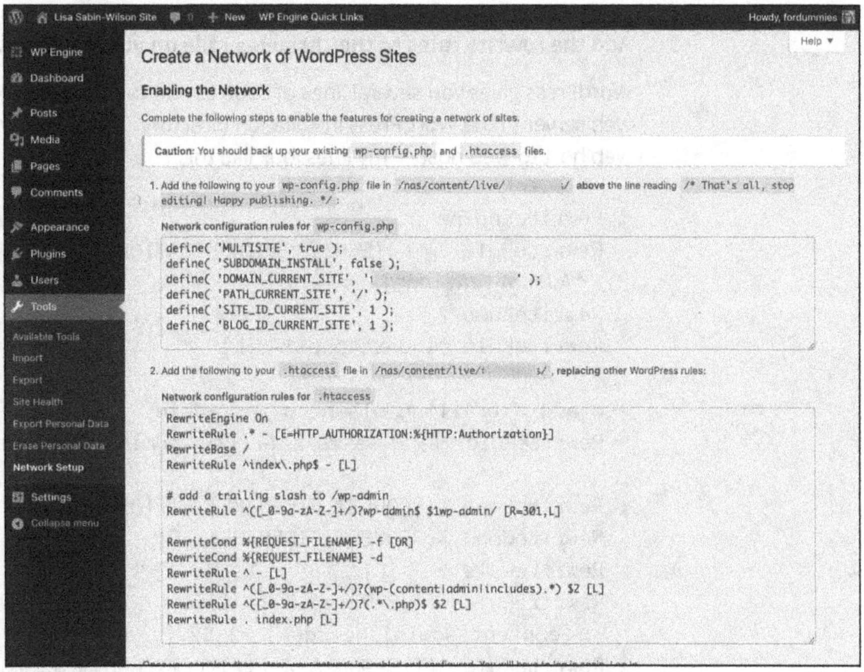

FIGURE 2-2: The Enabling the Network screen.

2. **Add the required network-related configuration lines to the `wp-config.php` file following the `define( 'WP_ALLOW_MULTISITE', true );` code you added earlier.**

   On the Enabling the Network screen, WordPress gives you up to six lines of configuration rules that need to be added to the `wp-config.php` file. The lines of code you add may look like this:

```
define( 'MULTISITE', true );
define( 'SUBDOMAIN_INSTALL', false );
define( 'DOMAIN_CURRENT_SITE', 'domain.com' );
define( 'PATH_CURRENT_SITE', '/' );
define( 'SITE_ID_CURRENT_SITE', 1 );
define( 'BLOG_ID_CURRENT_SITE', 1 );
```

   The lines of code that appear on the Enabling the Network screen are unique to *your* installation of WordPress. Make sure that you copy the lines of code that are given to you on the Create a Network of WordPress Sites page on *your* installation, because they are specific to your site's setup.

3. **Add the rewrite rules to the .htaccess file on your web server.**

   WordPress gives you several lines of code to add to the .htaccess file on your web server in the WordPress installation directory. These lines may vary from web host to web host — my lines look like this:

```
RewriteEngine On
RewriteRule .* - [E=HTTP_AUTHORIZATION:%{HTTP:
  Authorization}]
RewriteBase /
RewriteRule ^index\.php$ - [L]

# add a trailing slash to /wp-admin
RewriteRule ^([_0-9a-zA-Z-]+/)?wp-admin$ $1wp-admin/ [R=301,L]

RewriteCond %{REQUEST_FILENAME} -f [OR]
RewriteCond %{REQUEST_FILENAME} -d
RewriteRule ^ - [L]
RewriteRule ^([_0-9a-zA-Z-]+/)?(wp-
  (content|admin|includes).*) $2 [L]
RewriteRule ^([_0-9a-zA-Z-]+/)?(.*\.php)$ $2 [L]
RewriteRule . index.php [L]
```

REMEMBER

In Book 8, Chapter 1, I discuss the required Apache module `mod_rewrite`, which you must have installed on your web server to run WordPress Multisite. The rules that you add to the .htaccess file on your web server are `mod_rewrite` rules, and they need to be in place so that your web server tells WordPress how to handle things like permalinks for posts, pages, media, and other uploaded files. If these rules aren't in place, the WordPress Multisite feature won't work correctly.

4. **Copy the lines of code that you entered in Step 3, open the .htaccess file, and paste the code there.**

   Replace the rules that already exist in that file.

5. **Save the .htaccess file, and upload it to your web server.**
6. **Return to your WordPress Dashboard, and click the Log In link at the bottom of the Enabling the Network screen.**

   You're logged out of WordPress because by following these steps, you changed some of the browser cookie-handling rules in the `wp-config.php` and .htaccess files.

7. **Log in to WordPress by entering your username and password in the login form.**

With the Multisite feature enabled, you see a link to My Sites in the top-left corner of your screen. If you hover your mouse pointer over that link, the Network Admin link appears on the drop-down menu in the top-left corner of the Dashboard. The Network Admin Dashboard is where you, as the site owner, administer and manage your multisite WordPress network. (See Book 8, Chapter 3.)

Disabling the Network

At some point, you may decide that running a network of sites isn't for you, and you may find that you want to disable the Multisite feature. Before disabling the network, you want to save any content from the other sites by making a full backup of your database. Book 2, Chapter 6 has detailed information about backing up your site.

The first step is restoring the original `wp-config.php` file and `.htaccess` files that you saved earlier. (Refer to the "Enabling the Network Feature" section, earlier in this chapter.) This step causes your WordPress installation to stop displaying the Network Admin menu and the extra sites.

You also may want to delete the tables that were added, which permanently removes the extra sites from your installation. Web hosts provide you with different tools to allow you to access and work with your database. The most popular tool is called PHPMyAdmin. You can use that tool to delete the multisite tables from your WordPress database when you want to deactivate the feature. The extra database tables that are no longer required when you aren't running the WordPress Multisite feature include

- **`wp_blogs`:** This database table contains one record per site and is used for site lookup.
- **`wp_blog_versions`:** This database table is used internally for upgrades.
- **`wp_registration_log`:** This database table contains information on sites created when a user signed up if they chose to create a site at the same time.
- **`wp_signups`:** This database table contains information on users who signed up for the network.
- **`wp_site`:** This database table contains one record per WordPress network.
- **`wp_sitemeta`:** This database table contains network settings.

Additionally, you can delete any database tables that have blog IDs associated with them. These tables start with prefixes that look like wp_1_, wp_2_, wp_3_, and so on.

REMEMBER

WordPress adds new tables each time you add a new site to your network. Those database tables are assigned unique numbers incrementally.

IN THIS CHAPTER

» Getting familiar with the Network Admin Dashboard

» Managing your network

» Preventing spam blogs

Chapter 3
Becoming a Network Admin

After you enable the WordPress network option and become a network admin, you can examine the various settings that are available to you and go over the responsibilities you have while running a network.

As a network admin, you can access the Network Admin Dashboard, which includes several submenus, to manage the sites in your network, as well as the overall settings for your network. This chapter discusses the menu items and options on the Network Admin screen, guides you in setting network options, and discusses the best ways to prevent spam and spam blogs (splogs).

Exploring the Network Admin Dashboard

When you visit the Dashboard after activating the Multisite feature, the toolbar includes the My Sites menu, which contains the Network Admin link.

WordPress has separated the Network Admin menu features from the regular (Site Admin) Dashboard menu features to make it easier for you to know which part of your site you're managing. If you're performing actions that maintain your main website — publishing posts or pages, creating or editing categories, and so on — you work in the regular (Site Admin) Dashboard. If you're managing any of the network sites, plugins, and themes for the network sites or registered users, you work in the Network Admin section of the Dashboard.

REMEMBER

Keep in mind the distinct differences between the Site Admin and Network Admin Dashboards, as well as their menu features. WordPress does its best to know which features you're attempting to work with, but if you find yourself getting lost on the Dashboard, or if you're not finding a menu or feature that you're used to seeing, make sure that you're working in the correct section of the Dashboard.

The Network Admin Dashboard (see Figure 3-1) is similar to the regular WordPress Dashboard; however, the modules pertain to the network of sites. Options include creating a site, creating a user, and searching existing sites and users. Obviously, you won't perform this search if you don't have any users or sites yet. This function is extremely useful when you have a community of users and sites within your network, however.

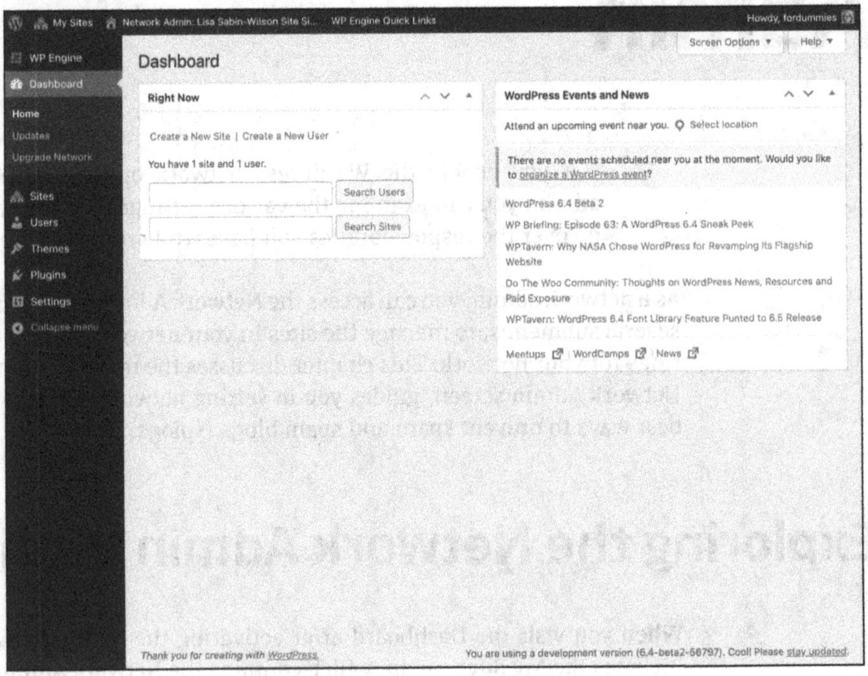

FIGURE 3-1: The Network Admin Dashboard.

TIP

The Network Admin Dashboard is configurable, just like the regular Dashboard; you can move the modules around and edit their settings. Refer to Book 3, Chapter 1 for more information about arranging the Dashboard modules to suit your tastes.

The Search Users feature allows you to search usernames and user email addresses. If you search for the user *Lisa*, for example, your results include any user whose username or email address contains *Lisa*, so you can receive multiple results when using just one search word or phrase. The Search Sites feature returns any blog title or URL within your community that contains your search term, too.

The Network Admin Dashboard has two useful links near the top of the screen:

- **Create a New Site:** Click this link to create a new site within your network. When you click the link, the Add New Site screen appears. Find out how to add a new site in the "Sites" section, later in this chapter.
- **Create a New User:** Click this link to create a new user account within your community. When you click this link, the Add New User screen appears. Find out how to add a new user to your community in the "Users" section, later in the chapter.

Additionally, the Network Admin Dashboard gives you a real-time count of how many sites and users you have in your network, which is nice-to-know information for any network admin.

Managing Your Network

As mentioned, the Network Admin Dashboard has its own set of menus separate from the regular Site Admin Dashboard. Those menus are located on the left side of the Network Admin Dashboard. This section goes through the menu items and provides explanations and instructions for working with the settings and configurations to manage your network, sites, and users.

The menus available on the Network Admin Dashboard offer these options:

- **Sites:** View a list of the sites in your network, along with details about them.
- **Users:** See detailed info about current users in your network.
- **Themes:** View all the currently available themes to enable or disable them for use in your network.

» **Plugins:** Manage (activate/deactivate) plugins for use on all sites within your network.

» **Settings:** Configure global settings for your network.

All the items on the Network Admin Dashboard are important, and you'll use them frequently throughout the life of your network. Normally, I'd take you through each of the menu items in order so it would be easy for you to follow along on your Dashboard, but it's important to perform some preliminary configurations of your network before you do anything else. Therefore, the following sections start with the Settings menu and then go through the other menu items in order of their appearance on the Network Admin Dashboard.

Settings

Click the Settings menu link on the Network Admin Dashboard. The Network Settings screen appears (see Figure 3-2), displaying several sections of options for you to configure to set up your network the way you want.

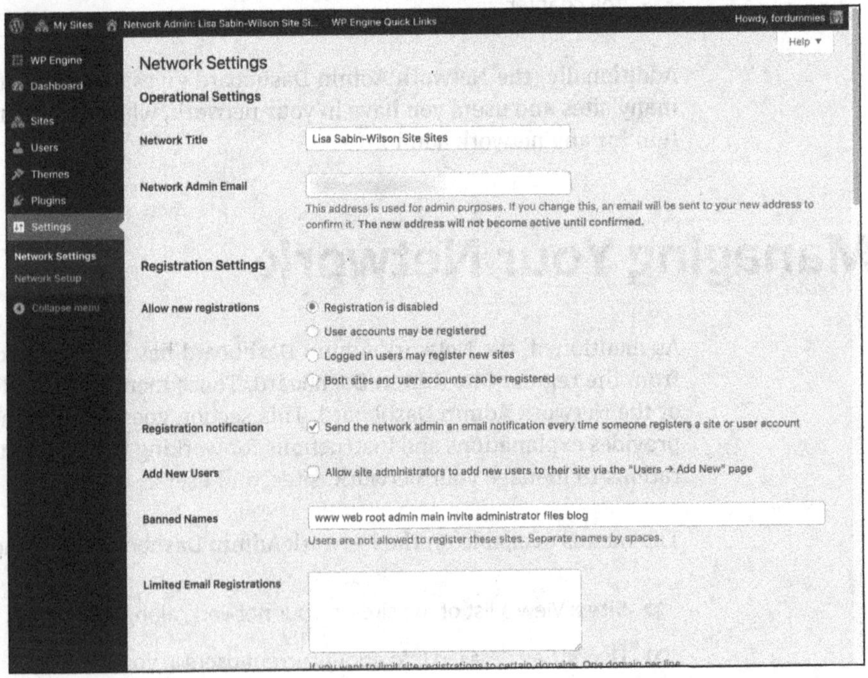

FIGURE 3-2: The Network Settings screen.

WARNING

When you finish configuring the settings on the Network Settings screen, don't forget to click the Save Changes button (scroll down to the bottom of the screen), below the final Menu Settings section. (See Figure 3-6 later in the chapter.) If you navigate away from the Network Settings screen without clicking the Save Changes button, none of your configurations will be saved, and you'll need to go through the entire process again.

Operational Settings

The two options in the Operational Settings section, shown in Figure 3-2, are

- **Network Title:** This setting is the title of your overall network of sites. This name is included in all communications regarding your network, including emails that new users receive when they register a new site within your network. Type your desired network title in the text box.
- **Network Admin Email:** This setting is the email address that all correspondence from your website is addressed from, including all registration and signup emails that new users receive when they register a new site and/or user account within your network. In the text box, type the email that you want to use for these purposes.

Registration Settings

The Registration Settings section (see Figure 3-3) allows you to control aspects of allowing users to sign up to your network. The most important option is whether to allow open registration.

To set one of the following options, select its radio button in the Allow New Registrations section:

- **Registration Is Disabled:** Disallows new user registration. When selected, this option prevents people who visit your site from registering for a user account.
- **User Accounts May Be Registered:** Allows people to create only user accounts, not create sites on your network.
- **Logged In Users May Register New Sites:** Allows only existing users (those who are logged in) to create a new site on your network. This setting also disables new user registration. Choose this option if you don't want just anyone registering for an account. Instead, you, as the site administrator, can add users at your discretion.
- **Both Sites and User Accounts Can Be Registered:** Allows users to register an account and a site on your network during the registration process.

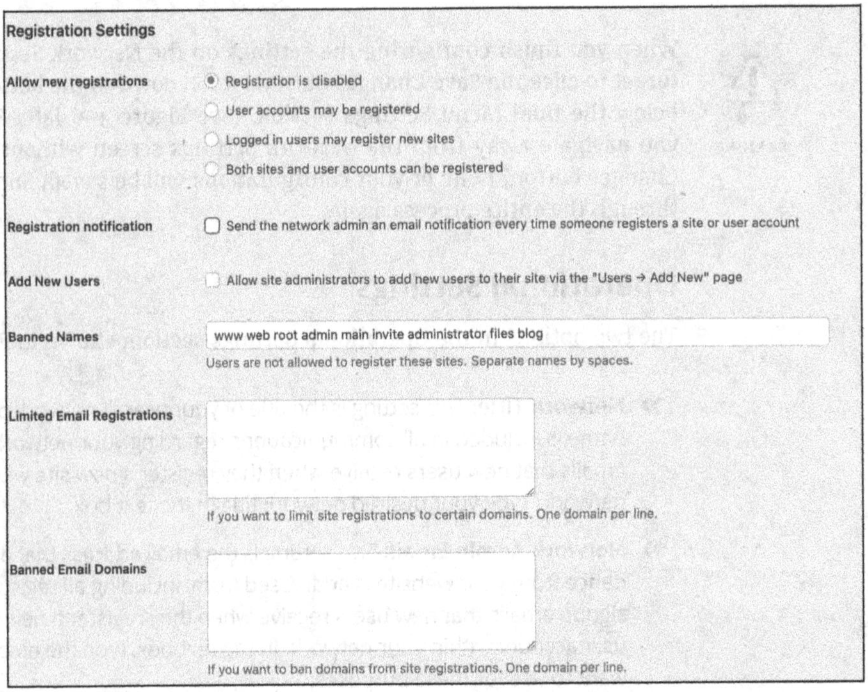

FIGURE 3-3: The Registration Settings section of the Network Settings screen.

These options apply only to outside users. As a network admin, you can create new sites and users any time you want by setting the necessary options on the Network Admin Dashboard. (For information about creating users, see the "Users" section, later in this chapter.)

The remaining options in the Registration Settings section are as follows:

- **Registration Notification:** When this option is selected, an email is sent to the network admin every time a user or a site is created on the system, even if the network admin creates the new site.
- **Add New Users:** Select this check box if you want to allow your community blog owners (individual site admins) to add new users to their own community site via the Users page within their individual Dashboards.
- **Banned Names:** By default, WordPress bans several usernames from being registered within your community, including *www, web, root, admin, main, invite,* and *administrator* — for good reason. You don't want a random user to register a username such as *admin* because you don't want that person misrepresenting themselves as an administrator on your site. You can enter an unlimited number of usernames that you want to bar from your site in the Banned Names text box.

» **Limited Email Registrations:** You can limit sign-ups based on email domains by filling in this text box with one email domain per line. If you have open registrations but limited the email addresses, only the people who have an email domain that's on the list can register. This is an excellent option to use in a school or corporate environment where you're providing email addresses and sites to students or employees.

» **Banned Email Domains:** This feature, the reverse of Limited Email Registrations, blocks all sign-ups from a particular domain, which can be useful in stopping spammers. If you enter `gmail.com` in the field, for example, anyone who tries to sign up with a Gmail address will be denied.

New Site Settings

The New Site Settings section (see Figure 3-4) is a configurable list of items that WordPress populates with default values when a new site is created. These values include those that appear in welcome emails, on a user's first post page, and on a new site's first page.

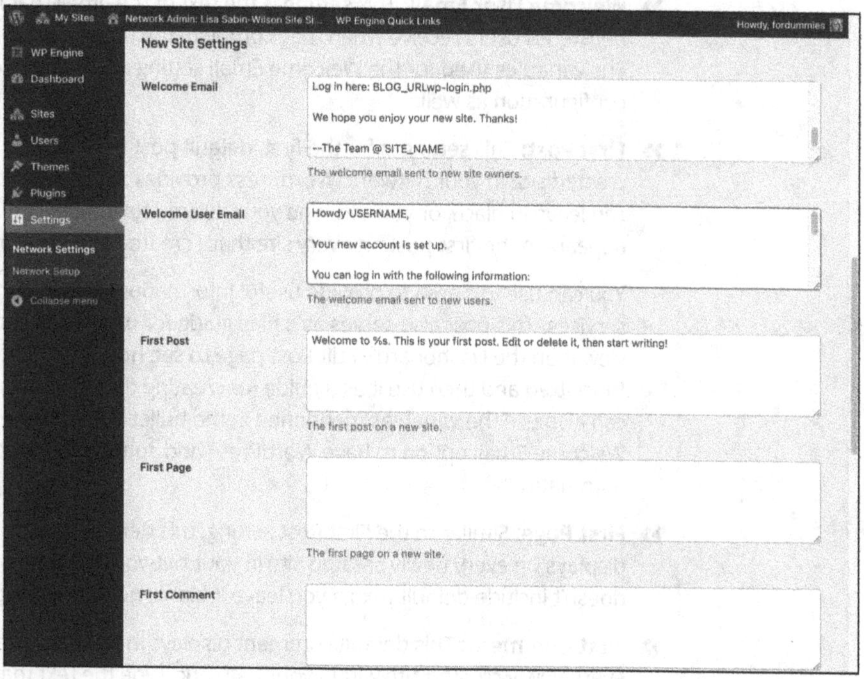

FIGURE 3-4: The New Site Settings section of the Network Settings screen.

The configurable list of items includes

- **Welcome Email:** This setting is the text of the email that owners of newly registered sites in your network receive when their registration is complete. WordPress provides a default message that you can leave in place, if you like. Or you can type the text of the email you want new site owners to receive when they register a new site within your network.

  A few variables you can use in this email aren't explained entirely on the Network Settings screen, including the following:

  - `SITE_NAME`: Inserts the name of your WordPress site
  - `BLOG_URL`: Inserts the URL of the new member's blog
  - `USERNAME`: Inserts the new member's username
  - `PASSWORD`: Inserts the new member's password
  - `LOGINLINK`: Inserts the hyperlinked login URL for the new member's blog
  - `SITE_URL`: Inserts the hyperlinked URL for your WordPress site

- **Welcome User Email:** This setting is the text of the email that newly registered users receive when they complete the registration process. The variables used for the Welcome Email setting apply to this email configuration as well.

- **First Post:** This setting is for the first, default post that displays on every newly created site in your network. WordPress provides some default text that you can leave in place, or you can type your desired text in the text box. This text appears in the first post on every site that's created in your community.

  You can use this area to provide useful information about your site and services. This post also serves as a nice guide for new users because they can view it on the Dashboard's Edit Post page to see how it was entered and formatted and then use it as a guide for creating their own blog posts. You can also use the variables mentioned in the bullet points in the earlier Welcome Email option to have WordPress add some information for you automatically.

- **First Page:** Similar to the First Post setting, this default text for a default page displays on every newly created site in your network. (The First Page text box doesn't include default text; if you leave it blank, no default page is created.)

- **First Comment:** This default comment displays in the first default post on every newly created site within your network. Type the text that you want to appear in the first comment on every site that's created in your community.

- **First Comment Author:** Type the name of the author of the first comment on new sites in your network.

- **First Comment Email:** Type the email address of the author of the first comment on new sites in your network.
- **First Comment URL:** Type the web address (URL) of the author of the first comment; this entry hyperlinks the first comment author's name to the URL you type here.

TIP

The last three items on this list — First Comment Author, First Comment Email, and First Comment URL — are not shown in Figure 3-4; you'll need to scroll down in your browser to see them.

Upload Settings

Scrolling down the Network Settings screen, you get to the Upload Settings section (see Figure 3-5), which defines global values pertaining to the type of files you'll allow the site owners within your network to upload by using the file upload feature in the WordPress Write Posts and Write Page areas. (See Book 3, Chapter 3.)

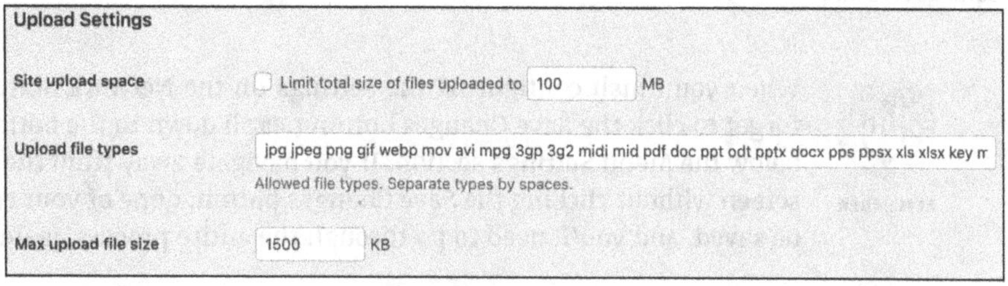

FIGURE 3-5: The Upload Settings section of the Network Settings screen.

The fields in the Upload Settings section have default settings already filled in:

- **Site Upload Space:** If you leave this check box unselected, users are allowed to use all the space they want for uploads; they have no limits. Select the check box to limit the available space per site and then fill in the amount in megabytes (MB); the suggested, default storage space is 100MB. This amount of hard drive space is what you give users within your network for the storage of files they upload to their sites. If you want to change the default storage space, type a number in the text box.
- **Upload File Types:** This text field defines the types of files that you, as the network admin, allow site owners to upload to their sites on their Dashboards. Users can't upload any file types that don't appear in this field. By default, WordPress includes the following file types: `jpg`, `jpeg`, `png`, `gif`, `mov`, `avi`, `mpg`, `3gp`, `3g2`, `midi`, `mid`, `pdf`, `doc`, `ppt`, `odt`, `pptx`, `docx`, `pps`, `ppsx`, `xls`, `xlsx`, `key`, `mp3`, `ogg`, `flac`, `m4a`, `wav`, `mp4`, `m4v`, `webm`, `ogv`, and `flv`. You can remove any default file types and add new ones.

- **Max Upload File Size:** This amount is in kilobytes (KB), and the default file size is 1500KB. This setting means that a user can't upload a file larger than 1500KB. Adjust this number as you see fit by typing a new number in the text box.

Menu Settings

The Plugins administration menu is disabled on the Dashboards of all network site owners, but the network administrator always has access to the Plugins menu. If you leave this check box unselected (see Figure 3-6), the Plugins page is visible to users on their own site's Dashboards. Select the check box to enable the Plugins administration menu for your network users. For more information about using plugins with WordPress, see Book 7.

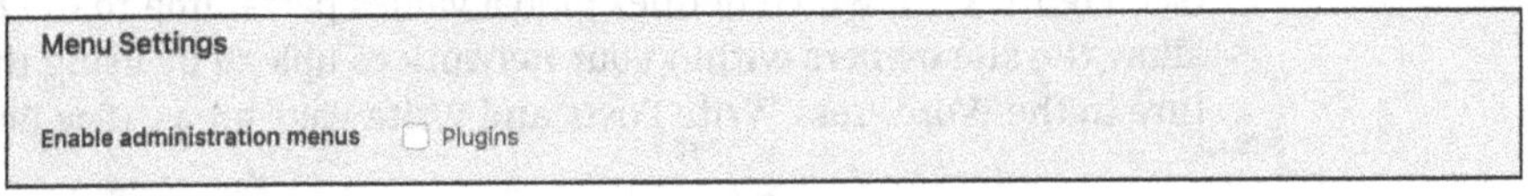

FIGURE 3-6: The Menu Settings section of the Network Settings screen.

REMEMBER

When you finish configuring the settings on the Network Settings screen, don't forget to click the Save Changes button (scroll down to the bottom of the screen), below the Menu Settings section. If you navigate away from the Network Settings screen without clicking the Save Changes button, none of your configurations will be saved, and you'll need to go through the entire process again.

Sites

Clicking the Sites menu item on the Network Admin Dashboard takes you to the Sites screen, where you can manage your individual sites. Although each site in the network has its own Dashboard for basic tasks (publishing, changing themes, and so on), the Sites screen is where you create and delete sites and edit the properties of the sites within your network. Editing information from this page is handy when you have problems accessing a site's back-end Dashboard.

The Sites screen (see Figure 3-7) also lists all the sites within your network, displaying the following statistics for each site:

- **URL:** The site's path in your network. In Figure 3-7, you see a site listed with the username `fordummies`. This path means that the site's domain is `fordummies.`*`yourdomain`*`.com` (if you're using a subdomain setup) or *`yoursite`*`.com/fordummies` (if you're using a subdirectory setup). I discuss subdomains and subdirectories in Book 8, Chapter 2.

- **Last Updated:** The date when the site was last updated (or published to).
- **Registered:** The date when the site was registered in your network.
- **Users:** The username and email address associated with the user(s) of that site.
- **ID:** The unique ID number assigned to the site. This ID number corresponds to the database tables where the data for this site are stored.

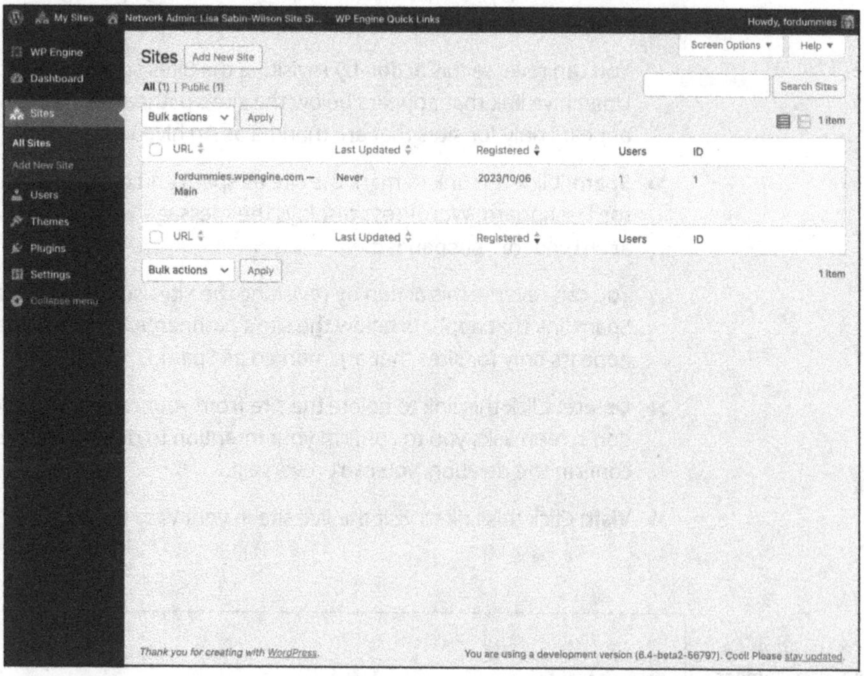

FIGURE 3-7: The Sites screen.

When you hover your mouse pointer over the URL of a site in your network, you see a handy listing of links that help you manage the site. Figure 3-8 shows the options that appear below a site listing when you hover your mouse pointer over a site name.

The management options for network sites, which are visible in Figure 3-8, are as follows:

- **Edit:** Click this link to go to the Edit Site screen (see Figure 3-9), where you can change aspects of each site.
- **Dashboard:** Click this link to go to the Dashboard of the site.

» **Deactivate:** Click this link to mark the site for deletion from your network. A message appears in a pop-up window, asking you to confirm your intention to deactivate the site. Click the Yes button to confirm. The user's site displays a message stating that the site has been deleted.

You can reverse this action by revisiting the Sites screen and clicking the Activate link that appears below the site pathname. (The Activate link appears only for sites that are marked as Deactivated.)

» **Archive:** Click this link to archive the site on your network and prevent visitors from viewing it. The user's site displays a message stating `This site has been archived or suspended.`

You can reverse this action by revisiting the Sites screen and clicking the Unarchive link that appears below the site's pathname. (The Unarchive link appears only for sites that are marked as Archived.)

» **Spam:** Click this link to mark the site as spam and block users from accessing the Dashboard. WordPress displays the message `This site has been archived or suspended.`

You can reverse this action by revisiting the Sites screen and clicking the Not Spam link that appears below the site's pathname. (The Not Spam link appears only for sites that are marked as Spam.)

» **Delete:** Click this link to delete the site from your network of sites. A confirmation screen asks you to confirm your intention to delete the site; after you confirm the deletion, you can't reverse it.

» **Visit:** Click this link to visit the live site in your web browser.

FIGURE 3-8: Site management options on the Sites screen.

Generally, you use the Edit Site screen (see Figure 3-9) only when the settings are unavailable from the Dashboard of that particular site. Configure these options on the four tabs of the screen:

» **Info:** On this tab, you can edit the site's domain, path, registered date, updated date, and attributes (Public, Archived, Spam, Deleted, or Mature).

» **Users:** On this tab, you can manage the users who are assigned to the site, as well as add users to the site.

» **Themes:** On this tab, you can enable themes for the site. This capability is particularly useful if you have themes that aren't network-enabled. (I cover themes later this chapter.) All the themes that aren't enabled within your network are listed on the Themes tab, which allows you to enable themes on a per-site basis.

» **Settings:** The settings on this tab cover all the database settings for the site that you're editing. You rarely, if ever, need to edit these settings, because as network administrator, you have access to each user's Dashboard and should be able to make any changes in the site's configuration settings there.

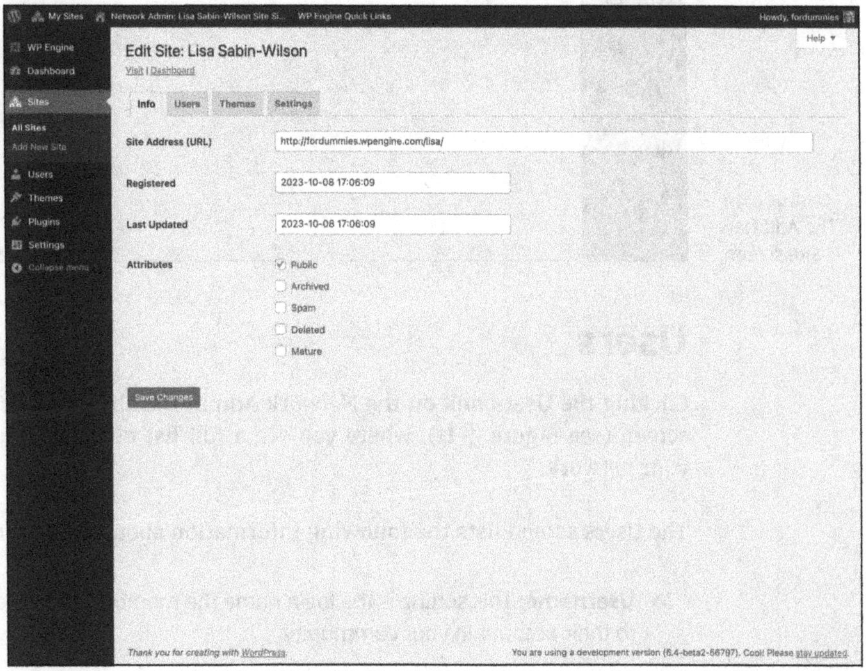

FIGURE 3-9: The Edit Site screen.

The Sites screen (refer to Figure 3-7) also includes a link called Add New Site. Click that link to load the Add New Site screen (see Figure 3-10) on your Network Admin Dashboard. Fill in the Site Address (URL), Site Title, Site Language, and Admin Email fields and then click the Add Site button to add the site to your network. If the Admin Email you entered is associated with an existing user, the new site is assigned to that user on your network. If the user doesn't exist, WordPress creates a new user and sends a notification email. The site is immediately accessible. The user receives an email containing a link to their site, a login link, and their username and password.

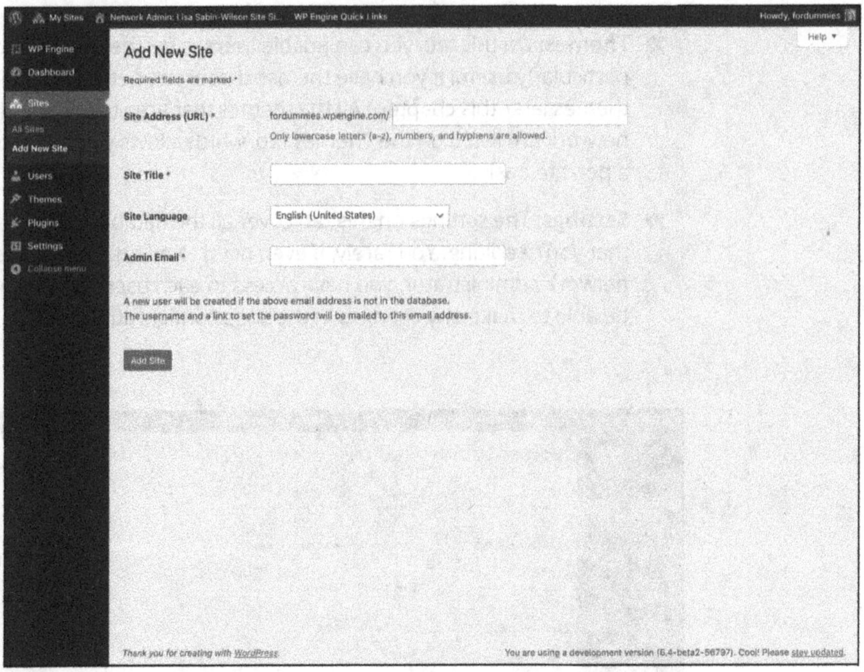

FIGURE 3-10: The Add New Site screen.

Users

Clicking the Users link on the Network Admin Dashboard takes you to the Users screen (see Figure 3-11), where you see a full list of members, or users, within your network.

The Users screen lists the following information about each user:

- **Username:** This setting is the login name the member uses when they log in to their account in your community.
- **Name:** This setting is the user's real name, taken from their profile. If the user hasn't provided their name in their profile, this column is blank.
- **Email:** This setting is the email address the user entered when they registered on your site.
- **Registered:** This setting is the date when the user registered.
- **Sites:** If you enable sites within your WordPress network, this setting lists any sites of which the user is a member.

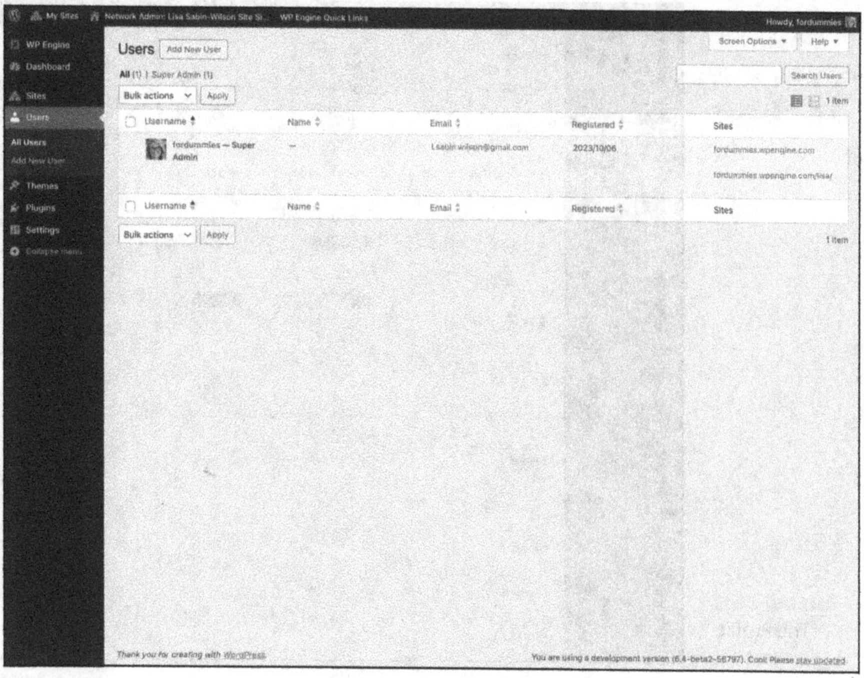

FIGURE 3-11: The Users screen.

You can add users to the network, manage users, and even delete users by clicking the Edit or Delete links that appear below their names when you hover over them with your mouse pointer (the same way you do with sites on the Sites screen).

To delete a user, simply hover your mouse pointer over the username in the list that appears on the Users screen. Click the Delete link. A new screen appears, telling you to transfer this user's posts and links to another user account (yours, most likely). Then click the Confirm Deletion button. WordPress removes the user from the network.

WARNING

This action is irreversible, so be certain about your decision before you click that button!

You can also edit a user's profile information by clicking the Edit link that appears when you hover your mouse pointer over their name on the Users screen. Clicking that link takes you to the Profile screen, shown in Figure 3-12, which presents several options. These options happen to be (mostly) the same options and settings that you configured for your own profile information (as discussed in Book 3, Chapter 2).

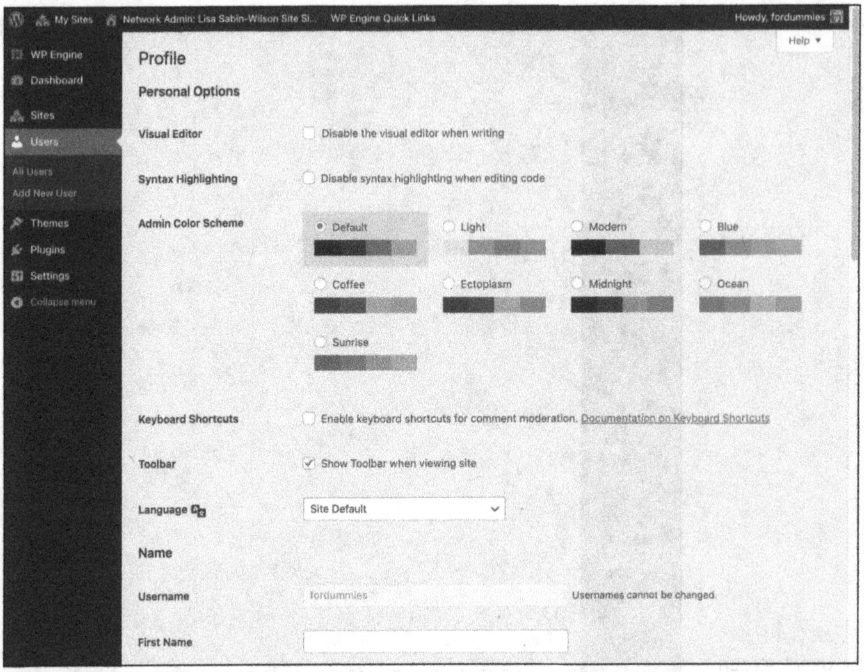

FIGURE 3-12: The Profile screen.

The only difference with the Profile screen within the Network Admin Dashboard is the setting labeled Super Admin, which is deselected by default (not shown in Figure 3-12; scroll down to view it in your browser). If you select this check box, however, you grant this user network admin privileges for your entire network, which means that the user has exactly the same access and permissions as you. See the nearby sidebar titled "Super admin versus network admin" for information about admin roles in the WordPress Multisite network.

TECHNICAL STUFF

As of this writing, the terms super admin and network admin are interchangeable. When WordPress merged the WordPress MU code base with the regular WordPress software back in 2010 (in version 3.0), the term it used to describe the network admin was super admin. Now network admin is the standard term, but areas within the Network Admin Dashboard and regular Dashboard still use the super admin label. That situation will most likely change in the near future, because WordPress will realize the discrepancy and update later versions of the software.

You can add a new user by filling in the Username and Email fields and then clicking the Add User button. WordPress sends the new user an email notification of the new account, along with the site URL, their username, and their password (randomly generated by WordPress at the time the user account is created) (shown in Figure 3-13).

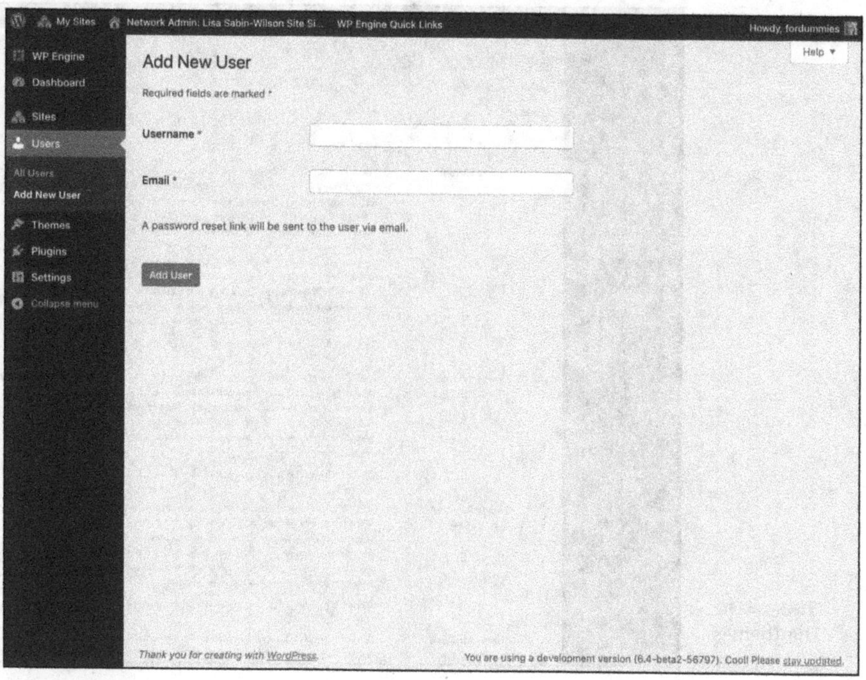

FIGURE 3-13: The Add New User screen.

Themes

When a network is enabled, only users who have network admin access have permission to install themes, which are shared across the network. You can see how to find, install, and activate new themes in your WordPress installation in Book 6, Chapter 2. After you install a theme, you must enable it on your network to have the theme appear on the Appearance screen of each site. To access the Themes screen (shown in Figure 3-14), click the Themes link on the Network Admin Dashboard menu.

TIP

Turn to Book 8, Chapter 5 to see how to enable a theme on a per-site basis.

Plugins

By and large, all WordPress plugins work on your network. Some special plugins exist, however, and using plugins on a network involves some special considerations.

TIP

For details on finding, installing, and activating plugins in WordPress, see Book 7.

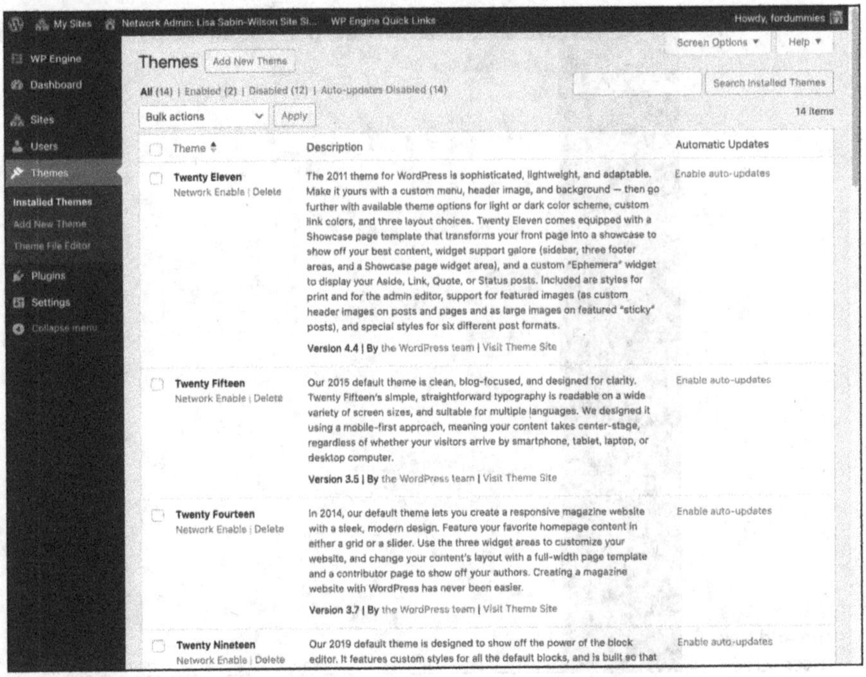

FIGURE 3-14: The Themes screen.

Browse to the Plugins screen of your WordPress Network Admin Dashboard by clicking the Plugins link. Check out the Plugins screen shown in Figure 3-15, and look below the name of the plugin. Do you see the Network Activate link? That link is the big difference between plugins listed on the regular Site Admin Dashboard and those listed on the Network Admin Dashboard. As the network administrator, you can enable certain plugins to be activated across your network. All sites on your network will have the network-activated plugin features available, in contrast to plugins that you activate on the regular Site Admin Dashboard, which are activated and available only for your main website.

TIP

If you select the Plugins administration menu (see the "Menu Settings" section, earlier in this chapter) on the Network Settings screen, users see the plugins listed on their Plugins screens of their Dashboard. In their list of plugins, they see only the plugins that you haven't network-activated — that is, all the plugins you installed in your WordPress installation but not activated on those users' sites. Users can activate and deactivate those plugins as they desire.

Only network administrators can install new plugins on the site; regular users within the network don't have that kind of access (unless you've made them network administrators in their User settings).

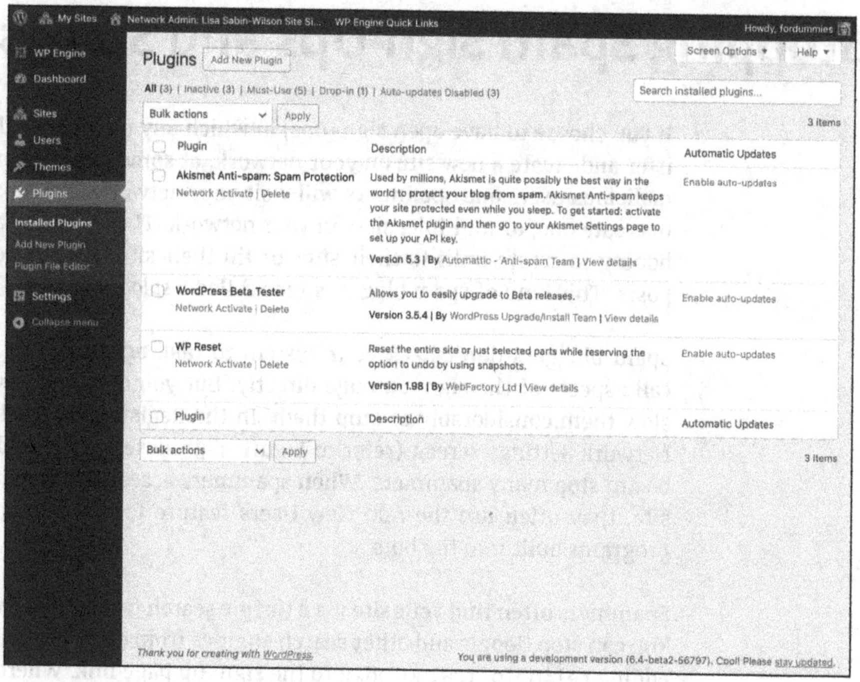

FIGURE 3-15: The Plugins screen.

Also located on the Plugins menu of the Network Admin Dashboard are two other links: Add New and Editor. Click the Add New link to load the Plugins screen (shown in Figure 3-15), where you can add and install new plugins by searching the WordPress Plugins page within your Dashboard. (I cover this topic in Book 7, chapters 1 and 2.) The Editor link gives you access to the Plugin File Editor.

WARNING

The Plugin File Editor is found on the Network Admin Dashboard under the Plugins menu, and only users at the network admin level can access this page. The Plugin File Editor gives you the ability to modify and save plugin files from within your Dashboard. This is something I highly recommend *not* doing, because there is no such thing as undoing an action once you've saved changes. Instead, if you're a developer, or if you employ a developer to help you with highly technical things, use a code editor and version control to modify and manage plugin files for your website. The same advice goes for the Theme File Editor link that you find under the Themes menu on the Network Admin Dashboard — don't make any changes unless you know what you're doing.

Stopping Spam Sign-Ups and Splogs

If you choose to have open sign-ups, in which any member of the public can register and create a new site on your network, at some point automated bots run by malicious users and spammers will visit your network sign-up page and attempt to create one, or multiple, sites in your network. They do so by automated means, hoping to create links to their sites or fill their site on your network with spam posts. This kind of spam blog or site is called a *splog*.

Spam bloggers don't hack your system to take advantage of this feature; they call aspects of the sign-up page directly. But you can do a few simple things to slow them considerably or stop them. In the Registration Settings section of the Network Settings screen (refer to Figure 3-3), deselect the Add New Users check box to stop many spammers. When spammers access the system to set up a spam site, they often use the Add New Users feature to create many other blogs via programs built into the bots.

Spammers often find your site via a Google search for the link to the sign-up page. You can stop Google and other search engines from crawling your sign-up page by adding `rel=nofollow,noindex` to the sign-up page link. Wherever you add a link to your sign-up page inviting new users to sign up, the HTML code you use to add the `nofollow,noindex` looks like this:

```
<a href="http://yoursite.com/wp-signup.php" rel="nofollow,noindex">Get your own
   site here</a>
```

You can add this code to any page or widget as a normal link to instruct legitimate visitors to sign up for a site on your network.

IN THIS CHAPTER

» Understanding default user management

» Changing default user behavior

» Exploring user access to site features

Chapter 4

Managing Users and Controlling Access

In Book 8, Chapter 3, I discuss the Network Admin menu of your Dashboard, which allows you to manage aspects of your network. In this chapter, I explain how to manage users across the network, including changing some of the default management options to suit your needs.

One of the hardest things for new network admins to understand is that although each site is managed separately, users are global. That is, after a user logs in, they are logged in across the entire network and have the ability to comment on any site that has commenting enabled. (See Book 3, Chapter 2.) The user can visit the Dashboard of the main site in the install to manage their profile information and can access the Dashboard's My Sites menu to reach sites that they administer. The user also registers at the main site — not at individual sites in the network.

Setting Default User Permissions

When you enable the Multisite feature, new site and new user registrations are turned off by default. But you can add new sites and users from the Network Admin Dashboard. To allow users to sign up for your network, follow these steps:

1. **Log in to the Network Admin Dashboard and then click the Settings menu link.**

   The Network Settings screen loads in your browser window.

   REMEMBER

   The Network Admin Dashboard is different from the Site Admin Dashboard. For reference, you can find your Network Admin Dashboard at this URL: `https://`*`yourdomain.com`*`/wp-admin/network/settings.php`. (Replace *`yourdomain.com`* with your actual domain name.)

2. **In the Registration Settings section, select User Accounts May Be Registered (shown in Figure 4-1).**

   This setting allows users to register on your network. It also assigns them to the main site as Subscribers, but doesn't allow them to create new sites.

3. **Click the Save Changes button at the bottom of the page.**

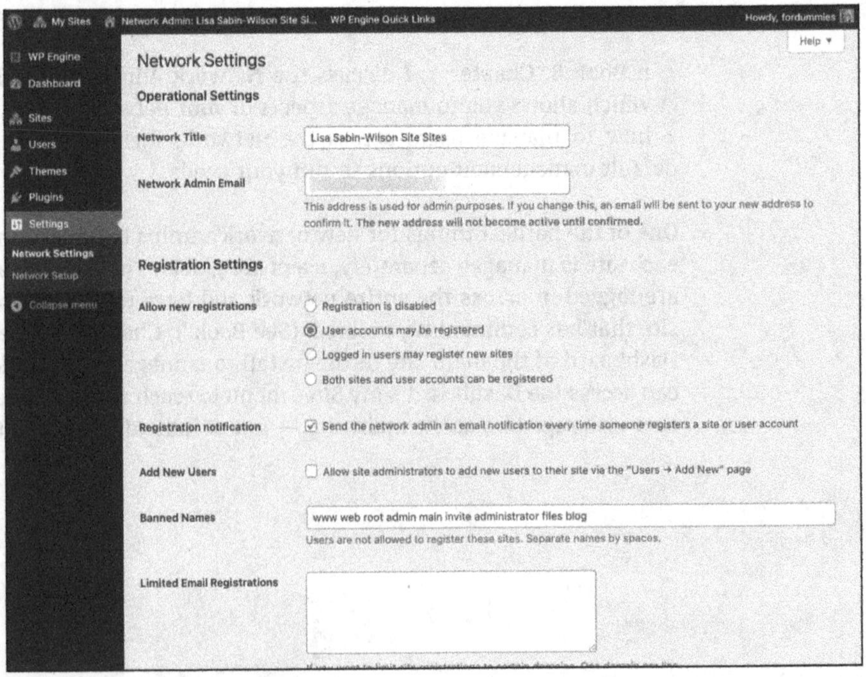

FIGURE 4-1: User registration options.

TIP: If you select Both Sites and User Accounts Can Be Registered on the Network Settings screen, you not only allow users to register a new account, but also give them the option to create a new site on your network.

Registering users

When signing up, the user is directed to the main site of the installation and then added to one of the child sites. This site may be the user's site (if they chose to have a site when registering) or an existing site. If it's any existing site other than the main site, you, as the network admin, must add the user to that site manually. The user who owns the site can manually add users as well if you enabled the option in the Network Settings screen that allows site admins to add users to their sites.

The registration page (see Figure 4-2) is located at `http://yourdomain.com/wp-signup.php`. This sign-up page bypasses the regular WordPress registration page. (See Book 3, Chapter 3.)

TIP: The registration page shown in Figure 4-2 may look different from the one on your own site, and that's because it uses the styling and design from the activated theme you are using. In Figure 4-2, the site I am using has the Twenty Twenty-Four theme activated, so it is using the styles from that theme. See Book 6 for more information on themes.

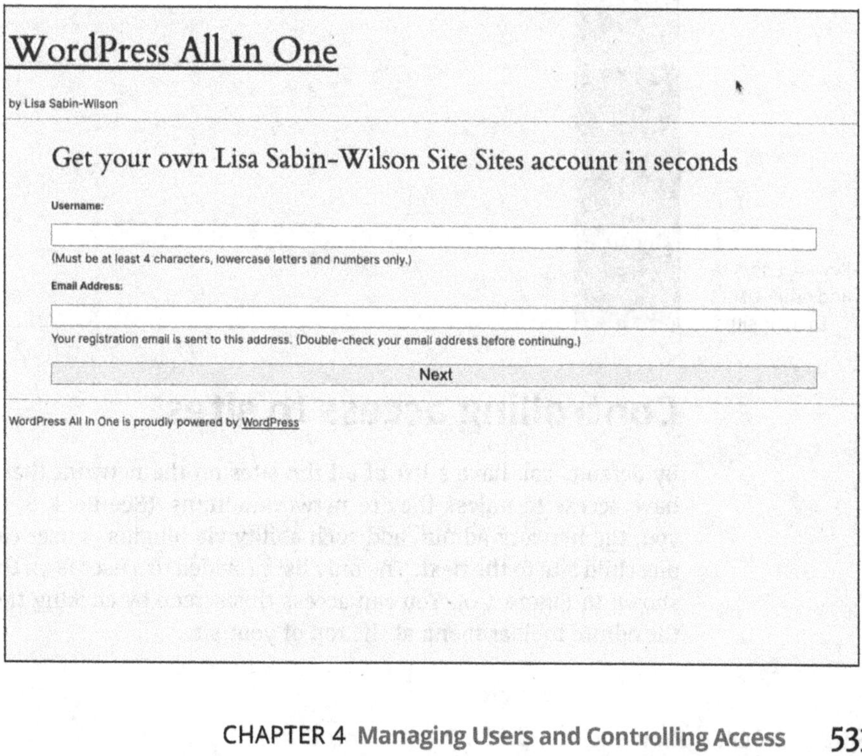
WordPress All In One
by Lisa Sabin-Wilson
Get your own Lisa Sabin-Wilson Site Sites account in seconds
Username:
(Must be at least 4 characters, lowercase letters and numbers only.)
Email Address:
Your registration email is sent to this address. (Double-check your email address before continuing.)
Next
WordPress All In One is proudly powered by WordPress

FIGURE 4-2: Network registration page.

After filling out the form, the user receives an email with a link to activate their account. When they do so, they can immediately log in and manage their details; they're directed to their primary site, which is the main site if they have no site to administer.

You also can add users to existing sites in the network. You can always assign users to specific sites on a per-case basis. When you set up a network and select Allow Site Administrators to Add New Users to Their Site via the "Users ⇨ Add New" Page (shown in Figure 4-3), you allow site admins to add other users in the network to their sites. Although the Add New Users setting is turned off by default, you can enable it by selecting the Allow Site Administrators to Add New Users to Their Site via the Users⇨Add New Page option on their Dashboard.

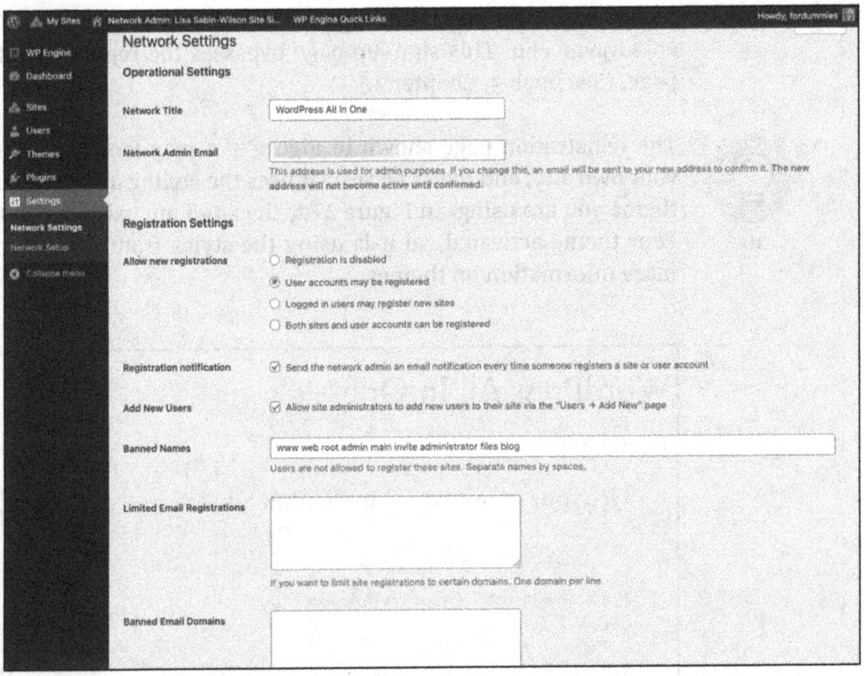

FIGURE 4-3: Allowing users to add other users to their sites.

Controlling access to sites

By default, you have a list of all the sites on the network that other users don't have access to unless they're network admins. (See Book 8, Chapter 3.) Unless you, the network admin, add such ability via plugins, a user can't navigate from one child site to the next. The only list provided to a user is on the My Sites screen, shown in Figure 4-4. You can access this screen by clicking the My Sites link on the admin toolbar menu at the top of your site.

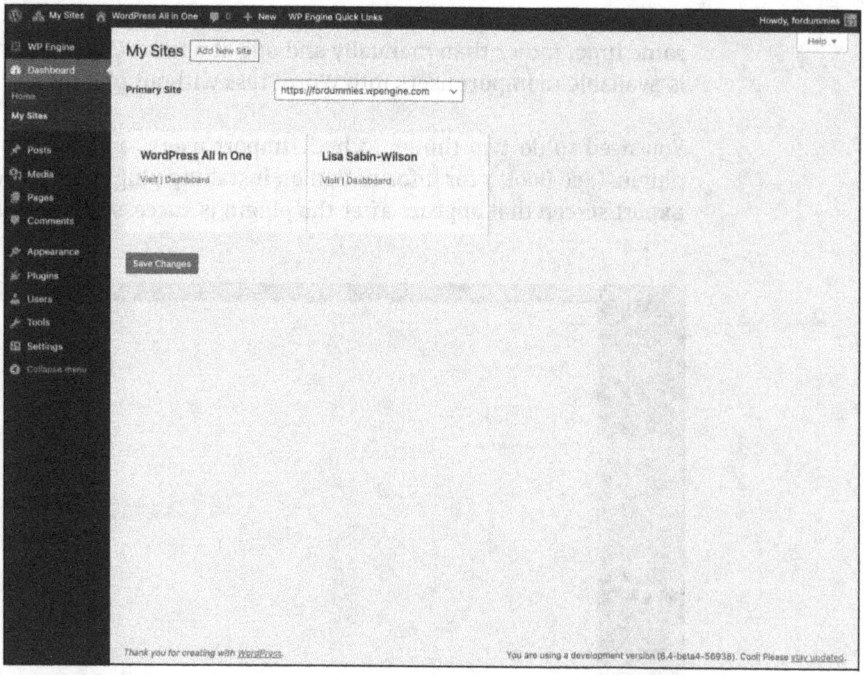

FIGURE 4-4: My Sites screen shows sites that the user manages.

The My Sites screen lists only sites of which the user is the administrator, not sites on which the user has a lesser, or no, role. Additionally, the My Sites screen has Add New Site button that allows the user to create more sites (if the network admin allows that access via the Network Settings screen of the Network Admin Dashboard).

TIP

If you're running (or planning to run) a network of sites and want to display a public-facing list of sites in your network, a plugin called Multisite Site Index gives you access to a widget, or a shortcode, that you can use to display a list of sites within your network on a page of your own website. Users and visitors can click through that list to easily discover sites within your network. You can find the Multisite Site Index plugin on the WordPress site at `https://wordpress.org/plugins/multisite-site-index`.

Importing users

You may have an existing pool of users you want to add to the network if, for example, you had a website before your network existed and collected registrations or sign-ups. (Even newsletter programs give you a downloadable list of users that you can import into your network.) You can use the Import Export WordPress Users plugin, available at `https://wordpress.org/plugins/users-customers-import-export-for-wp-woocommerce`, to import a large group of users at the same time, rather than manually and one at a time. Currently, no default method is available to import users into WordPress without plugins.

You need to do two things to bulk-import users, and the first is to install the plugin. (See Book 7 for information on installing plugins.) Figure 4-5 displays the Export screen that appears after the plugin is successfully installed.

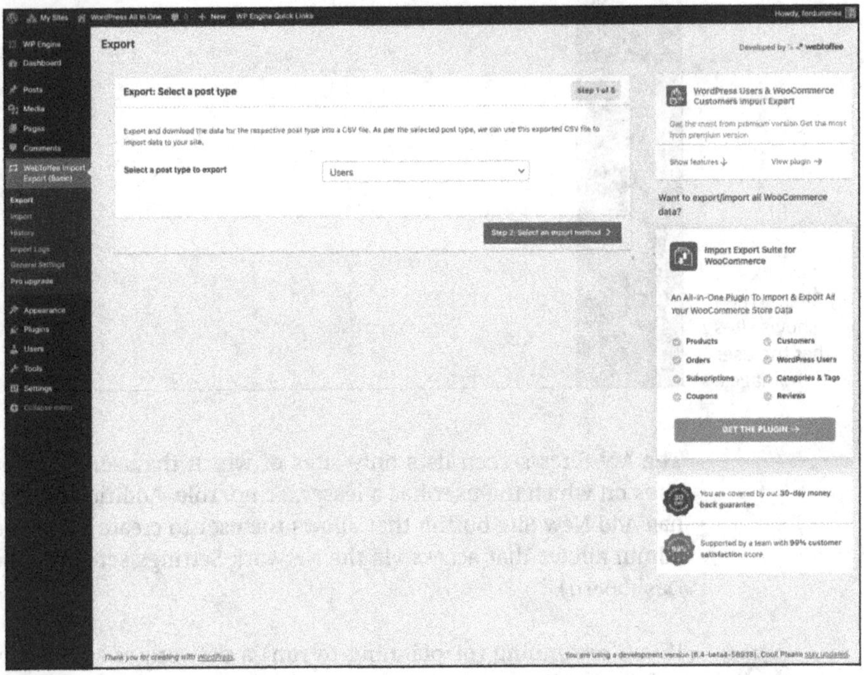

FIGURE 4-5: Export screen.

After you have successfully installed the plugin, you need to get your list of users in CSV (comma-separated value) format. Figure 4-6 shows the CSV file that I created to run a test import of users. Using Google Sheets (`https://www.google.com/sheets/about`), I created the following columns in a spreadsheet (note that you don't see all of the columns in Figure 4-6):

- ID
- user_login
- user_pass
- roles
- user_email

- first_name
- last_name
- display_name
- user_url

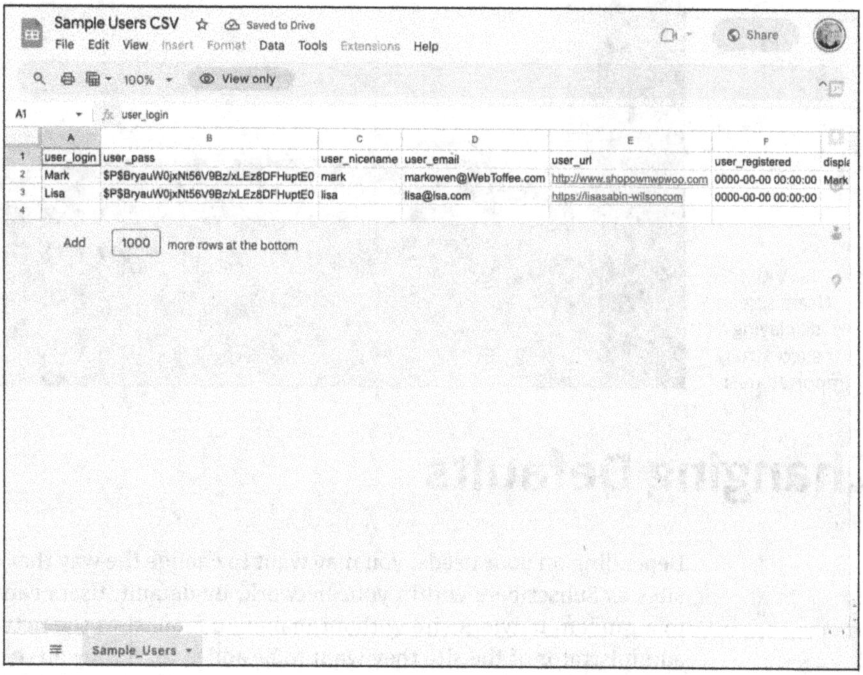

FIGURE 4-6: CSV file containing user data ready to import.

TIP

While I used Google Sheets for the CSV example, you do need to have a Google account in order to be able to sign into Google and use their Sheets feature. Alternatively, you can use any spreadsheet editor to create and manage CSV files, like Microsoft Excel or Apple's Numbers application.

After I created these columns, I populated the rows with user data (in Figure 4-6, my data is dummy data used to test the functionality of the plugin) and then saved the file on my computer as a `.csv` file.

Click the Import link in the WebToffee Import Export (Basic) menu (refer to Figure 4-5), and then click the Upload File and Import button. Figure 4-7 shows the Users screen of the WordPress Dashboard with successfully created user accounts after you perform the import by using the Import Export WordPress Users plugin.

FIGURE 4-7: Users screen displaying a successfully imported user.

Changing Defaults

Depending on your needs, you may want to change the way that users are added to sites as Subscribers within your network. By default, users can't add themselves to a random network site without making a request to the network admin or the administrator of the site they want to be added to. If they do register on your site, by default they're added as users only on the main site. This setup may work fine for most sites, but if you want your users to be able to register with existing sites within your network, read on.

Site-specific sign-up

For many people, signing up on the main site and then asking to be added to a subsite by a network admin can be a confusing experience. Plugins, however, can make the process easier and less confusing for everyone.

If you want existing users to be able to add themselves to existing sites on the network, the Network Subsite User Registration plugin, available at `https://wordpress.org/plugins/network-subsite-user-registration`, allows users to sign up on any site within your network. Install this plugin as a regular plugin, as outlined in Book 7, chapters 1 and 2.

After the plugin is installed, choose Users ⇨ Registration on any site within the network to enable public registration on that site. (See Figure 4-8.)

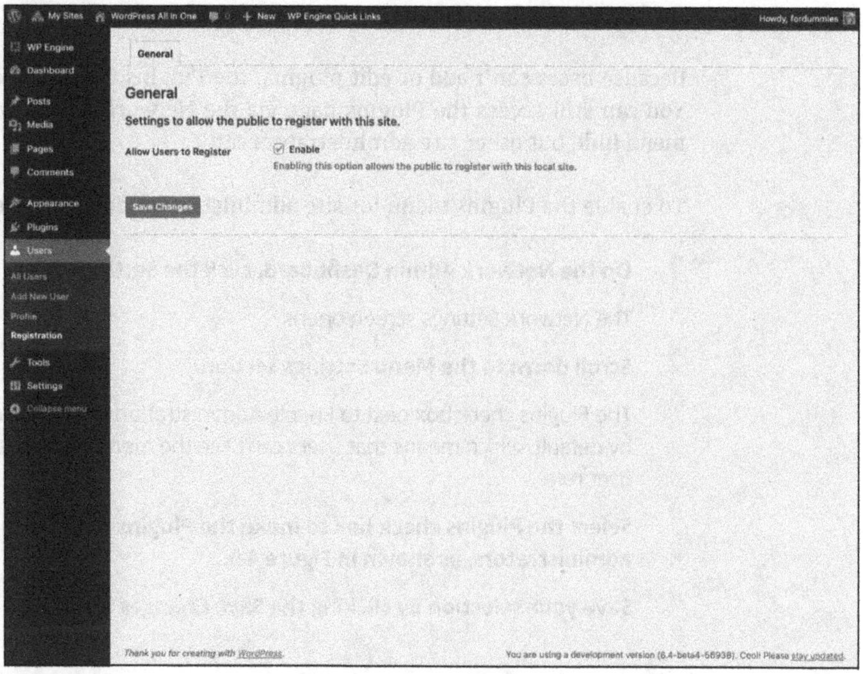

FIGURE 4-8: Enabling public registration on a network site.

User role management

When a user is added to a network or a site, they are assigned the role of Subscriber by default. You may want to assign a different role to the user and automatically add them to your other sites in the network. (Book 3, Chapter 3 explains roles and permissions.)

When a user signs up for their own site, for example, you may want to assign them a non-administrator role. You may want to set their role to Editor, for example, to restrict the menus they can access on the Dashboard and to prevent them from using some of the functionality of WordPress. You may want to have new site owners sign up as Editors of the sites to give them fewer permissions on their Dashboards. You may also want to create custom roles for the users in your network, roles that aren't covered by the default user roles in WordPress.

The Members – Membership & User Role Editor Plugin (`https://wordpress.org/plugins/members`) allows you to manage the roles of all the users in your network from their site Dashboards. This plugin saves you a lot of time in managing user roles and access in your network.

Exploring Default Site Settings

Default settings can control user access to things such as menus, themes, and the Dashboard. Book 8, Chapter 2 discusses the network settings in detail.

Because users can't add or edit plugins, the Plugins menu is disabled by default. You can still access the Plugins page via the Network Admin Dashboard Plugins menu link, but other site administrators can't.

To enable the Plugins menu for site administrators, follow these steps:

1. **On the Network Admin Dashboard, click the Settings menu link.**

   The Network Settings screen opens.

2. **Scroll down to the Menu Settings section.**

   The Plugins check box next to Enable Administration Menus is deselected by default, which means that users can't see the menu regardless of their user role.

3. **Select the Plugins check box to make the Plugins menu available to site administrators, as shown in Figure 4-9.**
4. **Save your selection by clicking the Save Changes button.**

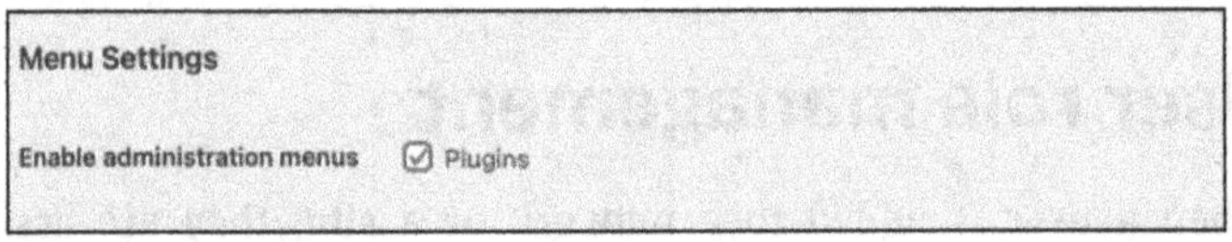

FIGURE 4-9: Enabling the Plugins menu for site administrators.

REMEMBER

Similarly, you must enable any themes installed on the network before a site administrator can choose the theme from the Appearance menu. I explain how to manage and enable themes in a Multisite WordPress site in Book 8, Chapter 5.

IN THIS CHAPTER

» Understanding theme management

» Gathering and displaying content from sites across your network

» Understanding network-wide plugins

» Finding multisite plugins

Chapter 5
Using Network Plugins and Themes

When you add new plugins and themes to your Multisite WordPress installation, you add new functionality and aesthetics. But you don't just multiply your choices; the possibilities become endless. You can gather and display information from across the network, for example, or make the same features available to all users. You can choose to have the same theme on all sites or different themes. You can not only manage plugins and themes on a global level, but also have site-specific control.

In this chapter, I show you how certain functionality appears across the network and how certain plugins look by default on all sites for all users. I also cover controlling access to different themes for different sites.

One of the interesting features of a network is the extensive use of the `mu-plugins` folder. In this chapter, I describe exactly how this folder processes plugin code. I also cover the Network Activate link on the Plugins page, which is very similar to the Activate link, but has important differences in a Multisite install.

REMEMBER

This chapter doesn't cover installing plugins and themes. I cover installing plugins in Book 7, Chapter 2 and installing themes in Book 6, Chapter 1.

Using One Theme on Multiple Sites

In certain situations (such as when you want consistent branding and design across your entire network), each site in a network is used as a subsection of the main site. You could set up WordPress networks with a magazine-style design on your main site and populate the content with different posts from sites within your network, aggregating all the content to the main site. You can see an example on the Academics page, in the Colleges and Schools section of the Bose State University website at `https://www.boisestate.edu/academics-landing`. (See Figure 5-1.)

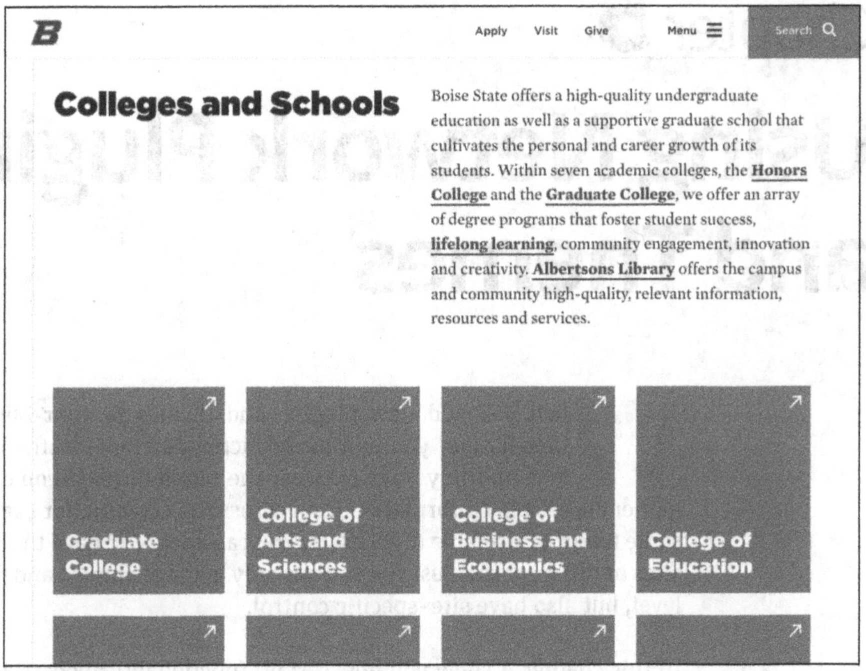

FIGURE 5-1: Boise State University uses the WordPress Multisite feature.

Boise State University is Idaho's largest university, offering over 200 degrees and certifications. Their main site serves as a primary portal of information about their schools, programs, news, and activities. They host over 200 subsites in their Multisite installation, where they are able to aggregate content from each of those sites into their main site, whenever they need to.

The sites within the Boise State University network use the same theme to display their content, making the branding consistent across the network sites — a good example of a theme that aggregates content from sites within a network.

Although each site in the network operates separately from the main (network admin) site, you may want each site to look the same as the main site because it ties into the main site visually, through design and branding, and provides a consistent branding experience for visitors to any site within the network. You may have a custom theme specially made for the main site, with added features to display network-wide content. If consistency and network branding are your goals, you may want to create a single theme to be used on all sites within your network (not just your main site).

REMEMBER

Book 6 discusses how WordPress accesses themes that are stored on the web server. When the network is enabled, these themes are shared among all sites and are available on the site administrator's Dashboard. If a theme file is changed, every site in the network that uses the theme experiences the change, because only one copy of the theme is being served. When a theme is enabled, it appears on the Manage Theme screen of the administrator's Dashboard (accessed by hovering the mouse pointer over the Appearance menu of the Network Admin Dashboard and clicking the Themes link). Users can choose to activate this theme so that it displays on the front side of the site. You must activate a theme for use across all sites in a network by clicking the Network Enable link on the Themes menu in the Network Admin Dashboard. (Access the Themes screen by clicking the Themes menu link on the Network Admin Dashboard.)

The main network site could have 20 themes installed in the main WordPress installation, but if you haven't enabled these themes for use across the entire network, site administrators can't see network-disabled themes on their Dashboards and, therefore, can't use them on their sites.

If a consistent network design is what you're after, you'll run into a few troubles with the WordPress network because by default, no matter what themes you've activated, the default WordPress Twenty Twenty-Four theme gets activated whenever new sites are created within your network. It would be nice if WordPress provided a global setting on the Network Admin Dashboard that allowed administrators to assign the default theme to every site that's created. Currently, however, that feature is available only by adding a small line of code to the WordPress configuration file. (If you are someone who isn't afraid to edit a little code, I cover this in the "Setting the default theme for sites" section, later in this chapter.)

Enabling themes for individual sites

You may have a customized theme for one particular site that you don't want other sites within the network to use or access. You, as network admin, can edit each site in the network. You can perform basic tasks such as enabling, disabling, or adding themes to the network without leaving your Dashboard. If you want to make a theme available for use on only one site and unavailable for other sites, follow these steps:

1. **Click the Network Admin link on the My Sites menu in the top-left corner of your Dashboard and then click the Sites link.**

   The Sites screen appears, showing a list of all sites in the network, sorted by creation date. (See Figure 5-2.)

2. **Hover your mouse pointer over the site you want to enable a theme for and then click the Edit link.**

   The Edit Site screen displays on your Dashboard.

3. **Click the Themes tab of the Edit Sites screen.**

   The screen lists themes that you can enable for the site you're editing. (See Figure 5-3.)

4. **Click the Enable link for the theme you want to use for the site you're editing.**

   The Edit Site screen refreshes with the Themes tab still active and displays a message stating that the theme has been enabled.

5. **Repeat these steps for any other sites on which you want to enable a theme.**

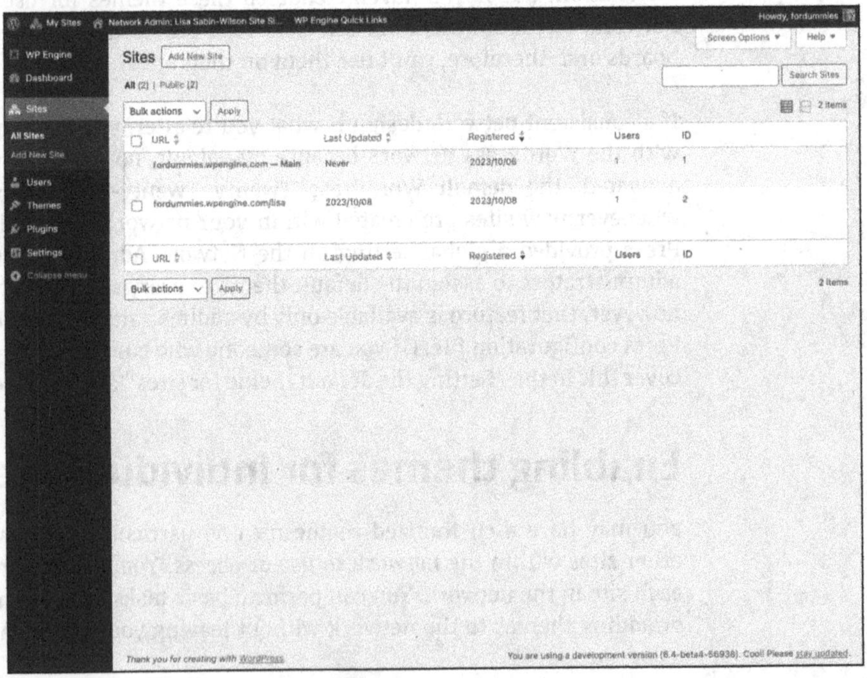

FIGURE 5-2: A list of sites in the network.

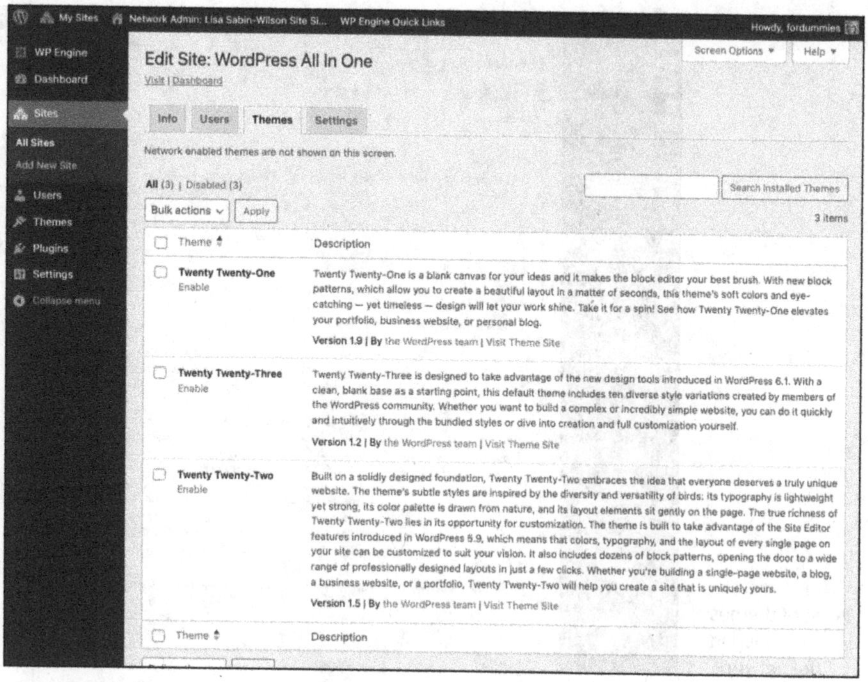

FIGURE 5-3: The Edit Site screen with the Themes tab active.

Installing themes for network use

Installing a theme for use on your network involves the same process you use to install a theme on your individual site (see Book 6, Chapter 1), but with an extra step: You have to enable each theme on the Network Admin Dashboard to make it available on the Appearance menu of the individual site administrators' Dashboards. Here's how to enable a theme so that all your site owners can use it on their sites:

1. **Click the Network Admin link on the My Sites menu in the top-left corner of your Dashboard and then click the Themes menu link.**

   The Themes screen appears, displaying a list of installed themes. (See Figure 5-4.) Each theme installed in the `/wp-content/themes` folder is listed on this screen.

2. **Click the Network Enable link for the theme you want to use.**

   Enabling a theme causes it to appear in the list of available themes on each network site's Dashboard, but doesn't change any user's active theme; it merely makes this theme available for use.

3. **Repeat these steps to enable more themes on your network.**

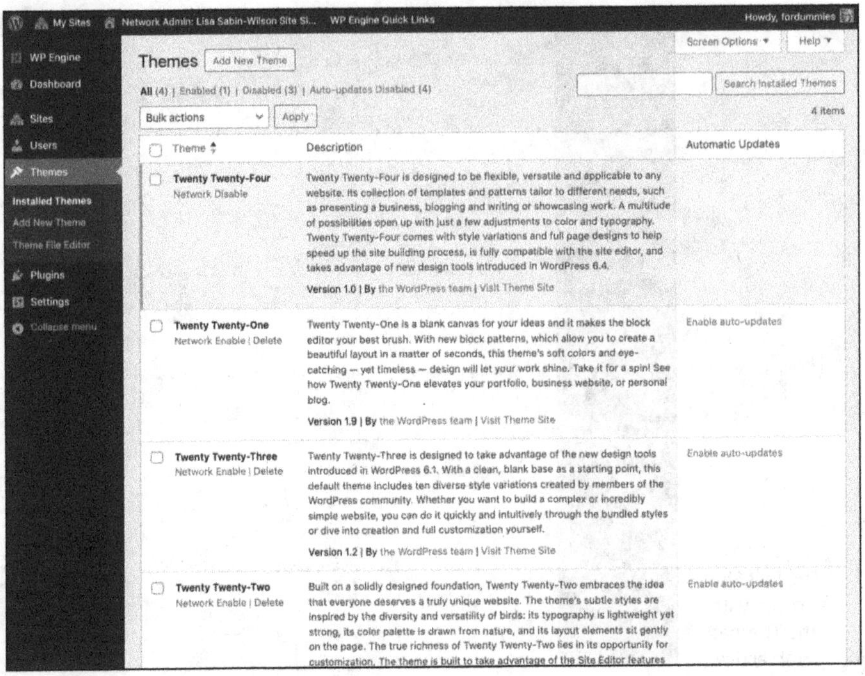

FIGURE 5-4: A list of themes installed in the network.

REMEMBER

Just installing a new theme in your main WordPress installation doesn't make it available for use network-wide. As the network admin, you always have to enable a theme before your site owners can use it.

Setting the default theme for sites

When a new site is created on the network, by default it displays the Twenty Twenty-Four theme provided within WordPress, which is the default theme for all new WordPress installations. If you want to use a different theme for all new sites, you can add a `define` statement to the `wp-config.php` file of your WordPress installation.

Install your theme on the server, as I outline in Book 6, Chapter 1. You may also want to enable the theme network-wide, as outlined in the previous section, "Installing themes for network use." This step isn't necessary, but if you have other themes available, and if the active theme is disabled, a user who switches away from that theme won't be able to switch back to it.

Because the Twenty Twenty-Four WordPress theme is already the default, I use another popular WordPress theme (the default theme before Twenty Twenty-Four was released) called Twenty Twenty-Three (`https://wordpress.org/themes/twentytwentythree`). To set this theme as the default theme for all sites within a network, follow these steps:

1. **Log in to your web server via SFTP.**

   Book 2, Chapter 2 discusses using SFTP.

2. **Open the `wp-config.php` file in your favorite text editor.**

   On a Mac, you can use TextEdit, or on a PC you can use NotePad.

   TIP

   Save a copy of your original `wp-config.php` file to your desktop before editing it in case you make any mistakes in the next few steps.

3. **Locate the following line of code in the `wp-config.php` file:**

```
define( 'DB_COLLATE', '' );
```

4. **Add a new blank line below it.**
5. **Type** define('WP_DEFAULT_THEME', 'twentytwentythree');

   This one line of code tells WordPress to use the Twenty Twenty-Three theme as the default theme for all new sites within your network.

   TIP

   The part of the line of code in Step 5 that looks like this — `twentytwentythree` — is the name of the folder that contains the theme in the `/wp-content/themes/` folder in the file directory on your web server. The name within quotes should be identical to the name of the folder where the theme files reside.

6. **Save the `wp-config.php` file and upload it to your web server.**

   All new sites created now display the Twenty Twenty-Three theme.

Gathering and Displaying Network-Wide Content

Depending on your needs, you may want to gather content from sites across your network to display on the front page of the main site. Although some plugins can perform this task for you, you can accomplish the same thing by placing a few lines of code in your theme template file.

The main page of your network is controlled by the theme that's active on the Themes screen of your regular Dashboard (which you access by hovering your mouse pointer over Appearance and clicking the Themes link). You can customize this theme with the code samples provided in the next section, "Adding posts from network sites."

Adding posts from network sites

One of the best ways to pull visitors into your site is to display a short list of headlines from posts published on other sites within your network. If you have a single WordPress site, the recent posts widget can handle this task. When you're running a network, however, you have no built-in way to pull a list of posts from across all the sites in your network. But the Network Posts Extended plugin (`https://wordpress.org/plugins/network-posts-extended`) allows you to share posts and pages from across your entire network on any given page on your main site through the use of a shortcode. The shortcode provided by the plugin has a variety of parameters you can use to customize the display of the content. You can specify the number of posts to display, for example, or display content only from certain sites. You can use several parameters and custom HTML elements with the shortcode; all the options available to you are listed at `https://wordpress.org/plugins/network-posts-extended`.

Listing network sites

To list all the sites in the network, use the Multisite Site Index plugin, available for free on the WordPress website at `https://wordpress.org/plugins/multisite-site-index`. You install this plugin just as you do any other plugin in WordPress; see Book 7, Chapter 2 for information on installing WordPress plugins.

To display a listing of sites from your network, you must include a shortcode that the plugin developer provides within the body of a page or post published to your main site. The most common and most useful method is to create a page that includes the plugin shortcode. To list all network sites, follow these steps (which use the default Twenty Twenty-Four theme):

1. **Log in to the WordPress Dashboard of the main site.**
2. **Hover your mouse pointer over Pages and click the Add New link.**

   The Add New Page screen appears.

3. **Fill in a title for your page.**

   You might type something like *Network Sites List*.

4. **Click the Add Block icon.**

   This step loads the blocks you can use to create content on a page.

5. **Select the shortcode block below the Widgets heading.**

6. **Add the `[site-index]` shortcode in the text field (See Figure 5-5).**

   This shortcode displays the titles of all the sites within your network in a list.

7. **Publish the page.**

   Now when you visit the page on your website, you see that it displays the list of sites in the network. (See Figure 5-6.)

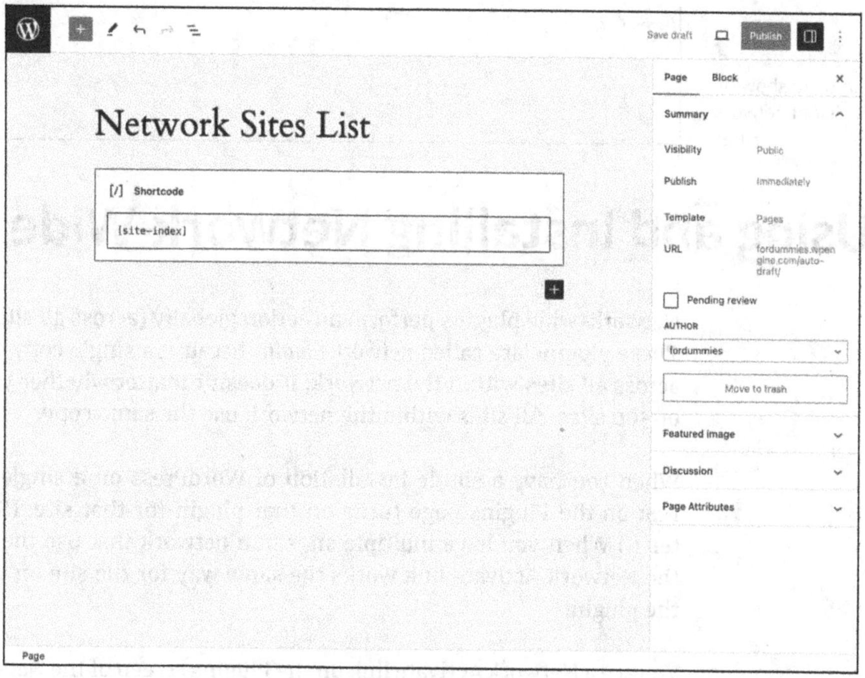

FIGURE 5-5: Adding a shortcode to a page by using the shortcode widget block.

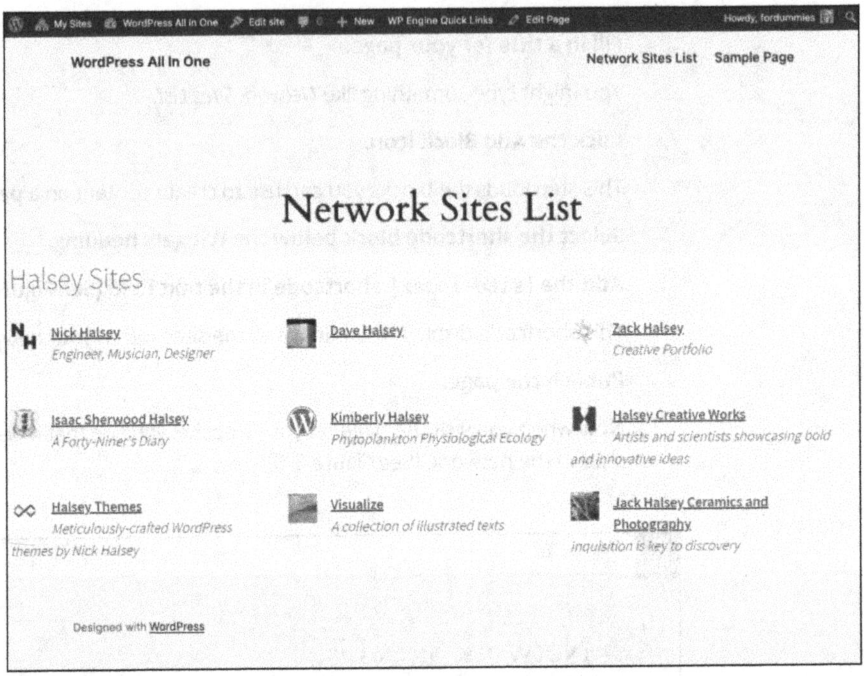

FIGURE 5-6: A page showing the list of network sites.

Using and Installing Network-Wide Plugins

Network-wide plugins perform an action globally (across all sites in the network). These plugins are called *network plugins* because a single copy of a plugin is used across all sites within the network; it doesn't matter whether your network has 5 or 500 sites. All sites within the network use the same copy.

When you have a single installation of WordPress on a single site, the Activate link on the Plugins page turns on that plugin for that site. (See Book 7, Chapter 1.) When you have multiple sites in a network that use the Multisite feature, the Network Activate link works the same way for the site on which you activate the plugin.

You see a Network Activate link on the Plugins screen of the Network Admin Dashboard. This link activates the plugin on all sites in the network (that is, it turns on the plugin for all network sites). You can't manage plugin options globally, however, unless the plugin itself is coded to let you do so. A list of network-activated plugins appears on the Plugins screen of the Network Admin Dashboard (which you access by clicking the Plugins menu link).

REMEMBER

Any changes made in a plugin affect every site within your network.

A special breed of plugins — called *Must-Use* — gets installed in the `/wp-content/mu-plugins` folder on your web server. Any plugin file placed inside this folder runs as though it were part of the WordPress core installation; it does not need to be activated and it cannot be deactivated unless you remove it from your installation completely. The plugins in this folder execute automatically without the need for activation in your Dashboard.

WARNING

You can't install or access the plugins in the `/wp-content/mu-plugins/` folder from the WordPress Dashboard. If you use the Install Plugins screen (hover your mouse pointer over Plugins and click the Add New link) to find and install a plugin, you're required to move the plugin files from the `/wp-content/plugins` folder to the `/wp-content/mu-plugins` folder via SFTP.

Generally, plugins placed in the `/wp-content/mu-plugins` folder are for network-wide features or customizations that users can't disable. An example is a custom-branded login page on each site in your network. If a plugin design adds a new menu item, the menu item appears as soon as the plugin is placed in the `/wp-content/mu-plugins` folder, without further need for activation from the Dashboard.

Not all plugins placed in the `/wp-content/mu-plugins` folder appear in the plugins list on the Plugins screen, because not all of them require activation. You can see the Must-Use link on the Plugins screen in Figure 5-7. This link displays the plugins that are included in the `/wp-content/mu-plugins` folder, but you will notice there are no options for you to activate, deactivate, or edit them.

REMEMBER

You still control plugin settings on a per-site basis; you must visit the back end of each site if you want to alter any settings provided by the plugin.

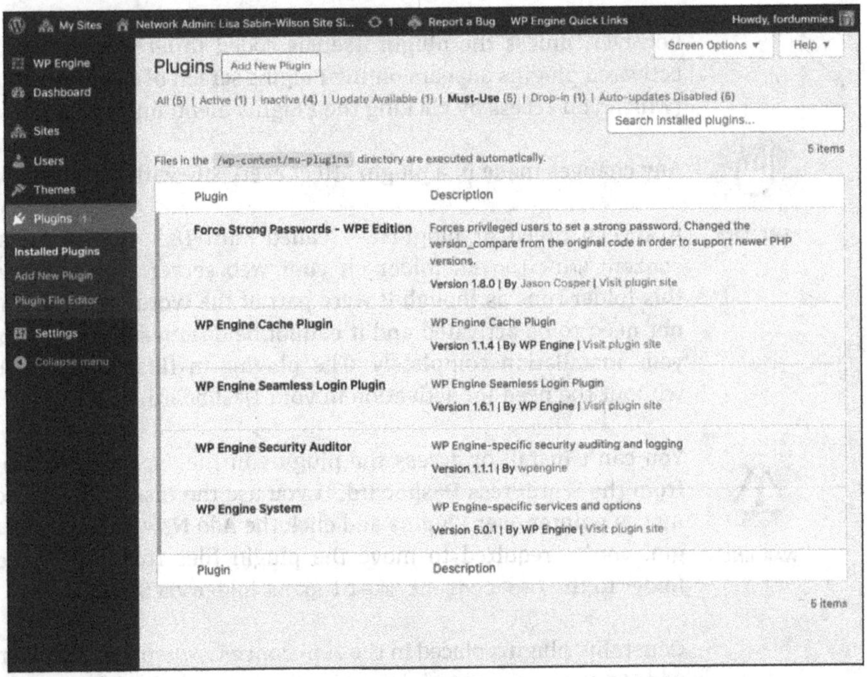

FIGURE 5-7: The Must-Use link on the Plugins screen.

Discovering Handy Multisite Plugins

You can find multisite plugins that take advantage of WordPress's multisite functionality on the WordPress Plugins page at `https://wordpress.org/plugins`.

Usually, multisite plugins are tagged with certain keywords that help you find them, such as *multisite* and *network*. Use the search field on the Plugins page to search for a plugin by keyword. The WordPress website displays a page that lists the related plugins, such as `https://wordpress.org/plugins/search/multisite` or `https://wordpress.org/plugins/search/network`.

TIP

You can find more plugins by searching in search engines and by searching the WordPress Support page (`https://wordpress.org/support`).

IN THIS CHAPTER

» Discovering domain mapping

» Understanding how to map domains

» Setting up multiple networks

Chapter 6 Using Multiple Domains within Your Network

With a network of multiple sites easily available in WordPress, many people prefer to run multiple sites on their own separate domain names through one install.

In this chapter, I discuss using multiple domains and a feature called *domain mapping*, which enables you to not only run multiple sites, but also multiple sites with unique domain names that aren't tied to the main site's installation domain.

To tackle this chapter, you need to understand basic information about domain names (see Book 2, Chapter 1).

Finding Your Way with Domain Mapping

Domain mapping means telling your web server which domains you want WordPress to answer to and which site you want to be shown to visitors when they request that domain. This process is more than domain forwarding or masking, because the URLs for your posts have the full domain name in them. Instead of the child site's being in `secondsite.`*`yourdomain`*`.com` format, it can be in *`myotherdomain`*`.com`.

Domain mapping isn't possible in certain cases, however. If your WordPress install is in a subfolder, and this folder is part of the URL, any mapped domain will also contain this folder name. In that case, it would be better to move the install so that it isn't in a subfolder.

You also need to access your web host's control panel (where you manage DNS records on your web server) and the control panel for your domain-name registrar, which is often a different company.

REMEMBER

By default, the network install lets you choose between a subdirectory setup and a subdomain setup. This step is still required before you can specify a domain for that site. I cover how to enable the network in Book 8, Chapter 2. Be sure to set up the network and make sure that it's functioning properly before you attempt to map domains.

Setting up a custom domain

You need to set up your web server to accept any incoming requests for the domain you want to map and the location to send your site visitors to. For the following steps, I am using the admin portal provided to me by my web host at WP Engine (`https://wpengine.com`). Every web host has a different interface, so if you are not hosting your WordPress site on my recommended host, WP Engine, you need to discover where this interface is located within our web host's portal.

Follow these steps to set up domain mapping in your WP Engine portal:

1. **Log in to your WP Engine account.**

   The address is provided by your web host and usually is available at `https://my.wpengine.com`.

2. **Click the Sites link in the left side navigation menu.**

   The My Sites page displays in your browser window, displaying a list of all the sites you have set up on your account.

3. **Click the name of the site you want to add your domain mapping to.**

   The settings for the site displays in your browser window.

4. **Click the Domains link.**

   This loads the Domains page in your browser window. (See Figure 6-1.)

5. **Click the Add Domain button.**

   The Add Domain page displays, as shown in Figure 6-2.

6. **Enter your domain name in the Domain field.**

   Leave the rest of the settings filled in with the default selections.

7. **Click the Add Domain button.**

   A message appears that the domain has been added to your hosting environment. The message also tells you that the verification of the domain will be made once you point the DNS of the domain to WP Engine. The verification process can take up to 24 hours.

8. **In the Choose Verification Method section on the Add Domain page, select Skip Pre-Verification.**

9. **Click the Continue button.**

   The Update DNS page displays in your browser window with the information you need to add to your domain registrar. This step is covered in the following section, "Editing DNS records."

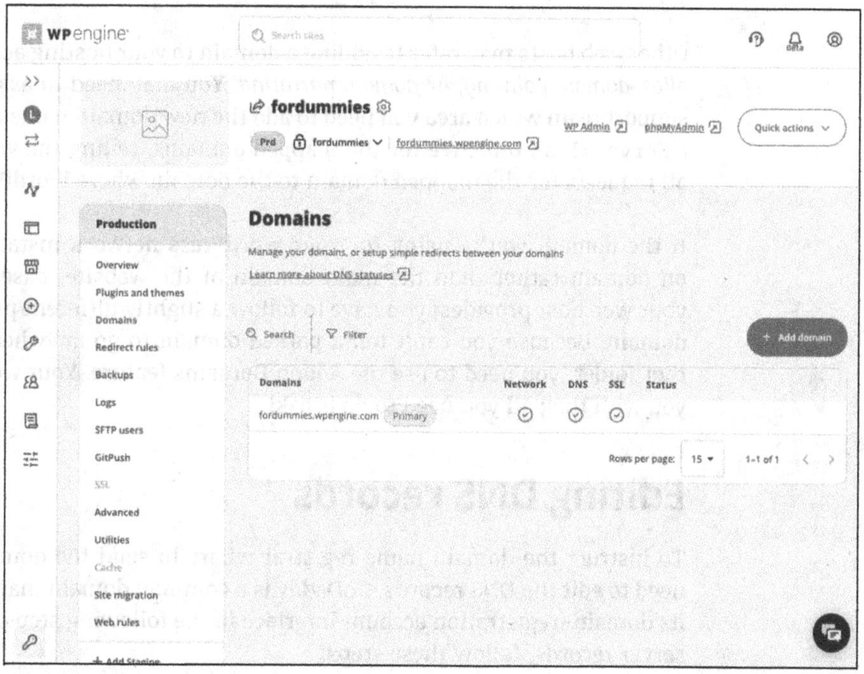

FIGURE 6-1: The Domains page in the WP Engine portal.

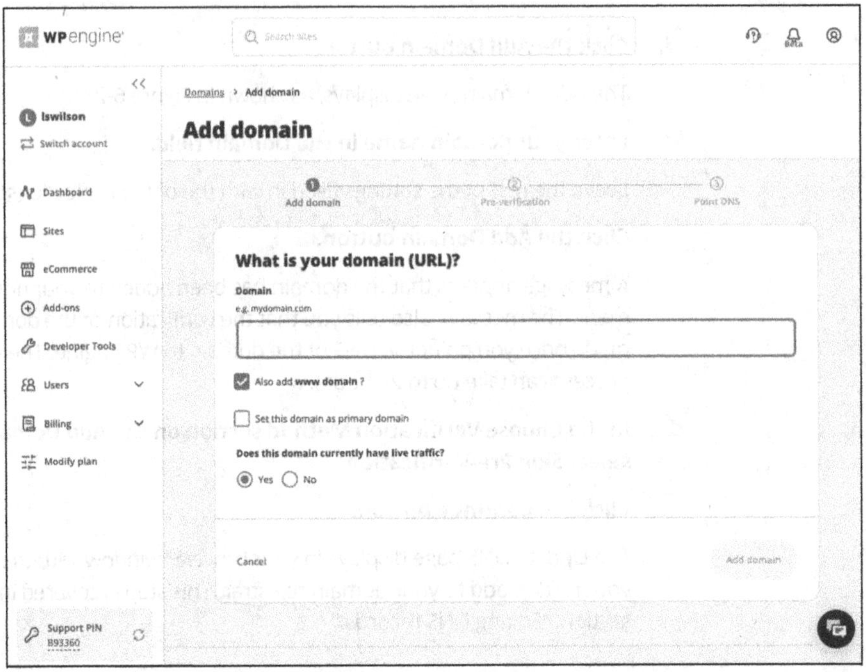

FIGURE 6-2: The Add Domain page in the WP Engine portal.

Other web hosts may refer to adding a domain to your hosting account as a *domain alias, domain pointing,* or *domain mirroring.* You may need to ask your web host's support team which area you need to add the new domain name into. You're using a `ServerAlias` directive for the mapped domains, telling the web server to send all requests for the mapped domain to the domain where WordPress is installed.

If the domain you're using for your WordPress network installation is an add-on domain rather than the main domain of the website, based on the method your web host provides, you have to follow a slightly different process to park the domain. Because you can't tell a parked domain to go anywhere other than the root folder, you need to use the Addon Domains feature. Your web host can assist you with this; all you need to do is ask!

Editing DNS records

To instruct the domain name registrar where to send the domain name to, you need to edit the DNS records. GoDaddy is a common domain-name registrar, I use its domain-registration account interface in the following steps. To edit the name server records, follow these steps:

1. **Log in to your domain-name registrar.**
2. **Click the DNS management tools.**

   Figure 6-3 shows the information for the domain to map.
3. **Click the Add New Record button.**

   Several form fields appear on the screen, where you will configure new DNS records for your domain.
4. **Select CNAME in the Type drop-down menu.**
5. **In the Name field, type the symbol @.**

   This tells your registrar that you want the CNAME to point to your custom domain.
6. **In the Value field, type in the name provided by your web host.**

   Figure 6-4 shows the value my WP Engine portal gave me to set as my CNAME at my domain registrar: `wp.wpenginepowered.com`.
7. **Click the Add More Records button.**
8. **Select A in the Type drop-down menu.**

   This creates the A Record for your domain DNS.
9. **In the Name field, type the symbol @.**

   This tells your registrar that you want the A Record to point to your custom domain.
10. **In the Value field, type in the numbers provided by your web host.**

    Figure 6-4 shows the values for the A Record provided by my web host.
11. **Repeat steps 7 through 10 to add a second A Record.**

    Most web hosts will give you two sets of numbers to set as A Records, so repeat the steps to add another A Record.
12. **Click the Save All Records button.**

    This saves all of your DNS changes. Now servers around the world know that your domain "lives" at this web server location. DNS changes may take up to 24 hours to propagate.

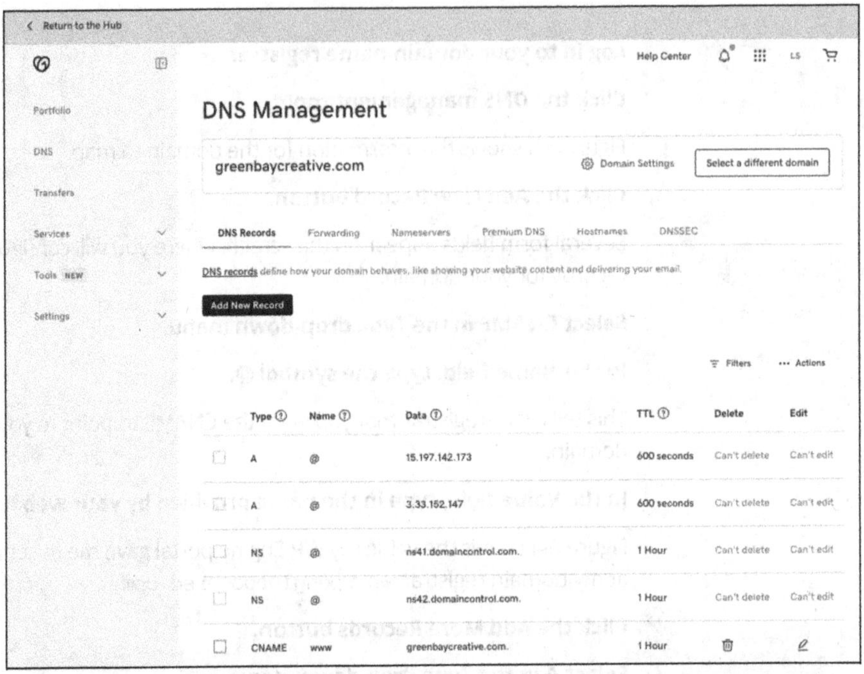

FIGURE 6-3: The DNS Management tool in the GoDaddy portal.

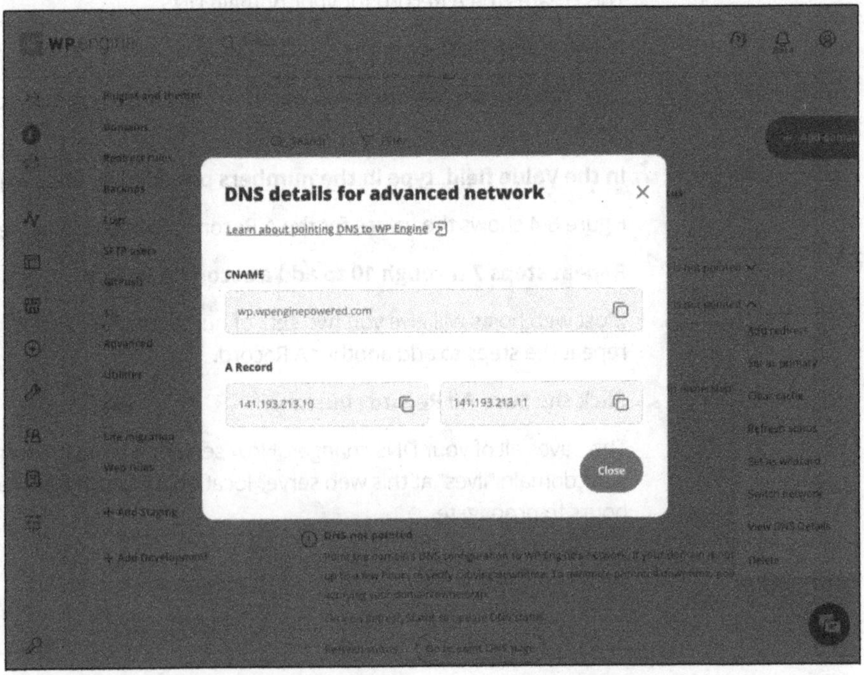

FIGURE 6-4: The DNS information provided for a custom domain.

Setting the Site Domain

Now that you have your custom domain registered and the DNS set up correctly to point to the web server where you have your WordPress multisite set up, you need to make sure that the site you are mapping the domain for is set up to use that domain. Follow these steps to make sure your domain is added to the site in your network:

1. **Log in to your WordPress Dashboard.**
2. **Click the Network Admin link in the My Sites drop-down menu, located at the top-left corner of your Dashboard.**
3. **Click the Sites link in the Network Admin menu.**

   The Sites page loads on the Network Dashboard.
4. **Hover your mouse pointer over the site title that you want to add the custom domain to.**
5. **Click the Edit link that appears.**

   The Edit Site page loads on your Dashboard. (See Figure 6-5.)
6. **Type your custom domain name in the Site Address (URL) field.**
7. **Click the Save Changes button.**

   This saves the Site settings with the custom domain name.

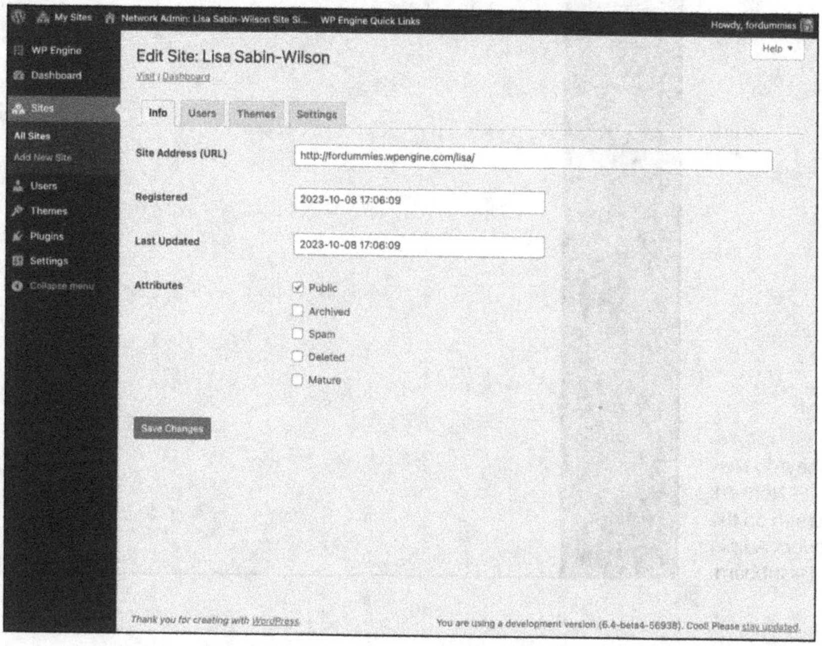

FIGURE 6-5: The Edit Site page on the Network Dashboard.

Setting Up Multiple Networks

Multiple networks are supported in the WordPress code base, but there's no built-in menu or interface on the Dashboard. Running multiple networks in one install is an advanced feature that allows you to have another network in the same installation act as a second independent network of sites. That network can use its fully qualified domain name or a subdomain. The extra networks inherit the same type of sites. If your original network was installed with subdomain sites, the extra network will also have subdomain sites. The network admin carries over to the new network, too. You can add other network admins to the second network without giving them network-admin access on the original network.

The plugin that helps you perform this task is WP Multi Network (available at `https://wordpress.org/plugins/wp-multi-network`). You install and manage the WP Multi Network plugin in a way that's similar to how you install and manage the WordPress MU Domain Mapping plugin. The domain for the new network still needs to be added to the install, but the creation of the network is done on the add New Network screen after you install the WP Multi Network plugin. You can't turn an existing site on the network into a second network; you must set up a new site when the new network is created. Figure 6-6 shows the Add New Network screen.

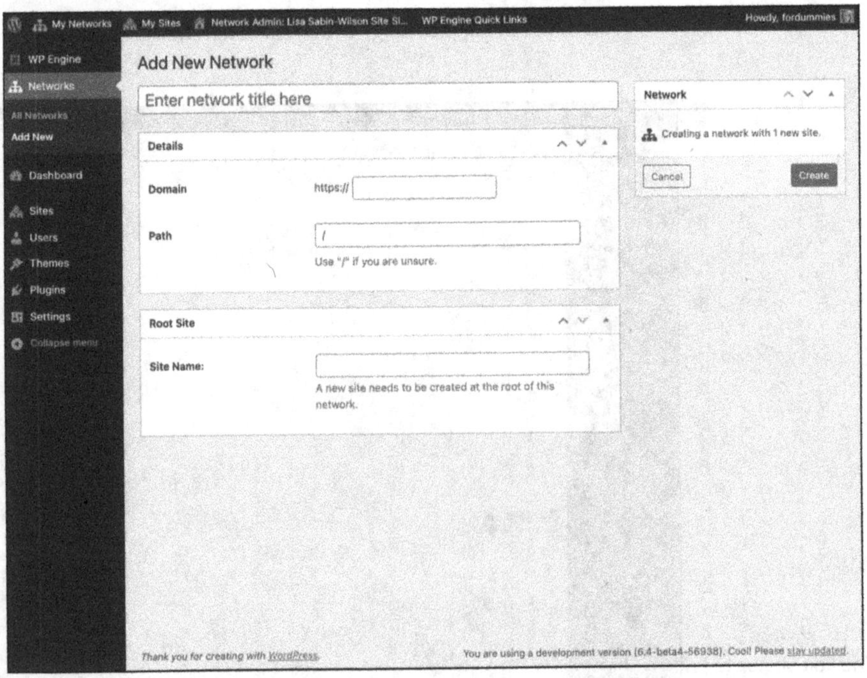

FIGURE 6-6: The Add New Network screen on the Network Admin Dashboard.

When this plugin is installed and the network is activated, you see a new menu on the Network Dashboard called Networks. Click the Add New link on the Networks menu to load the Add New Network screen.

To create a new network, fill in the fields on the Add New Network screen:

- **Network Title:** The name of the network you're creating (such as My New Network)
- **Details:** The settings for the Domain and Path
- **Domain:** The domain name you'll use for this new network (such as `mynewnetwork.com`)
- **Path:** The server path your new network will use (such as /home/*mynewnetwork*/public_html/)
- **Site Name:** The name of the site that will serve as the main site of this network (such as Network Main Site)

When you're done, click the Create button on the right side of the Add New Network screen. WordPress creates your new network, and you can assign child sites to it.

Index

B

C

D

E

F

G

H

I

J

K

L

M

N

O

P

S

T

U

V

W

X

Y

Z

About the Author

Lisa Sabin-Wilson (*WordPress For Dummies*, *WordPress Web Design For Dummies*) has 20 years' experience working with the WordPress platform, having adopted it early in its first year of release in 2003. Lisa is the co-owner of a successful WordPress design and development agency, WebDevStudios (`http://webdevstudios.com`), and is a regular speaker on topics related to design and WordPress at several national conferences. You can find Lisa online at her blog at `lisasabin-wilson.com` or on Twitter at `@lisasabinilson`.

Dedication

To WordPress . . . and all that entails, from the developers, designers, forum helpers, bug testers, educators, consultants, plugin makers, and theme bakers.

Author's Acknowledgments

Every person involved in the WordPress community plays a vital role in making this whole thing work, and work well. Kudos to all of you! Also, big thanks to my wonderful husband, Chris Wilson, for his incredible support, backbone, and ability to put up with my crazy days of writing — I could *not* have done it without you!

Special thanks to the co-authors of the first edition of this book who helped form the framework of the publication and ensured its initial success: Cory Miller, Kevin Palmer, Andrea Rennick, and Michael Torbert.

Publisher's Acknowledgments

Acquisitions Editor: Elizabeth Stilwell
Project Editor: Lynn Northrup
Copy Editor: Lynn Northrup
Technical Editor: Mitch Canter
Production Editor: Pradesh Kumar
Cover Image: © dubassy/Shutterstock